www.letsgo.com

EUROPEAN RIVIERA

researcher-writers
Christa Hartsock
Jocelyn Karlan
Taylor Nickel
Julia Rooney
Mark Warren
William N. White

staff writers
Adrienne Y. Lee
Dorothy McLeod
Taylor Nickel
Sara Joe Wolansky

research managers
Anna E. Boch
Joseph B. Gaspard
Chris Kingston

editors
Teresa Maria Cotsirilos
Bronwen Beseda O'Herin
Jonathan Rossi

managing editor
Marykate Jasper

CONTENTS

RESEARCHER-WRITERS

CHRISTA HARTSOCK. Christa's love affair with Barcelona began with her extensive research on the city's urban planning for her senior thesis. An art and architecture scholar, she was powerless to resist the likes of Gaudí's Manzana de Discordia. After her immaculate research was finished, Christa embarked on an epic biking trip to Amsterdam, where she snored loud enough to wake up the whole town.

JOCELYN KARLAN. After spending part of last summer stranded on top of a mountain in Ecuador, Jocey chalks up her time with Let's Go as a success. A student of psychology, Jocey may have used hypnosis to charm the locals—or maybe she's just incredibly amiable. Her editors think it's the latter; Jocey's enthusiasm to research every nook and cranny (and cave) in Andalusia made her indispensable.

TAYLOR NICKEL. From the shores of SoCal to the French Riviera, 20-year-old Taylor has already traveled to over 50 countries. When he wasn't researching the best hostels in Marseille, he was working the tables at a casino in Monte Carlo or riding a scooter from Saint-Tropez to Cannes. His winning smile and enviable tan made it hard for anybody, from hotel managers to customs officials, to say no to Taylor.

JULIA ROONEY. This veteran of *Let's Go Italy 2009* demonstrated a prodigious knowledge of Italian culture that put her editors—and probably even a few locals—to shame. From surviving the Amalfi Coast's treacherous cliff-top bus rides to devouring dangerous amounts of gelato, Julia kept her cool with perfect prose and *perfetto italiano.*

MARK WARREN. Traipsing along the Camino in northern Spain and scooting south into Portugal, Mark circumnavigated nearly half of the Iberian Peninsula. This modern-day Magellan's route was a whirlwind of port wine, seafood, and learning that Portuguese is really not that similar to Spanish.

WILLIAM N. WHITE. An experienced sailor, William proved himself no ordinary **boat** nerd, displaying additional talents as a hiker, pizza critic, and—of course—star RW. While the beach bums around him soaked up the sun in Monterosso, William spent his time bringing subtle wit and a travel-savvy perspective to his research.

THE EUROPEAN RIVIERA

Between David Guetta's music videos and Daniel Craig's impressive torso (that scene? With the so-not-there swimsuit? In *Casino Royale?)*, we admit that our expectations were pretty high for the Riviera, and after 50 years in this business we didn't think we could still be surprised. Talk about getting schooled. During seven weeks of caffeinated hostel-hopping, we dodged tear gas canisters in riots, got (wo)man-handled at Drag Nights, passed out on the yachts of strangers, discovered that butt-pasties do in fact exist, and may or may not have stolen a rental scooter. It's no secret that the young bourgeois of the world flock to the Riviera to bum, binge, and break it down at a safe distance from prospective employers. From its pristine beaches to its legalized gambling, the Riviera appears to be designed for it. Folks have been migrating here for some R and R since Hercules, and you're just as likely to find a Mediterranean god or goddess sipping absinthe here today as you were way back then.

Spring-break stereotypes aside, the Riviera's debauchery is rooted in something much deeper. Like most places people escape to, this region is defined by an astonishing lack of rules, and as such has long been a haven for uncompromising people, from tax-evaders to Catalan anarchists to alcoholic visionaries. It's not a coincidence that Gaudí, Picasso, Miró, Chagall, and Matisse all have such a rich presence here.

It's also not a coincidence that one of the most socially liberal places in the world is also home to one of the few remaining monarchical city-states. This fierce streak of iconoclasm makes the Riviera a hotbed for wild ideas and fosters a work-hard-play-hard attitude that's hard to resist. Not that you should.

top five enactments of fantasy

5. FORMULA 1 GRAND-PRIX: Get ready for fast cars, fast women, and €500 bills. A funfest for drivers with a death wish and the robber barons that fund them, Monaco's most famous drag race pits Mercedes-McLauren against Ferrari every June and sends Formula 1 racers careening through Monaco's historic streets.

4. LA SAGRADA FAMÍLIA: It may still be a work in progress, but Gaudí's melting sand castle of a cathedral is the crowning jewel of Barcelona. The undulating walls of its towers look like something out of someone else's dream.

3. CARNIVAL: France might bill itself as a proudly secular country, but when it comes to church-condoned feathers, falsies, and masquerade balls, Nice conveniently becomes a Catholic stronghold again. You can't really blame them. Nothing brightens up a winter better than a little Vatican-approved T and A.

2. DISSENY HUB BARCELONA: Ever dream of making a chair simply with a beam of light? Chances are you haven't, but just in case you have (or you're curious how it's even possible), this contemporary art museum will show you said chair, let you touch it, and even explain every single step of its magical creation.

1. ÎLE D'OR: Talk about your own private universe. This small island off the coast of St-Raphaël was won by a French doctor in a high-stakes card game in the early 20th century. Ever the down-to-earth type, he proceeded to rename himself Augustus I, built himself a castle, and crowned himself king of an uninhabited island. The guy went as far is to print stamps and mint his own currency—all of which, naturally, featured pictures of himself. His descendents still live in the castle today.

when to go

Ah, the Mediterranean—its weather and its men are equally lovely at any time of year. If you want to undergo that treasured rite of passage of the American college student and (ahem) "backpack through Europe," we recommend that you visit over spring break or during the summer. Hotel rates can skyrocket come summer, and lots of locals take their vacation time in August, so the sea of humanity can get overwhelming. If you want to do something unprintable with a beautiful person whom you never plan to see again, the sun, sand, and rollicking vibe of the Mediterranean in August is more than worth the price.

The French in particular seem to think that visiting a beach in the winter is indicative of mental illness, but the late fall, winter, and early spring remain relatively temperate around the Mediterranean, despite periodic cold or rain. If you're not made of money, are here for the museums, or are annoyed by high numbers of Teva-wearing camera-snapping tourists like yourself, then this is the time to go. Be sure to keep in mind the European vacation schedule when you plan your trip. France, Spain, and Italy are all European welfare states with (gasp!) government-mandated vacation time; local families flock to the costs for vacation during the winter holidays, Easter, July, and August.

student superlatives

- **BEST GENDER-BENDING.** Talk about a toss-up, but we're going with the club Vogue in Cannes (p. 163).
- **BEST "ASSASSINATION OF PAINTING."** Juan Miró's work might look like cheerfully-colored Surrealist distortions to you, but this loyal son of Barcelona viewed his work as an "assassination of painting" itself; a Catalan nationalist oppressed by Franco's fascist regime, his work was intended to assault bourgeois conceptions of reality. See it today in the Fundació Miró (p. 222).
- **MOST SATISFYING CALORIE INTAKE.** The pizzas of Naples (p. 29).
- **MOST SATISFYING CALORIE BURN.** A hike along the Cinque Terre (p. 80).
- **MOST SERENE FLOATING WOMAN.** She's definitely somewhere in Nice's famed Musée National Mesage Biblique Marc Chagall (p. 104).
- **BEST PLACE TO SPOT DESIGNER CLOTHING.** Anywhere in Monaco.
- **BEST PLACE TO BURN DESIGNER CLOTHING IN PROTEST.** Anywhere in Barcelona.
- **BEST BLOW.** By which we mean glass-blowing. Head to Biot.
- **BEST PLACE TO ACQUIRE A TONED MEDITERRANEAN.** Ibiza.
- **BEST PLACE FOR A TONED MEDITERRANEAN TO ACQUIRE YOU.** Um, yeah: Ibiza.

what to do

I'M ON A BOAT

We thought that MTV music videos were just mass-produced Hollywood daydreams, but the parties along the Riviera make them look like BBC documentaries. We're talking boozefests on yachts, cage dancing, retro jazz clubs, and the most famous casino in history. From bros and their accessory women to fashionably disaffected vegans, there's really something here for everyone. If you were ever planning on getting yourself into a *Hangover*-esque situation, this is definitely the place to do it.

- **ST-TROPEZ:** You'd better acquire a sugar daddy—the wealth per square km in this town might outdo the Vatican, and docking your yacht alone might run you €5000 (p. 176).
- **IBIZA:** Between the strobe lights, the costumed performers on stilts, and the occasional visits from Lady Gaga, the famed hot spots of Ibiza exist in an alternate reality of their own (p. 288).
- **CANNES:** Stalk Matt Damon on the red carpet, then escape to the strobe lights and wacked-out decor of the chic local clubs (p. 157).

TAKE A HIKE

Though the Riviera may be a study in excess, the Lohan look-alikes aren't what earned this region so many UN World Heritage Sites. The smaller towns that dot the Riviera's coastline preserve the peaceful provincialism of Old World Europe. Crooked buildings cling to cliffsides overlooking the sea, and winding cobbled streets yield spectacular views of the ocean. Some of the most renowned Roman ruins in the world are also in this area, including Pompeii. A short trek or bus ride outside of the main towns yield hiking trails, scuba-diving opportunities, and other delights for the adrenaline junkie.

- **CINQUE TERRE:** We think this might be one of the most beautiful hikes in Europe, so take a day to walk along the cliffs between the Italian coast's sleepy villages (p. 80).
- **HERCULANEUM:** Most tourists go gaga over Pompeii, but this smaller collection of ruins is less touristed, more compete, and just as exquisitely preserved by the shenanigans of Mt. Vesuvius (p. 42).
- **GROTTA AZZURRA:** The crowning glory of Italy's Isle of Capri, the neon aquamarine waters of this surreal sea cave are more than worth a trip (p. 48).

BEYOND TOURISM

Maybe you want to do some good in the world, or maybe you didn't get lucky at Monte Carlo and need some way to pay for the rest of your trip. Either way, there are ample opportunities for volunteer work and part-time jobs along the Riviera. There is also an array of language immersion and academic programs in Barcelona and the South of France, for those of you looking for an excuse to stay longer.

- **ECOVOLUNTEER, COMMON DOLPHINS:** Sleep on a 17.7m cutter in the Bay of Naples and save the whales and dolphins too! (p. 365).
- **AUPAIRCONNECT:** Potential au pairs and families can sign up to this service that matches them up for free (p. 367).
- **ESCAPE ARTIST:** This listings website allows employers to post right on its directory and allows you to search listings by location, employment type, and your work experience. It also posts many articles on living and working abroad (p. 367).

FROMAGERIE
NICOLE
BARTHELEMY
ABRICOT
CASSIS
GRIOTT

suggested itineraries

BEST OF THE EUROPEAN RIVIERA

1. IBIZA: It's a UN World Heritage Site, but that's probably not why you're here.

2. BARCELONA: Welcome to Spain's glorious beacon of art, late-night tapas, and Catalan commies.

3. ST-TROPEZ: If MTV created the universe, it'd probably look something like this.

4. CANNES: While Cannes is the definition of glamour during the summer, it's actually one of the more laid-back towns along the Riviera for much of the rest of the year. If you go in the low season, hit up the open-air fish markets and free local movie tickets.

5. NICE: Combining a wealthy reputation with an affordable underbelly, Nice neatly condenses everything amazing about the Côte d'Azur into one sizzling metropolis.

6. MONACO: About the grittier side of Monaco...does a used Ferrari dealership count?

7. CINQUE TERRE: Wind through the hills and quiet beaches that hem an improbably blue strip of Mediterranean.

8. BAY OF NAPLES: No, Naples is not full of trash—we don't know who started that one, but for the record it's chock-full of pizza, Roman ruins, and hiking trips instead.

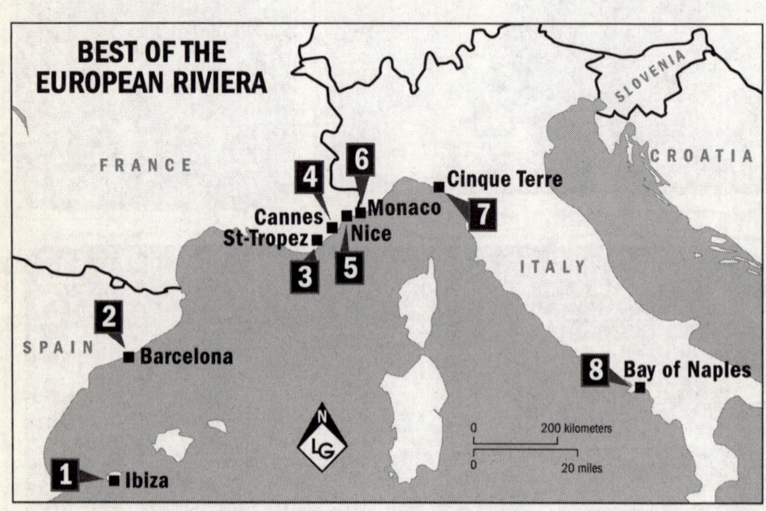

THE BUDGET BACKPACKER

1. VALENCIA: With the energy of Madrid, the warmth of Sevilla, and the artsy spunk of Barcelona, Valencia is a smaller city that combines the best of its neighbors through a mix of extremes. It's also a much better deal than the rest of the Riviera and fosters a hip and alternative bar scene.

2. BARCELONA: This city takes pride in its youthful vibe and innate sense of cool and provides plenty of quirky hostels for the budget traveler.

3. MARSEILLE: France's Tijuana is colorful, chaotic, and gritty. Take in a view of the city from the windswept Notre Dame de la Garde, then hike to the nearby calanques for some choice skinny dipping or cliff jumping territory.

4. NICE: This city's been on the backpacker must-see list since the youth of the world discovered beaches and cheap wine.

5. MENTON: Known as the "Secret Riviera," this city is graced by Côte d'Azur sunshine without the gouging prices and snobby club scene.

6. CINQUE TERRE: While the area's recently become much more touristed, you can still find the provincial peace and quiet you came here for, as well as some decent deals.

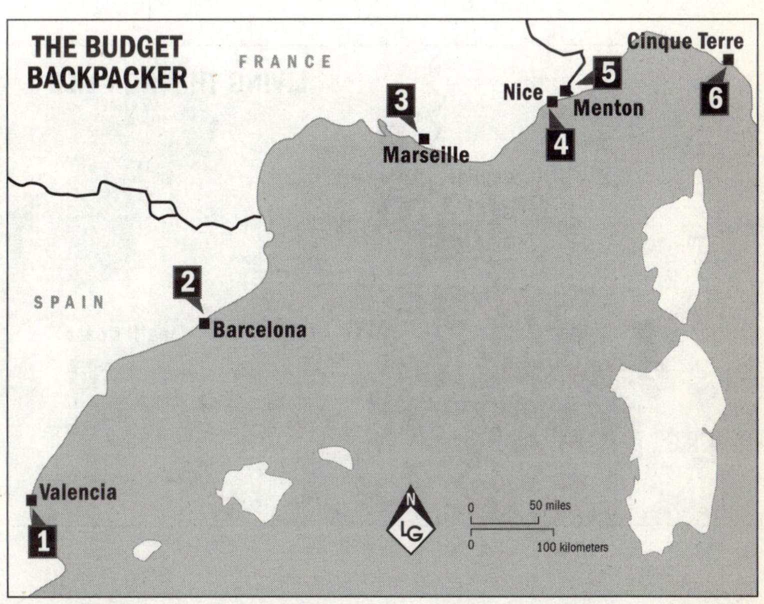

LIVING THE HIGH LIFE

1. IBIZA: You might not remember much of your trip to Ibiza, but the hazy flashbacks you do have will probably involve a lot of mojitos. And go-go dancers. And maybe some leather.

2. SITGES: This small town outside of Barcelona boasts crystalline waters, a whopping 300 days of sun a year, and regular "sausagefest" foam parties at the local gay club.

3. ST-TROPEZ: Funny story: we discovered St-Tropez's high concentration of topless beaches here. Then we missed our ferry home.

4. CANNES: Dress to impress and then get down with Clooney.

5. MONACO: Not every country proudly counts yacht hopping, gambling, and tax evasion among its national pastimes—Monaco's a rich man's fantasy and a pretty special place.

6. AMALFI COAST: The small towns that dot this strip of Italy's coastline are low on bars and debauchery, but the spectacular views and small-town cafes make for an ideal breather after a week of cheap drinks and all-nighters.

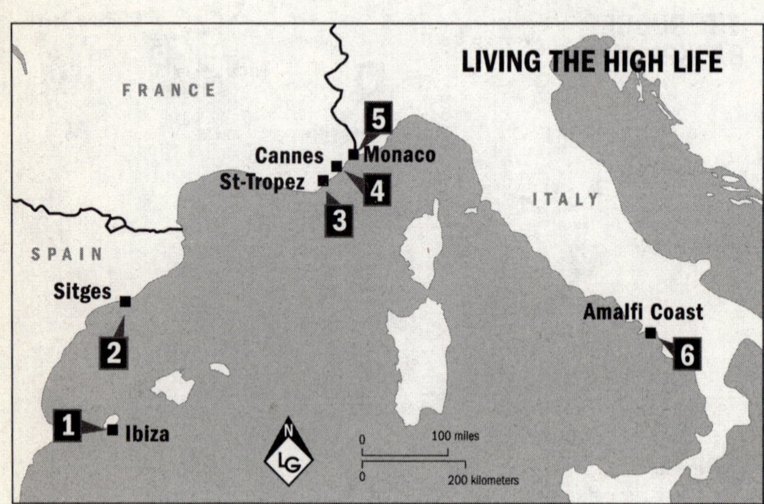

THE SCENIC ROUTE

1. MÁLAGA: Burn off your hangover by basking on the white sand of the city's famed beaches.

2. ALICANTE: The town's craggy mountains and lush pine forests make for an outdoorsy complement to lazy days in the sand.

3. ANTIBES: F. Scott Fitzgerald vacationed here for a reason, you know. The beaches are free and the snorkeling's unparalleled.

4. BIOT: The glassblowing capital of France, Biot hasn't changed much since the 1400s, and the townspeople have clung to the old Provençal architecture of white-washed walls and tiled floors, making every hotel, restaurant, and cafe the most adorable place you've ever seen.

5. VENCE: A mid-size medieval village in the hills between Nice and Cannes, this peaceful haven is most famous for the healing properties of its drinking water. Laugh all you want, but its powers were "proven" when it healed Nero's wife, Poppaea.

6. CINQUE TERRE: Come on now: you just really need to go here. It's not like we haven't said it enough times already or anything.

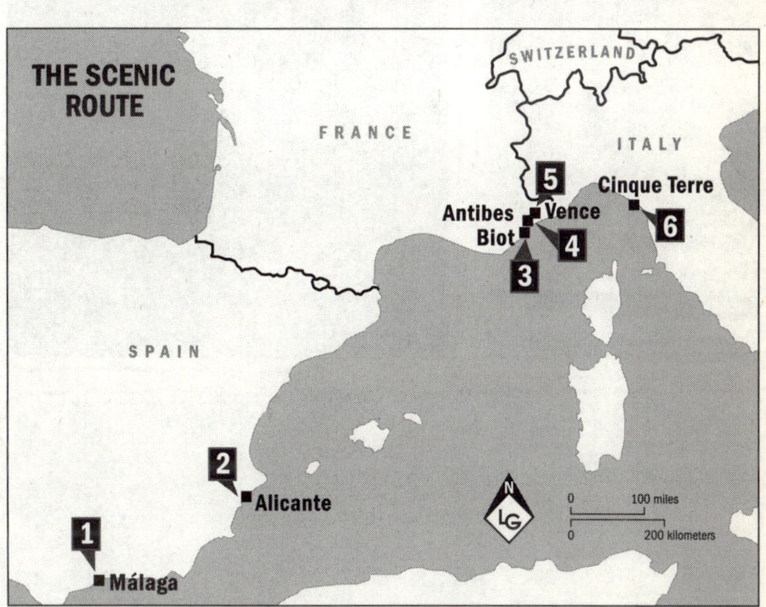

how to use this book

CHAPTERS

In the next few pages, the travel coverage chapters—the meat of any *Let's Go* book—begin with the Bay of Naples. From Italy's ankle, we'll move northwest along the Italian coast to Cinque Terre, then on into France, where we'll don our sunglasses and hobnob with the glitterati in Nice and Monaco before hitting the beaches of the Côte d'Azur. Our first Spanish stop is the big city of Barcelona. Never fear: it too has beaches. So does Sitges, the resort town whose chapter follows Barcelona's. After Sitges, we make a quick venture off the coast and into the Mediterranean Sea with a chapter on Las Islas Baleares, which consist of Majorca and Ibiza. Returning to the mainland, we drop anchor in Valencia and proceed south along the Spanish coast to nearby Alicante. We continue along the shore to our last destination (and chapter), Spain's intriguing Costa del Sol. But that's not all, folks. We also have a few extra chapters for you to peruse:

CHAPTER	DESCRIPTION
Discover the European Riviera	Discover tells you what to do, when to do it, and where to go for it. The absolute coolest things about any destination get highlighted in this chapter at the front of all Let's Go books.
Essentials	Essentials contains the practical info you need before, during, and after your trip—visas, regional transportation, health and safety, phrasebooks, and more.
European Riviera 101	European Riviera 101 is just what it sounds like—a crash course in where you're traveling. This short chapter on the European Riviera's history and culture makes great reading on a long plane ride.
Beyond Tourism	As students ourselves, we at Let's Go encourage studying abroad, or going beyond tourism more generally, every chance we get. This chapter lists ideas for how to study, volunteer, or work abroad with other young travelers in the European Riviera to get more out of your trip.

LISTINGS

Listings—a.k.a. reviews of individual establishments—constitute a majority of *Let's Go* coverage. Our Researcher-Writers list establishments in order from **best to worst value**—not necessarily quality. (Obviously a five-star hotel is nicer than a hostel, but it would probably be ranked lower because it's not as good a value.) Listings pack in a lot of information, but it's easy to digest if you know how they're constructed:

ESTABLISHMENT NAME ▼ type of establishment ❶

Address ☎phone number website

Editorial review goes here.

Directions to the establishment. ***i*** *Other practical information about the establishment, like age restrictions at a club or whether breakfast is included at a hostel.* ⓢ *Prices for goods or services.* *Hours or schedules.*

ICONS

First things first: places and things that we absolutely love, sappily cherish, generally obsess over, and wholeheartedly endorse are denoted by the all-empowering **Let's Go thumbs-up.** In addition, the icons scattered throughout a listing (as you saw in the sample above) can tell you a lot about an establishment. The following icons answer a series of yes-no questions about a place:

	Credit cards accepted		Cash only	♿	Wheelchair-accessible
	Not wheelchair-accessible		Internet access available		Alcohol served
❄	Air-conditioned		Outdoor seating available	▼	GLBT or GLBT-friendly

The rest are visual cues to help you navigate each listing:

☎	Phone numbers	🖥	Websites	⇄	Directions
i	Other hard info	$	Prices	⏰	Hours

OTHER USEFUL STUFF

Area codes for each destination appear opposite the name of the city and are denoted by the ☎ icon. Finally, in order to pack the book with as much information as possible, we have used a few **standard abbreviations.** In Italian destinations, you'll see these generally in addresses or directions, where Via becomes V., Viale becomes Vle., Piazza becomes P., and Corso becomes C. In French destinations, pl. stances for *place*, or plaza, bld. stands for boulevard, and av. stands for avenue. *Entrées* mean appetizers in French, whereas *plats* are main dishes. In Spain, c. stands for *calle*, or street. Av. stands for *avenida*, or avenue.

PRICE DIVERSITY

A final set of icons corresponds to what we call our "price diversity" scale, which approximates how much money you can expect to spend at a given establishment. For **accommodations,** we base our range on the cheapest price for which a single traveler can stay for one night. For **food,** we estimate the average amount one traveler will spend in one sitting. The table below tells you what you'll *typically* find in the European Riviera at the corresponding price range. The leftmost column contains ranges for Italy, the middle column contains those for France, and the rightmost column contains those for Spain. Keep in mind that no system can allow for the quirks of individual establishments.

ACCOMMODATIONS	RANGE			WHAT YOU'RE LIKELY TO FIND
❶	under €20	under €25	under €20	Campgrounds and dorm rooms, both in hostels and actual universities. Expect bunk beds and a communal bath. You may have to provide or rent towels and sheets.
❷	€20-30	€25-40	€20-29	Upper-end hostels or lower-end hotels. You may have a private bathroom, or there may be a sink in your room and a communal shower in the hall.
❸	€31-45	€41-60	€30-37	A small room with a private bath. Should have decent amenities, such as phone and TV. Breakfast may be included.
❹	€46-65	€61-80	€38-50	Should have bigger rooms than a ❸, with more amenities or in a more convenient location. Breakfast probably included.
❺	over €65	over €80	over €50	Large hotels or upscale chains. If it's a ❺ and it doesn't have the perks you want (and more), you've paid too much.
FOOD	**RANGE**			**WHAT YOU'RE LIKELY TO FIND**
❶	under €7	under €15	under €6	Probably street food or a fast-food joint, but also university cafeterias and bakeries (yum). Usually takeout, but you may have the option of sitting down.
❷	€7-15	€15-25	€6-12	Sandwiches, pizza, appetizers at a bar, or low-priced entrees. Most ethnic eateries are a ❷. Either takeout or a sit-down meal, but only slightly more fashionable decor.
❸	€16-25	€26-35	€13-17	Mid-priced entrees, seafood, and exotic pasta dishes. More upscale ethnic eateries. Since you'll have the luxury of a waiter, tip will set you back a little extra.
❹	€26-33	€36-45	€18-25	A somewhat fancy restaurant. Entrees tend to be heartier or more elaborate, but you're really paying for decor and ambience. Few restaurants in this range have a dress code, but some may look down on T-shirts and sandals.
❺	over €33	over €45	over €25	Your meal might cost more than your room, but there's a reason—it's something fabulous, famous, or both. Slacks and dress shirts may be expected. Offers foreign-sounding food and a decent wine list. Don't order a PB and J!

ITALY

BAY OF NAPLES

If there's one thing unifying the smorgasbord of cities that fills the Bay of Naples, it might just be the traffic—buses whipping around Amalfi's winding cliffs recall the omnipresent motorcycles that zoom through Naples's equally twisting streets. With no traffic lights in either case, only honks and vrooms let you know if something is coming round the bend. Watch out.

Equally as hard to anticipate are the immense contrasts in scenery and character you'll find throughout the region. Indeed, you may be wondering how such a diverse assortment of locales can all be packed in the same chapter—it's hard to equate Naples's piles of trash with Capri's piles of sand. You'll find that in many ways, this diversity's a good thing, for the plastic-looking streets and colorful trinkets of Amalfi beach towns don't possess quite as much staying power as *Napoli*'s century-old churches and catacombs. Head to the dirty and practical big city for cultural riches and treat the rest of the Amalfi Coast like a dollhouse—pretty, popular, but not all too habitable. Somewhere between the grime and glitz sit Pompeii and Herculaneum, cities which unexpectedly combine the best of their southern and northern neighbors: as the footprints of once bustling cities, their remains contain both the quaint streets of the bay's beach towns and the artistic masterpieces of a metropolis like Naples.

In short, the Bay of Naples could be its own Italy—it has enough scenic variety and sights to keep any itinerary fresh for well over a week. And when we said transit unifies the place, we weren't just talking about the ready-to-run-you-over kind: frequent buses and trains make the whole region easily navigable, even during short stays.

greatest hits

- **PIZZA PIONEERS.** Naples invented pizza, and by now they've definitely figured out how to make a good pie. Pretty much anywhere in Spaccanapoli will prove stunningly delicious (p. 29).
- **RUINED FOR LIFE.** Pompeii might be more famous, but Herculaneum is our pick of the cities that got on the wrong side of Mt. Vesuvius (p. 42).
- **COASTING.** The postcard cities of the Amalfi Coast are all spectacular, but move a little away from the beach to reach Ravello, a hilltop town with a phenomenal music festival (p. 65).

student life

For student life around the bay, it's best to stick to the big cities. Sorrento is a remarkably friendly city for young people. Though it attracts its fair share of seriously wealthy Western tourists, it's also home to great bars and the famed *limoncello*. C. Italia is lined with great options. Amalfi and Positano are great towns to visit during the day, hang out on the beaches and enjoy yourself, but you'll quickly notice these aren't really places where people study. Similarly, Capri is just a little too beautiful for anything as real as a university to take hold there–so your best bet might be the enigma that is Naples. Avoid the area around the train station, but a little further west in the *centro storico* you'll find plenty of young people at the bars along V. Enrico de Marinis. This area is right next door to the University of Naples Federico II, the world's oldest state university which still boasts a huge student body. And, of course, while in Naples remember to enjoy some of every student's favorite: pizza. Next time you're back at college and ordering a late-night pie, you'll remember your visit to the home of this greatest of inventions, and probably wish that you were back there. So eat up now, and make your friends jealous with all the stories later.

naples *napoli* ☎081

Naples is a bustling, hectic city—revel in it if you like, revile it if you must, just don't be scared by it. Travelers who know where they're going (or just look like they do) will fare best. Traffic zooms through the streets in lanes half the width of the painted lines. Red lights are mere suggestions. Crossing the street is a battle of wills—one of which has a V8 engine on its side. Yet Neapolitans take it all in stride. Cheerful chaos is a lifestyle they have eagerly adopted, though they now take out the trash, and much of the crime and grime has gone with it. Laughing together in one hearty chuckle, locals seem to spend every waking hour on the town, drinking, smoking, carousing, and eating.

Especially eating. This city invented **pizza,** and it sure knows how to make a good slice. The challenge is less finding the best than finding something else to eat: with pies so savory and inexpensive, it's hard to try something a little different. Still, the seafood that has defined the Mediterranean diet for centuries overflows fishermen's holds in the picturesque bay.

It's a shame tourists often treat this city as a mere stopover while exploring nearby attractions. All they see is the train station—unruly and unclean, the worst of stereotypical Naples, but many areas have the beauty of a resort town. Scrub off the grime and graffiti, and there's much to be found in the city's architecturally masterful *centro*. Don't trust us? Trust UNESCO, which recently deemed Naples's historical center a **World Heritage Site.** For millennia, the city has been an outpost for the world's greatest civilizations, so forgive Naples its untidiness and petty crime: the continent and, really, the world as they stand in the modern era owe a lot to this scrappy city.

ORIENTATION

The *centro* and the most interesting areas of Naples are arranged roughly in an "L" shape along the coast. To the northeast, in an unappealing and unsafe neighborhood, is Stazione Centrale on **Piazza Garibaldi.** From the corner of the *piazza* opposite the

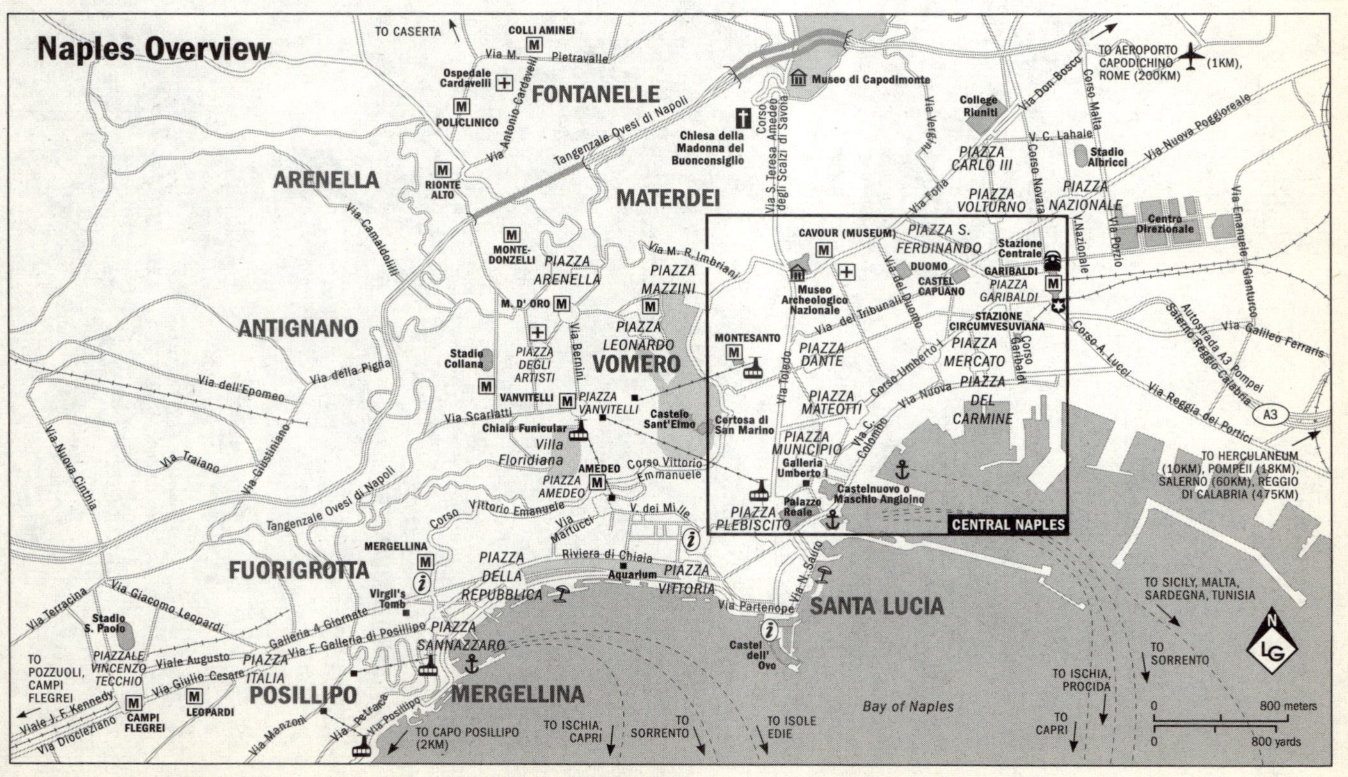

Naples Overview
TO CASERTA
COLLI AMINEI
Via M. Pietravalle
Ospedale Cardavelli
POLICLINICO
Via Antonio Cardavelli
FONTANELLE
Tangenziale Ovesi di Napoli
Museo di Capodimonte
Chiesa della Madonna del Buonconsiglio
Corso Amedeo
Via S. Teresa degli Scalzi di Savoia
Via Vergini
College Riuniti
Via Don Bosco
Corso Malta
TO AEROPORTO CAPODICHINO (1KM), ROME (200KM)
V. C. Lahale
Stadio Albricci
Via Nuova Poggioreale
PIAZZA CARLO III
PIAZZA VOLTURNO
Corso Novara
PIAZZA NAZIONALE
V.Nazionale
Via Porzio
Centro Direzionale
Via Emanuele Gianturco
ARENELLA
RIONTE ALTO
MATERDEI
Via Camaldolilli
Via Foria
MONTE-DONZELLI
PIAZZA ARENELLA
Via M. R. Imbriani
PIAZZA MAZZINI
CAVOUR (MUSEUM)
PIAZZA S. FERDINANDO
Stazione Centrale
GARIBALDI
PIAZZA GARIBALDI
DUOMO
CASTEL CAPUANO
Museo Archeologico Nazionale
Via del Duomo
Via dei Tribunali
STAZIONE CIRCUMVESUVIANA
Corso Garibaldi
Autostrada A3 Pompei Salerno Reggio Calabria
Via Galileo Ferraris
ANTIGNANO
M. D' ORO
Via Bernini
PIAZZA LEONARDO
VOMERO
MONTESANTO
PIAZZA DANTE
PIAZZA MERCATO
Corso Umberto I
Corso A. Lucci
Via Reggia dei Portici
A3
Stadio Collana
PIAZZA DEGLI ARTISTI
Via della Pigna
Via dell'Epomeo
VANVITELLI
PIAZZA VANVITELLI
Via Toledo
PIAZZA MATEOTTI
Via Nuova
PIAZZA DEL CARMINE
Via Scarlatti
Chiaia Funicular
Castelo Sant'Elmo
Certosa di San Marino
PIAZZA MUNICIPIO
Via C. Colombo
Villa Floridiana
AMEDEO
Corso Vittorio Emanuele
Galleria Umberto I
Castelnuovo o Maschio Angioino
TO HERCULANEUM (10KM), POMPEII (18KM), SALERNO (60KM), REGGIO DI CALABRIA (475KM)
Via Traiano
Via Giustiniano
Via Nuova Cinthia
PIAZZA AMEDEO
V. dei Mille
PIAZZA PLEBISCITO
Palazzo Reale
CENTRAL NAPLES
Tangenziale Ovesi di Napoli
Corso Vittorio Emanuele
Via Martucci
MERGELLINA
FUORIGROTTA
PIAZZA DELLA REPUBBLICA
Riviera di Chiaia
Aquarium
PIAZZA VITTORIA
Via N. Sauro
Via Partenope
SANTA LUCIA
TO SICILY, MALTA, SARDEGNA, TUNISIA
Via Terracina
Via Giacomo Leopardi
Stadio S. Paolo
Virgil's Tomb
Galleria 4 Giornate
Via F. Galleria di Posillipo
PIAZZA SANNAZZARO
Castel dell' Ovo
TO SORRENTO
TO POZZUOLI, CAMPI FLEGREI
PIAZZALE VINCENZO TECCHIO
Viale Augusto
PIAZZA ITALIA
Via Giulio Cesare
CAMPI FLEGREI
LEOPARDI
POSILLIPO
MERGELLINA
TO ISCHIA, PROCIDA
Bay of Naples
TO CAPRI
0
800 meters
800 yards
Viale J. F. Kennedy
Via Diocleziano
Via Manzoni
Via Petrarca
Via Posillipo
TO CAPO POSILLIPO (2KM)
TO ISCHIA, CAPRI
TO SORRENTO
TO ISOLE EDIE
N
LG

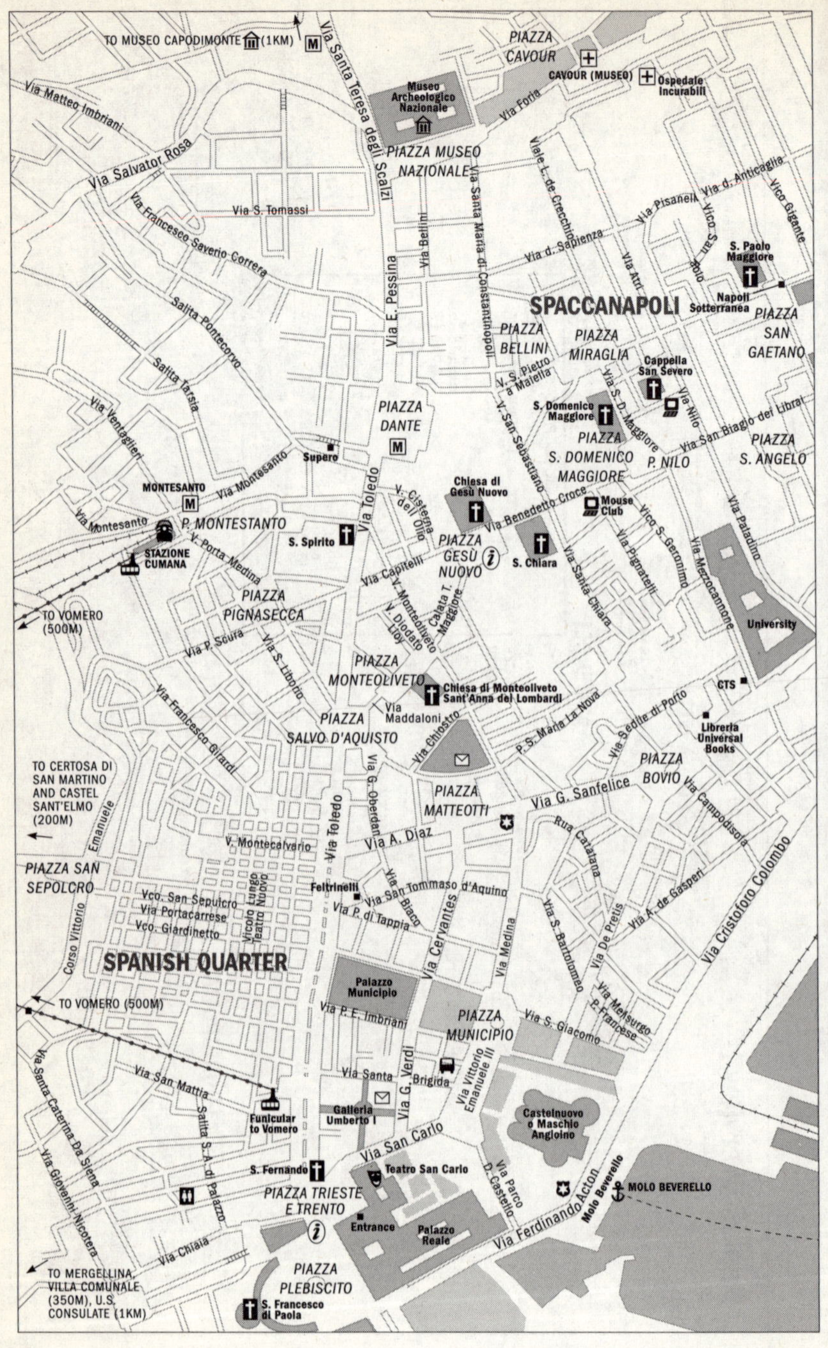
TO MUSEO CAPODIMONTE (1KM)
Via Santa Teresa degli Scalzi
PIAZZA CAVOUR
CAVOUR (MUSEO)
Ospedale Incurabili
Museo Archeologico Nazionale
Via Foria
Via Matteo Imbriani
PIAZZA MUSEO NAZIONALE
Via Salvator Rosa
Via Santa Maria di Constantinopoli
Viale L. de Crecchio
Via d. Anticaglia
Vico Gigante
Via Pisanelli
Vico San Paolo
Via S. Tomassi
Via Francesco Saverio Correra
Via Bellini
Via d. Sapienza
Via Atri
S. Paolo Maggiore
Via E. Pessina
Salita Pontecorvo
Napoli Sotterranea
SPACCANAPOLI
PIAZZA SAN GAETANO
PIAZZA BELLINI
PIAZZA MIRAGLIA
Cappella San Severo
V. S. Pietro a Maiella
Salita Tarsia
Via Ventaglieri
PIAZZA DANTE
S. Domenico Maggiore
Via Nilo
Via S. D. Maggiore
V. San Sebastiano
Via San Biagio dei Librai
PIAZZA S. DOMENICO MAGGIORE
P. NILO
PIAZZA S. ANGELO
Supero
Via Montesanto
MONTESANTO
Via Toledo
V. Cisterna dell'Olio
Chiesa di Gesù Nuovo
Mouse Club
Via Benedetto Croce
Vico S. Geronimo
Via Paladino
Via Montesanto
P. MONTESTANTO
S. Spirito
PIAZZA GESÙ NUOVO
S. Chiara
Via Pignatelli
Via Mezzocannone
STAZIONE CUMANA
V. Porta Medina
Via Capitelli
Via Santa Chiara
TO VOMERO (500M)
PIAZZA PIGNASECCA
V. Monteoliveto
V. Diodato Lioy
Calata T. Maggiore
University
Via P. Scura
Via S. Liborio
PIAZZA MONTEOLIVETO
Chiesa di Monteoliveto Sant'Anna dei Lombardi
CTS
Via Francesco Girardi
Via Maddaloni
Via Chiostro
PIAZZA SALVO D'AQUISTO
P. S. Maria La Nova
Via Sedile di Porto
Libreria Universal Books
TO CERTOSA DI SAN MARTINO AND CASTEL SANT'ELMO (200M)
Via G. Oberdan
PIAZZA MATTEOTTI
Via G. Sanfelice
PIAZZA BOVIO
Via Campodisola
Emanuele
V. Montecalvario
Via A. Diaz
Rua Catalana
Via Cristoforo Colombo
PIAZZA SAN SEPOLCRO
Feltrinelli
Via San Tommaso d'Aquino
Vco. San Sepulcro
Via Portacarrese
Vco. Giardinetto
Vicolo Lungo Teatro Nuovo
Via P. di Tappia
Via Cervantes
Via S. Bartolomeo
Via De Pretis
Via A. de Gasperi
Corso Vittorio
SPANISH QUARTER
Via Medina
Palazzo Municipio
TO VOMERO (500M)
Via P. E. Imbriani
PIAZZA MUNICIPIO
Via S. Giacomo
Via Melisurgo
P. Francese
Via Santa Caterina Da Siena
Via San Mattia
Via Santa Brigida
Via G. Verdi
Via Vittorio Emanuele III
Castelnuovo o Maschio Angioino
Salita S.A. di Palazzo
Funicular to Vomero
Galleria Umberto I
Via San Carlo
Via Giovanni Nicotera
S. Fernando
Teatro San Carlo
Via Parco D. Castello
Molo Beverello
MOLO BEVERELLO
PIAZZA TRIESTE E TRENTO
Via Ferdinando Acton
Entrance
Palazzo Reale
Via Chiaia
PIAZZA PLEBISCITO
TO MERGELLINA, VILLA COMUNALE (350M), U.S. CONSULATE (1KM)
S. Francesco di Paola

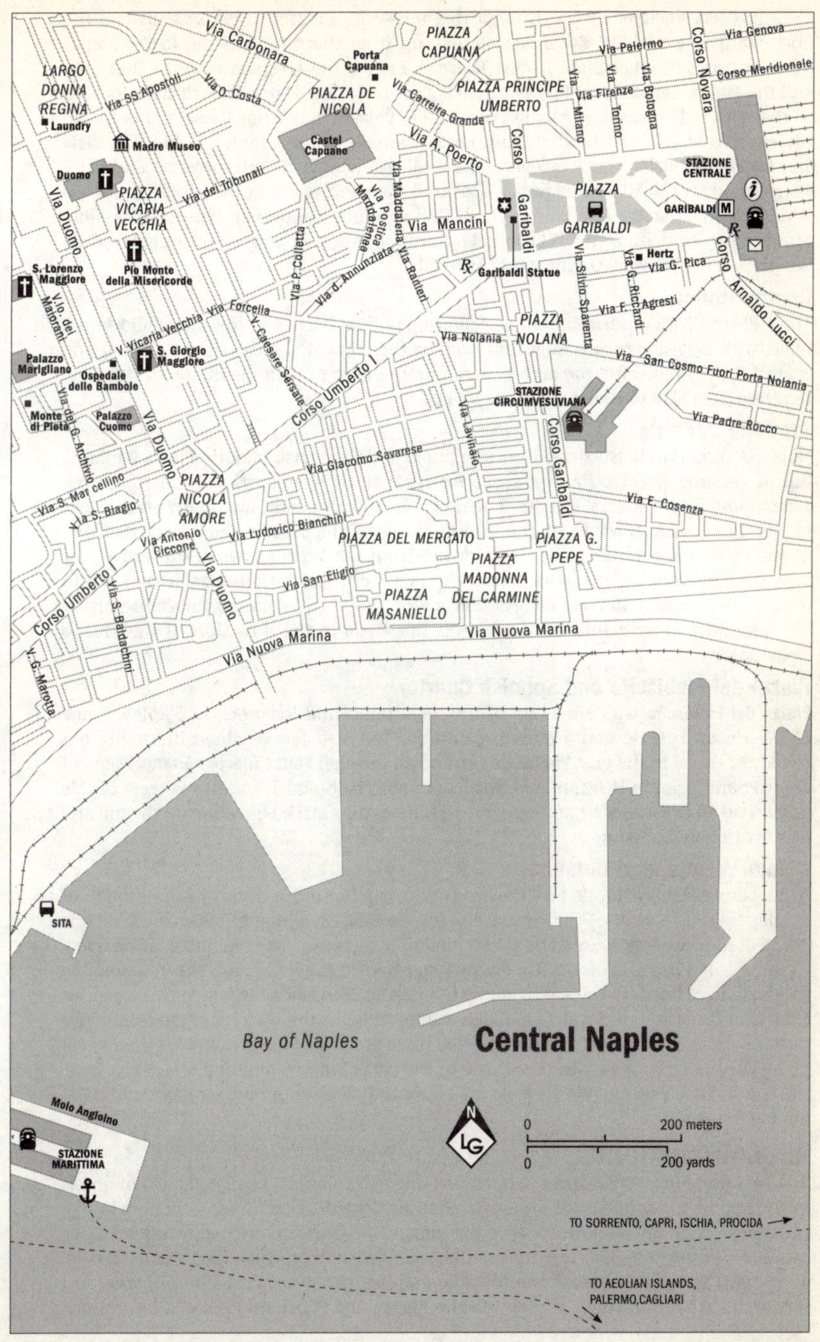

naples . orientation

station, **Corso Umberto I** runs through the university district to **Via Depretis** and the port. **Via Duomo** and **Via Mezzocannone** lead up from there toward the **Centro Storico** (also known as Spaccanapoli). **Via Toledo** connects the western edge of that area and the **Museo Nazionale** to the historical sights, including **Piazza del Plebiscito,** located to the south. The fashionable, shop-lined **Via Chiaia** leads from these sights to the Riviera-like waterfront hidden from many tourists, along which run **Via Caracciolo** and **Riviera di Chiaia.** These streets extend all the way to the picturesque and calm **Mergellina** district. All of this unfolds around the soaring hill at the city's center, on which sits the **Vomero** and where you'll find stunning panoramic views. Accessible primarily by funicular, this hilltop neighborhood is a shopping district centered on the perpendicular **Via Scarlatti** and **Via Bernini.**

Centro Storico

The Centro Storico, also known as Spaccanapoli, is Naples's oldest neighborhood, filled with tiny alleys and beautiful architecture. Located west of the station and east of P. del Plebiscito, the area is much more pleasant than the chaos by Stazione Centrale. It is also paradise for pizza lovers.

Stazione Centrale

Naples's transit hub, Stazione Centrale opens onto the vast, chaotic **Piazza Garibaldi,** full of vendors and traffic that stops for no man or woman. Hotels surround the *piazza* and fill its nearby streets. The neighborhood is seedy, and many streets are, in fact, lined with trash. From the far left corner of the *piazza*, **Corso Umberto I,** one of the city's main boulevards, leads away from the bustle toward the university area and, eventually, the port. From the same corner, **Corso Garibaldi** runs south to the sea, passing **Stazione Circumvesuviana** on the way. From the far right corner, V. Alessandro Poerio follows the line of the **Metro** in the direction of the Museo Nazionale.

Piazza del Plebiscito and Spanish Quarter

Piazza del Plebiscito was once one of the most important locations in Naples, home to the Palazzo Reale and a stunning church. Today, it has declined in vitality but remains central to the city. **Via Toledo** runs north through **Piazza Trieste e Trento,** home of Teatro San Carlo, to P. Dante and Spaccanapoli. The Spanish Quarter is west of this main road and features a number of small but bustling streets heading up the hill and lined with hanging laundry.

Chiaia, Vomero, and Outskirts

Numerous neighborhoods less known to tourists but more beautiful than much of Naples lie to the west of the *centro storico*. **Vomero,** on a high hill above the city, is connected to its lower areas by three funicular railways. The one most often used, Centrale, departs V. Toledo for **Piazza Fuga.** Back near sea level, the fashionable **Chiaia** district borders the seafront, as does quiet **Mergellina** farther to the west. **Via Francesco Caracciolo** and **Riviera di Chiaia** run parallel to the water and surround **Villa Communale,** one of the city's finest parks, palm trees and all. Nearest to the *centro* along the water is Castel dell'Ovo, one of the city's famous monuments. Away from the water, **Via Chiaia** and **Via dei Mille** are sleek and clean shopping streets that bustle all day long.

ACCOMMODATIONS

The first thing most travelers see upon arriving in Naples is a neon junkyard of hotels in the hectic and unpleasant area near **Stazione Centrale.** Don't trust anyone who approaches you in the station—people working on commission are happy to lead naive tourists to unlicensed and overpriced hotels seedier than those you could find on your own. There are several comfortable and inexpensive options in this area; just be careful when returning at night. **Centro Storico** and **Piazza del Plebiscito** have much better-located options, though at noticeably higher prices. Progressing further west, **Vomero, Chiaia,** and **Mergellina** boast numerous hospitable bed and breakfasts in quiet areas that provide excellent views of the city or the sea.

Centro Storico

Accommodations in Naples's historical heart are more convenient and thus pricier, but they'll put travelers just a dough's throw away from the ancient streets that are the pizza capital of the world.

6 SMALL ROOMS — HOSTEL ❶

V. Diodato Lioy 18 ☎081 79 01 378 www.6smallrooms.com

Modesty may be a virtue, but the Australian owners of this beautiful hostel seem to be taking it a bit far with the name of this place. Most of the "small" rooms are huge, with high ceilings and fun, elaborate murals of the city and ancient Roman gods. A tremendous communal kitchen doubles as a breakfast room where guests gather to chat—when they're not in the spacious common room with flatscreen TV, DVD and music collection, and even guitars on which to strum the night away.

Ⓜ1: Dante. Walk down V. Toledo, turn left onto V. Tommaso Senise, and make the 1st right onto V. Diodato Lioy. i Breakfast included. Free lockers. Some rooms with A/C. No bunk beds. Free Wi-Fi. Resident cats and dogs. Ⓢ Dorms €20; singles or small doubles with bath and A/C €25-45; doubles €50-55, with bath €55-65; triples €60-75; quads €80-95. 10% Let's Go discount. Reception 8am-midnight. Keys provided after hours.

NAPLES PIZZA HOSTEL — HOSTEL ❶

V. San Paulo ai Tribunali ☎081 19 32 35 62 www.naplespizzahostel.com

When guests open the door to their room, it's clear this hostel is a step above the rest. Most chambers have loft beds up a set of steps above the other bunks, creating a secret, secluded single within a dorm. One guest apparently enjoyed her stay so much that she painted a mural of—what else?—happy students eating Neapolitan pizza on the orange walls of the common room.

Taking V. Tribunali from the station, turn right onto V. San Paulo ai Tribunali. i Breakfast included. Laundry €5. All-female dorms available. Communal kitchen. Free Wi-Fi. Ⓢ 5-bed dorms €15-18; singles €25-35, with bath €35-40; doubles €35-45/€45-55; triples €49-65/65-70, quads €65-70/71-79. Reception 24hr.

HOTEL NEAPOLIS — HOTEL ❸

V. Francesco del Giudice 13, 3rd fl. ☎081 44 20 815 www.hotelneapolis.com

It's easy to stay connected at this luxurious budget hotel, which not only takes reservations via Skype but has computers with free internet in every room, from the smallest single to the superior doubles. Even with a large computer desk, the 24 rooms are spacious and have fine draperies and bedding.

Ⓜ1: Dante. From P. Dante, head through Porta Alba down V. dei Tribunali and turn left onto V. Francesco del Giudice. Enter the courtyard and take the elevator. i Breakfast included. Skype name: Hotel Neapolis Ricivimento. Ⓢ Singles €35-50; doubles €60-90.

ALLOGIO MIRAGLIA — PENSIONE ❷

P. Luigi Miraglia 386 ☎081 45 53 82 www.bedandbreakfastmiraglianapoli.it

This bed and breakfast takes travelers on a quick trip to paradise—if the palm-lined desert-island bedspread counts. There's no real sandy beach, but a few comfortable rooms and a breakfast served in bed or the small dining room help whisk away lingering memories of the hectic Naples below.

Take V. dei Tribunali to P. Miraglia. i 1 double has toilet inside, all others outside; all showers outside rooms. Ⓢ Singles €25; doubles €40; triples €60; quads €75.

Stazione Centrale

The area around P. Garibaldi is littered with cheap hotels, their bright signs glaring enough to fill a Las Vegas junkyard, so you're virtually assured that rooms will be available. Just exercise caution when returning after dark.

HOTEL GINEVRA HOTEL ❷

V. Genova 116 ☎081 28 32 10 www.hotelginevra.it

Exiting Naples's train station is always an adventure, but few expect a full-blown safari. Get ready for it as you walk into this hotel and encounter the jovial staff behind the desk—or is that a tiki bar? This is no joke (well, maybe it is a *little* tongue-in-cheek kitschy): the "ethnic" rooms come with elephant carvings on the door, bamboo on the walls, and vines on the ceiling—not to mention a flatscreen TV. Superior rooms have more amenities, including minibars and A/C. Some have murals of the Amalfi Coast.

Take the 1st right out of the station onto C. Novara, then the next right onto V. Genova. Singles €25-35, with bath €35-45; doubles €35-50, "ethnic doubles" €40-65, superior €45-70; triples €45-65, with bath €50-75. 10% Let's Go discount.

HOSTEL PENSIONE MANCINI HOSTEL, PENSIONE ❶

V. P.S. Mancini 33 ☎081 55 36 731 www.hostelpensionemancini.com

The helpful owners make this hostel, located in a distinctly average building, stand out. Bedrooms are comfortable, some with balconies. But the overwhelming hospitality of an owner who organizes outings for and shares extensive knowledge of the city with his guests makes it stand out.

Directly across P. Garibaldi from the station. i Breakfast included. Free luggage storage and lockers. Free Wi-Fi. Dorms €13-16; singles €25-30, with bath €40-45; doubles €35-45/40-50; triples €54-66/60-70; quads €60-68/70-80. 10% Let's Go discount. Reception 24hr.

HOTEL ZARA HOTEL ❷

V. Firenze 81 ☎081 28 71 25 www.hotelzara.it

Comfy common areas with deep couches, large TV, and a fish tank make socializing easy, while the simple rooms make for a good night's sleep.

Walk down the right side of P. Garibaldi from the station and turn onto V. Milano, then right onto V. Firenze. Singles €25-35; doubles €30, with bath €35; triples €50/60.

Piazza del Plebiscito and Spanish Quarter

Find hostel central in the clean area near the port just a few minutes walk from P. del Plebiscito. Other accommodations, from luxury hotels to petite B and Bs, await discovery on the surrounding steep streets.

HOSTEL OF THE SUN HOSTEL ❶

V. Melisurgo 15, 7th fl. ☎081 42 06 393 www.hostelnapoli.com

This hostel is quite simply the most fun place you can stay in Naples. The exuberant—somehow even that strong word seems too weak—staff begins everyone's stay with an in-depth and amusing introduction to the city and a collection of free maps to stuff in pockets. They keep it going by hosting several outings weekly, occasionally cooking for guests, and relaxing with them in the colorful and comfortable common room which features a flatscreen TV, DVDs, computers, and Nintendo Wii. (The owner has been known to challenge guests; those who beat him get a free stay, though he claims an undefeated record.)

Take the R2 bus from C. Umberto I near the station, get off at the 2nd stop on V. Depretis. i Breakfast included. Private rooms with ensuite A/C. Free lockers. Free internet and Wi-Fi. 5- to 7-bed dorms €16-20; doubles €55-60, with bath €60-70; triples €75-80/€70-90; quads €80-90/€85-100. 10% Let's Go discount. Reception 24hr.

HOTEL AND HOSTEL BELLA CAPRI HOSTEL ❶

V. Meilsurgo 4, 6th fl. ☎081 55 29 494 www.bellacapri.it

The ground-floor hotel for people over 30 here is kept well-hidden from the groups of students who occupy the upper floor. Every night is a social occasion, with guests cooking in the communal kitchen, chatting, and gathering for near-nightly outings to bars in the *centro*. Satellite TV and three computers beckon to keep them in, but the excitement of Naples outside of the port area usually succeeds in drawing students from their rooms and to the streets.

R2 bus from C. Umberto I near the station to the 2nd stop on V. Depretis. After hours, ring bell. i Lockers with €5 deposit. All-female dorms available. Free internet and Wi-Fi. Dorms €15-21; singles €40-50, with bath €50-70; doubles €50-60/€60-80; triples €70-80/€80-100; quads €80-90/€90-110. 10% Let's Go discount. Wash and dry €7. Reception 24hr.

I FIORI DI NAPOLI

B AND B ❸

V. Francesco Girardi 92, 3rd fl. ☎081 19 57 70 83 www.ifioridinapoli.it

This inn is a mighty fine place for travelers who don't mind being surrounded by vines. Flower murals decorate the walls, and the real things grow in the hallways and on the sunny rooftop terrace. The seven rooms are named after various species of flora and appointed brightly to match. Two dining-and-sitting rooms, a communal kitchen, plus the local knowledge of a kind owner makes this B and B a great value.

From V. Toledo, take V. Montecavalo and turn right onto V. Francesco Girardi. The B and B is on the left, with no sign. Ring bell and take stair A to 3rd fl. i Some rooms with ensuite A/C. Internet available on 1 computer in breakfast room. Doubles used as singles €35, with bath €40; doubles €60/€70.

HOTEL TOLEDO

HOTEL ❹

V. Montecalvario 15 ☎081 40 68 00 www.hoteltoledo.com

The peaceful rooftop terrace is just one highlight of this Spanish Quarter property's common areas. They also include a large bar with throne-like dining chairs and couches that guests sink into while enjoying a nightcap.

From P. Dante, walk down V. Toledo and turn right onto V. Montecalvario. i Breakfast included. Free Wi-Fi and internet point in bar. Singles €50-65; doubles €70-100; suites €100-120. Reception 24hr.

Chiaia, Vomero, and Outskirts

Farther from the city center, the neighborhoods get nicer and the rooms pricier. Seek out smaller B and Bs for the best rates and most personal service.

CAPPELLA VECCHIA 11

B AND B ❹

Vicolo Santa Maria a Cappella Vecchia 11, 1st fl. ☎081 24 05 117 www.cappellavecchia11.it

Meeting other travelers has never been easier than at the communal breakfast table of this well kept B and B. The common room has comfortable couches and a public computer, while bedrooms with comfortable beds and large bathrooms come in a pleasantly shocking purple-and-green color combo.

From V. Santa Caterina just before P. dei Martiri, turn onto the small alleyway of Vicolo Santa Maria a Cappella Vecchia. Take the stairs to the right. i Breakfast included. Free Wi-Fi. Singles €50-70; doubles €80-110.

OSTELLO MERGELLINA (HI)

HOSTEL ❶

V. Salita della Grotta 23 ☎081 76 12 346 www.ostellonapoli.com

Far from the bustle that makes Naples what it is, this hostel is a little out of the way. Nonetheless, the sun shines brightly and the turquoise water beckons just steps away in the quiet Mergellina neighborhood, where the hostel provides small bedrooms and a comfortable but spare lobby with flatscreen TV.

Ⓜ Mergellina. Make 2 sharp rights onto V. Piedigrotta, then a right onto V. Salita della Grotta. Turn right onto driveway after overpass. i Breakfast included. Wi-Fi available in lobby. Dorms from €15; singles from €25; doubles from €40. Reception 24hr.

HOTEL CIMAROSA HOTEL ❹

V. Cimarosa 29 ☎081 55 67 044 www.hotelcimarosa.it

Up the steps of this hotel, ascend into the Space Age. There's a wavy, blue ceiling light that casts the entire hall in an eerily hip light, not to mention the illuminated sculptures that fill wall nooks. Who doesn't need that extra artsy touch? Inside, 19 spacious rooms feature floor-to-ceiling windows—eight of which have views of the bay—plasma TVs, and large showers.

From the funicular in P. Fuga, turn right onto V. Cimarosa. Singles €60-70; doubles €90-110.

SIGHTS

Been there, done that. So the Greeks, Romans, and Spanish have each said about the city of Naples, and each of their conquests has left a unique mark on this remarkably historical metropolis. Home to a world-renowned antiquarian museum and an ancient underground system that remains a remarkable feat of engineering, Naples has got the really-old thing covered. Meanwhile, the **Palazzo Reale** gives an uncensored glimpse into the life of an 18th-century royal and a reminder of the steps the city has taken into the modern age.

Centro Storico

Part wide boulevards with ornate architecture, part Roman alleys, Naples's Centro Storico has a history that is palpable. Churches hold exquisite art, while museums offer a glimpse into the city's Roman and Greek past. Many churches with free admission provide small historical tidbits as well. Note that modest dress is required for all churches.

NAPOLI SOTTERANEA (UNDERGROUND NAPLES) ANCIENT ROME

P. San Gaetano 68 ☎081 29 69 44 www.napolisotterranea.org

Get down and dirty 35m below the city exploring ancient Greek aqueducts, WWII bomb shelters, and more. Before moving underground, the fascinating guided tours begin with a visit to an ancient Roman theater now built into apartment houses. **Emperor Nero,** noted psycho but not a recognized virtuoso, twice performed here, insisting to an audience that the earthquake they felt as he sung was merely applause of the gods. Beneath the historical center, Mussolini-era graffiti remain as signs of the 3000 Neapolitans who made the tunnels their home for three years during the Allied bombardment of the city. Visitors wander through passageways, grottoes, and catacombs, and while most of the tunnels are cavernous and well lit, the last part of the tour has patrons shimmying through a tiny tunnel in the rock with only candles illuminating the way.

Take V. Tribunali and the entrance is to the left of San Paolo Maggiore church. i Tours offered in English. €9.30, students €8. 10% Campania Artecard discount. 90min. tours depart every 2hr. M-F noon-4pm, Sa-Su 10am-6pm.

MUSEO ARCHEOLOGICO NAZIONALE MUSEUM, ANCIENT ROME

P. Museo Nazionale 19 ☎081 29 28 23

museoarcheologiconazionale.campaniabeniculturali.it

Even if the prospect of more archaeological specimens has no appeal for you, you've got to be intrigued by the more salacious stuff on display at this museum. It's home to the ever-popular **Gabinetto Segreto** ("Secret Cabinet"), a trove of sexual artifacts recovered from the ash-entombed archaeological site at Pompeii. Of course, the entire museum is not pornographic—heck, some of it's even good for kids—as it contains the most significant collection of artifacts from the nearby towns that were destroyed by Vesuvius's famed eruption. One of Europe's oldest and best-regarded museums, the Museo Nazionale is expansive, and an audio tour or guidebook is worth the price.

Check out the **Farnese Bull,** one of the largest surviving statues from antiquity. It's sculpted from a single slab of marble that was reworked by Michelangelo. The mezzanine level contains exquisite mosaics from Pompeii, notably the **Alexander Mosaic,** with a young and fearless Alex the Great routing the Persian army.

Ⓜ Cavour. Turn right from the station and walk 2 blocks. Ⓢ €10, EU citizens ages 18-24 €5, under 18 and over 65 free. Open M 9am-7:30pm, W-Su 9am-7:30pm.

CAPPELLA SAN SEVERO CHURCH, MUSEUM

V. de Sanctis 19 ☎081 55 18 470 www.museosansevero.it

Here's one fewer church in a city full of them—this 1590 chapel has been converted to a private museum. Several remarkable 18th-century statues, of which Giuseppe Sanmartino's **Veiled Christ** is by far the best known, fill the corridors.

To the right when walking away from P. San Domenico Maggiore on the street of the same name. Ⓢ €6, ages 10-25 €4, with Artecard €5. Open M 10am-5:40pm, W-Sa 10am-5:40pm, Su 10am-1:10pm.

COMPLESSO MONUMENTALE DI SAN LORENZO MAGGIORE ANCIENT ROME

V. dei Tribunali 316 ☎081 37 23 720 www.sanlorenzomaggiorenapoli.it

Now why would those silly Romans put a market underground? In short, they didn't, but the built-up city around their old stomping ground has left an ancient bazaar—with shops, a bakery, and tavern—beneath Naples's streets. It's on display here, along with the delicately frescoed cloister and relatively barren nave of the church under which the market was found.

As you come from P. Dante on V. Tribunali, the entrance is on the right across from Napoli Sotteranea. Ⓢ €9, students €7. Open M-Sa 9:30am-5:30pm, Su 9:30am-1:30pm.

Stazione Centrale

The hubbub that engulfs Stazione Centrale is a sight in itself. Beyond that, you'll have to head toward the *centro storico* for more to see.

PIO MONTE DELLA MISERICORDIA MUSEUM

V. Tribunali 253 ☎081 44 69 44 www.piomontedellamisericordia.it

Life on the run was good to Caravaggio, or so it appears. After killing a man in a 1606 duel, the master became a fugitive from justice and fled to Naples, where he was commissioned to paint one of his masterpieces, **The Seven Works of Mercy,** for this small chapel. That painting is the centerpiece of a round nave surrounded by works of art. More hang above, in the former offices of the centuries-old charitable organization that commissioned the chapel. Works by **Mattia Preti** and **Francesco de Mura** fill several rooms, while a balcony in one office offers a superb view of Caravaggio's work from above.

On V. Tribunali, before V. Duomo when coming from the station. Ⓢ €5, students €4. Open M-Tu 9am-2pm, Th-Su 9am-2pm.

PIAZZA GARIBALDI ♿ PIAZZA

P. Garibaldi

Don't worry about missing this *piazza*—it truly is a sight to behold, if not the prettiest picture to put on a postcard. P. Garibaldi is to Naples as Naples is to Italy: its most incomprehensibly chaotic outpost. Street vendors stake out their sidewalk claims like 1849 California miners, only here the Gold Rush comes from tourists' pockets in exchange for cheap sunglasses and knockoff bags. A spider web of roads and Neopolitan drivers who won't stop add to the disorder. Unlike the streets in much of Naples, the ones here really are lined with trash. At the end of the *piazza* farthest from the trains, **Garibaldi** himself watches over the scene.

Outside Stazione Centrale and at the end of C. Umberto.

DUOMO ♿ CHURCH

V. Duomo 149 ☎081 44 90 97

Hearing about hidden beauty gets old in Naples—why can't some of the good stuff be out in the open on the city's streets? Yet in the city's cathedral, here it is again: an ornate 13th-century interior behind a 19th-century facade. The church has been altered many times over the centuries, but the Baroque paintings and gold metal fittings of its **Cappella del Tesoro di San Gennaro** remain the main attraction. Two containers of congealed blood from the saint for whom the chapel is named (in English, St. Januarius, a former bishop of Naples) sit in the requilary. Keep your eyes on those vials: according to legend, if they do not liquefy on the day of the **Festa di San Gennaro,** it's time to start running, as disaster is about to strike the city. (Not scared? Go visit Pompeii.)

From Stazione Centrale, take C. Umberto I to V. Duomo and turn right. Church free. Archaeological site €1.50. Museum €6, students €4.50. Church open M-F 8:30am-noon, Sa-Su 8:30am-1pm and 5-7pm. Excavations open M-F 9am-12:30pm and 4:30-7pm, Sa-Su 9am-1pm. Last entry 30min. before close. Museum open M by group reservation, Tu-Su 9:30am-5pm.

Piazza del Plebiscito and Spanish Quarter

PALAZZO REALE — MUSEUM

P. del Plebiscito 1 — ☎081 40 05 47

King in the castle! Err, *palazzo*, that is. Whatever the name, visitors can play royalty for a day wandering through the magnificent halls of this sprawling structure, once the seat of Bourbon kings and Spanish viceroys in Naples. Wander through artwork-filled rooms and see—but don't dare sit in—the velvet-draped golden throne of former kings, whose exploits are recounted in the aptly but not succinctly named fresco, *The Splendor of the House of Spain and Some Episodes in the Life of Ferrante of Aragon*, on the ceiling in a subsequent room. The palace is also an intellectual Mecca, as it contains the 1,500,000 volume **Biblioteca Nazionale,** which holds carbonized scrolls from the Villa dei Papiri in Herculaneum. As if this *palazzo* wasn't packed with enough stuff already, the **Teatro di San Carlo,** Europe's oldest continuously active theater, calls the place home as well. Its acoustics are reputedly better than those of Milan's **La Scala.**

In P. del Plebiscito, across from the basilica. €4, students €2. Audio tour €2.50, though we advise against it since, in all rooms, you'll find informative signs in English. Open M-Tu 9am-8pm, Th-Su 9am-8pm. Last entry 1hr. before close.

CASTELLO NUOVO O MASCHIO ANGIONO — MUSEUM

V. Vittorio Emmanuelle II at P. Municio — ☎081 42 01 241

When **Charles of Anjou** needed a castle in 1279, beachfront property was cheap, so he took up a lot of it and had this large castle constructed. Today, it's still an integral part of the city's skyline. The castle once had seven towers, but **Alfonse of Aragon** (he called himself the Magnanimous—no big deal) did some remodeling, leaving the building with the five turrets it sports today. He also added the most impressive part of the structure, an intricately carved, arched entrance inspired by Roman architecture. Inside, the castle's exhibitions are limited, though you'll find a decent collection of medieval art and royal artifacts on the first floor. Don't miss the bronze doors that once guarded the castle. They survived destruction during a successful Genoese siege of the city but were scarred by a cannonball when the Genoese hauled them back home as booty. **Baron's Hall,** up steps to the left of the courtyard, is a former meeting place with a stunning dome, while the splendid **Cappella Palatina** provides a cool retreat from the sun-baked courtyard.

Take the R2 bus from P. Garibaldi or walk from V. Toledo or the centro storico. €5. Open M-Sa 9am-7pm.

BASILICA DI SAN FRANCESCO DI PAOLO — CHURCH

P. del Plebiscito 10 — ☎081 76 45 133

Designed to mimic the Pantheon in Rome, this towering domed church is no copycat. Its interior is soaring—54m high and 34m in diameter—and bright like its Roman counterpart, but the basilica is not exactly like its pagan counterpart, as it features carved statues of saints surrounding the nave (though we could get into an interesting conversation about Catholicism's use of sainthood as a way to appeal to pagan polytheism here if we really wanted to get deep). The building dominates P. del Plebiscito.

The building with the large dome. i Modest dress required. Free. Open M-Sa 8am-noon and 3:30-7pm, Su 8:30am-1pm and 4-7pm.

Chiaia, Vomero, and Outskirts

CASTEL SANT'ELMO — CASTLE, MUSEUM

V. Tito Angelini 20 ☎081 22 94 401 www.polomusealenapoli.beniculturali.it

Stop, gulp in some air, and step up to the wall and gaze out. You'll need that oxygen, because this view—standing eye level with airplanes—truly takes the breath away. Sweeping from the hills, across the *centro storico* and port to Chiaia and Mergellina along the turquoise water, the vista is amazing. Then, in the distance, there are Vesuvius and Capri, ferries leaving foamy white streaks between them. Once a defensive outpost, the ramparts of P. d'Armi atop this castle are one of Naples's loveliest places. They're also now part of a creative art installation by **Giancarlo Neri** which uses lighting to artificially "compete" with the moon in certain parts of the city. **Napoli Novecento,** an extensive modern art museum featuring canvases and sculpture from the last century of Neapolitan modern art, can be found in the old fortress as well.

In Vomero. From the funicular at P. Fuga, turn right up the steps and follow the signs along V. Morghen to the castle. The ticket office is to the right in the gate. €5, EU students ages 18-25 €2.50. Open M 8:30am-7:30pm, W-Su 8:30am-7:30pm. Guided tours of the museum offered hourly 9am-6pm.

MUSEO NAZIONALE DI CAPODIMONTE — MUSEUM

V. Miano 2 ☎081 74 99 111 www.museo-capodimonte.it

Here is a true rarity among museums, especially in Italy: a collection that features classical works alongside contemporary art. Though it's famous for its **Farnese Collection,** once owned by a family of the same name, the museum has much more going for it than that. Formerly a royal palace, the *museo* boasts many rooms that are precious artifacts in themselves, though unlike 2D paintings, these works of art can hold visitors inside them. In the second floor's Neapolitan collection, works by **Caravaggio** and numerous 19th-century masters from the city are on display.

In the north of the city. ⓂCavour, then bus C63 or R4. €7.50, EU students ages 18-25 €3.75. Open M-Tu 8:30am-7:30pm, Th-Su 8:30am-7:30pm.

CASTEL DELL'OVO (EGG CASTLE) — CASTLE

Borgo Marinari ☎081 24 00 055

All that fuss over an egg? Yes indeed, throughout the city's history one measly egg has caused a string of panics. According to legend, the enchanted egg in question was placed in this castle's foundation by **Virgil.** If its fragile shell were to break, the city of Naples would crumble. After the yellow-brick castle sustained significant damage when one of its arches collapsed, none other than the queen herself had to reassure the public that the egg was safe. Originally a monastery, the castle was later converted to be used for defensive purposes but is now mostly used for its beautiful views, especially at sunset.

In Chiaia. Walk down V. Santa Lucia from south of P. del Plebiscito. Free. Open M-Sa 8:30am-7pm, Su 8:30am-2pm.

SPAGGIA ROTONDA DIAZ BEACH

V. Francesco Caracciolo

Capri and Ischia, Sorrento and Amalfi—they're all so far away. Spaggia Rotonda is right here in the heart of Naples, and it's a Neapolitan **beach** at its finest. This is the perfect spot for working on the southern Italian tan you see on everyone around you.

Walk down V. Caracciolo along the waterfront from Mergellina or Chiaia. Free. Open daily sunrise to sunset.

FOOD

When in Rome, do as the Romans do. When in Naples, eat **pizza.** If you ever doubted that Neapolitans invented the crusty, cheese-covered pie, the city's pizzerias will take that doubt, beat it into a ball, throw it in the air, spin it on their collective finger, punch it down, cover it with sauce and mozzarella, and serve it *alla margherita.* Centro Storico is full of excellent choices, especially along **Via Tribunali,** the pizza corridor of the world.

Centro Storico

GINO SORBILLO PIZZERIA ❶

V. dei Tribunali 35 ☎081 44 66 43 www.sorbillo.eu

Making pizza and children since 1935, Gino Sorbillo has created a dynasty: a family of 21 pizza-making children, several of whom own their own shops nearby. His eponymous shop also gave birth to the *ripieno al forno* (literally "fried in the oven"), a.k.a. the calzone. Twenty-one scrumptious specialty pizzas bear the names of the family's numerous offspring.

Between V. Arti and Vico San Paolo. Pizza €3-8. Service 10%. Open Sept-July M-Sa noon-3:30pm and 7-11:30pm.

PIZZERIA DI MATTEO PIZZERIA ❶

V. dei Tribunali 94 ☎081 45 52 62 www.pizzeriadimatteo.it

This place has its priorities straight: while diners at Pizzeria Di Matteo have to take the stairs, the pizza rides to the dining room in an elevator. The Neapolitans that fill the tables aren't bothered by the unhurried service, and tourists who are shouldn't be. If they could just imagine the fluffy dough of Matteo's standout marinara pie melting in their mouths, they'd be more than happy to wait for it.

On V. dei Tribunali near V. Duomo. The only door seems to lead into the kitchen, but this is indeed the entrance. Pizza €2.50-6. Open M-Sa 9am-midnight.

ANTICA TRATTORIA DEL CARMINE RISTORANTE, SEAFOOD ❸

V. dei Tibunali 330 ☎081 29 43 83

Recommended by locals as a great date spot or stop for some quality fish or pasta, this trattoria with a multi-level dining room under brick arches retains the rustic, ancient charm of Naples's historic center. Try the linguine with seafood *(€13)* or go for a simpler pasta or fish from the extensive menu.

Directly across from Napoli Sotteranea. Primi €4-13; secondi €7-10. Fish €7.50-13. Open Tu noon-4pm, W-Su noon-4pm and 7-11pm.

SORRISO INTEGRALE VEGETARIAN ❷

Vico S. Pietro a Maiella 6 ☎081 45 50 26 www.sorriosointegrale.com

Naples making you feel like you're becoming round and sprouting tomato sauce and mozzarella? At some point, take a break from pizza and pasta to try this small, hidden organic and vegan restaurant with a constantly changing menu

Near P. Miraglia, on the small connecting street between Vico S. Pietro a Maiella and P. Bellini. Inside the gate on the right when heading to P. Bellini. Cover €2. Primi €4.50; secondi €5.50-7.50. Open daily noon-4pm and 7-11pm.

FANTASIA GELATI GELATERIA ❶

V. Toledo 381 ☎081 55 11 212 www.fantasiagelati.it

The podium for this proud gelato gold medalist is the place it's always been: the streets of Naples. There's no need for a flashier showcase, as Fantasia earns admirers enough among the locals and visitors who wander in off the street to sample fruit flavors made from real juices. There are also many creatively titled scoops like Cuore Nero ("Black Heart"), a deep, dark chocolate.

ⓂDante. On V. Toledo south of P. Dante. i Other locations at P. Vitelli 22, V. Gilea 80, Largo Lala 30, and V. Fragnito 39. Ⓢ Cones €1.50-5, gluten-free €2. Open in summer daily 7am-1am; in fall, winter, and spring Tu-Su 7am-11pm.

"everywhere else"

This was how my itinerary was described when I took the job of researching in Italy for *Let's Go.* Others had research routes that focused on a single city (Rome, Venice, Florence) and its environs. I went to the "other" places, bouncing around the country's north before landing in very southern Naples. What has become abundantly clear to me over the past eight weeks is that "everywhere else" is, in fact, somewhere after all. Destination by destination, here's what I learned:

Milan is more than a financial capital. It's a sprawling metropolis with hopping nightlife, gourmet restaurants (some at less than gourmet prices), and collections of exquisite art.

Turin, a city I knew nothing about, has a modern history to rival Rome's ancient one. It's home to opulent Savoy palaces and domed basilicas perched on verdant green hills. It seems that nothing more than a river separates this cosmopolitan city from the rugged beauty of the Alpine foothills.

Cinque Terre is touristed, but even its tiny, jewel-like towns that sit perched on rocks contain more than turquoise water and beaches. Intimate restaurants set in the hills above town and rocky trails offering stunning vistas make these villages so much more than your average seaside resort.

Bologna is a student paradise—100,000 of them call the city home, eating high-quality, cheap grub, then partying until 4am in medieval piazze and waking up in time for class the next day.

And Naples is not really full of trash. Much of it is beautiful and better explored over the course of a few days before you run off to the islands and coastline nearby.

Of course, as soon as I finish my route I'll be off to spend some time in the "Big Three" Italian cities, taking the train up to Rome, Venice, and Florence. But that doesn't mean the best of Italy is yet to come. I'm pretty sure I've found that already.

—William White

LEOPOLDO BAKERY ❶

V. Toledo 8 ☎081 55 12 909 www.leopoldo.it

This tiny shop fills little blue boxes with kilos of Neapolitans, all tied up with their signature yellow ribbon. The packaging is a nice touch, but it's hard to imagine the individual who doesn't promptly tear off that ribbon and devour the box's contents soon after arriving home. If you count yourself guilty of such self-indulgence, you're not to be blamed, for from Leopoldo's simple cannoli to its cartoonish frosted animal cakes, everything here is irresistibly sugary and oh-so-delicious.

Ⓜ Dante. South of P. Dante. ⓢ Pastries from €0.50. Open daily 10am-7pm.

Stazione Centrale

As many takeout places and cafes line **Piazza Garibaldi** as do street vendors. Most food here is grab-and-go for travelers on the move, though there are a few sit-down spots for visitors with more time before the train arrives.

ANTICA PIZZA DA MICHELE PIZZERIA ❶

V. Cesare Sersale 1/3 ☎081 55 39 204 www.damichele.net

All the people here must know something. They take numbers from the chef inside, then wait around in the hot midday sun, sometimes for 1hr. What they're waiting for has been called, by some, the best pizza in the world. The options may be limited to margherita and marinara *(€4.50)*, with the option of double cheese *(€5.50)*, but once a pie is in front of you, you know it's the real deal. Thin, crispy, and just right, the pizzas emerge from the oven at the back and, needless to say, their stays on the plates are short-lived.

Walk down C. Umberto I and turn right. i Takeout available. ⓢ Sodas €1.50. Open M-Sa 10am-11pm.

MIMI ALLA FERROVIA SEAFOOD ❸

V. Alfonso d'Aragona 19/21 ☎081 55 38 525 www.mimiallaferrovia.it

Many of the diners here may arrive by train, but the seafood comes by **boat,** fresh from the bay. Chefs waste no time cooking the salty harvest in delicious shellfish dishes and *secondi* plates to serve here at Mimi alla Ferrovia, one of the few full-service restaurants near Stazione Centrale. Served by black-tied waiters in an elegant dining room, the professionals and tourists who dine here must find it a refreshing retreat from the summer heat.

Across the piazza from the station, take V. Poerio and turn right onto V. Alfonso d'Aragona. ⓢ Primi €7-10. Meat and fish dishes €8-13. Service 15%. Open M-Sa noon-3pm and 7-10:30pm.

RISTORANTE BERGANTINO RISTORANTE ❷

V. Milano 16 ☎081 55 38 996

Pass through these doors and the inevitable end is coming—for the rather vulnerable-looking fish in this restaurant's big tank, that is. Though, truthfully, those sea creatures will likely see Bergantino's doorway once more when they're sitting in the stomach of one of the restaurant's satisfied patrons. Even those who don't speak Italian will find the friendly banter and laughter of the servers here entertaining, though the low din resonating throughout the dining room might remind you of your high school's cafeteria.

From the station, walk along the right side of the piazza and turn right. ⓢ Cover €1.50 plus 12% for service. Pizza €3.50-12. Pastas €5-8. Open M-Sa 11:30am-4pm and 6-10:30pm.

Piazza del Plebiscito and Spanish Quarter

The area has its share of touristy cafes, mostly on **Via Toledo.** Step into the Spanish Quarter's alleys for something more authentic—and for an alternative to pizza, too.

HOSTERIA TOLEDO RISTORANTE ❷

Vicolo Giardinetto 78/A ☎081 42 12 57 www.hosteriatoledo.it

If you doubt that this place has its fair share of happy customers, step inside Hosteria Toledo, which calls itself a landmark, and allay your suspicions. Postcards from admirers dangle from the ceiling and taped-up photographs of happy eaters line the walls. Specializing in pasta and seafood, this homey spot has axed pizza from its menu in a dramatic, anti-establishment move largely unheard of in the Neapolitan culinary scene. Those who are flustered by this shocking development can try the chef's surprise—it rarely disappoints, though the price will be a surprise as well.

Take Vicolo Giardinetto off V. Toledo. Restaurant is at the intersection with V. Sperzanella. Primi €6.50-8; secondi €7-14. Service 10%. Open M 1-4pm and 7pm-midnight, Tu 1-4pm, Th-Su 1-4pm and 7pm-midnight.

TRATTORIA NENNELLA RISTORANTE 2

Vicolo Lungo Teatro Nuovo 105 ☎081 41 43 38

From construction workers to bankers, Neopolitans gather here for long and leisurely lunches at unbelievably low fixed prices from a menu consisting of a *primo*, *secondo*, *contorno*, fruit, and wine. In summertime, patrons sit outdoors in the street, where views of the unchoreographed neighborhood hubbub should be fascinating for the uninitiated.

Walk up Vicolo Teatro Nuovo and look for the signs near Vicolo Lungo Teatro Nuovo Prix-fixe menu €10. Open M-Sa noon-3pm and 7-10:30pm. Closed in Aug.

LA SFOGLIATELLA MARY BAKERY 1

Galleria Umberto I ☎081 40 22 18

The summer weather may be scorching (hey, it's the South) but somehow, a piping hot *sfogliatelle* still hits the spot. Naples's signature pastry is a flaky, triangular puff of dough filled with a variety of tasty pastes. Mary makes some of the city's best, though it has to be eaten on the run—there's not a single seat at this tiny stand.

Just inside the entrance of Galleria Umberto I off V. Toledo. Pastries from €0.80. Sfogliatelle €1.50. Fruit tarts €2.50. Open M-Sa 8am-8pm, Su 8am-3pm.

LA BOTTEGA DELLA PASTA TAKEOUT 1

Vico D'Afflitto 41 ☎081 41 00 06

If you don't want to do to a real restaurant, skip the supermarket and get some fresh, genuinely Neapolitan pasta at this local shop. Though they may not speak English, the helpful ladies behind the counter will help you pick the best type for what you're cooking, no matter what culinary creations are floating through your head.

Take Vico D'Afflitto from V. Toledo. The shop is about halfway up on the right. Pasta €5-7 per kg. Lasagna €10-12 per kg. Open Tu-F 9:30am-8pm, Sa 9:30am-2pm and 4:30-8pm, Su 9:30am-2pm.

7 SOLDI RISTORANTE 1

Vico Tre Re a Toledo 6 ☎081 41 87 27

The name means "seven pence," but more than seven Neapolitans—and foreigners—are fans of this Spanish Quarter restaurant if the lunchtime crowd is any indicator. The chatty staff serve up massive salads *(€5-7),* some with whole crustaceans piled on top, beady eyes begging not to be eaten and all, plus pizzas fresh from an oven near the entrance.

Turn onto Vico Tre Re from V. Toledo near P. Trieste e Trento. Pizza €3-7. Secondi €5-8. Open Tu-Su noon-4pm and 7pm-midnight.

Chiaia, Vomero, and Outskirts

FRIGGITORIA VOMERO BAKERY 1

V. Domenico Cimarosa 44 ☎081 57 83 130

Super-quick, super-cheap, and about as Neapolitan as a place can be, this no-frills fast-food joint fills its flour-dusted display cases with fried dough creations. Sweet **arancino di riso** is a Neapolitan classic and local favorite, but the biggest crowd-pleaser has to be the dirt-cheap pricing: most items are under €1, so buy a whole bunch.

In Vomero. Head away from the funicular at P. Fuga and look across the square. i No seating available. Fried foods €0.20-2. Panini €2.50. Open M-Sa 9:30am-2:30pm and 5:30-8:30pm.

PIZZERIA GORIZIA PIZZERIA ❷

V. Bernini 29-31 ☎081 57 82 248

From late lunch through late at night, this place is packed with local diners taking a break from work or, more likely in this quarter, from an afternoon of serious shopping. Their hard work is rewarded with a delicious pizza *crudaiola (€8),* a piping-hot and distinctly Italian pie with *mozzarella di bufala,* tomato, prosciutto, oregano, and olive oil. A selection of *contorni* includes not only traditionally cooked vegetables, but also unique specialties such as... french fries.

In Vomero. From the funicular at P. Fuga, take V. Cimarosa to the left and turn right onto V. Bernini. Ⓢ Cover €1. Pizza €5-8. Primi €6-13; secondi €8-15. Open Tu-Su 12:30-4pm and 6:30pm-midnight.

HAPPY MAX KEBAB KEBAB ❶

P. Giulio Rodino 35

Try what locals call the best kebab in Naples—just don't look for any seating or superfluities.

In Chiaia. Take V. Chiaia from V. Toledo and turn right onto the small piazza and V. Filangieri before P. dei Martiri. Ⓢ Sandwiches €3.50. Open daily 11:30am-midnight.

GRAN CAFFÈ CIMIRINO CAFE ❶

V. Gonzaga Filangieri 12/13 ☎081 41 83 03

Grab a cappuccino and croissant to-go or an espresso and brioche to savor at the outdoor tables. Savor you should, for the brew here is locally lauded as the best coffee in the city. Pay first at the register to the right, then step right up and experience the aroma you're enjoying in liquid form.

In Chiaia. Take V. Chiaia from V. Toledo and turn right onto V. Filangieri before P. dei Martiri. Ⓢ Pastries €0.60-2.50. Coffee drinks €1-2. Open M-Th 7am-10pm, F-Su 7am-1am.

NIGHTLIFE

The discos in Naples may be few and far between—literally—but the city is not without after-hours activity. Its *centro* and fashionable outer neighborhoods bustle with bars and, better yet, students in *piazze* drinking cheap beer from—where else?—local pizza joints. **Piazza Gesù Nuovo** and **Piazza Duomo** are filled with students, some of whom firmly believe in the healing power of certain botanicals, but the most popular *piazza*, known as **Kesté,** is also one of the more obscure to outsiders. *(From C. Umberto I, walk up V. Mezzocannone and take the 1st left onto V. Enrico di Marinis.)* The environs of **Piazza del Martiri** contain tons of bars, though unlike those in the previous *piazze*, the ones here are less convenience store and more the Ritz. Some nightclubs call the place home as well, though they're virtually all closed in July and August. **Piazza Bellini** is relaxed and bookish, with computers and Wi-Fi replacing the DJ booth and bass. If a short funicular or longer Metro ride is in the cards, you could join the young and hip in Vomero's **Piazza Vanvitelli.** Avoid the area around **Stazione Centrale,** it is very sketchy at night.

Centro Storico

The *centro* offers a pleasing selection of bars scattered throughout the area. Students gather nightly at a *piazza* on **Via Enrico de Marinis,** just off V. Mezzocannone and conveniently only a few minutes walk from some of Naples's best hostels. At bars and pizza joints in this area, a large beer starts at €2 or less.

TROPICANA CLUB, LATIN

V. San Giuseppe dei Ruffi 14 ☎338 23 08 288

Whether they come from Buenos Aires or Bolivia, Brazil or Bogota, they're welcome here. Those who don't speak a Latin language are warmly welcomed too, but their nation's flag won't be on the wall at this salsa and Latin music club, one of Naples's most hopping hidden spots. A packed, small dance floor moves into a frenzy when the DJ starts spinning, and the sardine-smooshed patrons make the most of it by dancing with whomever's nearby.

Just off V. Duomo. When walking uphill, turn left. 1st drink €5, €3.50 per drink thereafter. Open daily midnight-6am.

LEMME LEMME BY INTERNET BAR BAR

P. Bellini 74 ☎081 29 52 37

Sway to the beat, check your email, grab a drink, or check the score—the free internet at this popular bar is great for everything except your social life. Stay away from the screen and mingle with the locals who gather on this pretty *piazza.* You can friend them all on Facebook later.

ⓂDante. Walk through Porta Alba and turn left onto V. Santa Maria di Constantinopoli; the piazza is immediately to the right. Beer €3-5.50. Cocktails €6. Open M-Sa 9am-3am, Su 5pm-3am.

ARTS CAFE CLUB

V. San Giuseppe dei Nudi 9 ☎081 21 88 467 www.artscafe.eu

An older crowd gathers for an old-school spectacle nightly at this club featuring everything from jazz quartets to Vaudeville-esque shows in its simple venue near the Museo Nazionale.

From V. Santa Teresa degli Scalzi (V. Roma) across from the museum, take the zigzagging street upward to the cafe. Drinks €5, with dinner €20. Open daily 6pm-1am, though the owners say they are often open later.

CAFFÉ LETTERARIO INTRA MOENIA BAR

P. Bellini 70 ☎081 29 07 20 www.intramoenia.it

A more relaxed, literary crowd gathers here in an attempt to escape the nightly beat on the bar-filled *piazza.* This place's interior might appeal to those with an insatiable desire to drink in a library—it's filled with shelves, wood paneling, and an interesting collection of old clocks.

ⓂDante. Walk through Porta Alba and turn left onto V. Santa Maria di Constantinopoli; the piazza is immediately to the right. Beer €4-5. Cocktails €7-8. Open daily 10am-1am.

Chiaia, Vomero, and Outskirts

GOODFELLAS BAR

V. Morghen 34 ☎340 92 25 475 www.goodfellasclub.com

This is a good old sports bar—except there's hardly any sports on TV. Screens show MTV along with the occasional soccer match, while cover bands take to the stage three nights weekly at 11pm. Sports-wise, the Chicago Bulls jerseys and baseball posters on the wall could still get any red-blooded soul into the mood for a beer and some football (of whichever variety you prefer).

In Vomero. Up the stairs from the funicular in P. Fuga and to the left. 0.5L wine €3.50. Beer €5. Cocktails €7. Open Tu-Su 8pm-2am.

S'MOVE BAR

Vico dei Sospiri 10/A ☎081 76 45 813 www.smove-lab.net

This bar is the closest one can come to getting groovy in summertime Naples, as a DJ spins house, funk, or rap most nights to create the feeling of being at a disco, without most of the dancing. Young patrons cluster at the bar and around high outdoor tables with their mojitos and crushed drinks—the bartender's specialties.

In Chiaia. From P. dei Martiri, take V. Alabardieri, then make the 2nd left. Beer €5. Cocktails €7-8. Open daily 7pm-4am. Aperitivo 7-9pm.

VINTAGE ENOTECA

V. Bernini 37/A ☎081 22 95 473 www.vintageweb.it

Vomero's first wine bar makes quite an impression. On nights when a DJ plays inside, the sound bursts onto the street and draws in a line of young people who would otherwise stay at the tables outdoors. Then the dance floor gets hot and sweaty in an almost anti-*enoteca* way. (This is not your mother's wine bar.) Couples should check out the romantic restaurant in the back, which serves light fare of cheese plates and salads, plus seasonal specialties from a small kitchen.

In Vomero. From the funicular at P. Fuga, take V. Bernini past P. Vanvitelli. i DJ on W, Sa-Su. Wine €5. Cocktails €7. Open M-Th 7pm-1am, F-Sa 7pm-3am. Happy hour 7-9:30pm. Closed 2 weeks in Aug.

L'OCA NERA — IRISH PUB
V. Bernini 17 — ☎081 55 81 649

This place has the classic look of an Irish pub and the extensive beer selection to match. Satellite TVs in every room keep diners' minds off the table conversation. Play darts but *please* be accurate—in keeping with Neapolitan safety standards (or lack thereof), there is no backboard to stop errant needle-nosed objects from zooming past the target and hitting people sitting behind.

In Vomero. From the funicular at P. Fuga, turn left onto V. Cimarosa, then turn right onto V. Bernini. Beer €4-6; gourmet varieties up to €15. Cocktails €6. Open daily 7:30pm-1:30am.

ARTS AND CULTURE

Naples is known more for carefree lifestyles and a disregard for rules than arts and refinement, yet the city presents a number of opportunities to experience something a bit more unique than a red-light-running scooter. On September 19 and the first Saturday in May, the city stops all its scooters to celebrate its patron saint in the **Festa di San Gennaro.** Join the crowd to watch the procession on V. Duomo in May and see San Gennaro's blood (normally kept in the city's Duomo) miraculously liquefy, keeping the former settlement safe for another year.

Opera, Theater, and Classical Music

TEATRO DI SAN CARLO — PIAZZA DEL PLEBISCITO
V. San Carlo 98 — ☎081 79 72 331 or 79 72 412 www.teatrosancarlo.it

La Scala's southern foil, Teatro di San Carlo puts on magnificent productions in Europe's oldest operating opera house—a theater that many say has better acoustics than the jewel of Milan. This is an argument in which you might not want to engage with a resident of that northern city, but stopping in here for a show will let you see if the claims are true. The symphony *(Oct-May)* and opera *(Dec-June)* seasons both offer great opportunities to put those ears to good use and hear sound on a grand scale.

In P. Trieste e Trento, near P. del Plebiscito. i All tickets go fast, buy in advance. Gallery tickets from €12. Box office open M-Sa 10am-7pm, Su 10am-3:30pm.

TEATRO STABILE DI NAPOLI — PIAZZA DEL PLEBISCITO
P. Municipo — ☎081 55 13 396 www.teatrostabilenapoli.it

Shakespeare is on the menu—in English, with subtitles—of Naples's most renowned theater company, which performs primarily at Teatro Mercadante in P. Municipo. Unlike American theater, Italian shows run for just a few weeks, so check the schedule and plan your stay according to what strikes your dramatic fancy.

From Stazione Centrale, take bus R2. From €15. Box office open M-Sa 10:30am-1pm and 5:30-7:30pm, Su 10:30am-1pm.

TEATRO NUOVO — SPANISH QUARTER
V. Montecalvario 16 — ☎081 49 76 267 www.nuovoteatronuovo.it

Try something a bit more modern at this theater, a showcase for new productions in the Spanish Quarter. Featuring occasional dramatic laboratories in which the public can participate, the theater has made a name for itself by differing from establishment venues like the two listed above.

Ⓜ Dante. Walk down V. Toledo and turn right onto V. Montecalvario. Ⓢ Tickets from €10. Season runs Oct-Apr.

Festivals

AMALFI COAST MUSIC FESTIVAL — SUMMER

Locations in Naples and Amalfi Coast towns ☎+1 301-587-6189 www.musicalstudies.com

Annually in June and July, Naples and the Amalfi coast open their theaters and music venues to a group of outsiders looking to learn about music from the best of the best. While they do so, these musicians stage nightly classical music concerts throughout the region, from solo piano to full orchestra performances. Mozart's ballets have been a highlight in past years, and of course, the surroundings delight no matter what the performance.

Most shows in Naples take place at the Complesso Monumentale di San Lorenzo Maggiore, V. dei Tribunali 316. Ⓢ Tickets free-€10. June-July. Concerts nightly at 9pm.

NEAPOLIS FESTIVAL — SUMMER

Mostra d'Oltremare, P. Tecchio www.neapolis.it

Perfect for students, this festival attracts local and international pop and rap artists to show off their skills on outdoor stages near the soccer stadium. With thousands of people packed in, travelers can't help but party with some Neapolitans while swaying to the synthesized beats.

Ⓜ Mostra. On the piazza outside the station. Ⓢ €30. Mid-July. Doors open daily at 4pm.

Sports

STADIO SAN PAOLO — OUTSKIRTS

Piazzale Vincenzo Tecchio ☎081 23 95 623 www.sscnapoli.it

If it's game day, light blue is the color of choice in this bustling metropolis. The Neapolitan football club lacks the international following of many Italian teams, but what it loses there, it more than makes up for with rabid home crowds who still have a crush on their late-1980s hero, Argentine **Diego Maradona.** For the semifinal of the 1990 World Cup (held in the stadium), Maradona went so far as to ask the Italian fans to cheer for Argentina (who were playing *against* Italy), which the Italians politely declined. Maradona answered with the game-winning penalty kick. Hardly fazed, today the city council has sought to rename the stadium after Maradona—with a minor snag being an Italian law forbidding the naming of buildings after anyone who hasn't been dead for at least 10 years. Whatever it's called, however, the stadium filled with 60,000 screaming Neapolitans is a snapshot of true city life that cannot be rivaled.

Ⓜ Mostra, in the Fuorigrotta area. Directly outside the station. Ⓢ Tickets from €15. Season runs Sept-June; most games Su afternoons.

SHOPPING

Very low prices can make Naples an enticing place to score that killer deal—as long as you remember that there's a reason the street vendor grabs his wares and runs when a police car turns the corner. His livelihood depends on his craftiness, and given the opportunity to outwit you, he will. If a transaction seems too good to be true, **it is.** On that note, **never buy electronics from street vendors.** Many tourists, even those who checked the name-brand packaging, have ended up with the most expensive bag of salt they ever bought. What should you do? Haggle, bargain, and barter to your heart (and wallet's) content. Where haggling *won't* get you too far is at designer stores, which are surprisingly abundant in the city's nicer areas, including **Piazza Martiri, Via dei Mille,** and **Via Scarlatti.**

Designer Stores

Designer shops line the streets near **Piazza dei Martiri,** particulary **Via dei Mille.** Fashionable locals flock to Vomero's pedestrian-only **Via Scarlatti** for a much calmer, window-gazing stroll.

ASCIONE — PIAZZA DEL PLEBISCITO

Angiporto Galleria Umberto I 19 — ☎081 42 11 11 www.ascione.it

This glittering jewelry store proves that, in Naples, "fruits of the sea" don't just end up on restaurant plates. Here, beautifully colored coral from the Mediterranean ends up in silver and gold settings. Made in nearby Torre San Greco, these coral baubles are ready to be worn as a conversation-starting necklace or romantic ring.

In the galleria, off V. Toledo *Jewelry from €200.* *Open M-Sa 9:30am-1pm and 3-6pm.*

CANE ROSSO — CHIAIA

V. Carlo Poerio 42 — ☎081 24 05 207

From Naples to Milan, sneakers are a crucial element of the Italian outfit. They can be worn with jeans or with a suit, but if they don't catch the eye immediately, something must be wrong. This store sets out to solve that problem in an explosively colorful fashion, with brand-name sneakers in canary yellow, fuchsia, and every point on the rainbow in between.

From Riviera di Chiaia, turn onto Vle. Ravaschieri and then turn left onto V. Carlo Poerio. *Sneakers €75-200.* *Open M-Sa 10am-1:30pm and 4:30-8pm.*

Bargain Stores

Via Chiaia has a concentration of stylish but inexpensive clothing outlets en route to the more expensive area near **Piazza dei Martiri.** Vomero offers other shops exploding with color, but prices jump in this well-off enclave.

CERAMICHE DI VIETRI — VOMERO

V. Sergio Abate 14 — ☎081 57 86 924 www.ceramichedivietri.com

The colors of Naples are here to take home and enjoy. The blue of the sea, yellow of the sun, purples, reds, and millions of coral colors. This small shop next to a bustling outdoor market keeps the Neapolitan artisan tradition alive by selling hand-painted ceramics with cartoonish, bubbling fish and waving, delicate reefs. Step inside to take home a fragile but beautiful piece of this gorgeous coastline.

Ⓜ Medaglie d'Oro. Walk down V. Fiore and turn right. *Small plates €6.50; extra-large €32. Bowls €12.* *Open M-Sa 9:30am-1:45pm and 4:30-7:45pm.*

IL CAMICIAIO — CHIAIA

V. Chiaia 180 — ☎081 41 57 65

The shirt you get will probably be gray, but on the bright side, shopping here means saving more of those colorful euro bills. With a selection biased toward beige and that color's dull friends, this men's shop offers a selection that's sleek and fitted but certainly doesn't jump out of the window display.

Take V. Chiaia from V. Toledo. *Pants from €10. Shirts from €20.* *Open M-Sa 9:30am-2:30pm and 4-6:30pm.*

BIBLO — VOMERO

V. Giovanni Merliani — ☎081 55 84 685

Under the shimmering sunlight, equally gleaming and artistically patterned sundresses flow in the considerable hilltop breeze. That is, they would be flowing if bought (for unbelievably low prices) off the mannequins and worn out into the summer day.

From Funicolare Centrale in P. Fuga, turn left onto V. Cimarosa and then right onto V. Merliani. *Dresses from €10.* *Open M-Sa 10am-2pm and 4:30-6pm.*

Markets

ARTIGANO — VOMERO

Between V. da Camaino and V. Fiore

If you're ready to haggle but maybe not to fight with the vendor as you attempt to buy that nice souvenir T-shirt, it's better to avoid P. Garibaldi and head to Vomero. Everything, even the markets, are a little cleaner up here, and the crowd is a little less rough. Many of the same wares at similar prices are available despite the significantly higher-class digs. After all, a street market is a street market is a street market.

Ⓜ Medaglie d'Oro. The streets in the triangle just to the southwest of the piazza contain the market. Ⓢ Dresses from €3. Fresh fruits and vegetables from €1 per kg. Open M-Sa 8:30am-2pm.

FIERA ANTIQUARIA NEAPOLITANA — STAZIONE CENTRALE

Villa Communale, V. Caracciolo — www.fierantiquarianeapolitana.it

Filled with artisans and vendors selling ancient artifacts and more recent antiques, this *fiera* is a feast for the eyes, though the hefty price tags discourage purchases of the exquisite items. Hundreds of would-be shoppers wander through aisle after aisle to browse rare stamps, books, coins and art.

From V. Chiaia, walk through P. dei Martiri and onto V. Calabritto, which emerges at the eastern end of Villa Communale. Ⓢ Prices vary widely, but many rare antiques can be expensive. Open 3rd Sa-Su each month 8am-2pm. Also open on the 4th Sa-Su except June-Aug.

ESSENTIALS

Practicalities

- **TOURIST OFFICES: EPT** offers booking services, free maps, and the indispensable guide **Qui Napoli,** which includes abundant hotel and restaurant listings. *(P. dei Martiri 58 ☎081 41 07 211 www.eptnapoli.info Open M-F 9am-2pm.)* There is another, often crowded, branch in Stazione Centrale. *(☎081 26 87 79 Open M-Sa 9am-7pm, Su 9am-1pm.)* Friendly **AASCT** provides info on accommodations, transportation, and things to do. *(V. San Carlo 9 ☎081 40 23 94 www.inaples.it Outside Galleria Umberto I, near P. Trieste e Trente. Open daily 9am-7pm.)*
- **CONSULATES: Canada.** *(V. Carducci 29 ☎081 40 13 38 In Chiaia, 2 blocks from V. dei Mille. Open M-F 9am-1pm.)* **UK.** *(☎081 42 38 911; emergency ☎06 42 20 23 54 Open M-F 9:30am-12:30pm and 2-4pm.)* **USA.** *(P. della Repubblica 2 ☎081 53 88 111; emergency 033 79 45 083 At the far west end of Villa Communale, on the waterfront. Open M-F 8am-1pm and 2-5pm.)*
- **INTERNET:** Internet points are clustered around V. Mezzocannone and P. Bellini. **Lemme Lemme by Internet Bar** offers computer terminals and free Wi-Fi. *(P. Bellini 74 ☎081 29 52 37 Ⓢ Computers €0.05 per min. Open M-Sa 9am-3am, Su 5pm-3am.)*
- **POST OFFICES:** Head here for a window into true Neapolitan life. The defunct telecommunications hall next door has an oddly library-like atmosphere in which to relax in the shade. As may be obvious, you can also mail things from here. *(P. Matteoti ☎081 55 24 233 Open M-F 8:15am-6pm, Sa 8:15am-noon.)*

Emergency!

- **POLICE: Polizia Municipale** *(☎081 75 13 177).* **Polizia del Stato** can be found at V. Medina, near P. Matteoti, or at P. Garibaldi 22, directly across the *piazza* from the station.
- **HOSPITALS/MEDICAL SERVICES: Incurabili** is more helpful than its name might suggest. *(P. Cavour ☎081 25 49 422 Ⓜ Cavour (Museo). The emergency ward is directly up V. Maria Longo.)*

Getting There

By Plane

Aeroporto Capodichino (NAP) *(Vle. Ruffo Fulco di Calabria ☎081 84 88 87 73 or 081 75 15 471 www.gesac.it Open daily 5:30am-11:30pm.)* is located in the northeast of the city and is a great point of access to the whole Bay of Naples area. Twenty airlines operate from the airport, including Alitalia, British Airways, Lufthansa, and EasyJet. The red and white **Alibus** shuttle travels from the airport arrivals terminal to the seaport near P. Municio and to P. Garibaldi. *(€3.10. 15-20min.)* City bus **3S** *(€1.10. Every 30min.)* also runs from the arrivals terminal to P. Garibaldi but has many more stops and can be a target for pickpockets. **Taxis** to and from Stazione Centrale and most destinations in the *centro* should not have fares higher than €23—confirm with the driver before getting in.

By Train

Stazione Centrale is in the crazy part of Naples, by P. Garibaldi. **Trenitalia** *(☎199 30 30 60)* runs from **Rome.** *(From €12. 1-3hr., every 30min. 5:40am-10:10pm.)* **Eurostar** trains operated by Trenitalia arrive from **Milan** via **Bologna, Florence,** and **Rome.** *(€98. 5hr., every hr. 6:30am-5:15pm.)* **Circumvesuviana** *(☎081 77 22 111 www.vesuviana.it)* trains are used primarily to access outlying tourist sights such as Pompeii. Trains originate in **Sorrento.** *(€3.40. 50min., every 30min.-1hr. 5am-10:25pm.)* Stazione Centrale is not the final stop: trains continue one more stop down C. Garibaldi to **Stazione Nolana.**

Getting Around

The **UnicoNapoliticket** *(☎081 55 13 109 www.napolipass.it)* is valid for all modes of transportation in the city. Tickets come in three varieties: 90min. *(€1.10)*, full-day *(€3.10)*, and weekend *(€2.60)* and can be bought at newsstands and *tabaccherie.* All regional buses and trains are included in the **UnicoCampania** system *(www.unicocampania.it)*. Prices depend on the zone of your destination. *(€1.70-8.20; daily tickets €3.50-16.40.)* Schedules change frequently and are published in the daily newspaper *Il Mattino*.

By Bus

Public bus lines crisscross the city; most accommodations and tourist offices provide maps. Most buses run from 6:30am to just before midnight. **R1** runs from P. Bovio to Vomero, while **R2** connects the train station at P. Garibaldi to P. Municipio along C. Umberto I. Cleverly-named **3S** connects the three stations: the airport, train station, and the ferry port at Molo Beverello.

By Metro

Currently, the Metro *(☎800 56 88 66 www.metro.na.it)* is useful for reaching far-away destinations (such as P. Cavour, Montesanto, P. Amedeo, or Mergellina) but not for exploring the *centro*, though it is being expanded. Trains run 6am-11pm. The lines extend west from P. Garibaldi to **Pozzuoli** from underground at Stazione Centrale. Line 1 stops at **Piazza Cavour** (Museo Nazionale), **Piazza Amedeo** (from which the funicular runs to Vomero), and **Mergellina.** Transfer at P. Cavour for Line 2 to P. Dante and P. Medaglie d'Oro.

By Funicular

Three funicular lines connect the lower city to elevated Vomero: **Centrale** runs from V. Toledo to P. Fuga; **Montesanto** from P. Montesanto to V. Morghen; and **Chiaia** from V. del Parco Margherita to C. Cimarosa. Centrale and Cimarosa make intermittent stops at C. Vittorio Emanuele. *(Every 10min.; M-Tu 6:30am-10pm, W-Su 6:30am-12:30am.)*

By Taxi

A number of companies operate the city's white taxis *(☎081 88 88; 081 570 70 70; 081 55 60 202; 081 55 15 151)*. Only take official, licensed taxis with meters and always ask about prices upfront; even recognized companies have been known to charge suspiciously high rates. Meters start at €3 Monday through Saturday 7am-8pm, €5.50

Sunday and nights. Each additional 65m costs €0.05. There may also be surcharges for luggage. Fees double for trips beyond city limits.

pompeii *pompei*

Sailing around the Bay of Naples, you'll see Mt. Vesuvius from nearly all vistas. It lurks formidably as though to say, "Don't forget about me." Well, given the crowds that stream to Pompeii annually, we hardly think the massive volcano is being forgotten (even if it *has* been dormant more than half a century). On August 24, 79 CE, it earned its infamy, erupting and blanketing the nearby city of Pompeii in a cloud of ash. Tragic though the eruption was for the residents of this ancient metropolis, the preservation of its streets, artifacts, and even people is unparalleled, making this frozen snippet of life nearly two millennia ago a gold mine for archaeologists and a sort of morbid historical "playground" for tourists. Excavations of Pompeii, which started in 1748, have revealed an entire city, most of which is walkable in a day. Streets covered in large, stone blocks, fading frescoes, chipped mosaics, and a labyrinth of small rooms may get repetitive after a few hours—eerie how much it resembles a circa-2011 suburb in that way—but nonetheless spark some thoughts about what this ancient city must have been like. Chances are it was more interesting than its modern-day reincarnation: the small *centro* about 1km away doesn't offer too much to the traveler, except possibly a cheaper meal than what can be found by the ancient city. Head to the ruins in the morning and, if hunger calls, stroll down to the new city for a meal and to escape from the crowds.

ORIENTATION

The ruins cover 66 hectares of land extending east to west, though only 45 are accessible to the public. The area around the **Circumvesuviana,** the **Porta Marina** entrance, and **Piazza Esedra** is full of expensive restaurants and souvenir shops. A 20-25min. walk down V. Plinio and then V. Roma will lead you to the modern city's *centro.* There, the Trenitalia train station is down V. Sacra in P. XXVIII Marzo. Inside the ruins, many of the most important sights are located on the western side, closer to the Porta Marina entrace. These sights include the **Forum** and the **House of the Faun.** A little to the east is the old city's **brothel,** and in a rather peaceful spot at the far eastern corner, you'll find Pompeii's **amphitheater.** Working your way back from there toward the entrance, you'll pass the **Great Theater** on the southern edge of the ruins.

SIGHTS

For the price of one ticket at Pompeii, you'll have the run of an entire ancient city, but that doesn't mean touring the ruins is a simple undertaking. Pompeii was a true metropolis, complete with basilicas, bars, and brothels, and that kind of scope can be intimidating. Plenty of tour guides will try to coerce you into joining their group *(most €10-20).* Rather than shelling out the money to become one of the crowd, opt for an informative audio tour *(€6.50, 2 for €10).* While both options will teach you a lot, one of the most fun ways to experience Pompeii is to navigate its maze-like streets solo—you'll likely get lost even with a map. Before heading out, pick up a free map and guidebook at the info office by showing your ticket. *(€11, EU citizens age 18-24 €5.50, EU citizens under 18 and over 65 free. Valid 1 day; no re-entry. If you plan on seeing more sights, a combined ticket allows entry to Herculaneum, Oplontis, Stabia, Boscoreale and Pompeii over the course of 3 days for €20, reduced €10. Ruins open daily Apr-Oct 8:30am-7:30pm; Nov-Mar 8:30am-5pm. Last entry 90min. before close.)* Of course, the pleasure of going it alone can be mitigated when the city is packed, and at times it's hard to walk down one of Pompeii's cobbled streets without running into another visitor. Come in the early summer or fall for slightly less crowded circumstances.

Near The Forum

Entering from Porta Marina, you first hit the **Basilica,** the remains of a building originally used for legal purposes and business matters. Now an open space occupied by columns that resemble tree stumps, it's a small taste of the many columned structures to come. Immediately beyond the Basilica, the **Temple of Venere** provides a great view of the surrounding landscape. To the left is the grassy **Forum,** the first-century city's political, religious, and economic center. Head to the **Granai del Foro** on the left for a startling peek at four body casts created by pouring plaster into air pockets in the ash that were formed by disintegrated bodies. You may not be able to tell that one of them is a dog, but the three human figures, one of whom is a pregnant woman, are contorted in heart-wrenching positions of fear. Passersby throw coins of prayer through the metal gates in memory of these individuals' awful ends. For a look at less disturbing human forms, head to the **Tempio di Apollo,** where copies of Apollo and Diana statues that once dominated the area stand. (The originals are in Naples's **Museo Archeologic Nazionale.**) As this area is closest to the main entrance and the cafeteria, it is predictably the most crowded. Head elsewhere for a quieter walk.

Near the House of the Faun

The wide V. delle Terme and V. della Fortuna surround the area around the stunning **Casa del Fauno,** the biggest and perhaps best preserved residence in the ruins. Your attention will undoubtedly be drawn to the bronze faun statue at the house's center, but don't miss the mosaic-covered surrounding rooms—unfortunately, these mosaics can only partially make up for the absent Alexander mosaic now displayed at the Naples Museo Archeologico Nazionale. At the time of its discovery, that tiled decoration suggested some relation between the house's wealthy owner and Alexander the Great. Head to the intimate **House of the Small Fountain** for a peek at a beautifully decorated fountain, complete with mosaics, frescoes, and petite sculptures. The smallish **House of the Vettii** is home to frescoes of Priapus and his biggish member—as the god of fertility, he can be forgiven for weighing his crowning "jewel" on a scale. If you can take your eyes off the amusing picture, admire the brighter-than-usual red walls which have immortalized the color "Pompeii red," a warm earthy hue.

Near The Brothel

While all of Pompeii's ruins are full of strolling tourists, none are as packed as the **Lupanare,** the ancient city's brothel. Looks like it's just as popular now as it was centuries ago. If you can squeak past the tourist groups, take notice of the explicit frescoes lining the walls, which show popular bedroom positions as a source of "inspiration" for the men who frequented the place. The small rooms, occupied only by stone beds which were luckily covered in comfier mats, leave more to the imagination. The upstairs rooms are not accessible but were used for more expensive transactions. Nearby, the large **Stabian Baths** feature a body cast and a wall of impressive mosaics.

Near The Amphitheater

That big green block on your map indicates the **amphitheater,** a massive structure that could hold 20,000 spectators and hosted Colosseum-like gladiator battles in its day. Much quieter now, the arena stands as another vivid reminder of what this city used to be. The adjacent **Great Palaestra** provides a nice break from the hard-to-navigate stone blocks scattered about the rest of the city and some shade under its trees. Less serene is the **Garden of the Fugitives,** where you'll find more plaster casts of the bodies of individuals who didn't flee the city in time. The **House of Octavius Quartio** and **House of Venus** are more peaceful. At these ancient abodes, gardens have been planted based on modern knowledge of ancient horticulture.

Near The Great Theater

Though less impressive in size than the amphitheater, the **Great Theater** has a bit more culture to it—both ancient and modern. Originally a stage hosting plays, it now serves as a performance space for summer music concerts, giving it some life apart from the tourist hordes. The nearby **Small Theater** was the site of ancient poetry readings. An acoustically designed rooftop surrounding the theater's rim amplified the voice of the reciting poet. Nearby, the **Botanical Garden** provides a nice punch of greenery, shade, and pleasant smells.

ESSENTIALS

Practicalities

- **TOURIST OFFICES:** Tourist Offices are located at V. Porta Marina Inf. 12 *(☎081 85 07 255 At the Circumvesuviana station.)* and at V. Sacra 1. *(☎081 536 32 93 www.pompeiturismo.it Near the Trenitalia station.)* Both offer information on and maps of the modern city of Pompeii, sell tickets for sightseeing buses around Campania, and stock pamphlets about museums in the area. *(Both open daily 8:30am-6:30pm.)*
- **LUGGAGE STORAGE: Bag check** at the archaeological site is free and mandatory for large bags.
- **POST OFFICES:** *(P. Esdera 1 ☎081 85 06 164 Right near the V. Porta Marina Inferiore entrance. Open M-F 8am-1:30pm, Sa 8am-12:30pm.)*

Getting There

The best way to get to Pompeii's archaeological site is by the **Circumvesuviana train** from Naples's Stazione Centrale *(€2.40. 20-30min., every 15min.)* or from Sorrento. *(€1.90. 20-30min., every 20min.)* Get off at Pompei Scavi. From the train, the ruins' main entrance, **Porta Marina,** is to the right. If you proceed onward down V. Villa dei Misteri, you can enter at the less crowded entrance at **Piazza Esedra.** Instead of the Circumvesuviana, you can take a **Trenitalia** train. *(€2.40. 20-40 min., every 30min. Ticket office open daily 6:40am-8:28pm, with 3 15min. midday closings.)* The train will drop you off in modern Pompeii's *centro.* From the station, walk up V. Sacra until you reach P. Bartolo Longo. Turn left down V. Colle San Bartolomeo. It's a 20-25min. walk to the archaeological site's main entrance, so it is better to enter at the less crowded **Piazza Anfiteatro,** a short way down V. Plinio.

herculaneum *ercolano*

Once you've gotten over Herculaneum's hard-to-pronounce name, there's very little to begrudge this delightful ancient Roman town. A smaller archaeological site than the more famous Pompeii, Herculaneum is much easier on the sightseer than its big sib—you can cover its grounds in an afternoon without fatigue or boredom ever setting in. Not only is it better preserved and less crowded than good old Pompy, but it's also situated in a beautiful natural enclave. Sparkling water less than 1 mi. away and lush green trees surrounding the ruins make Herculaneum worth a daytrip even if you're not an archaeological fanatic. Best of all, the modern city that cradles the ancient one has not become a tourist trap, meaning you'll find plenty of residential life, shops, and cheap restaurants if you want to spend the afternoon. Slow down and gear up for this undiscovered lost city.

ORIENTATION

From the train station, head down the hill onto **Via IV Novembre.** The ruins are a 5min. walk away.

HERCULANEUM (ERCOLANO SCAVI)

ANCIENT ROME

At the intersection of C. Resina and V. IV Novembre ☎081 732 4338 www.pompeiisites.org

Herculaneum is a city upon a city. You'll know you've reached the ancient Ercolano when cotton-candy pink houses suddenly cede to dusty, copper-colored ones. Even before buying a ticket to enter the ruins, take a moment to look around. The public walkway leading to the information desk provides one of the best views of the city in its entirety. To the right is the 4½ hectare region open to the public. (Another 16 or so hectares are not visible.) From this elevation, you get the best sense of how deeply the city was buried by the explosion and of how much was vertically preserved. About 16m of pyroclastic rock covered the region, making its second-story structures even better preserved than those of Pompeii.

The large archways directly below the elevated promenade provide a good introduction to the city's tragic fall—or, rather, what fell upon it. In these cavities lie the skeletons of over 300 victims, likely those who were waiting for **boats** to take them from the city before the volcano hit. Luckily for squeamish visitors, the skeletons are not available for viewing. Instead of skeletons, you get the pots, beds, and even baths the skeletons used back when they were covered in flesh. Descending into the ruins, you'll come across frescoes and mosaics that rival those of intact churches, baths where you could later retreat to clean off all that Roman soil, and roofs that could shelter you from the rain. Walking around Herculaneum is a bit like walking through a functional city. If you feel like an intruder or a diary-reader...well, you should.

Though this city (really more of a town) is smaller than Pompeii, you could easily spend hours exploring its nooks and crannies. Make sure not to miss the **Casa del Tramezzo di Legno,** one of the site's largest and most detailed complexes: large frescoes, a marble table at its center, and wooden dividers give the room its name. The **Casa della Cervi** (House of the Deers) is a bit like a museum: still-life frescoes (now covered in Plexiglas) line the walkway, while the central courtyard was once home to life-size statues depicting dogs destroying deer. (No evidence that Herculaneum's citizens were alliteration authorities.) Just across the way, **Casa del Relievo di Telefo** contains a beautiful line of columns and an incredible relief of Telephus, Hercules's son. (Among his many accomplishments, Hercules was also a hotshot here, as he was the town's supposed founder.) Not only were they artistically inclined, but the people of Herculaneum knew how to live: the **Larga Taberna** contains a series of holes that were used for serving food and wine. They cleaned themselves in style too—the **Terme Suburbane** (Suburban Baths) is a three-room complex whose middle area contains an intricate black-and-white mosaic on its floor. If you're still upset about not seeing those skeletons, visit the **Casa dello Scheletro** (House of the Skeleton) and the adjoining rooms, which contain a stunning turquoise mosaic and meditative altarpiece.

Appreciate the age of this sight, but allow the modernity that rubs up against old Herculaneum to enrich your experience of the ancient town. Rooftops of modern dwellings peek out beyond the ruins' perimeter, and the sounds of city residents penetrate the otherwise silent streets of the remains. Like a remarkable mini-Rome, where rubble and modern brick live side by side, Herculaneum is maybe not as much a city upon a city, as it is two cities in one.

See **Orientation** *above.* ***i*** *Mandatory and free bag check by the ticket window. Free map and guide at the information point beyond the ticket window. Audio tours (available in English) can be obtained past the park entrance. Gift shop, bathrooms, and snack bar past park entrance. €11, EU citizens ages 18-24 €5.50, EU citizens under 18 or over 65 free. Access to 5 sites (valid 3 days) €20/10/free. Audio tour €6.50, 2 for €10. Open daily Apr-Oct 8:30am-7pm; Nov-Mar 8:30am-5pm. Last entry 90min. before close. Information point open daily 8:30am-1:30pm and 2-5pm.*

FOOD

While most people make their way down to the archaeological site as though unable to resist gravity, we advise that you take a slower stroll through the neighborhood as a precursor to your visit. The streets are full of residents, cheap shops, and trattorias dishing up stellar food at uninflated prices. To tide yourself over for the tour ahead, stop by **Luna Caprese** for a delicious pizza made exactly to your liking. *(V. Quattro Novembre 68 ☎081 77 71 543 Ⓢ Pizza €3-4.50. ⏰ Open M-Sa noon-3:30pm and 6:30-10:30pm.)*

ESSENTIALS

Practicalities

- **TOURIST OFFICES:** At Herculaneum's tourist office you can pick up a small map of the modern city and ruins, though the excavation sight provides much more information. *(V. IV Novembre 82 ☎081 78 81 243 www.comune.ercolano.na.it 3min. down the hill from the train station. ⏰ Open M-Sa 8am-6pm. Occasionally closes in the afternoon.)*

Emergency!

- **POLICE: Carabinieri** *(V. Nicolo Marcello Venuti 30 ☎081 77 76 022).* **Local Police** *(☎081 78 81 400).* **State Police** *(☎081 78 87 111).*

Getting There

To get to Herculaneum, take the **Circumvesuviana train** from Naples's Stazione Centrale to Ercolano Scavi *(Ⓢ €1.80. ⏰ 17min., every 15min.)* or head to the same destination from Sorrento. *(Ⓢ €1.90. ⏰ 45min.)* From the station, head downhill 500m to the main gate. The ticket office is 200m further to the left.

Getting Around

Taxis can be found near the train station in Piazzale della Stazione Circumvesuviana *(☎081 73 93 666).*

isle of capri ☎081

Capri certainly qualifies as an oasis. Before even landing at its dock, visitors have their cameras going, snapping postcard shots of the aquamarine water and pastel houses dotting the island's cliffs. Pebble beaches, stunning vistas, and rocky hikes add to this escape's at times unbelievable beauty. Yet walking around the narrow streets of the isle's residential area, you may feel as though you're in a Disneyland for the Bill Gateses of this world. Narrow streets split off the main thoroughfares and lead to dollhouse-like homes labeled not with street numbers, but rather with endearing names painted on ceramic tiles. It's hard to believe these residences are inhabited by real people and not characters out of a glossy Hollywood film. Find yourself in the people-ridden *centri* of Capri and Anacapri, where sparkling jewelry and equally shiny menus lure in tourists, however, and you'll discover that this "oasis" is only really that for the select few with the means to access it. Don't let us get you too down, though. Spend a day here swooning at gorgeous vistas and daydreaming about a life more glamorous than your own. Surrender to the fantasy of it all, and you'll leave Capri with the Cinderella feeling of having been princess for the night in your very own private oasis.

ORIENTATION 

The Isle of Capri consists of two towns: **Capri,** closer to the port, and **Anacapri,** higher up and further west.

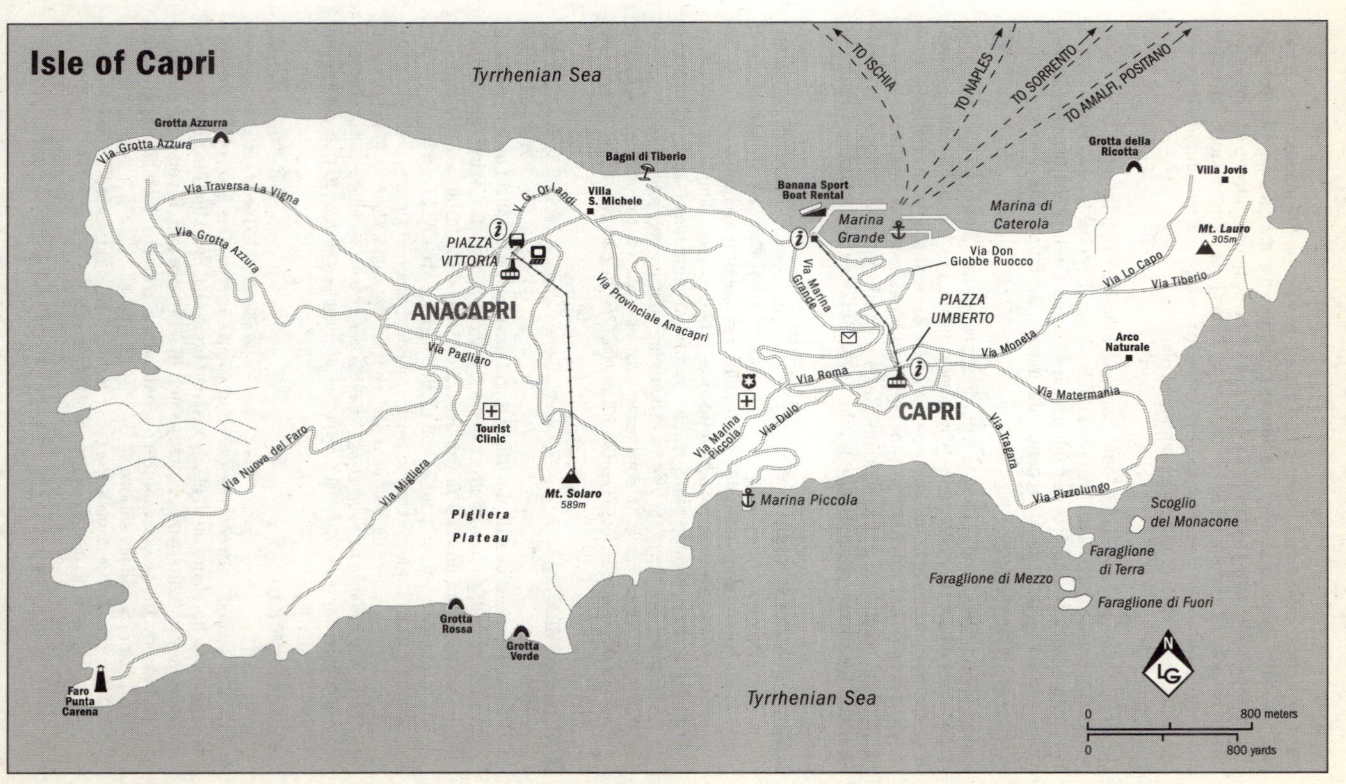
Isle of Capri
Tyrrhenian Sea
TO ISCHIA
TO NAPLES
TO SORRENTO
TO AMALFI, POSITANO
Grotta Azzurra
Via Grotta Azzurra
Via Traversa La Vigna
Via Grotta Azzura
Bagni di Tiberio
Villa S. Michele
V. G. Orlandi
PIAZZA VITTORIA
ANACAPRI
Via Pagliaro
Via Provinciale Anacapri
Banana Sport Boat Rental
Marina Grande
Via Marina Grande
Marina di Caterola
Grotta della Ricotta
Villa Jovis
Mt. Lauro
305m
Via Don Giobbe Ruocco
Via Lo Capo
Via Tiberio
PIAZZA UMBERTO
Via Moneta
Arco Naturale
Via Roma
Via Matermania
CAPRI
Via Tragara
Via Dulo
Via Marina Piccola
Via Pizzolungo
Marina Piccola
Tourist Clinic
Via Nuova del Faro
Via Migliera
Mt. Solaro
589m
Pigliera Plateau
Grotta Rossa
Grotta Verde
Faro Punta Carena
Scoglio del Monacone
Faraglione di Terra
Faraglione di Mezzo
Faraglione di Fuori
N
LG
0
800 meters
0
800 yards

Capri

Capri centers around **Piazza Umberto I.** Radiating from here, the main streets are **Via Roma** (mostly practical stores), **Via Vittorio Emanuele** (designer shops), **Via Botteghe,** and **Via Longano** (mostly restaurants). Off these thoroughfares, dozens of unmapped streets branch off, though most are residential lanes lacking merchants. Pay attention to the painted tile signs that indicate street names as well as commercial stores and restaurants when looking for unmapped places.

Anacapri

The prefix "ana" means "above," and Anacapri is indeed well up a hill from Capri. Once you've made the trek up (or taken the bus), you'll probably be in **Piazza Vittoria,** the upper town's center. Most of the action is down the long **Via Giuseppe Orlandi,** which is full of restaurants, merchants, and most of the interesting places to visit.

ACCOMMODATIONS

Rooms in both Capri and Anacapri are pricey year-round, thanks to the popularity of the lovely island they call home. The most conveniently located hotels also tend to be the most expensive, making any stay here at least a bit of a splurge for the budget traveler. Seek out harder-to-find bed and breakfasts and smaller side-street *pensioni* for somewhat reduced prices. Reserve in advance and arrange a check-in time with the owner, as, quite often, 24hr. reception does not apply.

Capri

HOTEL QUATTRO STAGIONI — HOTEL ❸

V. Marina Piccola 1 ☎081 83 70 041 www.hotel4stagionicapri.com

The humorous and hospitable staff make this one of the sunniest spots on the island, even if its look isn't as refined as other options. Simple furnishings, a relatively unfrequented patio, and a removed location make Quattro Stagioni a break from the glitz of the *centro*. Rooms are sunny, clean, and quiet.

Bus to V. Marina Piccola. i Breakfast included. All rooms with bath ensuite. 10% Let's Go discount M-F. Free Wi-Fi. Singles €40-70; doubles €70-130. Extra bed €20-30. Reception 24hr.

VILLA PALOMBA — B AND B ❸

V. Mulo 3 ☎081 83 77 322

Possibly the best deal on the island if you can manage the slight trek to get here. A vine-covered patio with great views gives you plenty of relaxing space, while the wicker furniture and flower-decorated sheets' old-fashioned feel matches the motherly attention paid to you by the hostess. Free Wi-Fi is a huge plus and will keep you connected to the world outside this secret garden.

From V. Marina Piccola, walk down stairs on the right onto V. Mulo; walk through tunnel and slightly downhill, following signs. i Breakfast included. All rooms with bath ensuite. A/C €10 per day. Free Wi-Fi. Singles €45-65; doubles €80-130. Door service until 8pm.

HOTEL IL PORTICO — HOTEL ❹

V. Truglio 1/C ☎338 18 28 700 www.ilporticocapri.com

Ideally located between the port and Capri's *centro*, this spot offers the reliability of a hotel and the feel of a bed and breakfast. Sparkling clean rooms (and since they're white, you can tell) smell like flowers and, if you step out onto the balcony, the sea. A canopy-covered patio surrounded by plants is great for breakfast or a midday snooze.

Off V. Marina Grande on the way to Capri's centro. i Breakfast included. All rooms with bath ensuite. Free Wi-Fi. Doubles €80-160; triples €140-190.

Anacapri

VILLA MIMOSA BED AND BREAKFAST — B AND B ❸

V. Nuova del Faro 48/A ☎081 83 71 752 www.mimosacapri.com

Anacapri might already resemble a fairy-tale land, but if you had any doubts, Villa Mimosa's hanging bird cages and antique sculptures adorning the garden will do the trick. Save for the occasional food run, you won't want to leave this retreat: rooms are even equipped with private terraces. Lack of Wi-Fi is a bit inconvenient, but it just adds to the escape, right?

*100m down the hill on the right from the last stop of the Marina Grande-Anacapri bus. **i** Breakfast included. All rooms with bath ensuite. Public computer with free internet. Doubles €70-100. Call to arrange check-in time.*

SENARIA HOTEL — HOTEL ❺

V. Follicara 6 ☎081 83 73 222 www.senaria.it

Senaria retains the perks of a hotel without becoming a generic rest stop. With only 12 rooms and a public terrace, it's small enough that you might get to know your temporary neighbors. Especially large rooms with tall ceilings and simple white curtains should put you at peace, and if you haven't gotten enough exercise from the island's hills, take advantage of the discount at the nearby gym.

*Take Marina Grande-Anacapri bus to V. Caprile. Follow signs downstairs, just off the piazza. **i** Breakfast included. All rooms with bath ensuite. Free Wi-Fi. Doubles €100-170. Reception 24hr.*

BAR DUE PINI RESIDENCE — APARTMENTS ❹

P. Vittoria 3 ☎081 83 71 404 www.2pini.com

You can easily pay these rates for a room half the size. Due Pini's six apartments located on the surrounding streets of P. Vittoria are thus steals, offering extra-spacious "doubles" and "triples," if you want to call them that. Make up the extra euro by cooking your own meals in the adjoining kitchenette. Access to a Jacuzzi and park are added perks that make these residences worth the cost.

*In P. Vittoria. **i** Most apartments have fully equipped kitchen; all have private bath. Wi-Fi downstairs in bar for a fee. Doubles €90-135; triples €170-180. Reception 8am-6pm at bar downstairs.*

SIGHTS

Capri is hardly a cultural experience to rival Rome or even Cinque Terre. The best things to see here are the island's natural beauty and its posh buildings and shops. Walk down V. Le Botteghe and V. Vittorio Emanuele to see every designer store known to Milan lining streets half as wide as those of the big city. In addition, there are churches—this is Italy, after all. Most churches are small, free, and pastel-colored like the houses surrounding them. One worth visiting is the **Chiesa di San Michael,** a Baroque church with a stunning Majolica tile floor. The depiction of Adam and Eve in Earthly Paradise actually recalls the views from Anacapri, reminding you that you're in a paradise of your own. *(In P. San Nicola, off V. Giuseppe Orlandi. €2. Open daily 9am-7pm.)*

VILLA SAN MICHELE — VILLA, ANCIENT ROME

Vle. Axel Munthe 34 ☎081 83 71 401 www.villasanmichele.eu

If free views aren't enough for you, then you can pay for one. The Villa San Michele does have something on the rest of the island though—actual history. Originally an ancient Roman villa, its remains were maintained by Axel Munthe, who used them as a home (and quite likely a retreat to nurture his literary and scientific inclinations) at the end of the 19th century. Here, he wrote the famous *The Story of San Michele*—see if you can trace the story's origin while walking through its birthplace's beautiful gardens and sculpture loggia.

A 5min. walk down V. Capodimonte out of P. Vittoria; the street becomes Vle. Axel Munthe. €6. Open May-Sept 9am-6pm; Oct Apr 9am-5pm; Nov-Feb 9am-3:30pm; Mar 9am-4:30pm; Apr 9am-5pm.

THE GREAT OUTDOORS

Beyond Capri's rampant commercialism lies its stunning natural beauty—and that's the best reason to come. Most **hikes** are hilly but not terribly rugged, making a pair of sneakers enough for hitting the paths. The **Arco Naturale,** a triumphant stone arch, can be reached by starting in P. Umberto I, heading down V. le Botteghe, and finally veering right onto V. Matermania. Head down a steep staircase, and you'll hit the spot. Turn back around and make your way left, passing the Grotta di Matermania and the **Villa Malaparte,** a rare work of modern architecture in a country filled with ancient and Renaissance-era buildings. When the road opens out onto V. Pizzolungo, the **Faraglione,** Capri's famous three rocks, is around the way. The walk is about 1½hr. Head to the tourist office for detailed maps of other suggested hikes.

GROTTA AZZURRA — CAVE

On the island's northwest coast, below Anacapri ☎081 83 70 973

Despite being blue, this is Capri's golden star—and when we say blue, we mean swimming-pool aquamarine. The walls of this water-filled cave shimmer almost artificially when sunlight beams through from beneath the water's surface. Though you can appreciate the grotto without knowing a stitch of history, anyone bitter about paying the hefty entrance fee may be interested to know that Roman statues were discovered here (they now reside in the **Museo Archeologico Nazionale** in Naples). Legend has it that spirits reside in the caves—if the authorities don't catch you taking a prohibited swim, maybe the ghosts will.

A popular option for reaching the Grotta Azzurra is to take a cruise with the Grotta Azzurra company. Boats leave from Marina Grande every hr. 10am-1pm (€14). A cheaper option is the bus from Anacapri to Grotta Azzurra leaving from Vle. de Tommaso (15min., every 10-20min. 6:30am-10:30pm). You can also walk from Anacapri down V. Pagliara, V. Tuoro, V. Damecuta, and V. Grotta Azzurra for 50min. Once there, catch a Cooperativa Battellieri rowboat to the entrance. Ⓢ Coop. Battellieri boat €7.50. Entry €4. Last boat at 5pm.

MONTE SOLARO — PANORAMIC VIEWS

V. Caposcuro 10 ☎081 83 71 428 www.capriseggiovia.it

It might be nearly as expensive as the ferry to Capri, but the ascent 589m above the island is worth it. For 13min., titillate or tremble as your chairlift climbs up to the summit. From the island's highest point, you can enjoy an unrivaled panorama of land and sea: Ischia, Naples, and the Appenines loom in the distance, though standing there you wouldn't wish yourself anywhere else.

*The chair lift leaves from V. Caposcuro 10, just off P. Vittoria in Anacapri. **i** Cafe and terrace at the top. Ⓢ Round-trip €9. Ticket office open 9:30am-5pm. Last ride to Monte Solaro at 5pm; last ride back to Anacapri at 5:30pm.*

FOOD

The Isle of Capri is famous for the **Caprese salad**—rich mozzarella balls tossed with sweet red tomatoes and fresh basil. *Limoncello*, a lemon-flavored yellow liqueur, seems to epitomize the island's sweetness and bright feel. It's hard to find a budget meal here, but cafes often have decently priced panini to tide you over.

Capri

Pricey restaurants and cafes in the *centro* cater to tourist crowds. High-quality spots can be found on smaller streets, though that doesn't mean they're any cheaper. If you want a picnic for your day, head to well-stocked **Supermarket Deco** at V. Marina Grande 35/37, which has good prices and, by Italian standards, great hours. *(☎081 83 77 221 Open M-Sa 8am-9pm, Su 8am-1pm.)*

TINELLO — SEAFOOD ❷

V. L'Abate 3 ☎081 83 76 578

Finally, a restaurant without a photo-supplemented (dear Italy: we know what pasta carbonara is; we don't need a picture), touristic, or pages-long menu: this tiny spot feels like it could be in an old city center rather than ritzy Capri. The only thing reminding you of the water is the exquisite seafood menu, featuring fish of the day served grilled or baked in "*acqua pazza*" (crazy water). Eight small tables keep it classy without being flashy.

From Chiesa Santo Stefano, walk up stairs to the covered V. L'Abate. Primi €7-15; secondi €10-15; dolci €5-7. Open daily noon-2:30pm and 7:30-11pm.

VERGINIELLO — RISTORANTE ❸

V. Lo Palazzo 25 — ☎081 83 70 944

The whole package: terrace seating for a view, straw covering for some shade, and great value for some help re-padding that dented wallet. Despite its central location and amazing panorama, this large restaurant retains the feel of a family-run trattoria, with its light-hearted staff (who might crack a joke before cracking open the wine) and generous portions. The excellent ravioli Capri *(€10)* makes mainland variants feel heavy.

Take V. Roma from P. Umberto I and walk down the stairs on the right past the post office. Cover €2. Pizza €3-8. Primi €7-14; secondi €12-22. Open daily noon-3pm and 7:30pm-midnight.

Anacapri

More budget-friendly, though less fancy, options make Anacapri a good spot when hunger calls. **Galardo** doubles as a supermarket and convenience store if you need basics. *(V. Giuseppe Orlandi 299 Open daily 8am-1:30pm and 4:30-8:30pm.)*

PASTICCERIA GELATERIA SAN NICOLA — BAKERY, GELATERIA ❶

V. San Nicola 7 — ☎081 83 72 199

Size *does* matter. What this shop lacks in square footage, it makes up for in the size of its pastries. Unlike more glamorous spots, this closet-sized bakery makes treats that are actually fresh and well-priced. Try their massive *biscotto all'amerena*, a long cookie stuffed with a mix of nuts and amaretto flavoring and topped with crunchy meringue *(€1)*.

Take V. Giuseppe Orlandi away from P. Vittoria and turn right onto V. San Nicola. Pastries €0.80-3. Cannoli €1.50. Gelato €2.50-3. Open daily 7am-9pm.

TRATTORIA IL SOLITARIO — PIZZERIA ❷

V. Giuseppe Orlandi 96 — ☎081 83 71 382 www.trattoriailsolitario.it

Tucked away behind a garden and sporting its *own* garden inside, this pizzeria feels miles away from the commercial flare of Anacapri. It has probably the best prices on the island for a sit-down pizza, yet it isn't lacking in flavor or creativity as a result: the *ammiraglia* is a white pie topped with an unusual combo of mussels, calamari, clams, shrimp, and mozzarella (just to remind you it's still pizza). Homemade bread makes the €1.50 cover charge actually worth it.

A short walk down V. Giuseppe Orlandi from P. Vittoria; follow signs to the right. Cover €1.50. Pizza €3.50-8. Primi €5.50-15. Caprese salad €6. Open in summer daily noon-3pm and 7:30-11:30pm; in fall, winter, and spring M noon-3pm and 7:30-11:30pm, W-Su noon-3pm and 7:30-11:30pm.

AGORÁ — RISTORANTE, ENOTECA ❸

P. Caprile 1 — ☎081 83 72 018 www.agora-capri.com

Fine Mediterranean food meets live music and wine. Sounds like Italy to us. Along with "normal" pizzas (though when they're this good, normal seems like an understatement), more creative brick-oven specialties set this place apart from its neighbors. Vegetarians will cave for the *pane* pizza stuffed with veggies, provola, and *fior di latte* cheese *(€6)*. Anyone will cave for the wine selection which justifies Agorá's status as an *enoteca*. With tall ceilings and a white theme going, the place is light-feeling without being in the sun.

On the left in P. Caprile. Pizza €5-7.50. Salads €5.50-7.50. Primi €8-14. Open daily 6:30-11:30pm.

SNACK BAR ORLANDI CAFE ❷

V. Giuseppe Orlandi 83/83A ☎081 83 82 138

Just a step from P. Vittoria, this bright cafe has all the standards—pizza, salads, and liquid pick-me-ups—but combines them in a lunch menu that makes the value better than standard. At €10, their midday combo of salad, *primo*, drink, and service is a steal. They're not on the menu, but helpful hints from the friendly staff are part of the deal.

A short walk down V. Giuseppe Orlandi from P. Vittoria; on the left. Primi €8-10; secondi €8-12. Pizza €6-7. Fixed lunch €10. Open daily 9am-8pm.

NIGHTLIFE

With ferry and hotel costs what they are, the Isle of Capri is not the young traveler's party town that other beach locales sometimes are. People who can afford to stay here head to expensive lounges and discos. The economically minded might consider the ridiculously early 5:40am ferry back to Naples, which means you can "stay the night" partying in Capri instead of booking a hotel room. Given the cost of most spots however, sleeping in Naples or living it up in Capri will probably end up costing about the same.

Capri

BYE BYE BABY CLUB

V. Roma 6 ☎081 83 75 065 www.byebyebabycapri.com

Funky furniture sits in the lounge areas of this downstairs disco, though you won't be doing much sitting as the night wears on. The nightly DJ spins mostly commercial beats under a giant disco ball and across from stunning views of the water. The hefty price of drinks draws a sophisticated crowd, so don't expect to get in donning beachwear and flip-flops.

Take V. Roma from P. Umberto 1 and descend steps on right. Entry M-F with purchase of drink. F-Sa and special events cover €20; includes 1 drink. Cocktails €10. Open Tu-Su 11pm-5am.

NUMBER 1/NUMBER 2 CLUB

V. Vittorio Emanuele III 53/55 ☎081 83 77 078

Follow the blue lights down to this spectacular double-whammy of a spot—but only if you're prepared to rub shoulders with a pretty crowd and their pretty pennies. The two adjoining rooms let guests drift seamlessly between live vocals and jazz (Number 1) and commercial and house (Number 2)—neither runs the regular gamut of tunes, but instead both feature eclectic styles to suit high-styled folks. Gold ceilings in Number 1 give way to a blacklight-lit hall in Number 2. If you have any intention of feeling tipsy on something other than great music, grab some drinks beforehand—at €20 a glass, you might feel lightheaded for a reason other than the alcohol.

*Take V. Vittorio Emanuele III from P. Umberto I. **i** Dress to impress; bouncers are discerning. M-Th entry with drink; F-Su cover €30+. Cocktails €20, at a table €40. Open daily 11pm-3am.*

MEDJ PUB PUB

V. Oratorio 9 ☎081 83 75 148

The cheapest spot to get a cocktail or beer, even by non-resort standards. Without the hip decor or nightly DJ of nearby clubs, it attracts a younger crowd looking for good conversation loosened up by a few too many drinks—the more you order the cheaper they get. If you need a little bit more entertainment than your tipsy friends, sports games aired on the flatscreen TV are a good distraction.

From P. Umberto I, take V. P.S. Cimino and turn left onto the small V. Oratorio. Beer €2.50-4. Shots €4. Cocktails €5-6. Panini €4-7. Open in summer daily 8pm-2am; in fall, winter, and spring Tu-Su 8pm-2am.

Anacapri

Quieter than its downstairs sister, Anacapri has little else than late-night cafes and pubs in the way of nightlife. The view from your terrace better be beautiful.

BOCCADILLOS PUB

V. Giuseppe Orlandi 208 ☎081 83 73 783

The wooden interior of this pub and "game room" stays open during the day for customers at the adjacent cafe (owned by the same family). At night, customers move from outside tables to stools or head to the floor to play pool or foosball or watch soccer. Cheap food and cocktails attract an unpretentious crowd that can't stomach the clubs of Capri. There's not much in the way of music, so bring your bar voice.

At the end of V. Giuseppe Orlandi, as it intersects with V. Pagliaro. Beer €3-4. Cocktails €5-6. Panini and pizza €3-5. Open daily 7pm-1am.

BLOOM BAR

V. Caprile 5/B ☎081 83 71 716

It's actually just as good to come here during the day for their cheap and filling panini (even a New York-style hot dog with mustard and sauerkraut), but with late hours and great cocktail deals to match, Bloom is an OK place to bring some friends and settle down at a wooden bench. Low-key music and a big interior make this a good hangout spot, but don't expect the action to get too hot.

From the end of V. Giuseppe Orlandi veer left to the start of V. Caprile; Bloom is just past the post office. Beer €3-5. Cocktails €5-6. Panini €5-5.50. Pastas €7-10. Open M 5:30pm-3am, Tu-Su noon-3am.

ESSENTIALS

Practicalities

- **TOURIST OFFICES: Info points** offer free maps, a list of accommodations and restaurants, and information on sights and tours. There are three locations: to the right of the dock at **Marina Grande** *(☎081 83 70 634)*, in **Piazza Umberto** in Capri *(☎081 83 70 686)*, and in Anacapri just off P. Vittoria at **Via Giuseppe Orlandi 59** *(☎081 83 71 524 www.capritourism.com, www.infocapri.molti All branches open M-Sa 8:30am-8:30pm, Su 9am-3pm.)*
- **CURRENCY EXCHANGE:** There's only one on the island. *(P. Vittoria 2, Anacapri ☎081 83 73 146 Open M-Sa 8:30am-6pm.)*
- **LUGGAGE STORAGE:** In Capri. *(Once you've taken the funicular into Capri, walk down the steps from P. Umberto I. Each bag €3 per day. Open daily 8am-10pm.)* In Anacapri. *(P. Vittoria 5 Each bag €2 per day. Open daily 9:30am-5pm.)*
- **INTERNET: Capri Graphic** offers internet and office supplies in Capri. *(V. Listrieri 17 ☎081 83 75 212 From P. Umberto I walk down V. Longano and make a right onto V. Listrieri. €2 per 10min., €6 per hr. Open M-Sa 9am-1pm and 4-8pm.)* In Anacapri try **Hotel Due Pini.** *(P. Vittoria 3 ☎081 83 71 404 €1 per 10min., €5 per hr. Open daily 8am-6pm.)*
- **POST OFFICES:** In Capri. *(V. Roma 50 ☎081 97 85 211 3min. from P. Umberto I. Open M-F 8am-6:30pm, Sa 8am-12:30pm.)* In Anacapri. *(Vle. de Tommaso 8 ☎081 83 71 015 Open M-F 8:30am-1:30pm, Sa 8:30am-noon.)*

Emergency!

- **POLICE: Carabinieri** has offices in Capri *(V. Provinciale Marina Grande 42 ☎081 83 70 000 By the port. Open until 8pm.)* and Anacapri *(V. Caprile ☎081 83 71 011).* There is also **City Police** in Capri *(V. Roma 70 ☎081 83 74 211).*

- **HOSPITALS/MEDICAL SERVICES: G. Capilupi** in Capri. *(V. Provinciale 2 ☎081 83 81 205 At the 3-pronged fork at the end of V. Roma. ⏰ 24hr. service for emergencies.)*

Getting There

By Ferry

Capri is an island and has no airport; therefore, it's time for **ferries** and **hydrofoils.** Capri's main port is Marina Grande. Various companies run ferries to and from Naples and Sorrento. **Caremar** *(☎89 21 23 www.caremar.it)* is the cheapest option but not the most frequent, running both ferries and hydrofoils to and from **Naples** *(Ferries €10, hydrofoils €14.50. ⏰ Ferries 80min., hydrofoils 50min.; depart Naples every 2-4hr. 5:40am-9:10pm, depart Capri every 2-4hr. 5:45am-10:20pm.)* and hydrofoils to **Sorrento.** *(€9.80. ⏰ 25min.; depart Sorrento 7:45, 9:25, 2:30, 7pm; depart Capri 7, 8:40am, 1:40, 6:15pm.)* **SNAV** *(☎081 42 85 555 www.snav.it)* runs the most frequent hydrofoils to and from **Naples** *(€16. ⏰ 45min., every 30-80min. 6:50am-7:10pm.)* and **Sorrento** *(€13.50. ⏰ Every 20-85min. 7:35am-6:30pm.)*

Once There

Once you've actually arrived on the island, the fastest way to get to Capri's *centro* from the port is by funicular. *(⏰ Every 15-30min. 5:25am-1:45am.)* For information on tickets, see **Getting Around,** below. If you want to walk, it'll take about 20min. up the winding streets. To get to Anacapri directly from the port, take the hourly bus leaving from outside the ticket office in Marina Grande. *(⏰ Every 30min. in the afternoon, otherwise every hr. 5:45am-9:05pm.)*

Getting Around

Once in Capri and Anacapri's town centers, navigating the narrow and steep streets is only practical on foot. To get between major points, take **buses** or the **funicular** *(€1.40 per ride)*. You can buy a €1 rechargeable card and fill it with €2.20 for 1hr. (includes one bus and one funicular ride) or €6.90 for the week. Rechargeable cards are rarely worth it for daytrips but are practical if you're here for a while and planning to bus around the island a lot. The ticket office is to the right of the port. *(☎081 83 89 515 i Cash only. ⏰ Open daily 6:30am-11pm.)* From Capri *centro*, ATC buses run to **Anacapri.** *(⏰ Every 10min. during the day, 20min. early and late, 6am-2am.)* All buses depart from the start of V. Roma in Capri. From Anacapri *centro*, buses head to other island destinations like Grotta Azzurra and Faro. All buses stop in P. Vittoria in Anacapri. For a **taxi,** head to the hubs at the Marina Grande port, P. Umberto I in Capri *(☎081 83 70 543)*, or P. Vittoria in Anacapri *(☎081 83 71 175)*.

sorrento ☎081

Sorrento is the practical traveler's paradise. Located on a train, bus, and ferry route that connects it with the Amalfi Coast's other cities, Sorrento makes dazzling, high-cliffed Bay of Naples beauty easily accessible. While many travelers use Sorrento as a springboard for daytrips, its mix of paved streets and urban grit with shopping and beach bumming—the epitome of leisure—make it worth exploring in its own right. Before hopping on that train to more serene destinations, kick back with a glass of *limoncello* (as common as water here) and a *cono* of mint gelato for some daytime relaxation. Don't forget your heels, though—staying out into the wee hours of the morning is as popular with Sorrento's young crowds.

ORIENTATION

With its flat layout and paved sidewalks, Sorrento is very easy to navigate. Circumvesuviana trains and SITA buses pull into **Piazza de Curtis.** From there, head up the steps to **Via degli Aranci,** which has plenty of cheap accommodations and stores along its sidewalks, or down the hill to **Corso Italia,** which leads into the *centro.* A short walk will take you to the palm-tree-filled **Piazza Tasso** and the parallel **Via San Cesareo,** which is cluttered with souvenir and *limoncello* shops. From the *piazza*, steep stairs lead to the waterfront, a small public beach, and the port.

ACCOMMODATIONS

Being a beach town, Sorrento has its fair share of hotels—sometimes it feels as though they make up a third of the buildings here. With so many cheap hostels and one-star hotels only a few minutes from the *centro*, Sorrento is a great base for hopping around the Amalfi coast. Though not as conveniently located, one train stop away in Sant'Agnello, **Seven Hostel** is a great option. The clean and spacious dorms there are complemented by free Wi-Fi, breakfast, and fun common areas. *(V. Iommella Grande 99 ☎081 878 6758 www.sevenhostel.com* **i** *Credit cards accepted. Ⓢ Dorms €19-30.)* If you can't get enough of the beach and sky, there is also a campsite, **Nube D'Argento,** a 15min. walk from central Sorrento. *(V. Capo 21 ☎081 878 1344 www.nubedargento.com Ⓢ €8-11 per person; €5-10 per tent. Bungalows €9-11.)* For more options, check the tourist office's extensive list.

ULISSE DELUXE HOSTEL

HOSTEL ❶

V. del Mare 22 ☎081 87 74 753 www.ulissedeluxe.com

With its air-conditioned rooms, marble foyer, and discounted access to its private fitness center, Ulisse Deluxe is not easily reconciled with conventional expectations about hostel living. Doubles are more like those of a hotel, with their spacious rooms (yes, multiple rooms) and sparkling-clean ensuite bathrooms. Dorms may be bunked but they're well-kept and have fashionable wooden armoires. It's close to the beach, though with the on-site pool, you might opt to stay sand-free.

Walk down C. Italia nearly to its end and then head downstairs just before the hospital. Walk 3min. toward the right down V. del Mare. i Breakfast €5. All rooms with ensuite bathroom. Free Wi-Fi. Public internet point €10 per day. Ⓢ Dorms €18-25; doubles €60-80; triples €90-120; quads €120-160. Reception 24hr.

BED AND BED DIANA CITY

HOTEL ❸

C. Italia 5 ☎081 80 74 392 www.dianacity.com

You don't have to veer out of central Sorrento or resort to dormitory living to find an affordable room: this newly opened spot is as convenient as it is cheery. Colorful rooms decorated with bright paintings and linens remind you of the beach, though the memory-jolt isn't really necessary as the sand is only 10min. away. There's no breakfast provided, but complimentary tea and coffee are in all the rooms.

From P. Tasso, head 10min. down C. Italia, away from the train station. i All rooms with ensuite bathroom. Free Wi-Fi. Ⓢ Doubles €59-79. 10% discount at downstairs bar. Reception 8am-9pm. Key lets you enter or leave whenever.

OSTELLO LE SIRENE

HOSTEL ❶

V. degli Aranci 160 ☎081 80 72 925 www.hostellesirene.com

The bunk beds in the small rooms at this hostel don't allow for much wiggle room, but le Sirene's proximity to the beach and train is convenient. Rooms have ensuite baths, which would be a plus if the floors weren't wet and a bit dirty. Still, the friendly staff working with the adjacent bar (where breakfast and happy hours are held) give a bit of pep to the place, as does the perpetual disco music playing in the common space. Rooms don't have lockers, so either take your stuff with you or leave it in the public baggage room.

From train station, follow signs down V. degli Aranci and walk 5min. i Breakfast included. Sheets included. Towels €0.50. All-female and all-male dorms available. Free Wi-Fi. Ⓢ 10-bed (male-only) and 8-bed (women-only) dorms €16; 6- to 7-bed (co-ed) €18; 4-bed (co-ed) €19-20. Doubles €45-60. Reception 7am-9pm, though someone at the bar is always there.

SIGHTS

Beaches

Sorrento doesn't offer much in the way of religious and artistic must-sees, but its location on the coast makes it a great starting point for scenic hikes and leisurely days on the sand. Most visitors hit the **beach,** head up **Corso Italia** for shopping, or hop on a SITA bus to hit nearby cities on the Amalfi coast. Sorrento's main beach is the **Marina Grande,** easily accessible by walking down V. de Maio and climbing down 100 steps to the winding road. From there, the port is to the right and a sizeable stretch of private beach is to the left. The tiny public area, which will undoubtedly be crowded, is just beyond. Alternatively, walk down C. Italia in the direction of St. Agnello, the smaller neighbor of Sorrento. (You can also get there by taking the 5min. train ride from Sorrento). From P. Municipio by the Circumvesuviana station in St. Agnello, head left onto Vle. dei Pini and then veer left again onto C. Marion Crawford (yes, that is actually the name of the street, and no, she was not Italian) to reach **Marinella Beach.** Marinella Beach is considerably smaller than Marina Grande, though arguably more serene. The best and farthest beach is **Puolo Beach,** accessible by a 45min. walk from P. Tasso or by the A bus. To reach it on foot, follow V. del Capo for 30min., turn right onto V. Marina di Puolo, and head down the path to the shore. Unlike the nearby **Punta del Capo,** this beach is actually sandy.

Other Sights

If you don't just want to lie around in the sun (who are you?), you can check out the sight listed below or head to the tourist office, which offers walking maps and booklets with sight-seeing itineraries.

CAPO DI SORRENTO — BEACH, RUINS

On the coast, 10-15min. northwest of V. del Capo.

For a break from the tourist crowds and crowded beaches near the *centro,* head down C. Italia to the Capo di Sorrento, a small protrusion of beach and cliff off the otherwise flat coast. Either walk 30min. up the paved V. Capo, passing mostly hotels and greenery, or take the EAVBUS A line. When you reach Calata di Punta del Capo, head right down the steep cobblestone road which eventually becomes soil and winds to the coast. Near the base, you'll pass a small sign marking the **Ruins of Villa di Pollio Felice.** They truly are ruins—without the post, you would barely know they existed. Continue on past the few crumbling arches and make the steep descent to an aquamarine pool of water which will most likely be occupied by swimmers, though far fewer than fill Sorrento's main beaches. A short walk further leads to flat rocks and more water, where a family-heavy crowd switches off between sunbathing and swimming.

Facing the water, take C. Italia left and continue as it winds into V. del Capo. i The walk is easy and doesn't require sneakers.

FOOD

Eating good food and staying cool in Sorrento is easy—*gelaterie* and *limoncello* merchants seem to come in pairs. If you've never tasted the sweet yellow drink, pop into **Limonoro** for a free sample and a piece of *limoncello*-filled chocolate. *(V. San Cesareo 49/53 ☎081 807 2782 www.limonoro.it. i Accepts credit cards. Open daily 8am-9pm.)* Sit-down restaurants line the touristy C. d'Italia, and while they're not as expensive as those in most beach towns, better spots can definitely be found on peripheral streets. Likewise, fruit stands and *salumerie* are plentiful, but your best bet for stocking the picnic basket is either the **STANDA** supermarket *(C. d'Italia 225 i Accepts credit cards. Open M-Sa 8:30am-1:55pm and 5-8:55pm, Su 9:30am-1pm and 5-8:30pm.)* or the **SISA,** which has even better prices. *(V. degli Aranci 157. i Cash only. Open M-Sa 8:30am-1:30pm and 5-8:30pm.)*

PRIMAVERA GELATERIA — GELATERIA, PASTICCERIA ❶

C. Italia 142 — ☎081 80 73 252 www.primaverasorrento.it

When the Pope and bikini-clad supermodels can agree on something, you know it's good: photos of each line the walls of this famed *gelateria,* where proud owner Antonio Cafiero dishes up over 70 flavors of gelato and sweets. Try his invention, the *caffe al nocciola,* a liquid concoction of hazelnut and coffee served in a chocolate-lined cone. Or do like countless movie stars have and devour a *delizia al limone,* a sponge cake smothered in lemon-flavored cream, though you probably won't end up with your photo on the wall unless you can manage a 3 ft. high stack of them. Believe it or not, some people have.

5min. down C. Italia from P. Tasso. Pastries €1.50-3. Cones €2.50-12. The €12 cone is unimaginably large. Open daily summer 9am-1am; fall, winter, and spring 9am-midnight.

IL GIARDINIELLO — RISTORANTE ❷

V. dell'Accademia 7/9 — ☎081 87 84 616 www.giardiniellosorrento.com

Retreat from the sun and crowds to this leaf-covered restaurant while watching Nonna Luisa mix dough for her namesake *torta di nonna.* The garden, filled with funny statues, adds a bit of spunk to the otherwise classic setup. Be assured of high-quality ingredients from start to end—everything from the olive oil to the *limoncello* is homemade. Classic *Sorrentina* dishes, like gnocchi with tomatoes and basil, are accompanied by a large selection of wine and often served by the owners themselves.

From P. Tasso, head down V. de Maio, turn left onto V. Santa Maria Grazie, and continue as the street becomes V. Accademia. Cover €1. Pizza €4.50-7. Primi €4-7. Fish and meat €6-14.50. Open in summer daily 10:30am-midnight; in winter M-W 10:30am-midnight, F-Su 10:30am-midnight.

SALTO — PIZZERIA ❶

V. degli Aranci 147 — ☎334 31 22 016

Portions and menu sizes are rarely this gigantic, even in Naples. Drop by Salto's miniscule shop before hitting the beach or the train for a pizza, made any way you like it. *Primi (€3.50)* may be served on a plastic plate but are better and bigger than anything in the *centro*. Plenty of smaller eats like Nutella-filled brioches *(€0.80)* and *sfizi (€0.80)* are great on the go, especially if your wallet is light.

From the train station, head down V. degli Aranci away from the centro. Across the street from hostel. Pizza €2.50-4, slices €0.80. Panini €3-3.50. Primi €3.50. Open daily 9am-1am.

NIGHTLIFE

For such a small town, Sorrento is home to a surprising number of hopping evening spots. Head down **Corso Italia** for a lively array of bars and cafes teeming with gelato-lickers and cocktail-sippers. Though this town doesn't boast the beach discos of other coastal cities, you can still break it down at spots like **Daniele's Club,** which has a small dance area and caters to a distinctly tourist crowd. *(P. Tasso 10 and down the steps ☎081 877 3992 www.bagattelle.net Open daily 9pm-4am.)*

ENGLISH INN — CLUB, BAR, RISTORANTE

C. Italia 55 — ☎081 807 4357 www.englishinn.it

English keeps the crowd hustling every night and well into the morning. Customers consistently pack its downstairs restaurant for English grub like fish and chips *(€10)*, but the real action happens upstairs in the vine-covered rooftop garden. A nightly DJ, plenty of TVs, and a cheap bar (with bartender's choice happy hours) give rowdy guests their choice between dancing, drinking, or watching it all unfold. The fun and laid-back staff are happy to take requests on anything from music to group drink discounts. When the wee hours start to set in, treat yourself to a hot breakfast in classic English fashion—nice and big.

5min. from P. Tasso. Shots €2. Beer €3-3.50. Cocktails €5. Pizza, pasta, and panini €5-9. Open daily 8am-4am. Kitchen closes at 2am. Upstairs garden open 7:30pm onward. Happy hour 10pm.

INSOLITO — BAR, CLUB

C. Italia 38/E — ☎081 87 72 409 www.insolitosorrento.it

For those who want to disguise their foreign status and slip in with a sleeker Italian crowd, Insolito's cool glass bar and modern mini-disco will fit the bill. Despite its "prettier-than-thou" look (and bartenders to match), the place stays down-to-earth thanks to its cheap happy hours. Live music early in the evening gives way to DJ'd beats for anyone wanting to move their hips, though don't expect the raucous crowd that can be found at other touristy spots.

*5min. down C. Italia from P. Tasso. **i** Internet €1 per 10min. Cocktails before 10pm €5, after €8. Open daily 8am-5am.*

ESSENTIALS

Practicalities

- **TOURIST OFFICES: Info Points** are the most convenient sources of information and are scattered throughout the town. They provide free maps, a small guidebook on Sorrento, and bike rental. Locations at the **Marina Piccola** *(near the port)*, in **Piazza de Curtis** *(outside the train station)*, in **Piazza Tasso,** and in **Piazza Andrea Veniero** *(near the end of C. Italia). (☎ All open daily at 10am; some close at 8pm, others at 9pm.)* The main **Tourist Office** provides free maps, train and bus schedules, and small guides about Sorrento. *(V. Luigi de Maio 35 ☎081 807 4033 www.sorrentotourism.com From P. Tasso, take Luigi De Maio to the end of P. Sant'Antonino and continue toward the water. Open M-Sa 8:30am-4pm.)*
- **CURRENCY EXCHANGE:** The *centro* is full of exchange places, but **Golden Store** has better rates than most. *(V. del Corso 38C ☎081 878 1413 5min. from P. Tasso. Open daily 8am-10pm.)*
- **INTERNET: Insolito.** *(C. Italia 38/E ☎081 877 2409 www.insolitosorrento.it Wi-Fi €4 per hr. Open daily 8am-5am.)*
- **POST OFFICES:** *(C. Italia 210 ☎081 877 2429 Open M-F 8am-6:30pm, Su 8am-1pm.)*

Emergency!

- **POLICE: Carabinieri** *(Vicolo III Rota ☎081 80 73 111).* **Police** *(Vicolo III Rota ☎081 80 75 311)* right off C. Italia heading toward St. Agnello.
- **HOSPITALS/MEDICAL SERVICES: Santa Maria della Misericordia** keeps miserable hours. *(C. Italia 129 ☎081 533 1112 Open to public for appointments M-Sa 1-3pm and 7-8:30pm, Su 1-4pm and 7-8:30pm.)*

Getting There

By Train

Chances are you're traveling to Sorrento from Naples. That's the closest big city and, therefore, the closest airport. Circumvesuviana trains roll into the station in P. de Curtis 6. *(☎800 05 39 39 Every 15-30min. 5:01am-11:26pm.)* The train runs to **Naples** *(€3.40. 1hr.)* and makes stops along the way in **Pompeii** *(€1.90. 20-30min.)* and **Herculaneum.** *(€1.90. 45min.)*

By Ferry

If taking the Circumvesuviana scares you too much (sure, Mt. Vesuvius is dormant, but who knows when that might change?), you can take the ferry across the Bay of Naples. Ferries arrive at the port on the Bay. Take the B or C city bus to P. Marina d'Italia or walk from P. Tasso down the steps to the port. Ticket offices open and close in accordance with the first and last boats of the day. **Linee Marittime Partenopee** *(☎081 80 71 812 www.consorziolmp.it)* runs hydrofoils from **Naples** *(€10. Every 2hr. from Naples 9am-6:25pm, from Sorrento 7:20am-4:25pm.)* and **Capri.** *(€14. Roughly every hr. from Capri 8am-7pm, from Sorrento 7:20am-6:20pm.)* **Metro del Mare** *(☎199 60 07 00 www.metrodelmare.net)* runs ferries from **Positano** *(€9. 4-5 per day from Positano 9am and 12:30-6:10pm, from Sorrento 9:30am-1:15pm and 6:05pm.)* and **Amalfi.** *(€11. 1hr.; 4-5 per day from Amalfi 8:35am, noon, 1:50, 5, 5:40pm; from Sorrento 9:30am-1:15pm and 6:05pm.)*

By Bus

SITA buses *(☎089 405 145 www.sitabus.it)* stop in P. de Curtis in front of the Circumvesuviana train station and are the best way to travel to Sorrento from the Amalfi Coast. Buy tickets from **Unicocampania** bus drivers or the kiosk in P. de Curtis. For prices and logistics see the box below. Buses run to **Positano** *(45 min., every 30min. 6:30am-midnight.)* and **Amalfi.** *(1½hr., every 30min. 6:30am-midnight.)*

bay of buses

To get around Sorrento and the Amafi Coast, buses are your friend. Tickets work on a system where you buy them for a given amount of time, and then are entitled to unlimited rides within that timeframe. Tickets are also valid for EAVBUS service within Sorrento, and the Circumvesuviana trains. A 45min. ticket costs €2.40, 1½hr. €3.60, 24hr. €7.20, and a 3-day pass €18. For information on where to buy them, check the **Getting There** section for each town.

Getting Around

Though walking is easy, **EAVBUS** does run orange buses throughout the city *(Ⓢ One-way ticket €1)*. Integrated SITA tickets (see box above) are also valid on EAVBUS lines. For information on finding your way around the city, see **Orientation**.

positano ☎089

Like the two-piece bathing suit that originated here (a.k.a. the bikini), Positano is a city in two parts. In one, you have the hot, crowded coast and, in the other, the cool cliffs which cushion it on either side. The divided layout matches the cultural clash that seems to define this small town: literati like **Jack Kerouac** and **Tennessee Williams** famously celebrated the beauty here, and now countless tourists simply bundle it into their rounds along the Amalfi Coast. Though Positano's unique geography makes it harder to navigate than surrounding cities, hiking, tanning, shopping, or hitting the town after dark are equally feasible options in its diverse landscape. Just don't expect to do any of those activities in the solitude Kerouac might have enjoyed—Positano's history and beauty have cemented its status as one of the coast's most popular destinations.

ORIENTATION

Though not huge, Positano is tricky to navigate. The *centro* sits nestled on the coast between two high cliffs but is not accessible by SITA buses—coming from other cities, you'll have to walk or take a local bus down. From the **Chiesa Nuova** stop, the winding **Viale Pasitea** and a few short-cut staircases lead to the **Spiaggia Grande,** the town's recreational and commercial heart. Alternatively, from the **Positano Sponda** stop, **Via Cristoforo Colombo** is a gentle slope which winds into **Via dei Mulini** and heads to **Piazza Flavio Gioia,** which is full of shops and close to the tourist office. A footpath from Spiaggia Grande leads along the coast to **Spiaggia del Fornillo,** a somewhat less crowded option. Be prepared for winding, pedestrian streets near the water and curving car-ridden roads farther up the cliffs. The area around Chiesa Nuova may not be the city center, but it has great restaurants, cheaper accommodations, and the best views.

ACCOMMODATIONS

Expect anything from expensive four-star hotels to charming and cheap bed and breakfasts. The most affordable spots are located on the hill descending from the **Chiesa Nuova** SITA bus stop. Closer to the coast and up the other side around **Positano Sponda,** bigger and costlier hotels are more common.

OSTELLO BRIKETTE — HOSTEL ❷

V. Guglielmo Marconi 358 — ☎089 87 58 57 www.brikette.com

Positano's only hostel delivers with a laid-back staff, a social and panoramic terrace to rival those of nearby hotels, and bright, spacious dorms. Though you can't use the kitchen, cheap bar grub and beer and a communal refrigerator should save you from Positano's more expensive options. That's not to mention the bountiful breakfast options, including America's two favorite morning foods: pancakes and eggs *(€2-4)*. The only thing you don't have is the beach lapping at your door, but the hostel's location near the bus actually makes it more convenient for travelers than central hotels.

From Chiesa Nuova stop, walk 100m to the left of Bar Internazionale and climb steps. i Breakfast €2-4. Bag storage after checkout €2 per bag. Free Wi-Fi. $ 8-bed dorms €22-24; doubles €65, with bath €75; triples with bath €120. Reception 24hr.

CASA COSENZA — PENSIONE 4

V. Trara Genoino 18 — ☎089 87 50 63 www.casacosenza.it

Tiled floors, arched ceilings, and stripped wooden doors set this lovely guesthouse apart from other accommodations this close to the coastal center. Casa Cosenza's only single is snug but great if you like simplicity and ocean views. Doubles are much more spacious and feature terraces or balconies with views that make them feel even bigger. Plants and a tiled walkway leading to the rooms might remind you of the countryside instead of the ocean. Though breakfast is expensive, the continental offerings could be satisfying enough to last you through lunch.

From the tourist office, exit onto V. Trara Genoino, heading up stairs in the direction of V. Pasitea. Look for signs on the right of the small street. i Breakfast €10. All rooms with ensuite bathroom. Free Wi-Fi. $ Singles €50-60; doubles €100-120. Extra bed €40.

B AND B VILLA PALUMBO — B AND B 4

Vle. Pasitea 334 — ☎089 87 59 82 www.villapalumbo.it

If you're thinking about staying in one of Positano's hotels, consider the five bedrooms offered at this small bed and breakfast instead. Lace curtains lead to private terraces with unbelievable views of the coast and cliffs. Though rooms aren't huge, they are well cared-for, and the sunny vistas make them feel airy. The friendly owner serves home-cooked breakfast on the public terrace and even leaves a bottle of wine and snack in each room upon arrival.

From Chiesa Nuova stop, walk downhill for 5min. and look for sign on the left. i Breakfast included. Rooms have private bath. $ Singles €50-70; doubles €60-80; triples €70-90. Reception 8am-9pm. Call ahead to arrange arrival time.

THE GREAT OUTDOORS

More than other cities along the Amalfi coast, Positano offers great outdoor opportunities ranging from lazing on the beach to sweating your way up the surrounding hills. After taking a stroll through the center's bustling boutiques, head to **Fornillo Beach,** Positano's most secluded and scenic. Tucked away past the Torre Trasita and the main docking area, it's a bit quieter than the rest. To reach it, take V. Positanese d'America, a footpath starting at the port's right side and winding down the coast. The more centrally located **Spiaggia Grande** has only a small public area near the docks, making for a less-than-clean swim. Nearby, **Blue Star** rents motorboats and rowboats if you want to drift down the water on your own. Or, consider taking a tour of the Blue and Emerald Grottoes in a more directed itinerary *(☎089 81 18 88 www.bluestarpositano.it)*.

If you've had enough water, head inland for some **hiking.** A 45min. climb will take you up the side of **Montepertuso,** which is pierced by a huge hole. From its top, you can take the **Path of the Gods** *(about 4hr.)*. Hit up the tourist office for maps and information on the excursions—but before setting out, get ready with water and good shoes. The trails are not for the light of heart *or* flip-flops.

FOOD

Positano's *centro* is full of elegant restaurants—or at least, restaurants disguising tourist-trappery with elegance. While it won't be hard to satisfy seafood cravings near the coast, head up the hill toward Chiesa Nuova for great views, fewer people, and slightly better prices. The **Mini Market A.D.** stocks basics and is close to Chiesa Nuova bus stop. *(V. Pasitea 352 ☎089 81 23 437 i Credit cards accepted. Open M-Sa 7:30am-1:45pm and 4:30-9pm, Su 8am-1pm.)*

C'ERA UNA VOLTA — RISTORANTE ❷

V. Guglielmo Marconi 127 ☎089 81 19 30 www.ristoranteceraunavolta.info

When they're not scribbling down takeout orders from hungry backpackers and locals, the busy waiters will be running to your table, delivering piping-hot plates in record time. This place has excellent pizza that will fuel you up for a day of rushing or resting—though, when you see the views of the coast from C'era una Volta's rooftop terrace, you'll probably choose the latter. It may be an uphill trek from the beach, but, with lower prices and that fabulous view, it's all the better for its elevated locale. Luckily for hostelers, all they have to do to get here is roll out of bed.

Down the street from the Chiesa Nuova bus stop. Cover €1. Pizza €4-7. Primi €6-8.50; secondi €7-18. Open M-W noon-3pm and 7-11pm, Th 7-11pm, F-Su noon-3pm and 7-11pm.

SARACENO D'ORO — RISTORANTE ❸

V. Pasitea 254 ☎089 81 20 50 www.saracenodoro.it

Under soft red arches and twinkling lights, indulge in a meal that perfectly captures this part of Italy—everything from the coastal view to the homemade *scialatielli allo scoglio* (finely-cut pasta with seafood) shouts, "Amalfi!" Large doors open out onto small sidewalk tables, making the restaurant as airy as it is aromatic—you can be assured, that fish smell is drifting from the kitchen, not the ocean below. Though half the joy comes from lingering a while, margherita pizzas on the go *(€5)* can save you some time and money.

Halfway up V. Pasitea between the Chiesa Nuova SITA stop and the tourist office; walk up the hill or take an orange city bus. Cover €2. Pizza €6-10, takeout €4-8. Pasta €10-15. Meat and fish €9-15. Open daily Mar-Dec noon-3pm and 6pm-midnight.

TRATTORIA GROTTINO AZZURRO — SEAFOOD ❷

V. Guglielmo Marconi 303-305 ☎089 87 54 66

Seafood restaurants often have a somewhat stuffed-shirt attitude, perhaps thanks to their usually elevated prices. Fortunately, with its white walls and wooden tables, the simple interior of this laid-back trattoria looks more like a tugboat than a cruise ship. There's no need for aesthetic flair because, as the natives of Positano know, this spot has the best seafood around. No pizza means you'll have to content yourself with a proper spoon, fork, and plate. Don't worry: with food this good, it won't be hard.

Outside the Chiesa Nuova SITA bus stop. i No reservations. Primi €6-10; meat entrees €10-12, seafood entrees €12-24. Open M-Tu 11am-3pm and 7-10:30pm, Th-Su 11am-3pm and 7-10:30pm.

ESSENTIALS

Practicalities

- **TOURIST OFFICES: Azienda Autonoma di Soggiorno e Turismo di Positano** provides free maps of the city as well as information on hotels, restaurants, and transportation options. *(V. del Saracino 4 ☎089 87 50 67 www.aziendaturismopositano.it Near the end of V. dei Mulini, in Positano's centro. Open M-Sa 8:30am-8pm, Su 8:30am-2:30pm.)*

- **CURRENCY EXCHANGE: Angela Collina** exchanges currency and has a **Western Union.** *(P. dei Mulini 6 ☎089 87 58 64 At the start of V. dei Mulini. Open daily 9am-2pm and 4-9:30pm.)* The most **ATMs** and **banks** are clustered around V. dei Mulini.
- **LUGGAGE STORAGE: Blu Porter** has baggage pickup and deposit. *(In front of the pharmacy at Vle. Pasitea 22 ☎089 81 14 96 www.positanobluporter.it i Cash only. $ €5-10 per day, per bag. Open daily 7am-7pm.)*
- **POST OFFICES:** *(V. Guglielmo Marconi 320 ☎089 87 51 42 Near the Chiesa Nuova SITA stop. Open M-F 8am-1:30pm, Sa 8am-12:30pm.)*

Emergency!

- **POLICE: Police.** *(V. Guglielmo Marconi 111 ☎089 87 50 11 At the intersection with V. Pasitea.)* **Municipal police.** *(Località Mulini ☎089 87 52 77).*
- **HOSPITALS/MEDICAL SERVICES: Red Cross.** *(Vle. Pasitea 246 ☎089 81 19 12).*

Getting There

By Bus

Positano is best reached by blue **SITA** buses. There is no central bus station: Positano's many bus stops all sit on the elevated road above the coastal *centro*. From the stops, either walk 10-20min. down the steps or road, or take a small orange bus marked "Positano Interno" to the coast. *($ €1. Every 10-15min.)* Arriving in Positano, either get off at **Chiesa Nuova** (in front of "Bar Internazionale") or **Positano Sponda** (near V. Cristoforo Colombo and closer to the *centro*). From any of Positano's stops, buses run to and from **Sorrento** *(1hr., 31 per day 7:10am-12:40am.)* and **Amalfi.** *(45 min., 31 per day 6am-12:50am.)* Buy tickets at *tabaccherie*. The cost of the ticket depends on the length in time of your trip. *($ 45min. €2.40, 1½hr. €3.60, 24hr. €7.20, 3-day €18.)*

By Ferry

By water, ferries and hydrofoils arrive at the port on **Spiaggia Grande. Metro del Mare** *(☎089 19 96 00 700 www.metrodelmare.net)* runs ferries between Positano and **Amalfi** *($ €9. 6-7 per day, from Amalfi 8:35am and 11:45am-5:40pm, from Positano 10:15am-6:35pm.)*, **Naples Molo Beverello** *($ €14. 4 per day, from Naples 8:25-9:20am and 3:10pm, from Positano 12:15-6:10pm.)*, and **Sorrento.** *($ €9. 4-5 per day, from Sorrento 9:30am-1:15pm and 6:05pm, from Positano 9am and 12:30-6:10pm.)* **Alicost** *(☎089 81 19 86 www.lauroweb.com/alicost.htm)* runs ferries and hydrofoils to **Capri.** *($ €14.50-16.50. 30-60min.; from Capri 3:30, 4:25, 5, 5:30pm; from Positano 8:50, 10, 10:55am.)*

Getting Around

Walking is pretty much the only option for getting around Positano, which, given its small size, is not really a problem. There are many steps and uneven paths, though, so exercise caution or you could end up looking really stupid. For more information on getting around or how to get from the bus stops to the town center, see **Orientation** or **Getting There**.

amalfi ☎089

Amalfi is the cool kid on the block—universally known, the subject of wild rumors, the one everyone else wants to be. Not surprising, as it's the perfect marriage of waterfront and commercial *centro* yet somehow escapes becoming either fully urban or completely beach resort. More than any other coastal spot, Amalfi walks the line between artificial and natural beauty—the Escher-like Duomo and Disneyland-style houses sit beside sparkling blue waters, jagged cliffs and lush green trees. This unique combo makes this town highly sought-out (read: expensive and crowded). To escape, head to the neighboring Atrani, 10min. away on foot, which offers cheaper options and some originality of its own. No, it's not just the copycat kid fawning over the hotshot, even though it's name *is* awfully similar.

ORIENTATION

Amalfi is shaped like an upside-down T: its base lying on the waterfront and its thin center extending slightly uphill. It's all easily walkable in an hour. **Piazza Flavio Gioia** (the bus and boat hub) leads into **Piazza Duomo,** which funnels into the narrow **Via Lorenzo d'Amalfi** and **Via Pietro Capuano.** These two central thoroughfares are lined with merchants, small food shops, and cafes; while most of the nicer restaurants can be found up steps on either side; look for signs. **Corso delle Repubbliche Marinare** runs along the coast and becomes **Via Pantaleone Comite.** Follow this road to get to neighboring **Atrani,** a 10min. walk around the large cliff. Atrani's much quieter center is located down a circular ramp in **Piazza Umberto.**

ACCOMMODATIONS

Cheap accommodations in Amalfi are few and far between. For better prices, head to **Atrani.** If you do want to shell out your euros, you'll likely get good services and great views of the water, though you'll still have to pay to step on the sand.

HOTEL LA CONCHIGLIA — HOTEL ❹

Piazzale dei Protontini ☎089 87 18 56 www.amalfihotelconchiglia.it

The bright aquamarine shutters and decorative tiling of this hotel match Amalfi's beautiful water. This family-run place 10min. from the *centro* is secluded from crowds but still provides guests with beach proximity and plenty of relaxing space on the terraces and garden. Eleven clean rooms aren't fresh-and-crispy new, but they have charming white curtains and painted tile accents that give the place the feeling of an old-fashioned summer home. Owner Alfonso speaks little English but if you can muster up broken Italian, he'll be happy to tell you the secrets of Amalfi, his lifelong hometown.

*Facing the water from the bus stop, walk right on the waterfront along Lungomare dei Cavalleri for 10min. Look for hotel sign when you reach Salita S. Caterina. **i** Breakfast included. Rooms with ensuite bathroom and fan. Free Wi-Fi. Singles €55; doubles €80-90; triples €110-120. Beach access, 2 chairs, and umbrella €18. Reception 8am-8pm; call ahead to arrange arrival time.*

A SCALINATELLA HOSTEL — HOSTEL ❷

P. Umberto I ☎089 87 14 92 www.hostelscalinatella.com

Helpful staff and cheap prices are the only appealing thing about an otherwise bare-bones hostel. Its location in the more secluded Atrani is a plus, though you won't have anything near hotel-like amenities. Dorm rooms aren't terribly private, don't have lockers, and some don't have windows. As the crowd is mostly backpackers, though, the vibe is laid-back, if slightly quiet.

*From Amalfi, walk 10min. along V. Pantaleone Comite overlooking the waterfront; after the tunnel, head down the circular ramp on the right into Atrani's centro. Reception in P. Umberto I until 10am. After that, head up V. dei Dogi and follow signs to the right up the steps. **i** Breakfast included. Laundry €7. 4-bed dorms €25; doubles, triples, and quads €70-140. Call about arrival time to make sure staff is around. Showers open 6-10am and 5-10pm.*

HOTEL LIDOMARE — HOTEL ❸

V. Piccolomini 9 ☎089 87 13 32

The nearly silent surrounds of Hotel Lidomare will make you wonder if you're still in Amalfi. Get a room with a terrace, though, and you'll have no trouble remembering how close the ocean is—great views of the water await. Antique bookshelves, curious wall decorations, and beautiful mosaics distinguish

Lidomare from more generic hotels. You can't use it, but ask to see the old-fashioned kitchen anyway for a peek at where your breakfast fixings are carefully prepared. Prices are surprisingly good for the area.

*Head out of P. Duomo through the alleyway and up the steps to the left. **i** Breakfast included. All rooms with ensuite bathroom. Wi-Fi €5 per 3hr. Singles €45-60; doubles €80-120. Reception 24hr.*

SIGHTS

DUOMO DI SANT'ANDREA, CLOISTER OF PARADISE AND CRYPT — CHURCH

P. Duomo ☎089 87 13 24

After you utter your first "wow" at seeing Amalfi's blue waters, your second one will come when you pass its Duomo, the proud star of the city's busiest *piazza*. Admire the peculiar black-and-white facade and its strong geometric patterning before climbing over 60 steps to the top. The interior might not be worth the wait if you arrive after the free "hours of prayer," but the quiet **Cloister of Paradise,** with its arcade of interlaced white columns, makes for a nice stroll. Get your money's worth by popping into the **crypt,** which holds the body of St. Andrew, and the small museum, which displays intricate jewelry and ornamentation from the church's treasury.

To enter basilica during prayer, go through main doors up the stairs; to enter midday, head up the stairs and left to the ticket desk. Basilica free during hours of prayer; €3 midday entry only with combined ticket to museum, crypt, and cloister. Basilica open for prayer daily 7:30-10am and 5-8pm. Open with museum, crypt, and cloister 10am-5pm.

PAPER MUSEUM (MUSEO DELLA CARTA) — MUSEUM

V. delle Cartiere 23 ☎089 83 04 561 www.museodellacarta.it

Compared to others in Italy, this museum is as lightweight as, well, a piece of paper. Nonetheless, the town takes pride in the place, which is housed in a 14th-century paper mill that may become more notable once you know that Amalfi is famed for its artisan production of a certain kind of thick paper. The included tour adds a bit of amusement to the place and lets you watch this miraculous thing—paper—being made.

*10min. up V. delle Cartiere from the P. Duomo. **i** Admission includes tour (available in English). €4, students and groups €2.50. Open daily 10am-6:30pm.*

THE GREAT OUTDOORS

Beaches are the reason most people come to Amalfi. The town's main beach is the **Marina Grande,** which, though unremarkable, is well-loved and easily accessible (translation: crowded). Head around the Torre di Amalfi to neighboring **Atrani,** where a much quieter sandy stretch awaits. If lying in the sun and dipping into the calm waters isn't your idea of fun, try a rigorous **hike** through Amalfi's stunning countryside. One of the most popular hikes connects Amalfi to Ravello through Pontone. The 2hr. uphill climb starts at the **Museo della Carta.** From here, continue on the partially paved path, following signs for Ravello. Monuments you'll pass on the way include the churches of **San Giovanni Battista** and **Santa Maria del Carmine.** The shorter 1hr. hike from Atrani to Ravello consists mostly of steep stairs and provides a scenic route ending up beside the **Villa Cimbrone.** The tourist offices in both Ravello and Amalfi provide detailed hiking maps.

FOOD

Most higher-quality restaurants are located up side steps off the main streets. The local favorite dish is *scialatelli* (a coarsely cut pasta), often topped with excellent seafood. **La Grande Mela** supermarket offers a better and less expensive selection of basic foodstuffs than the specialty grocers which line V. Pietro Capuano *(V. dei Curiali 6 ☎089 87 11 60 Turn right into the alley at the start of V. d'Amalfi. Open M-Sa 8am-1:30pm and 5-8:30pm, Su 8am-1:30pm.)*

BAR BIRECTO — CAFE ❶

P. Umberto I ☎089 87 10 17 www.ilbirecto.com

You've had pizza, gelato, and beer before—the first two are practically Italy's middle names—but finding them on the cheap, especially in Amalfi's touristy streets, is another story. Bar Birecto's happy hour combos *(all the above for €5)* is nothing less than spectacular. Combine the sweet food and drink deal with free Wi-Fi and chill service from longtime owner, Luigi, and you've got a winner. One liter pitchers of cocktails *(€7)* and mixed beer drinks like the cielo blue *(beer, rum, and Blue Caracao; €4)* will have you wondering if that's the blue Amalfi water or just a similarly colored cocktail before you. Either way, you'll want to dive in.

In Atrani. From Amalfi, walk 10min. along V. Pantaleone Comite overlooking the waterfront; after the tunnel, head down the circular ramp on the right into Atrani's centro. i Free Wi-Fi. Gelato €2-3.50. Pizza €4-6. Primi €5-7. Beer €2.50-6. Cocktails €4-5. Open daily 7am-2am. Happy hour 3-7pm.

TRATTORIA E PIZZERIA DA MEMÉ — RISTORANTE ❸

Salita Marino Sebaste 8 ☎089 83 04 549

This family restaurant is set back away from Amalfi's beach-going crowds. Locals gather at small tables scattered on stone steps leading to the fresh interior. Though the brick-oven pizza is a real steal, their specialty is homemade pasta topped with fresh seafood. You can't go wrong with the regional favorite, *scialatielli allo scoglio*.

Walk up V. Lorenzo d'Amalfi from P. Duomo. As it becomes V. Pietro Capuano, look for signs on the left of the street and turn up the stairs. Cover €1.50. Pizza €3.50-10. Primi €6.50-15; secondi €8-15. Open in summer daily noon-3pm and 6:30pm-midnight; in fall, winter, and spring Tu-Su noon-3pm and 6:30pm-midnight.

PIZZA EXPRESS — PIZZERIA ❶

V. Pietro Capuano 46

Pop into this tiny joint for the best prices and quickest service in town. Its hole-in-the-wall status, however, means you'll have to head elsewhere with your goods. If standing with a pie in your hand doesn't sound appealing, grab a smaller *fagottini (sauce, cheese, and veggies or meat stuffed in a pizza-dough crust; €2)*, which is filling and easier to eat. This is the kind of place you find on every block in Naples, but here in Amalfi, Pizza Express is one-of-a-kind.

From P. Duomo, walk up V. Lorenzo d'Amalfi and continue as it becomes V. Pietro Capuano. Pizza €2.50-5, slices €1-1.50. Calzones €4. Open in summer daily 9am-10pm; in fall, winter, and spring M-Th 9am-10pm, Sa-Su 9am-10pm.

ESSENTIALS

Practicalities

- **TOURIST OFFICES:** The **Azienda Autonoma Soggiorno e Turismo di Amalfi** provides free maps of the city and surrounding area (including hiking maps), bus and ferry schedules, and hotel and food listings. *(C. delle Repubbliche Marinare 27, through the courtyard. ☎089 87 11 07 www.amalfitouristoffice.it 5min. from P. Flavio Gioia, in the direction of Atrani. Open M-Sa 9am-1pm and 2-6pm, Su 9am-1pm.)*
- **POST OFFICES:** *(C. delle Repubbliche Marinare ☎089 83 04 831 i Also has currency exchange. Open M-F 8am-6:30pm, Sa 8am-12:30pm.)*
- **POSTAL CODE:** 84011.

Emergency!

- **POLICE: Carabinieri.** *(V. Casamare 19 ☎089 87 10 22 To the left of V. delle Cartiere's start, on the way to the Museo della Carta.)* **Police.** *(In P. Municipio ☎089 87 16 33 Around the corner from Tourist Office.)*
- **HOSPITALS/MEDICAL SERVICES: Guardia Medica** *(V. Casamare before the Carabinieri ☎089 87 14 49).*

Getting There

By Bus

Amalfi is best reached by blue **SITA** buses which run up and down the coast *(☎089 87 35 89 www.sitabus.it).* Buses arrive in and depart from P. Flavio Gioia near the port. There is no central office, but tickets can be bought at nearby *tabaccherie* or at the **Touring Point** at Vico dei Pastai 9, just off the *piazza.* The cost of the ticket depends on the length in time of your trip. *(€2.40 for 45min., €3.60 for 1½hr., €7.20 for 24hr., €18 for 3 days.)* Buses run between Amalfi and **Sorrento** *(1½hr.; depart M-Sa every 30min., slightly reduced on Su, 6:30am-midnight.),* **Ravello** *(25min., every 15-30min. 6:30am-midnight.),* and **Salerno.** *(75min., depart every 15-4 min. 5:15am-12:45am.)* To get between Amalfi and **Positano** (45min. away), just hop on an Amalfi-Sorrento bus—they all stop in that other coastal town.

By Boat

Ferries and hydrofoils (docks beside the bus stop) are a more expensive option, but provide nice views and service some places buses don't reach. **Metro del Mare** *(☎199 60 07 00 www.metrodelmare.net)* runs ferries to **Salerno** *(€8.50. Depart Salerno 8, 11:30am, 5:15pm; depart Amalfi 10:40am, 4:45, 7pm.),* **Positano** *(€9. 6-7 per day, from Positano 10:15am-6:35pm, from Amalfi 8:35am and 11:45am-5:40pm.),* **Naples** *(€14-15. 2hr.; 6 per day; from Naples 8:25-9:20am, 3:10pm, and 5:20pm, from Positano 8:35am-5:40pm.),* and **Sorrento.** *(€11. 1hr.; 4-5 per day; from Sorrento 9:30am-1:15pm and 6:05pm; from Amalfi 8:35am, noon, 1:50, 5, 5:40pm.)* **Alicost** *(☎089 87 33 01 www.lauroweb.com/alicost.htm)* runs ferries and hydrofoils to and from **Capri.** *(€15-17. 50-80 min.; 5 per day; from Capri 9:30-9:40am and 3:30-5:30pm; from Amalfi 8:25-11:35am.)*

Getting Around

The biggest transportation decision most travelers face in Amalfi is dive or belly-flop. Walking will get you around quite easily. Atrani is a 10min. walk away, although if that's too far, you can get there in half the time (save five whole minutes!) by catching a Ravello- or Salerno-bound bus, which will drop you off in Altrani. For information on schedules, ticket purchase, and prices, see **Getting There** .

ravello ☎089

If the Amalfi Coast is a house, Ravello is the attic a lot of visitors don't see but actually stores much of the coolest stuff. This tiny town sits quite literally above all of Amalfi's coastal cities and offers phenomenal views down on them. It has beautiful gardens, elegant villas, and a classical music festival that makes you think the place might be heaven itself (it certainly has enough altitude to make you wonder). Come here to get away from the bustle—everything from the music to the older crowds begs you to slow down.

ORIENTATION

Ravello is a small hilltop town, easily walkable in an hour. After getting off the bus at **Via G. Boccaccio,** walk through the tunnel into **Piazza Duomo.** From there, a few main streets, including **Via Roma** and **Via della Francesca** (headed for **Villa Cimbrone**), branch off, leading to stunning views and Ravello's outdoor sights.

SIGHTS

Like the aforementioned attic, Ravello packs a lot of cool stuff into a small space. If you don't want to go the more cultural route, consider doing some hiking around the area. Routes are well marked and fairly easy to do; the tourist office provides detailed maps.

VILLA RUFOLO

GARDENS

P. Duomo ☎089 85 76 21 www.villarufolo.it

Ravello is most renowned for its yearly music festival, much of which is performed in the serene grounds of the 13th-century Villa Rufolo. There's a reason the festival is based here—these grounds are so stunning that they inspired **Richard Wagner:** it was in his honor that the town initiated the festival. The villa's lands, once the possession of Ravello's wealthiest family, feature a cloister and the **Torre Maggiore** (visible from outside the walls), but the natural beauty is its most obvious and pleasing element. A garden full of diverse and rare flora complements the blue seascape gleaming below.

Right off P. Duomo. €5, under 12 and over 65 €3. Open daily 9am-9pm. Last entry 15min. before close.

VILLA CIMBARONE

GARDENS, PANORAMIC VIEW

V. Santa Chiara 26 ☎089 85 74 59 www.villacimbrone.com

Not that you need a break from anything (Ravello's streets are that calm), but if you want a bit more beauty, head to the Villa Cimbarone, a short walk from P. Duomo. The six-hectare expanse of land was once coveted for its relative fertility in comparison with the rockier expanses in most of Ravello, but was eventually abandoned. In the 20th century, **Ernest William Beckett** bought the neglected land and determined to turn it into a work of landscape art—his revitalization of the grounds is one of the most stunning manifestations of English design in Italy. Though he didn't sculpt the views of the coast with his own hands, they are just as beautiful as his more contrived design.

From P. Duomo, head down V. San Francesco and continue as the street becomes V. Santa Chiara. The villa is about 10min. away. €6, children €4. Open daily 9am-8pm.

FOOD

The restaurants in musical Ravello serve up some seriously delicious food that'll have you singing their praises, but you may end up singing the blues when the bill arrives—things here aren't cheap.

CUMPÀ COSIMO

RISTORANTE ❸

V. Roma 44/46 ☎089 85 71 56

After 81 years of business, this family-run trattoria has carved itself a spot in Ravello's cliffs and in the hearts of its residents. On top of top-notch service to locals, the friendly owners show their love for their coastal neighbors, printing business cards on handmade paper from Amalfi's **Paper Museum**. You're here for food, though, not history. Rich crêpes with ham and cheese are a family specialty *(€11)*, but for those who can't make up their mind, the testing plate *(€15)* may be the better choice. The platter lets you sample some of Ravello's best pasta, all house-made. Between bites, chat with the longtime owners and learn more about Ravello lore.

Down V. Roma, just past the tourist office. Pastas €9-15; meat/fish €9-40; cheese €9-10. Open Mar-Sept daily noon-3:30pm and 6:30-10:30pm; Oct-Feb Tu-Su noon-3:30pm and 6:30-10:30pm.

RISTORANTE PIZZERIA VITTORIA

RISTORANTE ❷

V. dei Rufolo 3 ☎089 85 79 47 www.ristorantepizzeriavittoria.it

For a twist on the old pie, try the 0.5m pizza "plank," with your choice of three toppings *(€18)*. The inner garden's small tables may barely accommodate the giant-sized entree, but with a friend, you'll have no trouble finishing it off. Decent-sized pies are best devoured solo. For a lighter plate and reminder of the sea, try the popular sliced octopus drizzled with olive oil and lemon juice *(€10)*.

From P. Duomo, head out onto V. dei Rufolo for 2min. Cover €2. Pizza €5-9. Primi €9-12; secondi €15-18. Open daily 12:15-3pm and 7:15-11pm.

FESTIVALS

RAVELLO FESTIVAL

SUMMER

P. Duomo 7 ☎089 85 84 22 www.ravellofestival.com

Ravello really spoils us sometimes. As if the view wasn't enough, the town goes and gives us one of the world's largest classical music festivals each summer. If classical music's your thing, you'll probably be in heaven. If it's not, you can just look at the view. After witnessing Ravello's stunning beauty during a visit here in 1880, German composer Richard Wagner based some of his **Parsifal** on the Villa Rufolo gardens. Cashing in on this (really rather minor) legacy, the town has for more than 50 years hosted an annual series of concerts that attracts renowned performers. The festival has expanded to encompass dance, art shows, and discussion groups as well. In a small town, having a festival so grand that it gets a new theme each year—2010's was "Madness"—is quite an achievement, and one of the two things (yes, the other is indeed the view) that sets Ravello apart from other Amalfi Coast destinations.

*Most performances take place in Villa Rufolo gardens, although the reach of the festival extends over the whole town. **i** Check the website, ticket office at the above address, or the tourist office for a schedule of events. Concert tickets €20-70. Festival runs July-Sept. Ticket office open daily May-Sept 10am-8pm.*

ESSENTIALS

Practicalities

- **TOURIST OFFICES: Azienda Autonoma Soggioro e Turismo di Ravello** provides free maps of the town and surrounding area (including hiking maps), information on the Ravello Festival, and hotel and restaurant listings. *(V. Roma 18 ☎089 85 70 96 www.ravellotime.it A 2min. walk from P. Duomo. Open daily 9:30am-1pm and 2-6pm.)*
- **INTERNET: Bar Calce** provides internet and Wi-Fi. *(V. Boccaccio 11 ☎089 85 71 30 Beside SITA bus stop. **i** Cash only. €1.50 per 15min., €5 per hr. Discounts on internet if you buy food. Open daily 8:30am-1:30pm and 3:30-10pm.)*
- **POST OFFICES:** *(V. Boccaccio 21 ☎089 85 86 61 Beside SITA bus stop. Open M-F 8am-1:30pm, Sa 8am-12:30pm.)* Also has an **ATM,** though others are throughout the town.

Emergency!

- **POLICE: Carabinieri.** *(V. Rogadeo 1 ☎089 85 71 50 At the end of V. Roma, make a right.)* **Polizia Locale.** *(P. Fontana Moresca ☎089 85 74 98 At the end of Vle. Gioacchino D'Anna.)*
- **LATE-NIGHT PHARMACIES:** Unlike most Italian towns, Ravello does not have many pharmacies. Try **Farmacia Russo** if you need one. *(V. Boccaccio 15 ☎089 85 71 89 Right by the SITA bus stop. Open daily 9am-1pm and 5-8:30pm.)*

Getting There

Ravello is a 25min. ride from **Amalfi** on a blue **SITA bus.** Buses arrive and leave from the end of V. Giovanni Boccaccio regularly. *(Every 10-30min. 5:45am-12:25am.)* You can also call a **taxi** *(☎089 85 80 00)* from the bus stop. Alternatively, **hike** 1hr. up fairly even stairs from **Atrani** (through Castiglione and Scala) or 2hr. from Amalfi (through Pontone). For more information, see **Amalfi Sights.**

Getting Around

Ravello is small and navigated almost exclusively by foot. For more information on how to navigate by foot, see **Orientation.**

CINQUE TERRE

Once an undiscovered paradise, the Cinque Terre now offers a break to backpackers tired of city-hopping through Europe. Frequent train service makes the five charming cliffside villages that dot this stretch of the Italian Riviera easily accessible, yet the region's unique landscape, characterized by terraces built up over thousands of years of grape and citrus farming, prevents this Italian Shangri-La from becoming a tourism-fueled playground-by-the-sea. Yes, out-of-town visitors are a large majority of the summertime population, and English at times feels like the area's first language. But visitors willing to trek along the trails that connect the region's five towns find that a number of unrivaled vistas and secluded beaches remain. The tourist office says the walk, which winds through vineyards, along cliffs, and into forests, takes 5hr., but experienced hikers claim it can be done in less than four.

Part of the pleasure of exploring the area on foot comes from getting to know each of the five villages' distinct personalities. **Monterosso,** blessed with a welcoming expanse of sand, is the modern beach town, **Vernazza** the quieter but more beautiful sister by the sea. Hilltop **Corniglia** is tiny but offers the most stunning vistas of all five towns. **Manarola** has the best (and wackiest) swim spot, and **Riomaggiore** sees backpackers trying, successfully or not, to find last-minute rooms.

It would be a lie and a cliché to say that, in the Cinque Terre, there's not a car in sight. They're here, along with scooters and motorboats too. But in the face of all the beachfront hustle and tourist bustle, it's still possible to slip away into the vineyards, look down on the towns, and witness the beauty and majesty that make the Cinque Terre seem too perfect to be real.

greatest hits

- **I LIKE HIKE.** Leave your train ticket behind and hit the hiking trails to get between the five picturesque villages. Check out our walking tour for the best places to admire the scenery (p. 80).
- **TAKE A BREATHER.** Backpacking can be hard, we know that. So take it easy and lie on Monterosso's beach for a few minutes. Or a week (p. 73).
- **JAM BY THE MED.** La Cantina da Zio Bramante in Manarola is one of the best destinations for nightlife and surprising ensemble musical performances you'll find in all of Italy (p. 88).

student life

Cinque Terre may not have any actual universities, but that certainly doesn't mean it's short on students. The villages, particularly Monterosso, are packed with young people throughout the spring and summer. Many are American tourists here for everything from spring break partying to...summer partying. Check out the bars on P. Garibaldi for a good time once the sun has gone down. During the day, students can be found on the villages' beaches, the hikes between them, or maybe just still in bed sleeping off their hangovers.

monterosso ☎0187

The biggest and most bustling of the towns on Cinque Terre's verdant stretch of coast, Monterosso feels the least like Italy and the most like the Bahamas, or Delaware, or, well...any other coastal places to which English-speakers flock in the summertime. It's a resort town through and through, with the added bonus of some quaint cobblestoned streets and colorful old buildings. The sheer number of restaurants, hotels, and shockingly bright umbrellas (that can be yours for just a small fee!) that line the long beachfront sets this town apart from the rest.

ORIENTATION

Divided in two by a steep hill, Monterosso can nonetheless be walked from end to end in less than 10min. From the train station, turn left onto **Lungomare di Fegina,** where the sea view is obstructed (how rude!) by the umbrellas of beachside cafes. Free and private beaches are interspersed below this boardwalk-like avenue. Pass through the tunnel or take the slightly longer scenic route climbing to the right and enter **Piazza Garibaldi,** from which the tiny **Via Vittorio Emanuele,** inaccessible to cars, splits off to the left. Just further right is **Via Roma,** Monterosso's "Main Street" beneath which runs its **underground river.** Home to numerous restaurants, shops, and accommodations, V. Roma runs up the hill to parking and one of the roads that leads out of town.

ACCOMMODATIONS

Monterosso contains most of the Cinque Terre's hotels—probably as many as fill all the other villages combined.

HOTEL SOUVENIR HOTEL ❷

V. Gioberti 24 ☎0187 81 75 95

Though the owners urge their guests to party on the beach, the groups of backpack-lugging students who stay at Souvenir seem content to hang out in the in the hotel's large and comfortable rooms, many with bunk beds to accommodate bigger groups.

Head up V. Roma from the waterfront; turn right onto V. Gioberti, and walk to the end. Dorms €25-35; singles €45.

HOTEL AMICI  HOTEL ❹

V. Buranco 36 ☎0187 81 75 44 www.hotelamici.it

Far, far away from the touristy world of Monterosso, there is a secret garden of terraces, citrus trees, and bright flowers. That garden just happens to be this hotel's roof. After going up five floors in the elevator, guests can keep going up and up through the foliage if the lounge chairs and patio tables aren't good enough. The hotel also has spacious rooms with large bathrooms to match.

From the waterfront, take V. Emanuele to P. Matteotti, turning left onto V. Buranco. Hotel has a

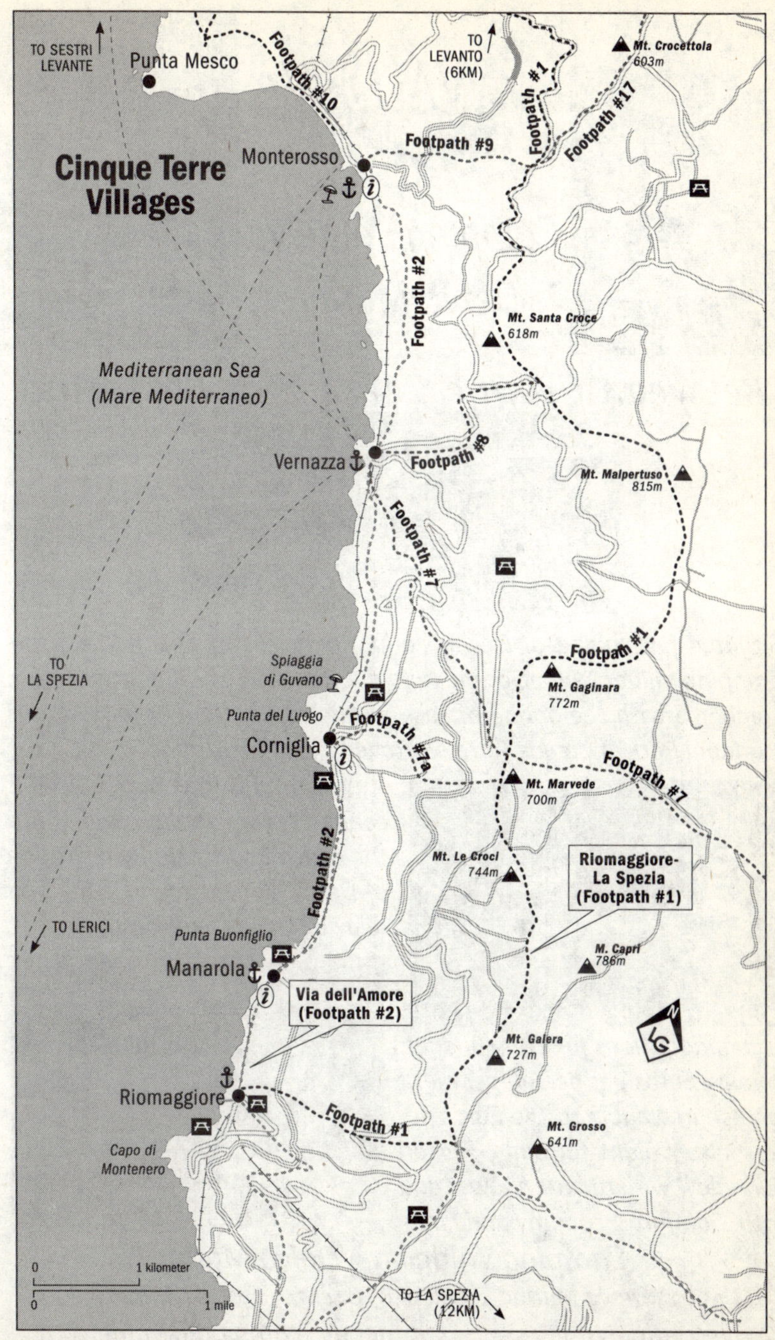
Cinque Terre Villages
TO SESTRI LEVANTE
Punta Mesco
Footpath #10
TO LEVANTO (6KM)
Footpath #1
Mt. Crocettola 603m
Footpath #17
Footpath #9
Monterosso
Footpath #2
Mt. Santa Croce 618m
Mediterranean Sea (Mare Mediterraneo)
Vernazza
Footpath #8
Mt. Malpertuso 815m
Footpath #7
TO LA SPEZIA
Spiaggia di Guvano
Footpath #1
Mt. Gaginara 772m
Punta del Luogo
Corniglia
Footpath #7a
Mt. Marvede 700m
Footpath #7
Footpath #2
Mt. Le Croci 744m
Riomaggiore-La Spezia (Footpath #1)
TO LERICI
Punta Buonfiglio
M. Capri 786m
Manarola
Via dell'Amore (Footpath #2)
Mt. Galera 727m
Riomaggiore
Footpath #1
Mt. Grosso 641m
Capo di Montenero
0
1 kilometer
0
1 mile
TO LA SPEZIA (12KM)

large sign on the right. ***i*** *Breakfast included; board plans including lunch (available year-round) and dinner (June-Aug) available. Wi-Fi €2.50 per hr., €3.50 per 2hr.* Ⓢ *Bed in double or triple €50-70; singles €60-80. €5 surcharge per night for stays under 3 nights.*

APPARTAMENTINI CINQUE TERRE AFFITTACAMERE ❹

V. Molinelli 85/6 ☎366 50 85 150 www.appartamentini.it

Once guests manage to ascend the three-dimensional labyrinth of staircases snaking up the side of the building (the chaos you're envisioning is probably about right), they will find these three new apartments absolutely gleaming with modern cabinetry, flatscreen TVs, and ensuite kitchens with stove and fridge. An outdoor grass patio with table and chairs makes for a perfect romantic hangout.

Turn right from the train station and then right onto V. Molinelli opposite the parking lot. The apartments are in the tall pink buildings to the left up the hill. Ⓢ *Doubles €80.*

ALLE 5 TERRE AND CINQUE TERRE GUESTHOUSE AFFITTACAMERE ❷

V. Molinelli 87 ☎0187 81 78 28 www.alle5terre.com

V. Gioberti 25 ☎0187 81 78 28 www.guesthousecinqueterre.com

The one-stop shopping isn't limited to wine and sauces, as the owners of **Cantina di Sciacchetrà** also rent rooms in two different properties. These guesthouse chambers are modern and sleek, with eye-popping zebra bedspreads, while some of the homier rooms at Alle 5 Terre feature leather furniture.

To Alle 5 Terre, turn right from the station and then right onto V. Molinelli. The rooms are in a larger apartment building on the left. Cinque Terre Guesthouse is located on V. Gioberti, to the right off V. Roma. Ⓢ *€25-35 per person. Apartment from €75.*

SIGHTS

IL GIGANTE ♿ MONUMENT, BEACH

V. Mollina, near V. Fegina

He's the best-looking lifeguard on the beach. Too bad he's so hard to get into bed. That's because he's a stone giant carved from a cliff, watching over one of Monterosso's **free beaches.** Beyond the giant's gaze, you'll be able to view more of the town's public shores, the most of any of the Cinque Terre towns. The uncontrolled stretches tend to be mixed in with roped-off private areas for hotel guests and paying customers. Look for the *ingresso libero* signs by the stairs or beach access to be sure that no cabana boys will come chasing you down with a bill.

Turn right out of the train station onto Lungomare Fegina. Ⓢ *Free.*

CHIESA DEI CAPPUCINI CHURCH, PANORAMIC VIEW

Above Monterosso

Climb to a point high above Monterosso—a Monterosso on the hill that most beachgoers never see, covered in foliage and cut off from the sounds of the world. From the Jesus statue halfway up, the full panorama of Cinque Terre is visible—all five towns and a swathe of ocean. Higher up, though, the view begins to be obscured by leaves, and a hiker gets different angles of Monterosso itself, fit snuggly into a valley that rises much higher than its peach-colored buildings. Finally, at the summit, the 17th-century church contains a magnificent golden cross by the Dutch artist, **Van Dyck,** who spent his most productive years in the Cinque Terre.

Turn left from the train station and then left again onto V. Bastoni at the yellow sign for "Chiesa." Then climb up many flights of uneven steps to reach the church. Ⓢ *Free.*

FOOD

Monterosso's food offerings are as broad and varied as can be found in the Cinque Terre. This means nothing exotic, but a selection of Italian-style restaurants from several pizzerias and Ligurian seafood shops as well as focaccerias and *gelaterie* lining the waterfront streets. To make a picnic, visit **SuperConad Margherita.** *(P. Matteotti 9 Open June-Sept M-Sa 8am-1pm and 4:30-8pm, Su 8am-1pm.)*

CANTINA DI SCIACCHETRÀ

ENOTECA ❶

V. Roma 7 ☎0187 81 78 28

The one stop on V. Roma required for wine connoisseurs and thirsty students alike, this bottle-filled shop offers regional wines including its namesake, the world-renowned sweet wine, at dirt-cheap prices. Plus, samples are available at the lowest price of all: zero. The enthusiastic and kind English-speaking staff are always eager to pour something but will also help customers navigate the selection of marmalades and sauces *(€5-10).* For many backpackers, this place's outdoor seating is the beach (just ask the staff to open the bottle before you leave).

On the left before the first underpass over V. Roma. Cinque Terre wine €5-20. Sciacchetrà €27. Open daily 9am-11pm.

RISTORANTE L'ALTAMAREA

SEAFOOD ❸

V. Roma 54 ☎0187 81 71 70

Fresh fish and even fresher homemade pasta are the hallmarks of this well-loved restaurant's traditional Ligurian menu. Most locals already know the chef and his scrumptious creations, but tourists just discovering them for the first time come away equally satisfied. Fish ravioli is among the unique dishes recommended by diners and the staff alike.

On the right after the 1st underpass on V. Roma. Primi €10; secondi €14-18. Open M-Tu noon-3pm and 6-10pm, Th-Su noon-3pm and 6-10pm.

PIZZERIA LA SMORFIA

PIZZERIA ❷

V. Vittorio Emanuele 73 ☎0187 81 83 95

A huge selection of 50 different pizzas (and 16 white pizzas, plus 10 calzones) draws locals, including workers from other nearby restaurants, to this crowded joint. Three employees frantically wait tables, cut pizzas, and make change to keep up with the rush and calls for beer that flow from the groups of young people under the awnings. The large pizzas will feed an army. The calzones shaped like bloated croissants are filled with deliciously melty cheese and sauces.

Take the 1st left on the piazza after the tunnel onto V. Vittorio Emanuele. The pizzeria is up on the left. Pizzas €4.50-7, large €9-14. Calzones €8. Open daily 10:30am-3pm and 6-11pm.

PASTICCERIA LAURA

CAFE ❶

V. Vittorio Emanuele 59

Quick and easy, Pasticceria Laura serves some of the sweetest pastries around to locals who eat them at the bar and outdoor tables while reading the newspaper pink pages (sports section). Paired with a warm cappuccino, not much can beat a sugary cannoli. Here, that isn't cold cream in a crusty casing, but rather an airy, cream-filled puff of dough.

Pass through the tunnel, then take V. Vittorio Emanuele to the left from the piazza. Pastries €1. Espresso €1-2. Open M 7:30am-10pm, W-Su 7:30am-10pm.

FOCACCERIA IL FRANTOLO

BAKERY ❶

V. Gioberti 1 ☎0187 81 83 33

The bread here comes piping hot out of the oven and straight into your hands, where the wonderful grease will stain the napkin and possibly your hands with that indelible mark of focaccian (is that a word? It should be) goodness. Il Frantolo serves an excellent brand of this special bread stuffed with olives, peppers, cheese, and more.

cinque terre

V. Gioberti to the right from V. Roma. Focaccia €1-3. Open M-W 9am-2pm and 3:30-8pm, F-Su 9am-2pm and 3:30-8pm.

NIGHTLIFE

It seems difficult to call a collection of three bars a nightlife "hub," but, in Monterosso, that's what **Piazza Garibaldi** is. A few other bars, including one filled with raucous travelers, can be found on **Via Roma.** Many of the restaurants near the train station or past P. Garibaldi on the shoreline offer quieter spots where you can drink *sciacchetrà* while the sea breeze ruffles your hair.

FAST BAR — BAR

V. Roma 13 — ☎0187 81 71 64

It's fast times at Cinque Terre in this all-American bar, where it is the rare customer who speaks Italian rather than English. Visiting students chat at tables and mingle by the bar over draft beers and colorful cocktails sipped from long neon straws (apparently they weren't flashy enough already).

After exiting the tunnel, pass under the railroad bridge and head left onto V. Roma. The bar will be on the left. Shots €3. Beer €4-4.50. Cocktails €5-6. Open daily 10am-2am. Aperitivo 6:30-8pm. Closed 2 weeks in Dec and all of Jan.

CA DI SCIENSA — BAR

P. Garibaldi 17 — ☎0187 81 82 33

Don't worry about missing any of the action of the sporting world at Ca di Sciensa. TVs are everywhere you go and every way they come—outside, upstairs, flatscreen, big-screen, and even vintage versions with knobs. Join your friends in the extensive but frequently full outdoor seating for once-a-week live music.

From the tunnel, walk along the opposite side of the railroad bridge to P. Garibaldi. Beer €2-4. Cocktails €5. Sandwiches €5. Open May-Sept daily 10:30am-2am; Oct-Apr M 10:30am-2am, W-Su 10:30am-2am. Aperitivo 7-8:30pm.

SCIUSCETTÚA CAFE — BAR

P. Garibaldi 22 — ☎0187 81 84 57

The restaurant is stone, arched, and cave-like, but that doesn't mean it's cold. The friendly staff, including three brothers who own the place, keep nights lively and patrons feeling welcome, but they guard their top-shelf liquors with care. You'll have to pay the premium to sip that sweet stuff.

From the tunnel, walk along the opposite side of the railroad bridge to P. Garibaldi. Cocktails €5-7.50. Appetizers €2.50-4.50. Open daily Apr-Oct noon-2am. Aperitivo buffet 5:30-8:30pm.

HIKING

The hike from Monterosso to Vernazza *(1½hr.)* is the most challenging of the four town-linking hikes, but without question, the pain is worth the gain: breathtaking vistas of the towns and spectacular panoramas of the sea crown the uphill journey. The start on the far-left side of Monterosso lulls hikers into a false sense of security with gradual ramps, before throwing them—BAM!—straight into a wall of steep, uneven, and seemingly unending steps. At higher elevation, the climb gives way to a relatively flat track notable for its wildflowers, butterflies, and gorgeous views over terraced vineyards back to Monterosso. Eventually, you'll begin to see the town of Vernazza. Watch the whitewashed ferryboats zipping by and pity them. Only the landlubbers have the privilege of this vista. The descent into Vernazza mirrors the ascent from Monterosso, struggling over rocky and uneven steps. This last stretch leads directly onto a tiny alley off a street in Vernazza's upper section.

cinque terre card

Cinque Terre Cards can be bought in the train stations and Cinque Terre National Park offices in each of the five towns. If you have any intention of hiking while in the area, you will need to purchase one, as they are required for access to the paths. They also grant reduced entry fees to various attractions in the towns and access to the bus routes within each town. A one-day pass costs €5, two-day is €8, three-day is €10, and seven-day is €20. You also have the option of buying an obviously-titled "with train" pass that includes unlimited access to the trains connecting the villages. This pass costs €8.50/€14.70/€19.50/€36.50, and is not worth the extra money since a) a train ride costs €1.40, so you'd have to ride it three times in one day to make it worth your money and b) you're buying what is essentially a hiking pass, who needs trains?

ESSENTIALS

Practicalities

- **TOURIST OFFICE: Cinque Terre National Park Office** provides information on trails and sells **Cinque Terre Cards,** which are necessary for hiking. *(P. Garibaldi 20 ☎0187 81 70 59 or 0187 80 20 53 www.parconazionale5terre.it i Also in the train station. Open daily 8am-8pm.)* **Pro Loco** offers information on hiking and accommodations as well as **currency exchange.** *(V. Fegina 38 ☎0187 81 75 06 www.prolocomonterosso.it In front of the train station. Open daily 9am-7pm.)*
- **ATMS: Banca Carispe.** *(V. Roma 49 and V. Roma 69 Open daily 8:05am-1:15pm and 2:30-3:45pm.)* Also **Bancomat** has an ATM on the ground floor of the train station.
- **INTERNET: The Net** has computers and Wi-Fi. *(V. Vittorio Emanuele 55 ☎0187 81 72 88 www.monterossonet.com €1.50 1st 10min., €0.10 per min. thereafter, or €10 per 2hr. Open daily 9:30am-9pm.)*
- **POST OFFICE:** *(V. Roma 73 Open M-F 8am-1:30pm, Sa 8am-12:30pm.)*

Emergency!

- **POLICE: Carabinieri** *(☎0187 81 75 24).* Also **Polizia Locale** in the Municipal Building *(P. Garibaldi ☎335 62 09 462).*
- **LATE-NIGHT PHARMACIES:** The pharmacy at **Via Fegina 44** posts after-hours rotations outside. *(☎0187 18 18 394 Outside the train station. i Cash only. Open M-Sa 8:30am-12:30pm and 4-7:30pm, Su 9am-12:30pm and 4-7:30pm.)*
- **HOSPITALS/MEDICAL SERVICES:** There is a **doctor's office** in the municipal building *(P. Garibaldi).* Check the bulletin board for numbers of doctors on call. Obviously, in a serious emergency call an **ambulance** *(☎118).*

Getting There

By Train

The station is on the waterfront on V. Fegina. *(☎0187 81 83 23 Ticket office open daily 6:30am-7:25pm.)* The town lies on the Genoa-La Spezia line, and, as is not the case for some of the Cinque Terre villages, most trains stop here. Trains arrive directly from **Genoa.** *(€5. 1½hr., about every hr., departing Genoa 5am-10:20pm.)* A few trains come from **Turin** *(€18. 4hr.; 5:20am, 1:20, 5:20pm.)*, **Milan,** and **Florence,** but most arrivals from these cities transfer in one of the two points above. Local trains run between **Levanto** and **La Spezia,** with stops at each of the five villages *(M-F €1.40, Sa-Su €1.50. 2-19min., every 30min. or less 4:51am-11:39pm.)* Train schedules to the towns are available at tourist offices.

By Ferry

From **La Spezia** *(€12. 2hr., 4 per day)*. Ferries by **Navigazione Golfo dei Poeti** *(☎0187 81 84 40 or 0187 73 29 87)* connect the five towns. Departures from the dock to the right after exiting the tunnel run to **Riomaggiore** or **Manarola,** *(Round-trip €11.50.)* or to **Vernazza** *(Round-trip €6).*

Getting Around

Walking is the best way to do it.

Boat Rental

For where most mortals can't walk. Try **Samba.** *(☎0187 33 96 81 22 65 Across from the train station, on the beach. i Cash only. 2-person kayaks €25 per 3hr. Open daily 9am-6pm.)*

By Bus

National Park Buses, a.k.a. green vans, run through town regularly, connecting it to points in the hills. *(Free with Cinque Terre Card.)* Bus #1 connects the *centro sportivo* on the waterfront to Pietrafiore. *(About every 45min., 8:10am-6:35pm.)* Bus #2 goes from *centro sportivo* to Bivio and the church at Soviore, on top of the mountains. *(Every 30min.-1hr. 10:35am-6:30pm.)*

vernazza ☎0187

Judging by a quick walk down its primary street, Vernazza is a small haven for seafood restaurateurs, colorful umbrellas, and tourists who like to be in bed by 10pm. Revolving around the central streets of **Via Roma** and **Via Visconti,** the town is mostly door after door of apartments occupied by welcoming Italians ready to take in the lonely wayfarer and his or her all-too-heavy luggage. The *piazza* by the beach is surrounded by restaurants serving up anchovies—a local specialty—in salads, soups, and pastas. When that's all been washed down with a cool wine from one of Vernazza's gourmet stores, only a dip in the fresh blue waters of the town's petite but oh-so-fine beach will do. Squished on three sides by pastel-colored buildings and on the other by a field of bobbing fishing **boats,** the sand here may nonetheless blanket Cinque Terre's most renowned swimming spot. Though there are tourists here, as is typical in these parts, a trip to Vernazza during the day can still feel like an escape from the over-hyped beach resort aura.

ORIENTATION

One street, three names, and 100 million postcards. That's Vernazza in a nutshell, with the help of some hyperbole. The town's main street, **Via Roma,** runs from the train station and becomes **Via Visconti** about halfway to the water. Above the train station, it's called **Via Gavino** and is where you'll find many of the village's essential services. At the bottom of V. Visconti, restaurant-lined, umbrella-shaded **Piazza Marconi** overlooks Vernazza's tiny, picturesque harbor. From V. Roma/V. Visconti, many smaller "streets"—really staircases—and the trails to Monterosso and Corniglia connect with the homes and *affittacamere* (room rentals) above.

ACCOMMODATIONS

With a few exceptions, Vernazza's accommodations are almost all rental rooms owned by private citizens. Look for signs advertising *camere* in front of stores, restaurants, and doorways all over town.

ALBERGO BARBARA — HOTEL ❹

P. Marconi 30, top fl. ☎0187 81 23 98 www.albergobarbara.it

Ahoy there! Lifting that giant suitcase up a spiral staircase with only a rope to cling to may not be fun (though it really makes the nautical theme work), but it's worth it to get to the rooms above. Many have sea views and wooden rafters, and even those that look out the back are bright and airy.

To the right when coming from V. Roma. i No elevator. Several flights up. Doubles €50, with bath €60-65, with sea view €100. Closed Dec-Feb. Check-in until 5pm; later, call ahead.

PENSIONE SORRISO — PENSIONE ❹

V. Gavino 4 ☎0187 81 22 24 www.pensionesorriso.com

While the toddler who runs the place is busy checking people in, his mother plays with blocks—wait, something's wrong there. This hotel's youngest resident is just one indication of the homey feel at Pensione Sorriso, where rooms are tucked away from the bustle of P. Marconi. Breakfast served in a communal dining room, free Wi-Fi access, and comfortable, brightly painted rooms make this humble *pensione* one of the best values in the village. The downstairs cafe is a lively gathering spot for young visitors as well.

Head uphill from the train station; the hotel will be on the right after the playground. i Breakfast included. Free Wi-Fi. Singles €60, with bath and A/C €70; doubles €85, with bath €110, with bath and A/C €125.

CAMERE DA MARTINA — AFFITTACAMERE ❹

P. Marconi 26 ☎0187 81 23 65 or 329 43 55 344 www.roomartina.com

The one and only Martina herself shows patrons to whichever of the four rooms they have chosen, each located in one apartment building next to the harbor on Vernazza's main square. What they may lack in thought-out and up-to-date design—one poster of the New York City skyline still has the Twin Towers on it—they make up for in comfort and practicality. Each room has a fridge, great for storing that vintage bottle from the shop downstairs.

On the right side of P. Marconi when facing the water. 2- and 4-person rooms from €30-35 per person. No reception; call ahead.

SIGHTS

CASTELLO DORIA — CASTLE

V. G. Guidoni

The Cinque Terre and its seas were a playground for the powerful families of Vernazza early in the last millennium, and from this castle, they observed and manipulated their domain...with the help of a strategic location and some artillery. (And thank goodness someone was protecting this harbor: at one point in the 13th and 14th centuries it was the primary port exporting the region's wine.) Today, though, the power is gone, and the thought of Vernazza controlling the sea—influencing anything, really—seems marvelously quaint. But the view, the commanding and description-defying view, remains for all to see. From the grassy deck of the castle roof, climb the foot-wide spiral staircase to the top of the tower, where a low stone wall is the only thing keeping viewers from tumbling to the rocks and sea below. (In America, this would have been shut down long ago with the help of a roomful of lawyers. Fortunately, we're in Italy.) The wall, well out of sight, is also the only thing between camera-toting travelers and the surrounding region's natural and historic beauty, all topped off with the colorful sprinkles of five cute little towns.

Turn left onto V. G. Guidoni and walk up many steps, following the signs for "Castello." €1.50. All proceeds benefit local charity. Open daily 10am-7pm.

VERNAZZA PORT — BEACH

P. Marconi

Once upon a time, this miniscule inlet was home to much of the wine shipping on the Italian Riviera. Now it sees a lot of toddlers in swim diapers taking their first dip with mom and dad. The small strip of sand located right in the heart of Vernazza has no services or lifeguard, but its small size and protected water mean it remains very family friendly.

At the end of P. Marconi. Free. Open daily sunrise-sunset.

FOOD

Vernazza is the perfect place for budget travelers to pack a picnic. Its gourmet shops, from delis to *pescherie* (fish shops), offer significant discounts over its many restaurants, which are concentrated around the waterfront in **Piazza Marconi. Salumi e Formaggi** *(V. Visconti 19 ☎0187 82 12 40 i Cash only. Open M-Sa 8am-2pm and 5:20-7:30pm, Su 8am-1:30pm.)* sells produce and other staples, while just up the street, the small **Coop** *(V. Roma 25 Open M 8am-1pm and 5-8:15pm, Tu 8am-noon, W-Su 8am-1pm and 5-8:15pm.)* stocks groceries of all kinds.

liguria n ambrosia

Wine bars and shops line the tiny capillaries of the Cinque Terre's streets, advertising the *produtti tipici* of the Liguria region—the famous Cinque Terre *bianco.* This wine is cultivated from grapes grown in the hillsides by the hiking trails through which tourists regularly meander. Those very trails began as crucial arteries for transporting grapes and other staples (and here, wine is a staple) to the central port at Vernazza. The scent of lemon and thyme perfuming the route reveals that the region's vineyards and farms are still very much committed to a traditional way of life. After a tough day of hiking or an even tougher one of reclining in the sun, try a cool glass of *sciacchetrà,* a sweet, thick, amber vintage that is the region's most famous product. At this point, you may never want to return to the modern (or sober) world.

BAIA SARACENA — PIZZERIA ❶

P. Marconi 16 ☎0187 81 21 13 www.baiasaracena.com

The location—in an arcade next to Vernazza's quaint fishing port—is special, and so is the pesto pizza. For just €5 (€4.50 for margherita), patrons can get a large and amazingly filling slice as well as a soda. Even when it's raining, dozens of visitors gather with their slices to eat on the rocky sea wall as waves crash at their back. For table service (when it's sunny), sit on the patio and savor the majestic view from a table.

Far down on the left side of the piazza, right before the seawall. Whole pizzas €6.50-8.50. Bruschetta €5-6. Salads €5-8. Open M-Th 10:30am-10:30pm, Sa-Su 10:30am-10:30pm.

BLUE MARLIN BAR — CAFE ❶

V. Roma 43 ☎0187 82 11 49 bluemarlin2@lycos.it

Here's something many travelers haven't seen in a while: eggs and bacon. And what a relief it can be to find those two staples on one's breakfast plate, as is possible here in the heart of Vernazza. And if eggs *(€4)* keep Americans happy, adding sausage or bacon *(€2)* should really put them in hog heaven. Despite a cuisine that seems particularly suited to Uncle Sam, this bar fills with patrons of all nationalities by mid-morning and tends not to empty out until just before

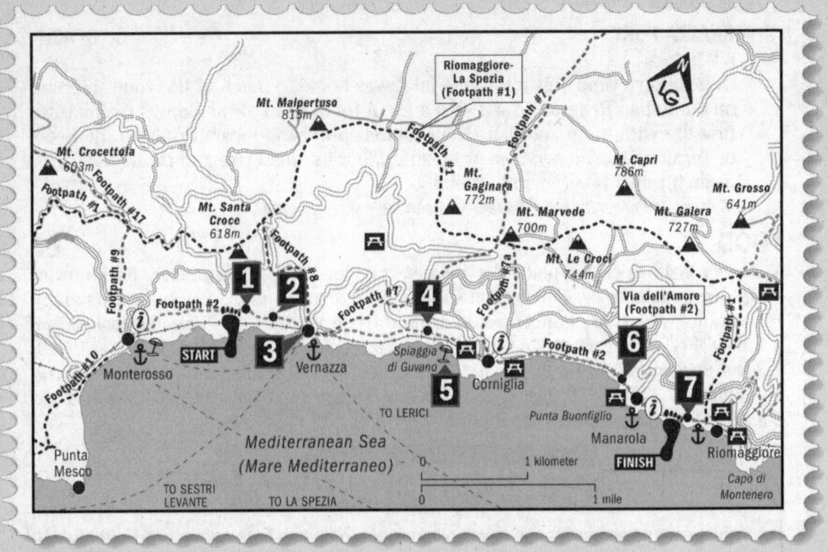

hiking the cinque terre

The five villages on this stretch of the Ligurian coastline offer the perfect potential for enjoyable, and not particularly difficult hikes. For our descriptions of each hike, see the hiking section of each town. Here, we pick out our absolute favorite moments of the paths stretching from Monterosso to Riomaggiore. We hope you appreciate the beauty of this area as much as we did.

1. MONTEROSSO ASCENT WATERFALL. One more step. One more step. And then a few more. And then, before you get to the breathtaking views over the whole region, you get beauty on a miniature scale. As you cross over a small slate footbridge, a waterfall flows to the left and under the bridge. As most hikers pass right on by, take a short detour down below the bridge, where the noise of falling water drowns the din of footsteps from above. For the slow or step-climbingly-challenged, the rocks and roots here make a perfect spot for the first sit-down water or snack break (you're less than 20min. outside of Monterosso). For those who feel that, nah, we can keep going, stop and savor nature for a moment anyhow.

2. PUNTA LINA OVERLOOK. Come on, Vernazza, stop playing hard to get. From here, more than three-quarters of the way to the second town, hikers finally get their first glimpse of that fruit basket of buildings peeking out from behind its protective hill. Since the overlook is in a clearing at a bend in the trail, it's a spot where a number of people take a break—and photos—by taking a few steps down to gaze between the brush. A closed trail leads downhill here, but it is impassible, and plus, though it brings you closer to Vernazza on the map it also heads downhill, meaning the perspective is lost and photos get worse, not better.

3. LAST CHANCE BEFORE VERNAZZA. Ladies and gentlemen, the captain has indicated that the town is in sight and we've been cleared to make our final descent. We remind you that those wishing to avoid the chatty tourist throngs in the *centro* should consider stopping at this one little bench, after the guard shack and before the street begins. It does provide a close-up view of the bobbing **boats** and stone-cold castle, without all that hastle. Meal service will be provided by picnic basket.

4. MARKER 15 OVERLOOK. No need to mince words: this view is simply the best on the trail. Emerge from behind the brush and whoa—the gasps are audible (this is almost true, we swear). Across the valley, floating high above the azure sea on a pillow of green foliage is Corniglia, with its beautiful sister Manarola just a few kilometers beyond.

5. GUVANO BEACH. Both clothing and decency seem to be optional at this beach, a steep 20min. climb down to the cove from the main trail. Lovers have been known to do more than simply suntan in the buff on the sands of Guvano. Geographically, it is known to locals as one of the most pristine and secluded spots around due to its fine sand beaches and turquoise water undisturbed by swim-diapered toddlers. The seclusion, however, may be better explained by its accurate but somehow untrustworthy rickety white sign from the trail that belies its not-quite-official status with park authorities.

6. PUNTA BUONFIGLIO. Just around the corner from Manarola is a quiet overlook that should be teeming with people. But it isn't, as the luxuries of town lure from so close. Above a rock wall, Punta Buonfiglio is the best-maintained stopping point on the trail, with grassy lawns perfect for croquet (you did bring your set, didn't you?) or picnics and a view over Manarola and the sea. A small playground keeps the little ones occupied, while amateur meteorologists amuse themselves analyzing one of the more quirky features, a windsock. But everyone, big and small, benefits from the first free public bathroom on the trail (donations accepted).

7. TUNNEL OF LOVE. The trail's final portion is famous as the "Via della'Amore." No spot on the walk says why better than the tunnel of love, where couples pause to leave a small mark on the concrete walls and a big smooch on each others' lips. Covered in painted, scratched, and drawn outlines of hearts and padlocks (the unbreakable bond, ya know?), in a big city the tunnel's mercilessly graffitied concrete might indicate a part of town you'd rather not be in, but on the Lover's Trail, after miles of magnificent scenery, this somehow seems a touching way to be re-acclimated from the paradise of the trail to something a little more familiar to city dwellers.

closing, when the day's first meal is a distant memory.

Down the hill from the train station; on the right. Pastries €1. Bruschetta €3-4. Pizza €5-7. Espresso drinks €1-2. Open daily 7am-6:30pm. Hot breakfast served 8:40-11:30am.

TRATTORIA GIANNI FRANZI RISTORANTE ❷

P. Marconi 5 ☎0187 82 10 03 www.giannifranzi.it

Serving as a coffee bar, hotel lobby, and lounge for local hangers-on, Gianni Franzi's front room seems to be bustling with activity at all hours of the day. In its stone-walled back room, however, the dining area is a quiet escape into a world of savory pastas and meats. The chefs are known locally for their pesto-making prowess.

Walk down V. Roma/V. Visconti to the piazza and look to the left. Primi €8-15; secondi €10-20. Open Mar 11-Jan 9 M-Tu 8am-11pm, Th-Su 8am-11pm.

PANIFICO DA GINO BAKERY ❶

V. Vinsconti 3 ☎0187 81 22 95

Sometimes you just need it quick and easy. Lunch, we mean (get your mind out of the gutter there, reader). That's what this bakery serves in its warm focaccia sandwiches, wrapped up and easy to eat during a stroll towards the waterfront. The store also carries a variety of loaves and rolls useful for backpackers who made a perfect picnic before setting out but forgot that all-important sandwich ingredient: bread.

Down V. Roma on the right. Breads and rolls €1-3. Sandwiches €3, on focaccia €4. Open M-Tu 7am-1pm and 5-7pm, Th-Su 7am-1pm and 5-7pm.

HIKING

The trail from Vernazza to Corniglia *(75min.)*, while still difficult due to a significant number of steps throughout, is more open than the previous walk. It begins along a wide trail with continuous views of the ocean over a brush-covered hill. With less shade comes more cacti (in Italy, who knew?). The hike's most impressive point is near **Marker 15**, over 200m up, where the trail overlooks Corniglia—itself a city on a hill—with Manarola's orange and pink hues standing out against the many azure inlets in the distance. After winding along above the turquoise water that sparkles like glittery sidewalks, you'll be about 15min. outside of Corniglia. Here, the terrain changes, and walkers wander through a working agricultural landscape, the air scented with thyme and lemon that grows on the surrounding trees. The trail spills onto a road outside of town. Turn right to head toward Corniglia's *centro*.

ESSENTIALS

Practicalities

- **ATMS: Banca Carispe** has a stand-alone machine at V. Roma 37. Also **Banca Carige** *(V. Gavino 18 Open M-F 8:05am-1:20pm and 2:30-3:45pm.)*
- **LAUNDROMATS: Lavandara il Cargetto.** *(V. Carugetto 15 ☎333 78 99 499 Turn right at V. Ettore Vernazza across from the pharmacy, then take the first left. Wash €5, dry €6. Open daily 8am-10pm.)*
- **INTERNET: Phone Home Internet Point** has computers and Wi-Fi. *(V. Roma 38 €0.15 per min. 1st 30min., €0.10 per min. thereafter. Wi-Fi €3 per 30min. Open daily May-Oct 9:30am-10pm; Nov-Apr 9:30am-8pm.)*
- **POST OFFICES:** Also includes a currency exchange. *(V. Gavino 30 Open M-F 8am-1:30pm, Sa 8am-12:30pm.)*

Emergency!

- **POLICE: Municipal** *(P. dei Caduti 34 ☎0187 82 11 47 Just uphill from the train station.)*

- **LATE-NIGHT PHARMACIES: Dott. Elena Niccolo** posts after-hours emergency numbers. *(V. Roma 2 ☎0187 81 23 96 Down the hill from the station; on the left. Open M-W 9:30am-1pm and 4-7:30pm, Th 9:30am-1pm, F-Sa 9:30am-1pm and 4-7:30pm.)*
- **HOSPITALS/MEDICAL SERVICES: Ambulatorio Medico di Vernazza** *(V. Gavino 5 ☎335 65 56 845 i Call 6-9pm for appointments. Open M 11am-noon, Tu 5-7pm, W 4:30-5:30pm, Th 10:30am-noon, F 5-6pm.)*

Getting There

By Train

Vernazza is located on the line between Genoa and La Spezia. Trains arrive directly from **Genoa** *(€5. 1½hr., approx. every hr., departing Genoa 5am-10:20pm.)* and **La Spezia** *(€1.40. 20min., every 30min. or more, departing 4:30am-12:50am.)*, just four stops away. A few trains come from **Turin** *(€18. 4hr.; 5:20am, 1:20, 5:20pm.)*, **Milan,** and **Florence,** but most arrivals from these cities transfer in one of the two points above. Local trains run between **Levanto** and **La Spezia** with stops at the five villages *(M-F €1.40, Sa-Su €1.50. 2-19min., every 30min. or less, 4:51am-11:39pm.)*

By Ferry

Boats run by **Navigazione Golfo dei Poeti** *(☎0187 81 84 40 or ☎0187 73 29 87)* connect Vernazza to **Monterosso.** *(€6 round-trip. 15min., 8 per day departing Monterosso 10:30am-5:50pm.)* From Monterosso, ferries also connect to Manarola and Riomaggiore.

Getting Around

Cars are not allowed within the village, which only has one road wide enough to fit them. While this rule (and hundreds of steps) work to thwart delivery people, it's great for pedestrians. **National Park Buses** run to San Bernardino-Muro church high above the town. *(9:45am, noon, 3, and 6pm.)*

corniglia ☎0187

There's no beach in Corniglia, and to a significant extent, that—and the nearly 400 steps up from train to town—keeps the tourists away. As a result, this village at the center of the Cinque Terre provides a stunningly beautiful and refreshingly quiet respite from its neighbors down the coast.

ORIENTATION

From the train station, walk to the left along the tracks to the back-and-forth steps that lead to the town center. At the top of the climb, travelers find themselves on the very appropriately named **Via alla Stazione,** which leads into the town's **centro storico,** to the left. From the *centro,* follow **Via Fieschi** to many *affittacamere* and panoramic views on the left as well as a few restaurants to the right. The main trail to Vernazza and Manarola also crosses through this central intersection.

ACCOMMODATIONS

Although Corniglia is best as a daytrip because of its small size and inconvenient hilltop location, there are a number of *affittacamere* that tend to be more affordable than those in other towns.

OSTELLO CORNIGLIA HOSTEL ❷

V. alla Stazione 3 ☎0187 81 25 59 www.ostellocorniglia.com

Among a sea of signs advertising rooms, the bright yellow *ostello* stands out, and for good reason. This two-year-old, 24-bed hostel offers the most affordable accommodations in town, with colorful common spaces to match.

In the yellow building to the right before the centro storico. i Breakfast €3. Single-sex 8-person dorms €24; doubles €55. Extra bed €20.

B AND B DA BEPPE

B AND B ❹

V. Serra 2 ☎0187 82 11 63 or 338 49 52 022

Located on a small but well-lit street, the doubles and one apartment of this simple bed and breakfast don't offer sea views but bright rooms with table and chairs that invite relaxation away from much of Cinque Terre's bustle. The helpful elderly couple who own and run the B and B go back and forth offering advice, though sadly, non-Italian speakers will miss much of the banter's nuance.

To the right and then up the steps from the centro storico. Doubles €90.

SIGHTS

Corniglia's precarious position on a steep hill means that nearly every corner offers a beautiful vista or other enchanting discovery.

PANORAMIC VIEWS

PANORAMIC VIEW

V. Solferino and V. Fieschi

Rapunzel's hair is not required to climb to the top of the **Torre** (tower), though some stamina might be needed to conquer even *more* stairs. Those who take on this low-tech Stairmaster will be rewarded with the highest view in town, which looks over Manarola to the left and down upon the turquoise waves. The busy sea lanes to La Spezia are also visible, with mammoth ships appearing like water-walking ants on the horizon. On clear days, even the hulking mound of Corsica is visible. Just down the road (and more steps—get used to it), **Terrazzo Panoramico Santa Maria** one-ups the tower from a lower vantage point, though the waves still crash far below. More than 180 degrees are visible in a panorama that includes Monterosso. Camera-shy Vernazza and Riomaggiore, however, hide behind their hills.

To reach the tower from V. Fieschi, turn left at Largo Turagio and head up 2 flights of stairs, then up a 3rd flight to the right. The Santa Maria viewpoint is at the very end of V. Fieschi.

MARINA

BEACH

Below V. Marina

No sunbathing here, unless any prospective tanner is OK with being fried by the sun and pummeled by the waves that crash on the steaming rocks. This beach, located far below Corniglia, still draws a few adventurous fishermen (wearing unfortunately tiny swimsuits) and tourists willing to climb down—you guessed it—more steep and zigzagging stone steps, these not as well maintained as those leading to town. For a place to picnic with the waves' white noise as the only break to the peace, however, there are few better locations. Park it on one of the several benches along the steps to the water.

From V. Fieschi, turn right onto V. Marina and follow it down to steps that lead to the water's edge below.

FOOD

A **Butiega** sells a variety of fresh fruits and vegetables, meats, and cheeses, plus essentials like soap, batteries, and beer. *(V. Fieschi 142 ☎0187 81 22 92 Open daily in summer 8am-7pm.)*

TERRA ROSSA ENOTECA

ENOTECA ❷

V. Fieschi 58 ☎0187 81 20 92

At the bottom of a terraced vineyard, under a nearly opaque awning of vines, seven tables sit hidden and waiting for weary patrons. With a postcard-like view of the town, valley, and sea below, Terra Rossa draws hikers, tourists, and locals seeking rest and a sip of Corniglia's *Polenza*, a dry white wine, or another Cinque Terre vintage *(€4-5)*. As if further enticement could possibly be needed, the restaurant also offers sweet delights at all hours of the day, from homemade breakfast cookies *(€3)* to *scriocco*, a selection of cheeses with honey and chutney *(€10)*.

To the right from centro storico, overlooking the valley. "Finger food" €7-10. Wine €4-5. Open M-Tu 8am-8pm, Th-Su 8am-8pm.

LA GATA FLORA PIZZERIA ❶
V. Fieschi 109 ☎0187 82 12 18

Once the trail-fatigued backpacker realizes it's not vertigo that's making her see pots and pans hanging from the ceiling—they've been recycled as lights—she must deal with another sight quite uncommon in these parts: a rectangular pizza. Yes, with corners. The thick crust makes a filling meal, while the focaccia, also square, with toppings including tomato and olives can hold you over as a tasty snack.

From centro storico, turn right onto V. Fieschi; the pizzeria will be on the left. Whole pizzas €4.50-7, slices €2.50-3.50. Focaccia €1.80-3. Open M 10am-3pm and 6-8pm, W-Su 10am-3pm and 6-8pm.

CANTINA DI MANANAN RISTORANTE ❸
V. Fieschi 117 ☎0187 82 11 66

Whether it's a desire to create exclusivity or a European dislike of working that keeps this restaurant open for just over 4hr. per day doesn't really matter: make time to visit the small stone-walled restaurant during its operating hours. The front entrance is covered in chalkboards scrawled with the dishes of the day, including the popular stuffed pastas.

From centro storico, turn right onto V. Fieschi; the restaurant will be on the left. Cover €1.80. Primi €10-12; secondi €12-18. Open M 12:45-2:30pm and 7:45-9:15pm, W-Su 12:45-2:30pm and 7:45-9:15pm.

HIKING

Talk about an inauspicious start to this trail *(40min.)*. Even after climbing down 382 steps from Corniglia (a good reason to do the trail in this direction), the scenery scarcely improves, as the entry to this portion of the trail is past the train station, through a bunker-like concrete gully, and past a number of abandoned warehouses. A rope bridge marks the exit from these unfortunate surroundings, but don't get too excited. Compared to the first two sections of trail, the scenery here is only decent. The trail is much flatter and paved with gravel in many places, making it easier for hikers of all abilities. Near Manarola a few rocks at water's edge are perfect for sunbathing, as many have discovered—that's if you don't mind taking what the park calls a "dangerous descent," to reach them. Picnic areas are also plentiful at this end of the trail, which soon swoops around a rocky point and reveals a gradual ramp into the heart of Cinque Terre's fourth town.

ESSENTIALS

Practicalities

Corniglia's services are limited, so you better hope your lodging has things like laundry or you'll be lugging along a bag of dirty clothes to the larger towns.

- **TOURIST OFFICES: National Park Tourist Office** has information on trails and trains. *(☎0187 81 25 23 In the train station. Open daily 7am-7pm.)*
- **ATM: Banca Carispe** *(V. alla Stazione 35).*
- **POST OFFICE:** *(V. alla Stazione 5 In the yellow municipal building. Open M-F 8am-1:30pm, Sa 8am-12:30pm.)*

Emergency!

- **POLICE: Municipal** *(☎0187 82 11 47).*
- **HOSPITALS/MEDICAL SERVICES: Guardia Medica** *(☎338 376 0007).*

Getting There

By Train

Stazione Corniglia, a 15min. uphill walk from the village itself, is along the Genoa-La Spezia line, though a number of the trains that stop at other points bypass this small town. Trains arrive directly from **Genoa** *(€5. 90min., approx. every hr., departing Genoa 5am-10:20pm.)* and nearby **La Spezia.** *(€1.40. 15min., 30 per day, 4:30am-12:50am.)* A few trains come from **Turin** *(€18. 4hr.; 5:20am, 1:20pm, 5:20pm.)*, **Milan,** and **Florence,** but most arrivals from these cities transfer in one of the two points above. Local trains run regularly to connect the five towns of the Cinque Terre.

By Bus

Green National Park shuttle buses run from the train station to town. *(☎0187 81 25 33 €1.50, round-trip €2.50. Free for holders of Cinque Terre Cards. Every 30min.-1hr., 7:35am-8pm.)*

By Stairs

Three hundred and eighty-two of them, each one closer to the top than the last, guaranteed. Walk along the promenade by the rail tracks—not the bus road—to reach them.

Getting Around

Cars are not permitted within the village, so **walking** is basically the only option. Be warned that due to the town's geography, steep climbs are part of navigating Corniglia. Even bikes take up too much room for the narrow streets—and unless the rider is a "that's totally sweet dude" BMXer, your favorite two-wheeler wouldn't handle the steps all that well, anyway.

manarola ☎0187

One of the smallest of the five towns, Manarola concentrates the Cinque Terre's back-in-time Italian feel within just a few short blocks. With a rocky cove as the centerpiece for both local fishermen and out-of-town swimmers, Manarola offers a large dose of maritime charm. Though its main street may not seem to present a wide variety in the way of restaurants or nightlife, the town keeps its cards close to its chest. You'll need to give this village a more thorough examination to find the jewels, hidden in its basements and hills, that make the place unique.

ORIENTATION

Manarola has one primary street that's known as **Via Birolli** toward the water and **Via Discovolo** on the other side of the train tracks. A tunnel leads from the train station to the central *piazza*, where stairs and a ramp lift pedestrians over the buried rail lines. To the right, V. Discovolo winds up past a number of *affittacamere* to the church, hostel, and some restaurants. To the left, over the hulking *piazza*, V. Birolli shoots straight down to the water past a number of restaurants.

ACCOMMODATIONS

Manarola is home to one of the few hostels in Cinque Terre, but numerous *affittacamere* provide most of the lodging for budget travelers.

OSTELLO CINQUE TERRE — HOSTEL ❷

V. Riccobaldi 21 — ☎0187 92 02 15 www.hostel5terre.com

It may have a summer camp atmosphere, but this is no wood-board bunkhouse. All rooms look out over Manarola and the sea beyond, and an airy restaurant with terrace serves as a gathering spot. What's more, an extensive board game collection and snorkel equipment for rent keep patrons entertained.

From the train station tunnel, turn right and walk 300m uphill to the church, where the hostel will be to the left. ***i*** *Wi-Fi €1 per 15min.* Ⓢ *6-bed dorms €23; doubles €65; quads €100.* ⏰ *Reception 7am-1pm and 4pm-1am. Lockout 10am-5pm. Closed Nov-Feb.*

CAPELLINI AFFITTACAMERE AFFITTACAMERE ❹

V. Birolli 88 ☎0187 92 04 10

Although she doesn't own a computer, the kind, motherly keeper of these simple but comfortable rooms literally goes out of her way to make guests feel at home, as she has to descend from the fourth floor for every request. The rooms, on Manarola's main street, each have a few pieces of antique furniture like leather armchairs, plus a table, chairs, and fridge: perfect for a quiet night in.

Turn left from the tunnel, over the piazza; the property is on the right. Ⓢ *Doubles €60; triples €75.*

LA TORRETA B AND B ❺

Vico Volto 20 ☎0187 92 03 27 www.torretas.com

The digits before that decimal point may scare some (the entire villa can be rented for a mere €2000 a night), but they come with some serious luxury. Free nightly tastings of wine and local specialties are held on the breezy terrace, which has one should-be-more-common amenity: a telescope for stargazing. Check out those celebrities sunbathing on their yachts out at sea—or the heavens, if you want. Inside, canopied beds and large rooms are attended by a professional staff befitting such a hip boutique bed and breakfast.

Turn right from the tunnel and then right at the church piazza at the top of the hill. Entrance to the B and B is by the overlook fence. Ⓢ *Singles €100; doubles €120; quads €190.*

SIGHTS

ROCKY BEACH BEACH

At the end of V. Birolli

A boat putters by, a swimmer uses it to screen the defender, and—he scores! Yes indeed, water polo is one of the primary pastimes—after fishing from small, enthusiastically colored boats, of course—practiced in Manarola's compact cove. The rock face leading down from the town doesn't dissuade swimmers from nearby homes or from two continents away, and neither does the occasional marine traffic. Sunbathers populate the hard surfaces, both slanted and flat, along the boat ramp, while more adventuresome types jump 15 ft. from the central outcropping.

Turn left from the tunnel and head down to the water on V. Birolli. Ⓢ *Free.*

MUSEO DI SCIACCHETRÀ MUSEUM

V. Discovolo 203

This one-room museum showcases the history of the Cinque Terre region, a story very intertwined with wine. The now-famous trail linking the towns was once a trade route through which grapes, lemons, and thyme were brought to the wider world. Also, see the tools used to harvest the tens of kilos of delicate grapes needed to produce just one liter of *sciacchetrà*. A 15min. video on the process *(available in English)* is played on request.

Turn right from the tunnel; the museum is up the hill on the right. Ⓢ *Free with Cinque Terre Card, which is required for admission.* ⏰ *Open daily 9:30am-1pm and 1:30-7pm.*

FOOD

TRATTORIA DAL BILLY RISTORANTE ❷

V. Rollandi 122 ☎0187 92 06 28

Maybe it's the local's choice of restaurant because of the view. It certainly could be because of the food. Or perhaps it's just because residents are the only ones who want to make the hike up the steep road in order to dine at Trattoria dal Billy. If it's the latter—**lightbulb!**—visitors should take the hint: the walk is worth it. Locals love the fresh seafood (caught by a fisherman whose gleaming mug adorns the walls) and homemade Ligurian pastas. Many are so large, even with whole lobsters in the dish, that they are best consumed by two, but the staff can prepare dishes for lonely parties of one.

Turn right from the tunnel, then follow the road uphill 300m to the church piazza. Then turn right up the steps at the far side of the piazza and follow the small street to the trattoria. Cover €2. Primi €6-10; secondi €9-17. Open M-W noon-2:30 and 6-10:30pm, Th 6-10:30pm, F-Su noon-2:30pm and 6-10:30pm.

LA CAMBUSA — PIZZERIA 1

V. Birolli 110 — ☎0187 92 10 29

The display case is always full. Maybe that's because there are so many choices that no customer can bear to pick just one dish. Beneath the hand-painted sign and fake ivy of this seatless establishment (not counting a few benches outside) every bread product and delicacy known to humanity awaits, from cannoli *(€1)* and pastries to focaccia with tons of different toppings.

Turn left from the tunnel and cross the piazza. The pizzeria is on the right. Focaccia €1.80-2.50. Panini €3. Pizza slices €2. Open daily 8am-8pm.

IL PORTICCOLO — RISTORANTE 2

V. Birolli 92 — ☎0187 92 00 83 www.ilporticcolo5terre.com

One of Manarola's most prominent restaurants, Il Porticcolo isn't shy, putting itself out there with a large, protruding patio that extends some ways into the street. While the prices catch many a visitor's eye, divine dishes like the *gnocchi al pesto* keep some locals coming back as well.

Turn left from the tunnel; the restaurant will be on the right past the piazza. Primi €5-9; secondi €7-16. Open M-Tu 11am-11:30pm, Th-Sa 11am-11:30pm.

NIGHTLIFE

The Cinque Terre's undiscovered hotspot is here in Manarola, but it's close to the only game in town.

LA CANTINA DA ZIO BRAMANTE — BAR

V. Birolli 110 — ☎0187 76 20 61

How much more fun would elementary school music class have been with a few bottles of wine? Ignore the flagrant illegality of that proposal for a moment, then look to this cantina for the answers. The owner and friends jam on the guitar (or didgeridoo) nightly at the front of the room cluttered with microphones, amps, and songbooks. Patrons join in on the bongos, tambourines, and the tables. Music starts at 9:30pm, and the crowd—locals young and old and tourists who become regulars over the course of their vacation—arrives soon after, but it has to stop by midnight. The owner says his mom is sleeping above the family-run business.

Turn left from the tunnel and cross the piazza; it is on the right. Wine €2.50-4.50. Cocktails €5-6. Open M-W 9:30am-1am, F-Su 9:30am-1am.

HIKING

All's fair in love and walking, as the final stretch of Cinque Terre's famous "Trail #2" (the blue line on the tourist-office map) demonstrates. Known as **Via dell'Amore,** or the "Lovers' Trail," this 20min. walk can be completed by anyone, and with elevators at both ends, it is nearly wheelchair accessible except for a few steps in the middle. *(Disabled visitors should call the park in advance at ☎0187 76 00 91 for lift information.)* Smooth and paved, this hike provides more than just a mild introduction to the sea views further along. Its uniqueness comes from the so-called "tunnel of love" graffitied with sappy hearts and Cupid's arrows by countless paramours over the years, though some have painted elaborate murals. A cheesy but nonetheless popular trail tradition is to affix a lock to the park fences with your one and only and throw away the key as a symbol of everlasting affection.

ESSENTIALS

Practicalities

- **ATM: Banca Carispe.** *(275 V. Discovolo # Just outside the tunnel.)*
- **POST OFFICES:** *(216 V. Discovolo # To the right outside the tunnel. Open M-F 8am-1:15pm, Sa 8am-12:30pm.)*

Emergency!

- **PHARMACIES:** *(238 V. Discovolo ☎0187 92 01 60 Open M 9am-1pm and 4-7:30pm, Tu-Th 9am-1pm, F-Sa 9am-1pm and 4-7:30pm.)*
- **HOSPITALS/MEDICAL SERVICES: Croce Bianco Riomaggiore** *(☎0187 92 07 77).*

Getting There

By Train

Trains arrive directly from **Genoa** *($ €5. 1½hr., approx. every hr., departing Genoa 5am-10:20pm.)* and nearby **La Spezia.** *($ €1.40. 15min., 30 per day 4:30am-12:50am.)* A few trains come from **Turin** *($ €18. 4hr.; 5:20am, 1:20, 5:20pm.)*, **Milan,** and **Florence,** but most arrivals from these cities transfer in one of the two points above. Local trains run regularly to connect the five towns of the Cinque Terre.

By Ferry

Ferries operated by **Navigazione Golfo dei Poeti** *(☎0187 81 84 40 or ☎0187 73 29 87)* connect the town to **Monterosso** and **Riomaggiore.** *($ Round trip €6. 15min., 8 per day, departing Monterosso 10:30am-5:50pm.)* From Monterosso, ferries also connect to Vernazza.

Getting Around

National Park **buses** connect the center of town to **Volastra** in the hills above. *(About every hr. 7am-11:30pm. Check the schedule in the tourist office for specific times, which change frequently.)* Other than this, your feet are all you'll need.

riomaggiore ☎0187

Riomaggiore, the touristy town at the other end of the Cinque Terre from Monterosso, lacks a beach but is intimately connected with the sea. The water's not even visible from the village's main drag—but don't tell the fishermen rinsing their **boat** hulls or the nearby boat rental companies trawling for customers. Those visitors who set up camp in Riomaggiore and prefer not to tan on rocks and swim in the wake of passing boats take the train to the sandy beaches of Monterosso each morning. As the sun sets (and with it the opportunity for soaking up the rays) they return in droves to descend upon the town's numerous seafood restaurants and affordable bars, adding to this town's vibrant culture.

ORIENTATION

From the train station, a tunnel leads to the center of town at **Piazza del Vignaiolo.** The town's central street, **Via Colombo,** heads steeply upward past numerous bars, restaurants, and hotels, eventually becoming **Via de Santuario** and reaching the intersection with **Via de Gasperi,** which circles the valley and boasts marvelous views of the buildings below. Between V. Colombo and V. de Gasperi and accessible by a number of staircases lies the town's main church, accompanied by its **Castello,** from which visitors can marvel at spectacular views of the sea. At the lower end of V. Colombo across from the tunnel exit, a staircase leads down to the marina, which is invisible from the main square and home to colorful, bobbing skiffs, a number of seafood restaurants, and the ferry terminal.

ACCOMMODATIONS

At the extreme end of Cinque Terre, Riomaggiore has more than its fair share of room rentals and *locanda* (inns), meaning that this is the best place to look for last-minute lodging (though that doesn't guarantee anything will be available if you arrive in mid- to late summer). Most hotels and room rentals are on **Via Colombo,** but looking on a few back streets and above the town center can yield rewards.

MAR-MAR — AFFITTACAMERE ❷

V. Malborghetto 4 ☎0187 92 09 32 www.5terre-marmar.com

Talk about assorted flavors—from student dorms to vast apartments, this room rental company seems to have it all. Each room includes an ensuite bath, but beyond that, little is shared by the 30 different properties. Some have TV, others balconies, and prices vary accordingly. Those who choose to spend less can still benefit from the community terrace, a space for all renters that overlooks the water.

After the tunnel, turn left up V. Colombo. Mar-Mar is ahead on the left. Dorms €15-20; doubles and apartments €60-120. Office open daily 9am-1pm and 2-5pm.

EDI — AFFITTACAMERE ❹

V. Colombo 111 ☎0187 92 03 25

With many boasting full kitchens and terraces, Edi's apartments are dressed to impress and priced to please. (One-bedroom apartments with living room and bathtub for €60?! It's a real possibility.) The best deals, however, are on the couple of rooms reserved for young people, which include many of the same amenities—minus the sea view, but you can find that at the beach—for even lower rates.

From the tunnel, head about halfway up V. Colombo, where Edi is on the right. Student rooms for 2-3 people €50-75; doubles €60-100; apartments €60-180.

LOCANDA DALLA COMPAGNIA — B AND B ❹

V. del Santuario 32 ☎0187 76 00 50 www.dallacompagnia.it

The most popular accessory at this cheery bed and breakfast should probably be a skateboard for guests to zoom down the steep hill of V. Colombo. Though perched at the top of the road, this *locanda* is still only minutes (perhaps seconds for those on wheels) from the water and restaurants in the lower end of the town. It features five brightly colored rooms and an open breakfast area as well as a few "mini-apartments" farther from the main building but with similar amenities.

At the top of V. Colombo, in the small piazza on the right. i Breakfast included in most rates. Doubles outside the hotel €30-50, in main building €60-100. Small discount for payment in cash. Check-in noon-6pm.

HOTEL CA DEI DUXI — HOTEL ❺

V. Colombo 36 ☎0187 92 00 36 or 0187 76 05 63 www.duxi.it

Ca dei Duxi's six rooms have a rustic feel. If it weren't for the sea breeze on the terrace (available in several rooms), the wood beams, beds, and arched stone breakfast area could have travelers believing they were in Tuscany, not Cinque Terre. But hotel guests keep coming back, not just for the water and sunshine but for the young, friendly staff and rooms with A/C and fridge. The owners also rent rooms and apartments with fewer amenities at lower prices.

Up V. Colombo at the steps on the left. Breakfast included. Wi-Fi available in lobby. Hotel doubles €70-120; triples €90-130. Rooms outside hotel €50-60, with private bath €60-75. Apartments outside hotel €60-80. Lobby area open 11am-9pm.

SIGHTS

ARTWORK OF SILVIO BENEDETTO — PUBLIC ART

In P. Rio Finale, the tunnel, and all over town — www.silviobenedetto.it

Buenos Aires native Silvio Benedetto has made it his mission to beautify Riomaggiore through monumental works of art, and all visitors to the town are beneficiaries of his project. From the moment one exits the station, a striking mural catches the eye. Benedetto's *Storia di Uomini e de Pietre (History of Man and Stone)* immortalizes the region's hardworking farmers in dramatic poses and eye-catching colors, showing how they created the unique terraced landscape over thousands of years by stacking eight million cubic meters of sandstone. Benedetto's installation in the train tunnel also focuses on the landscape, representing the changes in the Cinque Terre over time and through the seasons in a mosaic that begins with small natural elements and ends with more durable, modern terra cotta. The starfish marks the tunnel's exact center. Exploring the rest of town, visitors will unexpectedly find Benedetto's influence in many places, including Riomaggiore's municipal building, lending a little bit of whimsy to this less secluded sea town.

First admire the mural outside the train station. Then proceed through the tunnel to town, focusing on the mosaic to the right, and don't miss the tile installation outside the tunnel's end. Above town, the municipal building on V. T. Signori also has a mural. Free.

CASTELLO — CASTLE

Above V. T. Signori and P. della Chiesa

Mother nature has a kind reward for those hearty travelers who, having made the hike from Manarola or even Monterosso, are willing to climb a few more steps to Riomaggiore's ancient *castello*. After the bustle of V. dell'Amore, this is a quiet retreat with an even more magnificent sea view, the same one that allowed sentries defending the city hundreds of years ago to see for miles. Look down on the trail below, Riomaggiore's pink and yellow buildings, and the village's protected, rocky harbor.

From V. Colombo, follow the signs for "Castello" up the steps to P. della Chiesa. Outside the front doors of the church, take the steps up to the right, which lead to the castle. For those less inclined to walk (see the altitude pun?) a lift rises 38m from the station to a promenade just below the Castello. Castle free. Lift €0.50 per person or €1 per family. Open daily 8am-8pm. Lift closes at 7:45pm.

FOOD

The lower one goes, the more restaurants one finds in Riomaggiore. They line the bottom of **Via Colombo** and the marina, but a few worthwhile places are also high above town. Those looking for a picnic or an inexpensive bite should stop at one of the many *alimentari* (grocery stores) that occupy lower V. Colombo.

TE LA DO IO LA MERENDA — PIZZERIA, TAKEOUT 1

V. Colombo 161 — ☎0187 92 01 48

Can the menu at this tiny hole-in-the-wall takeout joint get any bigger? Sure it can: the staff hangs handwritten pages of new dishes and specials all over the outside and from the clotheslines inside. Serving more than typical pizza and pasta, this quick and scrumptious spot draws patrons all day with local specialties including crispy *farinata* and vegetarian Ligurian pastas, even without giving their hungry guests a single place to sit down.

At the bend in V. Colombo, on the right. Medium pizzas €5-7, slices €2-3. Ligurian dishes to go €5-8. Open daily 8am-8pm.

DAU CILA

SEAFOOD ❸

V. San Giacomo 65 ☎0187 76 00 32

Some townspeople say that this is not only their favorite restaurant in town, but it is also the only restaurant that serves fresh fish brought into the town's harbor. While that's probably not true, great fresh fish is certainly to be had.

From the tunnel, take the steps down toward "Marina." Once outside, Dau Cila is on the left. Salads and primi €9-12; secondi €12-18. Open daily noon-3pm and 6-11pm.

RIPA DEL SOLE

RISTORANTE ❸

V. de Gasperi 282 ☎0187 92 01 43 www.ripadelsole.it

Removed from the conglomeration of touristy spots in the valley below, this place has a fancier feel without fancier prices. That means good eats, good views, and better company. (Please, no Hawaiian shirts or cameras around the neck.) The restaurant's menu focuses on seafood-based pastas, plus the occasional special addition from the chef, such as the popular truffles.

Walk all the way up V. Colombo and V. del Santuario and turn left. Or, take the new public elevator from P. Chiesa to V. de Gasperi. Primi €10-11; secondi €10-20. Open Tu-Su noon-2pm and 6:30-10pm.

GELATERIA CENTRALE 2

GELATERIA ❶

V. S. Giacomo 105 ☎0187 76 00 66

It's not often that *Let's Go* recommends the number two of anything. But in this case, being the second twin doesn't make this seafront ice cream shop second-best. An unbeatable view of the harbor helps this shop dethrone its sister *(on V. Colombo)*, which serves the same treats, all made in-house.

From the tunnel, take the steps down toward "Marina." Once outside, take the ramp on the left upward . Gelato €1.50-3.50. Open daily 10am-10pm.

cinque terre

NIGHTLIFE

Not to be confused with that other Rio (look a few thousand miles west), this Cinque Terre town certainly lacks a hard-partying club scene, but has a couple of nice bars.

BAR CENTRALE

BAR

V. Colombo 144 ☎0187 92 02 08

The central gathering point for Riomaggiore's visiting international crowd isn't much to see on its own (except for caffeine-junkies itching to see its high-tech espresso machine). When the people start flowing in and the backpacker crowd begins to swap travel tales, however, it becomes easy to see why visitors return night after night.

Up V. Colombo on the left. Beer €3.50-5. Cocktails €5.50-7. Open daily 7am-1am.

A PIE DE MA, BAR AND VINI

BAR

V. dell'Amore ☎0187 92 10 37

Who knows how many lovers have taken a break from smooching on the path above for a cocktail overlooking the sea—a pretty romantic location in itself? The A Pie de Ma drinks can't hurt the relationship either.

*From the train station, take the steps up to V. dell'Amore. Turn right at the sign just before the ticket booth. **i** Live music most F-Sa at 9pm or 9:30pm. Wine €2-6. Beer €2.50-4.50. Cocktails €5-6. Open daily 10am-midnight.*

ESSENTIALS

Practicalities

- **TOURIST OFFICES: National Park** is next to the train station. Sells **Cinque Terre Cards** and has **Wi-Fi internet access** as well as 6 computer stations on upper level. *(☎0187 76 07 15 Ⓢ Internet access €0.80 per 10min. ⏰ Open daily 8am-7:30pm.)*
- **ATM: Banca Carige** offers currency exchange. *(V. Colombo 215 ⏰ Open M-F 8:20am-1:20pm and 2:30-4pm.)*
- **LAUNDROMATS: Wash and Dry Lavarapido.** *(V. Colombo 109 **i** Cash only. Ⓢ Wash and dry both €3.50 per 30min. Detergent €1. ⏰ Open daily 8:30am-7:30pm.)*
- **POST OFFICES:** *(V. Pecunia 7 ☎0187 80 31 60 ⇞ Up the stairs from V. Colombo and to the left. ⏰ Open M-F 8am-1pm, Sa 8am-noon.)*

Emergency!

- **POLICE: Municipal.** *(V. Santuario 123c ☎0187 92 09 75 ⇞ Above V. Colombo on the right.)*
- **LATE-NIGHT PHARMACIES: Farmacia del Mare** posts late-night pharmacy information outside. *(V. Colombo 182 ☎0187 92 01 60 ⏰ Open M-Sa 9am-1pm and 4-8pm, Su 9am-1pm.)*
- **HOSPITALS/MEDICAL SERVICES: Croce Bianca** *(V. Colombo 68 ☎92 07 77).*

Getting There

By Train

Riomaggiore is a stop for almost all regional trains. Trains arrive directly from **Genoa** *(Ⓢ €5. ⏰ 90min., about every hr., departing Genoa 5am-10:20pm.)* and nearby **La Spezia.** *(Ⓢ €1.40. ⏰ 15min., 30 per day 4:30am-12:50am.)* A few trains come from **Turin** *(Ⓢ €18. ⏰ 4hr.; departing Turin at 5:20am, 1:20, 5:20pm.)*, **Milan,** and **Florence,** but most of the time, travelers from these cities must change trains. Frequent local trains connect the five villages of Cinque Terre.

By Ferry

From **La Spezia** *(Ⓢ €12. ⏰ 2hr., 4 per day.)* Ferries operated by **Navigazione Golfo dei Poeti** *(☎0187 81 84 40 or ☎0187 73 29 87)* connect the five towns. Departures are from the marina. Take the steps down from the station tunnel, then keep left and walk back up on V. San Giacomo, where the ticket office is located. To **Monterosso** or **Manarola.** *(Ⓢ Round-trip €11.50.)* To **Vernazza.** *(Ⓢ Round-trip €6.)*

Getting Around

By Bus

National Park Buses run from the town center on V. Colombo to the hilltop parking lot, *castello*, and cemetery. Some travel to Biassa, several kilometers away in the mountains. *(Ⓢ Free for Cinque Terre Card holders. ⏰ Every 30min.-1hr. 7am-10:30pm.)*

On Water

Il Corsaro Rosso, "the red pirate," rents kayaks and snorkel equipment and recommends the best spots to visit. *(Riomaggiore Marina ☎328 17 86 457 or ☎328 69 35 355 ⇞ Down the stairs toward "marina" and to the right by the boats. Ⓢ Single-person kayaks €5 per hr., €25 per day; 2-person €10/€45; 3-person €15 per hr. ⏰ Open daily May-Sept 9am-6pm.)*

Under Water

Diving Cinque Terre offers daily snorkeling and scuba excursions. *(V. San Giacomo ☎0187 92 00 11 ⇞ Down the stairs in the corridor toward the marina. Ⓢ Snorkeling excursions €18. ⏰ Open daily Easter-Sept 9am-6pm. Scuba and snorkel boat trips depart M-F 2:30pm, Sa-Su 10am and 2pm.)*

FRANCE

NICE AND MONACO

When that rich friend of yours utters the words "Côte d'Azur" you immediately think of these twin cities of fame and fortune. OK, one is a country, but it's no bigger than a city. Linked by a 20min. rail trip, these millionaire meccas have even the most well-funded backpackers cowering in the hills that line the PACA region. While undoubtedly adorable, they can get tame and repetitive, which is when you double-dog-dare your wallet to venture into the coastal region. After the initial shock of yachts, gambling, and real-life celebs, you'll start to see the grittier side of Nice that's full of bars, backpackers and cheap finger foods. And about the grittier side of Monaco... does a used Ferrari dealership count?

Despite umbrella rental prices that make Disneyland seem affordable, the cheapest and most reliable activity is the beach and sun. After all, if you're going to travel somewhere to sunbathe for free, you might as well do it in the most expensive place possible—the story you tell after will be that much better. The appeal of the sun is what brought Americans to the southern shores in the 1920s and it's still what keeps tourists and backpackers from all over the globe coming here year after year. When the sun goes down, these two cities are famous for the even gliztier nightlife. Despite the commonplace €10 cocktail, finding a cheap beer is no further than the closest British or Irish pub which always seems to be a couple blocks away.

greatest hits

- **FROM RUSSIA WITH LOVE.** Not really, but Matisse was famously obsessed with a Russian girl, who inspired an impressive percentage of his artwork. Check it out at the Musée Matisse (p. 103).
- **DRIVERS WITH DEATH WISHES.** Monaco's most famous drag race pits Mercedes-McLauren against Ferrari every June and sends Formula 1 racers careening through Monaco's historic streets (p. 125).
- **VATICAN-APPROVED T AND A.** France might bill itself as a proudly secular country, but when it comes to church-condoned feathers, falsies, and masquerade balls, Nice conveniently becomes a Catholic stronghold again (p. 113).

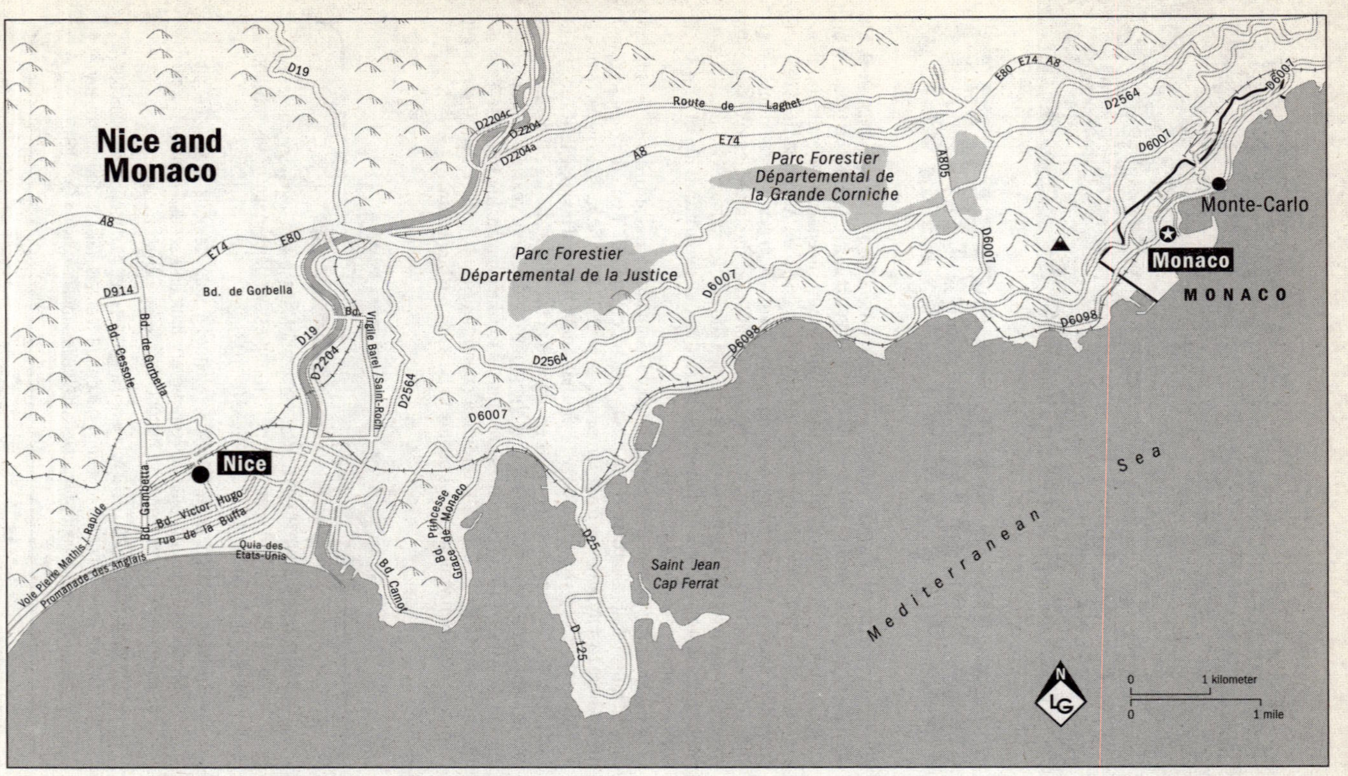
Nice and Monaco
Monte-Carlo
Monaco
M O N A C O
Mediterranean Sea
Parc Forestier Départemental de la Grande Corniche
Parc Forestier Départemental de la Justice
Route de Laghet
Saint Jean Cap Ferrat
Nice
Bd. de Gorbella
Bd. de Gorbella
Bd. Cessole
Bd. Gambetta
Bd. Victor Hugo
rue de la Buffa
Quia des Etats-Unis
Promenade des Anglais
Voie Pierre Mathis / Rapide
Bd. Virgile Barel / Saint-Roch
Bd. Princesse Grace de Monaco
Bd. Camot
D6007
D2564
D6098
D25
D 125
D19
D2204
D2204a
D2204c
D914
A8
E74
E80
A805
0
1 kilometer
0
1 mile
N
LG

nice ☎04

Nice has been on the backpacker must-see list since the youth of the world discovered its beaches and cheap wine. Combining a wealthy reputation with an affordable underbelly, Nice neatly condenses everything amazing about the Côte d'Azur into one sizzling metropolis. While those of you who'd like to escape the tourists will groan when you see the busloads of cruise-shipping retirees and loudmouthed Anglophones in the Vieille Ville, you'll cheer when you see the rock-bottom happy hour prices at the local bars, and grin when you interact with the well-established youth culture that goes out of its way to make travelers feel welcome (a rarity in France). Daytime activities revolve around the rocky beaches and immense seaside promenade; extensive shopping opportunities and an unparalleled array of museums are available for those of you who can't just lie around all day. The city just about explodes at night, with live music in almost every bar and club and non-stop parties that make it hard to keep from dropping dead with exhaustion.

ORIENTATION 

Vieux Nice

Vieux Nice is bounded by **Boulevard Jean Juares** to the north, the **château** to the east, and the **Jardin Albert I** to the west. Its winding steets are sometimes confusing for the tourists that invade the area around lunchtime and after sunset. The **cours Saleya** hosts local markets during the day that give way to cafes at night. Some of the largest crowds gather around the **Église Saint Jeaques** and the **Palais du Justice** for street performers. This is also where you'll find most of Nice's nightlife, backpackers, and cruise ship tourists. Small shops selling liqueurs, oils, and soaps are interspersed amongst the small boutique restaurants and hookah lounges.

Massena

Bounded by the **train station** to the north, the **Jardin Albert 1er** to the southwest, and the **bus station** and **old city** to the east, Massena is one of the busiest areas for any commerce that extends beyond tourism in Nice. The **tram** runs right through the middle of the neighborhood along **Jean Medecin,** and stops in front of the **main square,** the **shopping center,** and the **train station.** The closer you get to the train station, the higher the frequency of sex shops and neon lights. On the plus side, the hotels around here are cheaper. Closer to the old city, you can find row upon row of cheap clothing outlets (or at least cheap compared to other towns on the Riviera). Massena also hosts most of the city's metropolitan **museums;** almost all of them are free, though a couple of the private museums, such as the **Musée National Mesage Biblique Marc Chagall,** are not. The local restaurants and bars mostly cater to residents, and you'll be hard pressed to find fellow tourists.

Sea Front

The Sea Front is the easiest part of Nice to navigate. Step one: face ocean. Step two: walk either left or right. Boom, you have just oriented yourself along the only axis of this neighborhood. Dotted with the Massena Museum and the Opera, with the Hotel Negresco standing in the middle, the Sea Front is the least budget-friendly place to be in Nice. The hotels are pricey, the restaurants are formal, and the beaches are private. If you walk along any of the streets that run perpendicular to the ocean, you can find cheap food stands and two-star hotels. By doing so, you will have to give up the ocean view, unless you want to kink your neck in a manner befitting a circus performer to get a whiff of the salt air. A block up from the ocean runs streets parallel to the ocean, where you find more laid-back bars and cafes, as well as some affordable shopping. For those who want to escape the tourist-infested Vieux Nice at night, this is the perfect area to wander the boulevards in search of a more undiscovered Nice, one without the unattractive fanny packs and unwashed backpacks.

ACCOMMODATIONS

Vieux Nice

You'll pay more for a smaller room in the Vieux Nice, but you can't get any closer to the action than these hotels. It might be worth the credit card bill to keep from relying on Nice's tram to get you from where you want to be to where you want to pass out.

HOTEL VILLA LA TOUR — BOUTIQUE HOTEL ❹

4 rue de la Tour — ☎04 93 80 08 15 www.villa-la-tour.com

An adorable boutique hotel in a former 18th-century monastery, La Villa de la Tour is a classier place for travelers who don't mind paying a little extra for convenience and luxury. Check out the rooftop terrace for an intimate view of Vieux Nice.

Take the Tram (dir. Pont Michel) to Catedral Vieille Ville. Walk in same direction as tram for 2-3 blocks and turn right onto rue de la Tour. Singles €49-129; doubles €52-139; triples €150.

AU PICARDY HOTEL — HOTEL ❷

10 bld. Jean Juares — ☎02 93 85 75 51

This budget traveler's favorite is easy to find and centrally located in the Vieux Nice. The family-run hotel offers simple rooms and a shared terrace that connects all the rooms to each other.

Take the tram (dir. Pont Michel) to Catedral Vieille Ville. Walk in same direction as tram for 1 block. Hotel on your right. Singles and doubles €25-38; triples and quads €40-54.

HOTEL DE LA MER — HOTEL ❹

4 pl. Massena, 1st fl. — ☎04 93 92 09 10

A slightly more expensive, traditional hotel on the border of Massena and Vieux Nice. With exceptional views of the pl. Massena and the fountain, l'Hotel de la Mer is for those who want proximity to shopping and the beach, and don't mind the added cost.

Take the tram (dir. Pont Michel) to Massena. Walk around the fountain and toward the ocean. Hotel is on the right. Singles and doubles €65-95; triples €90-129; quads €110-159.

Massena

While the sex shops and neon lights might be a turnoff, Massena hosts the cheapest hotels in Nice. Don't worry: the hotels we've included here don't rent by the hour.

VILLA SAINT EXUPERY — HOSTEL ❷

22 av. Gravier — ☎08 00 30 74 09 www.vsaint.com

One of Europe's coolest hostels, Villa Saint Exupery boasts one of the most extensive lists of organized activities we've ever seen, including sailing trips to St-Tropez and "Anything But Clothes" parties in its newly renovated monastery-turned-social-space. The place used to be one of the farthest hostels from the Vieille Ville, but all that changed in 2010 with the opening of its sister hostel in the pl. Massena. Family-run with English-speaking staff.

From the Comte de Falicon tram stop, walk toward the post office and walk up av. du Ray. Continue straight as the road turns into av. Gravier. Walk 2 blocks and make a sharp left turn up the steep hill to the hostel on your left. Prices change frequently depending on occupancy. Dorms €16-30; doubles €54-90. Reception open 8am-noon and 6pm-2am.

HOTEL BELLE MEUNIERE — HOSTEL ❶

21 av. Durant — ☎04 93 88 66 15 www.bellemeuniere.com

This manor-turned-hostel is a backpacker's dream. Forget about the kitsch and the coin-operated soap dispensers; this place is unapologetically simple in its design and home-makeover feel. The rooms are all different and packed with loud social youth, who are attracted by the hostel's ideal location and "Backpacker special." New apartments with kitchenettes are also available for weekly rent not far from hostel.

*From the train station, walk across the street and down the stairs to av. Durant. Walk half a block and hostel is on your right. **i** Backpacker Special: Breakfast, linens, and shower €18. Ⓢ Doubles €49-52; triples €45-60; quads €80. Reception until midnight.*

PETIT LOUVRE — HOTEL ❸

10 rue Emma et Phillip Tiranty — ☎04 93 80 15 54

Hidden on a side street off the main drag, this hotel is centrally located and one of the best budget options for a long-term stay. The small but clean rooms offer baths, beds, and kitchenettes equipped with pots, pans, and silverware. While it may look like an Ikea catalogue, the prices are much more budget-friendly.

*From the tram stop Thiers, walk away from the train station down av. Jean Medecibout 4 blocks past the Notre Dame cathedral. Turn left onto rue Emma et Phillip Tiranty. Hotel is on your left. **i** Kitchenettes available. Ⓢ Singles €45-51, weekly €288; doubles €57/369; triples €68.50/440.*

HOTEL CRILLON — HOTEL ❸

44 rue Pastorelli — ☎04 93 85 43 59 www.crillon-hotel-nice.com

This old hotel has certainly been around the block a couple of times. While the halls smell of the good old days when smoking indoors was kosher, the newly renovated clean rooms are a nice surprise, and the steel cage of an elevator completes the archaic vibe.

From the tram stop Medecin, continue along av. Jean Medecin 2 blocks and make a left onto rue Pastorelli. Hotel is on your left. Ⓢ Singles €49-60; doubles €60-80; triples €70-90.

HOTEL INTERLAKEN — HOTEL ❸

26 rue Durant — ☎04 93 88 30 15 www.hotelinterlaken.fr

Once upon a time, Picasso and Andy Warhol had a love child. That love child was then asked to decorate a hostel in Nice. This is that hostel. Seemingly random stripes, colors, mismatched kitschy chandeliers, and shiny objects are scattered among the brightly colored and spacious rooms. Just to make everything groovier, the hotel comes with a bar.

Opposite the train station. Ⓢ Singles €44-55; doubles €49-62; triples €69-81; quads €84-104.

AUBERGE DE JEUNESSE — HOSTEL ❶

3 rue Spitalieri — ☎04 93 62 15 54 www.fuaj.org

Finally, a branch of the AJ hostel chain that's not in the middle of nowhere. This centrally located AJ is just as warm and welcoming as all the others, and features the cheapest beer at the most international bar in town. Clean dorms and bathrooms push for environmental awareness with push activated showers.

From the tram stop Medecin, walk around the Nice Etoile shopping mall. Hostel is directly behind mall. Ⓢ Dorms €23. Lockout 11am-3pm.

Sea Front

Not to burst your bubble, but the hotels along the Sea Front are, well, expensive. Who would have thought that such a pristine location right next to the beaches in southern France would be expensive? Surely not us.

HOTEL CRONSTADT — HOTEL ❺

3 rue Cronstadt — ☎04 93 02 00 30 www.hotelcronstadt.com

One of the most down-to-earth hotels on the seafront, this establishment is run by an old lady who apparently still decorates like it's 1873. Old pictures, chandeliers, quilted bedspreads, and eerie silence add to the feel that this place might be haunted. The only question is, if you see Casper, who ya gonna call?

Bus #8, 11, 52, 60, 62 to Gambetta/Promenade. From the bus stop, along the promenade des Anglais, walk towards the Hotel Negresco and turn left onto rue de Cronstadt. Hotel is on your left. i Wi-Fi available. Singles €70-75; doubles 90-95; triples €110.

HOTEL ALBERT 1ER HOTEL ❹

4 av. des Phoceans ☎04 93 85 74 01 www.hotel-albert-1er.com

Your basic example of what a pricey, chain hotel will look like in the neighborhood. Nicely decorated and air-conditioned, this hotel will give you the buffet breakfast and comfy beds, so long as you're willing to put up with the demanding French and German families at the front desk.

Next to the Jardin Albert 1er, the side closest to the old city. i Wi-Fi available. Singles €69-89. €10 extra per person.

HOTEL CANADA HOTEL ❹

8 rue Halevy ☎04 93 87 98 94

A welcomed two-star hotel in this expensive neighborhood. Decorated with replicas of Fernand Leger paintings, this colorful and laid-back hotel has clean rooms and a calm breakfast terrace. If you can stand the heat without A/C, you can live the Niçois lifestyle here.

Bus #8, 11, 52, 59, 60, 62 to Gustave V. Facing direction of bus, walk across and down the street to the left of Le Meridien. Continue 1 block; hotel is on your right. Singles €52-60; doubles €65-85; triples €89-100.

HOTEL LE MEURICE BOUTIQUE HOTEL ❺

14 av. de la Suede ☎04 97 03 05 20 www.hotel-le-meurice.com

A cute boutique hotel that we would recommend to visiting parents or those with huge budgets. Adorable Belle Époque style complete with lacy breakfast area and light pink bedspreads in uniquely arranged rooms. All of the comforts of A/C, Wi-Fi, and TV, since you're paying for it. Old but classy and well-kept to meet the demands of picky clientele.

Bus #8, 11, 52, 59, 60, 62 to Gustave V. Facing direction of bus, walk across the street and down the street to the left of Le Meridien. Continue 1 block and turn right onto av. de Suede. Hotel is on your left. i Breakfast €7.50. Singles €98-125; doubles 115-153.

SIGHTS

Vieux Nice

MUSÉE D'ART MODERNE ET D'ART COMTEMPORAIN MUSEUM

promenade des Arts ☎04 93 62 61 62 www.mamac-nice.org

Located just blocks from the Vieux Nice, Nice's massive Museum of Modern and Contemporary Art offers minimalist galleries that pay homage to the French new Realists, as well as American pop artists like Warhol. Rotating contemporary exhibits showcase artists from around the world. Don't miss the collection of statues by Niki St-Phalle, which routinely frighten even the most hardcore hallucinogen users.

Promenade des Arts. Take the tram to Catedrale - Vieille Ville. Free. Tours €3, students €1.50. Open Tu-Su 10am-6pm.

CHÂTEAU CASTLE HILL FORTRESS

☎04 93 85 62 33

The remains of an 11th-century fort located on the hill overlooking Vieux Nice, this château is the oldest spot in the city. Celto-Ligurians claimed the sight until the Romans decided it would make a good spot for a fort in 154 CE. Centuries later, Provençal nobles built a castle and cathedral on the hill as a symbol of their authority. During King Louis XIV's great centralization of France, the fortress was destroyed. Today, all that remains is the large park and waterfall that were made from the ruins. The climb may be tiresome, but the view is well worth it, and offers 360° views of Nice and the Med.

Free. Open Jun-Aug daily 9am-8pm; Sept 10am-7pm; Oct-Mar 8am-6pm; Apr-May 8am-7pm. Info booth open July Aug Tu-F 9:30am-12:30pm and 1:30-6pm.

COURS SALEYA SQUARE, MARKET

cours Saleya

Built on the ramparts in the 18th century, the cours Saleya is now a bustling hub of activity ideally situated between Nice Vieille Ville and the beach. Nice's open-air market is located here by day, and a collection of hip cafes set out tables at night. The square is also home to the famous *Marche des Fleurs*, where you can buy opulent bouquets of local flora. A perfect spot to wander through Nice's winding alleyways.

Market daily 7:30am-1pm.

WAR MEMORIAL MEMORIAL

pl. Guynemer

At the foot of the castle hill, this enormous WWI memorial stands in honor of the 4000 Niçois who died in the line of duty between 1914 and 1919. Over 50m tall, this monument was erected in 1924, and cut directly into the old quarries. Some of the most spectacular views of the Mediterranean are along this promenade, which links the port to the Vieille Ville. Although there are signs that warn against it, don't be surprised to see local kids skateboarding on the memorial steps.

Free.

CATEDRALE ST. RÉPARATE CATHEDRAL

pl. Rossetti

Nice's largest and most opulent cathedral was inspired by early Baroque architectural models from Rome. It is not an accident that the design is a miniature version of the larger and more famous St. Peter's in Rome, complete with a triple nave and a transept.

Open daily 7am-6pm. Closed for visits during services.

ADAM AND EVE HOUSE HISTORIC SIGHT

rue de la Poissonerie

You'll walk right by this one if you're not careful. The Adam and Eve house, as it's called locally, is one of the last examples in Vieux Nice of the detailed facades that historically decorated the homes here. The house's bas-relief dates back to 1584, and depicts Adam and Eve, naked in the Garden of Eden, threatening each other with clubs. Apparently this WWE version of the Bible never made into the mainstream in English-language trasnlation.

PLACE GARIBALDI SQUARE

pl. Garibaldi

On the eastern end of the Vieille Ville, the large open space of pl. Garibaldi is lined by elegant, red buildings with green shutters and vaulted porticos. You can see the perfectly integrated Chappelle St-Sepulchre nestled amongst the buildings surrounding the statue and fountain of Garibaldi.

Massena

MUSÉE MATISSE MUSEUM

164 rue des Arenes ☎04 93 81 08 08 www.musee-matisse-nice.org

This expertly renovated Genoese villa displays decades of art by one of France's most elusive artists. The permanent collection includes Matisse's early sketches, as well as gouache 3D cardboard cut-outs...er...sorry...*"tableaux."* If you can't make it up to Vence to see Matisse's whimsical *Chapelle du Rosaire de Vence* for yourself, check out the museum's model of the chapel, and the exhibit that examines his creative process, including the artist's initial attempts to depict the Stations of the Cross in black and white finger paint. Temporary exhibits generally display more oblique aspects of Matisse's life and work, such as his decades-long artistic obsession with a Russian girl (he drew her and only her for 10 years) named Lydia.

Take bus #15, 17, 20, 22 or 25 to Arenes. Free shuttle between Chagall and Matisse museums. Tours in English by reservation. Free. Open M 10am-6pm, W-Su 10am-6pm.

MUSÉE NATIONAL MESAGE BIBLIQUE MARC CHAGALL MUSEUM

av. Dr. Menard 04 93 53 87 20 www.musee-chagall.fr

The museum showcases Chagall's interpretation of the Hebrew Bible, comprised of 12 massive canvases that the artist chose to arrange by color rather than chronologically. The adjacent rooms display his "creative" blending of the Bible and the Russian Revolution (because when you say Lenin, we think Crucifixion). The museum also includes an auditorium that hosts concerts and other events, with stained-glass panels by the artist depicting the story of creation.

Walk 15min. northeast from the train station or take bus #22 (dir. Rimez to Musée Chagall). €9.50 under 26. Art students and EU citizens free. Open May-Oct M 10am-6pm, W-Su 10am-6pm; Nov-Mar M 10am-5pm, W-Su 10am-5pm. Last entry 30min. before close.

MONESTERE CIMIEZ MONASTERY, MUSEUM

av. du Monestere

The monastery was a Franciscan hideout before it was confiscated by the Revolution. When the Revolution collapsed, Monestere Cimiez was returned to the church, and the monks expanded its gardens; they now overlook the port, and stretch to the cemetery where Matisse is buried. Inside the church is a nearly 6m tall marble cross, accompanied by small statues that portray figures from St. Francis's visions.

Take bus #15, 17, 20, 22 or 25 to Arenes. Walk across the park to the Monastery. Free. Open M-Tu 10am-5pm, Th-Sa 10am-5pm. Closed on Su during service.

SAINTE JEANNE D'ARC CHURCH CHURCH

11 rue Grammont

A modern wonder in its day, this church was built in the 1930s entirely out of concrete, then painted white to resemble some blend of sci-fi and Middle Eastern architecture. The domed Byzantine ceiling is laden with symbolism: pat yourself on the back if you can figure out the numerical significance of the seven mini domes supporting the church's three larger domes. Alright, well it has to do with a certain number of virtues supporting a trinity. The church is named after the small chapel to the side, which is dedicated to France's favorite 17-year-old saint (or witch, if you ask the English).

Take the T37 or bus 22 to Église Jean d'Arc. Open 8am-4:30pm.

MONT ALBAN FORT FORT

av. du Mont-Alban

Once a 16th-century fort, this massive and now defunct hilltop bastion boasts a stunning view of Nice, the nearby Cap d'Ail, and even Antibes. The brochure says that on a clear day you can see Corsica, but we sadly didn't. If you're yearning for a long uphill hike in hot weather, this fort's for you. Nice plans to convert the fort into a contemporary art museum in the near future, but for now you'll have to settle for a stroll around the battlements, as visitors are not allowed inside.

Take bus #14 to Chemin du Fort and walk downhill to the fort. Also a footpath exists near the bus stop Escalliers de Verre (bus #81 and 100).

PLACE MASSENA ♿ SQUARE

pl. Massena

One of the main centers of the city, this large town square is patterned like a checkerboard, and unlike many areas of Nice, remained relatively untouched during both world wars. The most recent renovations incorporated the tramway into the area, in addition to seven meditating statues perched atop a collection of large poles, designed by Spanish artist Juame Plensa (they supposedly represent each of the seven continents). These figures are joined by break dancers and street performers during the day and a grittier crowd at night. (Read: take the tram at night.)

Sea Front

The sights that line the Sea Front are largely architectural, with the exception of the villas and estates that have been converted into pretty impressive museums.

MASSENA MUSEUM ♿ MUSEUM

65 rue de France and 35 promenade des Anglais ☎04 93 91 19 10

Once home to (you guessed it!) the prominent Massena family, this giant seaside estate was donated to the city at the turn of the century by Andre Massena, much to the chagrin of the eldest son who had hoped to inherit it. Exhibits include paintings and photographs of Nice's old carnival pier and other neighborhoods, as well as a collection of elaborate dresses that would make Barbie blush. The ornate estate proves that France retained a nobility long after the Revolution.

Open M 10am-6pm, W-Su 10am-6pm. Free.

MUSÉE BEAUX ARTS ♿ MUSEUM

33 av. des Baumettes ☎04 92 15 28 28 www.musee-beaux-arts-nice.org

When you first see its inconvenient location in the far corner of the city, you'll be tempted to blow it off (we almost did). For art lovers, that would be a terrible mistake. This villa turned museum holds works by both Picasso and Rodin. One of the most macabre collections is a gallery by Niçois artist Gustav-Adolf Mossa, whose work includes the most nightmarish, surrealist paintings imaginable, including clowns with bloody knives and harpies on the piles of dead bodies.

Open M 10am-6pm, W-Su 10am-6pm. Free.

PROMENADE DES ANGLAIS ♿ PROMENADE

promenade des Anglais

Once a six-feet-wide dirt path, this main artery of Nice was expanded in 1820 by a wealthy Englishman, then inaugurated in 1931 by the Duke of Connaught, one of Queen Victoria's sons. Today it runs along the beach and connects the Sea Front to the Vieille Ville, and provides an easy footpath between private beaches.

BEACHES ♿ BEACH

promenade des Anglais

The public and private beaches alternate along the Baie des Anges from Vieux Nice as far as the Sea Front goes. Expect to pay for the umbrellas and chairs at the private beaches, bring multiple towels for padding, or buy a cheap beach mat—the beaches here are pretty rugged, and you don't want to end up sunbathing on jagged rocks. We recommend that you give up the search for sand and just go swimming.

HOTEL NEGRESCO — HOTEL, HISTORIC BUILDING

37 promenade des Anglais

There's a reason we didn't list Hotel Negresco under the accommodations—this place is over €400 a night. The classic Niçois architecture is pretty spectacular, though. The hotel has been classified as a historical building since 2003, ensuring that its bright white walls and pink dome will be in postcards well in the future.

FOOD

Vieux Nice

Food is plentiful and cheap in this part of town. You'll be able to find the expensive restaurants easily enough, but the charm of Vieux Nice lies in its small snack shacks, markets, and hole-in-the-wall *socca* joints. While heavy on the tourists, Vieux Nice still offers thriving local markets in the marche des Fleurs and the cours Saleya *(daily 7am-1pm)*, where flowers are sold at slashed prices alongside candied fruits, fresh produce, olives, and Italian cannolis. There are two large **Monoprix** supermarkets located on av. Jean Medecin *(open M-Sa 8:30am-8pm)* and in pl. Garibaldi. *(Open M-Sa 8:30am-8pm.)*

LA FERME SALEYA — TRADITIONAL ❸

8 rue Jules Gilly — ☎06 71 84 07 32

This traditional French restaurant will make you think that you're in the rural countryside of Bretagne or Angers. Cute pottery farm animals hint at the largely carnivorous meal that you're about to eat. Call ahead for a group, and the chef will prepare a personalized menu at prices that are comparable to the house *formule.*

Formule €15-22. Open Tu-Su noon-2:30pm and 7-10pm.

FENOCCHIO — ICE CREAM ❶

2 pl. Rossetti — ☎04 93 80 72 52

Serving the best ice cream in France, Fenocchio offers 96 flavors of Italian gelato, including more eccentric flavors such as beer, avocado, and rose. Traditional flavors like vanilla and pistachio are delicious here too. *Let's Go* recommends one of their decadent sundaes for €10-20.

1 scoop €2, 2 scoops €3.50. Open daily 10am-midnight.

RENE SOCCA — SOCCA ❶

2 rue Miralheti — ☎04 93 92 05 73

Forget the tourist-frequented *socca* joints—this is the only authentic one you'll find. The lines around the block indicate that this place serves some of the best quality fried Niçois dishes in the whole city. With a one drink minimum, terrace seating is available under signs that strongly advise against the use of silverware.

Socca €2.50. Plats €5-10. Open daily noon-9pm.

FLORIAN — CANDY SHOP ❷

14 quai Papacino — ☎04 93 55 43 50 www.confiserieflorian.com

Every sweet tooth's dream come true, this confectionery offers tours of its factory, where you learn how to make candied fruit, crystallized flowers, and candied orange peels. While the tour might make your mouth water, remain in control of you wallet, since you'll want to splurge (understandably so) in the pricey yet delicious boutique after being teased with samples.

In the New Port. Tours of factory on demand with video in English or French. Candied flowers €6. Candied fruit assortment €36. Open M-Sa 11am-8pm.

SNACK LA BANANE — CRÊPERIE, PANINI ❶

6 rue de la Poissonnerie — ☎04 93 79 07 54

Simple snack shack taken to the extreme with kitschy, banana-themed decor.

Provocative signs and pop art paintings make this a hip place for smoothies, paninis, or crêpes.

Panini €3.50-4. Crêpes €7. Open daily 8am-midnight.

L'ÉCURIE TRADITIONAL ❷

4 rue du Marché ☎04 93 62 32 62

A classic farm-themed French restaurant, this establishment serves traditional meat dishes (or wood-fired pizza for the less ambitious) in four different dining rooms; each one is decorated according to a different theme, ranging from beach cottage to countryside stable.

Plats €12-17. Menu €22. Open daily 9am-midnight. Kitchen open noon-11pm.

LA MERANDA PROVENÇAL ❷

4 rue de la Terrasse ☎08 92 68 06 89

A small 12-table gem on the edge of Vieux Nice, Le Meranda's chef Dominique le Stanc produces an outstanding menu that changes daily based on the local market fare. Ratatouille and pizza are regularly served here, in addition to traditional Provençal dishes.

Plats €9-13. i Reserve in person for lunch and dinner. Open M-F noon-1:30pm and 7-9pm.

SUR LE POUCE SOCCA ❶

4 rue St. François ☎04 93 13 98 23

This hole-in-the-wall restaurant serves traditional Niçois plates of *assiettes* and *socca* on its wooden benches outside the restaurant. Crêpes and other cheap French munchies are served in a low-key and informal atmosphere.

Pizza €2.50. Socca €2.50. Crêpes €3-6. Open daily noon-10pm.

BAR DU COIN PIZZERIA ❶

2 rue Droite ☎04 93 62 32 59

One of the best pizza joints in Nice, this colorful bar-cafe offers outdoor seating in a well-traveled corner of the Vieille Ville. The local favorite usually gets packed late at night, so get there before 10pm to get a table outside.

Pizza €7.50-11. Salads €10. Open daily noon-midnight.

Massena

Massena might not offer the backpacker staples of *socca* and cheap fast food, but if you have a little extra to spend on one night out, this is where you want to go. Classy, local, and cheap(er than Vieille Ville), Massena is not as infested with tourists as the rest of the city, and has the traditional cuisine you came to France for.

MANGEZ-MOI FRENCH ❸

9 rue Blacas ☎04 93 87 54 71 www.restaurantmangezmoi.com

This adorable French/seafood blend restaurant has all the kitschy decorations octogenarians go crazy for. Come for the taster menu of changing daily specials. Cozy garden seating on ivy-covered terrace.

€15 menu. €25 3-course. Open Tu-Th 9am-8:30pm, F-Sa 8:30-10pm.

SPEAKEASY VEGAN ❷

7 rue Lamartine ☎04 93 85 59 50

A throwback to the Haight-Ashbury circa 1967, this vegan restaurant is run by a friendly American expat hippie. Strangers share the small tables when it gets crowded. The menu changes frequently; cross your fingers and hope that Jane whips up her vegan pie.

€14 2-course menu. Specials €9-11. i Open M-F noon-2:15pm and 7-9:15pm, Sa noon-2:15pm.

LE NOLITA CRÊPERIE ❷

8 av. Durant ☎06 23 74 66 67

The small, New York-themed crêpe cafe serves lunch and breakfast specials on the small outdoor patio. Pasta specials accompany desserts *du jour* such as *Mousse au Chocolat* and sweet crêpes.

Midi menu €11. Crêpes €7-8. Open daily 8am-8pm.

COSY CAFE CRÊPERIE ❷

5 rue Clemenceau ☎04 93 88 92 99

If you're tired of the French but not their food, come to this popular hangout for English med students (thanks to the hospital across the street), who come in droves for the €10 crêpe specials; each special includes a free glass of cider.

Panini €4. Crêpes €2.50-7. Prix-fixe menu €10. Open daily 7:30am-6pm.

GRAND CAFÉ DE LYON BRASSERIE ❷

33 av. Jean Medecin ☎04 93 88 13 17 www.cafedelyon.fr

One of the oldest brasseries in Nice, this centrally located giant of a bar dominates the shopping area, and is a must for those craving the most elaborate sundae or people-watching combos. Crowds escape the heat by lounging in wicker chairs under rotating fans.

Ice cream €5-11. Cocktails €5.30-7.70. Open daily 7am-11pm.

LUNA ROSSA ITALIAN ❷

3 rue Chauvain ☎04 93 85 55 66 www.lelunarossa.com

While not the cheapest place for pizza or Italian food, this place is definitely worth a visit, if only for the murals of street art that decorates its walls. Luna Rossa closes early in the evening (by Niçois standards anyway), so up your blood alcohol content here at the chic wine bar before officially starting your night.

Plats €9.50-15. Salads €9.50-11. Open Tu-F noon-2pm and 7:30-10:30pm, Sa 7:30-10:30pm.

J. MULTARI BAKERY ❶

12 rue Pastorelli, 13 cours Saleya, 22 rue Gioffredo ☎04 93 85 08 43

Yes, it's a chain, but it's also both local and awesome. Marble countertops display the seemingly infinite desserts, sandwiches, and panini available as €5 specials. Like a bakery/sandwichery/*chocolatier* all rolled into one.

Sandwiches €5. Small plates €2-5. Open M-Sa 7am-8pm.

Sea Front

Most of the restaurants in this neighborhood are small cafes or more upscale brasseries. While eating out here along the promenade might be out of your reach, any of the small alleys that run perpendicular to the beach have cheap gyro stands and pizza places that sell by the slice. If you do happen to sit down at one of the pricey bistros, go for any of the fruit or ice cream cocktails that are frequently served up.

CAFÉ DE LA PROMENADE BRASSERIE ❶

3 promenade des Anglais ☎04 93 82 54 55

If you're aching for a real American or English breakfast (as real as France can provide, anyway), come to this cabana-esque diner, which features the plush vinyl booths of your local Denny's and the calorie intake to match.

Sandwiches and salads €7-12. Sundaes €7.70-9.70. American breakfast €13.50. Open daily 7:30am-2am.

LA CANNE A SUCRE BRASSERIE ❸

11 promenade des Anglais ☎04 93 87 19 35

This vaguely tropical cafe serves cool ice cream crêpes, cocktails, and smoothies.

The palm trees, fake fruit, and a certain Barry Manilow soundtrack are excessive enough to embarrass Chiquita Banana.

Pizza €9-14. Salads €6-15. Open daily 11am-11pm.

LE DOLCE MOMENTO BRASSERIE ❶

25 promenade des Anglais ☎04 93 80 90 18

This small brasserie-cafe by the sea serves an American-ish breakfast and traditional French food. The peaceful and informal setting is perfect for a quick bite after an exhausting day of sunbathing.

Breakfast €2.50-7.70. Plats €10. Open Tu-Su 8am-10pm.

NISS'TANBUL GREEK ❶

4 bld. Gambetta ☎06 23 12 66 32

A budget traveler's dream: renowned for its cheap gyros and Turkish fast food, Niss'tanbul whips up hot kebabs and baklava and pours out cheap Greek and Turkish wine.

Gyro €5. Plats €9-10. Open daily 11am-midnight.

POMODORISSIMO PIZZA ❶

2 rue Gambetta ☎04 93 02 43 67

Enabling the beach bums of the world one slice at a time, this hole-in-the-wall fast-food joint is ideally located for sunbathers. There's also a small seating area, if you aren't in a hurry to get back to the sand.

Pizza slice €2.50. Open daily 11am-8:30pm.

LES JARDINS DU CAPITOLE CAFE ❷

52 promenade des Anglais ☎04 93 94 78 81

Hipper than a lot of the local cafe joints, this brasserie serves mid-afternoon drinks as well as pizza, French salads and typical brasserie fare.

Menu formule €14. Open Tu-Su 11am-11pm.

LA SIRENA ITALIAN ❷

39 promenade des Anglais ☎04 93 80 88 39

For those lacking the appropriate language skills, "Sirena" is Italian for that cute half-female, half-fish on the front of the cafe. The staff here serves Italian fare and wood-fired pizza, offering a *formule* menu of pizza and dessert or *plat* and dessert.

Menu formule €13.50. Open Tu-Su 11am-8:30pm.

NIGHTLIFE

Vieux Nice

BULLDOG PUB POMPEII BAR, LIVE MUSIC

14, 16 rue de l'Abbaye ☎04 93 85 04 06 www.bulldogpub.com

One of Nice's best-kept secrets for locals and intrepid backpackers, this '60s and '70s rock-themed pub hosts live music every night. The house is regularly packed with young people, who resort to barstools and tabletops for standing room.

i Live music, smoking lounge upstairs. Beer €6. Cocktails €8. 6 shots €18. Open daily 8am-4am. Live music starts at 10pm.

WAYNE'S BAR PUB

15 rue de la Prefecture ☎04 93 13 46 99

Wayne's is a late-night institution in Nice, with an English-speaking staff that caters to rowdy, spitting crowds of unwashed backpackers. Huge crowds at night gather for pop-rock music and drunk, travel story-swapping (sounds like a *Let's Go* office party).

i Tourist bookings for bungee jumping, sailing, day trips to towns. Happy hour pints €3.90.

Beer €6.20. Cocktails €7.50. Open daily noon-2am. Kitchen open noon-11pm. Happy hour 5-8pm.

MA NOLANS PUB

2 rue François ☎04 93 81 46 90

Upscale and fun Irish pub that offers karaoke and trivia (with prizes for the winners). House specialty here is pear cider, if you happened to be debating a splurge on a pint or whiskey cocktail.

i Trivia night on M 8pm. Karaoke F 10pm-close. Beer €3.90. Cocktails €7.50. Open M-Sa noon-2am. Happy hour 5-8pm.

LE SIX GAY BAR

6 rue Raoul Bosio ☎04 93 62 66 64

One of the most opulent and creative gay bars in the Riviera. The large space dates back to the Belle Époque, with a room displaying the shower for its nightly shower show. Telephones scattered throughout the bar randomly connect to each other for secret chatting with anonymous patrons.

Beer €7. Cocktails €10. Open daily 10pm-5am.

3 DIABLES BAR

2 cours Saleya ☎04 93 62 47 00 www.les3diables.com

This bar has become a hopping youth hangout thanks to its Thursday night student prices; just flash your student ID for a dramatic reduction in prices. The two-story bar regularly serves both locals and backpackers. After midnight, DJs turn the bar upstairs into more of a club.

i Karaoke W night. Student night Th, pints €4. Liquor €3.50. Pints €6.80. Cocktails €8. Open daily 5pm-3am. Happy hour 5-9pm.

PADDY'S PUB PUB

40 rue Droite ☎04 93 80 06 75

Your typical Irish pub, Paddy's is a welcoming haven for backpackers and ex-pats; take a seat on the rough and beaten bar stools. The large TV screens show sporting events, and the bar features nine rotating beers on tap. Live music on the weekends.

i Happy hour drinks €4.50. Beer €6. Cocktails €7.50. Open daily 3pm-2am. Happy hour 6-8:30pm.

NOCY-BÈ HOOKAH

4, 6 rue Jules Gilly ☎04 93 16 93 20

This is a traditional Maghreb hookah bar with low lighting, low couches, and no alcohol consumption. Bright cushions, Moroccan lamps, and arched doorways allow you to take a trip across the Mediterranean without the 24hr. **boat** ride.

i No alcohol served. 1-drink min. (as in soda or tea). Hookah €10. Tea €4. Open M-Sa 3:30pm-12:30am.

PUB OXFORD PUB

4 rue Mascoïnat ☎04 93 92 24 54

The cheapest booze in town is served at this new English pub in the center of the old city. Walk through the red telephone booth in the doorway and enjoy the delightfully tacky atmosphere and good company.

i Happy hour shooters €1.50; cocktails €4; pints €3. Liquor €6.40. Beer €6.50. Open daily 7pm-5am. Happy hour 7-11pm.

HANIBAL LOUNGE HOOKAH, BAR

2 pl. Vieille ☎04 93 80 18 08

In the basement of a local bar, this social hookah joint encourages friend-making in its large cushioned booths. Designed to imitate the interior of a Roman bath, this lounge is decorated with mosaic tiles and offers a Western-friendly drink menu (read: booze).

Hookah €10.50. Cocktails €6. Tea €3.50. Open M-Sa 7pm-midnight.

THE PLEASURE BAR, SEX SHOP

27 rue Benoît Bunico ☎06 83 81 61 63

For the truly adventurous or hedonistic, this sex shop-bar should take you well past your limits, with its pink feathery decor and extensive drink list of suggestive cocktails such as "Sensual" and "Desire." Friendly owner has experience calming down visibly uncomfortable customers, and regularly reassures patrons that this is a "normal bar."

Cocktails €6-10. Open Tu-Su 6pm-12:30am.

LES DISTILLERIES BAR

24 rue de la Prefecture ☎04 93 62 10 66

Classy bar reminiscent of a turn-of-the-century brasserie. Belt-driven fans and antiquated radios complement the veteran adjoining brewery, reminding us that the Niçois have always drank like sailors, even in the classy Belle Époque.

Shots €3. Beer €7. Cocktails €7.50. Open M-Sa noon-2am. Happy hour 6-8pm.

BLAST AMERICAN BAR BAR

8 pl. Charles Felix ☎04 93 80 00 50

For homesick Americans looking for a comfy outdoor lounge, come to Blast in the *cours Saleya* for some good old-fashioned American breakfast, served until 3pm. Come back after sunset for a laid-back beer with the likes of Uncle Sam and the Mount Rushmore presidents.

Beer €4. Cocktails €9. Breakfast €6.50-8. Open daily 10am-2am. Kitchen open until midnight.

BLUE WHALES PUB

1 rue Mascoïnat ☎04 93 62 90 94

One of the cheaper pubs in the city, Blue Whales offers live music and a lengthy happy hour in an authentic bar scene reserved for budget backpackers and locals.

Beer €2. Shooters €3-4. 2 shooters for €10. Open daily 6:30pm-4:30am. Happy hour 6:30pm-midnight. Live music 11pm-4am.

LE CRAZY BAR

21 rue Droite ☎06 18 01 72 63

A flamboyant disco gay bar in the heart of the old city, Le Crazy has themed nights every night of the week; Tuesday's '90s Night, Thursday's '70s Night, and Saturday's "Crazy Night" are particular favorites. All sexes and sexualities welcome.

i Soirees and shows on themed nights every night of the week. Beer €4. Cocktails €10. Open daily 7pm-4am.

KING'S PUB PUB

15 rue de la Prefecture www.kingspub.fr.st

British medieval-themed pub is complete with iron railings and an overall dungeon feel. Large TV screens play sports games, and a live band performs every night after 10:30pm.

i Live music. Beer €4. Shots €4. Cocktails €8.50. Open daily 5pm-2am. Live music 10:30pm-midnight.

Massena

Massena might not be the backpacker's first choice for nightlife, but it might tickle your fancy if you're in town for longer than a week and in need of some serious cultural immersion. Few internationals venture beyond the realms of the Vieille Ville and the comfort of Wayne's, after all.

LA BODEGUITA DEL HAVANA — BAR

14 rue Chauvain ☎04 93 92 67 24

Papered with Che pics and with rum barrels as tables, this Cuban salsa bar and disco has the feel of a run-down bar in Havana. Serves Cuban dishes and an extensive list of mojitos *(€10.50).*

i Salsa dancing W-Th 7:30pm. Beer €3. Cocktails €10.50. Open Tu-Su 8pm-2am.

LE TONO — TAPAS, WINE BAR

18 rue Clemenceau ☎04 93 87 84 17

This laid-back wine bar was repeatedly recommended by locals, and serves tapas at an impressively reasonable €6. The menu is mostly vegetarian, but carnivores can find something to eat here too. The outdoor seating and relaxed jazzy vibe lure customers in for late lunches and drinks long after the sun sets.

Wine €3-4. Beer €5. Vegetarian tapas €6. Open Tu-Su 3pm-midnight.

LE TRENTE 7 — CAFE, BAR

37 rue Pastorelli ☎04 93 85 27 21

This somewhat typical bar is centrally located in the middle of an up-and-coming neighborhood. Extensively decorated with neon orange (in a good way), Le Trente 7 manages to be chic without raising its prices to match. It's not particularly popular with tourists or backpackers, so be prepared for some French immersion.

Beer €2.70-5. Cocktails €7-9.50. Open M noon-3pm, Tu-Sa noon-3pm and 6pm-late.

LE ROMAGNA — JAZZ BAR

22 rue d'Angleterre ☎04 93 87 91 55

La Romagna recently changed owners, and is now open infrequently. The dusty bar has the cheapest liqueur in town, and plays a diverse set list from the extensive collection of jazz records that line the shelves.

Beer €2.50. Shots €3. Open Sa 7-9pm.

ARTS AND CULTURE

Festivals and Carnivals

Nice is known for its summer music festivals, particularly the Fête de la Musique that occurs on the summer solstice. The bacchanalian Carnival takes place in February or March.

FÊTE DE LA MUSIQUE — CITYWIDE

This citywide festival is as unofficial as it is awesome. A treasured Niçois tradition since the mid-'80s, this celebration gets every bar, disco, and restaurant in the city to put on free live music in the streets, cafes and alleyways of the city on the summer solstice. Nice comes alive with everything from pop rock to DJ party music. The crowds get particularly rowdy in the *vieille ville*, so make sure to watch out for pickpockets and those who wish to ruin the fun, drunken times. Apart from that minor setback, this is Nice at its best; many of the bars open early and stay open well after 3 or 4am, and the fast food joints take advantage of the partiers and offer *socca* and pizza in the early morning as well. Head to the area around Wayne's and the cours Saleya for the best and most international bands.

Summer Solstice (June).

CARNIVAL

SEA FRONT
www.nicecarnaval.com

France might take pride in its secular society, but this annual excuse to get really drunk and dance around owes its existence to the Catholic culture of Nice. The Promenade des Anglais and the quai des Etats-Unis host two weeks of parades, fireworks, and concerts, while confetti falls like rain in Seattle. Flower processions, masked balls, and endless partying make this the liveliest time in Nice's winter.

Tickets €10-30.

NICE JAZZ FESTIVAL

CIMIEZ

arenes et Jardins de Cimiez ☎08 20 80 04 00 www.nicejazzfestival.fr

Every July, the quiet area of Cimiez and gardens outside of the Matisse Museum swell with over 55,000 spectators, who flock to the city for the eight-day festival, featuring 75 concerts and over 500 individual musicians.

i Free shuttle from the pl. Massena during concerts. €29-49 per night, students €22-36; 3-day passes €96-105; 8-day €185. Concerts 7pm-midnight.

Cinema, Opera, and Theater

CINEMATHEQUE DE NICE

MASSENA

3 espalande de Kennedy ☎04 92 04 06 66 www.cinematheque-nice.com

The historic theater screens old black-and-white films, documentaries, and art-house staples. The prices here are an absolute steal, but don't expect box office hits or convenient show times. Schedule changes weekly, and is available at the tourism office and local museums.

Tickets €2. Showings between 11am-8:15pm.

RIALTO CINEMA

SEA FRONT

4 rue de Rivoli ☎08 92 68 00 41

Rialto shows box office hits in their original (read: English) language. During the week-long *Fête du Cinema* in late June, movie tickets are only €3 if you've already paid full admission to a movie at one of the festival's participating theaters.

€9, students €6. Showings 2-10pm.

OPÉRA DE NICE

SEA FRONT

4-6 rue Saint-François de Paule ☎04 92 17 40 79

Produces stage performances September-May, and hosts visiting orchestras and individual soloists year round. Ballet and opera schedule changes and is available at the tourist office.

€7-40. Box office open M-F 8:30am-4:30pm.

THEATRE NATIONAL DE NICE

SEA FRONT

promenade des Arts ☎04 93 13 90 90 www.tnn.fr

Puts on concerts and plays. Check website for changing annual schedule.

€10-30, students €7.50-28. Box office open June-July Tu-Sa 1-7pm; Aug-May Tu-Sa 2-7pm. Su at 1pm for same-day entrance only.

ESSENTIALS

Practicalities

- **TOURIST OFFICE: Branch on Avenue Thiers** has hotel reservations, restaurant and sights guides as well as a city map and practical guide. (*Next to the train station. ☎08 92 70 74 07 www.nicetourisme.com Open June-Sept M-Sa 8am-8pm, Su 9am-7pm; Oct-May M-Sa 8am-7pm, Su 10am-5pm.)* Additional branches can be found at **5 promenade des Anglais** *(☎08 92 70 74 07 Open June-Sept M-Sa 8am-8pm, Su 9am-6pm; Oct-May M-Sa 9am-6pm.)* and at the

Airport. (*Terminal 1 ☎08 92 70 74 07 ⏰ Open June-Sept daily 8am-9pm; Oct-May M-Sa 8am-9pm.)*

- **CONSULATES: Canada.** *(10 rue Lamartine ☎04 93 92 93 22 ⏰ Open M-F 9am-noon.)* **UK.** *(Embassy in Monaco, 33 bld. Princesss Charlotte ☎377 93 50 99 54)* **US.** *(7 av. Gustave V ☎04 93 88 89 55 ⏰ Open M-F 9-11:30am and 1:30-4:30pm.)*
- **YOUTH CENTER: Centre Regional d'Information Jeaunesse (CRIJ)** posts summer jobs for students and provides info on long-term housing, study, and recreation. *(19 rue Gioffredo, near the Museum of Contemporary Art. ☎04 93 80 93 93 www.crijca.fr **i** Free internet access with Student ID. ⏰ Open M-F 10am-6pm.)*
- **LAUNDROMATS:** These are plentiful in Nice, so check to make sure you're not around the corner from one already before hitting these locations. *(7 rue d'Italie ☎04 93 85 88 14 $ Wash €3.50, dry €1 per 18min.); (11 rue de Pont Vieux ☎04 93 85 88 14 $ Wash €2.50-6.50, dry €.50 per 8 min. ⏰ Open daily 7am-9pm.)*

Emergency!

- **POLICE:** *(1 av. amrechal Foch ☎04 92 17 22 22)*
- **LATE-NIGHT PHARMACIES:** Check Nice Matin for rotating **Pharmacie de Garde** (24hr. pharmacy). Late-night service available by phone *(7 rue Massena ☎04 93 87 78 94).*
- **HOSPITAL:** *(5 rue Pierre Devoluy ☎04 92 03 33 75)*
- **INTERNET:** Internet access is available on almost every street corner in Nice, usually marked by neon signs in Arabic. Free internet at the CRIJ and Wi-Fi at select cafes and bars. The closest internet availability from the train station is on rue Theirs across from the Thiers tram stop.
- **POST OFFICES:** *(23 av. Thiers ☎04 93 82 65 22 www.lapost.fr ⏰ Open M-F 8am-7pm, Sa 8am-noon.)* Additional branches everywhere in the city.
- **POSTAL CODE:** 06033.

Getting There

By Plane

Aeroport Nice-Côte d'Azur (*NCE; ☎08 20 42 33 33*). Municipal Ligne d'Azur Buses leave ever 30min. for the airport from the train station. *($ €4. ⏰ #98 direct bus 8am-9pm.)* Before 8am, bus #23 *($ €1. ⏰ Every 15-25min.)* makes several stops, including at the train station. EasyJet flies to London, Vueling to Barcelona, and Air France to Paris and other domestic and international destinations.

By Train

Gare SNCF Nice-Ville is the more centrally located station. *(av. Thiers ☎04 93 14 82 12 www.sncf.com ⏰ Info and reservation center open M-Sa 8:30am-5:45pm.)* Trains to: **Cannes** *($ €6 ⏰ 40min., every 20min. 5:15am-midnight);* **Marseille** *($ €29-70. ⏰ 2½hr., 15 per day);* **Monaco** *($ €3.30. ⏰ 15min., every 20min.);* **Paris.** *($ €94. ⏰ 5hr., 6 per day.)* **Gare de Nice CP** *(☎04 97 03 80 80 www.trainprovence.com)* is located at 4bis rue Alfred Binet, 800m from Nice-Ville. Chemins de Fer de Provence runs to Digne-les-Bains *($ €18. ⏰ 3½hr., 5 per day, 6:25am-6:15pm.)* and Plan du Var. *($ €3.40. ⏰ 40min., 10 per day, 6:07am-6:15pm.)*

By Bus

Buses to regional, national, and international destinations are run by **Gare Routiere.** *(5 bld. Jean Juares ☎04 92 00 42 93 ⏰ Info booth open M-F 8:30am-5:30pm, Sa 9am-4pm.)* Bus #100 runs between Nice and **Menton** via **Monaco.** *(⑤ €1. ⏰ Leaves to Monaco M-Sa every 10-30min., 6am-8pm; Su every 20min., 6am-8pm.)* Buses also go to **Cannes.** *(⑤ €1. ⏰ 40min., every 20min.)*

By Ferry

Corsica Ferries *(☎04 92 00 42 93 www.corsicaferries.com)* and **SNCM** *(☎04 93 13 66 66)* send high-speed ferries from the new port. Reduced rates for those under 25 and over 60. Take bus #1 or 2 to the port. To Corsica *(5-6hr., €15-45; bikes €10; small cars €45-75.)* The two terminals are on opposite sides of the port, so check schedule ahead of time.

Getting Around

By Bus and Tram

Ligne d'Azur is the public bus company in Nice. *(3 pl. Massena ☎04 93 13 53 13 www.ligneazur.com ⏰ Office open M-F 7:45am-6:30pm, Sa 8:30am-6pm. ⑤ Individual passes €1, day pass €4, week-long pass €15. ⏰ Night bus runs 9:10pm-1:10am. Tram line runs through Jean Medecin and pl. Massena. Stops every 5min., 6am-2am along its 9km route.)* Buses operate daily 6am-9pm. Tourist office gives out bus schedule, and posted times are on bus stops.

By Taxi

Central Taxi Riviera *(☎04 93 13 78 78)* company runs throughout the city *(€20-40 from the airport to the center-ville).* Be sure to ask for the price before boarding and make sure the meter is turned on. Night fares are charged from 7pm-7am.

By Bike

Velo Blue *(www.velobleu.org)* is Nice's bike rental company. They require that you call or have a French credit card to rent the bike from bike stands. Stands are located all around the city *(30min. free, €1 per hr.).*

monaco ☎377

Not every country is synonymous with flashy cars, yachts, gambling, and income taxes—Monaco's a pretty special place. In the past, tax evasion was a national pastime, and the mega-rich flocked here for centuries, hoping to partake in material excess without being pestered by the IRS. While Monaco's fiscal policies have changed since then, the allure of this tiny principality still centers on its unmatched and unabashed celebration of wealth. Every year, the world stops spinning for the Monaco Grand Prix, where automotive companies and drivers compete to win the world's most difficult course, then party it up in the glamorous clubs near the first-place finish. One step off the train and you'll realize why Grace Kelly was so quick to ditch US citizenship for a life of luxury in this oasis of old-world royalty and nouveau riche jet setters.

ORIENTATION

Monaco-Ville

Monaco-Ville sits atop the **rocher de Monaco,** which François Grimaldi climbed and conquered while dressed as a monk (or *monaco*, in Italian) in 1297. Today, it overlooks the **Port of Hercules,** and houses the **Royal Palace** and everything else royal within the city limits. The royal aquarium, palace, car collection, and church are all located atop this neighborhood, which is barely larger than 5x9 blocks. There's a reason that this is the area of Monaco that's most densely packed with tourists. Take some pics, see the sights, then hurry back down the mountain—before you feel the need to push past the old lady who's holding back that extremely slow cruise-ship group.

comment t'appeles tu?

Determining how to refer to the **city/country/territory** of Monaco and its administrative areas is sometimes (read: almost always) confusing. Here are a few clarifications on what the heck this place is, and what it isn't.

Like Andorra and Liechtenstein, Monaco is an independent principality ruled by a prince (neither Fresh nor Purple), and it answers to no other government.

People often refer to Monte Carlo as the capital city, but it's a district. There is no capital city of Monaco, because it's a city-state with the entire country confined in the city limits.

It has no standing army, but France is willing to provide them with military protection–a provision which strangely comforts them.

Monte Carlo

OK, we've all heard of this place. Centered on the **Carre d'Or** and the **Monte Carlo casino,** Monte Carlo boasts the fanciest cars, fastest women, and most opulent clubs in Monaco. It might cost you a fortune just to step foot in this part of town, but if you don't mind being Monte Carlo's token plebeian you should put on your best and go people watch. Who knows—you might even find a rich sugar daddy. Keep going past the casino and you'll reach the only **beach** in the principality, as well as the **Forum** and **Sporting Complex.**

La Condamine

This neighborhood boasts the cheapest shops, bars, and general cost of living in Monaco. It's also refreshingly clear of tourists during the day, who are off on excursions to the *rocher;* at night, its laid-back bars provide a nightlife scene that's seriously lacking in the other parts of Monaco. Located below Monaco-Ville, La Condamine is also where the port's affordable hotels are, but keep in mind that "affordable" in Monaco requires a slight price adjustment, even from the already expensive Riviera.

Fontvieille

This neighborhood is the quiet western side of Monaco, home to private apartments and yacht clubs. The parties here happen behind closed doors, and there isn't much left for the common folk, unless you're looking for a job in the industrial sector. The area is also home to a large **shopping complex** and Monaco's **soccer stadium,** in case you were planning to see the home team.

ACCOMMODATIONS

Oddly enough, the cheapest place to stay in Monaco is in France; the best deals in the area are located in **Beausoleil,** a small town that overlooks Monte Carlo. If you're a purist and want to stay within the principality, **La Condamine** is your best bet for hotels under €100.

Monaco-Ville

There aren't any. Sorry. The Royal Palace and the private apartments of the über-rich are located here, and they don't want anyone renting a room with a sniper rifle and getting a shot at the prince (that's *Let's Go's* guess, anyway).

Monte Carlo

Actually, these hotels aren't even in Monaco. They're in France, but don't worry about it—Monaco's literally right across the street.

HOTEL VILLA BOERI BUDGET HOTEL ❹

29 bld. Leclerc ☎04 93 78 38 10 www.www.hotelboeri.com

It may look sketchy and overgrown from the outside, and the decorative mirrors may date back to the '70s, but this hotel is clean, simple, and cheap for the area. Small rooms have large beds and bath.

Take either the #4 or #1 bus to Église St. Charles. With the church on your left, walk along bld. des Moulins until coming to a stairwell on your left. Walk up the stairwell and turn right. Walk another 60m. Hotel is on your left. ***i*** *Free Wi-Fi and computer.* ⑤ *Singles and doubles €58-81; 3rd person €8; 4th person €12.*

HOTEL DIANA HOTEL ❹

17 bld. Leclerc ☎04 93 78 47 58 www.monte-carlo.mc/hotel-diana-beausoleil

Large comfortable rooms fill this classy hotel overlooking the Église St. Charles.

Take either the #4 or #1 bus to Église St. Charles. With the church on your left, walk along rue bld. des Moulins until coming to a stairwell on your left. Walk up the stairwell and turn left. Hotel is on your right. ***i*** *Parking and free Wi-Fi.* ⑤ *Singles €45-60; doubles €45-72. Prices vary depending on view.*

HOTEL OLYMPIA HOTEL ❺

17 bld. Leclerc ☎04 93 78 12 20 www.olympiahotel.fr

This is a more opulent boutique hotel, but because it's one street over from Monaco, it's *almost* within budget range by Monaco standards. Balcony and multi-balcony suites (yep, you can have two) overlook port as well as mountains behind Monaco.

Take either the #4 or #1 bus to Église St. Charles. With the church on your left, walk along bld. des Moulins until coming to a stairwell on your left. Walk up the stairwell and turn right. Hotel is on your immediate left. ***i*** *Free Wi-Fi.* ⑤ *Singles and doubles €85-130, with port view €95-135.*

La Condamine

HOTEL DE FRANCE HOTEL ❺

6 rue de la Turbie ☎93 30 24 64 www.monte-carlo.mc/france

This simple hotel is in the heart of the shopping district of the Condamine. Clean rooms feature bathrooms and A/C.

Follow direction "Fontvieille-Monaco Ville" through tunnel with moving walkway. At the exit, make a left to cross rue Prince Pierre and take stairs down to rue de la Turbie. Hotel is on your left. ⑤ *Singles €75-94; doubles €85-116; triples €105-140.*

NI HOTEL HOTEL ❺

1 rue Grimaldi ☎97 97 51 51 www.nihotel.com

This zany hotel is a cross between a funhouse and a madhouse. Crooked bright orange walls and oddly placed mirrors make Ni Hotel a challenge for the epileptic or criminally insane. Suites and apartments available.

From the train station, exit to La Condamine, making a right as you exit the tunnel rue Grimaldi. Continue as the road curves to the left. Hotel on your right. ⑤ *Singles €90-140; doubles from €170.*

HOTEL DE VERSAILLES HOTEL ❺

4 av. Prince Pierre ☎93 50 79 34 www.monte-carlo.mc/versailles

Closest hotel to the Grimaldi palace, as well as the train station. At these prices, you'd think you were staying at the real Versailles...

From the train station, exit to La Condamine and turn right onto rue Grimaldi. Walk as the road turns to the left, and turn right onto av. Prince Pierre. Hotel on immediate right. ⑤ *Singles €90-110; doubles from €140.*

HOTEL AMBASSADOR
HOTEL ❺

10 av. Prince Pierre ☎97 97 96 96 www.ambassadormonaco.com

Designed for business travelers, this hotel offers A/C, a newly renovated meeting room, and free Wi-Fi. Too bad this is a backpacker's guidebook.

From the train station, exit to La Condamine and turn right on rue Grimaldi. Walk as the road turns to the left, and turn right onto av. Prince Pierre. Hotel is on the right. Ⓢ Singles €150; doubles €170.

Fontvieille

HOTEL COLUMBUS
HOTEL ❺

23 av. des Papalins ☎92 05 90 00 www.columbusmonaco.com

Only a stone's throw from Monaco's heliport, this unparalleled chic hotel provides views of the Princess Grace Rose Garden, as well as three auditoriums for business or private cocktail parties.

If you arrive by helicopter, it's across the street (duh). i Breakfast €25. Ⓢ Singles €240; doubles €275.

SIGHTS

Monaco-Ville

THE PRINCE'S PALACE
PALACE

Monaco-Ville ☎93 25 18 31 www.palais.mc

The lavish palace is open to tourists when the flag is lowered and the prince is away, which, it turns out, is quite often. The free audio tour is offered in 11 languages, and will walk you past the silk tapestries, Royal Courtyard, and chambers that combine the opulence of Versailles with the shock of knowing that a monarch still lives here. Judging by the crowds, you could easily mistake the official portrait of Princess Grace for nothing short of the Madonna, herself.

Ⓢ €8, students €3.50. Open Apr 2-Oct 31 daily 10am-6:15pm.

MUSÉE OCÉANGRAPHIQUE
AQUARIUM

av. St. Martin, Monaco-Ville ☎93 15 36 00 www.oceano.mc

Originally a hobby of Prince Albert I, the monarchy's extensive collection of exotic Mediterranean fish is publicly displayed in a palatial, five-story aquarium. The aquarium's main attraction is the shark lagoon and naturalized marine mammals, both alive and stuffed as models. The permanent exhibit on the poles has an impressive section dedicated to global climate change, and each of the aquarium's 90 tanks manages to recycle 100% of the 250,000 gallons of water that the institution funnels from the marina every day; considering the 80ft. cliff that houses the museum and its restaurant, it's quite a feat of engineering.

Ⓢ €13, students €6.50. Open daily Apr-Jun 9:30am-7pm; July-Aug 9:30am-7:30pm; Sept 9:30am-7pm; Oct-Mar 10am-6pm.

NAPOLEONIC HISTORY MUSEUM
MUSEUM

pl. du Palais ☎93 25 18 31 www.palais.mc

Containing over 1000 items from France's First Empire, this museum was a gift to Albert II from his grandfather. Exhibits display letters of correspondence written by the megalomaniacal general concerning his conquest of Europe and even after his imprisonment on St. Helena. Not straying too far from Monegasque history, the museum also contains the charter granting Monaco's independence by Louis XII.

Ⓢ €4, students €2. Open daily Apr-Oct 10am-6:15pm; Dec-Mar 10:30am-5pm.

Monte Carlo

Let's be honest: you came to Monte Carlo for the casino, and we don't blame you. *Let's Go* won't advise you on how to play, but we can tell you that citizens of Monaco are banned from gambling—why take money from the rich?

CASINO MONTE CARLO CASINO

☎92 16 20 00 www.casinomontecarlo.com

The renowned gambling house was infamous well before it was Ian Fleming's inspiration for the first book in the **James Bond** series, *Casino Royale*, and continues to this day to conjure up images of Charles Wells breaking the bank at the turn of the century. While the well-dressed and optimistic can try their luck at any of the casino's table games or slot machines, the less intrepid can get a drink and hang out in the **Atrium du Casino** and marvel at the casino's opulence, which rivals the Royal Palace. Dress code is not in effect until 8pm, but jeans, sneakers, and T-shirts are frowned upon. The age restriction is strictly enforced, so bring photo ID.

Cover €10. i 18+. No jeans, sneakers, or T-shirts after 8pm. Slots open July-Aug daily from noon; Sept-Jun M-F from 2pm, Sa-Su from noon. Roulette daily from noon.

breaking the bank

If you feel the need to throw your hard-earned euro at one of the richest institutions in the world, do yourself a favor and go for the Roulette wheel. Several resourceful (read: cheating) men have made out quite successfully, including **Joseph Jagger** (distant cousin to Mick) in 1873.

Joseph discovered a slight advantage–one particular wheel landed on 7, 8, 9, 17, 18, 19, 22, 28 and 29 more often than on the other numbers. After placing 7 bets, he quickly made over $1 million on the first day. The casino figured out the flaw and quickly moved tables to throw Jagger off. He was able to find the wheel again in the sea of tables by identifying a chip in the wheel, continued winning, and left with over two million francs, or $5 million in 2005 USD.

Con man **Charles Wells** worked a similar steal, again on the Roulette wheel, in 1891. Wells **broke the bank** (winning more than the chips on the table) 12 times, winning $2.5 million in 11 hours. In one particularly absurd run, he bet the number 5 for five consecutive turns, and won each time. Despite hiring private detectives to investigate, the casino never found out his system. Wells chalked it up to **"luck."**

JARDIN EXOTIQUE GARDEN

62 bld. du Jardin Exotique ☎93 15 29 80 www.jardin-exotique.mc

This garden of rare plant species from around the world has been growing since the 16th century, when New World explorers brought over cacti and rainforest plants. Accompanying the garden are the Observatory Caves and the prehistory museum, which take visitors through a series of underground passageways and grottoes through the local lime-rich cave system. Forget which ones are stalagmites and stalactites? So do we.

€7, students €3.70. Open daily May 15-Sept 15 9am-7pm; Sept 16-May 14 9am-6pm (or until nightfall).

La Condamine

PORT OF HERCULES PORT

La Condamine

Home to more money floating on water than a Kevin Costner flop, this port is the main service center for the mega yachts that visit the area. Surrounding the port is the famous stretch of the **Monaco Grand Prix,** as well as a series of cafes and bars ideal for escaping the sun.

Fontvieille

HSH PRINCE RAINIER III'S CAR COLLECTION — MUSEUM

Terrasses de Fontvieille — ☎92 05 28 56 www.palais.mc

If you thought that the cars parked in front of the casino were impressive, think again—Prince Ranier III's antique car collection puts them all to shame. Highlights include the Cintroen Torpedo that crossed Asia for the Yellow Expedition race in the 1930s, and the sexy '56 Rolls Royce Silver Cloud that carried the prince and Grace Kelly on their wedding day. Don't miss the oldest specimen, the 1903 De Dion Bouton, one of the first widely manufactured steam engine cars.

€6, students €3. Open daily 10am-6pm.

LOUIS II STADIUM — SPORTS FACILITY

3 av. des Castelans — ☎92 05 40 11

One of the best-funded sports facilities in the world, the stadium is the home field of AS Monaco, as well as an Olympic swimming pool and multi-sport hall surrounded by a world-class athletic track.

€4, students €2. Tours M-Tu 10:30, 11:30am, 2:30, 4pm; W 10:30, 11:30am; F 10:30, 11:30am, 2:30, 4pm.

MONACO ZOO — ZOO

Terrasse de Fontvieille — ☎93 50 40 30 www.palais.mc

Home to 250 animals and 50 different species, this zoo was once the private animal collection of Prince Ranier III before he opened up the grounds to the public in 1954.

€4, students €2. Open daily June-Sept 9am-noon and 2-7pm; Oct-Feb 10am-noon and 2-5pm; Mar-May 10am-noon, 2-6pm.

BEACHES

PLAGE DU LARVOTTO

av. Princess Grace

Well, it's the best and worst beach in Monaco, since it's also the only one. Comprised of two manmade lagoons separated by a divider, this convenient sandy beach does not require a long hike or a daring leap over jagged rocks to reach. Larvotto is also one of Monaco's few great equalizers, since everyone in the country who wishes to sunbathe must either come here or, you know, stick to their private yacht's sunbeds.

i Lifeguard, toilets, and handicapped access.

FOOD

Monaco-Ville

CHOCOLATERIE DE MONACO — CHOCOLATIER ❶

pl. de la Visitation — ☎97 97 88 88

This *chocolatier* specializes in Monaco-themed chocolates and a Viennese chocolate drink that is richer than the Prince himself.

Average of €1 per 10g of chocolate. Chocolate drinks €4.10. Open daily 9am-6:30pm.

U'CAVAGNATU — MONÉGASQUE ❸

12 Comte Felix Gastaldi — ☎97 89 20 40

The traditional Monégasque cuisine here blends both French and Italian influences into a fusion of Mediterranean styles. Obscure foods include fried zucchini, and olive and onion omelets.

Lunch plates €12.50-15. Prix-fixe menu €25.50. Open daily noon-5pm and 7pm-1am.

COSTA MONACO CAFE, CRÊPERIE ❷

8-10 rue Basse ☎93 50 60 85

A small and relaxed cafe with low, blue couches in a low-ceilinged room, Costa Monaco serves tarts, crêpes and drinks.

Ⓢ Crêpes €3-3.60. Pizza €5.40. Sandwiches €2-5.70. Open daily 6am-8pm.

RESTAURANT L'AURORE MONÉGASQUE, ITALIAN ❷

6, 8 rue Princess Marie de Lorraine ☎93 30 37 75

Monégasque and Italian Restaurant L'Aurore is open to large groups by reservation. The menu is a little seafood-heavy, so if you're not into fish you might want to try eating elsewhere. Reserve in advance because the restaurant is packed at night.

Ⓢ Plat du jour €13. Menu €21. Open daily noon-2:30pm and 6:30pm-late.

LE PETIT BAR PANINI ❶

35 rue Basse ☎97 70 04 97

This small panini and sandwich cafe sells the cheapest fast food in Monaco Ville.

Ⓢ Panini €4. Sandwiches €5-10. Open daily 9am-8pm.

Monte Carlo

SAKURA SUSHI ❸

1 av. Henri Dunant ☎93 50 87 33

Sakura, a sushi restaurant and bar in the Carre d'Or of Monte Carlo, has an all-white interior and serves a specialty of fatty tuna and a variety of California rolls. You'll want to dress up to go anywhere near the Carre d'Or, and this chic sushi bar is no exception. Dress to impress.

Ⓢ Rolls €13. Pieces of sashimi €5. Open daily noon-2pm and 7-10:30pm.

IL TERRAZZINO ITALIAN ❸

2 rue d'Iris ☎93 50 24 27

A highly praised restaurant known for its festive interior, Il Terrazzino is designed to look like an outdoor market. Enjoy fine Italian cuisine while taking in a great view of the casino.

Ⓢ Prix-fixe €45. Plat du jour €12. Open M-Sa noon-2:30pm and 7:30-11pm.

LA MAISON DU CAVIAR FRENCH, TRADITIONAL ❹

1 av. St. Charles ☎93 30 80 06

Think your palate is refined enough for caviar? There's no better place to try it in Monaco than at this classy French restaurant and wine bar, which specializes in its namesake, as well as other traditional French dishes. If fish eggs aren't for you, don't worry. The four-course meal comes with *amuse bouche*, *foie gras*, an entree or soup or salad, and beef tartar or dessert. You certainly won't leave hungry, and for what you're getting the €28 price tag isn't too bad. For a meal this classy though, you'll want to look the part.

Ⓢ 4-course meal €28. Dishes €18-35. Open M-F noon-2:30pm and 7-10pm, Sa 7-10pm.

LA TAVERNE TRADITIONAL, BRASSERIE ❷

10 bld. de la Republique ☎04 93 35 07 87

Located in Beausoleil, this French bistro and brasserie has cheaper French options with a lunch menu for €15. Local and casual.

Ⓢ Lunch menu €15. Plates €9-16. Open Tu-Su noon-2:30pm and 5-11pm.

BISTROQUET ITALIAN ❸

Galerie Charles III ☎93 90 65 03

Italian restaurant situated on a terrace below the Casino. The canopy of bright lights that ring the terrace will make you think it's either Christmas or a scene from a certain canine-friendly Disney movie. Try a cocktail with your pasta *(€5.50).*

Ⓢ Pasta €14. Meat dishes €22-30. Open daily noon-midnight.

La Condamine

LA PROVENCE
PROVENÇAL ❸

22 rue Grimaldi ☎97 98 37 81

At this upscale Provençal restaurant in the Condamine, enjoy specialties like beef tartare in a classy atmosphere. You'll dine at wrought-iron tables that give La Provence a mix of traditional flair and modern architecture. This is the place to bring all the casual elegance you can muster.

Lunch menu €16. Plates from €9-18. Open daily noon-3pm and 7-10pm.

PLACE DU MARCHE
SANDWICH ❶

3 pl. d'Armes ☎97 77 73 40

If there were a French version of Quiznos, it would probably be something like this sandwich shop, which specializes in typical French combinations of goat cheese and ham. The varying menu also features salads named after American cities, although the city's theme doesn't always hold true. *Let's Go* gives them an A for effort (and an A+ for price).

Sandwiches €5.80-9. Salads €6-7. Open daily 11am-7pm.

BILIG CAFE CRÊPERIE
BRASSERIE, CRÊPERIE ❷

11 rue de la Princess Caroline ☎97 98 20 43

Cafe and crêperie that serves pizza, crêpes, and creative sundae-crêpe combos—we recommend the *"crêpe flambée,"* a crêpe doused in ice cream and rum and then set on fire. Badass. There is a modern bar inside, but it's much more pleasant to take your food outside and watch the promenade.

Crêpes €3.50-7. Pizza €9.50-11. Sundaes €6.50-7.50. Open Tu-Su 11am-10pm.

LA VILLA
ITALIAN ❸

4 rue Saffren ☎97 98 68 28

Upscale Italian-influenced restaurant that mixes modern and traditional decor. Specializes in complex meat dishes and Provençal specialites, as well as pasta.

Plates €19-65. Pasta €12-16. Open Tu-Sa noon-2:30pm and 7-10pm.

Fontvieille

ALDEN T
PASTA BAR ❷

rue de la Lüjerneta ☎97 98 57 57

This trendy pasta bar in the industrial section of Monaco opens for breakfast and lunch. The combo menu, which includes pasta, a drink, and a dessert *(€9)*, is a steal.

Pasta €6.50. Combo menu €9. Open daily 7am-6pm.

NIGHTLIFE

Monaco-Ville

Do you really want to be the backpacker that woke up the royal family? Didn't think so. Monaco-Ville is the sleepy side of town, with no bars or clubs to note.

Monte Carlo

This neighborhood hosts some of the glitziest parties and most expensive clubs in all of Monaco, not to mention the world. If you're not dressed like a count, be prepared to be turned away at the door (especially if you are a guy or group of guys). While the glam of the **casino** seems to rub off on the surrounding clubs and bars, there are some holdout low-key establishments here that still accept jeans and T-shirts; if it's a **pub,** you're probably in the clear. The **beach** is lined with lounges, and the **Princesse Grace** boasts some of Monaco's glitziest bars. The more laid-back pubs and wine bars run along **rue du Portier.**

MCCARTHY'S IRISH PUB

7 rue du Portier ☎93 50 88 10 www.mcpam.com

The last bastion of normalcy in the ritziest area of Monaco, this laid-back Irish pub serves Irish cocktails (read: whiskey-and-Bailey's inspired) and some staple Kilkenny and Guinness in a welcoming atmosphere. Whiskey barrels are used for tables, and the walls are covered with Irish road signs.

Beer €6. Cocktails €9-12. Happy hour prices up to 30% off. Open daily 5pm-5am. Happy hour M-F 5-8pm.

COSMOPOLITAN WINE BAR

5 rue Portier ☎93 25 78 60 www.cosmopolitan.com

Upscale wine bar where elite patrons blow the bank on €600 bottles of Bordeaux, and backpackers like us sit around and look classy with a €4 glass. Quiet outdoor seating provides an ideal space for a casual conversation and a laidback start to a wild night.

Wine €4-5. Cocktails €10-14. Open daily 12:30-2pm and 6-11pm.

LA NOTE BLEUE PIANO, JAZZ BAR

Plage du Larvotto ☎93 50 05 02 www.lanotebleue.mc

For those who as a general rule don't leave the beach if you can help it, this classy jazz and piano bar is spitting distance from the water. The whitewashed walls and low couches make for a comfy place to sip your "Pure Happiness" (vodka, peach) or "Pure Pleasure" (vodka, strawberry, champagne) cocktails.

Beer €7. Cocktails €12. Open daily 6:30pm-3am. Concerts W-Sa 6:30pm-midnight.

FLASHMAN CAFE BAR AND DISCO

7 rue Princesse Alice ☎93 30 09 03

Closest to the casino, this tiny disco bar gradually changes the music from jazz to club jams as the night goes on. The long dance hall in the back almost doubles the size of the bar, and the strategic happy hour and uncommonly late closing time ensures that people routinely start and end their nights here.

Beer €5. Cocktails €10. Open M 9am-5am, W-Su 9am-5am.

KARE(MENT) CLUB

10 av. Princess Grace ☎99 99 20 20 www.karement.com

Located in the Grimaldy Forum, this enormous homage to debauchery is comprised of three bars and a dance floor, and hovers 100ft. over the water. The views of the ocean from the third bar are particularly dramatic, and the nightly live DJs keep the party hopping. Thursdays are "Salsa Ladies Night"—and feature heavily discounted drinks—until 11pm, when the theme changes abruptly to '80s Night. Think those two themes fit well? Neither do we.

Open in summer daily 8am-5am; in winter M-F 8:30am-5am, Sa 6pm-5am.

THE LIVING ROOM PIANO BAR, CLUB

7 rue Speluges ☎93 50 80 31

Old-school piano bar and throwback to the 1920s and '30s, with a particularly casual patio deck. The DJ gradually incorporates modern music into the bar's repertoire as the night goes on, and expertly syncs modern mixes with the jazz piano.

Beer €10. Cocktails €15. Open M-Sa 11pm-5am.

CAFE SASS LOUNGE, BAR

11 av. Princess Grace ☎93 25 52 10 www.sasscafe.com

The name says it all. This sassy bar has all the attitude of the glitzy bars, minus the stuffy pretension. While still pricey, this bar teaches the other half how to have fun in the adjoining restaurant-bar, which hosts private parties and mixers for the snazzily dressed.

Beer €8. Cocktails €18. Open daily 8pm-5am. Kitchen open in summer until 1am.

ZELO'S RESTAURANT, LOUNGE

Grimaldi Forum ☎99 99 25 50 www.zelosworld.com

This stuffy top-floor bar of the Grimaldi Forum is redeemed by stunning views of the ocean and Monaco-Ville. The terrace seating and lounge area are the perfect place to consider ordering a drink, so long as its before 11pm, when the prices nearly double.

Beer €6, after 11pm €10; shooters €5/10; cocktails €9/15. Open daily 6:30pm-2:30am.

NI BOX BAR, CLUB, BOWLING ALLEY

35 bld. Louis II ☎97 98 77 77 www.nibox.mc

While you may not appreciate how much you'll have to pay for cover at this multi-story fun box, which includes a bar, disco, bowling alley, and video arcade, your inner Big Lebowski might appreciate the convenience of having all those fun things located in the same spot, or at least enjoy the views of the ocean from the top-floor bar. Membership required, and even then you still have to pay.

i 18+. Cover €10. Beer €5, after 11pm €8. Cocktails €10/12. Membership card €5. Club open Th 7pm-1am, F-Sa 11pm-4:30am.

La Condamine

The slacker hub of Monaco, La Condamine doesn't require you to dress up completely, though a collared shirt or heels would be nice. Most of the expat bars are located in this area, as well as some of the best happy hour deals.

SLAMMERS BRITISH PUB

6 rue Saffren ☎97 70 36 56

The name says it all. This British-run and Morrocan-designed pub with an open-mike jam session every Sunday. Low couches on the outdoor patio are packed with disaffected youth. Owner encourages ordering takeout for delivery to the bar from neighboring restaurants.

i Happy hour half-priced drinks. Beer €4. Liquor €10.50. Open M-F 5pm-1am, Sa-Su 1pm-1am. Happy hour 5-8pm.

STARS AND BARS BAR

6 quai Antoine 1er ☎97 97 95 95 www.starsnbars.com

The ideal guy hangout, Stars and Bars boasts an awesome collection of auto sports memorabilia, a collection of foosball tables, and crowds that regularly overflow onto the port. The bar serves killer beer cocktails—we recommend the "Exotic," a combo of light beer, pineapple and Malibu rum that will knock you on your ass.

i Happy hour half-priced drinks. Beer €5. Beer cocktails €8. Open daily 5:30pm-3am. Happy hour 5:30-7:30pm.

RASCASSE BAR, CLUB

quai Antoine 1er ☎93 25 56 90 www.larascasse.mc

One of the most upscale bars and clubs in this neighborhood, the Rascasse is well-known for its 5hr. happy hour and nightly DJs. The bar is located on the famous turn of the Grand Prix, and remains a sure bet for those who want some class in their evening without feeling intimidated or ripped-off.

i Happy hour half-priced drinks. Beer €6. Cocktails €10. Open daily noon-5am. Happy hour M-F 6-11pm. Music July-Aug Th-Sa 11:30pm until close; Sept-June F-Sa 11:30pm until close.

BRASSERIE DE MONACO BAR

36 route de la piscine ☎93 30 09 09

Right on the port, this bar and pseudo-club has all the traits of a strip club, from the dancing girls to the flatscreen TVs playing looped tapes of models' photo shoots. Don't worry; it isn't. The fun, young crowd gathers around long cafeteria-style tables for easy conversation and making friends.

Beer €6. Cocktails €15. Open daily 11am-3am.

FREDDY'S BAR BAR

20 rue de la Princess Caroline ☎93 30 86 30

Small, local bar with a '50s decor and a splash of the '70s (pink-and-green neon lighting was pretty unique to that decade). Outside sitting area and restaurant attached.

Beer €4. Cocktails €7. Open daily July-Aug 11am-midnight; Sept-June 11am-10pm.

Fontvieille

The only popular bar here is in the **Columbus Hotel,** but it's for stiffs and rich people, and probably not your idea of a good time. As multiple Bond movies suggest, the Columbus serves wicked martinis, but you need to dress up for it and be prepared to leave and catch a bus back to the fun side of town.

a day at the races

The **Formula One** race in Monaco may be the epitome of monetary excess, but it is possible to get by without spending thousands on gambling, drinking and jacuzzi parties with some self-control and clever budgeting.

- **WHEN TO GO:** The races are held over a three-day period in May. The upcoming dates are May 26-29, 2011 and May 24-27, 2012.
- **WHERE TO STAY:** No, not huddled on a park bench begging for a sniff of a champagne cork, but most reliably (and cheaply) in **Menton or Nice**. You can try and swing it at the Monte Carlo, but as of 2010, there are very few availabilities in 2011 (and you probably don't want to pay their rates anyway). Your best bet is to stay in Nice and take one of the frequent trains to Monaco. For those with a little pocket change, it is possible to rent the terraces of apartments that face the course for €3500 per week (jacuzzi not included).
- **TICKETS AND SEATING:** The official ticketing agency sells them online at www.monaco-grand-prix.com/en/TICKETS, but like the cars, they go fast. Keep in mind the best seating is in sections A1, A4, V, Z1 and Z2. Sections A and V cost $600-700 for the finals on Sunday, and Z sections cost around $150. Preliminary days are substantially cheaper ($200-300 for Saturday A sections, $106 for Thursday).
- **THE PRIX IS RIGHT:** Note the difference between the Grand Prix Historique vs. the Grand Prix F1. The F1 is the famous one, with the Formula One race cars featuring Mercedes-McLaren and Ferrari. In the Prix Historique, old race cars from before 1940 to current Formula Three cars tear through the town. It takes place 2 weeks before the Formula 1, races the same course as the big one, but the two-day package tickets only costs $88.

FESTIVALS

There are two **Grand Prix** in Monaco every year, despite what you have heard.

FORMULA 1 GRAND PRIX SPRING

The Formula 1 Grand Prix is the granddaddy of all that is fast and expensive. Flashy cars tear up the streets of Monaco during a three-day weekend in May every year, as the country plays host to ridiculous yacht parties and mind blowing hotel prices. Expect to shell out €600 for the good seats (€125 for nosebleed section) to watch Mercedes-McLauren or Ferrari battle it out for the title with their Formula 1 racers. Be aware that prices all the way to Cannes almost triple during this weekend, and transport becomes almost impossible by car. The best plan is to stay in France and commute to Monaco for raceday; to reduce the cost further, forego the finals on Sunday and attend the trials on Friday or Saturday instead, when the cost is almost halved.

In 2011, it'll be May 26-29.

HISTORIC GRAND PRIX SPRING

The Historic Grand Prix occurs exactly two weeks before the Formula 1 Grand Prix. This race takes place on the same track and involves the same car manufacturers, but the rides themselves are all shout-outs to years past. Cars made from the 1930s to the late 1980s that have ever participated in the Grand Prix are bracketed and raced; unsurprisingly, tickets to this event are much more affordable.

2 weeks before the Formula 1 Grand Prix.

ESSENTIALS

Practicalities

- **TOURIST OFFICES:** 2A bld. des Moulins *(☎92 16 61 16)* is uphill from the casino. The English-speaking staff provides city maps, extensive pocket guides for restaurants, hotels, nightlife, and attractions. *(Open M-Sa 9am-7pm, Su 11am-1pm.)* Annexes are in the train station at the ave. Prince Pierre exit, in the chemin des Pecheurs parking garage, in the port, and outside the Jardin Exotique. *(Open mid-June to Aug).*
- **EMBASSIES AND CONSULATES: Canada** *(1 av. Henry Durant ☎97 70 62 42).* **France** *(1 chemin du Tenao ☎92 16 54 60).* **UK** *(33 bld. Princess Charlotte ☎93 50 99 54).* Nearest **US** embassy is in Nice *(☎04 93 88 89 55).*
- **CURRENCY EXCHANGE:** The Bureau de Change is in Compagnie Monegasque de Change, in the chemins des Pecheurs parking garage. *(av. de la Quarantine ☎93 25 02 50 Cash advances €50 min. Open M-Sa 9:30am-5:30pm.)*
- **INTERNET: FNAC** is in Le Metropole Shopping Center. *(17 av. des Speluges ☎93 10 81 81 i Frequent lines. 20min. free. Open M-Sa 10am-5:30pm.)* **D@dicall Cyber Point** has Wi-Fi. *(1 impasse General Leclerc: Beausoleil ☎04 93 57 42 14 Internet €4 per hr. Open daily 10:30am-8pm.)*
- **POST OFFICES:** 23 av. Albert II *(☎98 98 41 41 Open M-F 9am-7pm, Sa 8am-noon.)* All mail posted in the principality must bear Monégasque stamps. An annex can also be found at av. Prince Pierre train station exit. There are four additional branches.
- **POSTAL CODE:** MC 98000 Monaco.

Emergency!

- **EMERGENCY NUMBERS: Ambulance:** ☎93 25 33 25.
- **POLICE:** *(3 rue Louis Notari ☎93 15 30 15).* There are five other stations in Monaco.
- **HOSPITAL: Centre Hospitalier Princesse Grace.** *(av. Pasteur ☎97 98 99 00 Accessible by bus #5, dir. Hospital.)*

Getting There

By Train

Gare SNCF has four main access points: galerie Prince Pierre, pl. St-Devote, bld. de Belgique, and bld. Princesse Charlotte. *(Open daily 4am-1am. Info desk and ticket window open M-F 5:50am-8:30pm, Sa-Su 5:50am-8:10pm.)* Trains run to: **Antibes** *(€6.30. 1hr.,* *every 30min.);* **Nice** *(⑤ €2.70. ⏰ 25min., every 30min.);* **Cannes** *(⑤ €7.50. ⏰ 1hr. 10min., every 30min.);* **Menton.** *(⑤ €1.70. ⏰ 11min., every 30min.).*

By Bus

Buses leave from the bld. des Moulins and av. Princesse Grace, near the tourist office. **TAM** and **RCA** *(☎93 85 64 44)* run lines to Nice *(45min.)* and Menton *(25min.)*. There is also a direct line from the Nice Airport (RCA) via the A8 motorway. *(⑤ €16.10, under 26 €11.50; round-trip €26. ⏰ 45min., every hr. 9am-9:15pm.)*

By Helicopter

Hey, you never know. It is Monaco, after all. **Heli Air Monaco** lands in Fontvielle at the Monaco Heliport. *(€7 per min., €120 per 30min.)*

Getting Around

The **bus** system in Monaco is a godsend from its hilly terrain built onto the side of a steep shoreline. The six lines run pretty much to wherever from wherever. *(⑤ Individual ticket €1, 24hr. pass €3. ⏰ M-F every 10min., Sa-Su every 20-30min.)* Buy tickets on board. **Taxis** *(☎93 15 01 01 ⑤ €10+)* run 24hr. and wait at 11 taxi stands throughout the city, including the casino, pl. des Moulins, and the train station. If you like control of your own wheels, you can also rent a **scooter** from Auto-Moto Garage. *(7 rue de Milo ☎93 50 10 80 i Credit cards accepted. ⑤ 50cc scooter €40 per day, €45 per 24hr., €260 per week. €1000 credit security charge. ⏰ Open M-F 8am-noon and 2-7pm, Sa 8am-noon.)*

villefranche-sur-mer ☎04 93

This small fishing village 10min. from Gare Nice is a haven for those trying to escape the noise and fellow backpackers of Nice. The much-appreciated sandy beach (in a region generally devoid of sand beaches) right off of the train tracks makes this village an ideal location for a daytrip—dig your toes into the sand and swim around without the crowds from neighboring towns. While the town itself is small, the sights are mostly free and feature local heroes and famous artists known only in this region. Be prepared for steep hills and winding alleyways in Villefranche's old town. Our advice: stock up on fruit and sandwiches in the old town and head to the harbor or beach for a day's picnic in this peaceful escape.

ACCOMMODATIONS

Villefranche-sur-Mer has ample accommodations for the budget traveler, but you can find cheaper and more backpacker-friendly locations in neighboring Nice (and a better nightlife, btw). The budget hotels are toward the top of the city's hill near the tourist office, while the quai boasts expensive waterfront properties crawling with older crowds looking to get away from loud noises and fun things in general.

LA REGENCE HOTEL ③

2 av. Marechal Foch ☎04 93 01 70 91

Simple hotel rooms with a prime location on top of the city's hill, near the Citadel and the Tourist office. The balconies overlook the port, and there's a lovely restaurant and bar on the ground floor. Simplicity is the name of the game here: think bare walls, white bedspreads. You'll get enough color on the beaches, anyway.

Across the street from the tourist office. i Breakfast €6.50. ⑤ Singles €58; doubles and triples €72.

HOTEL PROVENÇAL HOTEL ❹

av. Marechal Joffre ☎04 93 76 53 53 www.hotelprovencal.com

This clean hotel two blocks down from the tourist office hosts a classy restaurant and brightly colored rooms with A/C. Balcony and window views of the port and the citadel are a nice bonus.

With your back to the tourist office, walk to the intersection and turn right. Hotel is down the street 2 blocks on the right. i Breakfast €10. Ⓢ Doubles €59-90; triples €69-120. Prices higher in summer season.

SIGHTS

Villefranche is a small village whose sights don't exactly put it on the tourist map (not even the regional one). While its citadel is impressive enough, and its St. Peter's chapel is cute and historical, the most exciting sight in this town is the holy grail—no, not that one. We're talking about a sand beach devoid of private clubs or development. No rocky shores here.

PLAGE DES MARINIERS — BEACH

quai l'Admiral Ponchardier

Located steps from the train station, this long stretch of **sand** beach is exactly what the purists are dreaming about when they step foot on any of the rocky beaches in Nice or Cagnes. It's well worth the trip from Nice just to dig your toes into the warm, welcoming sand and swim in the calm, natural *baie La Rade.*

LA CITADELLE — FORTRESS

Fosses de la Citadelle, entrance at pl. Philibert

The imposing fortress was built in 1557 by the cunning military strategist Emmanuel Philibert, whose Machiavellian list of accomplishments included regaining Turin from the Spanish and French by exploiting a regional squabble. Today, the citadel houses Villefranche's numerous free museums, including a recreation of the town in the Middle Ages, the Volti Museum, and the museum of Goetz-Boumeester, a French-American surrealist painter whose little black book included Picasso and Miro.

Ⓢ Free. Museums open June-Sept M-Sa 10am-noon and 2:30-6:30pm, Su 2:30-6:30pm; Oct M-Sa 10am-noon and 2-5:30pm, Su 2-5:30pm; Dec-May M-Sa 10am-noon and 2-5:30pm, Su 2-5:30pm.

CHAPELLE SAINT-PIERRE PAR JEAN COCTEAU — CHURCH

quai de l'Admiral Courbert, at the end of rue Gabetta

This Romanesque Chapel was designed and painted by French Renaissance Man Jean Cocteau. This avant-garde poet, artist, playwright, director, and lover (his girlfriends included Edith Piaf and Coco Chanel) organized the town's craftsmen Wikipedia-style—everyone pitched in and added a bit of his own style to its construction and decoration. The interior was painted by Cocteau, and the ceramics and **boats** were built by local craftsmen and dedicated to local fisherman.

Ⓢ €2.50. Open June-Aug Tu-Su 10am-noon and 3-7pm; Sept to mid-Nov Tu-Su 10am-noon and 2-6pm; mid-Dec to May Tu-Su 10am-noon and 2-6pm.

FOOD

Food in Villefranche can be cheap, if you know where to look. The small alleyways in the old city harbor the cutest eats and best deals for a sit-down meal, while the quai has a more picturesque setting on the boardwalk (and higher prices). Picnics on the docks seem to be a popular choice; stop by the local Casino market *(1 rue Poilu Open M-Sa 9am-noon and 2-7pm.)* and then head towards the water, or try stocking up on fruit in Nice before you head to this small town.

L'ESCALE CRÊPES, BURGERS, TAPAS ❶

2 rue de l'église ☎04 93 55 35 27

Cute cafe and tapas restaurant located on a large patio at the bottom of an alleyway's narrow stairs. The menu is comprised of pretty basic fare, including kebab, burgers, and sandwiches.

Sandwiches €6.50. Plat du jour €13. Salads €8-11. Burgers €6. Open daily 10am-2am.

LES GARCONS PROVENÇAL ❷

18 rue Poilu ☎04 95 76 62 40

A modern Provençal restaurant with hints of rustic charm, Les Garcons has modern lighting that contrasts with the earth-tone walls and the rust-colored, wooden tables. The outdoor seating is in a quiet plaza near the cathedral. It's relaxed and chic at the same time, and the lunch menu (*entree*, *plat*, and dessert) is only €15.

Plats €13-15. Lunch menu €15. Open M-Sa noon-2pm and 7-10pm.

LA SERRE PIZZERIA, SANDWICHES ❶

rue de la May ☎04 93 76 79 91

This hole-in-the-wall pizzeria serves pizzas named after American States. Try the Texan or the Californian, but be warned that the theme doesn't really hold at all. When was the last time you had tuna and anchovies in either of the Dakotas?

Pizzas €5-6. Pasta €8. Open Tu-Sa 11am-2pm and 5-10pm.

LE ROXY PIZZERIA ❶

2 av. Grand-Bretagne ☎04 93 76 71 80

Pizzeria and cafe at the top of the city's hill that offers views of the port and Citadel. Cheap pasta and pizzas to go (and take to beach, hint hint).

Pasta €5. Pizza and drink €13. Open daily 12:30-4pm and 6:30-11pm.

NIGHTLIFE

There's a reason you don't need to go to this town for nightlife—Villefranche is smashed right between Nice and Monaco. If you want to get a leisurely beer after chilling all day in the sun, this one bar is the best place in town:

LOMBARDO'S BAR BAR

5 rue du Poilu ☎04 93 01 94 74

A local, laid-back sports bar with walls covered in soccer jerseys and scarves from teams all over France, Lombardo's is the perfect place to chat up Olympique Marseille's win in 2010 and the prospects of Paris Saint-Germain in the coming seasons.

Demis €1.50. Pints €5. Liquor €5. Open daily 11am-1:30am (or later).

ESSENTIALS

Practicalities

- **TOURIST OFFICE: Jardin Fraonçois Binon.** At the highest point in the city. Keep following signs going uphill, no matter if you think it's pointing downhill. *(☎04 93 01 73 68 Open July-Aug daily 9am-noon and 2-6pm; Sept-June M-Sa 9am-noon and 2-6pm.)*
- **TOURS:** Guided tour of the old town and Citadel organized by **tourist office.** *(€5, under 12 free.)* The "Citadel Mornings" tour includes light breakfast in Volti Museum courtyard and guided tour of old town and Citadel. *(€8 per person. May-Sept F 9am.)*
- **CURRENCY EXCHANGE: BNP Paribas.** ATM available *(1 av. Alber I ☎04 93 76 34 83).*

- **POST OFFICE:** av. Albert I and Sadi Carnot. *(☎04 93 76 30 80. ⏰ Open M-F 9am-noon and 2-5:15pm, Sa 9am-noon.)*

Emergency!

- **POLICE: Police Municipale** *(☎04 93 76 33 42).*
- **PHARMACY: Marchal Foch.** *(av. Laurent ☎04 93 01 70 10 ⏰ Open M-Sa 8:45am-12:15pm and 2:30-7:15pm.)*

Getting There

By Train

The **Gare SNCF** services the area. Automatic ticket dispensers are only for those with European bank cards. *(av. Georges Clemenceau ☎36 35 ⏰ Trains run 5am-9pm. Ticket office open 6am-noon and 1-7pm.)* Trains run to **Nice** *(Ⓢ €2.30. ⏰ 10min., every 30min.)* and **Monaco.** *(Ⓢ€5. ⏰ 15min., every 30min.)*

By Bus

The **#81** runs regularly to Villefranche from **Nice.** *(dir. Saint Jean Cap Ferrat. Ⓢ €5. ⏰ 20min., every 15min.)* The **TAM #100 bus** that connects Nice to **Menton** also stops in Villefranche.

menton ☎04 93

Often called the Secret Riviera, Menton is full of Côte d'Azur sunshine without the gouging prices and snobby club scene that pervades the coastline between Monaco and St-Tropez. Reminiscent of a time before discothèques, Menton is a quiet town with a slow pace of life; we don't think it's a coincidence that the city feels more Italian than French. With the Italian border just a couple of minutes away, you definitely feel the culture seeping in, with *gelaterie* and Italian cuisine frequently mixed with French menus and seafood. The town is still a popular destination for French and Italian tourists, so don't expect undiscovered bliss. Still, Menton's hybrid culture is more than worth a trip—any town that features pizza and gelato on the average *menu du jour* is a friend of ours.

ORIENTATION

Menton is neatly divided into three parts: the **Old Town,** the **New Town,** and the **beach** or **port.** While the beach is practically the only sight that is not in the Old Town, and the port de Garavan is mostly local and devoid of tourists, the **new port** on the border of the old city prominently features the **Bastion fort.** Head toward the **chapel tower** from the Bastion to enter the old city. The **place du Cap** with its slew of small restaurants is at its heart, while the **place Saint Michel** is the oldest part of town in front of the church. The two main walkways that snake through the old town and toward the new town are the **rue Saint Michel** and the **rue de la République,** which pass by the **Hôtel de Ville.** In the new city, the **avenue de Verdun** is the main road that clearly separates the new and old cities, and leads right to the doors of the casino and nightclub, passing by the **Palais de l'Europe** and the **Tourism Office.** Follow that road up and turn left to reach the **train** and **bus stations.**

ACCOMMODATIONS

HOTEL DE BELGIQUE BUDGET HOTEL ❸

1 av. de la Gare ☎04 93 35 72 66

Located close to the train station, this budget hotel offers 20 simple rooms with A/C and phones. The balconies provide great views of the new part of town.

Exit train station and walk straight. Hotel is on your right. i Book well ahead of time in summer. Singles and doubles €34-49; triples and quads €65-90. Reception 7am-2:30pm and 5:30-10pm.

AUBERGE DE JEUNESSE HOSTEL ❶

pl. Saint Michel ☎04 93 35 93 www.fuaj.org

Basic and backpacker-friendly, this local branch of France's most reliable chain of hostels comes complete with a full bar and cheap drinks, as well as clean bathrooms and sturdy bunks in the single-sex dorms. Be warned: walking here can be a challenge, and the area feels abandoned at night.

Take bus #6. Dorms €17.50.

L'AUBERGE PROVENÇAL HOTEL, RESTAURANT ❸

11 rue Trenca ☎04 93 35 77 29

Basic hotel in the heart of the old city. Located right off of rue St. Michel, the hotel offers free Wi-Fi, a bar, and A/C in 12 simple rooms.

Between rue St. Michel and rue de la République. i Restaurant and parking available. Singles and doubles €39-55.

RICHELIEU HOTEL ❹

26 rue Partouneaux ☎04 93 35 74 71 www.richelieu-menton.com

Simple hotel behind the Palais de l'Europe, removed from the main drag of nearby shopping stores. If you gamble, you'll appreciate its proximity to the casino, but hopefully you're a good gambler—if you're paying the rates to stay here, you can't afford to lose much more.

From the Palais de l'Europe, walk behind it onto rue Partouneaux. Hotel on the left. Singles €40-55; doubles €57-90; triples €80-115.

CAMPING SAINT MICHEL CAMPING ❶

route des Ciappes ☎04 93 35 81 23 www.tourisme-menton.fr

Nearby campsite with tent spots and caravans for rent. It's close to the Auberge de Jeunesse and shaded by rows of olive trees with awesome views overlooking Menton and the ocean. On-site restaurant offers pizzas *(€9)* and pastas *(€9-16)*. Foosball tables and pool are available as well.

Take bus #6. €4.45 per tent; €13 per car. Caravan €21.30. Electricity €2.80. Reception M-Sa 8:30am-noon and 3-7pm, Su 8:30am-12:30pm and 5-6:30pm.

SIGHTS

SERRE DE LA MADONE GARDEN

74 route de Gorbio ☎04 93 57 73 90 www.serredelamadone.com

One of the most spectacular gardens in a garden-packed city, the Serre de la Madone manages to be "Heaven on Earth" by organizing its repertoire of flowers so that there is always a flower bed in bloom. The pathways designed by American Lawrence Johnson take you past quiet pools and mazes of hedgerow, as well as the enormous **dragon tree** imported from the Canary Islands (though we didn't think it looked anything like a **dragon**).

Serre de la Madone stop on bus #7 (10min.) €8, under 18 and students €4. Open Tu-Su Apr-Oct 10am-6pm; Dec-Mar 10am-5pm. Guided tours 3pm.

MUSÉE JEAN COCTEAU MUSEUM

quai Napoleon ☎04 93 57 72 30

Located inside the Bastion, the museum's building is as much of an artistic triumph as the paintings it holds. In addition to his other work, Cocteau was known for applying his avant-garde aesthetic to decrepit historical buildings, and spent years revamping this abandoned fortress, which was originally built by the Prince of Monaco in 1616. The artist died before he could complete the renovations, but not before he could replace the windows with wrought iron, mosaic the hallways, and scatter zoomorphic statues throughout the rooms.

€3, students €1.50. Free 1st Su of the month. Open M 10am-noon and 2-6pm, W-Su 10am-noon and 2-6pm.

MONASTÈRE ANNONCIADE — MONASTERY

2135 cor André Tardieu — ☎04 93 35 76 92

A symbol of Menton, this monastery is perched 225m above the harbor and old city. The Virgin of the Annonciade allegedly cured Princess Isabella of Monaco's leprosy here, and the hike up is now peppered with 15 mini-chapels, each dedicated to one of the stations of the cross. You might never be this preoccupied with the Stations of the Cross ever again (unless you're Catholic, in which case you run through them every Friday in Lent); each chapel brings you closer to the awesome views from the top of the city below.

Take #4 bus from the Gare Routière at 8:30, 11:40am, 2:30, 6:35pm. Open daily 8am-noon and 2-6pm. Mass July-Aug M-Sa 7:30am, Su 10am; Sept-June M-Sa 11:15am, Su 10am.

BASILIQUE SAINT MICHEL — CHURCH

parvis St. Michel

The tower over the old city serves as a convenient landmark for tourists, and it should not be hard to locate the Baroque Chapel. The sheer grandeur of the church's glass chandeliers and suspended gold crown is somewhat undermined by its history; Menton didn't have any cemeteries until 1850, so poor locals were buried in a mass grave under the cathedral.

From rue St. Michel, turn left onto rue des Logettes, then go up the steps of the rue des Ecole Pie. Open June-Aug M-F 10am-noon and 2-6:15pm, Su 10am-noon and 2-6:15pm; Sept-May M-F 10am-noon and 3-5:15pm, Su 10am-noon and 3-5:15pm. Mass Su 10:30am.

PLAGES DES SABLETTES — BEACH

quai Bonaparte

Locals pack onto the only sand beach in the city. Next to two manmade lagoons, the **Baie de Garavan** provides an opportunity to swim in calmer waters.

FOOD

Menton's whole "my town is a garden" slogan is onto something. Numerous open-air markets line the ave. Sospel, including the bustling Marché Carei *(Open daily 7am-1pm)*. The Marché du Bastion offers a seaside shopping for produce on quai Napoleon III. Restaurants are packed in the old town along rue St. Michel and rue de la Republique. Local supermarkets line the rue de la Republique closer to the new city.

CAFE MENTONNAIS — MENTON CUISINE ❸

5 rue deu Vieux College — ☎04 93 35 43 08

A small cafe tucked away off of rue St. Michel, the Cafe Mentonnais serves a traditional fusion of Italian and French dishes with a heavy seafood influence. The walls are covered in sketches of the city and colorful modern art.

Formule €16. Lunch menu €13. Open Tu-Su noon-11pm.

MAISON HERBIN ET SON ARCHE DES CONFITURES — SPECIALTY MARKET ❷

2 rue Vieux College — ☎04 93 57 20 29 — www.confitures-herbin.com

The Maison Herbin is stacked wall-to-wall, floor-to-ceiling with jams, sauces, and honeys produced daily in the kitchen out back. Menton citruses are used to make the tangy jams, as well as the Liqueur de Menton *(€11.75)*, a French version of Limoncella. Flavors such as "lavender honey" or "dark chocolate orange jam" will run you more than the traditional flavors, but are worth the splurge.

Honey €4.30-7.70. Jams €4-6. i Free guided tours with free tastes M, W, and F 10:30am. Open June-Aug daily 9am-12:30pm and 3:15-7:30pm; Sept-May M-Sa 9am-12:30pm and 3:15-7:30pm.

THE LAST BEACH FAST FOOD, ITALIAN, ICE CREAM ❷

1563 promendade du Soleil ☎04 93 86 99 73

With seating right on the beach, this cheap fast-food cafe serves pretty much any kind of (Mediterranean) food you'll ever want, from ice cream to lasagna *(€11)*. A gluten-free menu is available, in addition to a wide array of salads and tarts for dessert.

i Staff speaks Italian. Ⓢ Plat du jour €11. Panini €4. Ice cream €2. Open daily in summer 9am-8pm; in winter 9pm-5pm.

LE GAMBAS ROUGE SEAFOOD ❷

rue de la Marne ☎04 93 28 54 75

Resembling a Louisiana shrimp house, this culinary blend of Italian and French cuisine serves a cheap *plat du jour* (€10) in an almost entirely outdoor seating area. Look for the large picture of a friendly-looking shrimp on the sign hanging over the tattered doors and windows.

Ⓢ €10 plat du jour. Open daily noon-2:30pm and 7-10pm.

PETIT TRAITEUR ROTISSERIE ❶

3 rue Trenca ☎04 93 57 29 86

This hole-in-the-wall French fast-food place specializes in rotisserie chicken, and also sells quiche, roast beef and bottles of port wine. While nothing fancy, the eatery is right next to the beach and serves as a one-stop shop for a high-class picnic at dirt cheap prices.

Ⓢ Whole chicken €3.50. Quiche and meats €2. Port wine €9. Open daily 10am-6pm.

YOGURTLANDIA FROZEN YOGURT ❶

9 rue St. Michel ☎04 93 45 82 33

Tiny frozen yogurt cafe serves crêpes, cheap sandwiches and, of course, its namesake. Yogurt cups come with a choice of two toppings, which range from raspberry to nutella to mint syrup. The colorful and fun interior is decorated with kindergarten colors and fake flowers that lighten the mood.

Ⓢ Small yogurt €2.50, medium €3.50, large €4.50. Sandwiches €3-4. Crêpes €3. Open daily noon-8pm.

TUTTI FRUTTI ICE CREAM ❶

24 rue St. Michel ☎04 93 35 26 97

As close to Italy as you can get without going a couple miles east and hopping the border. Serves gluten-free sorbet and original ice cream flavors, such as a cake-batteresque nougat and white chocolate.

Ⓢ One scoop €2, two scoops €2.50. Open daily 11am-8pm.

L'OLIMPO ITALIAN, SEAFOOD ❸

23 rue St. Michel ☎04 92 02 34 72

Italian seafood restaurant that serves a pricey but delicious two-person *paella (€48)*. Also serves more affordable pizza and pasta with seafood; the *spaghetti au fruit de mer* is a particular favorite. The blue exterior enhances the seafood theme.

Ⓢ Pasta and pizza €8-14. Calamari and zucchini €15. Open daily noon-2:30pm and 5-10pm.

NIGHTLIFE

LE TERRASSE BAR, LOUNGE

av. Felix Faure ☎04 92 10 16 16

The patio lounge and bar attached to the casino. The neon couches look out over the ocean and foster a pretty laid-back atmosphere, considering that most of the customers are here to get rich or die trying next door.

i 18+. Bring photo ID. Ⓢ Drinks €3-7, after midnight €6-14. Open M-Sa 7pm-4am.

LE BRUMMELL CLUB

av. Felix Faure ☎04 92 10 16 16

The nightclub attached to the casino. The large open dance floor is surrounded by low couches and leftover decorations from soirees past. The bright lights generate a clubby atmosphere that's less intimidating than the occasional elitism of neighboring Monaco or the seedy clubs of Nice.

i Soirees including '70s Night and White Party. Cover €15; includes 1 free drink. Free for women before 1am. Open 11pm-4am (or later).

CAFE DU MUSÉE BAR

25 quai Monleon ☎04 93 35 46 38

Seaside cafe and bar that is covered with old posters of Monaco's Grand Prix and Nice's celebs. Specialty drinks include Italian mojitos made with Italian sparkling white wine. The bar's closing hours are uncertain—it technically closes at midnight, but can stay open for hours afterwards until everyone leaves. The party really gets going on Fridays, when the DJ starts mixing popular music.

Beer €4. Cocktails €7-8. Open daily 8am-midnight. Friday DJ starts at 8:30pm.

LE BRAZZA BRASSERIE

2 pl. Clenencueau ☎04 93 35 73 12

This laid-back brasserie in the heart of the old town boasts a classic outdoor setting with TVs playing sports matches. The cheap beer and drinks make for an easy night out after a long day at the beach.

Beer €2.60. Cocktails €4.90-7.50. Open daily 11am-midnight.

STUDIO 29 TAPAS BAR

29 rue St. Michel ☎04 93 98 61 79

A trendy bar in the old city, Studio 29 serves tapas until 10pm under the spider-web-like chandelier hanging over diners. Outdoor seating is an alternative to the chic interior with low couches and a lounge area in the back. Drown yourself in its liter mugs of astonishingly well-priced beer *(€4)*.

Cocktails €7. Tapas and crêpes €8. Open daily 8am-12:30am.

ARTS AND CULTURE

Cinema

THÉÂTRE DU LAVOIR

63 bld. du Fossan ☎04 93 41 41 55 www.tourisme-menton-fr

In May, this theater hosts the annual Franco-Italian Street Theater's "Commedia dell'arte." This style of masked theater has its roots in the 1500s, when performers improvised lines from a planned scenario.

Contact tourist office for prices and tickets.

EDEN CINEMA

11 rue de la République

Eden screens French and American cinema dubbed in French.

€7, students €4. Open M 2:30-9pm, Tu 5-10pm, W 2:30-9pm, Th 5-10pm, F 2:30-9pm, Sa-Su 5-10pm.

Festivals

FESTIVAL DE MUSIQUE SUMMER

☎04 92 41 76 76 www.musique-menton.fr

Citywide music festival taking place in Menton's gardens, chapels and cathedrals. Starting in late July and running until mid-August, the festival allows visitors to appreciate the blooming gardens and charming town with a soothing soundtrack of classical music, opera, and chamber music.

Ticket prices vary with seating, students and under 25 up to 25% off. 1 concert €10-50, 3 €25-110, 6 €50-205, 9 €60-295.

FETE DU CITRON SPRING

04 92 41 76 76 www.feteducitron.com

Festival from mid-Feb to early March celebrating all things citrus, this Mentonnais party features parades with floats built from oranges, grapefruits, and lemons. Think Rose Bowl with lemons. Ward off scurvy with copious amounts of the town's famous lemon liqueur and enjoy the percussion bands and fire dancers in this sour Mardi-gras-esque revelry.

i Tickets available online. €9-23 depending on event, students up to 25% off. From mid-Feb to early March.

ESSENTIALS

Practicalities

- **TOURIST OFFICE:** Located inside the Palais de l'Europe. English-speaking staff offers free maps and restaurant and hotel guides, as well as festival information. *(8 av. Boyer 04 92 41 76 76 www.villedementon.com Open June-Sept M-Sa 8:30am-7pm, Su 9am-7pm; Oct-May M-Sa 8:30am-12:30pm and 2-6pm, Su 9am-12:30pm.)*
- **TOURS: Petit Train** covers major sights in the city with multilingual listening guides. *(departs from the promenade du Soliel, near the Bastion €7, under 9 €3. 40min.; Sept-June every 40min., 10am-noon and 2:15-5pm; July-Aug every 40min., 10am-noon, 2:15-5pm, and 7-11pm.)*
- **INTERNET: Le Café des Arts.** *(16 rue de la République 04 93 35 78 67 www.cafedesarts.com. i Credit card min. €10. €6 per hr. Open M-Sa 7:30am-8pm. Internet 7:30-11am and 2:30-8pm.)*
- **POST OFFICE:** cours George V. Currency exchange available. *(04 93 28 64 87 Open M-W 8am-6:30pm, Th 8am-6pm, F 8am-6:30pm, Sa 8:30am-noon.)*
- **POSTAL CODE:** 06500.

Emergency!

- **POLICE:** rue de la République *(04 92 10 50 50).*
- **HOSPITAL/MEDICAL SERVICES:** La Palmosa, rue Peglion *(04 93 28 77 77, emergencies 04 93 28 72 40).*

Getting There

From Gare SNCF *(pl. de la Gare Ticket office open M-F 8:40-11:50am and 2-6:30pm, Sa 9:30am-noon and 2-6:30pm.)*, **trains** run every 30min. *(5am-midnight)* to **Cannes la Bocca** *(€8. 1hr.)*; **Monaco** *(€1.70. 11min.)*; **Nice** *(€4.20. 35min.)*; **Genoa, ITA** *(€15-19. 2-3hr., 11-15 per day.)*; **Ventimiglia, ITA.** *(€4.60. 10min.)*

From promenade du Marechal Leclerc *(04 93 35 93 60 Open M-F 8:30am-noon and 1:30-6pm, Sa 10am-noon.)*, TAM **bus** #100 connects Menton to **Nice** through **Monaco** and the -sur-Mers. *(€1. Every 15min., 6:30am-7:30pm.)*

Getting Around

Menton is very pedestrian-friendly; most of the main roads are either entirely pedestrian or have ample sidewalk space. From the train station, walk straight and make your first right at the major intersection, and continue for a kilometer to reach the center of town.

Compagnie des Transports de la Riviera serves Menton and neighborhoods with 10 **bus** lines. *(€1, 10 trips €7.50, day pass €3.)* Most buses link the Marché to the Gare Routière. **Taxis** pick up from five stands throughout the city. *(04 92 10 47 02 i*

Reserve by phone on off-hours. ⏰ *Open daily 6:30am-7pm.)* You can rent **bikes** from 4 esplanade G. Pompidou. *(☎04 92 10 99 98 $ Bikes from €15 per day, €60 per week. 50cc scooters €40 per day; €500 deposit.* ⏰ *Open M-F 9:30am-12:30pm and 3-6:30pm, Sa 9:30am-noon and 5-6:30pm.)*

nice and monaco

CÔTE D'AZUR

A robber baron's daydreams fulfilled, Côte d'Azur is comprised opulent hubs of material excess and an accompanying sleeze factor no one's really supposed to see. For budget travelers, this is a good thing: if you can stand the grittier sides of residential Nice and Marseille, this strip of the Riviera can be enjoyed cost-effectively. Hedonism aside, the Riviera also boasts a cultural richness and vibrancy that give other French regions a run for their money. The Côte d'Azur has been the inspiration of artists from F. Scott Fitzgerald to Picasso, as well as the chosen resort of celebrities ranging from Brigitte Bardot to Bono. Many of the smaller towns that dot the coast feature a chapel, room, or wall decorated by artists like Cocteau, Chagall, or Matisse. The idyllic villas that overlook plunging cliffs are reminders that the Riviera is a mecca of international wealth. Each May, high society makes its yearly pilgrimage to the Cannes Film Festival; savvy travelers should comb through Cannes and St. Tropez's local theaters for cheap or free screenings of Cannes winners, which are sometimes released here long before they hit theaters back home. Despite the Côte d'Azur's reputation for glitz and glamor, penny-pinchers can soak up the spectacle and their share of sun, sea, and sand.

greatest hits

- **BEND THAT GENDER.** Soak up the vibrant gay nightlife in Cannes (p. 157).
- **SURF 'N' TURF.** Hike your way through the rocks of the calanques and cap off the adventure with a dive into the lagoon (p. 185).
- **CLOTHING OPTIONAL.** Funny story. A certain Let's Go researcher went to St-Tropez and discovered its high concentration of topless beaches. Then he missed his ferry home (p. 176).

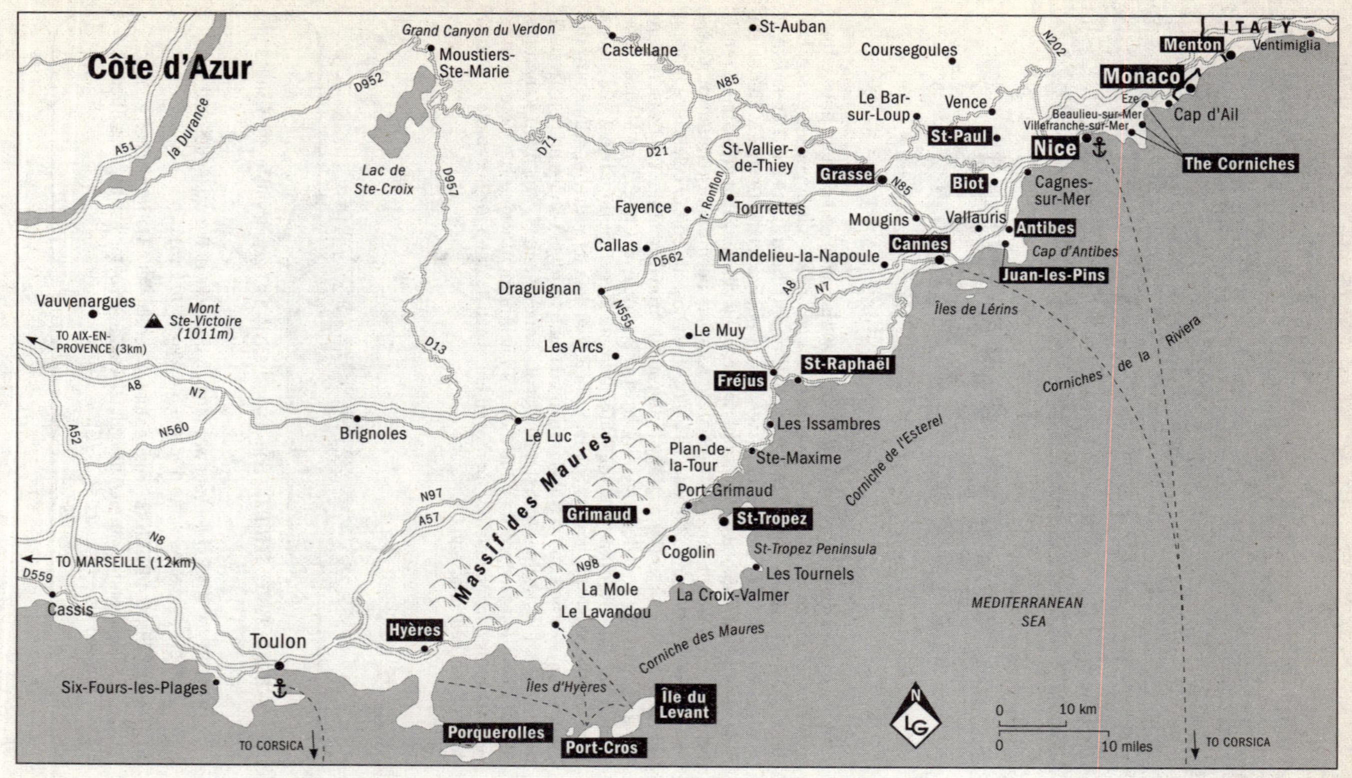
Côte d'Azur
ITALY
Ventimiglia
Menton
Monaco
Cap d'Ail
Eze
Beaulieu-sur-Mer
Villefranche-sur-Mer
The Corniches
Nice
Cagnes-sur-Mer
Antibes
Cap d'Antibes
Juan-les-Pins
Biot
Vallauris
St-Paul
Vence
Coursegoules
Le Bar-sur-Loup
Grasse
Mougins
Cannes
Mandelieu-la-Napoule
Îles de Lérins
St-Auban
St-Vallier-de-Thiey
Tourrettes
Fayence
r. Ronflon
Callas
Castellane
Grand Canyon du Verdon
Moustiers-Ste-Marie
Lac de Ste-Croix
Draguignan
Le Muy
Les Arcs
Fréjus
St-Raphaël
Les Issambres
Ste-Maxime
Corniche de l'Esterel
Corniches de la Riviera
Plan-de-la-Tour
Port-Grimaud
St-Tropez
St-Tropez Peninsula
Grimaud
Cogolin
Les Tournels
La Croix-Valmer
La Mole
Le Lavandou
Corniche des Maures
Massif des Maures
Le Luc
Brignoles
Hyères
Îles d'Hyères
Île du Levant
Port-Cros
Porquerolles
Toulon
Six-Fours-les-Plages
Cassis
TO MARSEILLE (12km)
TO AIX-EN-PROVENCE (3km)
Vauvenargues
Mont Ste-Victoire (1011m)
la Durance
MEDITERRANEAN SEA
TO CORSICA
TO CORSICA
A51
D952
D71
D21
N85
D957
D13
D562
N555
A8
N7
N202
A52
N560
N97
A57
N8
D559
N98
0 10 km
0 10 miles
LG

antibes ☎04 93

Antibes has the largest port on the Mediterranean, attracting sailors and scallywags of all varieties from around the world. A strange island of English-speaking visitors and residents, Antibes has its fair share of rugged British and Irish pubs, with very little of the hopping club scene found in Juan-les-Pins or Cannes. People are either here to drift or to look for work, so the crowd can range from drunk and entertaining to sketchy and intimidating. Antibes has the free beaches that you've been searching for, as well as some good SCUBA diving spots and snorkeling off of the Cap d'Antibes. While the museums, with the exception of the Picasso Museum, might be a tad on the dull side, the real attraction is the laid-back people and easygoing atmosphere, only 10min. from one of the craziest party cities on the Riviera.

ORIENTATION

Antibes is easy to navigate between the **port** and the **vieux ville,** even though the streets can be poorly labeled and the helpful tourist arrows can sometimes lead you into a wall. The easiest way to orient yourself is along the town's main streets: **rue de la Republique** and **boulevard d'Aguillon.** Both lead you right into the *Vieux Ville*, while offering totally different attractions along the way. Rue de la République is where you'll find upscale restaurants and shopping, while the sleazy port crowd will hang out at the laid-back pubs that line boulevard d'Aguillon. Unfortunately the **Cap,** where you'll find secluded beaches and nicer hotels, is either a 20min. walk or a bus ride away. The **#2 bus** goes along the coast. Within the *Vieux Ville*, no matter where you turn you'll almost always end up back at the **Marche Provençale,** a central square that sells fruits and vegetables during the day and turns into a flea market at night.

ACCOMMODATIONS

These are the cheapest ones in town. To find any hotels that are actually budget, you'll have to go to Juan-les-Pins or take a hike up the highway. These places get above €100 in the high season, and its over €200 for rooms of three to four. We don't want to subject our readers to such financial pain and suffering. Please go to Juan-les-Pins. If you're a trust fund baby, don't mind credit card debt, or absolutely must stay in Antibes for some reason, these are the best deals in town:

THE CREW HOUSE — HOSTEL ❷

1 av. St. Roch ☎04 92 90 49 39

Not the most luxurious place to stay, even by hostel standards, but definitely a fun experience for those willing to take a leap outside of their comfort zone and bunk with the rugged sailors and drifters who frequent this predominantly Anglophone hostel. For those used to the cramped living conditions and limited personal space of **boats** (or for those looking to give it a try).

From the train station, walk straight on down av. de la Libération, take 2nd right on the roundabout; the hostel is on your right. Apr-Oct dorms €25; Nov-Mar €20.

RELAIS INTERNATIONAL DE LA JEUNESSE — HOSTEL ❶

272 bld. de la Garoupe ☎04 93 61 34 40 www.clajsud.fr

Closer to Juan-les-Pins than Antibes, Relais International provides guests with clean rooms and an escape from the busy city center. Located next to the beach on the Cap, this English-speaking hostel also provides free breakfast and a youthful atmosphere.

Take bus #4 to the Telais de Jeunesse stop or the #2 to the Garoupe stop. Facing the water, walk to your right for 10min. i Breakfast included. Free bar and outdoor seating. Dorms €18. Open Apr-Sep.

HOTEL PETIT RESERVE BUDGET HOTEL ❸

20 bld. James Wyllie ☎04 93 61 55 86 www.petitreserve.com

Seven-room hotel on the Cap with ocean views. They've tried to liven up the simple rooms with mismatched colors and patterns (like light green and red plaid). While the decor might suggest color blindness, staff are very attentive to service detail, which calms the nerves of a predominantly German clientele.

From the train station, walk left onto Robert Soleau for 200m until you get to place du Général de Gaulle. Walk across the plaza onto bld. Albert 1er and follow it until you get to the beach (7 blocks). Turn right at the beach and walk for 700m. Hotel on your right. ***i*** *Traveler's checks accepted.* Ⓢ *Singles €31-51; doubles €48-98; 3-4-person suites €94-155.*

HOTEL LE RELAIS DU POSTILLON HOTEL ❹

8 rue Championnet ☎04 93 34 20 77 www.relaisdupostillon.com

Luxurious rooms with fancy bed curtains and antique painted furniture. Close to the center of town, but still separate from the bars and loud restaurants. Honeymoon level-rooms for cheap.

From the train station, walk straight on down av. de la Libération, take 1st right on the roundabout onto av. Mirabeau for 300m. Turn right onto rue Vauban, and take a left onto rue Championnet. Ⓢ *Singles €49-96; doubles €67-96.*

HOTEL L'AUBERGE PROVENÇALE BOUTIQUE HOTEL ❹

61 rue de la Republique ☎04 93 34 13 24 www.aubergeprovencale.com

It really says something that the cheapest room in Hotel l'Auberge Provençale comes with a four-poster double bed. This classy boutique hotel boasts a royal red theme wherever you go, from the drapes, to the bedspreads, to the place settings at breakfast.

From the train station, walk right down av. Robert Soleau until the pl. de Gaulle. Turn left onto rue de la République. Hotel is in the pl. Nationale. ***i*** *Restaurant on ground floor. Dinner €20.* Ⓢ *Singles and doubles from €65-120. Prices spike during the Monaco Grand Prix and Film Festival.* *Reception 8:30am-1:30pm and 5:30pm-midnight.*

HOTEL LE PONTEIL HOTEL ❹

11 impasse Jean Mensier ☎04 93 34 67 92 www.leponteil.con

Tucked away at the end of a cul-de-sac under the trees, this quiet hotel will have you itching to leave for the nearby beach, where there is more life and color than in this *hebergement*. The prices really make the establishment's bland character worth it.

From the train station, turn left onto Robert Soleau and walk 200m until you get to pl. du Général de Gaulle. Walk across the plaza onto bld. Albert 1er until one block before the beach (6 blocks). Turn right onto av. du Général Maizière (keeping to the left at the intersection) and walk 200m. Turn left onto impasse Jean Mensier. Hotel is at the end. ***i*** *Parking.* Ⓢ *Singles €58-87; doubles €58-105.*

SIGHTS

MUSÉE PICASSO MUSEUM

pl. Mariejol ☎04 92 90 54 20 www.musee-picasso.fr

Displays the artist's lesser-known paintings from the 1940s and video clips of him at work on sketches and paintings.

Ⓢ *€8.50, students €6, under 18 free.* *Open June 15- Sept 15 M 10am-6pm, W-Su 10am-6pm; Sep 16- June 14 M 10am-noon and 2-6pm, W-Su 10am-noon and 2-6pm.*

FORT CARRÉ FORTRESS

Sentier du Fort Carré ☎06 14 89 17 45

Once an important fortress guarding the port Vauban, the largest private marina in the Mediterranean, this fortress now serves as a showcase for swords and a statue of Napoleon on a horse. Yeah, it still doesn't compensate for his height. Maybe one of those 2400 yachts in the harbor, appropriately dubbed "Millionaire's Row," that would have eased his—well—Napoleon complex.

i Only by guided English or French tour. Ⓢ €3, under 18 free. ⏰ Open June 15-Sept 15 Tu-Su 10am-6pm; Sept 16-June 14 Tu-Su 10am-4:30pm.

MUSÉE D'ARCHÉOLOGIE — MUSEUM

On the waterfront in Bastion St-Andre-sur-les-Ramparts ☎04 95 34 00 39

If you thought the pottery museum in Biot was a hoot, you'll love the ancient Greek and Roman ceramics in this one. The temporary exhibits might be a little more interesting. Past exhibits included present-day objects aged 2000 years to look like archaeological finds from the future.

Ⓢ Students €3, under 18 free. ⏰ Open June 15- Sept 15 M 10am-noon and 2-6pm, W-Su 10am-noon and 2-6pm; Sept 16- June 14 M 10am-1pm and 2-5pm, W-Su 10am-1pm and 2-5pm.

MUSÉE PEYNET — MUSEUM

pl. Nationale

Features the drawings of the Lovers of Peynet. For those confused like us, Peynet was an illustrator for a Parisian newspaper who became famous for drawing the same two fictional lovers over and over again in different situations. His work went on to become a French symbol of love and humor in the 1950s.

Ⓢ Students €3, under 18 free. ⏰ Open June 15-Sept 15 M 10am-noon and 2-6pm, W-Su 10am-noon and 2-6pm. Sept 15-June 14 W-M 10am-1pm and 2-5pm.

MARCHÉ PROVENÇALE — MARKET

rue Aubernon

A market during the day, this covered area turns into a flea market during the evenings, and at seemingly random times during the summer months. Cafes line the market, so the area at the very least makes for good people watching in the shade.

⏰ Open June-Aug Tu-Sa mornings, some afternoons and evenings June-Aug; Sept-May Tu-Sa mornings.

BEACHES

PLAGE DU PONTEIL — BEACH

Antibes's largest public beach. The long stretch of sand is lined with street vendors and snack stands. It gets very crowded in summer during peak hours of the day.

Turn right from the vieux ville; walk along coast.

PLAGE DE LA SALIS — BEACH

Small public beach that's closer to the port, and the sunbathing hotspot that's closest to the *vieux ville*. The breakwater forms an almost enclosed cove for swimming in the calm, manmade lagoon.

Towards Port Vauban, right from vieux ville.

CAP D'ANTIBES — BEACH

A rocky beach surrounds the Cap, with crystal clear water that's perfect for snorkeling. Isolated and far from the crowds on the main public beaches.

Take the #2 bus from the bus station to Tour Gandolphe (M-Sa, every 40 min. 6:50am-7:30pm). Follow av. Monseigneurs-Lt. Beaumont to the end. Turn left onto pedestrian road, then right when a small door appears in the surrounding walls; take dirt path to the isolated beach cove.

PLAGE GAROUPE — BEACH

On the Cap. Sandy beach that was frequented by celebs such as F. Scott Fitzgerald, Picasso, and Cole Porter in the 1920s.

Cap d'Antibes.

FOOD

KEY WEST — COMFORT FOOD ❷

30 bld. d'Aguillon ☎04 93 34 58 20 www.lecapdantibes.com

This laid-back restaurant is your go-to place for comfort food like waffles and anything that you could possibly have a craving for. There's a sailing theme reminiscent of the Florida Keys, with whales and Hemingway featuring prominently on the lime green walls.

Breakfast food €1.80-6.50. Waffles €2.90-4.90. Cheesecake, salads, sandwiches €3-9. Open daily July-Aug 7:30am-2am; Sept-June 7:30am-7:30pm.

BRULOT WOOD FIRED ❸

3 rue Federic Isnard ☎04 93 34 17 76

Get rustic with wood-fired cuisine in this tavern-like restaurant. Farm implements hang from the ceiling, reminding you where your meat and fish dishes (€12) came from. Three-course *prix-fixe* (€19) features shrimp au pastis and crème brûlée to top it off.

Plats €12-17. Lunch €14. Dinner €19. Open daily 7pm-12am.

LE CRÊME BRÛLÉE PROVEN, FAMILY ❷

21 rue Thuret ☎04 93 34 56 58

Farm-themed Provençal restaurant serves crêpes, sandwiches, and *plats*, as well as its dessert namesake. Inside walls are painted to look as though cows are looking in on you while you eat. If that doesn't confuse or frighten you enough, check out the pots hanging from the ceiling that serve as lights.

Sandwiches €5.50. Crêpes €4-8. Plats €12-15. Open daily 9am-11pm.

LE VILLAGE PROVENÇAL ❸

31 rue James Close ☎04 93 34 19 66

This classy joint serves local mussels, roast duck, and escargots in a traditionally decorated Provençal establishment. Though the decor isn't remarkable, with whitewash plaster walls, the food is quite good. On a tight budget? Go for lunch to get the gourmet taste for almost half the price of the dinner menu.

Lunch €15. Dinner €28. Kid's menu €11.50. Open M-Tu noon-2pm and 7-10pm, Th-Su noon-2pm and 7-10pm.

CASA DEL PANINO PANINI ❶

20 pl. Nationale

Colorful panini bar serves 15 types of cheap, fast, and giant panini.

€4 for everything. Open M 7am-7:30pm, W-Su 7am-7:30pm.

LE KASHMIR INDIAN ❸

22 rue Thuret ☎04 92 94 00 03

Indian breads (€2) for incredibly cheap, although the elephants and camels painted on the wall are a bit tacky. Sit outside if it really bothers you.

Lamb €13-14. Dinner menu €19. Naan and bread €2. Open M-Sa noon-9pm.

MAISON ROLAR MARKET ❶

pl. Nationale

Old-school market with fresh veggies and fruit next to the town butcher.

Open M-Sa 7am-7:30pm, Su 8:30am-1pm.

NIGHTLIFE

LA BALADE ABSINTHE BAR

25B cours Massena ☎04 93 34 93 00

One of the world's few absinthe bars, La Balade is a famed subterranean hotspot that exclusively serves that one special drink. Don't look naive and ask if you hallucinate. You don't. Thanks to its 140+ proof, you'll be lucky if you see anything at all. Posters and bowler hats cover the walls in tribute to the 19th-centruy avant-garde, who guzzled the drink with a side of laudanum.

Open daily 9am-midnight.

THE HOP STORE — BAR

38 bld. d'Aguillon ☎04 93 34 04 06

Antibes's largest pub. With a giant patio that's almost always packed with a young crowd, this two-room bar hosts local rock bands and other live music performances every Wednesday, Friday, and Saturday. Although technically classified as an Irish pub, The Hop Store is the most international spot in all of Antibes.

Beer €2.50. Cocktails €7. Open in summer 9am-12:30am; in winter 3pm-12:30am.

THE BLUE LADY — PUB

Galerie du Port ☎04 93 34 41 00

Laid-back pub done up to look like the interior of a steamship in the American South. The wood and brass bar is decorated with entertaining signs referring to gamblers and loose women. Outdoor seating and live bands every other Friday. Don't miss out on their homemade pub grub, like hand-rolled sausage (€3.50).

Beer €3.40-5.50. Cocktails €7-10. Open 7:30am-midnight. Kitchen open until 3:30pm.

THE COLONIAL — BAR

36 bld. d'Aguillon ☎04 93 34 83 53

African colonial-themed bar complete with safari lounge upstairs (by reservation only) and elephant tusks and pictures of the "Big 5" (elephant, lion, rhino, jaguar, and the **cape buffalo**) on the walls. The outdoor seating is packed with wooden bar tables and stools, occupied by Anglophones.

Beer €4. Cocktails €8. Open daily 7pm-2:30am.

ESSENTIALS

Practicalities

- **TOURIST OFFICE:** Free maps, info on hotels, restaurants, and festivals. Help with hotel reservations. *(11 pl. de Gaulle ☎04 97 23 11 11 www.antibesjuanlespins.com. Open July-Aug daily 9am-7pm; Sept-June M-F 9am-noon and 1:30-6pm, Sa 9am-noon and 2-6pm, Su 10am-noon and 2:30-5pm.)*
- **TOURS:** The **Petit Train** covers both Antibes and Juan-les-Pins sights. *(Departure from pl. de la Poste ☎06 15 77 67 47 €7. July-Aug 10am-10pm; Mar-Oct 10am-6pm.)*
- **INTERNET ACCESS: Xtreme Cyber.** *(8 bld. d'Aguillon in Galerie du Port ☎04 89 89 93 88 €5 per hr. Open M-F 10am-8pm, Sa 10am-4pm.)*
- **POST OFFICE:** pl. des Martyrs de la Resistance *(☎04 92 90 61 00 Open M-F 8am-7pm, Sa 8am-noon.)*
- **POSTAL CODE:** 06600.

Emergency!

- **POLICE:** 33 bld. President Wilson *(☎04 92 90 78 00 or 92 90 53 12).*
- **PHARMACY:** Consult Nice Matin newspaper for rotating hours of Pharmacie de Garde *(63 pl. Nationale ☎04 93 34 01 63).*
- **HOSPITAL: Chemin des Quatres Chemins** *(☎04 92 91 77 77).*

Getting There

By Train

Gare SNCF *(pl. Pierre Semard. Ticket desk open daily 5:45am-10:45pm. Info desk open daily 9am-8pm. Station open 5:25am-12:10am.)* runs trains to **Cannes** *(€2.20. 15min., every 30min.)*; **Nice** *(€3.40. 15min., every 30min.)*, **Monaco** *(€6. 1hr., 5 per day.)*; **Marseille.** *(€24. 2hr., every hr.)*

By Bus

RCA *(☎04 93 39 11 39)* buses run from pl. de Gaulle to **Cannes** *(Ⓢ €1. ⏰ 20min., every 20-40min.)*, **Nice** *(Ⓢ €1. ⏰ 1hr., every 20-40min.)*, and **Nice Airport** *(Ⓢ €1.⏰ 30min., every 20-40min.)*

Getting Around

Walking is the easiest way to get around in the *vieux ville*. From the **train station,** turn left and walk for 5min., and you'll eventually hit the main drag of **rue de la République**, which takes you all the way to the port. To get anywhere farther away, such as the Cap, **buses** *(#2 to the Cap)* leave from **place Guynemer** *(☎04 93 34 37 60 Ⓢ €1, day pass €4, week pass €10. ⏰ M-Sa every 40min. 6:50am-7:30pm)*. The **free mini bus** connects the city to the beaches, train station and bus station. **Taxis** are also available from the train station *(☎04 93 67 67 67 Ⓢ €18 to Juan-les-Pins. ⏰ 24hr.)*

cagnes-sur-mer ☎04 93

Cagnes-sur-Mer is the halfway point between Nice and Cannes, and it provides access to all the provincial towns and medieval villages in between. It also features a medieval village of its own and the illustrious Grimaldi Castle, as well as a lively city center and beachfront fishing community. You can find more spectacular palaces and cuter fishing **boats** than those in Cagnes-sur-Mer, but you'll be hard-pressed to find all of those qualities in one city. If you're facing a time crunch, a stay here will ensure that you'll see all the major highlights of the region, even if you aren't seeing the best of the best. The cheap eats and hotels are a big draw for young travelers; just be warned that many establishments lower their prices at the expense of regional charm.

ACCOMMODATIONS

TURF HOTEL HOTEL ❸

9 rue des Capucines ☎04 93 20 64 0

Budget hotel near the beach. Simple rooms ranging from terrace suites to prison-cell-sized singles.

*Located along the Port de Cros-des-Cagnes in between av. de la Serre and av. Leclerc. **i** Parking available. Ⓢ Singles and doubles €40-82; triples €62-87.*

VAL DUCHESSE HOTEL ❹

11 rue de Paris ☎04 92 13 40 00 val.duchesse@wanadoo.fr

Beautifully tiled guesthouse that offers single rooms and apartments for rent. The modern decor is accented by bright traditional colors and furniture; facilities include a pool in case the 50m walk to the beach is too far for you.

Located along the Port de Cros-des-Cagnes in between av. de la Serre and bld. JFK. Ⓢ Studio €56-78; apartments €77-106. Prices change depending on season, getting more expensive in the summer months. 10% discount for a week stay. 20% discount for two-week stay between Oct-Apr.

LE MAS D'AZUR HOTEL ❸

42 av. de Nice ☎04 93 20 19 19

Provençal house run by a local family. The rooms are small but elegant, and the lobby nails that "homey" vibe with fireplaces and comfy couches. The furniture has an antique shop feel to it, which is fitting: the building dates back to the mid-18th century.

Located along the Port de Cros-des-Cagnes in between av. de la Serre and rue de la Pinede. Right as the highway divides. Ⓢ Singles and doubles €41-63; triples and quads €61-76.

LE COLOMBIER HOTEL ❶

35 chemin de Sainte-Colombe ☎04 93 73 12 77

Family-oriented campground, which includes 33 shady plots with concrete risers for tents.

1.5km from the train sation on the route de Vence. i Bar, pool, electricity, and washer/dryer. $ July-Aug singles €14; doubles €16.20. Sept-June singles €11.80; doubles €14.20.

SIGHTS

GRIMALDI CASTLE

CASTLE

Huat des Cagnes ☎04 92 02 47 30

Built by a distant relative of Monaco's royal family in 1300, the Grimaldi Castle now serves as the city's municipal museum and houses The Olive Tree museum, the Soldier Donation, and the local Modern Art museum. Additional rooms have been authentically restored to appear as they were in the Baroque era of Louis XIII. Swing by the top of the tower to see the stunning 360 degree view of Cagnes and the beach.

$ €4 for 2 students, under 18 free. Double ticket for Renoir Museum and Castle €6. Open July-Aug 10am-noon and 2-6pm; Sept-June Tu-Su 10am-noon and 2-5pm.

RENOIR MUSEUM

MUSEUM

chemin des Collettes ☎04 93 20 61 07

The museum harbors 11 original paintings, sculptures, and sketches by the town's most famous resident. Hoping that some ocean air would help with his arthritis, Renoir retreated to Cagnes-sur-Mer towards the end of his life. He immortalized the beauty of the coastline in paintings until 1919 when he died. Renoir's estate is still preserved to this day with rooms containing his wheelchair and easel as they would have been.

$ €4 for 2 students, under 18 free. Double ticket for Renoir Museum and Castle €6. Open July-Aug Tu-Su 10am-noon and 2-6pm; Sept-June Tu-Su 10am-noon and 2-5pm.

FOOD

L'ILOT

PANINI, SALADS ❶

rue du Captitaine de Fregate Henri Vial ☎04 93 31 80 97

Cheap panini stand right on the ocean. Sick view of the water and rock beach below.

$ Paninis €4. Salads €5. Open M-Sa 11am-10pm.

AUBERGE DU PORT

MEDITERRANEAN ❸

95 bld. de la Plage ☎04 93 07 25 28

Conveniently located right on the bord du Mer, this restaurant specializes in fish and Mediterranean dishes. A nice place to eat well without breaking the bank; the outdoor seating overlooks the promenade.

i If fish grosses you out, this probably isn't the place for you. $ Lunch menu €15; 3-course dinner menu €24-31. Open M-Sa noon-11pm.

LE PROVENÇAL

PROVENÇAL, BURGERS ❸

4 pl. du Château ☎04 93 20 08 86

This outdoor cafe in the shadow of the Grimaldi Castle specializes in Provençal cuisine, but also an impressive range of burgers. It might take a French palate to tell, but each type of burger is prepared with specific types of beef; some of the patties are even made with *foie gras*. Try ordering that at Burger King.

$ Burgers €8-18. Open M-Sa 11am-11:30pm.

BRASSERIE DES HALLES

BAR, TAPAS ❷

8 rue J. Raimond Giacosa ☎04 92 02 77 29

At this brasserie in the pedestrian center of town, customer ages range from the young and pierced to the old and walker-bound. Sandwiches, tapas and 12 different beers on tap.

$ Plat du jour €10. Menus €12-14.90. Open Tu-Sa 11:30am-11:45pm.

ESSENTIALS

Practicalities

- **TOURIST OFFICE:** Visit the office for free bus schedules, maps, and restaurant and hotel guides. *(6 bld. Marechal Juin ☎04 93 20 61 64 www.cagnes-tourisme.com Open Jul-Aug M-Sa 9am-12:30pm and 2-6pm; Sept-Jun M-F 9am-noon and 2-6pm, Sa 9am-noon.)* Other locations are on the beach at 99 promenade de la Plage *(☎04 93 07 67 08)*, and on Huat-des-Cagnes in pl. Docteur Maurel *(☎04 92 02 85 05)*.
- **YOUTH CENTER:** Beach sports center including beach volleyball, windsurfing, kayaking, and sailing. *(bld. de la Plage ☎04 93 07 33 04 Open daily Jul-Aug 9:30am-6pm).*

Emergency!

- **POLICE: Police Municipale** *(21 sq. des Grands Plans ☎04 93 22 19 22).*
- **HOSPITAL: Clinique Saint Jean** *(92 av. du Dr. Maurice Donat ☎04 92 13 53 33).*
- **PHARMACY: Pharmacie Centrale** *(4 av. Auguste Renoir ☎04 93 20 61 08).*

Getting There

By Train

Gare SNCF is located on the corner of Cros-des-Cagnes and bord de Mer. *(☎04 92 35 35 35).* To **Cannes** *(€6. Every 30min.)*, **Nice** *(€3.20. Every 30min.)*, and **Marseille** via Cannes *(€25).*

By Bus

TAM line #200 *(€1)* runs between Cannes and Nice stops at the Cagnes-sur-Mer train station, Gare Routiere. From **Nice** *(35min., every 15min. between 6:30am-6pm, every 30min. between 6-8pm.)* from **Cannes** *(1¼hr., every 15min. 6:15am-6pm, every 30min. 6-8pm).*

Getting Around

Free **shuttle bus** *(#44)* runs between gare routière and Haut-des Cagnes *(daily 7am-8pm).*

côte d'azur

vence ☎04 93

A mid-sized medieval village in the hills above Cagnes-sur-Mer, this peaceful haven is most famous for the healing properties of its drinking water; laugh all you want, but its powers were "proven" when it healed Nero's wife, Poppaea, and preserved the life of Henri Matisse, who designed and painted the nearby Chapelle du Rosaire. While the sights here might not be much of a draw for young travelers, it's certainly worth visiting this town to deliberately do nothing and relax in its small peaceful squares, or sample one of the ubiquitous open air markets. Make a mental note to come back here when you're old and feeble, because something about the city is incredibly calming, even with its lively underbelly and riotous, month-long music festival.

ACCOMMODATIONS

LA LUBIANE HOTEL ❸

10 av. Marechal Joffre ☎04 93 58 01 10

A cheap guesthouse run by a little old lady. The rooms all have similar flowery wallpaper, which will repeatedly remind you that someone over 70 did the decorating for the whole hotel. If you can get past that, though, this is a great option for a quiet stay in Vence. Since it's a former restaurant, La Lubiane has a large dining area and an awesome terrace view of the valley.

From the tourist office, walk towards the city entrance, taking the first right onto av. Elise. Turn left onto av. des Poilus and continue past the intersection. The hotel is on the right. Singles €36.60-41; doubles €51-62.20; triples and quads €70-77.40.

LA CLOSERIE DES GENETS — HOTEL 3

4 impasse Macellin Maruel ☎04 93 58 35 18 www.closeriedesgenets.com

Hotel and restaurant with 10 rooms for rent. The funky modern art made from household metal scraps hangs throughout the hallways, and the simple rooms are painted sherbet hues that range from aqua to pink.

From the tourist office, turn left and walk towards the old city. Walk 3 blocks on Marcellin Maurcel and make a right onto impasse Marcellin Marucel. i Bar and Wi-Fi. Singles €40; doubles €80; triples €95; quads €110.

LA COLOMBE DE VENCE — BED AND BREAKFAST 4

1458 chemin de Saint Colombe ☎06 25 61 52 47

B and B run by old lady who might not know what the internet is and speaks no English. The garden terrace overlooks an amazing view of the valley, though. Have the tourist office check availability and book your room here for you; the B and B is this woman's house, and she is not kind to strangers just showing up without prior notice. Seriously though.

From the tourist office, walk around the old city until you reach chemin St. Colombe. Walk about 1km to 1458; it's on your right. i Breakfast included. 3 night min. stay. Rooms €49. 3-night min. stay.

DOMAINE DE BERGERIE — CAMPGROUND 4

route de la Sine ☎04 93 58 09 36 www.domainelabergerie.fr

Camping grounds in the middle of the forest. Complete with small water park and mobile homes for rent.

From gare routière, take the #46 bus to Bergerie. i Pool, electricity, parking, and grocery store. Low-season site for 1-2 people with electricity €18.90; high-season €39.

SIGHTS

CHAPELLE DU ROSAIRE — CHURCH

466 av. Henri Mattisse ☎04 93 58 03 26

Small chapel run by Dominican nuns who look like they'll break your fingers if you attempt to take a picture—and we can understand why they're so protective: these are Matisse originals. Black-and-white stick figure drawings, sure, but these are the famous artist's Stations of the Cross. Nod politely when the 146-year-old nun talks about each interpretation and try not to look confused.

Admission €3.20. Open M 2-5:30pm, Tu 10-11:30am, W 2-5:30pm, Th 10-11:30am, Sa 2-5:30pm.

CATHEDRALE — CATHEDRAL

Cité Historique

Impressive cathedral in the center of town that was built in the fourth century AD; the site was previously occupied by a pagan Roman temple. Contains "Moses saved from the Nile," a baptistery mosaic by Marc Chagall.

Free. Open daily 9am-6pm, except during religious services.

PEYRA GATE FOUNTAIN — FOUNTAIN

Cité Historique

The current quatrefoil fountain was erected in 1822, on the site of a fountain dating back to 1578. The Fontaine de Peyra was one of only three sources of drinking water in Vence until the city was piped in 1886, and remains drinkable today. If you're looking for a Biblical miracle, this is (allegedly) the place to go—the waters of the Foux have very low sodium content, and as a result may be particularly good for you. They became famous for their healing properties when Nero sent his fragile wife Poppea to drink from the waters of Vence. She left the town in good health. Our personal theory is that she just needed a little time off from Nero.

FOOD

LA TAVERNE SAINT VERAN
PIZZERIA ❶

9 pl. Surian ☎04 93 24 00 98

Pizzeria in the heart of the old city. The wooden outdoor furniture and large stucco painting of Vence as it once was in the Middle Ages make it seem like they've been cooking pizza here since before the revolution.

Pizza €11. Open T-Sa 11am-2pm and 5-10pm.

CRÊPERIE BRETONNE
CRÊPERIE ❶

6 pl. Surian ☎04 93 24 08 20

A charming little traditional crêperie with a classic menu; try the classic ham, cheese, and egg over easy. Also serves its own brewed cider. The indoor seating area can get a little stuffy, so take your crêpes outside to bask in the sunlight.

Crêpes €3-9. Menu €10.90. Open Tu-Sa noon-11pm.

LE CRAB ENRAGÉ
SEAFOOD ❷

4 impasse Marcellin Maurel ☎04 93 58 35 18

Seafood restaurant in the hotel Closeire des Genets. Covered terrace or garden seating. Wednesday is "Mussel Day," when fresh mussels go for €12.50 per plate. Weird art made from scrap metal is scattered throughout the restaurant.

Prix-fixe €15. Open Tu-Sa noon-2pm and 5-10pm.

BAR DE L'ETOILE
CAFE, BAR, FAST FOOD ❶

204 av. des Poilus ☎04 93 58 25 81

More of a bar than a restaurant, this place serves traditional Provençal dishes as well as the occasional burger. Cheap plates and a great three-course menu make this place attractive; l'Etoile's curb appeal doesn't do much for it.

Plates €6.50-9.50. Menus €13-15. Open daily 11am-2:30am.

ARTS AND CULTURE

Festivals

NUITS DU SUD
SUMMER

Vence

World music festival that takes place every summer, and stretches from the beginning of July to the beginning of August. The music is usually more Latin influenced. If you don't want to pay, you can sit at any cafe along the place and be an eavesdropping freeloader.

€10-18. Some performances free. July-Aug.

ESSENTIALS

Practicalities

- **TOURIST OFFICE:** Provides maps and restaurant and hotel guides as well as same-day hotel and B and B reservations for free. *(8 pl. de Grand Jardin ☎04 93 58 06 38 Open M-Sa 9:30am-6pm, Su 10am-2:30pm.)*
- **BANK: BNP Paribas** has ATMs available. *(pl. du Grand Jardin ☎08 20 82 00 01 Open M-F 9:30am-noon, 2-7pm, Sa 10am-noon.)*
- **INTERNET: SOS Informatique** *(147 av. des Polius ☎04 93 24 37 97)* offers Wi-Fi.
- **POST OFFICE:** *(av. Tuby ☎04 93 58 44 00.)*

Emergency!

- **POLICE MUNICIPAL:** *(pl. Marechal Juin ☎04 93 58 03 20).*

• **PHARMACY: Pharmacie du Frene.** *(1 pl. du Frêne ☎04 93 58 03 04.)*

Getting There

TAM **bus** line #400 goes between Nice and Vence, stopping at the Cagnes SNCF train station *(€1. 22min., runs every 30-40min. M-F 7:23am-3:10pm, Sa 8:20am-2:40pm, Su 8:30am-8:57pm.)*

îles des lérins ☎04 92

Ever wonder what it would be like to be stranded on a desert island? The Îles des Lérins are about as close as you'll want to get (and you probably won't want to stay long). A 15-20min. **boat** ride from Cannes, the two small islands, Sainte-Maguerite and Saint-Honorat, have no accommodations; they quite literally close at night, so bring a tent if you don't think you'll make the last boat back. If you're having flashbacks to Jurassic Park or nightmares about **dragons,** we feel you. We really, really do.

FOOD

Sainte-Maguerite and Saint-Honorat each host a few food stands, in addition to several restaurants. The stands are the better deal, and serve sandwiches, ice cream, and other types of fast food.

LA GUERITE SEAFOOD, PROVENÇAL ❺

Sainte-Marguerite

Pricey and picturesque, La Guerite is only accessible by private dock or by a trek in the woods. The restaurant is broken into a cafe and beachfront dining area, in the shadow of Fort Royal. This luxurious setting comes at a hefty price though—the grilled lobster special will set you back €60. The restaurant stays open late for those who docked their yachts off the coast of the island.

Plats €30-60. Prix-fixe menu €55. Open daily 11am-8pm.

L'ESCALE PIZZERIA ❸

Sainte-Marguerite

The cheaper of the two prominent restaurants on the island. It's easy to get to from the dock, and serves pizza and melon *assiettes* on a covered patio overlooking the sea.

Pizzas €13-14. Open daily noon-6pm.

LA TONNELLE PROVENÇAL ❺

Saint-Honorat

This restaurant and snack shack is open only for lunch, serving traditional Provençal cuisine, as well as an extensive seafood grill.

Plats €19-30. Open Mar 10-Nov daily noon-4pm.

SIGHTS

Sainte-Marguerite

FORT ROYAL MUSEUM, FORT

An impressive old fort that now serves as museum of underwater archaeology, the Fort Royal is most famous for its stint as a prison—the man in the Iron Mask was held here for 11 years. No, he's not just a fictional character played by Leonardo DiCaprio. To this day, no one knows the identity of the nameless man jailed by Louis XIV, whose face remained covered by a velvet cloth for the duration of his imprisonment (sorry, the iron mask is only a legend, introduced by Dumas's swashbuckling fictions). Over 60 names have been proposed, including everyone from Richard Cromwell (son of Oliver Cromwell of England) to Louis XIV's half brother. Our guess? It was Colonel Mustard in the Library with the candlestick. The mysterious man was later moved to the Bastille in Paris, where he died in 1703.

i Admission includes guided tour. ⓢ €3.20, under 26 free. Open June-Sept 10am-5:45pm; Oct-May 10:30am-1:15pm and 2:15-5:45pm. Tours June-Sept 11am, 2, 3:30pm.

LA MONESTÈRE FORTIFIÉ MONASTERY

Saint-Honorat

The monastery has been in continuous use since the year 400 CE, in spite of small interruptions like the invasion of the Saracens and WWII. While the modern monastery is closed to visitors, the abbey is open to the public, though modest dress is required for entry. The adjoining shop sells wine produced by the monks on the island's vineyards.

ⓢ Free. Open daily 8am-6pm.

ESSENTIALS

Getting There

To get to Sainte-Marguerite, take the **Trans Côte d'Azur** from **Cannes** *(☎04 92 98 71 30 www.trans-cote-azur.com. ⓢ €11.50, students €9.50. 15min., every 30min. 9am-5:30pm. Last departure from island 6pm Sep-Jun, 7pm Jul-Aug.)* **Planeria** runs ferries from **Cannes** to Saint-Honorat *(☎04 92 98 71 38 www.cannes-ilesdeslerins.com ⓢ €11. 20min. Departures May-Sept every hr. 8am-3pm, 4:30-5:30pm; return trips every hr. 8:30am-3:30pm, 5-6pm. Departures Oct-May every hr. 8am-4:30pm; return trips every hr. 8:30am-3:30pm, 5pm. Ticket booth open Sept-May M-Sa 9:30am-5pm, Su 8:30am-5pm; June-Aug M-Sa 9:30am-6pm, Su 8:30am-5pm.)*

biot ☎04 93

Biot is the glassblowing capital of France. While it has some less than interesting museums on pottery, the real attractions are the modern day artisans, who mold molten glass with the same tools used centuries ago. The town itself hasn't changed much since the 1400s, and the townspeople have clung to the old Provençal architecture of whitewashed walls and tiled floors, making every hotel, restaurant, and cafe the most adorable place you've ever seen. While at first you might be met with suspicion by locals who are highly aware that you're a foreigner, they are more than eager to open up, especially the many restaurateurs and artisans. Getting around in the city is pretty easy, since the town is no more than a couple hundred meters across. Because you could walk Biot in under 30min., it's best to explore the town slowly, wander through some shops, and enjoy the long lunches.

ACCOMMODATIONS

HOTEL DES ARCADES HOTEL ❸

16 pl. des Arcades ☎04 93 65 01 04 www.hotel-restaurant-les-arcades.com

Located in the heart of the old city, this charming hotel and restaurant feels more like a warm guesthouse than a hotel. The large rooms with whitewashed walls and painted antique furniture will make you think this place costs a fortune, but it's actually the only affordable place in the city.

From the entrance of town, walk until the rue de la Calade and turn right. Hotel is in the place on your left. i Restaurant on ground floor. ⓢ Singles and doubles €55-100.

L'AUBERGE DE LA VALLÉE VERT HOTEL ❸

3400 route de Valbonne ☎04 93 65 10 93 nicodex@wanadoo.fr

A converted farmhouse in the hills above the city. The small rooms are part of a large house with a huge dining area, designed for banquets and wedding receptions. A little far from the old city, but the peace and quiet is well worth it, especially by the pool in summer.

From the town center, take the #7 or 10 bus to chemin des Soulières. Hotel is across the street. Singles and doubles €60-70; triples and quads €80; quints €90.

LE CAMPING L'EDEN — CAMPGROUND ❷

63 chemin du Val de Pôme — ☎04 93 65 63 70 www.campingleden.fr

"Camping" is a relative term when the campsite comes with a full bar and pool complex that resembles a water park. Eden indeed. The campground also offers a restaurant, grocery store, and mobile homes for rent. Avoid the place in July and August, when prices more than double.

Next to the Verrerie du Val de Pôme. From the train station, take the #10 bus to chemin Pres. Walk in the direction of the bus line until chemin du Val de Pôme. Turn right and walk 300 m. Camping on your left. i Wi-Fi €5 per 30min., €8 per hr. Tent sites June-Aug €32-45; Sept €20; Apr €20. Each additional person €4-7. Open Apr 1-Oct 30.

SIGHTS

VERRERIE DE BIOT — GLASSBLOWER

chemin des Combes — ☎04 93 65 03 00 www.verreriebiot.com

Oldest and most impressive of all the glassblowers. This is the place that created the bubble glass effect, now endlessly replicated by plastic knock-offs at Crate and Barrel. A large open pathway ushers tourists into the factory, as well as a glassblowing museum that will tempt you to buy everything at the gift shop, so long as it doesn't break in your backpack.

Free. Workshop open daily June-Aug 9:30am-8pm; Sept-May 9:30am-6pm.

MUSÉE NATIONAL FERNAND LÉGER — MUSEUM

chemin Val du Pome — ☎04 92 91 50 30 www.musee-fernandleger.fr

Museum featuring the work of Ferdinand Léger. We guarantee that you saw his stuff in an art history book. He's the one with the curvy black and white images of women with random swaths of bright color that seem to be random...er... artistically brilliant.

€2, ages 26 and under free. Free first Su every month. Free audio tour available in English. Open May-Oct. M 10am-6pm, W-Su 10am-6pm; Nov-Apr M 10am-5pm, W-Su 10am-5pm.

ARTISIANS OF BIOT — SHOPPING DISTRICT

Biot is a condensed artisan capital, packed with jewelers, glassblowers, painters, and sculptors. They all have their own stores, which are treasure troves of art for tourists, ranging from your average sculpture to Moroccan leatherwork to plaster-of-Paris figurines. Stop by the tourist office for a large brochure on where to find all of them.

Generally open M-Sa 10am-7pm. Times may differ.

MUSÉE D'HISTOIRE ET DE CÉRAMIQUE BIOTESSE — MUSEUM

9 rue St. Sebastien — ☎04 93 65 54 54

Museum of the ceramic history of Biot (really). It's exactly as interesting as it sounds. Entire rooms are reconstructed to show visitors how pottery was fired way back when. Exhibits feature large pots and iron works that look like ancient torture devices. Or they fall under the "art" category.

€2. Open daily June-Aug W-Su 11am-7pm; Sept-May 2-6pm.

FOOD

LA CRÊPERIE DU VIEUX VILLAGE — CRÊPERIE ❷

2 rue Saint Sebastien — ☎04 93 65 72 73

Cottage-like crêperie with flowers laid out on the tables and painted on the walls, and a cute reading nook by the window. The *menu classique (€12.50)* includes ham and cheese crêpe, salad, and dessert crêpe, as well as a big kiss and hug from the cheery owner. The neighborhood favorite will be changing locations in mid-2011 and moving to 29 rue St. Sebastien; the new premises will feature a terrace and shiny new alcohol license.

Crêpes €8-10. Sweet crêpes €3-5. Open July-Aug W 9am-10pm, F-Su 9am-10pm; Sept-May W 9am-6pm, F-Su 9am-6pm.

LA GALERIE DES ARCADES

PROVENÇAL ❸

16 pl. des Arcades ☎04 93 65 01 04

Cheap, traditional Provençal menu under the shade of an ivy-covered terrace, on the bottom floor of an adorable hotel that you cannot afford. Modern art covers walls and jives well with the traditional architecture.

Plats €15. 3-course menu €32. Open July-Aug Tu-Su 11am-10pm; Sept M 11am-2:30pm, Tu-Sa 11am-10pm.

PIZZERIA DU SOLEIL

PIZZERIA ❷

9 passage de la Bourgade ☎04 93 65 74 74

Tiny (really tiny) pizzeria hidden away from the main street. If you have no need for personal space, this restaurant and its 4 tables will suite your needs well. Cramped? Try standing next to the bar and scarfing down your oven-fired pizza.

Pizzas €7.50-9. Plat and entree €9. Open M 11:30am-10pm, Tu 11:30am-3pm, W-Sa 11:30am-10pm.

LA CAFE DE LA POSTE

CAFE ❸

24 rue St. Sebastien ☎04 93 65 19 32

La Poste's huge banquet-hall-sized seating area and bar make the term "cafe" something of a misnomer here. There's relaxing outside seating in the middle of the square, but the interior's tiled tables and cozy feel will drag you inside for at least a look.

Mussels €12.50. Plats €13. Prix-fixe menu €30. Open in high-season daily 10am-midnight; low-season M-Th noon-3pm, F-Sa 5pm-midnight, Su noon-3pm.

NIGHTLIFE

CAFE BRUN

BAR, CAFE, VEGETARIAN

44 impasse St. Sebastien ☎04 93 65 04 83

Welcoming bar with the jerseys of different sports teams hanging on the walls. The shiny brass bar and wooden tables are a throwback to another century, and exude some good old small town charm. And if you don't particularly like sports, small towns, or other centuries, you'll probably end up drinking here anyway; this is the only bar in town.

Beer €3. Cocktails €6. Vegetarian dishes €12. Plats from €10. Open M-Th 11am-7pm, F-Sa 11am-12:30am. Happy hour 6-8pm.

ESSENTIALS

Practicalities

- **TOURIST OFFICE:** Offers maps, brochures and advice on glassblowers and walking routes depending on interests. *(46 rue St. Sebastien ☎04 93 65 78 00 www.biot.fr Open daily 9am-6pm.)*
- **BANK:** **Caisse d'Espargne**. ATM available *(1 chemin Neuf ☎04 93 65 11 78.)*
- **POST OFFICE:** rue St. Sebastien, next to tourist office *(☎04 93 65 11 49 Open M 9am-noon and 2-5:15pm, Tu 9am-noon, W-F 9am-noon and 2-5:15pm, Sa 9am-noon.)*
- **POSTAL CODE:** 06018.

Emergency!

- **POLICE MUNICIPALE:** 7 calade des Bachettes *(☎04 93 65 06 66).*
- **PHARMACY:** 1 chemin Neuf *(☎04 93 65 00 16 Open daily 10am-7pm.)*

- **HOSPITAL: Centre Medical,** chemin des Bachettes *(☎04 93 65 00 23).*

Getting There

Gare SNCF trains run to **Biot train station (TER)** *(Open 6am-11pm.)* Trains to **Cannes** *(15min., every 30min. €3);* **Antibes** *(9min., every 30min. €1.20);* **Nice** *(25min., every 30min. €3.40);* **Marseille** via Cannes *(€28.30).* From the train station, **bus** lines #7 and 10 go to city center. *(€1 last return at 7:39pm.)*

TAM line #200 (€1) that runs between Cannes and Nice stops at the Biot train station. From **Nice** *(45min., every 15min. 6:30am-6pm, every 30min. 6-8pm.)* from **Cannes** *(1hr. 25min., every 15min. 5am-6pm, every 30min. 6-8pm.)* Arrives at Gare SNCF. Take bus #7 or #10 to town center. For **taxis**, call Biot Taxi *(☎06 09 65 96 48.)*

Getting Around

Within the town, walk any direction for 3min. and you'll have left town. To get to the *verreries* (glassblowing workshops), there are frequent buses *(#7 and 10, €1).* Consult tourist office for exact timetables. As a general rule, buses run every 10-15min. 7am-8pm.

juan-les-pins ☎04

Whenever Cannes outprices the Riviera's Spring Break crowd (think Film Festival), Juan-les-Pins subs in as the life of the party. In July and August, the clubs stay open until breakfast—or lunch—and the warm beach welcomes the excessively tan and hungover back into the relaxed rhythm of town life. Situated on the east side of the Cape of Antibes, Juan-les-Pins differs from its historic sister city in that there is little to do other than party, soak in the sun, and play in the water. You'll find actual young people on the beach here, and a very vibrant nightlife that isn't choked by glitz and exploit (cough, Cannes, cough). Be sure to still dress up when you go out—despite the sun and fun, the people here dress to impress, especially during the summer months.

ORIENTATION

Juan-les-Pins is pretty easy to get around; any street from the **train station** leads directly to the beach. A walk down **avenue Docteur Favre** takes you right into the middle of the *bar du nuits* and clubs, with the casino conveniently nearby. Walking straight out of the train station down **avenue Marechal Joffre** leads you to the main beach and **tourist office,** while **avenue l'Esterel** takes you to the budget hotels and cheaper restaurants before hitting the beach on the other side of the train tracks.

ACCOMMODATIONS

HOTEL DE LA PINÈDE — HOTEL ❸

7 av. Georges Gallice — ☎0648 29 52 74 www.hotel-pinede.com

This classy but funky boutique hotel is a stone's throw from Juan-les-Pins's party district. Don't worry about shut-eye; the windows are soundproof. We're not sure what to make of the paintings of the New York skyline or the Buddha statues, but with a breakfast terrace that's this prime for sunbathing, we don't mind the non sequiturs.

From the train station, walk down on av. du Doctueur Fabre. When you reach bld. de la Pinede, make a right. When you reach a 5-point intersection, make a slight right onto av. George Gallice. Hotel is on your immediate right. ***i*** *Breakfast €5.50. Soundproof windows. Singles €45-50; doubles €60-90; triples €90-120. Prices are higher in summer season.*

HOTEL CECIL — HOTEL ❹

rue Jonnard BP 51 — ☎04 93 61 05 12 www.hotelcecil-France.com

Tucked away on the opposite side of town, this quiet Belle Époque hotel will have you thinking about putting some pink furniture in your own house.

From the train station, turn right and walk down av. de Esterel 3 blocks. Turn right onto rue

Jonnard. Hotel is halfway down the street on your left. ***i*** *Breakfast €6.50. Prices increase in summer months.* Ⓢ *Singles €55-76; doubles €58-89; triples €105.*

PARISIANA

HOTEL ❷

16 av. l'Esterel ☎04 93 61 03 hotelparisiana@wanadoo.fr

This budget hotel is close to the train station, and has a breakfast terrace and skylights in the central stairwell. The small rooms make for a cozy experience, especially in the triple room.

Take a right out of the train station down the street 2-3 blocks. Hotel on your right. Ⓢ *Singles €32-48; doubles €45-62; triples €57-74; quads €67-82. Prices increase in summer.* *Reception 8am-10pm.*

TRIANON HOTEL

HOTEL ❷

14 rue l'Esterel ☎04 93 61 18 11

This budget hotel's rooms are a pleasant surprise, considering the ridiculously low prices. The yellow and lavender paintings of flowers add a domestic touch. If it didn't face away from the beach, the bright breakfast terrace would be perfect, but at least it's close to the train station.

From the train station, turn right onto rue l'Esterel. Hotel is 2-3 blocks down on your right. ***i*** *Breakfast €5.* Ⓢ *Singles €30-43; doubles €40-62; triples €64-74; quad €73-82.* *Quiet hours from 10:30pm-8:30am.*

BEACHES

The beaches are ordered from east to west.

PLAGE D'ANTIBES-LES-PINS

bld. du Littoral.

The furthest from the city center (it's almost closer to St-Raphaël), Plage d'Antibes-les-Pins is less crowded than its sister beaches. This is particularly noticeable during the summer months, when it's usually impossible to see any sand in Juan-les-Pins because the umbrellas are so packed together.

PLAGE DU PONT DULYS

bld. Charles Guillaurmont.

One of the most youth-centric beaches in town. It's far enough from the city's center to keep out the elderly and children, but not quite out of the reach for lazy teenagers.

PLAGE LA GALLICE

bld. Boudoin

The closest beach to the town, La Gallice is right next to the port, so you can watch the **boats** sailing in and out of the harbor. You can also get some good people watching in, since this beach is also the most crowded.

PLAGE EPI HOLLYWOOD

bld. Boudoin

Just out of reach of the city, this beach is where you'll most likely find skinny dippers around 5am who've just been kicked out of the nearby clubs. During the day it's pretty quiet and provides some escape from town.

PLAGE DES ONDES

bld. Marechal Juin

In Juan-les-Pins, less sand equals lighter crowds, but it also means less comfortable sunbathing. Some of the coastline at Ondes is more like loose gravel, and no part of the beach is quite like the picturesque white sands that line the coast.

FOOD

LE SWEET CAFE

DINER ❷

16 bld. Baudoiinâ ☎04 93 67 82 12

This relaxing cafe and diner lies on the edge of Juan-les-Pins's party district. Come here after leaving the party early to munch on everything any other restaurant in Juan-les-Pins has to offer, but at lower prices. The outside patio is lively at night.

Pizzas €8.40-11. Crêpes €3.30-9. Salads €7-13. Cocktails €8. Ice cream cocktails €8. Open May-Sept 8am-2am or later; Nov-Apr 8am-7pm.

LE RUBAN BLEU — BRASSERIE ❸

promenade du Soleilâ ☎04 93 61 31 02 plage.rubanbleu@wanadoo.fr

Beachfront brasserie and restaurant that is ideal for watching the young and the fabulous strut their stuff down the boardwalk. You'll pay for the awesome view, unfortunately; the prices here get pretty high. An outdoor seating area opens up on the beach as the night wears on.

Plates €19-25. Crêpes €3.50-5. Open M-Sa noon-3pm, Su noon-4pm. Beach restaurant open F-Sa 7:30-10:30pm.

LA BAMBA — PIZZERIA ❸

18/20 rue Docteur Datheville ☎04 93 61 32 64

Upscale pizzeria and restaurant a block away from the shopping and party center of Juan-les-Pins. Open air restaurant where you can still feel the heat from the wood-fired stoves in the back.

Dishes €13-15. Pizza €7.80-14. 3-course prix-fixe menu €17.50. Open daily noon-10:30pm.

LA PÂTE À CRÊPES — CRÊPERIE ❷

24 av. de l'Estelâ ☎04 93 61 33 14

If crêpes were ever a classy dining option, this place would collect Michelin stars like no other. Chic blue lighting and metal tables add to the modern experience without hurting the wallet.

Prix-fixe galette, crêpe, and carafe of wine €12.50. Crêpes €2.50-3.50. Open July-Aug Tu-Su noon-10:30pm; Sept-June Tu-Su 11:45am-2:30pm and 6:30-10:30pm.

L'HORIZON — SEAFOOD ❸

37 bld. Charles Guillaumont ☎04 93 67 23 11 www.horizon-restaurant.com

This unassuming, quiet restaurant serves seafood right on the beach. Tucked in between a beach shop and smaller restaurant, this marina-themed establishment serves whatever the local fishermen caught fresh that day, including lobsters and shellfish on occasion.

Plates €18-28. Plat du jour €12. Open Jan-Nov 23 M-Tu 11:45am-2pm and 6-10:30pm, Th-Su 11:45am-2pm and 6-10:30pm.

NIGHTLIFE

PAM PAM — BAR

137 bld. Wilson ☎04 93 61 11 05 www.pampam.fr

Brazilian bar that serves drinks out of tiki statues. Bright-colored and life-sized tiki gods take the stage with festively dressed dancers at 10pm. Outdoor seating allows some escape from the bongo drums.

Apértifs €5. Cocktails €8-12. Open daily 3pm-3am.

L'IDEM — BAR, LOUNGE

6 bld. de la Pinede ☎06 09 53 02 49 www.lidem06.unblog.fr

There's 24/7 salsa dancing at this lounge and bar, a block away from the crazy clubs and parties. Skills range from beginner to the pros, who are all too happy to take a greenhorn onto the floor. Lessons are available, and include a night with your instructor or partner on the floor every Thursday night (€12-22).

Beer €6. Liqueur €5-10. Cocktails €9. Open M-Th 7pm-1am (or later), F-Sa 7pm-4am (or later), Su 7pm-1am (or later).

HEMINGWAY COCKTAILS AND CIGARS

BAR

carrefour de la Nouvelle Orléans

Formerly known as the Che Cafe, this *bar du nuit* kept the Cuban decor, added some Hemingway books, and renamed itself. Two stories of Cuban maps and pictures of the famous author make their rum specials seem slightly more authentic.

i Cigar cave. Beer €4. Mixed rum drinks €9-15. Open Apr-Sept daily 3pm-5am.

LE CRISTAL

BAR

av. Georges Galliceâ ☎04 93 61 62 51

A chill crowd gathers on the terrace to watch local clubbers strut by, or they surround the bar to watch the barmen (literally) juggle bottles as they mix their special ice cream cocktails *(€10)*.

Ice cream cocktails €10. Open daily 8:30am-2:30am.

ZAPATA

BAR

av. du Docteur Dautheville www.juanbynight.com

Think you'll only see someone order 10 shots for himself in Mexico? Think again. We saw it at this Mexican bar, which specializes in shots of "fuego" (gin, run, vodka, spices and lime). Walls covered in old pre-Revolution photos of Zapata and Hidalgo.

Tequila shots €6. Beer €7. Open daily 7pm-3am.

LE VILLAGE

DISCOTHÈQUE

1 bld. de la Pinede ☎04 92 93 90 00

Crowds line up early and stretch across the street for this Cuban-themed discothèque and *bar du nuit*. Anticipation for nightly DJ mixes and live performances throughout July and August keeps the city buzzing all year.

Cover €13. Drinks €9. Open July-Aug daily midnight-5am; Sept-June F-Sa midnight-5am.

MILK

DISCOTHÈQUE

av. George Gallice ☎04 93 67 22 74

Swanky bar and discothèque entirely decorated in white. Dress up if you think you'll be let in, and get here early to avoid the long lines at the doors, especially on weekends.

Cover €16; includes 1 drink. Drinks €12-18. Open July-Aug daily noon-6am; Sept-June F-Sa noon-6am.

EDEN CASINO

CASINO

bld. Edouard Baudouin ☎04 92 93 71 71 www.casinojuanlespins.com

Underground casino made to look like a literal cave. The fake plants and colorful lighting add to the Vegas factor, while the prices remind you that you're still in Europe. Blackjack *(€5 per min.)*, roulette *(€5 per min.)* and poker are played regularly, as well as slot machines (no craps, unfortunately). Present passport for entry. Must be 18+ and well-dressed for table games (for the Apatow-esque out there, that means no sneakers, jeans, or T-shirts).

i 18+ for table games. Beer €4. Cocktails €8. Open noon-4am.

FESTIVALS

FESTIVAL DE JAZZ A JUAN

SUMMER

☎04 97 23 11 19 www.antibesjuanlespins.com

Ten-day jazz festival where the town population triples as beatniks and old timers alike flood the streets to jam. Oh yeah, and it's the longest-running jazz festival in Europe. The jam fest is usually held in mid to late July, but its dates, the location of its concerts throughout town, and each concert's admission prices vary each year depending on who's performing. As of this writing, Juan-les-Pins has yet to set its 2011 program; check the city's website for more information.

A good percentage of the performances are free; check website for more information. Expected 2011 dates July 14-25.

ESSENTIALS

Practicalities

- **TOURIST OFFICE:** 51 bld. de Charles Guillaumont. From the train station, walk down av. Maréchal Joffre and turn right when you hit the beach. Tourist office is 2min. away on the right, at the intersection of av. de l'Admiral Courbet and av. Charles Guillaumont. *(☎04 97 23 11 10 www.antibes-juanlespins.com Open M-Sa 9am-noon and 2-6pm, Su 10am-5pm.)*
- **LAUNDROMAT:** On the corner of av. de l'Esterel and av. du Docteur Fabre. *(☎04 93 61 52 04 Wash €3.90, dry €0.50 per 15min. Open daily 7am-10:30pm.)*
- **INTERNET:** **Mediterr@net,** 3 av. du Docteur Fabre. *(☎04 93 61 04 03 €3 per hr. Open M-Sa 9am-10pm, Su 10am-9pm.)*
- **POST OFFICE:** av. de Maréchal Joffre. *(☎04 92 93 75 50 Open M-F 8am-noon and 2-5:45pm, Sa 8:30am-noon.)* ATM available on opposite side (av. Doctuer Fabre).
- **POSTAL CODE:** 06160.

Emergency!

- **POLICE:** ☎04 97 21 75 60.
- **PHARMACY:** 1 av. de l'Admiral Courbet. *(☎04 93 61 12 96 Open daily 8am-12:30pm and 2-6:30pm.)*

Getting There

To get to Juan-les-Pins by **train,** go to the Gare SNCF station *(av. de l'Esterel. Open daily 6:30am-8:55pm. Ticket window open 8:50am-noon and 1:30-5pm.)* To **Antibes** *(€1.25. 5min., 25 per day.),* **Cannes** *(€1.75. 10min., 25 per day.);* **Monaco** *(€6.80. 1hr., 10 per day.);* **Nice** *(€4.10. 30min., 25 per day.).* You can also get to Juan-les-Pins by **bus** *(☎04 93 34 37 60).* **Bus #1** *(€1. 10min., every 20min. 7am-8pm)* runs from Sillages to pl. Guynemer in Antibes, where you can transfer to the Gare Routiere (regional buses). Night bus #1 between pl. de Gaulle in Antibes and Juan-les-Pins in summer only *(Jul-Aug 8pm-12:30am).* **Taxis** *(☎04 92 93 07 07 or 08 25 56 07 07)* t the Jardin de la Pinede and outside the train station. The bus from Juan-les-Pins to Antibes is €14-16.

Getting Around

Most of Juan-les-Pins is very walkable; the only problem that we suspect will arise is deciding which beach you should settle on before you start breaking a sweat. If you are completely averse to exercise, the **tourist train** is more than happy to shuttle you around to see the surrounding sights, in case you don't want to walk there yourself. *(☎06 15 77 67 47 i Runs from bld. Boudoin to Antibes, then the vieille ville, and back again to Juan-les-Pins. 30min.; Mar-Oct Mo-Su every hr. 10:30am-6:30pm, Jul-Aug runs every hr. 7:30-11:30pm).*

cannes ☎04 93

This star-studded and glitzy city on the water definitely has its pricey side, especially during the film festival. If you plan your trip carefully, though, Cannes is probably one of the cheapest places for backpackers to go on the French Riviera. Defined by a distinctly laid back atmosphere for 10 months out of the year (July and August see massive swells in millionaires and their paparazzi, of course), Cannes harbors some of the best that Côte d'Azur has to offer in shopping and beaches, not to mention the fresh shellfish at any of its open air markets. The club scene can be a little intimidating at first, but dressing up just a little bit will go a long way when it comes to getting past the bouncers. In fact, dressing up in general is a good idea here, if only to fit in. Between the hours of 7 and 8pm, locals and tourists magically go from topless and nude (always in vogue here) to full makeup or sports jackets. Don't get caught on the wrong side of this unspoken dress code.

Everyone knows about the Cannes Film Festival, and the city's residents more than benefit from it; local movie theaters here are able to show Palm d'Or winners before anywhere else in the world. The Palais des Festivals hosts additional expos and concerts throughout the year, which puts Cannes in the party mood almost all the time. You might have to splurge on accommodations—a centrally located place in the city and near the beach is worth the price. Hostels have yet to find their way to the pricey coast of Southern France.

ORIENTATION

Cannes is a very easy city to get around; it's a lot smaller than you imagined it was in that last dream of yours where you won Palme d'Or and exchanged room keys with **Matt Damon.** The town can be easily divided into two areas—the expensive part of town and the normal part, where the actual residents live. To the **East of the Palais des Festivals,** the hotels, prices, and breast augmentations get bigger. With names like Dior and Chanel scattered around the private beaches (and where you have to pay to go to the beach), it's easy to get overwhelmed. If the bling is too much for you, head back towards **the Castre**—the large castle on hill to the West—back to the **Suquet,** where the restaurants are intimate, the prices are lower and people in general are a little more mellow. The nightlife thrives around **rue Doctuer Gerard Monod,** but residents generally stick to the cafes and brasseries that line **rue Felix Fauvre.** The best (and free) bacchanalias are further West past the **Vieux Port,** where you'll find the local population of the young and the restless partying it up almost year round.

ACCOMMODATIONS

HOTEL ALNEA

HOTEL ❹

20 rue Jean de Riouffe ☎04 93 68 72 77 www.hotel-alnea.com

Upscale hotel with walls covered in paintings reminiscent of Gaugin's Tahiti phase. Bright colors make this place come alive, and the beach theme will soon have you dying to go to work on your tan line. Large, clean rooms are each themed according to a famous tropical island or locale.

From the train station, turn right and walk to the MonoPrix. At the intersection, keep going straight one block to rue Jean de Riouffe. Turn left. Hotel is on your immediate left. ***i*** *Breakfast €7.50.* Ⓢ *Singles €60; doubles €70; twin €80.* *Check-in 2pm; checkout 11am. Reception 8am-8pm.*

HOTEL 7

HOTEL ❹

23 rue Maréchal Joffre ☎04 93 68 66 66

This star-studded hotel opened in January 2010 and still has that new car smell. Pictures of old movies and movie stars are framed on the silver, chic walls. The minimalist decor in the rooms make them feel less small. Handicapped room on ground floor is opened up into a TV lounge when not occupied.

From the train station, turn right and walk until the highway entrance. Walk up the sidewalk to the highway and make a left onto Maréchal Joffre. Hotel will have movie posters on the side facing the train station. ***i*** *Breakfast €6. Handicapped room on ground floor.* Ⓢ *Singles €60; doubles €70-80; family room (4-person) €90.*

HOTEL PLM

HOTEL ❹

3 rue Hoche ☎04 93 38 31 19 www.hotel-plm.com

Boutique hotel with deals if you stay for a while. Clean, nice smelling rooms with purple bathtubs make this simple hotel worth the extra euros, if only to avoid the local dumps.

From the train station, walk right down Juan Juares. Turn left at rue de 24 Aout. Walk for one

côte d'azur

block until at rue Hoche. Turn right and walk 1 block. Hotel on right. **i** *3rd night is 25% off, 6th night is 50% off. Breakfast €8.* Ⓢ *Singles €46-71; doubles €54-79; superior doubles €59-85.*

HOTEL MIMONT HOTEL ❷

39 rue Mimont ☎04 93 39 51 64 www.canneshotelmimont.com

Still the best budget option in town. Large, clean rooms for relatively cheap, and special *petit chambres* with bed and sink (shared toilet and shower) upon request. On the other side of the train tracks, but still 5min. from town. The Incredibly hospitable hosts speak English and are very welcoming to *Let's Go* readers and Americans, who seem to be the majority of their clients.

From the train station, turn left and take the underpass next to the tourist office to rue Mimont. Turn right, and walk for 3 blocks past the post office. Hotel is on your left. **i** *Breakfast €6.20.* Ⓢ *Petit chambre €30; singles €37-43; doubles €42; triples €58.*

LA VILLA TOSCA HOTEL ❺

11 rue Hoche ☎04 93 38 34 40 www.villa-tosca.com

Amazing, spacious, and centrally located, but prohibitively expensive for most students. Lavish boutique hotel that is probably the best quality for what you pay in all of Cannes. Huge rooms with armoires and couches, and a breakfast area that looks like something Louis XIV would approve of.

From the train station, walk right on Juan Juares. Turn left on rue de 24 Aout and walk for 1 block. Turn left on rue Hoche, hotel is on your left. **i** *Free Wi-Fi.* Ⓢ *Singles €61-98; doubles €82-125; triples €109-161; quads €131-183.*

HOTEL ASCOTT HOTEL ❸

27 rue des Serbes ☎04 93 99 18 24 www.canneshotel.com

Budget hotel that's a little pricey for what you get. Decor is from the early '90s (read: lingering '80s vibe), and the metal panels that cover the windows from the outside make the rooms dark and dreary, but at least the bathroom is clean.

From the train station walk left half a block and turn right down rue des Serbes. Hotel is 2-3 blocks down on your right. Ⓢ *Singles €46-61; doubles €51-72; triples €68-90.*

HOTEL L'ESTEREL HOTEL ❹

15 rue de 24 Aout ☎04 93 38 82 82 reservations@hotellesterel.com

Boutique hotel that's easy to find and close to the market and train station. The large, well-lit rooms are standard, but what sets this place apart is the rooftop terrace, which provides a breakfast with a view of all of Cannes.

From the train station, turn right and walk half a block until rue de 24 Aout. Turn left and walk 1 block down the street. Hotel is on your right. **i** *Breakfast €8.* Ⓢ *Singles €50-80; doubles €63-80; deluxe doubles €74-90.*

MODERN WAIKIKI HOTEL HOTEL ❹

11 rue des Serbes ☎04 93 39 09 87

Funky hotel with bright pinks, zany lavender shapes, and pictures of celebrities covering the walls. Chic rooms with dark bedspreads and carpet each come with private bathrooms, and a shower with nine shower heads.

From the train station, walk left half a block until rue des Serbes. Turn right and walk 4 blocks, past rue d'Anitbes to the hotel on your right. Ⓢ *Singles €50-60; doubles €65-85; triples €75-95.*

CAMPING PARC BELLEVUE CAMPING ❶

67 av. Maurice chevalier ☎04 93 47 28 97

Camping is the cheapest option in Cannes if you are not sharing a room, so pitch a tent and live life as a beach bum going from campground to beach and back. If you do decide to go into town though, please take a dip in the pool or shower on site before doing so; the French don't smell *that* bad.

Take the #2 bus to Les Aubépines and walk 500m, following the signs to the campground. **i** *Pool and restaurant on site. Showers and laundry.* Ⓢ *July-Aug single tent €16, doubles €19. Sept-June single tent €13, doubles €15. Laundry €3. Electricity €3.* *Reception from 8am-8pm.*

ATLANTIS HOTEL
HOTEL ❸

4 rue de 24 Aout ☎04 93 39 18 72 www.cannes-hoel-atlantis.com

Like Atlantis, this hotel should have sunk to the bottom of the ocean a long time ago—at least that would excuse the water damage in every bathroom we saw. Be sure to spring for the expensive room, so your single doesn't smell like mold. Rough around the edges, which is good for a dive bar, but not a hotel thats €50 per night.

From the train station, turn right and walk down Jean Juares. Make a left at rue de 24 Auot and walk 2 blocks. Hotel on the left. i Jacuzzi and sauna. Singles €42-44; doubles €53-90.

SIGHTS

L'ÉGLISE DE LA CASTRE
CHURCH

Towering over the old city and Vieux Port, this church provides crystal clear views of Cannes all the way to Palm Beach on a clear day. The local landmark nearly bankrupted the city, which had to constantly fundraise for 80 years to complete the structure and commission its glass and crystal chandeliers, not to mention the neo-Gothic organ that puts Notre Dame's to shame.

Free. Open daily June-Aug 9am-noon and 3:15-7pm; Sept-May 9am-noon and 2:15-6pm.

MUSÉE DE LA CASTRE
MUSEUM

☎04 93 38 55 26

Formerly the private castle of the monks of Lérins, this museum houses a permanent collection of ancient relics from the Americas, as well as a display of musical instruments from around the world. The only thing relevant to Cannes is its Provençal art collection from the late 19th and early 20th centuries, which feature depictions of day-to-day life in the city.

€3, students €2. Open Tu-Su July-Aug 10am-7pm; Sept 10am-1pm and 2-6pm; Oct-Mar 10am-1pm and 2-5pm; Apr-June 10am-1pm and 2-6pm.

CENTRE D'ART/MALMAISON
EXHIBITION SPACE

47 bld. de la Croisette ☎04 97 06 44 90

Hosts multiple temporary exhibits that change depending on what's politically popular at the time. Issues like green living and globalization are popular.

€4, under 25 €2. Open June-Sept M-Th 11am-8pm, F 11am-10pm, Sa-Su 11am-8pm; Oct-Nov Tu-Su 10am-1pm and 2-6pm.

CASINO CRIOSETTE
CASINO

1 espace Lucien Barrière ☎04 92 98 78 00

The most accessible casino in the area, Criosette features slot machines, blackjack, craps, and roulette, as well as a series of fake statues of Greek gods. Kinda like Vegas, only less sleazy. Wait, never mind: a bunch of guys with slicked hair and their shirts unbuttoned to their belly button just walked in.

i No dress code for slots. No jeans, sneakers, or T-shirts for table games. Slots open at 10am, tables open 8pm-4am.

PLAGE DE LA CROISETTEN
BEACH

Between Vieux Port and the Port Canto

A series of private beaches where you will have to shell out €20 for a sunbrella or beach chair. Pure heresy, in our opinion. The beaches are lined with even pricier restaurants, so you don't need to wander far from your towel to give away even more money.

PLAGES DU MIDI
BEACH

East of the Croisette.

Beautiful sandy beach that's free to the public. Packed in the summertime, this is where you go to meet locals and brush up on some volleyball skills, assuming you know how to say "serve" in French.

PALM BEACH BEACH

East past the Croisette

A ways away from the Croisette, this family friendly beach has a much more laid-back atmosphere, as evidenced by the local windsurfers and kite boarders.

FOOD

BELLIARD — BAKERY ❷

1 rue Chabaud ☎04 93 39 42 72

The 75-year-old *boulangerie* has maintained its humility in one of the priciest areas of Cannes. The neighborhood institution sells an array of charming and affordable *assiettes (€9.50)* as well as tarts, cakes, and a rum raisin ice cream that will put hair on your chest.

Assiette du Jour €9.50. Tarts and cakes €2-3.50. Open daily 7am-8pm.

AKWABAMO EXOTICK — AFRICAN ❷

36 rue Mimont ☎04 93 99 89 10

This awesome Côte d'Ivoire restaurant specializes in West African cuisine of chicken and beef *brochettes (€10).* Pick from six unpronounceable sauces or indulge in the fish dish with rice *(€13).* Down it with homemade pineapple and coconut rum. Baskets and crafts cover the walls of this simple establishment.

Dishes €9-18. Open Tu-Th 11am-10pm, F-Sa 11am-midnight.

LE FREATE — ITALIAN ❸

26 rue Jean Hibert. ☎04 93 39 45 39

In business since '47, this Cannes staple sates its clients with grilled meats and pizza, and provides its patrons with that perfect opportunity to escape the hustle in the glitzy part of Cannes for some laid-back cafe action near the beach.

Plates €7.50-15. Open June-Sept 6:30am-2am. Oct-May 6:30am-1pm.

LES MAREYEURS DU SUB-EST — MARKET ❶

rue Docteur Pierre ☎04 96 39 39 23

Just cause you're on a budget doesn't mean you can't get lobster. You'll just have to cook it yourself, since this market specializes in live blue lobsters from the daily catch. Make sure you get a fighter, they have the most meat.

€15 per kg. Open daily 8am-noon.

MARCHÉ FORVILLE — MARKET ❶

rue Marché Forville

Large, covered market sells everything from fruit to eels to flowers to dairy products. Get up early, since the best products go fast.

Open Tu-Su 7am-1pm.

LA CRÊPERIE — CRÊPERIE ❷

66 rue Maynadier

Small crêpe place in the heart of the cheap stores on rue Maynadier. Outdoor seating provides the opportunity for judging passersby based on which fake brands they bought. Cheap crêpes at a humble restaurant.

Crêpes €2.80-8.70. Open Tu-Su 1pm-8pm.

CARREFOUR — MARKET ❶

Intersection of rue Maynadier and rue Docteur Pierre

The Costco of France. Cheap everything, especially liquor and wine in the back of the store.

Varying. Open daily 9am-8pm.

LAETITIA PASTA — ITALIAN ❷

18 av. Maréchal Joffre ☎04 93 39 52 79

Incredibly cheap pasta and salads for students and budget travelers alike.

Student menu gets you a pasta and drink for ridiculously reasonable prices *(€6.50)*. The simple interior decor matches the simplicity of its menu, while a small stand outside proudly boasts its main dish of the day.

Students menu €6.50. Normal menu €8 for pasta and drink. Salads €5.90, pastas €5.50-7.10. Open M-Sa 8:30am-7:30pm.

JEAN-LUC PELÉ — BAKERY ❷

26 rue Maynadier — ☎04 93 38 06 10 www.jeanlucpele.com

Chic bakery that specializes in 20 different flavors of macaroons. Also serves the most elaborate cakes, crème brulees, and tarts you'll ever see. Free samples!

1 macaroon €1.10 or €9.50 per kg. Tarts, cakes, and crème brulees from €5. Open daily 9:30am-8pm.

AUX BONS ENFANTS — RESTAURANT, FRENCH ❸

80 rue Meynadie

Upscale restaurant where the chef creates the menu based on the day's catch of fish. Outdoor seating in narrow alley makes for intimate dining experience.

Provençal menu €22. Plates €10-25. Open May-July noon-2pm and 7:15-9:30pm; Sept noon-2pm and 7:15-9:30pm; Oct-Apr M-F noon-2pm, 7-9pm, Sa noon-2pm.

NIGHTLIFE

THE STATION TAVERN — BAR

18 rue Juan Juares — ☎04 93 38 34 91

A godsend for young budget travelers. Cheap beer and karaoke is all you need to fill a small lounge with every under-25 in Cannes. The karaoke nights *(Th-Sa 9pm)* are completely unpretentious, and totally awesome in their unabashed cheesiness.

i Karaoke Th-Sa 9pm. Beer €3.50, 10 beers for €16, 10 shots for €16. M-Sa 6pm-2am.

MORRISON'S — PUB

10 rue Teisseire — ☎04 92 98 16 17 www.morrisonspub.com

Laid-back pub that gets mobbed early in the evening and stays packed until closing. The walls are covered with the quotes from Irish playwrights, as well as the drunken musings of local patrons. Irish and British staff breathe a sigh of relief when they get to converse in English.

i Live music W-Th and Su at 9:30pm. Ladies night on Su, unlimited beer and wine for women €8. Happy hour 5-8pm. Pints €6. Whiskey €8. Open from 5pm-2am.

BROWN SUGAR — BAR, RESTAURANT

17 rue des Frères Pradignac — ☎04 93 39 70 10

Kooky Holland-themed bar goes all out with bicycle wheels, accordions, skis, pots and sleds hanging from ceiling. Noticeable family clientele that tapers off as the night goes on. Come before 9:30pm and you get a free tapa with the purchase of a drink. How come you taste so good?

Beer €4-7. Shooters €5. Cocktails €8. Open daily 6pm-2:30am.

CARRE D'OR — BAR

16 rue des Frères Pradignac — ☎04 93 38 91 70

Bar and small club whose walls of mirrors makes it seem bigger than it is. Center bar is an island in the middle of the dance floor that is often used to dance upon, but you won't see this upscale crowd anywhere up there before 1am, or before going through a €700 bottle of Absolut.

Cocktails €10. Beer €7. Open 7pm-2:30am.

SPARKLING AND 4U — NIGHTCLUB

6/8 rue des Frères Pradignac — ☎04 93 39 71 21

And sparkle it does. This joint bar and club is what a club looks like in everyone's wildest dream. Multiple rooms, colors, and textures are enough to keep even the most ADD child interested and focused on this club for the night. A large circular bar (4U bar) sits in the center of the main room, and additional bars are scattered throughout the establishment. Thursday is theme-night. First Thursday of the month is GLBT night. Member of the Cannes Rainbow GLBT association.

Shooters €4. Cocktails €12. Open M-Sa 6pm-5am.

ZANZIBAR BAR

85 rue Felix Fauvre ☎04 93 39 30 75 www.lezanzibar.com

Europe's oldest official gay bar, Zanzibar showcases a classic sailor theme. Small and barrel-like room is covered in images depicting jolly young men drinking and singing on the waterfront. The bar attracts a somewhat older crowd early on in the night, but beckons Americans and youth after midnight.

i GLBT info at www.hexagonegay.com. Beer €4.50. Cocktails €9-10. Open daily 7pm-5am (or later).

LE 7 CABARET, NIGHTCLUB

☎04 93 39 10 36 www.discotheque-le7.com

Get prepared for a raunchy all-nighter: this local legend's outrageous drag shows start at 2am, and the drinks and fabulously dressed performers continue until 5am. Cannes's most famous caberet club, Le 7 caters to all genders and sexual orientations.

Cover Fri-Sa €12, includes 1 drink. Drinks €9.50. Shooters €7. Open Th-Su 11:30pm-5am.

VOGUE BAR

20 rue du Suquet ☎04 93 39 99 18

Prepare to be (wo)man-handled. This *fabulous* Hollywood GLBT bar in the heart of the Suquet compensates for its small size with sparkling mirrors, images of red carpet divas, and a soundtrack fit to accompany your strut down the runway. Come here to play guess-what-gender, then be told very proudly that gender is a construct.

Cocktails €8. Open daily 8:30pm-2:30am.

SOON BAR

3 rue Commandant André ☎06 23 59 98 12 www.lesoon.fr

If the giant champagne bottles don't get you thinking that you've made it in life, maybe the light-up bar or silver faux alligator cushions will. If you find that's too much for you to handle, the outside seating provides a slight escape from pretentiousness, but the people reel it back in.

Beer €5-8. Cocktails €13. Open M-Sa 7pm-2:30am.

LE MUST BAR, NIGHTCLUB

14 rue du Batéguier ☎06 68 14 27 40

Like a scene out of a '70s porn flick, this *bar du nuit* has chic, glittery plastic barstools, private alcoves in dimly lit areas, and a giant picture of Marilyn Monroe. Outside seating has low couches and a hookah water pipe when you reach sparkly overload. Theme nights include a Russia Night where vodka is discounted.

Shooters €5. Beer €6-8. Cocktails €10. Open Mar-Oct daily 7pm-2:30am; Nov-Feb F-Sa 7pm-2:30am.

PEOPLE BAR BAR

6 rue des Frères Pradignac ☎04 93 68 65 66 www.lepeople-bar.fr.

Small and simple, classy bar is completely silver, right down to the large picture of Marilyn Monroe (she's a favorite in Cannes, apparently).

Shooters €5. Cocktails €10. Open M-Sa 6pm-2:30am.

SOF: SPIRIT OF FOOD RESTAURANT, BAR

4 pl. Gambetta ☎04 93 38 38 10

More of a restaurant that's just open really late than an actual bar, this hip establishment refuses to be pinned down. American, Italian, Chinese, French... whatever kind of cuisine you're craving, they probably have it. That goes for the international beer selection too. Laid-back crowd and family atmosphere, or people who just want a break between clubs. Come before 9:30pm and get a pint and tapas *(€12)*. Live music on the weekends.

Beer €3.50. Cocktails €8.50. Open daily 6am-2:30pm and 6pm-2:30am.

AU BUREAU BAR

49 rue Felix Fauvre ☎04 93 39 06 32

Beachy bar complete with sand covering the floor. Eleven different kinds of mojitos will drain your wallet and lift your spirits *(€11)*. This is where the swanky crowd comes to pretend that they're laid-back.

Mojitos €10. Cocktails €11. Open daily noon-2:30am.

CHATON BAR

11 rue Frères Pradignac

Brand new bar in the Carre d'Or district of town. Fun, small, and multicolored, the place was still unpacking when we checked it out in 2010. It fosters a younger, more care-free vibe than many of the uptight neighboring clubs.

Wine €5. Cocktails €12. Open daily 7pm-2:30am.

APERTIVO BAR

3 rue des Suisses ☎04 93 99 84 40

Funky wine bar that lets go of all its inhibitions, and the 30-40 year old crowd certainly follows. When the dance floor is too packed, middle aged roustabouts take to the street outside of the bar.

Beer €6. Cocktails €10. Open T-Su 6:30pm-12:30am. Soirees on W.

ARTS AND CULTURE

PALAIS DES FESTIVALS ET DES CONGRÈS FESTIVAL VENUE

bld. de la Croisette ☎04 93 39 01 01 www.palaisdesfestivals.com

Large venue that hosts every festival or expo that comes through Cannes. Everything from dance, to arts, to concerts to the film festival in May.

Prices vary. Open to visitors M-Sa 9am-noon and 2-6pm.

ARCADE THEATRE CINEMA

77 rue Félix Faure ☎08 92 68 00 39

Shows movies in their original version (English), and is right in the middle of the city, closer to the Suquet.

€8, students €6. All tickets €6 on W. Sa and Su morning show (10:30am) €4.50. Hours and show times vary.

FESTIVAL DE PLAISSANCE FESTIVAL, BOATING

Vieux Port ☎01 46 04 08 62 www.salonnautiquecannes.com

In case you wanted to feel worse about yourself for not having giggles of money, check out this aptly named **boat** show where the entire Vieux Port is filled with multimillion dollar yachts and megayachts during this week-long festival in September.

€15 entrance for the whole week.

FESTIVAL INTERNATIONALE DU FILM FESTIVAL, CINEMA

Palais des Festivals www.festival-cannes.com

What's Cannes without its film festival? Well sorry for you, but you can't go unless you're famous or connected. Either way you need an invitation. At least you can gawk at the celebrities and prices during this week-long festival in May.

Too much for you. Doesn't matter. You're not invited.

THEATRE ALEXANDRE III — THEATER

19 bld. Alexandre III ☎04 93 94 33 40 🖳www.theatredecannes.com

Small theater (176 seats) that has a regular schedule of both French and international plays.

ⓢ *€18, students €15.* 🕘 *See website for showtimes which vary*

ESSENTIALS

Practicalities

- **TOURIST OFFICE:** In the Palais des Festivals. Booking tickets for events and provides free maps of the city. *(1 bld. de la Croisette ☎04 92 99 84 22 🖳www.cannes.fr. 🕘 Open July-Aug 9am-8pm, Sept-June 9am-7pm).* Also a branch next to the train station. *(☎04 93 99 19 77 🕘 Open M-Sa 9am-7pm.)*
- **CURRENCY EXCHANGE: Trevelex.** €80 min. cash advance. *(8 rue d'Antibes ☎04 93 37 41 45 🕘 Open M-Tu 9am-6pm, W 9:45am-6pm, Th-F 8:50am-6pm, Sa 9:45am-6pm.)*
- **YOUTH CENTER: Cannes Information Jeuenesse.** Info on jobs and housing. *(5 quai St-Pierre ☎04 97 06 46 25 🖳lekiosque@ville-cannes.fr. 🕘 Open M-Th 8:30am-12:30pm and 1:30-6pm, F 8:30am-12:30pm and 1:30-5pm.)*
- **INTERNET: Cyber Atlas** *(Corner of Juan Juares and Helene Vagliano ☎04 93 69 42 86. ⓢ €3 per hr. 🕘 Open July-Aug 10am-11pm, Sept-June 10am-10pm.)*
- **POST OFFICE:** 22 rue de Bivouac Napoleon *(☎04 93 06 26 50 🕘 Open M-F 9am-7pm, Sa 9am-noon).* Branch at 34 rue Mimont *(☎04 93 06 27 00 🕘 Open M-F 8:30am-noon and 1:30-5pm, Sa 8:30am-noon).*
- **POSTAL CODE:** 06400.

Emergency!

- **POLICE:** 1 av. de Grasse *(☎04 93 06 22 22)* and 2 quai St-Pierre *(☎08 00 11 71 18).*
- **HOSPITAL: Hopital des Broussailles** *(13 av. des Broussailles ☎04 93 69 70 00).*
- **AMBULANCE:** ☎04 92 97 90 21.
- **PHARMACY: Pharmacie des Allees.** Staff speaks Russian, Italian, German, English and French. *(2 av. Felix Fauvre ☎04 93 39 00 18 🕘 Open July-Aug M-Sa 9:30am-9pm; Sept-June 9:30am-7:30pm.)*

Getting There

Buy **train** tickets at 1 rue Juan Juares. Automatic ticket booths if you have a European card. *(🕘 Station open 5:20am-1:10am. Ticket office open daily 5:30am-10:30pm. Info desk open M-Sa 8:30am-5:30pm.)* To **Antibes** *(ⓢ €2.75. 🕘 15min.)*; **Grasse** *(ⓢ €3.30. 🕘25min.)*; **Marseille** *(ⓢ €27.40. 🕘 2hr.)*; **Monaco** *(ⓢ €11. 🕘 1hr.)*; **Nice** *(ⓢ €6.20 🕘 45min.)*; **St-Rafaël** *(ⓢ €6.30. 🕘 25min.)*; **TGV** *to* **Paris** via **Marseille** *(🕘 5hr. ⓢ €80-100.).*

Rapide Côte d'Azur, pl. Hotel de Ville, runs **buses** *(☎04 93 48 70 30)* to **Nice** *(ⓢ €6. 🕘 1hr., every 20min.)* and **Nice Airport.** *(ⓢ €15. 🕘 1hr., every 30min. M-Sa 7am-7pm, Su 8:30am-7pm.)* Buses to **Grasse** *(ⓢ €1.50. 🕘 50min., every 45min.)* leave from the train station.

The closest **airport** is the **Nice-Côte d'Azur** *(NCE; ☎08 20 42 33 33).*

Getting Around

Walking is the easiest option in Cannes, since you'll find that its a much smaller city than in your Hollywood dreams and is incredibly manageable by foot. If you have to make it further than local campgrounds, take the **bus** *(€1)* in front of the train station. The Gare Routiere is in front of the Hotel de Ville, and is valid for one hour. The local **train station** leads to any city within reach. There are no subways or tram lines.

grasse ☎04

If your French hookup in Nice kind of smelled, you'd better thank Grasse. The perfume capital of France, Grasse is so famous for its fragrances that regional kings used to maneuver and fight for control over the rose fields back in the day. Blessed with the perfect climate, soil, and local species of rose, this is where they figured out that you could distill floral scents and apply it instead of bathing. While bathing has gained in popularity since the plague, the prevalence of perfume in France hasn't waned, and Grasse has supplied it for nearly 300 years. You'd think that the city might be a little more active due to the large influx of tourists, but Grasse maintains a colorful small-town vibe; the *perfumeries* are about the only things here that consistently stay in business, and the resulting cheap land and foreclosed buildings have recently provided opportunities to a large influx of immigrants in the tiny town. Situated on top of the hills overlooking the valley to Cannes, you can find a stunning sight at the edge of any street or balcony in Grasse. Come, smell, and leave, because after the last bus leaves town, Grasse goes to sleep, with the exception of a couple of local bars and clubs that remain open on the weekends. You won't find many tourists except during museum hours, but you'll struggle to find cheap accommodations that haven't already been booked up by old people in touring companies.

ORIENTATION

We're sorry. Orientation is hard in Grasse. One wrong left turn down the wrong alleyway could mean that you have to trek back uphill, only to find that the restaurant you wanted was at the bottom of the hill anyway. As far as basics go, the maps are hard to follow, since the numerous alleys and steps are not well marked, and may not qualify enough as streets to show up on a map. Asking for directions was never more utilized by our writers than here. Thankfully, the worthwhile museums are all centrally located, and the **bus station** will take you to the far away museums and **perfumeries.** The main areas that you must concern yourself with include the **place aux Aires,** where you'll find cafes and a weekend market of olive oils, dried fruits, and wine. The town's nicer restaurants are located in offshoots of this place. **Boulevard du Jeu de Ballon** has all of your bars and small cafes, as well as a theater and cinema. Hotels are located around the city, particularly around the **place de Patti** and in the **place des Cours.** The single most important place you must know is the **bus station,** at the top of the bld. du Jeu de Ballon, which will take you to the **Gare SNCF,** as well as Cannes, and all the campgrounds and *perfumeries* along the way.

ACCOMMODATIONS

Grasse is not very budget-friendly for hotelgoers. It seems that the only hotels that last are chains, since the ones that start up fizzle out due to either the difficult location or poor tourist attendance. The hotels that do last are in the center of the city, and they've used that as an excuse to jack up prices, let quality slide, or both. There's one hotel that we recommend, but it's a short walk from the center, and only recommended for groups of travelers. Otherwise, getting to and from camping locations will take you longer (and be more expensive) than just staying in Cannes and taking the train in for day trips.

MANDARINA — HOTEL ❺

39 rue Yves-Emmanuel Baudoin ☎04 93 36 10 29 www.mandarinahotel.com

Out of the way, but the views and cleanliness are worth staying uphill from the old town. Modern hotel with the comforts of lavender perfume (you are in Grasse, after all), comfy couches, and a terrace view of the valley that will take your breath away. Seriously, awesome view.

From the Gare Routiere, go up the steps toward the Odalys hotel and turn left. Walk up the street 200m; hotel is on your left. Ⓢ *Singles €80-85; doubles €85-95; triples €90-95; quads €95-100.*

HOTEL DU PATTI — HOTEL ❹

pl. du Patti ☎04 93 36 01 00 www.hotelpatti.com

Romantic (read: expensive) boutique hotel in the center of town. You pay for the convenient location, but are compensated with blue tile bathrooms and pink suites. Book ahead of time, since it's almost always booked by some group of septuagenarians touring the countryside before they die.

From the Gare Routiere, walk toward the road and turn left, going down the narrow alley next to the bus station to pl. des Faineants. Continue walking downhill until you get to pl. du Patti. Hotel on your left. i Breakfast €9. Ⓢ Singles and doubles €69-125; triples €105.

CAMPING DE LA PAOUTE — CAMPING ❷

160 route de Cannes ☎04 93 09 11 42 www.campinglapaoute.com

Camping option that is about three quarters of the way to Grasse from Cannes, or one quarter of the way to Cannes from Grasse, depending on whether you're a glass half full or empty type. Has ample space for parking and mobile homes for rent, for those who plan to "camp" like they do in Deliverance.

From the Gare Routiere, take the #600 bus to Cannes. Tell the driver you want to get off at Paoute for the camp site. Bus runs M-Sa every 30min., Su every hr. i 10% discount when you stay longer than 8 nights. Hot shower and pool use included. Ⓢ 1 person €12-17; 2 people €16-21. Electricity €4 per day.

ODALYS: HOTEL DES PARFUMS — HOTEL ❺

rue Eugene Charabot ☎04 92 42 35 35 www.hoteldesparfums.com

Chain hotel up the street from the Gare Routiere. Offers a pool, and mountain or valley views from the balcony rooms. Nice, but expensive.

From the Gare Routiere, look up the hill. You will see it. Walk up the steps to it. i Offers discounts on purchases at Galimard and golfing passes. Ⓢ Singles €88-104; doubles €115-147; triples €152-185; quads €178-214. Prices vary depending on season and mountain/valley view.

HOTEL PANORAMA — HOTEL ❺

2 pl. du Cours ☎04 93 36 80 80

Not the most spectacular of hotels for this price, but conveniently next to the tourist office, with balcony views (for a price) of the valley below. Don't expect luxury, or even boutique cuteness, and be willing to settle for budget hotel quality without the budget.

From the tourist office, 100m up the hill. i Breakfast €8. Ⓢ Singles and doubles €70-80.

SIGHTS

MOLINARD — PERFUMERIE

60 rue Victor Hugo ☎04 92 42 33 11 www.molinard.com

While not the most tourist-friendly place in the city, the 2km walk and lighter crowds that result from it is worth the extra attention. The free tour of this *perfumerie* will give you insight into the four famous flowers of Grasse, and how they have been combined at this factory, built by Gustav Eiffel, to make some of the most famous scents since the 1700s. You can make your own perfume here by reservation for 30min., 1½hr., or 2hr. session.

i Reservations required for workshops, held M-F 9:30am-4pm. Ⓢ Free. Workshops €27-96. Free tours in English available. Open July-Aug daily 9am-7pm; Sept daily 9am-6:30pm; Oct-Mar M-F 9am-12:30pm and 2-6pm, Sa 9am-noon and 2-6pm; Apr-June daily 9am-6:30pm. Tours July 9:30am-6pm; Aug-June 9:30am-noon and 2-5:30pm.

FRAGONARD — PERFUMERIE

20 bld. Fragonard ☎04 93 36 44 65 www.fragonard.com

Though perhaps less luxurious than Molinard, this *perfumerie* is accessible, and conveniently located in the heart of the museums and tourist office. Free tours are available of the exquisitely preserved, nearly 230-year-old factory. The top floor is a free museum on the history of perfume, where you can find international perfume bottles ranging from ancient Egypt and China to Chanel No. 5. Display of the old, retired distilling vats fill up an entire room.

Free tours in English. Open daily 9am-6:30pm.

GALIMARD — PERFUMERIE

73 routes a Cannes — ☎04 93 09 20 00 www.galimard,com

Opened in 1747, this was Louis XIV's royal source for perfume, located right next to the Grasse rose fields. Learn that not all roses are the same, and only the Grasse variety are used in high-class perfumes today. The factory offers 2hr. sessions with a professional nose, who will help you create your own perfume from a variety of base notes, heart notes and head notes. Ask your "nose" what that means.

*From the Gare Routiere, take the #600 bus to Cannes. Ask the driver to drop you off right in front of the perfumerie, also next door to a quick burger place. **i** Reservation required for perfume workshop. Free tours. Perfume creation €40. Open daily June-Sept 9am-6:30pm; Oct-May 9am-noon and 2-6pm.*

MUSÉE INTERNATIONAL DE LA PARFUMERIE — MUSEUM

8 pl. Cours — ☎04 97 05 58 00

Shows large displays of how perfume is made all around the world, from soaking things in animal fat to soak up the scent to boiling them in large vats to distill the smell. Apparently it's not just for good smells either, as evidenced by the 3000-year-old mummy's hand that has been preserved entirely by perfume.

€3, students €1.50, under 18 free. Open May-Sept M-F 10am-7pm, Sa 10am-9pm, Su 10am-7pm; Oct-May M 10am-12:30pm and 2-5:30pm, W-Su 10am-12:30pm and 2-5:30pm.

MUSÉE D'ART ET D'HISTOIRE DE PROVENCE — MUSEUM

2 rue Mirabelle — ☎04 93 36 01 61

Free museum that you wouldn't visit if it wasn't. It was a noble's residence from the 1600s until the Revolution, and now showcases a series of paintings and daily articles that would be interesting if they were in your great-grandparents' house but that don't really deserve their own museum. Hey, it's free.

Open May-Sept daily 10am-7pm; Oct-Apr M 11am-6pm, W-Su 11am-6pm.

MUSÉE JEAN HONORÉ FRAGONARD — MUSEUM

23 bld. Fragonard — ☎04 93 36 01 61

Another free museum where you can see what an old house looked like a long time ago. Large paintings dominate the residence of this Grasse artist, whose name the *perfumerie* adopted in 1923.

Open daily May-Sept 10am-7pm; Oct-Apr 11am-6pm.

CATHEDRAL NOTRE DAME DU PUY — CATHEDRAL

pl. du Cathedrale

This large old cathedral built in 1125 still uses its restored organ from the 1300s. Tower provides a view of both the city and the surrounding area.

Open daily 7am-8pm.

FOOD

EL TAPAS — TAPAS BAR, PIZZERIA ❸

2 av. Chiris — ☎04 93 36 33 19 eltapas@orange.fr

Tapas bar and pizzeria down the hill from the old city. The covered patio makes you feel like you're in Pamplona, waiting for the running of the bulls. It's impressive that at least one place in town has the "huevos" to offer cheap pizzas *(€5 each)*. Provençal theme mixed with some Spanish flair; just don't call it Spanish.

Pizzas €5. Tapas plate €8. Open daily 8pm-3am.

LA CRÊPERIE CRÊPERIE ❷

pl. aux Aires ☎04 93 11 23 84

Cheapest place in the pl. aux Aires. Sit outside and enjoy your cheap crêpes *(€3-8.50)* or go all out with an entree, *plat du jour*, and dessert *(€14.50)*. Casual and laid-back; no need to worry about what you're wearing.

Plates €5-12. Specials €14.50. Open Tu-Su 11:30am-7pm.

SPAGHETTERIA CAFE ❶

9 rue Jean Ossola ☎06 23 59 10 96

Cheap sandwiches and crêpes from this quick eatery. Croque monsieurs and baguette sandwiches on-the-go from a jolly old man that gives Santa a run for his money.

Crêpes €2-4.50. Sandwiches €5. Open M-Sa 10am-6pm.

LE PECHÉ GOURMANT BOULANGERIE ❸

6 rue de l'Oratoire ☎06 62 69 61 57

Le Peché serves its own dishes of Provençal cuisine, along with its macaroons and *galettes*. This small, jazzy place also scoops 90 different kinds of ice cream.

Plates and pastries €12. Cakes €1-5. Open W-Su 10am-7:30pm.

LOU CALENDON TRADITIONAL ❹

5 rue des Fabreries ☎04 93 60 04 49

Completely unrecognizable as a Michelin-rated restaurant, turn down an alley and through a back door to dine at this cozy upscale joint. The menu changes every three weeks according to what's in season.

Pl. aux Aires. Plat du jour, glass of wine, and coffee €19. Plats from €20. Open Tu-Su noon-2:30pm and 5-10pm.

ANGEL ICE CAFE, GLACERIE ❷

6 rue Jean Ossola

The weird totem pole signs will catch your attention, as well as the curious menu items that almost seem American. Hot dogs and milkshakes are served alongside croque monsieurs and crêpes. Totally off the wall and purely gimmicky, but definitely cheap.

Hotdogs €3.50. Milkshakes €4. 2 scoops of ice cream €3. Open daily 10am-7pm.

CAFE DES MUSÉES CAFE ❸

1 rue Ossola ☎04 92 60 99 00

This small cafe catches all the tourists coming out of the museums; you can infer that even from its name. Nonetheless, the place is pretty cute, with its shaded patio and barreled arch ceiling, and has reasonably priced *formules (€12)*.

Formule plat and dessert €12. Dessert du jour €4.50. Open M-Sa 9am-6:30pm, Su noon-6:30pm.

NIGHTLIFE

MANNEKEN PIS PUB BAR

37 bld. du Jeu de Ballon ☎04 93 40 03 72

An awesome little cave of a bar (literally; it's decorated like a cave). The central theme of this Belgian brewhouse is its namesake, a tiny peeing statue and replica of a famous Brussels landmark. Drink cheap beer and watch rugby and soccer on their two giant screens.

Drinks €5-7. Open Tu-Su 5pm-2am.

ZIG ZAG BAR BAR, CLUB

13 bld. du Jeu de Ballon ☎06 58 41 01 06

Trendy, two-story bar and club covered in zebra stripes with soirees every Friday and Saturday night.

Beer €4. Cocktails €7. Open noon-2am.

B.O. CAFE
BAR, CLUB

2 pl. de la Foux ☎04 93 40 07 18

An unfortunately named bar with a central location and large terrace seating. The funky decor reminds us of what the future looked like in 1959—but add a little glitter to a B-list movie and you've got B.O. Cafe. Sports on TVs and cheap beer almost don't go with the bar's decor, but it's appreciated by budget travelers.

i Happy hour 5-7pm. Ⓢ Beer €2.70. ⏰ Open M-Th noon-8:30pm, F-Sa noon-late, Su noon-8:30pm.

CAFE DES NEGOTIANTS
BAR

33 bld. du Jeu de Ballon ☎04 93 36 01 54

Local bar that's popular with Grasse's elderly population and budget travelers. Decorated like an old diner, with walls that are covered in Coke ads from the '50s and an old pinball machine that you'll be shocked still works.

Ⓢ Beer €3. Other drinks €6. ⏰ Open M-Sa 2:30pm-1:30am.

ARTS AND CULTURE

THEATRE DE GRASSE
THEATER

☎04 93 40 53 00 www.theatredegrasse.com

Everything from drama to the circus shows on Grasse's stage. Musical performances, dances and the occasional Hitchcock classic are also popular. Check website for rotating schedule.

Ⓢ Student prices €14-25, depending on the celebrity status of the actors, and popularity of performance. 3 spectacle pass €33.

CINEMA LE STUDIO
CINEMA

15 bld. du Jeu de Ballon ☎08 92 68 27 45

Only cinema in town that shows movies dubbed in French.

Ⓢ Students €8. ⏰ Open M-Sa 10am-10pm.

FÊTE DU JASMIN
FESTIVAL

☎04 97 05 57 92 www.ville-grasse.com

Giant festival in early August that celebrates the city's famous fragrant flower, powering all three of their *perfumeries*. The town uses an average of 150,000 blossoms a year in decorations alone.

Ⓢ Free. ⏰ Starting the 1st weekend in August.

ESSENTIALS

Practicalities

- **TOURIST OFFICE: Cours Honoré Cresp,** next to the Palais des Congrès. *(☎04 93 36 66 66 www.grasse.fr ⏰ Open June-Sept M-Sa 9am-7pm, Su 9am-1pm and 2-6pm; Oct-May M-Sa 9am-12:30pm and 2-6pm.)* Free maps in multiple languages, as well as suggested walking routes in the city. Provides hotel restaurant guides and 1hr. guided tours in English *(Ⓢ €2. ⏰ July-Aug Sa at 2pm).* A petit train runs to *perfumeries* and museums *(☎06 07 7563 60. Ⓢ €6, students €3. ⏰ Every 45min).*
- **INTERNET: Webphone,** 3 rue Fabreries *(☎04 93 77 78 62 Ⓢ €2 per hr. ⏰ Open daily 10am-10pm).*
- **POST OFFICE:** In garage under the Gare Routiere bus station *(☎04 92 42 31 11 ⏰ Open M-F 9am-noon and 2-5pm, Sa 9am-noon.)*
- **POSTAL CODE:** 06103.

Emergency!

- **POLICE:** 12 bld. Carnot *(☎04 93 40 31 60).*
- **PHARMACY:** 26 pl. aux Aires *(☎04 93 36 05 35).*

- **HOSPITAL:** chemin de Clavary *(☎04 93 36 05 35).*

Getting There

Traverse de la Gare runs trains through Grasse on a regular basis *(Ticket window open M-Sa 6:15am-8:55pm, Su 9:30am-noon and 1-5pm.)* Trains run to **Antibes** *(€5.50),* **Cannes** *(€3.50),* and **Nice** *(€8.20).* From the train station, there is a **free shuttle** that runs every 15min. to the *centre-ville.* You can also take the #1, 2, 3, or 4 bus to the Palais des Congrès *(€1.)* You can also get to Grasse by the **RCA** bus, pl. Notre Dame des Fleurs *(☎04 93 36 08 43 Open M-Th 7:30am-1:30pm and 2-5pm, F 7:30am-1:30pm and 2-4pm).* Services to **Cannes** *(€1. 50min.; M-Sa every 30min. 6am-8:15pm, Su every hr. 7:30am-7:30pm),* and **Nice** *(€1. 1hr.; July-Aug 15 per day, Sept-June 20 per day).* **Taxis** can be reached at ☎04 93 36 37 07.

Getting Around

No matter where you are in Grasse, it's always an uphill battle to get to your destination. Literally. Remember when your grandpa told you that in the old country he walked uphill both ways to get from home to school? Well, he grew up in Grasse. Unfortunately, the streets are so small that cars and buses cannot go through, so walking will have to do. To get anywhere outside the city, the **Gare Routiere** is around the corner from the theater and easy to find, and will take you along the routes to Cannes or Nice. The buses can also take you to the *perfumeries.* The easiest way honestly is the **Petit Train.** Save yourself the walking or bus-confusing; you don't want to get turned around and be heading the wrong direction, since it's uphill all the way back to the start.

saint-raphaël ☎04

St-Raphaël has all of the beaches, bikinis, and ensuing debauchery of its more popular neighbors, but at budget prices—by Riviera standards, anyway; the town's still not the rock-bottom deal you're probably looking for, but when you consider that Cannes and St-Tropez cater to counts, Clooney, and women who want Clooney, St-Raphaël starts to look like a steal. Midway through summer, the town boardwalk turns into a carnival in the evenings, and becomes packed with gaming booths and flirty teenagers. If you need to escape the crowds, the secluded beaches along the coast provide the perfect spot to avoid the crazy excesses of the Côte d'Azur. If nothing else, use this place as a launch point for a trip to St-Tropez—the ferry is definitely affordable and accessible from this point.

ORIENTATION

St-Raphaël is centered at its port and the **place Pierre Coullet,** where cute cafes and mom-and-pops rub elbows with big hotels and businesses. The **old city** lies between the train tracks and the water, while the newer part of the city (where you find lower prices) is on the other side of the tracks. The city gets confusing when it comes to addresses—two roads go by multiple names. **Cours Jean Bart** and **promenade Guilbaud** are the same thoroughfare, and businesses use either street name. The street is located on the **port,** closer to **Frejus.** The other main street in St-Raphaël runs along the **plage de Veillat,** and goes by one of three names: **promenade Rene Coty, boulevard de la Liberation,** or **promenade de Lattre de Tassigny.** Within the old port, the streets are neatly laid out in a grid, but lose their uniformity once you get into the newer part of the city.

ACCOMMODATIONS

St-Raphaël's choices are limited in terms of hostels. What would buy you a room in a nice hostel elsewhere gets you a low quality (read: run-down) hostel in this town. There are more budget options the closer you get to Frejus, just up the beach from St-Raphaël.

LES PYRAMIDES HOTEL ❸

77 av. Paul Doumer ☎04 98 11 10 10

Conveniently close to the beach and one of the cheapest places in St-Raphaël. There's a large covered patio for breakfast, and tiki masks on the wall that contribute to the hotel's vague island theme.

From the train station, turn left and walk to the end of the street. Turn right onto av. Henri Vadon and walk toward the beach. Make next immediate left and walk up 50m. Hotel is on the left. Singles €35-40; doubles €48-70; triples €70-75; quads €80-85.

HOTEL BELLEVUE HOTEL ❸

22 bld. Felix Martin ☎04 94 18 90 10

Another beach-themed hotel in the middle of the old town, close to the beach and the pl. Coullet.

From the train station, turn right and walk down rue Rousseau. Turn left onto bld. Felix Martin. Hotel is on your right 3 blocks down. i Breakfast €6. Singles and doubles €40-55; triples €55-90; quads €60-110; quints €70-140.

HOTEL D'EUROPE - GARE TERMINUS HOTEL ❹

358 pl. Pierre Coullet ☎04 94 95 42 91

Right across the street from the train station (hence the name). The clean rooms come with balconies that look over the pl. Coullet, if you're willing to shell out the extra cash.

Walk out of train station; the hotel is across the street to your right. i Breakfast €6. Singles €50-60; doubles €55-70; triples €75.

HOTEL PROVENÇAL HOTEL ❹

195 rue de la Garome ☎04 98 11 85 00 www.hotel-provencal.com

Motel-esque hotel where you can rent by the week as well as by the night. Simple rooms with weird patterned bedspreads and clean, private bathrooms.

From the train station, turn right and walk 2 blocks. Turn right onto rue Basso, walk to pl. Victor Hugo. Turn left onto rue de la Garome. Follow signs to the hotel on your left. i Breakfast €8. Singles and doubles €55-80. Weekly apartment rental €600.

LES PALMIERS HOTEL ❹

109 bld. de la Liberation ☎04 94 51 18 72

Upscale hotel right on the water. Yes, you'll pay through the nose for a room here, but the balconies, faux finish walls, and blue tile floors make Les Palmiers a refreshing change from the skeezy hostels you're probably used to staying in.

Closer to Frejus than St-Raphaël. Walk along beach for 20min. toward Frejus until arriving at hotel. i Half-board available. Singles and doubles €55-100. Half board €18 per day.

côte d'azur

NOUVEL HOTEL HOTEL ❹

66 av. Henri Vadon ☎04 94 95 23 30 www.nouvelhotel.com

A hole-in-the-wall hotel next to a gyro and shawarma stand, Nouvel is also close to the train station and beach. The rooms come with flowers and bright reds and blues, which attempt to offset the hotel's lack of curb appeal.

From the train station, turn left and walk 1 block. Turn right onto Henri Vadon. Hotel on your right. i Breakfast €6.50. Singles €49-60; doubles €54-69; triples €69-90. Half-board €25 per day.

SIGHTS

BASILIQUE NOTRE DAME DE LA VICTOIRE CHURCH

bld. Felix Martin ☎04 94 83 26 98

The basilica was built to commemorate the battle of Lepante in 1571, even though the church was built in 1883. The architecture is an odd synthesis of Roman and Belle Époque style, and features an impressive mosaic floor and 35m high ceilings.

Open daily 7am-9pm.

LA PYRAMIDE DE NAPOLEON MONUMENT

av. Guilbaud

Easy to miss in a crowd due to its small size—like its namesake—this pyramid commemorates Napoleon's landing in St-Raphaël before beginning his second attempt to become France's emperor and generally conquer the world. It's located at the major crossroads of the Port, so you won't have to go out of your way to see it.

MUSÉE DE PRÉHISTOIRE ET D'ARCHÉOLOGIE SOUS-MARINE MUSEUM

pl. de la Vieille Église ☎04 94 19 25 75

The museum showcases a collection of artifacts and professional analyses that examine the day-to-day life of ancient Roman settlers, including ancient fishing techniques. The lesson on harpoon work could come in handy if you're low on cash, but otherwise the museum is as exciting as ancient fishing sounds.

Free. Open Dec-Oct Tu-Sa 9am-noon and 2-6pm.

ÎLE D'OR ISLAND

Originally bought by a naval sergeant in 1897 for 280 francs, this private island off of the coast of St-Raphaël was subsequently lost to a doctor in a card game. That doctor built the tower you see here today in 1912. He then changed his name to Augustus I, crowned himself king of Île d'Or, and printed stamps and minted coins with his picture on them, and celebrated with a feast. We're serious. Apart from a temporary occupation by Allied forces using the beach to storm Provence in 1944, the island is still inhabited to this day; the "royal" family still lives in the tower and raises its flag whenever they're home. Because it's a private island, visitors are not welcome, but you can see the dramatic tower from St-Raphaël's coast.

JARDIN NAPOLEON GARDEN

quai Admiral Nomy

A public garden commemorating the man himself. Taking up over 20,000 sq. m on the old port, this area serves the purpose of open space for children's games, which is just what Napoleon would have wanted.

Open dawn-dusk.

BEACHES

The area's picturesque and secluded beaches are the main draw to both St-Raphaël and its neighboring twin city Frejus. While the coastline features a mix of sand and less accommodating rocks, you won't have any problems finding the water.

PLAGE DU VEILLAT ♿

Centre ville

The closest and easiest beach to get to, Veillat is also the most crowded. It's little wonder why; the coast is lined with a dense concentration of restaurants, and is the only prominent beach in the area with a lifeguard in July and August.

Walk toward Frejus; it's the large sandy beach expanse in front of you.

PLAGE DE LA TORTUE

Town of Valescure

A half-rock, half-sand beach that's popular with swimmers because of its protected bay.

Either bus #5, which leaves from St-Raphaël-Valescure SNCF, or the train station at Valescure.

PLAGE DE LA GARDE VIEILLE

Boulouris

Small, sand beach with absolutely no reminders of human life.

Either bus #8, which leaves from St-Raphaël-Valescure SNCF, or the train station at Boulouris.

PLAGE DU CAMP LONG

Dramont

A small, sand beach with a small, sandy restaurant. It's right around the corner from plage de Debarquement, where the Allies landed on the beaches of France in 1944. That beach is a little more crowded, though.

Either bus #8, which leaves from St-Raphaël-Valescure SNCF, or the train station at Dramont.

PLAGE D'AGAY

Agay

Large stretch of beach with swimming, restaurants, and on-duty life guards. Popular with local families.

Either bus #8, which leaves from St-Raphaël-Valescure SNCF, or the train station at Agay.

CALANQUE DE MAUBOIS

Le Trayas

Small bay with no beach, but large rocks for sunbathing. Recommended for strong swimmers, since there is no proper beach, lifeguard, or anything else to prevent you from getting hurt.

Train TER stop Le Trayas.

FOOD

CITIZEN PASTA BAR ❷

rue Vadon, right across from the train station ☎04 94 19 46 90 citizen.ctzn@live.fr

You'll want to perform your civic duty after visiting this godsend of cheap eating and drinking for budget travelers. Serves pasta and pizza in a youthful atmosphere. TVs, lime green chairs and a weird backwards logo advertise its quirky attitude. To top it all off, it's one of the few establishments in town with free Wi-Fi.

Pizza €7. Pasta €5. Beer €1.60. Open M-Sa 10am-3pm and 6-10pm.

LE GRILLARDIN PIZZERIA ❸

42 rue Thiers ☎04 94 17 11 41

Classy pizza joint that serves decent three-course *prix-fixe* menus or express lunches (pizza and coffee). Stone walls and wooden tables make you feel like you're in a cave.

Pizza €8-15. 3-course prix-fixe menu €14.50. Open M-Sa noon-3pm and 7-11pm.

LATIONS CAFE, ICE CREAM ❶

70 cours de Guilbaud

One of many ice cream shops in St-Raphaël with a line that stretches around the block, but the only one that serves unique flavors like Red Bull (in slushie form, too) and Bailey's. The free Wi-Fi and cheap crêpes complete the French budget traveler's three main food groups: ice cream, crêpes, and free internet.

2 scoops €3. Smoothies €2.50. Crêpes €3. Open M-Sa noon-10pm.

CRÊPERIE VIEUX PORT CRÊPERIE ❷

20 cours Guilbaud ☎04 94 19 44 88

Let this crêperie brighten your day with pretty (though synthetic) sunflowers on every table. Cool off with the signature ice cream crêpes. The outdoor seating is shaded by a giant, magical-looking tree; we suspect this is where the local elves churn the ice cream.

Salads €5-7. Crêpes €7-8. Open M-Sa noon-11pm.

CALDERON CHOCOLATIER ❶

89 pl. de la Mairie ☎04 94 83 68 08

Old, famous chocolaterie that specializes in macaroons and fruit-flavored chocolates, including flavors like orange or strawberry.

Macaroons €1. Chocolates €69 per kg. Open Tu-Sa 9am-12:30pm and 2:30-7pm, Su 9am-12:30pm.

HALLES RAPHAELOISE — OPEN MARKET ❶

rue Charles Hatral

Large open-air market for fruits and vegetables. Cheap and local.

Market prices. Open M-Th 6am-12:30pm and 3:30-7:30pm, F-Sa 6am-7:30pm, Su 6am-12:30pm.

CHEZ FRANK — PIZZA STAND ❷

311 av. Victor Hugo — ☎04 94 53 83 09 www.pizzerialacaleche.com

Cheap, fast, and reliable pizza in the more inland area of town. Frank's is one of the few places to serve pizza to-go and stays open exceptionally late. It's also open Sundays, which is a win for everyone.

Pizzas €6-11. Open daily 6-11pm.

NIGHTLIFE

ALBARIÑO — BAR, LOUNGE

105 bld. Gen. de Gaulle — ☎04 94 45 48 16

You'll think you're in the riotous medinas of Fez at this outrageous Morrocan and Spanish tapas bar, right across from the beach. Lounge on the bright red and orange carpets or the collection of low couches while indulging in chocolate fondue *(€9)* or, if you come on Tuesday's Zen soiree, a free massage.

Tapas €8-12. Fondue €9. Cocktails €8-10. Open June-Aug Tu-Su 8:30am-3am; Sept-May Tu-Su 8:30am-1am.

BLUE BAR — BAR

133 rue Jules Barbier — ☎04 94 95 48 16

A St-Raphaël institution, the large maritime *bar du nuit* specializes in blond beer, but serves beer from around the world, a selling point that they hammer home with the old world maps that paper the tables.

Beer €2.40, L of beer €9. Giraffes €24. Cocktails €7.50-8. Open daily June-Aug 7am-4am; Sept-Oct 7am-3am.

LOCH NESS BAR — PUB

15 av. Valescure — ☎04 94 95 49 49

Rugby jerseys, photos of hazy nights on the moors, and other Scottish paraphernalia cover the walls of this standard pub. Perfect for a laid-back night of aggressive drinking.

Beer €3-6. Giraffes €35. Cocktails €8. Open daily noon-2am.

LA FACTORY — CAFE, BAR

3 quai Albert 1er — ☎04 94 95 12 59

New York-themed, despite the misleading name. Relaxed outdoor seating allows for the usual people watching ops. A retractable canvas awning is used for shade.

Beer €3-5. Cocktails €7.50. Open Tu-Sa noon-1:30am.

ESSENTIALS

Practicalities

- **TOURIST OFFICE:** Located in the new port. Ignore signs that point to old tourist office. Free internet. *(99 quai Alber 1er ☎04 94 19 52 52 www.saint-raphael.com Open July-Aug daily 9am-7pm; Sept-June M-Sa 9am-12:30pm and 2-6:30pm.)*
- **BANKS:** Société Générale *(bld. Felix Martin ☎04 94 19 57 00 Open M-F 8:30am-noon and 1:45-5:30pm.)*
- **YOUTH CENTER:** Free condoms, job info, and resume counseling. *(21 pl. Gallienei ☎04 98 11 89 75 Open M-Th 8am-noon and 1:30-5pm, F 8am-noon and 1:30-4:30pm.)*
- **POST OFFICE:** av. Victor Hugo, behind station. *(☎04 94 19 52 00 Open M-F 8am-6:30pm, Sa 8am-noon.)*

- **POSTAL CODE:** 83700.

Emergency!

- **POLICE:** rue de Châteaudun *(☎04 94 95 24 24).*
- **PHARMACY:** 46 pl. Pierre Coullet. English spoken. *(☎04 94 95 04 05 Open daily 8:30am-7:30pm.)*

Getting There

St-Raphaël's **train station** is located at pl. de la Gare. *(Ticket booth open daily 6:30am-9pm.)* To **Cannes** *(€6.30. 25min., every 30min.),* **Marseille** *(€23. 2hr., 6 per day.),* **Nice** *(€12. 1hr., every 30min.)* **TER** also runs trains to Cannes that stop at Boulouris, Le Dramont, Agay, Antheor, and Le Trayas for beach access. **Buses** run from Navette to the **Nice Airport** *(☎04 94 76 02 29).* The bus service **Esterel Cars** run to to **Frejus** *(€1. 25min., every hr. 7:30am-6:40pm);* the bus service **Sodetrav** runs to **St-Tropez** *(€2. 1½hr., every hr. 6am-9pm);* and the bus service **Beltram** runs to **Cannes** via Trayas *(€7. 1 hr., 8 per day)* and to the airport in **Nice.** *(€22. 1 hr., 4 per day).* Buses run later Jul-Aug, but are infrequent during the year. Ferries depart from Les Bateaux de St-Raphaël to St-Tropez in the summer. *(☎04 94 95 17 46 €13, round-trip €22. 2 per day.)*

Getting Around

Again, tiny towns don't require (or provide) a lot of public transportation apart from walking. The old port pretty much has everything you could ever need within walking distance. To get to the further away beaches, use the **buses** at **Gare SNCF** *(#5 and 8, dir. Trayas. €1.),* rent a **scooter** *(Patrick Moto, 199 av. Gen Leclerc ☎04 94 53 65 99 €30 per day, €172 per week. Open M 9am-noon and 2:30-6pm, Tu 2:30-6pm, W-Sa 9am-noon and 2:30-6pm.),* or hire a **taxi** *(☎04 94 83 24 24).*

saint-tropez ☎04 94

St-Tropez is the excess capital of the world. You'd be stunned at the prices, if you weren't distracted by the beautiful yachts and beautiful people. Independent wealth thrives here, as evidenced by the numerous **boats** flying the flags of blacklisted tax havens. In a town where the tip to the dockmaster can run you as much as €5000, it can be hard to find deals. Apparently rich people just like spending money as a way to keep out the petty-folk. The real attractions here are the party beaches, which light up at night and continue until day break. Unfortunately, these parties are exclusive and hard to access without a yacht or some serious nighttime espionage. Beyond the money, St-Tropez is an incredibly beautiful town. Villas and small alleys make up the heart of the town, and it vaguely resembles a seaside village in Spain or Italy with its terra-cotta rooftops and colored tiles. It's easy to see why Hollywood and the mega wealthy fell in love with it, but that means making a serious dent in your wallet to enjoy it yourself.

ORIENTATION

Its wealth per square kilometer might outdo the Vatican, but St-Tropez is a very tiny town. Walking is the easiest way to get around here between the **old and new ports.** Unfortunately, the **beaches** are far away from the town center, requiring **shuttles** or a **scooter rental** (a good option for those who want freedom from tedious timetables) to get there. The most affordable restaurants, hotels, and shops are on the outskirts of town. The closer you are to the port or the quais, the higher the prices. From the **bus station** or **new port,** turn left and walk right into town. The **place des Lices** is the main square that is the most normal, local part of St-Tropez, with small stands for food, and banks and the market surrounding it. Most of the main roads lead to pl.

des Lices. To get to the beaches, either walk around the **citadel** past the cemetery on **chemin des Graniers,** or take the main road at the entrance of the town **(route des Plages)** where turning left at any intersection will take you to the beaches.

ACCOMMODATIONS

There are lots of places to stay in St-Tropez, so long as you have lots of money. The cheaper places are located in St. Maxime, the next town over, or just on the outskirts of St-Tropez. The hotels we listed are in the actual town, easy to get to, and under €100.

LE COLOMBIER — HOTEL ❺

impasse des Conquettes — ☎04 94 97 05 31

Beautiful, small hotel just on the edge of the old city. Small rooms, but a private breakfast available in the garden. Cheapest place in St-Tropez, but miraculously still very chic.

From the pl. des Lices (center of town), walk away from the citadel. Take the most left street (bld. Louis Blanc) from the sq. J. Moulin. Walk 1-2 blocks, turn left onto av. Paul Roussel. Turn left again onto impasse des Conquettes. Hotel is at the end of street. ***i*** *Cheapest rooms have no A/C and shared bath.* *Singles and doubles €63-110.*

LES PALMIERS — HOTEL ❺

24 bld. Vasserot — ☎04 94 97 01 61

Small, boutique hotel in the style of a Tropezienne villa. The orange walls and low, plastered ceilings make this affordable hotel even more attractive. Clean rooms and old-fashioned bar. The entry garden is overgrown, so it's an adventure just to find the reception. The villas overlook the garden.

From the pl. les Lices, walk away from the hill and rue joseph Quaranta on your slight right. Hotel is on your left. ***i*** *Breakfast €11.* *Singles and doubles €89-189.*

HOTEL MEDITERRANÉE — HOTEL ❺

21 bld. Louis-Blanc — ☎04 94 97 00 44

Old-school hotel with small singles and doubles and a 1940s vibe. The old Provençal-style wooden doors and furniture hint at the history of St-Tropez before Hollywood discovered it.

From the pl. Croix de Fer, head toward to the citadel, keeping to the right for 30m and then keeping to the left, onto bld. Louis-Blanc. Hotel is on your right. ***i*** *Last minute deals sometimes available in low season.* *Singles €82-101; doubles €102-144.*

FOOD

Food in St-Tropez is—surprise!—very expensive, especially for sit-down meals. There are some cheaper *prix-fixe* menus in the old city up near the Citadel, as well as closer to the new port (sailors gotta eat too). All over the pl. des Lices, you'll find cheap food options in the form of stands, and there is a local **Monoprix** (*Open daily 9am-6pm)* right as you walk into town from the new port.

CRÊPERIE BRETONNE — CRÊPERIE ❷

quai Frederic Mistral — ☎04 94 97 48 53

Authentic Breton crêperie that serves its own cider. Not your typical crêpes, though—these babies are crispy, folded halfway and left partially open, like they do it up north. Right on the port so you can feel like you're rich while you're dining on the patio. Old sailing paraphernalia cover the walls.

Crêpes €3.50-8. Cider €5. *Open daily noon-8pm.*

L'OLIVE — TRADITIONAL ❸

9 rue Aire du Chemin — ☎04 94 97 09 21

Finally, a three-course meal in St-Tropez that doesn't cost a fortune. Serves Provençal dishes near the citadel on a patio under a canopy of jasmine.

Prix-fixe 3-course meals €18. *Open M-Sa 7-10pm.*

LA TANNELLE PIZZERIA ❸
passage Gambetta ☎04 94 54 82 02
Rooftop pizzeria that has a view of the old port. The pizza is cheap, and the ivy growth on the patio provides ample shade. A warning though: the sign out front explicitly states that they don't accept €500 bills. Sorry, Richie Rich.
Pizza €11.50-13. Order for takeout €10. Open daily noon-9pm.

MIJO CRÊPES CRÊPERIE ❶
Marché Couvert, pl. des Lices
In the pl. des Lices, there's a covered market with permanent stands of cheap crêpes, which serve the cheapest and the sweetest in town.
Crêpes €2.50-5. Open daily July-Aug 9am-10:30pm; Sept-June 10am-7pm.

ROTISSERIE TROPEZIENNE CHICKEN ❶
Marché Couvert, pl. des Lices ☎04 94 54 85 04
Serves half or whole rotisserie chickens. A random Thai influence brings noodles and peanut sauce into the mix for some dishes.
Whole chicken €8.50, half €4.50. Thai chicken salad €3.50. Beer €2.50 Open July-Aug daily 10am-1:30pm and 5-9pm; Sept-June daily 10am-1:30pm and 5-7pm.

PAUSE-DOUCEUR CHOCOLATIER ❷
11 rue Allard ☎04 94 57 27 58
Searving Provençal syrup and *galettes* since the 1800s, this *chocolatier* is here to stay for a while, even if the owner decides to work whenever she wants, making the store's hours difficult to track. We suggest you stop by in the morning, when the proprietress is most likely to be there.
Chocolate €2-4. Galettes €5. Open M-Sa 9am-late (or whenever the owner wants).

LA FRÉGATE PIZZERIA ❸
52 rue Allard ☎04 94 97 07 08
Small pizzeria with a small patio, but the real attraction is the cozy air-conditioned dining room, with wooden chairs and tables under St-Tropez's traditional low ceilings. Serves 14 kinds of pizza.
Pizzas €10.50. Open daily noon-2:30pm and 5-10pm.

FRUITS N GO JUICE, CRÊPERIE ❶
22 rue Clemenceau
Juice and smoothie stand that also dabbles in crêpes, because everyone does. Prices of smoothies vary with market or in-season prices, but stay around €5-8 for almost a liter of smoothie.
Smoothies €5-8. Crêpes €2.50-3.50. Open daily 9:30am-7pm.

BARBARAC ICE CREAM ❶
2 rue Allard ☎04 94 97 67 83
Italian *gelateria* that makes its own ice cream. Elaborate decorations indicate the ice cream's flavor, such as coffee cup in one and Oreo cookies in another.
1 scoop €3, 2 scoops €4. Open 9:30am-midnight.

NIGHTLIFE

LE QUAI BAR
22 quai Jean Juares ☎04 94 97 04 07
Less pretentious lounge and bar that turns into a madhouse of packed bodies and pumping music. When the patrons start to climb onto the furniture, you're not sure if they are drunk or just trying to get out of the mosh pit. Expect absolutely debaucherous behavior.
Beer €5. Cocktails €13. Open Mar-Oct noon-4am.

CABANITO BAR

16 quai de l'Epi ☎05 14 12 28 60

Pound back shots underneath Che posters to the sounds of Cuban music and reggaeton. The super chill crowd gathers for Latin salsa, killer mojitos, and €4 beer. Soirees on Tuesday nights.

Beer €4. Cocktails €8. Open daily 5pm-3am.

KELLY'S IRISH PUB PUB

port du Saint Tropez ☎04 94 54 89 11

The only real laid-back bar in town. Unpretentious and unapologetic, Kelly's is the last stronghold of working locals and musicians that play classic American rock on the weekends. If barstools could talk...

Pints €6. Jagerbombs and shooters €6. Open daily midnight-3am.

PAPAGAYO CLUB

Résidence du Port ☎04 94 97 95 95

One of St-Tropez's most famous clubs, where bottles of booze cost more than your starting salary. If you can dress up and get past the bouncer, get ready for a packed house that vibrates with the bass, and keep your eyes out for what color a €500 bill is (hint: it matches the walls). Lounge seating by reservation only. If you forget, the large bouncer will remind you.

Cocktails €19. Open May-June F-Sa 12:30am-6am; July-Aug daily 12:30am-6am; Sept F-Sa 12:30am-6am.

MICASA SUSHI SUSHI, BAR

1 pl. Alphonse Celli ☎04 94 97 04 32

All-white interior sushi bar where everyone sits outside to enjoy the live rock music on the weekends. The older crowd jams and young crowd cases the lines at the exclusive clubs.

Beer €4. Cocktails €13. Open daily 6pm-2am (or later).

CHEZ MAGGIE BAR

7 rue Sibille ☎04 94 97 16 12

Clubby atmosphere without the stress of not getting in. Disco hits and '70s decor make this a popular location for soirees and a slightly older crowd.

Cocktails €12. Open daily 8:30pm-3am.

TSAR BAR

1 quai de l'Epi ☎06 11 95 76 43

Gay bar that is frequented by all genders and sexualities for the use of its hookahs. Pink, sparkly, and "fabulously" laid-back (think Claire's, only gay-er), this is the best place for a middle ground that's less than a club and more than a bar.

Beer €8. Cocktails €15. Hookah €20. Open daily 6pm-3am.

CHEZ LES GARÇONS GAY BAR

11-13 rue de Crepoun ☎04 94 43 68 70 www.chezlesgarcons.com

If the name didn't give it away, the small bar packed with older men will—this is one of the most popular gay bars in St-Tropez, and unlike the Tsar caters almost exclusively to gay men. Outside seating doubles the bar's size. Inside is a DJ and pink and blue arched ceiling.

Cocktails €12. Open June-Aug daily 7pm-3am, Sept-Dec Th-Su 7pm-3am; Feb-May Th-Su 7pm-3am.

CAFE DE PARIS LOUNGE, BAR

quai du Port ☎04 94 97 00 56 www.cafedeparis.com

Lavish interior reminds us of the Hall of Mirrors in Versailles, with chandeliers and mirrors everywhere. For the crowd that gets dressed, but is too busy anxiously looking at themselves to take the party to the next debaucherous step.

Cocktails €15-18. Open daily 8pm-1am (or later).

BAR DU PORT LOUNGE, BAR

quai Suffren ☎04 94 97 00 54

Modern lightshows meet white poofy outdoor lounge couches. This isn't a place that gets crazy, but it is a good option if you want to get your drink on outside. You might be denied entry if you aren't dressed well enough.

Cocktails €13. Open daily noon-2:30am.

SHOPPING

Real talk: shopping in St-Tropez is great. So is having a lot of money. Unfortunately, without a lot of money, there aren't any shopping options for you here. Really.

ESSENTIALS

Practicalities

- **TOURIST OFFICE:** On the corner of quai Jean Jaures and rue Victor Laugier. English spoken, free maps, and events guide. *(☎04 94 97 45 21 www.saint-tropez.st €1 bus schedules. Open daily June-Sept 9:30am-8pm; mid-Sept to early Oct 9:30am-12:30pm and 2-7pm; from mid-Oct to mid-Mar 9:30am-12:30pm and 2-6pm; late March-mid-June 9:30am-12:30pm and 2-7pm.)*
- **CURRENCY EXCHANGE: Societe Generale,** pl. des Lices. *(☎04 94 12 81 40 Open M-F 8:15am-12:15pm and 2-5:30pm, Sa 8:15am-12:25pm.)*
- **INTERNET: Kreatik Cafe.** *(19 av. Gen. Leclerc ☎04 94 97 40 61 www.kreatik.com €2 per 10min., €4 per 30min., €7 per hr. Open M-Sa 9:30am-noon, Su 2-10pm.)*
- **POST OFFICE:** pl. Alphonse Celli, between old and new ports. *(☎04 94 55 96 50 Open M-F 8:30am-noon and 2-5pm, Sa 8:30am-noon.)*
- **POSTAL CODE:** 83990.

Emergency!

- **POLICE MUNICIPAL:** av. Leclerc *(☎04 94 54 86 65).*
- **AMBULANCE:** ☎04 94 56 60 64.
- **PHARMACY: Pharmacie du Port.** *(9 quai Suffren ☎04 94 97 00 06 Open M-Sa 8:30am-8:30pm.)*

Getting There

St-Tropez is far from any train line, but there is a regular **ferry service** from **Les Bateaux de St-Raphaël** *(☎04 94 95 17 46 www.tmr-saintraphael.com 1-way €13, round-trip €23. 1hr.; twice daily at 9:30am and 2:30pm, return at 10:30am and 5:15pm.)* There is also a **bus ride** from the **St-Raphaël SNCF Gare** *(i Bus line #7601. €2. 1½hr., July-Aug arrivals every hr. 6am-8:15pm, return trips every hr. 6am-9pm; Sept-June arrivals every hr. 6am-8:15pm, return trips every hr. 6am-8:20pm.)*

Getting Around

This is a very easy city to walk. To get to the beaches, take the **shuttle service,** whose schedule you can pick up at the tourist office. You can also take a **taxi** *(☎04 94 97 05 27)*, or rent a **scooter.** *(Espace 83, across the street from Cafe Kreatik ☎04 94 55 80 00 Open M-Sa 9am-noon and 2-6pm.)*

marseille

We could call Marseille a "true immigrant city" with a "vibrant local culture," but we prefer to think of it as the Tijuana of France. A Tower of Babel, produced by the train-with-cut-brakes that is globalization, this (in)famous port town is the stomping ground of sailors, backpackers, mobs of immigrants, and (we suspect) unsavory characters involved in the import-export business. Expect color, chaos, and a lingering smell of trash. The city is most famous for its dense North African population, and parts of the city are more akin to Algiers or Fez than southern France. People from throughout the Mediterranean converge here to barter and argue loudly with each other in the downtown. Tourists generally observe them from behind the plastic windows of the dinky tour buses. Located in the center of Provence, Marseille is an ideal home base for visits to the *calanques* along the coasts, or to the Provençal cities of Avignon, Arles, or Cassis. This is not the prettiest town on the French Riviera, but it hosts the closest train station to the prettiest towns on the Riviera. Avoid certain neighborhoods, and schlep it to the sweet smell of lavender only an hour away.

ORIENTATION

Marseille is organized into three main districts. The area bounded by **rue Canebière** and the **calanques** to the East is **Vieux Port; Notre Dame de la Garde** is situated on its central hilltop. Up a few blocks and to the west is **Belsunce,** Marseille's immigrant quarter. Explore "Little" Algeria, Morocco, or Tunisia and people-watch from carpet shops and tea lounges. Just don't walk around there at night. The old quarter to the furthest West is **Le Panier,** where you'll find Marseille's oldest buildings and cramped 6ft.-wide alleys. The **quai du Port** is lined with expensive hotels, boutiques, and upscale seaside cafes.

Vieux Port

Bordered by Cours Julien to the east and the tourism office to the west, Vieux Port is where the bars, restaurants, shopping, and other vibrant parts of the city contain themselves. Crowned by **Notre Dame de la Garde** which overlooks its center, the neighborhood boasts the oldest *boulangerie* in Marseille, not to mention its most happening nightclubs. The port is hemmed by bars and cafes that turn into hotspots at night; upscale restaurants are situated further inland around **place aux Huiles.** Frustrated single men beware: at night in the Vieux Port, it can be particularly difficult to differentiate between clubs, bars, and strip clubs. The entrepreneurial young women beckoning you to come in at the door are a pretty good hint.

Le Panier

When the Greeks landed in Marseille 2,600 years ago, this is where they landed. Today, le Panier is the oldest and most cramped part of the city, though the area around La Vieille Charité might give it a run for its money. Mostly devoid of bars and clubs at night, this area is best to visit during the day, where the stores and the kooky cafes add charm to the winding narrow streets. At night, the same alleyways are shadowy and somewhat intimidating, since you might be the only one on them.

Belsunce

Little North Africa is bounded by **av. Belsunce** and the **Canebière**, and teems with little kebab stands and carpet stores; this is an ideal place to shop cheap, and perhaps stop in and enjoy a pastis with a group of old Algerian men. Once dark, the stores close, and the few bars in the area become packed with the city's local flair. Unless you're large, male, and handy in a knife fight, however, take the long way to the port and skip Belsunce at night.

ACCOMMODATIONS

Accommodations in Marseille range from the affordable to the absurd. Stick to Belsunce or on the city's outskirts for the cheapest hotels and hostels, or spend a little more at Vieux Port's quiet B and Bs and nicer, centrally located hotels. If you have money to burn, stroll over to Le Panier and quai du Port for some hotels that are as close to the marina as they are expensive. Unless you're splitting the cost of a terrace room, avoid the area if you're on a budget.

Vieux Port

BALAENA — HOTEL ❷

83 av. de la Pointe Rouge ☎06 68 42 21 22 www.hebergement-marseille.fr

Conveniently located next to the beach and attached to a wetsuit/dive shop, this spotless hostel remains happily unlisted on English sites because Celine, the owner, speaks no English. A must for those focused on outdoor activities such hiking the Calanques or diving/windsurfing/kiteboarding.

Ⓜ Metro line #2 to Castellene then take Bus #19 (dir. Madrogue de Montredon) to Tibulon. At the end of the alleyway. ***i*** *Wi-Fi, breakfast, and linens included.* Ⓢ *Shared rooms €22.50 per person; triples €81.*

AUBERGE DE JEUNESSE — HOSTEL ❶

impasse du Docteur Bonfils ☎04 91 17 63 30 www.fuaj.com

Far away from the city, but close to the beach. All the way out in the 8th arrondissement (something most FUAJ hostels have in common) the brightly colored, spacious reception welcomes you with a pool table and bar right as you walk in. Clean, but bare rooms. Organizes wind surfing (*€14 per person for a half day*) and kayaking half days on Saturday (€25) and full days on Su (€44).

Ⓜ Castellene. From there, take bus #44 to Clot Bey Leau. Walk in direction of bus to traffic circle and take a right onto av. Joseph Vidal. Pass the bike rental store and turn left onto impasse du Docteur Bonfils. Its at the end of the street. Look for Orange circle around blue triangle. ***i*** *FUAJ Card required. Bar, restaurant, Wi-Fi, kitchen, breakfast included.* Ⓢ *€19/night. Three nights maximum in summer.*

MONTGRAND — HOTEL ❺

50 rue Montgrand ☎04 91 00 35 20 www.hotel-montgrand-marseille.com

Clean and well-lit rooms with wide windows that let in lots of sunshine. Triples and quads available.

Ⓜ Estrangin, walk along rue Montgrand. Ⓢ *Singles €59-65; doubles €75; triples €85; quads €95.*

HOTEL RELAX — HOTEL ❹

4 rue Corneille ☎04 91 33 15 87 www.hotelrelax.fr

Boutique hotel that screams Belle Époque, but without the bankroll. Pink, upholstered, and slightly mismatched furniture is scattered throughout the reception. All rooms are doubles, so not the most affordable for the single traveler. Awesome location next to the Opera and many cafes. Book in advance in the summer.

Ⓜ Vieux Port. To the right of the Opera if facing colonnade. ***i*** *Parking available. Breakfast €7. Mini fridge and TV in each room.* Ⓢ *Rooms €60-65; triples €75.*

ST LOUIS — HOTEL ❺

2 rue des recolettes ☎04 91 54 02 74 www.hotel-st-louis.com

Quiet, easily accessible hotel near the Vieux Port. Tiled bathroom floor and comfy bed are welcomed amenities. Patio rooms overlook main Place as well as bright white dining room. Ask for student rate upon reservation.

Ⓜ Vieux Port ***i*** *Renovated in 2007. Breakfast €8.* Ⓢ *Singles €67; doubles €72; triples €90. Reduced prices in winter.*

Le Panier

The hotels in this area are freakishly expensive. A few of the better finds on the water sport exceptional views and will only cost you your right arm (unless you're left handed, in which case they will ask for that). For any of the other ones, come back when you've made it in life.

HOTEL HERMES HOTEL ❹

2 rue Bonneterie ☎04 96 11 63 63 www.hotelmarseille.com/hermes

Location, location, location. Hotel Hermes is right on the quai du Port, and next to an innocuous hotel that charges €180 per night. In light of these factors, the prices aren't that bad at this Greek-themed hotel with terrace rooms. While the rooms are reminiscent of a porno shot in a Motel 6 back in 1970's Miami (think pink sheets, loudly patterned carpets, and lingering smell of smoke in the halls), the proximity to cafes and the port more than make up for it.

Ⓜ Vieux Port. i TV, A/C, newly renovated. Breakfast €8. Ⓢ Singles €50; triples with terrace €90. We reccommend springing for the terrace.

Belsunce

LE VERTIGO HOSTEL ❷

42 rue des Petites Maries ☎04 91 91 07 11 www.hotelvertigo.com

Right next to the train station. Funky flea market finds decorate the walls and comprise the furniture at this dedicated, youthful hostel. The outside patio explodes with reds and blues and yellows, mimicking the festive streets of Marseille. Clean, cozy shared kitchen is a welcoming haven in this English-speakng, laid-back establishment.

From the train station, walk down the Grand Staircase onto bld. d'Athènes. Take the first right. Rue des Petites Maries will be on the left, hostel is 20 yards down on the left. i Wi-Fi, shared kitchen, 24hr reception, bar open til midnight. Ⓢ 2-6 person dorms €23.90; doubles €55-65.

HOTEL DU PETIT PARIS HOTEL ❷

33 rue Tapis Vert ☎04 91 90 89 94 www.hotelpetitparismarseille.com

Stay here when you want to stay someplace quality and close to the train station and Le Vertigo is fully booked, as Petit doesn't fill up as quickly. Not to be confused with the luxury Parisan hotel. Good for splitting a double or triple.

Ⓜ St-Charles Gare. Walk down stairs onto bld. d'Athènes for 5-6 blocks (depending on your defnition of a block) Make a right on rue Tapis Vert. Ⓢ Singles €40; doubles €50.

SIGHTS

Most of the must-see sights here are located in the Vieux Port of the city, which hosts **Notre Dame de la Garde** and the **Abbaye St.Vincent**. The museums are decent, and will hypnotize aficionados of 20th-century Cubism, Fauvism or any of those other "-isms" you studied in art school. If you are less than intellectually inclined (you are on vacation, after all), we recommend that you spend most of your time getting out of the city to see **Île d'If** or the **calanques**. **Le Panier** has the one of the oldest orphanages in France, which also served as a baroque church and now is a museum for Marseille's ancient history. To experience 1,000 years of North African culture in the Med, explore **Belsunce,** which is a sight and smell of its own.

Vieux Port

NOTRE DAME DE LA GARDE

Top of the hill ☎04 91 13 40 80

You simply won't get a better view of the city than this. As awesome as it is windy, this is where shipwreck survivors went to thank God, and it's where you will too, provided you survive the walk up (take the #60 bus instead). Towering over the Basilica is an 11.2m-tall golden Madonna and Child, which weighs just shy of 10,000 kilos. Services are still held in the crypt of the church, a tradition that's probably a holdover from the days when the Nazis were shooting at the basilica; you can still see the bullet holes in the east wall.

Take bus #60 from Vieux Port all the way to the end. Free. Open daily 7am-7:30pm.

MUSÉE CANTINI

19 rue Grignan ☎04 91 54 77 75 www.marseille.fr

Housed in a chic warehouse, this museum hosts a permanent collection of Picasso, Cezanne, and Dubuffet paintings. Focuses on Surrealist, Fauvist, and Cubist movements of the last century. The museum is currently undergoing renovations and is expected to be completed in 2013. The new and improved museum is expected to house French artists from all over the country as well as Europe (France is scheduled to be the EU's culture capital in that year).

ⓂPrefecture. €2.50 entrance fee. Under 10 free. Open daily 10am-5pm. Jul-Oct open til 7pm.

CHÂTEAU D'IF

quai des Belges ☎04 91 59 02 30

The legendary home to the **Man in the Iron Mask** and **Count of Monte Cristo**, this island fortress turned prison is less exciting than Alcatraz, but more exciting than just any rock in the middle of the harbor. Forget about the cool, fictitious noble prisoners, though since you were more likely to find Huguenot leaders jailed here during the religious purges of the 1600s. While it's an equally horrific story, somehow it just doesn't have the same ring to it.

ⓂVieux Port. Quai des Belges. Boat tickets €15, students €10. Château entrance €5. Studnets free. Open 9:30am-6:15pm, as a function of the last operating boats to the island.

ABBAYE ST-VICTOR

3 rue de l'Abbaye ☎04 96 11 22 60

An early Christian burial site for saints, the history of the Abbaye St-Victor is (naturally) characterized by power struggles, mob violence, and other things Jesus would totally do. The abbey was originally fortified against pagan invaders, and successfully repelled the barbarian hordes until part of it was destroyed and looted by **disgruntled** plebeians during the French Revolution. Though Napoleon attempted to restore the Abbey upon taking leadership, many of its treasures had been mysteriously misplaced. In their infinite respect for the dead that are buried here, the Christian faithful have more recently dug up the deceased saints and put their bones on display for tourists in the museum. Hallelujah. The Church also hosts a crypt that is way cooler than **Notre Dame de la Garde,** though you do have to pay for added awesomeness.

At the end of rue Sainte. i Serves F-Su. Free. Crypt entrance is €2. Open daily fro 7am-7pm. Will be closed until February 2011.

Le Panier

VIEILLE CHARITÉ

2 rue de la Charité ☎04 91 14 58 80 www.vieille-charite-marseille.org

The Vieille Charité was originally intended to be a tolerant place of worship for the homeless, but they tended to crowd the entrances and make church awkward for the other parishioners. The men and women of the cloth delicately transformed the church into an orphanage, perhaps in an effort to service more lovable charity cases. A wooden plank was strategically placed in front of certain windows so that the nuns couldn't see the local Mother or Father of The Year dropping their kid off in front of the Church. Today, the building hosts the **Baroque Chapel** and the **Musée des Arts Africains, Océaniens, et Amérindiens,** as well as the **Musée dArchéologie Méditerranée,** where you can peruse local ancient history from before and after Roman times.

Permanent exhibits €3, students €1.50. French university students (even exchange students)

and children under 12 free. Temporary exhibits €4, students €2.50 for students. ⏰ *Tu-Sa noon-7pm.*

Belsunce

MUSÉE DE LA MODE — MUSEUM

11 La Canebière ☎04 96 17 06 00 www.espacemodemediterranee.com

The ultimate window shopper's dream, this museum houses a history of clothing from the 1940s to the present, and boasts 6,000 garments. Lady Gaga's Kermit the Frog dress is sadly omitted. Closed until further notice in preparation for 2013.

ⓂVieux Port, walk up three block, on your left. *€2 entrance, students free.* ⏰ *Oct-May 10am-5pm, Jun-Sep 11am-6pm.*

LA CANEBIÈRE — MARKET

La Canebière

If you were expecting an open market with the local medicinal hash, we hate to disappoint: "la canabière" is a false cognate. Deriving its name from the Provençal for "hemp," this bustling shopping street is named after Marseille's historic ropemakers and sailors. Look for the really long street that separates Vieux Port from Belsunce.

ⓂVieux Port. Turn around and walk up.

THE GREAT OUTDOORS

Beaches

LA PLAGE POINTE ROUGE

Popular with local windsurfers and kite-boarders, and an oasis for SCUBA divers. Small but awesome windbreak, protected by a jetti.

#19 bus to Toulon.

PRADO PARC

When residents complained about not having easy access to local beaches, this park was created to provide both a community hangout and a buffer between more relaxed tanning beaches and the main road. Packed with both tourists and locals in summer, the park is pretty big, and is conveniently broken up into 4 smaller beaches: Benneveine, Borely, Roucas Blanc, and Vieille Chapele.

Either the #19 bus of #83 to La Plage bus stop.

Hiking

SORMIOU CALANQUE

One of the easiest and most breathtaking of the *calanques*, this trail leads down to a small cove where its just too pretty to not swim, even if it means donning your underwear or birthday suit to enjoy it.

Take the #23 bus to the end of the line, and follow the signs for Sormiou down a hike that is all downhill, and takes 25 min.

LUMINY CALANQUE

The *calanque* to the East of Sormiou, and equally pretty. Windy trail for 30min downhill to the water's edge where cliff jumpers are seen jumping from the high ledges into the lagoon.

End of bus #23, follow signs for Luminy.

CALLELONGE

☎08 11 20 13 13

Why go around the mountain when you can go over it? Hike across the peninsula from the end of the #19 bus (dir. Madrague de Montredon) up 432m to the port city of Callelongue (*1 ½hr. hike*).The path is paved with limestone, yields glorious views, and can be dangerous when windy; stick to the trail and follow the yellow brick road (read: stick to the yellow and black markers which mark the local trails, as opposed to bivouacking through any roads less traveled by). Be sure to pay attention to the trails' color-coding, since this trailhead is also the beginning of the 28km trail to Cassis. Optional detour to the summit of Marseilleveyre (*1.5hr.*).

Take #19 bus (dir. Madrogue de Montredon) all the way to the end from the Castellene Metro stop. **i** *Be sure to call about wind safety and closures regarding all of the calanques automated, multi-lingual. Black means closed, red means open 6-11am and green means open all day.*

MARSEILLE TO CASSIS

The adrenaline junkie's dream starts at the end of the #19 bus (dir. Madrague de Montredon). Follow the road up 100 ft. to the trailhead on the left. This "hike" is actually a 28km trek to the nearby town Cassis. Not recommended for beginners or whiners, the rocky trail winds up and over Marseilleveyre and into the small port town. Bring proper supplies and gear (read: water)—it's a long hike through dry areas.

Take #19 bus (dir. Madrogue de Montredon) all the way to the end from the Castellene Metro stop.

hollywood

They may look peaceful to you, but these oceanside promenades and narrow streets are the stomping grounds of spies, pirates, drug lords, international intrigue, and plain old-fashioned revenge (well, at least on the silver screen.)

- ***THE COUNT OF MONTE CRISTO.*** Edmond Dantès escaped Château d'If, the island prison off the coast of Marseilles, by dressing himself in his dead friend's burial shroud. (Ew.) Over 3500 Huguenots and scores of real-life political detainees found this feared fort-turned-prison escape-proof, but not so with our friend the Count. The prison is open today and frequented by tourists.
- ***THE FRENCH CONNECTION.*** Sit in a seaside cafe and await your shipment of smuggled heroin from Turkey. (*Let's Go* does not recommend smuggling drugs, because Doyle *will* find you. And he will shoot.) What most people don't know is that the ring leader, Paul Corbone, also smuggled Parmigiano-Reggiano cheese between Italy and France. But whether you're carrying illegal drugs or just illegal dairy products, you'll need to take a break and take in the harbor.
- ***THE BOURNE IDENTITY.*** If you manage not to fall off the ferry to Corsica, you will officially be more coordinated than Jason Bourne. No, seriously. He takes a spill off the ferry in the opening scene of the movie (two gunshot wounds may have had something to do with the fall, but *Let's Go* doesn't believe in excuses).

FOOD

Vieux Port

LE SUD DE HAUT — AFRICAN, HAITIAN ❸

80 cours Julien — ☎04 91 33 75 33

This hippie African/Haitian restaurant specializes in French attitude and American cinema, and is more than willing to provide a little kitsch whenever needed. Few other places offer sit down service with dessert for €10. The walls are painted in bright African colors and papered with American movie and music posters. Oddly enough, the Declaration of Independence too; we've just become more of a fan. The dessert is especially awesome—check out the chocolate covered fried banana.

ⓂNotre Dame-Cour Julien. Ⓢ €10.50 lunch menu with plat du jour and dessert du jour. Make it a three course for €16. Plats €11-16. Cocktails €7. Open T-Sa noon-2:30pm, 7-10:30pm.

AU FALAFEL — FALAFEL, SHAWARMA ❶

5 rue Lulli — ☎04 91 54 08 55

Kickass Israeli falafel and shawarma joint. The hummus is homemade, and the falafels are assembled in-house and served hot. The framed pictures of local graffiti art that line the walls are a particular treat, but we nonetheless recommend that you sit outside; the fryer is situated right by the entrance, and the place can get pretty hot. Take-out available.

ⓂVieux Port. Ⓢ €4.50 Falafel, Chicken curry and dishes €6. Open M-Th noon-midnight, F noon-4pm, Su noon-midnight.

FOUR DES NAVETTES — BOULANGERIE ❶

136 rue Sainte — ☎04 91 33 65 69 www.fourdesnavettes.com

Founded in 1781, the oldest *boulangerie* in Marseille is famous for its secret recipe of a lemony, hard biscuit that every February 2, the abbey of St-Victor blesses as they first come out of the oven at 6am. Almond cakes and other biscuits fill the air with aromas of marzipan and glazed sugar.

Down the street from the Abbaye St-Victor. Ⓢ 1 Navette €0.75, for a dozen €8. Open M-Sa 7am-8pm, Su 9am-1pm and 3-7:30pm. Aug daily 9am-1pm and 3-7:30pm.

CAFE LULLI — CAFE ❷

26 rue Lulli — ☎04 91 54 11 17 lecafelulli.over-blog.com

The tea jars stacked high behind the register demonstrate the number of available options at this tea cafe. As far as food goes, try the quiche and salad lunch combo (*€7.50*) or splurge on the dessert maison (*€2-6*).

ⓂVieux Port, near the Opera. Ⓢ Open Lunch menu from €7.50-11.

EATING — TRADITIONAL ❷

40 rue Montgrand — ☎04 91 33 76 88 www.ilove-eating.fr

Eating gets straight to the point. The ideal place to pick up a hefty picnic lunch before hitting the beach, the menu changes with the seasons, and the prices remain remarkably reasonable (*salad, cheese dish and wine; €7.80*). A large framed picture from Paris in the '20s takes you back to when people actually went on picnics.

ⓂVieux Port. Ⓢ Seasonal lunch menu €7.80. Bakery items €.50-3. Open M-F 8am-4pm.

LA KAHENA — NORTH AFRICAN ❸

2 rue de la République — ☎04 91 90 61 93

Tunisian restaurant which serves heaping bowls of couscous in hand painted blue plates. Map of Tunisia and mosaics of camels kick the kitsch up a notch to an almost annoying level.

ⓂVieux Port. Ⓢ Entres €5-6 while couscous plates will set you back €10-16. Open daily noon-2:30pm and 7:30-10:30pm.

Le Panier

CHEZ MANON — TRADITIONAL ❷

2 rue Rodillat — ☎06 21 42 30 91

This small cafe may only have 3 tables, but the light blue walls with yellow stripes are oddly soothing, and the proprietress Nacira is a sweetheart who goes out of her way to take care of you. Whether looking for a sandwich (*€3.50-4.50*) or a more substantial penne dish with salmon, or a combo of three French cheeses (*€9-12*), this is the perfect escape from the busy *quai du port*.

Ⓢ *Tucked away in plain sight 100m from the Vieille Charité.* ⏰ *Open daily 10:30am-6pm.*

LE SOUK NORTH AFRICAN ❸

100 quai du Port ☎04 91 91 29 29 www.restaurantlesouk.com

Tall people watch out in this low-ceiling-ed (we're talking 6' here) restaurant, which serves Maghreb style tea, *tahini*, and couscous. Tables are accompanied by small cushions in lieu of seats, and dishes served in traditional pottery from across the Med. Choose from wines from Morocco, Algeria, or France to accompany your menu du jour (€13.50).

Ⓢ *Plates from €8-25. Menu du jour offers plat du jour and dessert du jour or entree du jour and plat du jour.* ⏰ *Open Tu-Su noon-2:30 and 7:30-10:30pm.*

CHEZ MADIE LES GALENETTES PROVENÇAL ❸

138 quai du Port ☎04 91 90 40 87

A provençal cafe specializing in traditional Marseillaise cuisine, located in Marseille? Blasphemy! Not only that, but the beach theme trend applies here as well. Located right on the harbor, the fish tastes fresher and the tourists are louder. Splurge here for dinner when it's not as crowded on the boardwalk.

Ⓢ *Three course menu featuring local fish and lamb chops €25. Desserts €6.* ⏰ *Open M-Sa noon-2pm, 8-11pm.*

LE WICH ❶

passage Pentécontore, in between quai du Port and rue de la Loge.

A one window panini and crêpes shop identifiable by the light pink and green storefront and the long line that winds to the other end of the alley. The fare here is sweet and wicked cheap, and features sweet paninis that are rare in a world of grilled ham and cheese (*nutella and banana panini; €4*).

Ⓢ *Paninis and sandwiches from €3-5.* ⏰ *Open daily 10am-5:30pm.*

MIRAMAR PROVENÇAL ❺

12 quai du Port ☎04 91 91 10 40 www.bouillabaisse.com

If food is more important to you than housing, splurge here for over-the-top fish and lobster dishes and more over-the-top service. Named one of France's gourmet restaurants of the year in 2009, Miramar has sure taken pains to keep up its reputation; the outside seating is covered and enclosed, to keep out noise and riff-raff like yourself. Right on the water, reserve a table well in advance, preferably with someone else paying for you. This may well be the best meal you'll have in Southern France.

Ⓢ *Dishes between €25-44. Daily fish specials.* ⏰ *Open T-Sa noon-2pm, 7-10pm.*

Belsunce

MARCHÉ PROVENÇAL MARKET ❶

7 rue Vacon ☎04 91 54 44 87

Belsunce may well host a largely North African population, but we've noticed that there's plenty of cross-over between French and North African culture—and that most of these commonalities have to do with food. This open air fruit and vegetable market is the heart of Belsunce, and specializes in seasonal fruits from both sides of the Med. Incredibly, given the its size, the market is run by a single local Algerian family.

Ⓢ *Market prices.* ⏰ *Open daily 8am-8pm.*

ARABESQUE NORTH AFRICAN ❶

20A rue d'Aix ☎04 91 91 96 75

Algerian bakery and tea salon on a main, well-populated street in Belsunce. The neighborhood favorite boasts an array of finely decorated sweets covered in various amounts of caramelized sugar *(€1-3)*. A lunch menu comprised of your standard couscous and kebabs is also available *(€7)*. Try it with the mint tea, which is brewed with real mint leaves.

Bakery items €1-3. Lunch kebab or couscous €6.70. Open daily 6am-8pm, lunch from 12-3pm. Tea salon open after 3pm.

NIGHTLIFE

Most of the bars and clubs here are located in Vieux Port. The more artsy (read: kooky) watering holes are in the area around cours Julien, while the more hopping, and more expensive hotspots can be easily spotted along the port. Le Panier is devoid of bars, since it's devoid of people at night anyway. Belsunce is where you go when you want to get lost at night and quickly regret doing so.

Vieux Port

PETIT NICE — BAR

28 pl. Jean Jaurès

The giant covered patio seating dominates this local fixture of the Cours Julian neighborhood, and is almost three times the size of the bar itself. The inside is decorated with a seemingly random assortment of ropes, hats, Nice posters, and life rings that adhere to the restaurant's general Nice theme (we guess).

ⓂCours Julien. Half pints €2. Pints €4. Rum and cocktails €3.50. Open Tu-Th 11am-2am, F-Sa 8am-2am.

SHAMROCK — IRISH PUB

17 quai de Rive Neuve

A tried and true Irish bar where the city's students and youth hostel workers can always depend on to be open. In true **shamrock** fashion, the Shamrock encourages patrons to drink above and beyond the legal limit—on Mondays, all pints are half-off all night. Soccer and rugby scarves cover the walls.

i Happy hour Tu-Su 6-8pm. Pints €5.50-6. Open daily 4pm-2am.

DAN RACING — BAR

17 rue Andre Poggioli ☎06 09 17 04 07 www.dan-racing.tk

This Harley-themed bar is about as loose and fast as its owner, who never listens to a band before letting them play on stage. More often than not, this tolerant system of letting anyone play only adds to Dan Racing's fly-by-the-seat-of-your-pants vibe, but it occasionally results in the hiring of slasher headbanging groups who sound like some cross between Jacques Cousteau and Iron Maiden.

ⓂCours Julien. Free entry. Beer €2.50. Open F-Sa 6:30pm-2am.

EXIT CAFE — BAR

12 quai de Rive Nueve ☎04 91 54 29 43

The Euro-trashy Exit Cafe mixes loud electronic music with bright neon lights for a local clientele. Patrons are generally slicked-back-hair types who unbutton their shirts to their mid chest, so the inside is a bit to much to handle. The outside seating area is the perfect place to enjoy their 2 for 1 drinks deal at their generous happy hour.

Beer €5-6. Cocktails €8. 2 for 1 happy hours (5pm-10pm) Open Tu-Sa noon-2am.

TROLLEYBUS — CLUB

24 quai de Rive-Neuve ☎06 72 36 91 10 www.letrolley.com

One of the few clubs in Vieux Port that's not a strip club, this Trolleybus features different kinds of rock, electronica, and world beat in each of their three rooms. Whoever's in charge of the lights here should definitely get a pay raise: when this research-writer visited, a rock concert was projected onto the wall in the first room, fast-paced strobe light pulsed in another, and some moodier, groovier lighting was dappling the third.

€10, free drink with entry. Open Jul-Aug W-Sa 11pm-6am, Sep-Jun Th-Sa 11pm-6am.

BARBAROUSSE

CLUB

7 rue Glandèves ☎04 91 33 78 13 marseille.barberousse.com

The Marseille branch of this three-club chain is the original, and the pirate theme makes much more sense at this port city. A shooters bar of flavored rum and vodka, Barbarousse usually has a line out the door to get in, so arrive early, and preferably with a group of attractive females to get past the bouncers.

i No cover, just one mean line. Happy hour 7-10pm. Shooters €2, bottles for €23. Open Tu-Sa 6pm-2am.

LA POSTE A LA GALENE

CLUB, CONCERT VENU

103 rue Ferrari ☎04 91 42 16 33 www.lapostealagalene.com

This club/concert venue is a little out of the way and can charge steep covers, so check their website to see who's playing before heading out. Big open area on two floors and beer bar with large stage. Hosts local bands, DJs, and international groups. Themed nights vary from mask to '80s Nights.

Off of pl. Juan Juares. €1 membership required. Cover €5-18. Beer half-pint €3 full-pint €5. Open Tu-Sa 8pm-1am (concert nights start at 9, club nights start at 10:30pm). Closed from Jul-20-Sept 2.

Le Panier

BAR 13 COINS

BAR

pl. 13 Coins

Identifiable by its dark red exterior and the loud portraits of people painted in bright African yellows, greens, and reds along the walls, this chill bar is ideal for an early start in the afternoon or the first drink of the night. Posters advertising African and Maghreb music concerts paper the doors and windows. While the beer here is not the cheapest, the groovy vibe makes the place more than worth it.

Beer €3-4.50. Cocktails €5. Open daily 8am-midnight (or later depending on the scene).

ARTS AND CULTURE

Festivals

FESTIVAL DE MARSEILLE

SUMMER

Going strong since 1996, this ginormous music, dance, and movie festival features everything from ballet performances to special screenings to rock concerts. The festival is technically a celebration of Marseille's illustrious history, but appears to be more of an excuse for a two-month party. The festivities start in Le Panier and gradually move east across the city.

Prices vary according to event. June and July. Check out 6 place Sadi Carnot, or www.festivaldemarseille.com for specific information on times.

FÊTE DE LA MÉDITERRANEÉ

SPRING

pl. Bargemon (Hôtel de Ville) www.lafetedelamediterranee

Features music from France, le Maghreb and throughout the Mediterranean.

Free. Early May.

ESSENTIALS

Marseille is essentially an immigrant town, so if the local resources seem to be overwhelmingly intended for a North African/Arab population, that's because they are. Never fear! There is help for tourists here!

Practicalities

- **TOURIST OFFICE:** Free maps and accommodations bookings. Marseille City Pass includes RTM day pass, access to 14 museums, a walking tour, ferry to Île d'If and varying discounts for city music festivals and events *(4 La Canebière ☎04 91 13 89*

00 www.marseille-tourisme.com Vieux Port City Pass 1 day, €22; 2 day €29 Open M-Sa 9am-7pm, Su 10am-5pm.) Annex (*At train station* *04 91 50 59 18 Open M-F 10am-12:30pm, 1-5pm)*

- **TOURS:** Tourist office offers walking tours of the city in French daily (*One tour in English per week; ask for schedule*). **Petit Train:** Almost always full of families and tourist groups, this Disneyland-esque trolley takes tourists around the major sights of the city (*04 91 25 24 69* ***i*** Departs on 3 different tracks: Notre-Dame de la Garde basilica, Old Marseille, and Frioul archipelago. *From quai Belges every 30min.; from Port Frioul to the Saint Estève for the archipelago. The first two routes run Apr-Nov 10am-12:20pm and 2-6pm; the one to the archipelago runs Jul-Aug 10am-12:20pm and 2-6pm. €7/4 for children, €6/3 for children and the one to the archipelago runs Jul-Aug (€3.5/2.5 for children.)*
- **CONSULATES: UK** *(24 av. du Prado 04 93 15 72 10 Open M-F 9:30am-noon and 2-4:30pm by appointment only).* **US** (12 pl. Varian Fry *04 91 54 92 00 Open M-F 9:30am-noon and 2-4:30pm by appointment only).*
- **LOST PROPERTY:** Although it's probably already been resold or put on a ship to Algeria. Good luck. *(41 bld. de Briançon 04 91 14 68 97.)*
- **YOUTH CENTER:** Centre Régional Information Jeunesse (CRIJ) Information on long term housing, short term employment, vacation planning (once you get that job) and services for the disabled. *(96 La Canebière 04 91 24 33 50 www.crij.com Noailles Open M 10am-5pm, Tu 1-5pm, W-F 10am-5pm. Limited hours July and Aug.)*
- **GLBT RESOURCES:** *(www.gay-sejour.com)*
- **LAUNDROMATS:** Most hostels have laundry services, even if it's not listed; just ask. *(8 rue Rudolf Pollack. Open daily 9am-7pm.)*
- **INTERNET ACCESS:** Free internet at the CRIJ. There are also many internet cafes scattered around Belsunce and the Vieux Port. Look for the North African flags in the windows– they advertise that international calls can be made from that cafe.
- **POST OFFICE:** *(1 pl. Hôtel des Postes. Take La Canebière toward the sea and turn right on rue Reine Elisabeth as it becomes Hôtel des Postes. 04 91 15 47 00* ***i*** *Currency exchange available. Open M-W 8am-6:45pm, Th 9am-6:45pm, F 8am-6:45pm, Sa 8am-12:15pm. Branch at St-Charles as well scattered liberally around the city. Postal Code 13001.)*

Emergency!

- **SOS VOYAGEURS:** *(Gare St. Charles 04 91 62 12 80.)*
- **POLICE:** *(2 rue du Antoine Becker Branch at train station next to Platform A. 04 91 39 80 00).*
- **PHARMACY:** *(7 rue de la République 04 91 90 32 27* ***i*** *English and French spoken. Open daily 8:30am-7pm.)*
- **HOSPITAL:** Hôpital Timone, (264 rue St-Pierre Timone.*04 91 38 00 00).*

Getting There

By Plane: Aéroport Marseille-Provence *(04 42 14 14 14 www.mrsairport.com).* It's a popular destination, so many carriers offer service to Marseille (*airport code MRS*). Air France offers flights from Paris. Ryan Air also has service to London Airports and to various offshoots of main airports throughout Europe. Shuttles (*08 91 02 40 25 €.30 per min*) run every 20 minutes between the airport and Gare St-Charles (*€8 25min.*).

By Train: Gare St-Charles is the hub of the city, with frequent trains within France. International trains go through Paris (stations differing by ultimate destination). Trains to **Lyon** (*1 hr. 20 per day €58*), **Nice** (*2 hr. 20 per day €32*) and **Paris** (*3 hr., 15 per day €105*). For up-to-date, accurate fare information go to www.sncf.com. For those of you under 25, you can get a TER pass for €15, valid one year, and get a 50% discount on regional travel in Provence-Alps-Côte d'Azur (PACA), or anywhere else for that matter. Trust us, you don't want the TER from Marseille to Paris—its a long haul.

By Bus: pl. Victor Hugo, behind train station (*08 91 02 40 25. Gare St-Charles. Ticket counters open M-F 6:15am-7:30pm, Sa 6:30am-6:30pm, Su 7:45am-noon, 12:45-6pm.*) Depending on location, you can buy tickets on board the bus (i.e. the closer the destination, the more likely) but we recommend buying tickets at the window and follow ticket-window-guy's advice. To **Aix-en-Provence** (*every 10-15 min 6:30am-8:30pm, two per hour 9-11:30pm €5.50*), **Nice** (*2hr, 1 per day €28, students €19*), and **Cannes** (*2-3 hr. 4 per day €25, students €19*).

By Ferry: SNCM (*61 bld. des Dames 08 25 88 80 88 Open M-Sa 8:30am-8pm. Office open M-F 8am-6pm, Sa 8:30am-noon and 2-5:30pm*) **Corsica Ferries** (*7 rue Beauvau 08 25 09 50 95 www.corsicaferries.com Open daily 8am-8pm. To Corsica: €32-65; Algeria €105-315; Sardinia €60-85*)

By Taxi: Expensive, but if you must... **Marseille Taxi** (*04 91 02 20 20*). **Taxi Blanc Bleu** (*04 94 51 50 00*). 24 hr stands surround the Gare St-Charles and Vieux Port. To Vieux Port from Gare St-Charles €20-30. To airport €40-55.

By Car: Stand at the Gare St-Charles. **Avis** (*04 91 64 71 00 www.avis.fr i 21+ only. Under 25 surcharge €25 per day Open M-F 6:30am-10:30pm, Sa 7am-8pm.*)

Getting Around

Public transport is easily navigable here, with only two Metro lines, and two trams covering Belsunce and Vieux Port. Le Panier is only accessible by foot (which adds to the charm, we guess) but buses run along its perimeter. Bus passes can be bought for one journey *(€1.50)*, three days *(€10.50)* or 7 days *(€16)*. Solo passes can be bought on the buses, and are good for MetroTram or the bus for one hour after they are first validated. All public transport runs frequently Su-W 6am-11:30, Th-Sa 6am-1am. There are Le Vélo bike stands, but they only work with European bank cards, and require a €150 deposit on your credit card. If you do have a European bank card, though it's a screaming deal at €1 an hour (under 30min free, like in Paris). Buses that you'll care about leave from Gare St-Charles and from Castellene, as well as from Vieux Port. Around the Marina though, walking is your fastest and easiest option.

SPAIN

BARCELONA

Ask any local and they'll readily tell you—Catalonia is not Spain. As the fiesty gem and bubbling metropolis of the area, Barcelona fervently defends its region's status as a nation despite cries from the rest of Spain, and the resurgence of Catalan language (a mix of French and Castilian), culture, and pride after its violent repression by Franco sets it a world apart from its *castellano*-speaking countrymen. Don't worry, though; Spanish in a general sense is still spoken across the area, and even those whose Spanish doesn't extend beyond *cerveza* will find it relatively easy to be understood.

You don't need to sip from the famed fountain of **Canaletes** to fall forever in love with the city. Nestled in between the Montserrat mountains, Mediterranean waves, and the Rivers Bésos and Llobregat, the city offers a bit of the best of everything—incredible parks dotted by surreal architecture, mindblowing (and sleep-depriving) nightlife, mouthwatering tapas, quirky nooks and crannies, and culture oozing from every pore. And, if somehow the promise of **Gaudí 's architecture,** incredible museums, quirky bars, raging clubs, human towers, views from mountaintops, and free music galore wasn't enough, there's always the **beach.**

greatest hits

- **CAVA WITH A VIEW.** Grab a glass of the bubbly stuff while soaking in the view from Mirablau (p. 261).
- **CITY AT YOUR FEET.** Climb up the Columbus Monument (p. 209) at the end of Las Ramblas and gaze out over the entirety of Barcelona.
- **ART IS FOR LOVERS.** Stroll with your sweetheart along the *Manzana de la Discordia* (p. 219) and through the sculpture garden at the Fundació Miró (p. 222).

(art) student life

It doesn't matter if you're not a student of art history; everyone should learn about Antoni Gaudí's work in Barcelona. This isn't another boring church builder–this is the guy who decided a church needs bowls of fruit atop its spires. He tried to build a housing subdivision on a bare hill with a giant lizard fountain that did not attract enough buyers (Parc Güell); he designed whimsical, incredibly detailed houses with mosaics galore for Barcelona's business tycoons (Manzana de Discordia); and he began to construct his most well-known work, an exultant expression of his personal Roman Catholicism (Sagrada Familia). Gaudí's vision has proved so inspiring that construction has continued on the Sagrada Familia since its beginning in 1882 and may be completed in 2026, the centennial of Gaudí's death. Students often sketch Gaudí's creations, and Parc Güell is the perfect location for a picnic and beautiful view of the city.

orientation

BARRI GÒTIC AND LAS RAMBLAS

If there is one thing to know about Barri Gòtic, it's this: you will get lost. Knowing this, the best way to properly orient yourself to the neighborhood is to spend an entire day learning your way around. **Las Ramblas** provides the western boundary of the neighborhood, stretching from the waterfront north to Plaça Catalonia. **Vía Laietana** cuts through the city nearly parallel to Las Ramblas, running directly in front of the Catedral, through **Plaça de l'Angel,** and marks the eastern border of the Barri. The primary east-west artery, **Carrer de Ferran**, runs perpendicular to Las Ramblas and v. Laeitana, separating the Barri Gòtic into the **lower** (from C. de Ferran to the water) and **upper portions** (C. de Ferran to Carrer de Fontanella). Street names are located on plaques located on the upper stories of buildings, facing the named street, along with names of the squares. For these areas, the **L3 and L4 lines** of the Metro will be most helpful, with **ⓂDrassanes**, **ⓂLiceu**, and **ⓂCatalonia** dropping along Las Ramblas (L4), and **ⓂJaume I** located in the heart of the Barri Gòtic, at the intersection of **C. Ferran** and **Via Laietana.**

LA RIBERA

If you're looking for fashion-forward boutiques or cavernous *botegas* housed in medieval stone, Ribera is the place for you. For everyone else, the area may be incredibly frustrating for its lack of cheap options and tourist accessibility, but it does provide a more authentic alternative to the Barri Gòtic's crowded streets. For those looking for the most bang for their buck, **Passeig del Born** offers some cheap eats, as well as enough bars to make any pub crawl a night to remember—or to drunkenly forget.

EL RAVAL

Notorious as Barcelona's rougher neighborhood, Raval shouldn't be missed because of its bad rap. A healthy student population makes for quirky (and cheap) eateries as well as vibrant nightlife. Areas around **Rambla del Raval** and **Carrer Joaquim Costa** boast lots of smaller bars and late-night cafes frequented by Barcelona's alternative crowd. For daytime shopping, check out **Riera Baixa,** a street lined entirely with secondhand shops that also hosts a fleamarket on Saturdays, and the neighborhood around **Carrer**

Dr. Dou and **Carrer Elisabets** for higher-end (though still reasonably priced) shops. Be sure to take heed of the locals' warning: watch out for deserted streets and aggressive prostitutes during the night, and be aware that sometimes streets may still be eerily empty and filled with equally aggressive men or sneaky pickpockets during daylight hours.

L'EIXAMPLE

In this vibrant neighborhood, pronounced *eh-sham-plah*, big blocks and dazzling architecture means lots of walking and tons of exciting storefronts. The modernista building-lined **Passeig de Gràcia** runs from north to south, with the **Eixample Dreta** encompassing the area around **Sagrada Familia** and **Eixample Esquerra** comprising the area closer to the university. Though the former contains the notorious **Sagrada Familia,** as well as some surprisingly cheap accommodations for those willing to make the hike, the more pedestrian-friendly area is the Esquerra. While this neighborhood is notoriously posh, there are some cheaper and more interesting options as you get closer to **Plaça Universitat.** The stretch of **Carrer de Consell de Cent** boasts vibrant nightlife, where many "hetero-friendly" bars, clubs, and hotels help give "Gay-xample" its fitting nickname.

BARCELONETA

Barceloneta is a land of beaches and tourist traps that capitalizes on sunbathers flocking to beaches. A short walk from the Barri Gòtic along the water on **Passeig de Colon** will bring you to **Ⓜ Barceloneta. Passieg de Joan de Borbó** is the main road curving along the water toward the **beach,** housing museums and restaurants you want to avoid like the plague. Venture onto any of the streets off of **Passeig Joan de Borbó,** and you'll find a tight grid of little shops and more authentic (though by no means cheaper) haunts, with the plaza around **Calle del Baluart** being particularly luxurious. A 10-15min. walk along the packed beaches heading away from the **Gothic Quarter** will get you to the ritzy clubs and restaurants of **Port Olímpic.**

GRÀCIA

Gràcia is hard to navigate by metro. While this may at first seem like a negative, this poor municipal planning is actually a bonus. Filled with artsy locals and a few drunken travelers, Gràcia is best approached on foot. **Ⓜ Diagonal** will drop you off at the start of **Calle Gran de Gràcia,** which creates the eastern border of Gràcia up until **Ⓜ Fontana.** Take a right onto any road along this walk, and you'll be navigating Gràcia's plaza-centric **Calle de Ros de Olano/Calle de Terol,** which runs perpendicular to C. Gran de Gràcia, intersecting the restaurant and student-laden **Calle Verdi.** For bustling plazas both day and night, your best bets are **Plaza del Sol** and **Plaza de la Revolución de Septiembre de 1868,** both off of C. de Ros de Olano.

accommodations

BARRI GÒTIC AND LAS RAMBLAS

HOSTAL MALDÀ — HOSTAL ❶

C. Pi, 5 ☎93 317 30 02 www.hostalmalda.jimdo.com

Hostal Maldà provides a dirt-cheap home away from home, complete with your mother's cat, kitschy clocks, ceramics, and confusing knick-knacks. A comfy lounge with books and TV feels more like a living room than a dorm common space. Unlike many hostels, the price does not change with the season, nor will this hostal be booked months beforehand during the summer months; knowing their audience and popularity, the owners only accept 60% of capacity through reservations, so try stopping by if you're stranded or weren't quick enough to snag a room beforehand.

*Ⓜ Liceu. Begin walking in front of the house with the dragon and take an immediate left onto C. Casañas. Stay on this road as it passes in front of the church and through the Plaça del Pi. Enter the Galerias Maldà (interior shopping mall) and follow the signs to the hostel. **i** Sheets included. Luggage storage available. All rooms have shared bath. Ⓢ Singles €15; doubles €30; triples €45; quads €60. Reception 24hr.*

YOUTH HOSTEL ALBERGUE HOSTEL ❶

C. Palau, 6 ☎93 319 53 25 www.bcnalbergue.com

Clean dormitory-style rooms fitting 4-8 people with pleasant views onto the street and courtyard below. All rooms include cheerily colored ceilings and wooden floors, and some include balconies—perfect for scoping out fellow travelers, restaurants, or even the nearby trinket store. Common space provides a bright, albeit sterile seating area to veg out and watch TV, grab snacks from the vending machine, and even challenge fellow hostelers to a riveting game of chess.

*Ⓜ Liceu. Walk down C. Ferran toward Las Ramblas. Take the first left once reaching the Plaça Sant Jaume, onto C. de la Ciudad. Right onto C. d'Arai. Second left, onto C. del Palau. **i** Free breakfast 8-9:30am. Lockers included. Sheets €2. Kitchen open 7-10pm. Ⓢ 4- to 8-bed dorms €13-24.50. Reception 24hr.*

HOSTAL-RESIDÈNCIA REMBRANDT HOSTAL ❷

C. de la Portaferissa, 23 www.hostalrembrandt.com

Unlike most hostels, which only offer a practically infinite number of small, dark rooms that look exactly the same, the Hostal-Residència has a variety of large, spacious rooms with pleasant quirks and details. Many rooms include multiple large windows or balconies looking out over the corner of the street or into the courtyard, and one triple even has a loft. For once, it's worth the price to have a bathroom ensuite—even the ones that aren't equipped with jacuzzis are still big enough to spend an entire week in relaxing. The rooms are a real steal in the low season, and the location and charm are still worth it in the high season.

*Ⓜ Liceu. Walk down Las Ramblas toward Plaça Catalonia and take a right onto C. Portaferissa; the hostal is by Galerias Maldà. **i** Linens and towels included. Ⓢ Singles €20-30, with bath €20-35. Reception 9am-11pm.*

HOSTAL-RESIDENCA LAUSANNE HOSTAL ❸

Avinguda del Portal de l'Àngel, 14 ☎93 302 11 39 www.hostallausanne.es

An incredibly classy stairwell (marble stairs, blue- and gold-glazed tile) leads to an equally classy hostel. Each room sports excellent views, but try getting one that faces the patio—the view is better and it will be quieter at night, so long as your hostelmates aren't total hooligans. Enjoy the view from your own room, chat up some fellow travelers in the bohemian common space with free internet, microwave, and TV, or chill out on the back patio and look out over the neighboring rooftops.

*Ⓜ Catalonia. Exit the Metro and walk along the street toward the Corte Ingles, the rounded building with horizontal bands. Upon reaching the far corner of the square, turn right onto del Portal de l'Àngel. **i** Towels, sheets, and toiletries included. Fridge and luggage storage available. Ⓢ Singles €28-35; doubles €47-54; triples €68-75. Call for most up-to-date prices. Reception 24hr.*

QUARTIER GOTHIC HOSTEL ❷

C. Avinyó, 42 ☎93 318 79 45 www.hotelquartiergothic.com

Flags from many countries and the hostel's own propaganda and regalia deck the walls and halls of Quartier Gothic. Rooms overlooking the courtyard have the best views and the least noise from the nightlong babbling of the Gothic

Quarter. Though the attached baths are more spacious than in comparable hostels in the area, the shared bath is practically a room of its own (though only intended for one person at a time). With some rooms including TV and DVD players and a relatively impressive breakfast (selection of juices, coffee, tea, bread, and pastries), this hostel shows up many in its price range in terms of amenities while still being in a central location. Short-term apartment by Casa Milà also available through informal arrangement with one of the employees.

*ⓂDrassanes. Head toward Plaça de Catalonia on Las Ramblas. Turn right onto C. dels Escudellers, then right onto C. Avinyó. .* ***i*** *Breakfast €3. Safety box in room, lockers available for day after checkout for €2. Linens included. Rooms with private bath also have TV and DVD player.* Ⓢ *Singles €19-27; doubles €32-57; triples €42-75. Discount for booking online.* ⏰ *Reception 24hr.*

PENSIÓN CANADIENSE PENSIÓN ❸

Baixada de San Miquel, 1 ☎93 301 74 61 www.pensioncanadiense.com

Tucked away in the Gothic Quarter, the nine rooms of the Pensión Canadiense tempt the budget traveler with quiet rooms just seconds away from the bustling nightlife of the Barri Gòtíc. Each room has a private bath that will make you feel like backpacking royalty as well as balconies that face the street and interior courtyard for you to hold court.

*ⓂJaume I. Walk on C. Ferran towards Las Ramblas. Turn left on C. de Avinyó and take the first left onto Baixada de San Miquel. Hostel is immediately on your left. Upon entering building, take the right stairwell.* ***i*** *Sheets and towels included.* Ⓢ *Doubles €60-70; triples €95.* ⏰ *Reception 24hr. 4-night min. stay.*

PENSIÓN LA CALMA PENSIÓN ❷

C. Lleona, 8-10 ☎93 318 15 21 www.pensionlacalma.com

Ask to see the rooms yourself to find the one sporting the most beautiful

accommodations . barri gòtic and las ramblas

balcony view in all of the cheap hostels in the Gothic Quarter—hanging laundry, latticed gardens, terraced roofs, and all. A refreshing break from the nondescript, chain-like interiors being adopted by many hostels with private rooms, the Pensión La Calma instead promises sheets that look like they came out of the '70s, tile from the '80s, and paintings that would look at home in any secondhand store.

Ⓜ Liceu. Head toward the sea on Las Ramblas. Turn left onto C. Ferran, then right onto C. Raurich. Take the second left, C. Lleona. i Towels and linens included. Microwave and fridge available. Ⓢ Doubles €42, with bath €50, triples €63/€75. Reception 24hr.

ARCO YOUTH HOSTEL (ALBERGUE ARCO) HOSTEL ❷

Arco de Santa Eulalia, 1. ☎93 412 54 68

Offering rooms for six, eight, and 18 people with lockers ensuite, the Arco Youth Hostel provides a bunk in which to crash and food to wake up to in the morning. There's a communal kitchen with fridges, microwaves, a stove, and cookware for those looking to impress with culinary prowess. The smaller common space has couches, books, and a TV for enjoyment—just hope that no one is using their "gym," a.k.a. the exercise bike squeezed confusingly along the wall. Decent prices for the area, but be sure to abide by their extensive check-in and cancellation policies to avoid fees.

Ⓜ Liceu. Walk down C. Boqueria. Arco de Santa Eulalia is the third right. i Breakfast included. Lockers available with €10 key deposit. Towels included; sheets €1.70. Kitchen. Call if arrival time is different than originally noted. Fee for cancellation of reservation less than 48hr. in advance or no show; only accepts cancellation through email (not phone or fax). Ⓢ Dorms €20-23. Reception 24hr.

HOSTAL CAMPI HOSTAL ❸

C. Canuda, 4 ☎93 301 35 45 www.hostalcampi.com

Upon entering Hostal Campi, be prepared to navigate the labyrinth of well-lit, breezy social spaces—complete with balconies and sculpture-like bamboo shoots—to get to your room. Rooms are average size for the price and area, with singles, doubles, triples, and quads available for rent (for the latter, just ask them to add a bed to a triple). The more people staying, the better the deal, and with almost limitless common space, there's no need to worry about being stuck with your bros in an overcrowded room.

Ⓜ Catalonia. Walk toward the sea on Las Ramblas and take a left onto C. Canuda. i Internet €1 per hr. TV and computers available in living room. Ⓢ Singles without bath €30-34; doubles €52-67; triples €67-87. Reception 24hr.

PENSIÓN MARI-LUZ PENSIÓN ❷

C. Palau, 4 ☎93 317 34 63 www.pensionmariluz.com

Pensión Mari-luz offers large, spacious rooms at a modest price and is one of the most fashionably decorated hostels in its price range. Well-matched paint, bedspreads, and artwork (seems that the owners have a penchant for Dalí) offer a lively feeling that the nearly nonexistent social space lacks. With just a few chairs positioned in the alley-like foyer and a TV the size of a netbook, don't expect much socializing in this *pensión*.

Ⓜ Jaume I. Walk down C. Ferran toward Las Ramblas. Take the first left upon reaching the Plaça Sant Jaume, onto C. de la Ciudad. Right onto C. d'Arai. Second left onto C. Palau. i Lockers in dorm rooms; security boxes in doubles. Sheets and towels included. Kitchen, phone, and fax available. Ⓢ Dorms €15-23, with bath €16-24; doubles €50-60; triples €48-72; quads €60-92 (all with hall shower); quads with bath €64-96. Reception 24hr. Min. stay depends on season.

HOSTAL LEVANTE HOSTAL ❸

Baixada de San Miquel, 2 ☎93 317 95 65 www.hostallevante.com

Considering the rumors that the place used to be a haunt of Picasso when it was previously a whorehouse, Hostal Levante is now almost eerily clean and upstanding, with only a few stained chairs hinting dirtier days. Spacious yet simple private rooms cater to an older (or at least more mature) crowd than most similarly priced places in the area, and the hostel is much calmer as a result. If you don't mind shared facilities, save the €10 for the closet-sized bathroom.

*Ⓜ Liceu. Walk down Las Ramblas toward the sea. Take a left onto C. Ferran and a right onto C. Avinyó. Baixada de San Miquel is on the left, and Hostal Levante is right at the corner. **i** Lock box in room. Towels and linens included. Ⓢ Singles €35, with bath €45; doubles€55/65; triples €90.*

KABUL YOUTH HOSTEL — HOSTEL ❶

P. Reial, 17 ☎93 318 51 90 www.kabul.es

One of the biggest and most popular hostels in Barcelona, the Kabul Youth Hostel has hosted nearly one million backpackers since its establishment in 1985. The hostel offers bare-bones, dormitory-style accommodations and a rooftop terrace. Lower-capacity rooms are often cramped and more expensive, but if you can get one with a balcony (just ask), then it's worth the added expense. The common space boasts backpacker photo galleries, a pool table, other table games, music, and a never-ending swarm of chatty younger travelers that are genuinely excited about meeting other travelers. Free breakfast and dinner make the price of a room here a steal.

*Ⓜ Liceu. Walk toward the sea along Las Ramblas and turn left onto C. Ferran. Take the first right and enter the Plaça Reial. Kabul Youth Hostel will be on the far left, with well-marked glass doors. **i** Complimentary breakfast (8-10am) and dinner (8:30pm) first come, first served. Lockers included with €15 key deposit. Luggage storage available. Blanket included; sheets €2. Laundry facilities available. 20min. free internet per day. Guestlist access to local clubs. Ⓢ Dorms €15-29. Reception 24hr.*

HOSTAL FERNANDO — HOSTAL ❷

C. Ferran, 31 ☎93 301 79 93 www.hfernando.com

A bright, open reception area with friendly staff accurately portrays what travelers will find inside. While Hostal Fernando offers clean, spacious rooms, the decor of the private rooms feels almost like a Holiday Inn. Common room with TV, kitchen, and dining space on third floor.

*Ⓜ Liceu. Left onto C. Ferran from Las Ramblas. On left. **i** Breakfast included. Linens included. Towels €1.50. Internet €1 per 30min. Lockers included for dorms; safe box for private rooms. Credit card required for 1st night reservation. All private rooms have bath, dorms available with or without bath. Ⓢ Dorms €18-25; singles €45-55; doubles €60-75; triples €75-90; family rooms (fit 4-6) €90-160. Reception 24hr.*

HOSTAL SANTA ANNA — HOSTAL ❷

C. Santa Anna, 23 ☎93 301 22 46

Small, dark rooms, and almost medieval offerings—no internet, no wheelchair access, and cash only—mean you're paying almost exclusively for the location and customer service (which, barring technological progress, is superb). The shared baths are barely big enough to turn around in, so it's worth investing in one that's attached to the room. Besides having a helpful staff, you're also guaranteed to make some new friends—though there are no common spaces, there are a few friendly cats and small dogs ready and willing to receive your love if you can find them.

Ⓜ Catalonia. Walk down las Ramblas toward the water. Take a left onto C. Santa Anna. Ⓢ Doubles €50-60; triples €60. Reception 24hr.

HOSTAL PARISIEN — HOSTAL ❸

La Rambla, 114 ☎93 301 62 83

High ceilings and rooms that actually remind you that you're in the old city, complete with a parrot that will greet you in every language imaginable. Rooms are simple and somewhat pricey for the area (with bathrooms the size of small closets), but some have balconies that open onto La Rambla.

ⓂLiceu. Walk toward Plaça Catalonia on La Rambla. On right. i No alcohol permitted. $ Doubles €60, with partial or full bath €65. Short-term apartment also available. Prices may vary, call 7-10 days ahead to secure price for stay.

HOSTEL SUN + MOON — HOSTEL 2

C. Ferran, 19 ☎93 270 20 60 www.sunandmoonhostel.com

Though the crowded dormitory-style rooms seem like an utter sham price-wise, with travelers needing to rent sheets, blankets, and towels, the private rooms and apartments can be relatively economical and a fun place for larger groups to stay, provided you don't mind staying somewhere with the charm and decor of a kindergarten classroom. The hostel sports an incredibly lively atmosphere, filled with an endless stream of young travelers and located on one of the busiest streets in the Gothic Quarter. The common area feels more like a cafeteria than a living room, though, so you may want to take your revelries to the streets.

ⓂLiceu. Walk toward the water on Las Ramblas. Take a left onto C. Ferran. i Breakfast 8-9am. Sheets €2; towels €2; blankets €3. Luggage room €2. Free internet from 8am-midnight. $ Apartments from €130. Dorms €25-28. Reception 24hr.

LA RIBERA

PENSIÓN 2000 — PENSIÓN 2

C. Sant Pere Més Alt, 6 ☎93 310 74 66 www.pension2000.com

Brightly colored and well-lit rooms provide excellent views of the Palau de la Música Catalana across the street (and, reportedly, some complementary music performances on louder nights). High ceilings and a relaxed, college-living-room-like common space (without the empty beer cans and hookah, of course) make for a friendly home away from home, complete with concerned and super helpful hostel-owners-cum-parents.

ⓂJaume I. Walk on v. Laietana toward the Cathedral and take a right onto C. Sant Pere Més Alt, 6. Pensión 2000 is located directly across from the Palau. i Breakfast €5. Internet €1 per day. $ Doubles €55, with private bath €60. Extra bed €20, second extra bed €16. Reception 24hr.

GOTHIC POINT YOUTH HOSTEL — HOSTEL 1

C. dels Vigatans, 5 ☎93 268 78 08 www.gothicpoint.com

This youth hostel sports a social life as vibrant as its nearly fluorescent lime green walls, with a ping-pong table along the huge terrace for those nights when you just need to duke it out. The chutes-and-ladders-esque bedrooms provide standard youth hostel fare with one significant improvement: most are enclosed in their own wall of curtains for some semblance of privacy.

ⓂJaume I. Walk down C. Argenteria and take a left onto C. dels Vigatans. i Kitchen available. Inquire about working to pay for your stay. Sheets €2. Towels €2. $ Dorms €15-23. Reception 24hr.

HOTEL TRIUNFO — HOTEL 4

Psg. de Picasso, 22 ☎93 310 40 85 www.atriumhotels.com

Chic upscale rooms with curtains that actually match the covers, luxurious bathrooms with slick black tubs, and flatscreen TVs on the wall make this expensive option worth its price tag. A small common room with black leather couches, a contrasting white sculpture, and posters of worldwide art exhibitions provide the perfect place to prep before heading across the street to catch a classical performance in the Parc de la Ciutadella.

ⓂArc de Triumf. Walk on Psg. de Lluís Companys through the arch and toward the Parc. Follow the curve to the right once it meets the park to walk onto Psg. de Picasso. Hotel Triunfo is on the

right underneath the arcade. **i** *All rooms have private bath.* Ⓢ *Singles €40-45; doubles €60-70; triples €80-95. Discounts M-F.* ⏰ *Reception 24hr.*

HOSTAL RIBAGORZA PENSIÓN ❷

C. de Trafalgar, 39 ☎933 19 19 68 www.hostalribagorza.com

Brown- and blue-tiled floors paired with orange covers make for a funky color palette ensuite, while knick-knack ceramics make you feel as if you're staying with your Spanish grandmother. Let this place spoil you with clean rooms, balconies, and surprisingly large shared bathrooms.

Ⓜ Arc de Triumf. Stand on the far side of the Arc farthest from the Parc with your back to the arch. C. Trafalgar is the 1st street on your left. Ⓢ *Doubles €45, with bath €55-62; triples €60/€75.* ⏰ *Reception 24hr.*

HOSTAL DOS REINOS PENSIÓN ❷

C. de Trafalgar, 39, 4th fl. ☎60 618 54 98

Cheap private rooms compensate for the fact that some of the hostal's other amenities are hit-or-miss—be prepared for a reportedly weak Wi-Fi signal and the possibility of a non-functioning toilet covered by a sheet in one of the shared bathrooms. However, the price is rarely beat, and the place provides a clean spot to lay your head. Be sure to use the elevator unless you're training to climb Everest—Dos Reinos is located on the fourth floor.

Ⓜ Arc de Triumf. Stand on the far side of the Arc farthest from the Parc with your back to the arch. C. Trafalgar is the 1st street on your left. Ⓢ *Doubles €40; triples €60; quads €80. 10% additional fee for booking online, so call to make reservation.* ⏰ *Reception 24hr.*

HOSTAL NEW ORLEANS HOSTAL ❸

Av. del Marquès de l'Argentera, 13 ☎93 319 73 82 www.hostalorleans.com

Large rooms with ensuite bathrooms boast the nicest flatscreen TVs for a hostel in this price range—perfect for inviting your friends over to watch the game, since there isn't a common space.

Ⓜ Barceloneta. Walk on Plà de Palau away from the water and take a right onto Av. del Marquès de l'Argentera. **i** *Communal microwave and fridge available.* Ⓢ *Doubles €60-65; triples €70-75; quads €80-85.* ⏰ *Reception 24hr.*

PENSIÓN CIUDADELA PENSIÓN ❸

C. del Comerç, 33 ☎93 319 62 03 www.pension-ciudadela.com

Large air-conditioned rooms provide a pleasant retreat from the busy streets. There's no common room, so head to the Parc for socializing or make sure you get a room with a balcony to lounge on instead.

Ⓜ Barceloneta. Walk on Plà de Palau away from the water and take a right onto Av. del Marquès de l'Argentera. The pensión is on the left at the corner of C. Comerç. Ⓢ *Doubles €66; triples €72.* ⏰ *Reception 24hr.*

PENSIÓN PORT-BOU PENSIÓN ❷

C. del Comerç, 29 ☎93 319 23 67

With no kitchen or Wi-Fi and a TV that will leave you feeling as if you stepped back into the '80s, Port-Bou is a no-frills pensión. Clean, sometimes spacious accommodations provide a retro feel for those tired of glitz, glam, and the last few decades. If renting a room with an ensuite bathroom, just be sure it's one you can fit inside. Luckily, rooms come relatively cheap, so this is an affordable option if you're just looking to crash.

Ⓜ Barceloneta. Walk on Plà de Palau away from the water and take a right onto Av. del Marquès de l'Argentera. Take a left onto C. Comerç. Ⓢ *Doubles €45, with bath €55; triples €55/€60.* ⏰ *Reception 24hr.*

HOSTAL NUEVO COLÓN HOSTAL ❷

Av. del Marquès de l'Argentera, 19 ☎933 19 50 77 www.hostalnuevocolon.com

Newly renovated rooms provide motel-level charm without the underage drinkers partying illegally next door. Rooms range widely in size, so be sure to scope out the selection if you are claustrophobic.

Ⓜ Barceloneta. Walk on Plà de Palau away from the water and take a right onto Av. del Marquès de l'Argentera. Ⓢ Doubles €47; triples €87. Reception 24hr.

BARCELONA 4 FUN HOSTAL ❷

C. Ample, 24 ☎93 268 41 50 www.barcelona4fun.com

An unmarked door in an unmarked building hides private rooms with the social life (and shared bathrooms) of a hostel (if you can find the place, anyway). Young travelers pack this hostal's two- and three-person rooms, though most time is spent either in the kitchen or in the living room with a sunny view to the street, comfy furniture, and computers with free internet. Close to Barceloneta if you can't stay too far from the clubs.

Ⓜ Barceloneta. While facing the water, walk to your right along Psg. Isabel II/Psg. Colom. Walk for 5min. and turn right onto C. Avinyó. At the 2nd street (C. Ample), take a right. Look for a huge stone doorway on your left and doors leading into black-and-white checkered marble hallway. Go up grand staircase—door is unmarked, but it's door #2 on the 1st floor. i Free internet and Wi-Fi. Breakfast included. Towels €1. Ⓢ Doubles €54-60; triples €81-90.

EL RAVAL

HOTEL PENINSULAR HOTEL ❸

C. Sant Pau, 34 ☎93 302 31 38 www.hpeninsular.com

Four stories of rooms wrap around a well-lit courtyard with hanging plants. Comfortable rooms with little desks, and windows overlooking the picturesque surroundings make for a gigglishly quaint place to rest your head.

Ⓜ Liceu. On Las Ramblas, turn your back to Plaça Catalonia. C. Sant Pau will be on your right. i Free Wi-Fi and toiletries. Ⓢ Doubles €60; triples €85; quads €100. Reception 24hr.

IDEAL YOUTH HOSTEL HOSTEL ❶

C. la Unió, 12 ☎93 342 61 77 www.idealhostel.com

An industrial-chic common space with foosball and amoeba-like couches plays host to a revolving door of vibrant backpacking youth. The bathroom facilities in this standard youth hostel smell so soapy you know they're clean. Young, helpful staff will point you in the right direction and may even end up going with you to show you the ropes.

Ⓜ Liceu. Walk toward the water on Las Ramblas and take a right onto C. de la Unió. i Breakfast included. Safebox available. Ⓢ Dorms €18. €9.50 deposit. Reception 24hr.

HOSTAL GAT XINO HOSTAL ❸

C. l'Hospital, 155 ☎93 324 88 33 www.gatrooms.com

The super modern and stylish rooms with a white, black, and lime green color code will have you begging to buy one of their T-shirts to blend into the colorful surroundings. The interior decor even extends into the hotel's cafe and bathrooms. If you end up craving a chromatic world beyond this souped-up checkerboard, feel free to lounge in the courtyard's wooden benches.

Ⓜ Sant Antoni. Walk down C. de Sant Antoni Abat, which runs diagonally from the corner of the plaça. Stay right onto C. l'Hospital at the fork. i Breakfast, towels, and toiletries included. Ensuite bathrooms. Ⓢ Doubles €66-86.

CENTER-RAMBLAS YOUTH HOSTEL HOSTEL ❷

C. l'Hospital, 63 ☎93 412 40 69 www.center-ramblas.com

Though you won't be aching to call this place home, the social atmosphere and clean rooms make this place an attractive stay for a few nights. Industrial metal walls filled with photo murals of Barcelona will persuade you to head into the city with newly friends in tow.

Ⓜ Liceu. Walk down C. l'Hospital. i Breakfast and linens included. Lockers €2. Towels €2. Washer €2. Dryer €2. Ⓢ Dorms in summer €25, in winter €17-21. Breakfast 8:15-10am.

L'EIXAMPLE

SANT JORDI: HOSTEL ARAGO — HOSTEL ❸

C. Aragó, 268 ☎93 215 67 43 www.santjordihostels.com/hostel-arago

Sit back in their gloriously bright, home-like kitchen and common space, or gather round on one of the couches and listen to hostelmates play covers of Bob Dylan and Andrew Bird on the communal guitar. Any hostel with quotes from Guy Debord, Wittgenstein, and Nietzsche on its board has to be a little different, and this one is in the best way. Modern wooden and steel bunks offer a little more privacy and comfort than most hostels, though with nightly outings and a solid, exciting community, chances are you'll be spending little time in them.

Ⓜ Passeig de Gràcia. Walk along Psg. de Gràcia away from Plaça Catalonia and the Corte Ingles. Take a left onto C. d'Aragó. i Lockers and luggage storage included. Sheets and blankets included. Laundry available. Kitchen and computers with internet. Ⓢ Dorms €30-35. Reception 24hr.

SANT JORDI: APARTMENTS SAGRADA FAMILIA — APARTMENTS ❷

C. del Freser, 5 ☎93 446 05 17 www.santjordihostels.com/apt-sagrada-familia/

For those sick of dining on takeout, coffee, and beer, Sant Jordi's apartment-style lodging offers the chain's characteristic laid-back style, communal guitar, employee dedicated to arranging nightly parties, and guarantee of social hostelmates as cool as you (or as cool as you want to be). Each apartment includes a private bath (or two), a stylish and comfy living room, free washing machine, and stocked kitchen. With rooms for one, two, or four people, you can pick your privacy without *pensión*-style isolation.

Ⓜ Hospital Sant Pau. Walk along C. del Dos de Maig toward C. Corsega. Take a left onto C. Rosselló and stay left as the road splits to C. del Freser. i Apartments include living room, TV, washing machine, ensuite bath, and kitchen. Free Wi-Fi. Lockers, sheets, and blankets included. Ⓢ 4-bed dorms €16-28; singles €20-38; doubles €36-64. Towels €2. Quiet hours after 10pm.

HOSTEL SOMNIO — HOSTEL, HOSTAL ❸

C. de la Diputació, 251 ☎93 272 308 www.somniohostels.com

This ultra-sleek hostel offers the best of both worlds—beautifully decorated private rooms and budget dorm-style bunking. Cool wooden floors and modern decor will leave you expecting to pay the price, but you'll be thankfully disappointed. Super helpful and friendly staff will direct you to the best little tapas bar or the only cost-efficient driving tour in Barcelona. Watch for more locations in the near future, as they look to expand throughout Spain.

Ⓜ Passeig de Gràcia. Walk along Gran Vía toward the University and take the first right onto Rambla de Catalonia. Somnio is on the corner of C. Diputacio and the Rambla. i Breakfast €2. Lockers, towels, and linens included. Free Wi-Fi. Ⓢ Dorms €26; singles €44; doubles €78, with bath €87.

HOSTAL RESIDENCIA OLIVA — HOSTAL ❹

Passeig de Gràcia, 32 ☎93 488 01 62 www.hostaloliva.com

If you think the interior view of this modernista building from the wood-framed elevator is something, just ask for a room facing the street. Large windows facing the grandiose Passeig de Gràcia offer peep shows of the architectural orgasm of the *Manzana de Discordia*. Though lacking the fantastic views, interior rooms make up for their shortcomings with more room to move around. Large, bright rooms with marble floors and class suit the price range for amenities alone, and the near private view of Gaudí makes it well worth the extra cash.

Ⓜ Passeig de Gràcia. Walk along Psg. de Gràcia away from Plaça Catalonia and the Corte Inglés. Hostal Residencia Oliva is on the corner of C. Diputacio and Psg. de Gràcia, on your right. i Free Wi-Fi. Ⓢ Singles €38; doubles €66-85; triples €120.

EQUITY POINT CENTRIC HOSTEL ❷

Psg. de Gràcia, 33 ☎93 215 65 38 www.equity-point.com

Equity Point's location can't be beat, especially for its price. Though the expansive number of rooms and the gargantuan, but beautiful, reception area in this modernista building might intimidate you, their website puts it most accurately: this hostel is "like a cuckoo that's muscled into the very plushest of nests." Great views from the bunk-style rooms and a ton of amenities, including a terrace and bar, provide the perfect reprieve if somehow you don't feel like spending the day out front along Passeig de Gràcia.

*Ⓜ Passeig de Gràcia. Walk along Psg. de Gràcia away from Plaça Catalonia and the Corte Ingés. Equity Point is on the corner of C. Consell de Cent and Psg. de Gràcia. **i** Lockers available. Free Wi-Fi; computers with internet free for 20min. Top sheet and blanket €2 each. Towel €2 with €2 deposit. Ⓢ Dorms €18.50-30. Kitchen open until 10pm.*

GRAFFITI HOSTAL HOSTEL ❶

C. Aragó, 527 ☎93 288 24 99

True to its name, this hostel has graffiti, ranging from impressive works of art spanning entire walls to incredibly mundane scratchings by drunk hostelmates. An unmarked door hides the cheapest rooms in Barcelona complete with lockers, two outdoor terraces, and a common room. If you've visited before, be sure to stop by again—the hostel is under new management and has a facelift to show for it.

Ⓜ Clot or Ⓜ Encants. From Clot, face the rocket-shaped Agbar Tower and head directly to your right along C. d'Aragó. From Encants, walk along C. del Dos de Mag toward Agbar Tower and take a left onto C. d'Aragó. Ⓢ Dorms €10-13. Common areas closed midnight-8am.

BARCELONA URBANY HOSTEL HOSTEL ❷

Av. Meridiana, 97 ☎93 503 60 04 www.barcelonaurbany.com

The tons of young people flocking to this hostel guarantee a fun, social experience, and the free gym access and nightly clubbing outings provided by Barcelona Urbany simply greaten the potential. Rooms are supermodern, but don't be surprised if you want to spend most of your night on the terrace bar sipping super cheap beer and sangria *(€1)* instead.

*Ⓜ Clot. Walk along Av. Meridiana toward the rocket-shaped Agbar Tower. Urbany will be on your right, on the corner of Meridiana and C. de la Corunya. **i** Breakfast included. Luggage storage. Laundry available. Ⓢ All-female dorms €23-34; co-ed dorms €20-31. Singles and doubles €68-94. Reception 24hr.*

HOSTAL GIMÓN HOSTAL ❷

C. Mallorca, 557 ☎93 455 44 32 www.hostalgimon.es

Bright white modern rooms with wooden floors and furniture, each with a good-size attached bathroom. A comfortable and quiet place to return for the night, though not much more. While each room includes a TV, you'll need to head across the street to the locutori in search of internet access.

*Ⓜ Clot. Walk along Meridiana with your back to the rocket-shaped Agbar Tower and take a hard left onto C. de Mallorca. **i** Private bath and TV. Ⓢ Doubles €50; triples €65.*

HOSTAL EDEN HOSTAL ❷

C. Balmes, 55 ☎93 452 66 20 www.hostaleden.net

Don't expect another white-walled sleeping box—bright, pastel colored walls mimic the vivid blues, greens, yellows, and reds of the covers. The interior bathrooms are just big enough to get around in easily, and each comes with a hair dryer for when the windblown look isn't cutting it. The rooms aren't incredibly spacious, but also aren't closet-sized—just be nimble if you take the far side of the bed.

Ⓜ Passeig de Gràcia. Walk along Psg. de Gràcia away from Plaça Catalonia and the Corte Ingles.

Take a left onto C. d'Aragó just after Casa Battló. Take a left onto C. Balmes. ***i*** *Towels, safety boxes, and fans included.* Ⓢ*Singles €25-30, with bath €35-55; doubles €35-45/€50-60.*

BARCELONETA

There are very few budget accommodations in Barceloneta—it's better to stay in La Ribera or Barri Gòtic if you want to be near Barceloneta, and all its clubs and beachfront.

PENSIÓN PALACIO

PENSIÓN ❶

Psg. Isabel II, 10 ☎93 319 36 09 www.pensionpalacio.com

Bright, cheerful private rooms with dormitory-cheap prices. Just a few minutes' walk from the beach, this *pension* with a deceiving laundry list of rules and fees (they're actually laid-back, we promise) is just a 5min. walk from both the hip neighborhood of Born and the sandy beaches of Barceloneta.

Ⓜ Barceloneta. With your back to the beach, walk to the left on Psg. Isabel II. Pensión Palacio is under the arcade on the left side. ***i*** *Safety box included in each room. Laundry wash €5, dry €2. Kitchen €1 per day. Computers with internet available.* Ⓢ *Singles €15-22; doubles €30-44; triples €45-66.* *Computer room open 8am-11pm.*

SEA POINT

HOSTEL ❶

P. del Mar, 1-3 ☎93 231 20 45 www.equity-point.com

Offering Equity Point feel for an Equity Price, Sea Point is just seconds from San Sebastian beach, making it the only youth hostel bordering the water this side of Barceloneta. Tumble out of one of their solid metal bunk beds (no annoying midnight squeaks here) and onto the sand—though clean, bright, and lively, the accommodations aren't as spiffy as other Barcelona hostels in the chain.

Ⓜ Barceloneta. Follow Psg. Joan de Borbó until Pl. del Mar (near the beach) and enter the hostel through the cafe on the right side of the building. ***i*** *Breakfast included. Lockers €3. Sheets €2. Luggage storage. 20min. free internet access. Kitchen.* Ⓢ *Dorms €15-25.*

GRÀCIA

ALBERGUE-RESIDENCIA LA CIUTAT

HOSTEL ❶

C. de ca l'Alegre de Dalt, 66 ☎93 213 03 00 www.laciutat.com

Colorful dorm-style rooms offer a cheerily saturated, modern place to rest your head. Useful facilities dot every floor, including a fully equipped kitchen, common room with TV, and showers. Single and double rooms are also available, with discounts given to those who stay longer than seven days. The Disney-meets-graffiti murals lining the corridors exemplify the vibrant and young social atmosphere, and the terrace provides a welcome break for a breath of fresh air. Getting there from the city center may be a pain, but the bustling student-friendly (and cheap) nightlife of Gràcia is just a short walk away.

Ⓜ Joanic. Walk along C. de l'Escorial through the plaza and follow for 5-10min. Take a right onto C. de Marti before the clinic and take the first left onto C. de ca l'Alegre de Dalt. ***i*** *Lockers and towels included. Sheets €1.80. Free internet at public computers. Equipped kitchens and shared bathrooms on each floor. Laundry service available.* Ⓢ *4- to 10-bed dorms €17-20; singles €35-50; doubles €26-30. 1st night deposit required for online booking.* *Reception 24hr.*

HOSTAL LESSEPS

PENSIÓN ❸

C. Gran de Gràcia, 239 ☎93 218 44 34 www.hostallesseps.com

Recently renovated, this *pensión* boasts 16 larger rooms, all with huge baths and sleek flatscreen TVs. With these amenities, some people decide to not leave their rooms. Even for the area, this hostel is surprisingly quiet.

Ⓜ Lesseps. Walk away from the giant road along C. Gran de Gràcia. Hostal Lesseps is a few blocks down on the right. ***i*** *All rooms with ensuite bath. Free internet at public computers.* Ⓢ *Singles €40; doubles €65; triples €80.*

HOSTAL SAN MEDÍN HOSTAL ❸

C. Gran de Gràcia, 125 ☎93 217 30 68 www.sanmedin.com

Big beds and spacious rooms make this hostal feel more like a bed and breakfast than a budget *pensión*. Pictures of Barcelona's famous architecture dot the newly wallpapered walls, and mini chandeliers add some sparkle to your sleeping space. Snag a room with a balcony; otherwise you'll be looking out into a drab (though quiet) lightwell.

Ⓜ Fontana. Take a right onto C. Gran de Gràcia. San Medín is a block down on the right, just after Rambla de Prat. ***i*** *All rooms have a fan.* Ⓢ *Singles €30, with bath €45; doubles €50/60; triples €70/80.*

PENSIÓN NORMA PENSIÓN ❸

C. Gran de Gràcia, 87 ☎93 237 44 78

Meticulously maintained but somewhat bland rooms in an unbeatable location provide a relaxing place to return for the night after marching the *modernista*-studded Passeig de Gràcia nearby. To be safe, don't leave valuables in your room. Although the pensión is in a safe area, you'll need to turn in your keys before you leave, and at times the staff is less than diligent about watching guard over them at the reception desk.

Ⓜ Fontana. Take a right onto C. Gran de Gràcia. Pensión Norma is a few blocks down on the right. ***i*** *Sheets included.* Ⓢ *Singles €30; doubles with sink €45, with full bath €55; triples €66.* *Reception 24hr.*

OUTSKIRTS

Surrounded almost entirely by beautiful parks, Barcelona welcomes those adventurous backpackers who shy away from the touristy haunts of Las Ramblas. A number of camping sites and youth hostels are available, both of which are normally accessible by bus or metro. For camping, the **Associació de Càmpings de Barcelona** *(Gran Vía de les Corts Catalanes, 608 ☎93 412 59 55 www.campingsbcn.com)* has more info, while the **Youth Hostel Network of Catalonia** *(C. Calàbria, 147 ☎93 483 83 41 www.xanascat.cat)* features information about a few government-sponsored youth hostels in the city and surrounding areas.

The Great Outdoors

Almost all of Barcelona's campsites come equipped with baffling amenities, and even the more reserved campsites have basic bathing and laundry facilities as well as a supermarket and restaurant. If you're not the tenting type, affordable 4- to 6-person bungalows are usually available with kitchens and complete bathrooms. Many have minimum stay requirements, so be prepared to kick back and settle down for a few days.

CÀMPING TRES ESTRELLAS CAMPSITE ❶

Autovía de Castelldefells, km. 186.2, Gavá ☎93 633 06 37 www.camping3estrellas.com

If you got any closer to the beach, you'd be washed out to sea at high tide. Camping facilities dot the beautiful beach of Gavá, 12km from the city center *(35min. by bus)*. Extensive facilities boast not one but two swimming pools (in case you're afraid of sharks), volleyball nets, and a grill area, along with the expected supermarket, bar, and restaurant.

Gavá stop on bus L94 or L95 from Plaça Catalonia. Campsite 5min. walk from station. ***i*** *Pools, restaurant, supermarket, and barbeque area available.* Ⓢ *Camping €6-8 per person; €7.50-9 for tent. 2-person cabin €26-38; 4-person cabin €38-60.* *Open Mar 15-Oct 15.*

CÀMPING BARCELONA CAMPSITE ❶

Carretera N-11 km 650, Mataró ☎93 790 47 20 www.campingbarcelona.com

A coastal campsite along Martaró beach about 45min. from Barcelona by train boasts enough facilities to have you considering staying in some nights. A beachside restaurant doubles as a club at night, and shady, grassy plots give views of the nearby shore. The campsite covers all of the bases with a swimming pool, internet cafe, laundromat, restaurant, supermarket, and even a farm for those looking for a little animal companionship (by the way, pets are allowed so you can also bring your own).

Ⓜ Mataró and free shuttle bus from station to campsite outside the train station every 10min. N82 bus picks up outside of campsite every 1hr. Free bus to Plaça Catalonia from campsite Mar-June and Sept-Nov (35min.). i 6A power supply access. Pet-friendly. Swimming pool, restaurant, supermarket, laundry facilities, and bike rental available. Free shuttle to Martaró Beach every 15-30min. $ Camping €5-9 per person. 4-person bungalow and car €85-165; 6-person bungalow and car €110-165. Down payment of 35% and a deposit of €150 for bungalows. Open Mar 27-Nov. Check website for full availability.

CÀMPING MASNOU ♿ CAMPSITE ❶

Carretera N-11 km 633 Camil Fabra, 33. ☎93 555 15 03 www.campingsonline.com

A more rustic and down-to-earth alternative to many of the resort-esque campsites. Camping Masnou is close to the water, recommended for those looking to indulge in the outdoors or just rest their head inside a tent after sightseeing in the city. Cheap bungalows provide a warmer alternative to your frigid tent during the winter months.

Ⓜ Masnou or N80 bus from Plaça Catalonia. Campsite 5min. walk from station. i Bike rental, laundry, supermarket, pool, and restaurant available. Pet-friendly. $ Camping €5.20 per person. 4-to 6-person bungalows €60-90. Open year-round.

sights

BARRI GÒTIC AND LAS RAMBLAS

COLUMBUS MONUMENT — TOWER

Portal de la Pau ☎93 302 52 24

Located where Las Ramblas meets the water, the Columbus Monument offers an unbeatable view of the city and a certain heart attack for those afraid of heights for just €3. The 60m statue was constructed from 1882-1888 in time for Barcelona's World's Fair in order to commemorate Barcelona's role when Christopher Columbus met with King Ferdinand and Queen Isabella upon his return from the New World. Though it is said that the 7.2m statue at the top of the tower points west to the Americas, it actually points east, supposedly to his hometown of Genoa. Around the base of the column are reliefs depicting the journey, as well as bronze lions that are guaranteed to be mounted by tourists at any given hour.

Ⓜ Drassanes. Entrance located in base facing water. $ €3, children €2. Open daily May-Oct 9am-7:30pm, Nov-Apr 9am-6:30pm.

MUSEU D'HISTORIA DE LA CIUTAT — ♿ HISTORY

Pl. del Rei ☎93 256 21 00 www.museuhistoria.bcn.es

If you thought the winding streets of the Barri Gòtic were old school, check out the Museu d'Historia de la Ciutat nestled 20m underneath Pl. de Reial. Underneath this unassuming plaza lies the excavation site of **archaeological remains** of ancient Barcino, the Roman city from which Barcelona sprouted. One thing has remained the same—the people of this area love their booze, and huge ceramic wine flasks can be seen dotting the site, as well as intricate floor mosaics and strikingly well-preserved ruins ranging from the first to sixth centuries CE. The second part of the museum in the area features the comparatively new **Palacio Reial Major,** a 14th-century palace for Catalan-Aragonese monarchs that was built in part using the fourth-century Roman walls. Inside the palace, the expansive and impressively empty Gothic **Saló de Tinell** (Throne Room) is the seat of legend: here Columbus was received by Fernando and Isabel after his journey to the New World, while the **Capilla de Santa Àgata** avoids the fame of kitschy tales and goes right for the goods, hosting rotating exhibits about modern and contemporary Barcelona.

Ⓜ Jaume I. i Free multilingual audio guides. Ⓢ Museum and exhibition €7, students and under 25 €5, under 16 free. Museum €6, students €4. Exhibition €1.80/1.10. Open Apr-Sept Tu-Sa 10am-8pm, Su 10am-3pm; Oct-Mar Tu-Sa 10am-2pm and 4-7pm, Su 10am-3pm.

CITY HALL — GOVERNMENT

Pl. de Sant Jaume–Ciutat, 2 ☎93 402 70 00 www.bcn.es

The government-appropriate 18th-century Neoclassical facade facing the Plaça hides a more interesting 15th-century Gothic facade located at the old entrance to the left of the building (which is now also the tourist entrance). Inside City Hall are a myriad of treasures, both fantastical and more somber—the lower level is home to many pieces of sculpture from the Catalan masters (many of these same artists have work in the Museu Nacional d'Art de Catalonia), while the upper level boasts impressively lavish architecture and interiors such as the *Saló de Cent*, where the *Consell de Cent* (Council of One Hundred) ruled the city from 1372-1714. Around certain holidays, the Giants of the Old City may be seen lurking the halls—towering figurines representing past kings and queens, horses, indecipherable monsters, and **dragons.**

Ⓜ Jaume I. Take a right onto C. de Jaume I after exiting the station. Once in Pl. de Jaume I, City Hall is on your left. i Tourist info available at entrance. To enter, take alley to the left of City Hall and take a right onto C. Sant Miquel. Ⓢ Free. Tourist info open M-F 9am-8pm, Sa 10am-8pm, Su and holidays 10am-2pm. City Hall open to public Su 10am-2pm.

LA BOQUERIA (MERCAT DE SANT JOSEP) — MARKET

La Rambla, 89

If you're looking for the freshest tomatoes, leeks the size of a well-fed child's arm, fruit prickly enough that it could second as a shirukin, sheep's head (eyes included), or maybe just some nuts, the Boqueria has you covered in the most strikingly beautiful way. Though each neighborhood in Barcelona lays claim to its own *mercado*, Mercat de Sant Josep is not only the biggest and most impressive in the city, but it also claims the title of largest open-air market in all of Spain. As a consequence, expect to have to fight your way through wildebeest-like hordes of locals and tourists alike to get those cherished lychee for your picnic on the beach. If filling your stomach from the glowing rows of perfectly arranged, perfectly ripe produce doesn't satisfy your famished gut, restaurants surrounding the market offer meals made of fresh produce straight from the nearby vendors. For the frustrated vegans in the city, the market will be your godsend—just turn a blind eye to the ham legs hanging on the outskirts.

Ⓜ Liceu. Walk on Las Ramblas toward Pl. Catalonia and take a left onto Pl. de Sant Josep. Open M-Sa 8am-8pm, though some individual stands stay open after 9pm.

CATEDRAL DE CANTA CRUZ Y SANTA EULALIA DE BARCELONA — CATHEDRAL

Pl. de la Seu ☎93 315 15 54 www.catedralbcn.org

Behold: the Cathedral of the Holy Cross and Santa Eulalia (La Seu, for short) and its ever-present construction-related accoutrements, Barcelona's only cathedral and a marvel of beauty and perseverance. The impressive scaffolding rig and skeletal spire drawing attention away from the Gothic facade are actually signs of what you'll see advertised with the "Sponsor a Stone" campaign in the interior—costly renovations that began in 2005. The cathedral is no stranger to drawn out projects, however. Although construction on the cathedral began in

1298, the main building wasn't finished until 1460, the front facade until 1889, and the central spire until 1913.

Once you've been funneled through the scaffolding and into the main building's interior, almost all signs of construction disappear. Soaring vaulted ceilings mark the nave, and decadently decorated chapels—28 in all—line the central space. Most important, however, is the *cathedra* (bishop's throne) that designates this building as a cathedral and is found on the altar. Don't miss the crypt of Santa Eulalia, located at the bottom of the stairs in front of the altar.

To the right of the altar (through a door marked "Exit") is the entrance to the cloister, a chapel-laden courtyard enclosing palm trees and thirteen white ducks that are intended to remind visitors of Santa Eulalia's age at the time of her martyrdom. Here you will find the cathedral's museum, which hides various religious paintings and altarpieces in various stages of needing to be cleaned, a very gold monstrance (used during communion), and, in the Sala Capitular, Bartolomé Bermejo's *Pietà*. If you only have €3 to spend, pay to take the lift instead—you'll get up close and personal with one of the church's spirals and find yourself with a breathtaking view of the city.

Ⓜ Jaume I. Left onto V. Laietana and then left onto Av. de la Catedral. Ⓢ Catedral free. Museum €2. Elevator €2.50. Tours €5. Free admission M-F 8am-12:45pm and 5:15-7:30pm, Sa 8am-12:45pm and 5:15-8pm, Su 8am-1:45pm and 5:15-8pm. Visitor admission M-Sa 1-4:30pm. Inquire about guided visit to museum, choir, rooftop terraces, and towers.

PALAU DE LA GENERALITAT GOVERNMENT

C. de Sant Sever ☎90 240 00 12 www.gencat.cat/generalitat/eng/guia/palau/index.htm

Facing the Plaça Sant Jaume I and the Ajuntament, the Palau de la Generalitat provides a second reason this plaza is incredibly popular with protestors and petitioners. The Renaissance facade dates from the early 17th century, hiding a Gothic structure that was obtained by the Catalan government in 1400. Although the majority of visitors will be stuck admiring its wonderfully authoritative feel from the exterior, with a bit of magic in the way of good timing it is possible to see the interior. Inside, visitors will find a Gothic gallery, an orange tree courtyard, St. George's Chapel, a bridge to the house of the President, many historic sculptures and paintings, and the **Palau's carillon,** a 4898kg instrument consisting of 49 bells that is played on holidays and for special events.

Ⓜ Jaume. Take a right onto C. de Jaume I after exiting the station. Once in Plaça de Jaume I, Palau is on your right. Ⓢ Free. Open to the public on Apr 23, Sep 11, and Sep 24, and on 2nd and 4th Su of each month from 10am-2pm.

GRAN TEATRE DEL LICEU ♿❄ THEATER

Las Ramblas, 51-59 ☎93 485 99 00 www.liceubarcelona.com

Alongside the sometimes dirty paths, animal cages, and peddlers of Las Ramblas is one of the Europe's grandest stages that specializes in opera and classical performances. The Baroque interior of the auditorium will leave you gawking at the fact that it dates back only to 1999 when the interior was reconstructed after a 1995 fire (though, to be fair, it is an exact reconstruction of the previous auditorium). A 20min. tour provides a glimpse of the ornate *Sala de Espejos* (Room of Mirrors), where Apollo and the Muses look down upon opera-goers during intermission, and the five-layered bedazzled auditorium, where you may catch a director yelling furiously during a rehearsal if you are lucky. For a more in-depth tour that won't leave you spending half of your time looking at stackable chairs in the foyer or being told about the donors list (though it does include Placido Domingo), be sure to either come for the 1hr. tour at 10am, arrange a behind-the-scenes tour with the box office, or attend a performance in person.

Ⓜ Liceu. *i* *Discount tickets available.* *$ 20min. tour €4, 1hr. tour €8.* *Box office open M-F 10am-2pm and 2-6pm. 20min. tours start every 30min. daily 11:30am-1pm; 1hr. tour daily at 10am.*

P. DE L'ÀNGEL HISTORY

Corner of V. Laietana and C. de la Princessa

The square immediately surrounding the ⓂJaume I may now seem like nothing but a place to grab a good pastry, but in the days of Roman Barcino this spot was the main gate into the city. To revel in some of this seemingly absent history, simply walk parallel to **V. Laietana,** the busy street forming one side of the square's border. For a more contemporary piece of history (though still dating from the triple digits CE), look no further than the angel statue facing the street that happens to be pointing to her toe. This sculpture commemorates the event from which the plaza got its name—reportedly when carrying the remains of Santa Eulalia to the cathedral from Santa Maria del Mar, the caravan came to the plaça. Suddenly, the remains became too heavy to carry, and upon setting down the remains, an angel appeared and pointed to her own toe, alerting the carriers that one of the church officials had stolen Santa Eulalia's little digit.

ⓂJaume I. $ Free.

ROMAN WALLS HISTORY

Scattered throughout the Ciutat Vella, portions of the Roman remains are marked clearly with orange and black info plaques by the city, and it's hard not to run into at least one of them. For those history buffs looking for the most bang for their buck, walk down C. Tapineria (it's to your back as you exit the Metro station), a narrow street connecting Plaça de l'Àngel and Plaça Ramon Berenguer. This street holds the most concentrated number of fourth-century wall remains, though they may be hard to spot, as they are entirely incorporated into the base of the 14th-century Palau Reial Major. The second area of interest is the **Plaça Seu** in front of the Cathedral. To the left of the Cathedral is the only remaining octagonal tower, and to the right is a reconstruction of the Roman aqueduct and other smaller remains.

ⓂJamue I. $ Free.

Las Ramblas

Beginning along the sea and cutting straight through to Plaça Catalonia, Las Ramblas is Barcelona's world-famous main pedestrian thoroughfare that attracts flocks of visitors and herds of people attempting to draw money from said visitors. Lined with trees, cafes, tourist traps, human statues, beautiful buildings, and pickpockets, the five distinct promenades combine seamlessly to create the most lively and exciting pedestrian area in the city. The **Ramblas,** in order from Plaça Catalonia to the Columbus Monument are: **La Rambla de les Canaletess, La Rambla dels Estudiss, La Rambla de Sant Josepp, La Rambla dels Cataputxins,** and **La Rambla de Santa Monica.**

LA RAMBLA DELS ESTUDIS PROMENADE

Las Ramblas

Named for the university that was once located here (*estudis* means "studies" in Catalan), the path is now closer to a lesson in animal taxonomy than other scholarly topics. Known as "Las Ramblas dels Ocells" (literally, of the birds), the shops along this stretch of pavement sell everything from rabbits to guinea pigs, iguanas to turtles, ducks to parrots, and much more. Here is your place to pick up a pigeon, and with some good training, you may soon be able to sidestep Spain's postal service. This area justifiably becomes the target of Barcelona's active and outraged animal rights proponents, but there seems to be no indication that Las Ramblas will be any less furry, fluffy, or feathery anytime soon.

ⓂCatalonia. Walk toward the water.

LA RAMBLA DE SANT JOSEP ♿ PROMENADE

Las Ramblas

If you're looking for a bouquet for that special someone, or you've just decided that your hostel bathroom could really benefit from a few rose petals, La Rambla de Sant Josep is your place. Flower shops line this stretch of the pedestrian avenue, giving it the nickname "La Rambla de les Flors." Following the theme of living things now dead, the impressive Boqueria is found along this stretch, along with the once-grand and now practically gutted **Betlem Church.** The end of this promenade is marked by Miró's mosaic in the pavement at Plaça Boqueria.

Ⓜ Liceu. Walk toward Plaça Catalonia.

LA RAMBLA DELS CATAPUTXINS ♿ PROMENADE

Las Ramblas

La Rambla dels Cataputxins boasts access to ⓂLiceu and a straight shot to Plaça Sant Jaume I via C. Ferran, which runs directly through the center of the Gothic Quarter. Cafes and restaurants line this portion of Las Ramblas, and eager business owners will try desperately to pull you into their lair—if "tapas" and specials listed in English don't do it first. Littered with eye candy such as the **Casa Bruno Cuadros** (corner of C. Boqueria and Las Ramblas, the one with the **dragon** in front), Teatre Liceu, and a mosaic by Joan Miró, this portion of Las Ramblas is often the busiest.

Ⓜ Liceu. Walk toward the sea.

LA RAMBLA DE SANTA MÒNICA ♿ PROMENADE

Las Ramblas

Ending at the feet of Christopher Columbus himself, La Rambla de Santa Monica leads the boulevard to the waterfront. This portion of the path is the widest and, unlike its saintly name would suggest, the most packed with vices and temptation. Though filled with artists peddling their takes on Miró, your face, or dolphins in the shape of letters during the day, at night the area becomes thick with prostitutes aggressively looking for confused potential clients.

Ⓜ Drassanes.

LA RAMBLA DE LES CANALETES ♿ PROMENADE

Las Ramblas

The head of Las Ramblas when walking from Plaça Catalonia to the water, this rambla is named after the fountain that marks its start—Font de les Canaletes. Surprisingly unceremonious, the fountain is not a spewing spectacle of lights and water jets but instead a fancy drinking fountain with four spouts, rumored to make those who drink its water fall in love with the city. These days the fountain has amusingly run dry, so be sure to fill your Nalgene elsewhere.

Ⓜ Catalonia.

LA RIBERA

DISSENY HUB BARCELONA (DHUB) ♿ DESIGN, ART

C. Montcada, 12; Av. Diagonal, 686 ☎93 256 23 00; 93 256 34 65 www.dhub-bcn.cat

Ever dream of making a chair simply with a beam of light? Chances are you haven't, but just in case you have (or you're curious how it's even possible), Disseny Hub Barcelona will show you said chair, let you touch it, and even explain every single step of its magical creation. Split over two buildings nearly a town apart, Disseny Hub Barcelona focuses on showcasing Barcelona's cutting edge contemporary art with a commercial edge through amazing historical displays, video supplements, and a creative laboratory that fosters the budding designer in even the least creative visitor. The **Montcada branch,** located across from the Museu Picasso, houses temporary exhibitions and study galleries that test the limits of the imagination, including everything from heat sensitive wallpaper to an automated dessert printer. Just across town, the Palau de Pedralbes hosts the **Museu de les Arts Decoratives** and the **Museu Tèxtil i d'Indumentària,** both highlighting the evolution of art objects and fashion from the Romanesque to the Industrial Revolution with enough quirky artifacts and period dress to make it worth the trek. Currently, the price of admission provides access to both museums, but look for both to be housed under the same roof in the upcoming year as the primary home of the Disseny Hub Barcelona is finished in Plaça de les Glorièrs Catalanes in 2011.

Montcada: ⓂJaume I. From Metro, walk down C. de la Princesa and turn right onto C. de Montacada. Pedralbes: ⓂPalau Reial. i New combined museum to be opened in 2011 in Plaça de les Glories. Ⓢ Admission to both centers €5. Free Su 3-8pm. Montcada open Tu-Sa 11am-7pm, Su 11am-8pm. Pedralbes open Tu-Su 10am-6pm.

PICASSO MUSEUM ARCHITECTURE, ART

C. Montcada, 15-23 ☎93 256 30 00 www.museupicasso.bcn.es

Tucked away amongst the *bodegas* and medieval charms of Ribera is the Museu Picasso—five connected mansions dedicated to showcasing what Picasso's work was like before he was cool. His early years' collection is organized chronologically, providing insight into his development into the international star of Cubism. However, the collection is not completely Barça-centric. Paintings from after his time in Paris show the influence of the Impressionists he encountered, while several works from his Blue and Rose periods help to paint a picture of his past. The most sweeping gesture of influence is easily the room of the artist's 58 renditions of Velázquez's *Las Meninas*, where the iconic Spanish painter's work is spiked and contorted into a nightmare landscape of Cubist forms. Temporary exhibits highlight the work of Picasso's contemporaries, though the museum would easily attract the same droves of visitors without them. Expect a long wait along the crowded street of Montcada during any day of the week, especially on Sundays when the museum is free. To beat the throngs of people, try hitting up the museum early or waiting until the later hours.

ⓂJaume I. From the Metro, walk down C. de la Princesa and turn right onto C. de Montacada. i Free entrance on first Su of each month. Ⓢ €8.50 (valid for 2 days, only for permanent exhibits). Annual subscription (permanent and temporary exhibits included) €14. Open Tu-Sa 10am-7pm, Su 10am-2:30pm.

PARC DE LA CIUTADELLA PARK, MUSEUM

Between Psg. de Picasso, C. Pujades, and C. Wellington

Once the site of the Spanish fortress built by King Felipe V in the 18th century, the park was transformed into its current state after the citadel was destroyed in preparation for the Universal Exhibition of 1888. This sprawling complex designed by Josep Fontserè includes copious green space as well as various *modernista* buildings from the period. Points of architectural interest span from two areas: the antique fort holds the governor's palace, arsenal, and *capilla*, and the Exhibition in 1888 area showcases century-old gems, many of which are still in use today. The steel and glass **Hivernacle,** a greenhouse-turned-civic-space near the Pujades entrance, maintains its original function as well as its newer one as a concert venue. The **Natural History Museum** *(☎93 319 69 12)* continues educating crowds and completing conservation work between its two locations. The **Museu Martorell** functions as a geology museum, and the **Castillo de los Tres Dragones,** designed by Lluís Domènech i Montaner (of Palau de Música Catalana and Hospital de Santa Creu fame) comprises the **Zoological Museum** building and the entrance to the **Barcelona Zoo** *(☎90 245 75 45 www.zoobarcelona.cat).* The extravagant **Cascada Monumental** fountain located in the center of the park, designed in part by Antoni Gaudí, still provides a spectacle for any visitor. Though a newer addition, the **mastodon** near the entrance of the zoo makes for an excellent photo opportunity.

For those just looking to use the park as, well, a park, bike trails run around the exterior walls, and dirt pedestrian paths break up the lush grass and tree-shaded pockets. Expect to see nearly every corner covered in picnickers during the summer months, and be sure to stop by and join the locals for a bath in the fountain.

Ⓜ Arc de Triomf. Walk through the arch and down the boulevard to enter the park. i Free Wi-Fi available at the Geological Museum, Parliament building, and Zoological Museum. Ⓢ Park free. Museum €4.10-5.60, Su 3-8pm free. Zoo €16. Park open daily 10am-dusk. Natural History Museum open Tu-Sa 10am-6:30pm, Su 10am-8pm. Zoo open May 16-Sep 15 10am-7pm; Oct 10am-6pm; Nov--Feb 10am-5pm; Mar-May 15 10am-6pm;.

SANTA MARÍA DEL MAR

♿ CHURCH

C. Canvis Vells, 1 ☎93 319 23 90 www.santamariadelmar.es

Ribera is dominated by this church's stoic presence, but it's nearly impossible to get a good glimpse of the Santa Maria. Nearby streets only allow remotely satisfactory views of the exterior from the Fossar de les Moreres at the end of Psg del Born. The Plaça Santa Maria, located at the west entrance of the church, holds the best views of the church's impressive rose window (dating back to 1459) and the intricate relief and sculptural work of the main entrance.

Constructed between 1329 and 1838, this church exemplifies Catalan Gothic style—tough on the outside, light and airy on the inside. The inside is perplexingly spacious and open, with tall, slim octagonal pillars lining the main nave and no constructed boundaries between the nave and the altar area. Although there are three naves, it feels as if the interior is made of only one. Despite the beautiful proportions and effect of the architecture, the interior has little decoration, due to a conflagration there in 1936 during the Spanish Civil War.

Ⓜ Jaume I. Walk down C. de l'Argenteria to enter the plaza. Santa Maria del Mar will be in front of you to your right. Ⓢ Free. Open M-Sa 9am-1:30pm and 4:30-8:30pm, Su 10am-1:30pm and 4:30-8:30pm.

ARC DE TRIOMF

♿ ARCHITECTURE

Between Psg. de Lluís Companys and Psg. de Sant Joan

For a proper greeting from the city of Barcelona, be sure to arrive by bus and get dropped off at the **Arc de Triomf Station.** If you're coming by other means, cheat and come here anyway. Situated at the beginning of a wide boulevard leading to the **Parc de la Ciutadella,** the arch not only picturesquely frames the palm tree- and *modernista* building-lined road and its incredible terminating point, but also embraces visitors with a sculptural frieze by Josep Reynés with the inscribed phrase "Barcelona rep les nacions," or *"Barcelona welcomes the nations."* This seemingly incongruous ceremonious declaration stems from its construction for the 1888 Universal Exhibition, when the arc served as the main entrance to the fairgrounds in the Parc.

Nowadays the arc serves as little more than a historical artifact but is worth a gander if you are in the area. The triumphant brick arch was designed by Josep Jilaseca i Cassanovas in the Moorish revival style. Its exterior is decked out with sculptures of 12 women representing fame and a relief by Josep Llimona depicting the award ceremony.

Ⓜ Arc de Triomf. Ⓢ Free. Open 24hr.

EL RAVAL

CENTRE DE CULTURA CONTEMPORÀNIA DE BARCELONA (CCCB) ART

C. de Montalegre, 5 ☎93 306 41 00 www.cccb.org

A hub for anything involving the more contemplative ideas of the city, the Centre de Cultural Contemporània de Barcelona boasts everything from art exhibitions to lectures on Gilles Deleuze to theater to literature to help trying to figure out what the hell public and private space really means. Three exhibition galleries, two lecture halls, an auditorium, and a bookstore fill the striking architectural complex, consisting of an early 20th-century theater-turned-supersleek glass-expansion-wing. Paired with the thought-provoking collections of nearby MACBA, the CCCB offers everything you'll need to inspire that next existential crisis.

Ⓜ Universitat. Walk down C. Pelai and take the 1st right and then a left onto C. Tallers. Take a right onto C. Valldonzella and a left onto C. Montalegre, which will place you in front of the Museum complex. ***i*** *Guided visits in Spanish Th 6pm, Sa 11:30am.* *One exhibition €4.50. Two or more exhibitions €6, under 25 €3.40, under 15 free. €3.40 on W; free on 1st W of month, Th from 8-10pm and Su 3-8pm.* *Open Tu--Su 11am-8pm. Last entry 30min. before close.*

MUSEU D'ART CONTEMPORANI DE BARCELONA (MACBA) ARCHITECTURE, ART

P. dels Angels, 1 ☎93 412 08 10 www.macba.cat

If the teeny art galleries and student-studded eateries around El Raval have struck your fancy, consider checking out the culture hub that helped to spawn them all. Bursting out of the narrow streets and into its own spacious plaza, the bright white geometries of American architect Richard Meier's 1995 building have made an indelible mark on the land, both architecturally and culturally, by almost single-handedly turning the area into a regional cultural and artistic center. The stark, simple interior plays host to an impressive collection of contemporary art, with particular emphasis on Spanish and Catalan artists, including a world-renowned collection of interwar avant-garde art. Due to its prime location near the Universitat and its undeniable appeal to local youth, MACBA prides itself on hip happenings. During the summer, "Nits de MACBA" keeps the doors open until midnight on Thursday and Friday nights, with free guided tours and reduced admission. Students and art afficionados alike flock to the popular hangout to catch one of the more experimental rotating exhibits, exciting complements to the static permanent collection. As if this weren't enough, the museum completely transforms during Barcelona's Sonar music festival every year, magically converting into the Sonar Complex stage and denying admittance to all those without a festival ticket.

Ⓜ Universitat. Walk down C. Pelai and take the 1st right and then a left onto C. Tallers. Take a right onto C. Valldonzella and a left onto C. Montalegre, which will place you in front of the Museum complex. ***i*** *Guided tours in English included in ticket purchase.* *Entrance to all exhibits €7.50, students €6; temporary exhibits €6/4.50. One-year pass €12.* *Open June 24-Sept 24 M 11am-8pm, W 11am-8pm, Th-F 11am-midnight, Sa 10am-8pm, Su 10am-3pm; Sept 25-June 23 M 11am-7:30pm, W-F 11am-7:30pm, Sa 10am-8pm, Su 10am-3pm.*

L'ANTIC HOSPITAL DE LA SANTA CREU I SANT PAU ARCHITECTURE

C. de l'Hospital, 56

Not to be confused with Lluís Domènech i Montaner's Hospital de la Santa Creu in the Eixample, L'Antic Hospital de la Santa Crue i Sant Pau (or Old Hospital of Santa Cruz and Saint Paul) is a 15th-century Gothic building located in the middle of Raval. Although the main core no longer functions as a hospital, it does house an interior courtyard bedecked with beautiful trees, benches, and a restaurant. The interior theater rocks a rotating marble dissection table, and the archives boast a recording of famous Catalan architect Antoni Gaudí's death in

1926. At this time, the hospital was used to treat the poor, and Gaudí was mistaken for a homeless man and brought to the premises after being hit by a tram. The hospital also now houses the Reial Acadèmia de Farmàcia de Catalonia, the National Library of Catalonia, and an art museum in its chapel, the latter two of which is open to the public.

Liceu. Walk down C. de l'Hospital. Free.

LA CAPELLA DE L'ANTIC HOSPITAL DE LA SANTA CREU I SANT PAU — MUSEUM

C. de l'Hospital, 56 — ☎93 442 71 71 elnostremuseu.blogspot.com

The chapel of the Antique Hospital of Santa Cruz's rustic stone walls and arches provide fantastic views of the building's interior Gothic architecture. Though mostly gutted of all decoration, the upper balcony and dilapidated organ are still on view above the main entrance. The chapel now serves as a center for contemporary and experimental art with smaller rotating exhibitions.

Liceu. Walk down C. de l'Hospital. Free. Open Tu-Sa noon-2pm and 4-8pm, Su 11am-2pm.

NATIONAL LIBRARY OF CATALONIA — LIBRARY, ARCHITECTURE

C. de l'Hospital, 56 — ☎93 270 23 00 www.bnc.cat

Although once housed in the Palau de la Generalitat de Catalonia, the collection now known as the National Library of Catalonia found its home in the Old Hospital in 1940. The library was considered a general-use library during the Franco years and was declared the national library of Catalonia after his fall. Today, over 20,000 volumes are open to the public, including the soaring vaults of the general reading room.

Liceu. Walk down C. de l'Hospital. Free. Open M-Th 9am-8pm, Sa 9am-2pm.

RIERA BAIXA — FLEA MARKET, SECONDHAND

C. de la Riera Baixa — www.facebook.com/pages/Riera-Baixa

A street lined entirely with secondhand shops, Riera Baixa is a mecca for any bargain or vintage shopper. The main attraction happens on Saturdays when clothes, records, trinkets, cameras, and an unfathomable amount of other stuff combine with Raval's largely student population, giving birth to the most exciting flea market in the city.

Liceu. Walk down C. de l'Hospital and take a slight right onto C. de la Riera Baixa. Fleamarket Sa 11am-9pm. Shops open daily.

L'EIXAMPLE

FUNDACIÓ ANTONI TAPIES — ARCHITECTURE, ART

C. Aragó, 255 — ☎93 487 03 15 www.fundaciotapies.org

Housed in a building by *modernista* architect Lluis Domenech i Montaner, the Fundació Antoni Tapies is made unmissable by its mess of wire and steel atop a low brick roofline, a sculpture by its namesake Antoni Tapies entitled "Núvol i Cadira," or "Cloud and Chair" (1990) that supposedly shows a chair jutting out of a large cloud. Once inside, the lower two levels are dedicated to temporary exhibitions on incredible modern and contemporary artists and themes, recently holding work by Eva Hesse and Steve McQueen. Ascend to the top floor to find the gallery space dedicated to famous Catalan artists, including Antoni Tapies himself. Paintings and sculpture using found materials shed new light on Catalonia's turbulent past, while summer nights light up with DJ nights, free drinks, and after-hours galleries.

Passeig de Gràcia. Walk toward the mountain on Psg. de Gràcia and take a left onto C. Aragó. The museum has a funky mess of wire on top. €7, reduced €5.60. Free May 18 and Sept. 24. Open Tu-Su 10am-8pm.

SAGRADA FAMILIA — ARCHITECTURE

C. Mallorca, 401 ☎93 208 04 14 www.sagradafamilia.cat

If you know Barcelona, you know Sagrada Familia—its eight completed towers and fanciful forms befitting of its Gaudí nametag have been plastered on tourist magazines, highlighted in movie advertisements, and featured in every panorama of the city ever photographed in the modern era. And with over 120 years of construction, the cranes surrounding the Sagrada Familia complex have become as iconic as the temple itself.

Although still a work in progress, Sagrada Familia's construction began way back in 1882. The super-pious, super-conservative **Spiritual Association for Devotion to St. Joseph (or the Josephines)** commissioned the building as a reaction to the liberal ideas spreading through Europe in the decades prior. It was intended as an Expiatory Temple for Barcelona in commemoration of the Sacred Family—Mary, Jesus, and Joseph. When searching for an architect, the Josephines looked in-house and picked Diocesan architect Francisco de Paula del Villar as their main man, but the relationship quickly turned sour, and one year later the church replaced him with Gaudí after only the Gothic foundations had been laid.

At the time of employment, Gaudí was just 30 years of age, and he would continue to work on the building until his death over 40 years later. Modest private donations founded the construction of the church in the beginning, but after the completion of the **crypt** in 1889, the church received an incredibly generous private donation allowing Gaudí to step up his game. This extra cash gave birth to the design that would make the building both the most ambitious and the most impossible to complete in the city. After building the **Nativity Facade,** a drop in private donations slowed construction, and in 1909 temporary schools were built next to the church for workers' children. Gaudí set up shop on-site a few years later, living next to his incomplete masterpiece until his brutal death by tram just outside of the church's walls in 1926. Fittingly, he was buried inside the **Carmen Chapel** of the crypt.

Gaudí's bizarre demise marked the start of a tragic period for the temple. The Civil War brought construction entirely to a hault, and in 1936 arsonists raided Gaudí's tomb, mashed the plaster models of the site, and burned every document in the workshop, effectively destroying all artifacts of the architect's original intention. Since then, plans for the construction have been based off of the remaining reconstructed plaster models, with computers only recently being used to help understand their complex mathematics.

Currently, the building remains under the auspices of the Josephines, and architect Jordi Bonet, whose father worked directly with Gaudí, remains in charge of the overall direction. The Cubist **Passion Facade** (Passion being the crucifixion, death, and resurrection of Christ) faces Pl. de la Sagrada Familia, and was completed by Josep Marià Subirachs in 1998. Its angular and abstracted forms are a far cry from Gaudí's original plans for the facade in 1911 and provide a stark contrast to his own more traditional Nativity Facade on the opposite face. The first mass was held inside the gutted church in 2000 for celebration of the millennium, and the church's apse is projected for completion in the upcoming year thanks to a continuous stream of popular donations (read: your ticket price).

If all goes well, the projected completion date is 2026, coincidentally both the 100th anniversary of Gaudí's death and the date that hell is predicted to freeze over. Until then, paintings of the completed building line the adjacent **Casa Museu Gaudí,** and an exhibition dedicated to the mathematical models let you imagine the completed building that you'll probably never get to experience.

*Ⓜ Sagrada Familia. **i** Guided tours in English May-Oct at 11am, 1, 3, and 4pm; Nov-Apr at 11am and 1pm. Ⓢ €11, students €9, under 10 free. Elevator €2.50. Combined ticket with Casa-Museu Gaudí €13, students €11. Open daily Apr-Sept 9am-8pm, Oct-Mar 9am-6pm. Last elevator to the tower 15min. before close.*

CASA BATTLÓ ARCHITECTURE

Psg. de Gràcia, 43 ☎93 216 03 06 www.casabatllo.es

From the spine-like stairwell wrapping around the scaled building's interior to the undulating **dragon-esque** curve of the ceramic rooftop, the Casa Battló will have you wondering what kinds of drugs Gaudí was rectally injecting. This architectural wonderland was once the home of the fantastically rich and is now the most heavily frequented of the three *modernista* marvels in the **Manzana de la Discordia** lining Passieg de Gràcia. A self-guided audio tour lets you navigate the dream-like environs at your own pace, so be sure to spend some time with the curved wood and two-toned stained glass of each of the doors (from both sides—the glass changes color), the soft scale-like pattern of the softly bowed walls, and the charybdis-esque light fixture that pulls the entire ceiling rippling into its center. Gaudí's design spans from the incredibly logical to the seemingly insane, including a blue lightwell that passes from deep navy to sky as you descend in order to distribute light more evenly.

If you're having a problem parting with the cash to get in, just try this logic, heard in line at the box office: if your flight to Barcelona had cost €18 more than you paid, would you still have taken it? Then why miss this gem for the same price? Like the guy who needed convincing, you won't be disappointed.

*Ⓜ Passeig de Gràcia. Walk away from Pl. Catalonia on Psg. de Gràcia. Casa Battló is 2½ blocks down on the left. **i** Tickets available at box office or through TelEntrada. Entrance includes free self-guided audio tour. Ⓢ Tours €17.80, students and BCN cardholders €13. Open daily 9am-8pm.*

CASA MILÀ (LA PEDRERA) ARCHITECTURE

Psg. de Gràcia, 92 ☎93 484 59 00 www.lapedreraeducacio.org

No, this building's facade didn't melt in the Barcelona sun, though it has garnered some equally unflattering comparisons. Its nickname "La Pedrera" literally means "the quarry," and stems from popular jokes, criticism, and caricatures about the house upon its construction 100 years ago. Although wealthy businessman Pere Milà hired Gaudí after being impressed by his Casa Battló a few blocks away, his wife began to loathe her version of Gaudí's signature style as construction progressed, and eventually refused to let the costly venture proceed. Not one to let the difficult couple have the last word, Gaudí sued the rich pair over fees and gave his winnings from the suit to the poor. Not ones to have Gaudí have the last say, the couple then looked elsewhere to complete their home interior, making La Pedrera the only house designed by Gaudí that isn't graced by his furniture.

La Pedrera still functions as a home to the rich, famous, and patient—the wait list for an apartment is over 20 years long—as well as offices of the Caixa Catalonia. Many portions of the building are open to the public, including an apartment decorated with period furniture (and, true to the house, not designed by Gaudí) and the main floor. The attic, a space known as **Espai Gaudí,** boasts a mini-museum to the man himself, including helpful exhibits explaining the science behind his beloved caternary arches and what exactly it means for the architect to be "inspired by natural structures." Up top, a terrace holds the perfect photo opportunity, whether with the desert-like sculptural outcroppings or the view overlooking Barcelona to Gaudí's Sagrada Familia. During the summer the terrace lights up both literally and metaphorically with jazz performances on Friday and Saturday nights in a series known as *La Nit de Pedrera.*

Ⓜ Diagonal. Walk on C. Rosselló toward Psg. de Gràcia and take a right. La Pedrera is on the left at the corner of C. Provença. i Free audio tour with entrance. Ⓢ €9.50, students and seniors €5.50. Concerts €12; glass of cava included. Open daily Mar-Oct 9am-8pm; Nov-Feb 9am-6:30pm. Last entry 30min. before close. Concerts last weekend of June and July F-Sa 9pm-midnight.

CASA AMATLLER

ARCHITECTURE, CHOCOLATE

Psg. de Gràcia, 41 ☎93 487 72 17 www.amatller.com

The severe, rational counterpart to Gaudí's neighboring acid trip **Casa Batlló,** Casa Amatller was the first of the trio of buildings that has come to be known as the **Manzana de la Discordia.** In 1898, chocolate mogul Antoni Amattler commissioned **Josep Puig i Cadafalch** to spruce up the facade of his prominent home along Passieg de Gràcia, and out popped a mix of Catalan, neo-Gothic, Islamic, and Dutch architecture in a strict geometric plane. A carving of Sant Jordi battling the pesky **dragon** appears over the front door, accompanied by four figures engaged in painting, sculpting, and architecture. Amattler's peddling in the muses is more than just decorative. Inside the building, find the **Amattler Institute of Hispanic Art,** including a library accessible to visiting scholars and students of art history. Although the house is currently undergoing renovations, the main floor is still open to visitors by reservation every Friday at noon, though times will change as the work progresses. If you're in the area and feel like stopping by to take a look at this gem, the lower level gift shop includes a free exhibition of the house and its sculpture and informs you as to exactly how Amattler got so filthy rich, with bars of the company's delicious chocolate for sale on your way out the door.

Ⓜ Passeig de Gràcia. Walk away from Pl. Catalonia on Psg. de Gràcia. Casa Amatller is 2½ blocks down on the left. i Reservation by phone or email required for tour. Ⓢ Tours €10; chocolate tasting included. Guided tours F at noon.

HOSPITAL DE LA SANTA CREU I SANT PAU

ARCHITECTURE

C. Sant Antoni Maria Claret, 167 ☎90 207 66 21 www.santpau.es

Notoriously the most important piece of *modernista* public architecture, this hospital's practice is anything but *nouveau.* Dating back to 1401, the Hospital de la Santa Creu i Sant Pau is the newest embodiment of the medical practice formerly housed in the Antique Hospital de la Santa Creu in Raval. Wealthy benefactor Pau Gil bequested funds for the building upon his death with strict instructions, including the name appendage. Construction then began in 1902 under the design of **Lluís Domènech i Montaner,** who in almost Gaudían fashion (only made more appropriate by Gaudí's anonymous death in the old hospital), died before its completion. His son then saw the work to fruition, giving the hospital 48 large pavilions connected by underground tunnels and bedazzled with luxurious modernist sculptures and paintings. Although the hospital still functions as a world class medical facility today, you won't need to break a leg to appreciate its beauty. Guided tours are offered daily as a part of Barcelona's Ruta de Modernisme.

Ⓜ Hospital Sant Pau. Guided tours in English daily at 10, 11am, noon and 1pm. Information desk open daily 9:30am-1:30pm.

GRÀCIA

PARC GÜELL

PARK, ARCHITECTURE ❶

Gràcia

Now a mecca for countless tourists and outdoor-loving locals alike, Parc Güell was originally intended for the eyes of a select few. Catalan industrialist, patron of the arts, and all-around man of disgusting wealth Eusebi Güell called upon his right-hand man **Antoni Gaudí** in 1900 to collaborate on an endeavor completely unlike the previous Güell Palau. The patron envisioned a luxurious community of 60 lavish homes wrapped around an English-inspired, Ebenezer-Howard-esque garden paradise overlooking Barcelona—rich, elite, and pleasantly removed from the mundane realities of the city and its plebian people. Unfortunately for the complex, other members of Barcelona's upper class weren't convinced; they weren't about to abandon the amenities of the city for a cut-off hunk of grass dotted by Gaudí's seemingly deranged buildings, which at the time lacked even basic living luxuries. Construction came to a halt in 1914, and in 1918 the area became a park when the Barcelona City Council bought the property.

The park was opened to the public in 1923 and has since been declared a UNESCO World Heritage Site. Buses bring flocks of visitors directly to the **Palmetto Gate,** a structure flanked by a guardhouse-turned-museum and giftshop. Hand-drummers stationed outside of the facing alcove often provide a dreamlike soundtrack for walking through the gingerbread-esque architecture. Those with sturdy shoes lacking a fear of heights often choose to take the Metro and climb the escalators to the nature-clad side entrance. The main attractions of the park (and, consequently, the areas most packed with people) are the brightly colored mosaics and fountains, like the **salamander fountain** just across from Palmetto Gate. The pillar forest of the **Hall of One Hundred Columns (Teatre Griego),** dotted with sculptural pendants by **Josep Maria Jujol,** musicians, and people peddling fake handbags. The intricate vaults of the hall support **Plaça de la Nautralesa** above, enclosed by the winding **serpentine bench,** decked in colorful ceramics, including 21 distinct shades of white that were castoffs from the **Casa Milà.** If you catch yourself wondering how a ceramic bench can be so comfortable, thank the woman rumored to have sat bare-bottomed in clay for Jujol to provide the form.

Paths to the park's summit provide amazing views, and one in particular showcases what the park has left to offer: walk to the right when facing the salamander fountain from its base. Follow the wide path and veer right toward the shaded benches and continue climbing uphill to come across the **Casa-Museu Gaudí** *(C. d 'Olot, 7 ☎93 284 64 46 www.casamuseuGaudí.org.)* As you continue, the third and last original building of the complex, **Juli batllevell's Casa Trías** lays inconspicuously ahead, still privately owned by the Doménech family. **El Turo de Les Tres Creus** greets visitors at the top of the wide path. This, the park's highest point with appropriately incredible views, was originally intended to be the residents' church and now serves instead to mark the end of the ascent.

Ⓜ Lesseps. Walk uphill on Travessera de Dalt and take a left to ride escalators to safety. Bus #24 from Plaça Catalonia stops directly in front of the park. Free. Museum €5.50, students €4.50. Open daily Oct-Mar 10am-6pm; Apr-Sept 10am-8pm.

BARCELONETA

MUSEU D'HISTÒRIA DE CATALONIA — ARCHITECTURE, ART

Pl. de Pau Vila, 3 — ☎93 225 47 00 www.es.mhcat.net

If you're finally tired of having "Catalonia is not Spain" pounded into your head without a proper explanation as to what that could even possibly mean, stop by the Museu d'Història de Catalonia and be converted to the Catalan cause. Settled right before where the old city becomes the tourist-lined Barceloneta (purposefully so, perhaps?), this informative museum doubles as regional propaganda, attempting to inform anyone and everyone about Catalonia's history, politics, and culture in a way that is both inspiringly patriotic and amazingly informative. Detailed displays recount the city's history, complete with English captions and vivid dioramas, and shed light on the layers of history and ruins that you've seen throughout the city. But more than being a simple supplement to your tour guide, the museum provides something more helpful—a historical briefer as to what makes Barcelona and Catalonia as a whole just so unique. The museum recounts its history from flint tools to the harrowing, rollercoaster days of Castillian relations to the Catalan beatdown by Franco and the subsequent rise after his demise. One foot in the door and you'll be ready to track down your own independentist flag to take home.

Ⓜ Barceloneta. Museum is located along the water on Psg. Joan de Borbó. i Free admission on first Su of month. Ⓢ €4, students and under 18 €3. Open Tu 10am-7pm, W 10am-8pm, Th-Sa 10am-7pm, Su 10am-2:30pm. Last entry 30min. before close.

MONTJUÏC AND POBLE SEC

FUNDACIÓ MIRÓ — ARCHITECTURE, ART

Parc de Montjuïc ☎93 443 94 70 www.fundaciomiro-bcn.org

From the outside in, the Fundació serves as both a shrine to and a celebration of the life and work of Joan Miró, one of both Catalonia and Spain's most beloved contemporary artists. The bright white angles and curves of the Lego-esque Rationalist building were designed by Josep Lluís Sert, a close friend of Joan Miró. Since its first opening, the museum's holdings have expanded beyond Miró's original collection, with many works by those inspired personally by the artist being donated or acquired in the years after his death. A rotating collection of over 14,000 works now fills the open galleries with views to the grassy exterior and adjacent **Sculpture Park.** Highlights of the collection include paintings and gargantuine *sobreteixims* (paintings on tapestry) by Miró, as well as works by Calder, Duchamp, Oldenburg, and Léger. Like much of Barcelona, the foundation refuses to be stuck in its past—although an impressive relic of a previous era, the foundation continues to support the contemporary arts in the present day. Temporary exhibitions have recently included names such as Olafur Eliasson, Pipllotti Rist, and Kiki Smith, while the more experimental **Espai 13** houses exhibitions by emerging artists selected by freelance curators. Overwhelmed? You should be. This is one of the few times we recommend paying for the audio tour *(€4).*

Ⓜ Parallel and then take the Funicular to the museum. Ⓢ €8.50, students €6. Audio tour €4. Sculpture garden free. Open July-Sept Tu-Sa 10am-8pm, Su 10am-2:30pm; Oct-June Tu-Sa 10am-7pm.

NATIONAL ART MUSEUM OF CATALONIA — ARCHITECTURE, ART

Palau Nacional, Parc de Montjuïc ☎93 622 03 76 www.mnac.es

This majestic building perched atop the escalator summit of Montjuïc isn't quite as royal as it would at first appear. Designed by Enric Catà and Pedro Cendoya for the 1929 International Exhibition, the Palau Nacional has housed the Museu Nacional d'art de Catalonia (MNAC) since 1934. Though the sculpture-framed view over Barcelona from the museum's front can't be beat, more treasures await inside. Upon entrance you'll be dumped into the gargantuan colonnaded **Oval Hall,** which, although empty, gets your jaw appropriately loose to prepare for its drop in the galleries. The wing to your right houses a collection of Catalan Gothic art, complete with wood-paneled paintings and sculptures Pier 1 would die to duplicate. To your left in the main hall is the wing housing the museum's impressive collection of Catalan Romanesque art and frescoes, removed from their original settings in the '20s and installed in the museum space—a move for the best considering the amount of churches devastated during the Civil War just a decade later. Upstairs are the more modern attractions, with MNAC's collections of modern art to the left, numismatics (coins, for you non-collectors) to the slight right, and drawings, prints, and posters to the far right. For those intoxicated by the quirky architecture of the city, Catalan *modernisme* and *noucentisme* works dot the galleries, from Gaudí's 1907 *Confidant from the Batlló House* chair to Picasso's Cubist *Woman in Fur Hat and Collar*. Ranging from 1800-1940, the collection highlights both the shape of Barcelona's avant-garde movements at the time and paints a picture as to how they got that way. If art isn't your thing, check out the currency collection—though beauty may be in the eye of the beholder, this 140,000-piece brief in the history of Catalan coin will hardly have any detractors.

Ⓜ Espanya. Walk through the towers and ride the escalators to the top—the museum is the palace-like structure. ***i*** *Free entrance on first Su of each month. Permanent exhibits €8.50 (valid for two days). Annual subscription (permanent and temporary exhibits) €14. Open Tu-Sa 10am-7pm, Su 10am-2:30pm.*

POBLE ESPANYOL

ARCHITECTURE, ART

Av. de Francesc Ferrer i Guàrdia, 13 ☎93 508 63 00 www.poble-espanyol.com

One of the few original relics from the 1929 International Exhibition still dotting the mountain, the Poble Espanyol first aimed to present a unified Spanish village from its disparate, disjointed parts. Inspired by *modernista* celebrity Josep Puig i Cadafalch's original idea, the four architects and artists in charge of its design visited over 1600 villages and towns throughout the country to construct its 117 full-scale buildings, streets, and squares. Though intended simply as a temporary arts pavilion, the outdoor architectural museum was so popular that it was kept open as a shrine (or challenge) to the ideal of a united Spain that never was and never will be. Nowadays, the Poble Espanyol is all of this and more, with artists' workshops lining the winding roads peddling goods, spectacles during the day, and Terrazza and other parties raging on during the night.

Ⓜ Espanya. Walk through the towers and take a right after climbing the escalators to the top. €8.90, students €6.60. Night entrance €5.50. Open M 9am-8pm, Tu-Th 9am-2am, F 9am-4am, Sa 9am-5am, Su 9am-midnight. Shops open daily in summer 10am-8pm; in winter 10am-6pm.

the great outdoors

BEACHES

Let's talk *platges*—that's beaches in Catalan. For basic information on all of the city beaches, contact the **city beach office** *(☎932 21 03 48 www.bcn.cat/platges)*. Tents, motorcycles, soap, loud music, littering, and dogs (though we've only seen dogs and trash) are all prohibited. Showers, bathrooms, police, first aid, and basic info are available at each individual beach June-Sept 10am-7pm. Lifeguards are present at all beaches June-Sept daily 10am-7pm; Mar-June Sa-Su 10am-7pm. Lockers are available at the police station during certain hours. For the gym rats and juice heads, almost all beaches have some sort of outdoor workout facility.

PLATJA SAN SEBASTIÀ

BEACH

Mouth of the Port to C. del Almirall Cervera www.bcn.cat/platges

The first of Barcelona's public beaches when stumbling out of the Ciutat Vella, Platja San Sebastià, along with Barceloneta, is one of the oldest beaches in the city. Older residents of the Barri Gòtic fill the available sand and are joined by a mix of tourists attracted to its convenient location. Like all beaches closer to Las Ramblas and the center of the city, San Sebastià will fill up quickly, especially on weekends. If you're looking for a place a little more private, the end furthest from Barceloneta—near Torre San Sebastià—promises something at least remotely resembling peace and quiet.

Ⓜ Barceloneta. i Bathrooms, swimming area, and showers available. $ Free. Wheelchair-accessible bathing services available June and 2nd half of Sept on holidays and weekends. Open daily July-1st week of Sept 11am-6pm.

PLATJA BARCELONETA BEACH

From C. del Almirall Cervera to Port Olímpic www.bcn.cat/platges

The most popular (read: crowded) beach in Barcelona, Barceloneta attracts a vibrant mix of visitors, tourists, and brave locals regardless of the weather. In short, good luck finding a place to sunbathe even when there's no sun to be seen. With three volleyball courts, an outdoor gym, information center, various restaurants, a boardwalk, skating area, ping-pong, and a *biblioplaya* (beach-centric library), Barceloneta offers (nearly) everything but a spot to lay your towel.

Ⓜ Barceloneta or Ⓜ Ciutadella. i Info center. Book rental. Showers, public restrooms, volleyball courts, ping-pong tables, and gym available. $ Free. Open 24hr.

PLATJA DEL BOGATELL BEACH

From Bogatell Pier to Mar Bella Pier www.bcn.cat/platges

A rock wall protects a portion of Platja del Bogatell from the sea's sometimes perilous waves; however, the sport of choice here is not swimming, but marathon sunbathing on sand that resembles kitty litter when it gets wet. As with Platja San Sebastià, expect this beach to be frequented more heavily by an older crowd as teenagers and young adults flock to the busier Platja Barceloneta and more secluded Platja Nova Mar Bella. The adjacent Parc del Poblenou also offers a pleasantly green haven for those few that have grown tired of sand and waves.

Ⓜ Poblenou or Ⓜ Llacuna. i Swimming area, showers, volleyball courts, and ping-pong tables available. $ Free. Open 24hr.

PLATJA MAR BELLA BEACH

From Mar Bella Pier to Bac de la Roda www.bcn.cat/platges

Past the Bogatell naval base, rocky outcroppings provide cover for Barcelona's only designated portion of nude beach. Past this short stretch of plentiful skin is a gay beach, marked by a rainbow flag flying at the beachside restaurant. Mostly frequented by younger and local people, the two sections provide a perfect place to shed some inhibitions (among other things).

Ⓜ Selva del Mar. i Showers, public restrooms, ping pong tables, skating area, and basketball available. $ Free. Open 24hr.

PLATJA NOVA MAR BELLA ♿ BEACH

Bac de Roda Pier to Selva de Mar Pier www.bcn.cat/platges

The furthest of all the beaches and consequently the least crowded, Platja Nova Mar Bella is the stomping ground of local youth, teenagers, and students. Still easily accessible by metro, this beach boasts a more relaxing alternative to the tourist-pushing match of Barceloneta, especially on weekends.

Ⓜ Selva de Mar and Ⓜ El Marisme. i Showers and public restrooms available. $ Free. Wheelchair-accessible bathing services available on holidays and weekends during June and 2nd half of Sept. Open daily July-1st week of Sept 11am-6pm.

PARKS

PARC DE COLLSEROLA PARK

Crta. de l'Esglèsia, 92 ☎93 280 35 52 www.parccollserola.net

Just 20min. outside the center of Barcelona by train lies the largest metropolitan park in the world. At 84.65sq. km, Parc de Collserola makes Paris's Bois de

Boulogne look like a playground and New York's Central Park like a grade school shoebox diorama. The park stretches along the **Collserola mountain range** from the **Besos River** to the **Llobregat River,** with **Barcelona** and the **Vallés basin** forming its southern and northern boundaries, respectively. Although the park is easily accessible by public transportation, few people from outside of Barcelona and its environs make the short trek, so expect to find all signs and informational material in Catalan.

Collserola isn't your typical "city park." The city grid is nowhere to be seen, and there are more than pigeons and squirrels here. The park offers a refreshing dose of fresh air and wildlife that the gridded city misses. Due in part to straddling two distinct climates, the coastal **Mediterranean** and the more deciduous **Euro-Siberian,** Collserola shelters a wide range of flora and fauna, including the occasional wild boar. For a greatest hits showcase of the variety that the park has to offer, the trail from **Parc del Laberint** (Ⓜ Mundet) to **Sant Cugat** is highly recommended. Besides a relaxing place to birdwatch and improve your classification skills, the park also offers many opportunities for exercise, with a ton of hiking trails and the **Carrertera de les Aigües** (Water Road), a cycling track that follows the ridge of the mountain range.

For those who do not find never-ending delight in the birds and the bees, the park is littered with places to eat, benches to relax on, and historic pieces of architecture and ruins to mentally digest. History buffs will want to check out the 12th-century **Sant Adjutori** and **Sant Medir,** while modernists should be sure to make a stop at the **Collserola Tower,** a telecommunications tower designed by architect Normal Foster for the 1992 Olympic Games. Although the games have long passed, its 10th-floor observation room and unbeatable location on Vilana hill make it an ideal place to look out over all of Barcelona, Montserrat, and, if the day is clear, even the Pyrenees.

*Ⓜ Baixador de Valividvera for Information Center (S1, S2), Ⓜ Peu de Funicular (S1, S2), Ⓜ Les Planes (S1, S2), Ⓜ La Floresta (S1, S2, S5, S55), or Ⓜ Mundet (L3). **i** Tourist information center, museum, and restaurant near Ⓜ Baixador de Valvidvera entrance. Other museums and restaurants scattered throughout; see website for full listing. Ⓢ Free. Tours daily 10am-2pm. Info center open daily 10am-3pm.*

food

BARRI GÒTIC AND LAS RAMBLAS

ATTIC

FANCY ❸

La Rambla, 120 — ☎93 302 48 66 www.angrup.com

After a long day along Las Ramblas, Attic provides a soothing and incredibly orange world away from the performers, pickpockets, and never-ending construction. Serving fresh and utterly delectable food with prices downright reasonable for the quality of cuisine and mere presence of cloth napkins, Attic has no dress code, but it may be best to leave that pit-stained T-shirt and the pair of Tevas behind for the day.

Ⓜ Liceu. On La Rambla toward Plaça Catalonia. Ⓢ Appetizers €4.60-11; meat entrees €8-16.50, fish €10-13. Open daily 1-4:30pm and 7pm-12:30am.

LA COLMENA

PASTRY SHOP ❶

P. de l'Àngel, 12 — ☎93 315 13 56

Directly facing the Plaça de l'Àngel, *pastelería* and *bomboneria* La Colmena sweetly greets visitors as they appear bleary-eyed from the labyrinth of the Barri Gòtic and the Catalonian Sun. La Colmena offers a variety of pastries, chocolates, sweets, and hard drinks (of the dessert variety) to take the buzz off a day of continually getting lost. Mirrored walls and marble inlaid floors covered with confectioneries make you feel as if you've suddenly walked into an old-time mix between the shop in *Charlie and the Chocolate Factory* and the gingerbread house of Hansel and Gretel. Offerings range from the expected—chocolate *(€1.30)* and truffles *(€2)*—to those specific to Cataluña, like the *pastellitas de l 'Angel (€1.25),* a small and flaky pastry shell with sugary pumpkin filling. If you're overwhelmed (as you should be), just ask the knowledgeable staff.

Ⓜ Jaume I. La Colmena is at your back after exiting the metro. Sweets €1.30-4. Open daily 9am-9pm.

ESCRIBÀ DESSERT ❶

La Rambla, 83 ☎93 301 60 27 www.escriba.es

Grab a coffee and ogle the stained-glass peacock or one of the many just as impressive works of art waiting to be devoured in the front display case. With tarts, croissants, cakes, and deceivingly beautiful and life-like rings made of caramel, Escribà is waiting to tempt you from every corner of the store. If you're not in the mood for sweets, select one of their savory dishes, such as the croissant with blue cheese, carmelized apple, and walnuts *(€4.50)* or the "bikini" bread mold with ham and brie *(€3.50)*.

Ⓜ Liceu. Walk toward Plaça Catalonia. Escribà is almost immediately on the left. Sandwiches €3.50, salads €3. Menú €5.90. i Open Tu-Su 9am-9pm.

L'ANTIC BOCOI DEL GÒTIC CATALAN ❸

Baixada de Viladecols, 3 ☎93 310 50 67 www.bocoi.net

Enter the lair of L'Antic Bocoi del Gòtic, where walls of rustic stone are somehow made impressively classy. The restaurant specializes in Catalan cuisine with fresh, seasonal ingredients and prides itself on bringing new ideas to traditional food. The staff recommends their selection of cheeses and their own take on the *coques de recapte*, a traditional regional dish made of a thin dough with delicious fresh produce and thickly layered meats. This hip joint fills up quickly after opening.

Ⓜ Jaume I. i Reservations recommended. Appetizers €7-10, entrees €9-20. Open M-Sa 8:30pm-midnight.

CAJ CHAI TEA ❶

Sant Domenech del Call, 12 ☎610 33 47 12 www.cajchai.com

Pronounced Chai Chai and named after the Czech "caj," or teahouse, the interior gives off more of a pseudo-Japanese zen vibe than any eastern European bohemian affectations. Beg the waitstaff to help guide you through their overwhelming list of teas from around the globe, and be sure to ask if there are any teas that are particular to the season. A variety of Arab, Indian, and Japanese pastries (€1.50-2) provide the perfect complement to the international array of teas. Luckily, all teas come in a personal pot, so you'll have an excuse to lounge in the good vibes for awhile longer. Morning specials for chai and pastries also available.

Ⓜ Jaume I. Exit the Metro station and take a right onto C. Jaume I, walking through the square with administrative buildings. After passing through the square, the road becomes C. Ferran. Walk briefly down C. Ferran and take a right onto the narrow Sant Domenech del Call. Personal teas €2.50-7, pot for 4 €12-15; snacks €1.50-2. Cash only. M 3-10pm, Tu-Su 10:30am-10pm.

ARC CAFE FUSION, THAI ❷

C. Carabassa, 19 ☎93 302 52 04 www.arccafe.com

Down the narrow Carrer d'en Carabassa, Arc Cafe is easy to miss. For this reason, it's a great place to stop in when you're sick of the fanny packs and sneakers that crowd Las Ramblas—it's virtually guaranteed to be tourist-and bustle-free. The restaurant boasts a vegetarian-friendly menu that rotates every three months as well as popular Thai nights Th-F (regular menu still available). Luckily, their curries are always available—choose between chicken, bean curd, and jasmine rice *(€10.50-11.50)*—just be sure to order a mojito with Malibu to cool off *(€6)* if you're brave enough to go for spice. Cheaper midday menu also offered daily *(€9.60)*.

Ⓜ︎Drassanes. Walk toward the sea on Las Ramblas, take a left onto C. de Josep Anselm Clavé. Walk 5min. and stay on this road as it changes names to C. Ample. Take a left onto Carabassa. Arc Cafe on right. ***i*** *Reservations recommended on weekends.* *Appetizers €4.90-7.90, entrees €8.50-11.90. Wine €2. Beer €2-3.* *Open M-Th noon-1am, F-Sa noon-2am.*

LES QUINZE NITS MEDITERRANEAN ❷

P. Real 6 ☎93 317 30 75 www.lesquinzenits.com

Despite the restaurant's white tablecloths, leather chairs, and fabulous view of the Plaça Reial, the line outside of Les Quinzes Nits is enough to make any weary traveler looking for a classier dinner reconsider their priorities. Where else would you woo your most recent roadside romantic acquisition on a backpacker's budget? Try the duck confit with triaxat and pesto sauce *(€10)* or the leek pie with tomato and arugula *(€6.31)*. Expect a 30min. wait upon opening, but reportedly the line diminishes around 9pm.

ⓂLiceu, walk down Las Ramblas toward the sea and take a right on C. Ferran, then right onto Psg. Madoz. Restaurant on the left as you enter Plaça Reial. ***i*** *No reservations.* *Appetizers €3-6, entrees €6-10. Bread €.85.* *Open daily 1-3:45pm and 8:30-11:30pm.*

GOPAL VEGAN, DELI ❶

C. Escudeller, 42 ☎93 318 92 15

Located in the same plaça as Vegetalia, Gopal is a vegan deli that doesn't leave you guessing where its allegiances lie. Animal rights propaganda lines the walls, and a waitress in an Animal Liberation T-shirt mans the deli case filled with beautiful burgers of beans, lentils, seitan, and tempeh, as well as a variety of prepackaged veggie proteins and dairy substitutes for customers' home use. This spot is the perfect place to find more information on veggie-friendly restaurants and related events in the city as well as some dirt-cheap chow—€6 will get you a first and second course, soup, bread, and dessert. For a dessert that will leave you wondering why you ever bothered with other animals' secretions in the first place, be sure to pick up one of Gopal's cakes or muffins from Lujuria Vegana on your way out the door.

ⓂLiceu. Walk down Las Ramblas toward the sea. Take a left onto Carrer dels Escudellers and walk for about 5min. Gopal is on the right once you enter Plaça George Orwell. *Sandwiches €3.50. Produce and salads €3. Menú €5.90.* *Open daily 10am-midnight.*

XALOC TAPAS, MEAT ❷

C. de la Palla 13-17 ☎93 301 19 90

"Tapas, Mediterranean cuisine, Iberian Meats, Cheeses." What you see is what you get, and this phrase emblazoned across their menu header (combined with an entire epic wall of Iberian ham legs) does not disappoint. They know where they excel: high quality meats serve as the primary focus of simple dishes. Try one of their sampler plates of Catalan sausages *(€7)* or anything including *jamón* (ham). And, of course, vegetarians and vegans beware—you may be stuck with bread and salad.

ⓂLiceu. Walk down C. de la Boqueria and take an immediate left onto C. del Cardenal Casañas. Stay on this road in front of the church and through the Plaça del Pi, following it right as it leaves the square and becomes C. Palla. Xaloc is located where C. Palla merges with C. Banys Nous. *Tapas €2-7.* *Open daily noon-midnight.*

TUCCO PASTA ❶

C. d'Aglà, 6 ☎933 01 51 91

True to its name, Tucco "fresh pasta" offers just that—a selection of fresh pastas topped with your choice of sauce and cheese *(€4)*. The limited seating in the teeny store serves as a revolving door for hip, young locals and internationals wandering far off the beaten paths of the Gothic Quarter. If pasta isn't your thing, a selection of wallet- and veggie-friendly sandwiches, pizzas, desserts, salads, and snacks fill the nutritional void a meal of carbs creates. Don't expect to sit if you come at mealtime; instead, take your plasticware and hit the road.

Ⓜ Licue. Walk on Las Ramblas toward the water. Take a left onto C. Escudellers. Left onto C. d'Aglà. Ⓢ Pasta €4. Pizza from €9. Open M-F 1-11:30pm, Sa 1-6pm.

VENUS DELICATESSAN MEDITERRANEAN ❷

C. Vinyó, 25 ☎93 301 15 85

Ever-changing colorful local art and a laid-back staff make for a relaxed atmosphere, perfect for taking advantage of the free Wi-Fi. The deli is dotted both by laptop- and book-toting students as well as small groups looking for a calm place to relax and enjoy the afternoon. Though many of their salads are adventurous and refreshing, fresher fare for a similar price can be found in the area. If looking for something more substantial, there's always the gazpacho *(€5.50)* or moussaka *(€8)*, or go big with the day's *menú* *(€10)*.

Ⓜ Liceu. Right off of C. Ferran coming from Las Ramblas. i Free Wi-Fi for customers. Ⓢ Salads €5.50-8. Entrees €6.60-10. Menú €10. Open daily noon-midnight.

CAFE DE L'OPERA CAFE ❷

La Rambla, 74 ☎93 317 75 85 www.afeoperabcn.com

Beginning in the 18th century as a boarding tavern and later a chocolate shop, the cafe assumed its current form in 1929, adopting the amusing mix of modernist curves, Grecian women, and pastel paint colors that can be seen today. Don't be fooled by the fancy Parisian facade or the impressive historical pedigree—although famous as a Barcelonan post-opera institution, Cafe l'Opera offers affordable fare and a wide list of beer (including "Cannabis Club," *(€3.60)* which purportedly tastes like, well, you can guess), wines, drinks, and tapas.

Ⓜ Liceu. On La Rambla when walking toward the water. i Credit card only over €20. Ⓢ Tapas €2-4. Sandwiches €3-6.70. Specials €10.50-13. Open daily 8:30am-2:30am.

MAOZ VEGETARIAN VEGETARIAN, FALAFEL ❶

C. Ferran, 13 and La Rambla, 95 ☎65 384 76 53 www.maozusa.com

Short on time, cash, and patience? Stop into Maoz and grab a falafel with toppings buffet *(€4.20)* or fries *(€2.20)*. Don't expect to linger, though—this little corner restaurant barely has room for you to order. Instead, take your meal out onto the streets and walk proud knowing that even if it's chain fast food, at least it's not McDonald's.

Ⓢ Falafel €4.20. Fries €2.20. Open daily 11am-3am.

TRAVEL BAR BAR ❷

C. de Boqueria, 27 ☎93 342 52 52 www.travelbar.com

Predictably, this bar unabashedly caters to travelers. Unpredictably, it's a fantastic outside-the-hostel resource for people on the road, whether to meet fellow backpackers, chow down on a cheap meal, watch the game on the big screen, indulge in free internet, or browse their collection of travel books. Empty pockets? Stop in at 8pm for their €1 meals and to peruse their community bulletin board for deals on tours, rentals, and flamenco dance lessons. Older readers take note: complete with an endorsement from MTV, this place seems to cater almost exclusively to the college crowd. Menu is uncreative, overpriced, and downright cruel to vegetarians, but luckily it's near many delicious (and cheap) culinary alternatives.

Ⓜ Liceu. Exit and walk down C. de Boqueria. Bar on the left. Ⓢ Tapas €2-3. Entrees €6-12.50. Beer €3-5. €1 meals nightly at 8pm. 10% charge to sit on terrace. Open daily 12:30-11:30pm.

LA RIBERA

EL XAMPANYET — TAPAS ❷

C. de Montcada, 22 — ☎933 19 70 03

The cup doeseth overfloweth, with sheepskin wine bags, an overwhelming selection of *cava*, and crunchy old locals spilling out the door and onto the street at all hours. Inside is a museum of casks, blackened bottles, and kitschy bottle openers displayed against a hand-painted ceramic tile background. We recommend you try their cask-fresh *cerveza (€3.50)* or their house wine *xampanyet (€2)*, and pad your stomach with some of their delicious tapas *(€1.10-12.50)*.

Ⓜ Jaume I. Walk down C. de la Princesa and take a right onto C. de Montcada, towards the Museu Picaso. Xampanyet is on the right before reaching Plaçeta Montcada. Ⓢ Tapas €1.10-12.50. Beer €3.50. Wine and cava from €2. Open Tu-Sa noon-4pm and 7-11pm, Su noon-4pm.

PETRA — RESTAURANT ❷

C. dels Sombrerers, 13 — ☎933 19 99 99

With dark wood, stained glass, art nouveau prints, menus decaled onto wine bottles, and chandeliers made of silverware, Petra will have you expecting a high price for its eccentricity. Luckily, the bohemian feel is matched by bohemian prices. Pastas like the delicious gnocchi with blue cheese and asparagus *(€5.15)* and entrees *(€8)* are nice on the wallet.

Ⓜ Jaume I. Walk on C. Princesa and take a right onto C. del Pou de la Cadena. Take an immediate left onto C. de la Barra de Ferro and a right onto C. dels Banys Vells. Petra is located where C. dels Banys Vells terminates at C. dels Sombrerers. Ⓢ Menú €6.50. Appetizers €5-7; entrees €8. Open Tu-Sa 1:30-4pm and 9-11:30pm, Su 1:30-4pm.

LA BÁSCULA — VEGETARIAN CAFE ❷

C. dels Flassanders, 30 — ☎933 19 98 66

A working cooperative that serves cheap vegetarian sandwiches, *empanadas*, and salads. Doors serve as tables and a mixture of art, environmentally-friendly sodas, and protest flyers hanging up around the walls set this restaurant apart from the rest. Though discreetly robed in the same antique exterior as more expensive places, Báscula provides a cheaper alternative to the upscale eateries in other stone hideaways surrounding Ribera. Hours and seating availability may change as the restaurant fights for its right to serve in-house, but takeout is available no matter the outcome.

Ⓜ Jaume I. Walk down C. de la Princesa and take a right onto C. dels Flassanders. Ⓢ Entrees and salads €7-9. Sandwiches €4-4.50. Piadinas €6. Open W-Su 1-11pm.

HOFMANN PASTISSERIA — PASTRY SHOP ❶

C. dels Flassaders, 44 — ☎93 268 82 21 www.hofmann-bcn.com

Pastry school meets storefront in this Seussian mindbender in a French countryside setting. Artisans work on delectable goods in clear view on the mind-bending spiral staircase above, while glass cases and wooden cabinets filled with adorable gelatos *(€3.50)*, precious marmalade jars *(€8)*, and a selection of not-so-sickeningly-cute-but-utterly-delectable tarts and cakes wait below. For breakfast, try a coffee and one of the fresh croissants.

Ⓜ Jaume I. Walk down C. de la Princesa and take a right onto C. dels Flassanders. Hofmann is located immediately before crossing Psg. del Born. Ⓢ Croissants €1-1.50. Gelato €3.50.

Marmalades €8. Chocolates €1-5. Coffee €1.20-1.50. Open Tu-W 9am-2pm and 3:30-8pm, Th-Sa 9am-2pm and 3:30-8:30pm, Su 9am-2:30pm.

LA LLAVOR DELS ORIGENS

CATALAN ❷

C. Vidriería, 6 ☎93 453 11 20 www.lallavordelsorigens.com

La Llavor dels Origins serves typical Catalan fare with a picture menu that lets you see in almost excruciating detail what you will soon be eating. Seasonal menus rotate every two months, while the regular menu changes every six, ensuring that there will always be something new to scrutinize (and maybe cook on your own—all recipes are available on the website). Drawings from customers young and not-so-young deck the walls, belying the sleek, modern decor with homey charm.

*Ⓜ Jaume I. Walk down C. de la Princesa and take a right onto C. Montcada. Upon crossing the Psg. del Born, C. Vidriería is the street directly in front of you. **i** Organic meat available on request. Ⓢ Entrees €6-9.20. Beer €3. Wine €3.50. 15% discount for takeout. Open daily 12:30pm-1am.*

BUBÓ

BAKERY, CAFE ❶

C. Caputxes, 10 ☎93 268 72 24

Whether you're chilling in the outdoor seating with an up-close and personal view of Santa Maria del Mar or just gazing through the display case of the bakery next door, Bubó is sure to delight the eyes. Heartier fare includes reasonably priced sandwiches from its "world sandwich tour," while the perfectly glazed tarts and a rainbow of macaroons promise to deliciously tempt any sweet tooth.

Ⓜ Jaume I, Exit to C. de l'Argenteria and walk down C. de l'Argenteria away from V. Laietana. Once entering the plaza surrounding the church, take an immediate right onto C. dels Sombrerers and the first left onto C. Caputxes. Ⓢ Sandwiches €3.25-4. Tapas €2-6. Desserts €1-3.50. Cakes €20-30. Cocktails €4-8. Open M 4-10pm, Tu-Th 11am-10pm, F-Sa 10am-1am, Su 10am-10pm.

BODEGA LA TINAJA

WINERY, RESTAURANT ❸

C. de l'Esparteria, 9 ☎933 10 22 50 www.bodegalastinajas.com

With so much wine lining the walls that you'll feel tipsy just looking in, this dark, earthy den behind a huge Gothic door provides bottle after bottle, **jug after jug**, and even barrel after barrel for whatever your thirst (or just eyes) may desire. The smell of seasoned meat fills the air with typical Catalan entrees (€10-21).

*Ⓜ Barceloneta. Walk away from the water on Plà del Palau and turn right onto Plà del Palau at the end of the plaza. Turn left onto Plaça de les Olles and follow it as it veers into C. de les Dames. Turn right onto C. de l'Esparteria. **i** Sometimes hosts guitar and flamenco concerts. Ⓢ Salads €7.25-9. Full entrees €10-21, half €4.25-11. Open Tu-Su 8am-midnight.*

EL ROVELL

CATALAN ❸

C. de l'Argenteria, 6 ☎93 269 04 58 www.elrovelldelborn.com

Literally "the yolk" and not-so-literally "the place to meet," El Rovell satisfies both claims with a special egg-centric menu section and a large TV for congregating around the game. Don't be fooled by the screen in the back and the buckets hanging from the tables—this is no spit-your-shells-on-the-floor sports bar. Classy red leather stools and a clean wooded interior match equally refined clientele and cuisine, like *huevos rotos* (scrambled eggs) with *foie gras* (€9.25).

Ⓜ Jaume I. Exit to C. de l'Argenteria and walk down C. de l'Argenteria away from V. Laietana. Ⓢ Entrees €7.50-24. Salads €6.50-14. Tapas €5.50-11. Open daily 1-4pm and 7pm-midnight.

VA DE VI

CATALAN ❸

C. dels Banys Vells, 16 ☎93 319 29 00

This 15th-century tavern was once home to Christopher Columbus, though nowadays the rustic, earthy interior is caught in a decorating rift between 19th-century cellos and random fluorescent lightning bolts ripping through the main room. The menu hearkens back to its historic past with a selection of traditional Catalan dishes, cheeses from France and Spain, and enough wine and *cava* to get you to believe you discovered the **New World**.

Ⓜ Jaume I. Walk down C. de l'Argenteria and take a left onto C. Rossic. Take a right onto C. dels Banys Vells. Ⓢ Meats €4-14.20. Cheeses €4-9. Tapas €1.50-6.50. Wine €2. Cava €2.50. Beer €1.50. Open M-Th 6pm-2:30am, F-Sa 6pm-3am, Su 6pm-2:30am.

GADES FONDUES — FONDUE ❸

C. l'Esparteria, 10 ☎93 310 44 55 www.gadesfondues.com

For those who just can't get enough of sticking food in other food, Gades Fondues steps up to fill a role often neglected. A choice of chocolate, meat, and cheese fondues *(€14-16 per person)* lets you pick it and stick it in a much classier setting than the phrase would imply. Salads, carpaccio, and a selection of other dishes fill out the menu for those looking for a less interactive meal.

Ⓜ Jaume I. Walk down C. Princesa and take a right onto C. Montcada. Cross Psg. del Born and follow C. de la Vidrieria until you reach C. de l'Esparteria. i Fondues require min. 2 people. Ⓢ Salads €10. Fondues €14-16 per person. Tapas €6-12. Entrees €10-18. Menú €20-22. Open M-Th 8:30pm-midnight, F-Sa 8:30pm-1am.

LONJA DE TAPAS — TAPAS ❸

Placeta Montcada, 5 ☎93 315 14 47 www.cellerdelaribera.com

A long dining room with an arched arcade and dark wooden tables may appear like the cleaned-up, posh brother of every other tapas bar in the area. Lonja serves incredibly fresh, beautifully prepared Mediterranean-style tapas that range in price, and the pricey but comprehensive *menú de gustació* awaits if you can't make a decision on your own.

Ⓜ Jaume I. Walk down C. Princesa and take a right onto C. Montcada. Placeta Montcada is the small plaza at the end of C. Montcada. i Other location at Pl. de Palau, 7 with same hours. Ⓢ Tapas €4-11. Menú de gustació €36. Open M-Th noon-midnight, F-Sa noon-1am, Su noon-midnight.

EL RAVAL

SOHO — PITA, HOOKAH ❶

C. Ramelleres, 26

One of the most recent additions to Raval, Soho is also one of the most welcome, serving cheap and simple eats like pitas and pastas with meat and vegetarian options *(€2)* without sending you off in a rush. Low-slung seats with smaller, intimate rooms make the perfect setting for test-driving a hookah from the impressive wall of smoking paraphernalia *(€10)*.

Ⓜ Universitat. Walk down C. Tallers and take a right onto C. de les Ramelleres. Ⓢ Pitas €2. Pasta €3. Hookah €10. Open M-Sa 1pm-midnight.

JUICY JONES — VEGETARIAN ❷

C. Hospital, 74 ☎93 443 90 82 www.juicyjones.com

The big brother of the Juicy Jones in the Barri Gòtic, this version of the vegetarian eatery offers a Raval-inspired twist—daily specials of Indian dahl and curries spice up the normal selection of sandwiches, plates, and an impressive selection of juices. If you have ever wondered what M.C. Escher's art would have looked like in the times of LSD, the interior will satisfy your curiosity.

Ⓜ Liceu. Walk down C. de l'Hospital. Juicy Jones is on your right on the corner of C. Hospital and C. d'En Roig, before you hit Rambla del Raval. Ⓢ Menú €8.50. Daily thali plate €6. Tapas €2-3.50. Sandwiches €3.85-4.50. Open daily 1-11:30pm.

NARIN — MEDITERRANEAN ❶

C. Tallers, 80 ☎93 301 90 04

Sitting discretely along the shops and cafes of C. Tallers, Narin is hiding the best baklava in Barcelona and equally scrumptious falafel, shawarma, and kebabs. If you can't stand the heat, get out of the kitchen—the inside feels like a sauna with wooden walls and sweaty people. Luckily, beer comes cold and cheap *(€1.80)* for those looking to brave the bar area, and a tiled dining room provides a reprieve from the buzz of the kebab shaver.

Ⓜ Universitat. Walk down C. dels Tallers. Pitas €2.90-4. Snacks €2.50-4.80. Baklava €1. Beer €1.80. Open M-Th 11am-2am, F-Sa 11am-3am, Su 11am-2am.

HELLO SUSHI — SUSHI ❸

C. Junta de Comerç, 14 — ☎934 12 08 30 www.hello-sushi.com

The vaguely oriental interior with a modern, artsy twist provides sushi platters for a reasonable price, enticing a young clientele into its dark, pillow-padded lair. Dine at the bar, grab a table, or sit on the floor in the foyer and admire the paintings while the smell of *tempura* and *teriyaki* entice you to stay for another round.

Ⓜ Liceu. Walk down C. l'Hospital and take a left onto C. Junta de Comerç. i Live music at times; check website for schedule. Daily menú €8.50 or €14.50. Salad €4. Entrees €8-14. Sushi combos €12-32. Open Tu-Sa 12:30-4:30pm and 8:30pm-12:30am, Su 8:30pm-12:30am.

SHALIMAR — PAKISTANI, INDIAN ❷

C. Carme, 71 — ☎93 329 34 96

Shalimar serves authentic Pakistani and Indian dishes tandoori style. Generous portions and delicious meat-based curries including chicken *(€7)*, lamb *(€8.20)*, and shrimp *(€9)* punctuate a menu that would make any vegetarian happy. Hand-painted tiles and warm lighting perk up the interior as lace curtains block out the busy streets of Raval.

Ⓜ Liceu. Walk down C. de l'Hospital and take a right onto C. d'En Roig. Left onto C. del Carme. Shalimar is on the left before the fork in the road. Appetizers €2-8. Veggie specials €3.70-4. Shrimp curry €9.30. Chicken €7. Beer €2. Open M-Tu 8pm-midnight, W-Su 1-4pm and 8pm-midnight.

MADAME JASMINE — CAFE ❶

Rambla del Raval, 22

Allow yourself to be seduced either by the 19th-century French-brothel-chic interior or the scrumptious *bocadillos*. Orange and red lighting sets the mood, incense fills the nostrils, and a selection of sultry Latin, electro, and lounge music will get you in the mood to partake in the less literal red light activities lining the streets of Raval.

Ⓜ Liceu. Walk down C. de l'Hospital and take a right onto Rambla del Raval. Madame Jasmine will be on your left nearly two-thirds down. Sandwiches and salads €4.75. House vermouth €2.20. Cocktails €5.50. Shots €2. Open M-F 5:30pm-2:30am, Sa-Su 1:30pm-2:30am. Kitchen open daily until midnight.

MENDIZABAL — FOODSTAND ❶

C. Junta de Comerç, 2

A crowd of young, artsy students out front and vibrant multicolored tiles in the back make this otherwise inconspicuous foodstand hard to miss. Take your cheap eats to go, or grab a seat on the terrace in the neighboring plaza for an extra 10% (look for the coordinating chairs). Some veggie-friendly options are available—we recommend the tomato, brie, and avocado sandwich *(€3.60)*.

Ⓜ Liceu. Walk down C. l'Hospital. Mendizabal is at the corner of C. l'Hospital and C. Junta de Comerç. i Terrace seating located in plaça across the street, but will cost 10% extra. Bocadillos €3.60-4. Beer €2.50. Postres €1.50-3. Open daily 8am-12:30am.

KASPARO — CAFE ❷

Pl. Vincenç Martorell — ☎93 302 20 72

A veggie-friendly menu lays host to an incredibly busy indoor diner with enough outdoor seating to compensate for the handful of seats available inside at the bar. Sit on the metal-clad seating of the terrace to partially escape the clatter of dishes and silverware inside, and grab one of their veggie-friendly *platos del día* *(€4.50-8.50)* or just a beer *(€2.70-3.40)* to satisfy whichever appetite you've mustered.

Ⓜ Catalonia. When facing Las Ramblas, take the road to your right (C. de Petal) along the plaza. Turn left onto C. de Jovellanos at the end of the plaza. Follow C. de Jovellanos as it becomes C. de les Ramelleres, and Plaça de Vincenç Martorell is on the left. Ⓢ Tapas €3-11. Appetizers €1.40-5.30; entrees €4.50-8.50. Open daily 9am-midnight.

ORGANIC

CAFE, MEDITERRANEAN ❷

C. Junta de Comerç, 11 ☎93 301 09 02 www.antoniaorganickitchen.com

For once, you won't have to worry about space for seating—organic has enough room to fit an entire youth hostel and their luggage. A vegan buffet *(€7)* surprises and delights with croquettes, pasta, and salad fixings, while all vegetarian Mediterranean dishes will please even the most outspoken carnivores. Be sure to say thanks to Mother Earth as you leave—she'll be looking down on you approvingly, surrounded by peas, earth, and fire, to your left.

EN VILLE

BISTRO ❸

C. Doctor Dou, 14 ☎93 302 84 67 www.envillebarcelona.es

Marble-topped tables, terra-cotta floors, wicker chairs, and lamps that mimic the posts outside combine for a charming bistro-style restaurant that brings the outside in while still serving impressive dishes like the roasted pig with melon and cantaloupe tartare *(€14.50)*. Actual outdoor seating is available as well, if that's your thing, but be sure to sit inside to be serenaded by live flamenco, jazz, or bosanova on Tuesday and Wednesday nights.

Ⓜ Liceu. Walk toward Pl. Catalonia on Las Ramblas. Take a left onto C. del Carme and a right onto C. Doctor Dou. i Live music on Tu and W nights. Ⓢ Tapas €3.50-19.70. Appetizers €7-11.80; entrees €12.50-19.70. Open M 1-4pm, Tu-Sa 1-4:30pm and 8pm-midnight.

L'HORTET

VEGETARIAN ❸

C. Pintor Fortuny, 32 ☎93 317 61 89 www.hortet.es

An upscale vegan and vegetarian eatery for when Maoz and Gopal just aren't cutting it. Understated interior details will leave you guessing where its allegiances lie, with red faux-leather tablecloths and abstract paper lights that only vaguely resemble produce. Come hungry during the day—only the entire *menú* is available *(M-F €10, Sa €13, Su €15)*, while the restaurant offers up lighter fare a la carte on nights and Sundays.

Ⓜ Liceu. Walk on Las Ramblas toward Pl. Catalonia and take a left onto C. del Pintor Fortuny. i A la carte items only available on nights and Sundays midday. Ⓢ M-F midday Menú €9.80, Sa €13, Su €15; night menú €15. A la carte items €4.50-9.50. Open M-W 1-4pm, Th-Sa 8-11pm.

BIOCENTER

VEGETARIAN ❷

C. Pintor Fortuny, 25 ☎93 301 45 83 www.vegetarianobarcelona.com

Bright white walls and a modular grid make the perfect gallery-like setting for its rotating selection of paintings, sculptures, and dusty-looking antique books. Relaxing piano music contributes to the feel, and an entirely vegetarian menu specializing in healthy and ecologically friendly cuisine waits to please your inner, socially conscious yuppie.

Ⓜ Liceu. Walk on Las Ramblas toward Pl. Catalonia and take a left onto C. del Pintor Fortuny. Ⓢ Menú €15. Appetizers €5-7.50; entrees €7.50-9.25. Dessert €3.50-4.25. Open daily 1-11pm.

CHULO

CAFE ❶

Pl. Vincenç Martorell ☎93 302 40 95

Gold indoor couches and painted cherry trees inject a shabby chic upscale twist into the interior of this little cafe, but the real life is outside on the terrace in

Plaça Vincenç Martorell, where it helps form the trifecta of cafes lining the side of the courtyard. Cheap breakfasts like the *toasta* with brie and tomato *(€3.50)* and *bocadillos*, like salmon and cream cheese *(€4.90)*, make this cafe the best of the bunch.

Ⓜ Catalonia. When facing Las Ramblas, take the road to your right (C. de Petal) along the plaza. Turn left onto C. de Jovellanos at the end of the plaza. Follow C. de Jovellanos as it becomes C. de les Ramelleres, and Pl. de Vincenç Martorell is on the left. Ⓢ Breakfast €1.90-4.20. Sandwiches €4.50-5.50. Salad €5.75-7. Open daily 10am-midnight.

CAFE D'ANNUNZIO — CAFE ❷

Pl. Vincenç Martorell ☎93 302 40 95

Rainbow stickers mark the glass doors of the last of the three cafes that line the arcade of Plaça Vincenç Martorell. Pictures of Venice and sculptures of Roman heads dress up the otherwise generic interior that sells delicious coffee supplied by Cafe del Dog. Sit inside to find an anachronistic, ill-fitting mix of '80s alternative hits playing over the stereo.

Ⓜ Catalonia. When facing Las Ramblas, take the road to your right (C. de Petal) along the plaza. Turn left onto C. de Jovellanos at the end of the plaza. Follow C. de Jovellanos as it becomes C. de les Ramelleres, and Pl. de Vincenç Martorell is on the left. Ⓢ Appetizers €1.60-4. Platters €10-15. Beer €2.70-3. Sandwiches €5-8, small €3.25-5.50. Open daily 9:30am-1am.

CAFETARIUM — CAFE ❷

C. Tallers, 76 ☎66 764 01 11 www.cafetarium.com

Much classier and less horror-movie-esque than the name would imply, Cafetarium serves a mix of cheaper sandwiches and more filling *platos del día* for when the *bocadillos* and coffee aren't cutting it. For those missing the greasy comforts of home, a double hamburger *(€5.15)* will remind your arteries of the good old days. Quirky frames and cheap vintage-chic chandeliers make those creature comforts just hip enough to stomach.

Ⓜ Universitat. Walk down C. dels Tallers. Ⓢ Sandwiches €3.30-5.15. Menú €7.45. Tapas €4.10-6.10. Open M-Sa 8am-1am.

L'EIXAMPLE

OMEÍA — JORDANIAN ❷

C. Aragó, 211 ☎93 452 31 79

When you're (literally) sick of gorging yourself on cheap shawarma from stands, stop in to Omeía for some authentic Middle Eastern fare that will only make you regret not having a bigger stomach. Start off with their roasted red pepper soup *(€6.50)* and fill up with one of their traditional Jordanian dishes *(€9-13)*. A word of advice: be prepared to take a long walk around the long blocks of l'Eixample after you finish to ease digestion.

Ⓜ Universitat. Walk on C. d'Aribau to the left of the University. Take a right onto C. Aragó. Ⓢ Starters €5.95-7. Entrees €6-13. Menú €7.50. Open daily 10am-4pm and 8pm-midnight.

EL JAPONES — JAPANESE, SUSHI ❸

Passatge de la Concepció, 2 ☎93 487 25 92 www.grupotragaluz.com

This sushi costs more than the price of your hostel for the night, but it's more than worth shortening your trip. Bulk up on noodles or rice and order a mixed sushi platter *(€10.50-21.80)* for a cheaper (though by no means cheap) alternative. A sleek interior and romantic ambience makes for the perfect place to bring a date or make new friends.

Ⓜ Diagonal. Walk toward Psg. de Gràcia and take a right onto it. Take a right onto Passatge de la Concepció, the first smaller road on the right. Ⓢ Appetizers €5.70-10.20. Noodles €6-6.40. Sushi €5-10. Sushi platters €10.50-21.80. Open M-W 1:30-4pm and 8:30pm-midnight, Th-Sa 1:30-4pm and 8:30pm-1am, Su 1:30-4pm and 8:30pm-midnight.

CERVESERIA CATALANA TAPAS, CATALAN ❸

C. Mallorca, 236 ☎93 216 03 68

Tapas, *flautas*, seafood, burgers, beer, wine, and more—it's easy to see why locals flock to Cerveseria Catalana's warmly lit interior in the dark of night. During the evening hours, the bar and outdoor seats are abuzz with the lively chatter of 20-somethings, while the crowd gets older (though no less lively) as you move back through the proper tables. Plan on waiting to get a seat, or give in and join the barside party.

Ⓜ Diagonal. Walk away from Psg. de Gràcia and take a right onto Rambla de Catalonia. Take a right onto C. Mallorca. Ⓢ Starters €4. Salads €3-6. Tapas €3-12. Open daily 8am-1:30am.

CAFE CHAPULTAPEC MEXICAN ❷

C. Comte Borrell, 152 ☎93 451 92 85 www.cafechapultepec.com

Cheap, veggie-friendly burritos *(€4.15)* and other Mexican platters as well as free internet and an inside reminiscent of a coastal Mondrian painting make this cafe a pleasant retreat from the rest of the overpriced Eixample. Grab some *chilaquiles polls verdes* or *rojos* *(€6)*, or try one of their flavored hotcakes with tocino, ham, or maple syrup *(€4-4.50)*. Following its namesake, it's located a bit outside of the most heavily frequented areas, so it may require some traveling. But hey—isn't that what you're doing all this for?

Ⓜ Urgell. Walk along Gran Vía with your back to the rocket-shaped Agbar Tower and take a right onto C. Comte Borrell. Ⓢ Starters €3.30-4.60. Entrees €4.15-5.25. Dishes €5.90-7.90. Open Tu-F 10am-4pm and 7-11pm, Sa 12:30-4:30pm and 7-11pm, Su 12:30-4:30pm.

FRIDA'S MEXICAN RESTAURANT MEXICAN ❷

C. Bruc, 119 ☎93 457 54 09

Reportedly the most authentic Mexican restaurant in Barcelona, Frida's serves anti-TexMex quesadillas, *tostadas*, and a range of *platos*, including *cochinita pibil* *(€11.65)* and *michoacan carnitas* *(€11.35)*, generally for much less than they're worth. Kick back with a Jamaican-flavored margarita *(€5.70)* at the bar, sit under a fitting picture of Frida Kahlo, or take your food to go and picnic along nearby Passeig de Gràcia.

Ⓜ Girona. Walk on C. Girona toward C. Aragó and take a left onto C. de Mallorca. Frida's is on the corner of Mallorca and Bruc. Ⓢ 5 tacos €8.90 Th and F. Salads €5.90-6.30. Tostadas and quesadillas €2.85-2.95. Entrees €7.80-11.35. Margaritas €5.70. Open Tu-Sa 1-4pm and 8:15pm-midnight.

GINZA JAPANESE ❸

C. Provença, 205 ☎93 451 71 93

A tastier alternative to the multitude of all-you-can-eat Japanese-style restaurants in the area for a similar (or better) price. Fresh ingredients and delicious dishes are served in a somewhat bland but homey interior, though the portrait of Sumo wrestlers in a rainbow variety of suits is worth a look. Start with a miso soup *(€3)*, fill up on *tempanyaki* *(€6-12)*, and finish it all off with a shot of *sake*.

Ⓜ Diagonal. Walk on C. del Rosselló away from Psg. de Gràcia. Take a left onto C. Balmes and a right onto C. de Provenca. Ⓢ Appetizers €3-9.60; entrees €6-12. Sushi €6.50. Weekday lunch menú €10; weekends and nights €11. Open M-Sa 1-4pm and 8pm-midnight, Su 1-4pm.

MAURI PASTRY SHOP, TEA SHOP, DELI ❶

Rambla del Catalonia, 102 and 103 ☎93 215 10 20 www.pasteleriasmauri.com

This tripartite pastry-deli-dessert shop has something to enchant whatever your hunger. Dine in the 102 shop over little sandwiches, croquettes, and croissants, or order something from the deli next door and dine in the wood and plaster salon. Across the street you'll find their *bomboneria* and tearoom, offering adorable giftbaskets in case you're looking to woo a fellow traveler.

Ⓜ Diagonal. Walk away from Psg. de Gràcia and take a right onto Rambla de Catalonia. The pastisseria is on the right and the tea shop on the left. Ⓢ Pastries and snacks €1.50-2.50. Lunch menú €13. Open M-Sa 9am-9pm, Su 9am-3pm.

CAFE PARC BELMONT

CAFE, TAPAS ❷

C. Lepant, 256 ☎93 231 13 58

The friendly expat staff, collection of '60s hits from across the world (California Dreamin', anyone?), and pictures from Paris, New York, Barcelona, and more create the perfect setting to surround yourself in the idealized cultures you never knew. A selection of cheap sandwiches *(€2.55-3.10)* and delicious tapas keeps even the poorest starving artist happy.

Ⓜ Sagrada Familia. Walk downhill on C. Lepant. Cafe Park Belmont is on the left. Entrees €6.25-10. Sandwiches €2.55-3.10. Tapas €1-3.50. Salads €4-6.20. Open M-Sa 9am-11pm.

LAIE BOOKSTORE CAFE

CAFE, CATALAN ❸

C. Pau Claris, 85 ☎93 318 17 39 www.laie.es

Laie's is the perfect place to curl up with a purchased book after impressing your friends with your memorization of one of their literary quotes along the windows. Choose from a sunny yellow backroom with palm trees and burlap shades or chill out in the dark, shaded couches of the front. A veggie-friendly snack bar with gourmet mini sandwiches and pastries provides snacks during the odd hours, while an all-you-can-eat lunch buffet satisfies the hunger knowledge can't fill.

*Ⓜ Gràcia. **i** Internet €1 per 15min. Ⓢ Coffee and snacks €1.35-4.50. Beer €2-2.60. Wine €1.55-3. Lunch menú M-F €14; Sa-Su €17. Open M-F 9am-1am, Sa 10am-1am.*

COLMADO DE SOL

BEER, CAFE ❷

C. Consell de Cent, 383 ☎93 533 19 47 www.colmadodelsol.com

Although this little cafe offers a variety of deli-style items for takeout or enjoyment at one of their few tables, the real attraction is in their almost limitless selection of beer. Over 300 different types line the walls, all chilled and ready for your stomach. Knock back a few before heading to their tapas bar next door, or pick up a couple of classy brews so you're not stuck paying €1 for Estrella from a six-pack later in the night.

Ⓜ Girona. Walk along C. Consell de Cent toward C. del Bruc. Colmado de Sol will be right after the intersection. Ⓢ Plates of the day €8. Dinner menú €10. Open M-Sa noon-10pm.

EL ÚLTIMO AGAVE

MEXICAN ❸

C. Aragó, 193 ☎93 454 93 43 www.elultimoagave.com

Wrapped in brick and tastefully crumbling red plaster, this humbly named Mexican *rincón*, or corner, whips up tacos, *enchiladas*, and the *Último Agave (€14)*, which they claim is better (and more expensive) than most *fajitas*. Let the pole of *coronita* caps guide your path through their selection of Mexican beer, or simply opt for a margarita.

Ⓜ Universitat. Take C. Aribau, to the left of the University. Turn left onto C. Aragó. Ⓢ Appetizers €7-10.50; entrees €10-18. Desserts €4.50-5. Open M-Th 7pm-2:30am, F-Sa 7pm-3am, Su 7pm-2:30am.

BARCELONA-MADRID (PA AMB TOMÀQUET)

CATALAN ❸

C. Aragó, 282 ☎93 215 70 27

Named after the railroad line that used to run here, Barcelona-Madrid is the destination for delicious Catalan dishes and classy decor without the exclusivity imposed by lack of seating. Two floors of dark wood and bright plaster (and some little birdies) play host to shoppers and local businessmen during the lunchtime hours. Try the preserved duck with figs *(€10.20)* or the more adventurous marinated oxtail with herbs *(€10)*.

Ⓜ Girona. Walk toward C. d'Aragó and take a left onto the street. La Rita is a flew blocks down on

your left. Ⓢ *Appetizers €7-11; entrees €9-16.* ⏰ *Open daily 1-4pm and 8:30-11:30pm.*

LA FLAUTA TAPAS, SANDWICHES ❷

C. Aribau, 23 ☎93 323 70 38

La Flauta takes its name from the long, thin crusty Catalan sandwich that puts other *bocadillos* to shame. Bearing no resemblance to the stale bread and two slices of cheese you drunkenly paid €4 for at 3am, these sandwiches are stuffed full of mouthwatering veggies, meat, and cheese *(half €3.65-6.90; whole €4.75-8.75).* Lots of veggie options, tapas, and other plates fill out the menu in a decor that would never leave you believing that they're known for two pieces of bread and some filling.

Ⓜ Universitat. Walk down C. d'Aribau, the road to the left of the University. La Flauta is 1 block down on the left. Ⓢ *Weekday lunch menú €10.50. Entrees €4.50-7.90. Sandwiches €3.65-7.90.* ⏰ *Open M-Sa 7am-1:30am.*

THAI GARDENS THAI ❸

C. Diputació, 273 ☎93 487 98 98 www.thaigardensgroup.com

If you're just looking for some Thai food, grab their takeaway menu. If you're looking to impress, bring your date to the sprawling, city-like, overtly Thai interior, complete with a robed hostess and wooden bridge to greet you—in case you weren't already convinced you were walking into a parallel universe. To complete the experience, call ahead to sit at one of their traditional *kantok* tables—no chairs, just floor cushions.

Ⓜ Passeig de Gràcia. Walk along Psg. de Gràcia away from Plaça Catalonia. Turn right onto C. de la Diputació. Ⓢ *Appetizers €8.35-12.15; entrees €15.90-18.80. Daily lunch menú €15.* ⏰ *Open daily 1-4pm and 8-11:30pm.*

CAMPECHANO GRILL ❸

C. Valencia, 286 ☎93 215 62 33 www.campechanobarcelona.com

The great outdoors comes indoors at Campechano, which offers *carnes a la brasa* with a campfire setting to match. If you ever wondered what it was like to picnic at a '30s Barcelona *merendero*, Campechano may not satisfy your curiosity, but it'll try. Peek through the painted trees to peep at mountainside campers while saddling up and preparing to chow down on relatively cheap eats at picnic tables.

Ⓜ Diagonal. Walk to Psg. de Gràcia and take a right. Walk 3 blocks and take a left onto C. Valencia. Ⓢ *Lunch menú €10. Salads €4-6. Entrees €6-15.* ⏰ *Open M-W 9am-4pm, Th-Sa 9am-4pm and 9pm-2am.*

LA MUSCLERIA SEAFOOD ❷

C. Mallorca, 290 ☎93 458 98 44 www.muscleria.com

Would you eat them in a can, would you, could you, in a van? Would you eat them in a **boat,** could you eat them on a float? Although you probably won't be able to answer these questions, La Muscleria will let you try—they offer up more mussel options than a single mind can muster, though you'll have to order takeout (at a 20% discount) to experiment with eating locales. Ordering in gets you a bucket of mussels and a smaller dish of fries. Other seafoods (calamari and oysters, to name a few) round out the menu.

Ⓜ Girona. Walk along C. de Girona toward C. d'Aragó and take a left onto C. Mallorca. La Muscleria is located on the left, in a basement. ***i*** *20% discount for takeout.* Ⓢ *Salads €6.75-7. Mussels €9-11.* ⏰ *Open M-Sa 1-4pm and 8:30-11:30pm, Su 1-4pm.*

KIRIN JAPANESE, BUFFET ❷

C. Aragó, 231 ☎93 488 29 19

One of many Japanese all-you-can-gorge buffets in the area, only with two main advantages: the ambience doesn't feel like you're back in a high school cafeteria, and you don't even have to leave your seat to eat. Little conveyor belts bring

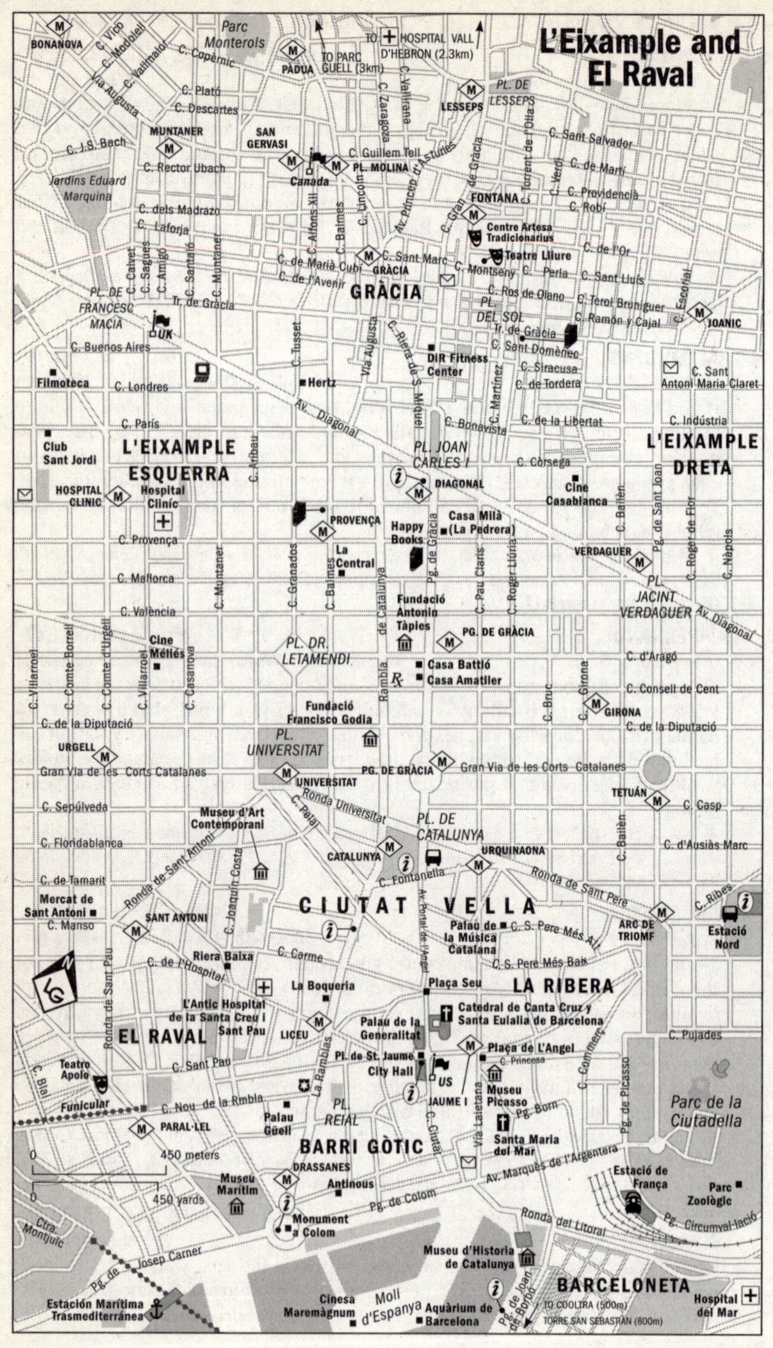
L'Eixample and El Raval
BONANOVA
C. Vico
C. Modolell
C. Vallmajor
C. Copèrnic
Parc Monterols
Via Augusta
PADUA
TO PARC GUELL (3km)
TO HOSPITAL VALL D'HEBRON (2.3km)
C. Plató
C. Descartes
C. Zaragoza
C. Vallirana
LESSEPS
PL. DE LESSEPS
C. Torrent de l'Olla
C. Sant Salvador
MUNTANER
SAN GERVASI
C. J.S. Bach
C. Guillem Tell
Av. Príncep d'Astúries
C. Gran de Gràcia
C. Rector Ubach
Canada
PL. MOLINA
C. de Martí
Jardins Eduard Marquina
C. Verdi
C. Providencia
FONTANA
C. Robí
C. dels Madrazo
C. Alfons XII
C. Balmes
C. Lincoln
C. Laforja
Centre Artesa Tradicionarius
C. de l'Or
Teatre Lliure
C. Sant Marc
C. Montseny
C. Perla
C. de Marià Cubí
GRÀCIA
C. Sant Lluís
C. de l'Avenir
C. Calvet
C. Sagués
C. Amigó
C. Santaló
C. Muntaner
GRÀCIA
C. Ros de Olano
C. Escorial
PL. DE FRANCESC MACIÀ
Tr. de Gràcia
PL. DEL SOL
C. Terol Bruniguer
C. Ramón y Cajal
JOANIC
UK
C. Tusset
Via Augusta
C. Riera de S. Miquel
Tr. de Gràcia
C. Buenos Aires
C. Sant Domènec
DIR Fitness Center
C. Siracusa
C. Sant Antoni Maria Claret
Filmoteca
C. Londres
Hertz
C. de Tordera
C. Martínez
Av. Diagonal
C. Bonavista
C. de la Libertat
C. Indústria
C. París
Club Sant Jordi
L'EIXAMPLE ESQUERRA
C. Aribau
PL. JOAN CARLES I
L'EIXAMPLE DRETA
C. Còrsega
DIAGONAL
Cine Casablanca
HOSPITAL CLINIC
Hospital Clinic
C. Bailèn
Pg. de Sant Joan
PROVENÇA
Casa Milà (La Pedrera)
Happy Books
C. Provença
C. Roger de Flor
C. Nàpols
C. Granados
La Central
Pg. de Gràcia
C. Pau Claris
C. Roger Llúria
VERDAGUER
C. Mallorca
C. Muntaner
C. Balmes
Rambla de Catalunya
PL. JACINT VERDAGUER
Fundació Antonin Tàpies
Av. Diagonal
C. València
PG. DE GRÀCIA
C. Comte Borrell
C. Comte d'Urgell
Cine Méliès
PL. DR. LETAMENDI
C. d'Aragó
C. Villarroel
C. Villarroel
C. Casanova
Casa Batlló
Casa Amatller
C. Girona
C. Consell de Cent
C. Bruc
GIRONA
Fundació Francisco Godia
C. de la Diputació
C. de la Diputació
PL. UNIVERSITAT
URGELL
Gran Via de les Corts Catalanes
PG. DE GRÀCIA
Gran Via de les Corts Catalanes
UNIVERSITAT
TETUÁN
C. Sepúlveda
C. Pelai
C. Casp
Museu d'Art Contemporani
Ronda Universitat
PL. DE CATALUNYA
C. Bailèn
C. Floridablanca
CATALUNYA
URQUINAONA
C. d'Ausiàs Marc
Ronda de Sant Antoni
C. Joaquín Costa
C. Fontanella
Ronda de Sant Pere
C. de Tamarit
C. Ribes
Mercat de Sant Antoni
CIUTAT VELLA
C. Manso
SANT ANTONI
Av. Portal de l'Àngel
Palau de la Música Catalana
C. S. Pere Més Alt
ARC DE TRIOMF
Estació Nord
Riera Baixa
C. Carme
C. de l'Hospital
C. S. Pere Més Baix
Ronda de Sant Pau
La Boqueria
Plaça Seu
LA RIBERA
L'Antic Hospital de la Santa Creu i Sant Pau
Catedral de Canta Cruz y Santa Eulalia de Barcelona
EL RAVAL
LICEU
Palau de la Generalitat
C. Pujades
Plaça de L'Angel
C. Princesa
C. Commerç
Teatro Apolo
C. Sant Pau
La Rambla
Pl. de St. Jaume
City Hall
US
Museu Picasso
Parc de la Ciutadella
C. Blai
JAUME I
Funicular
C. Nou de la Rmbla
Pg. Born
Pg. de Picasso
PL. REIAL
Palau Güell
Via Laietana
PARAL·LEL
C. Ciutat
Santa Maria del Mar
0
450 meters
BARRI GÒTIC
Av. Marquès de l'Argentera
0
450 yards
DRASSANES
Museu Marítim
Estació de França
Antinous
Parc Zoològic
Pg. de Colom
Ronda del Litoral
Monument a Colom
Pg. Circumval·lació
Ctra. Montjuïc
Pg. de Josep Carner
Museu d'Historia de Catalunya
BARCELONETA
Estación Marítima Trasmediterránea
Cinesa Maremàgnum
Moll d'Espanya
Aquàrium de Barcelona
Pg. de Joan de Borbó
TO COOLTRA (500m)
TORRE SAN SEBASTIAN (800m)
Hospital del Mar
LG

around an array of sushi, dumplings, and edamame for you to snag when hunger strikes, though you'll have to leave your seat to assemble a dish of raw meat, veggies, and seafood if you want a stir fry. Don't worry, though—the DIY aspect ends there, and their able chefs will take the plate off your hands and whip up a tasty dish in front of your eyes.

Ⓜ Universitat. Walk on the road to the right of the university, C. Balmes. Take a right onto C. d'Aragó. Ⓢ Buffet lunch M-F €8.60; Sa-Su €11.60; nights €13. Open daily 1-4pm and 8pm-midnight.

CAN CARGOL CATALAN ❸

C. València, 324 ☎93 458 96 31 www.cancargol.es

A fun selection of snail dishes *(including "grandfather" or "mother-in-law" style; each €9.25)* are complemented with a range of charcoal grilled veggies and meat-centric entrees, ranging from pig's feet *(€5.25)* to *bacalau* with garlic mousseline *(€7.50)*. Though obviously nicer than your average kebab stand, the relatively laid-back atmosphere with exposed rafters and blackened wine bottles won't make you feel too out of place when you show up in your shirt and cargo shorts.

Ⓜ Girona. Walk along C. de Girona toward C. d'Aragó and take a left onto C. de Valencia. ***i*** *Reservations recommended F-Su. Ⓢ Appetizers €3.75-8.75; entrees €5.75-18.25. Open daily 1:30-4pm and 8:30pm-midnight.*

SON HAO CHINESE, THAI ❷

C. Muntaner, 66 ☎93 453 83 03

An army of rainbow-colored Buddhas waits to usher you into the dragon-and-gold-bedecked shrine to Chinese stereotypes. Kitschy oriental paintings, Buddha heads, dangling red tassles, and lots of red predict a menu of pork stew in *huko* *(€8)* and shark fin soup *(€4)*, as well as noodle dishes, veggie-friendly platters, and other standard items for those sick of *jamón serrano*.

Ⓜ Universitat. Face the university. Take a left onto Gran Vía and a right onto C. Muntaner. Son Hao is before you reach C. d'Aragó. Ⓢ Soups €2.50-8. Salads €4-6.60. Entrees €5-14. Weekday lunch menú €12. Open M-Sa 1-3:45pm and 8-11pm, Su 1-3:45pm.

MOON CAFE CAFE ❷

C. Provença, 213 ☎93 488 17 21

One of the few places to find a veggie burger this side of Gran Vía (before hitting Gràcia, anyway), it's also one of the few places you'll find where said burger can live in peace with its veal counterpart on the menu. This brick-walled downstairs cafe stays dark, lush, and romantic at any hour of the day, but gets especially suave later in the evening.

Ⓜ Diagonal. Walk on C. del Rosselló away from Psg. de Gràcia. Take a left onto C. Balmes. Moon Cafe is a small door on the corner. Ⓢ Tapas €2.50-7. Salads €8-9. Sandwiches and rolls €3.50-7.50. Cocktails €6-7. Open M-Th 9am-2am, F-Sa 9am-3am, Su 9am-2am.

LA RITA CATALAN ❸

C. Aragó, 279 ☎93 487 23 76 wwww.laritarestaurant.com

The stomping ground of locals looking for an unbeatably priced midday meal. The cuisine spans a small range of traditional items with a twist, including potatoes and black sausage, duck breast with apples, raspberry *coulis*, and mango chutney. Though the price is near dirt cheap for the quality, the interior is anything but; expect an upscale but relaxed ambience that will make you question wearing that T-shirt—but not quite regret the decision.

Ⓜ Girona. Walk toward C. d'Aragó and take a left onto the street. La Rita is a flew blocks down on your right. Ⓢ Appetizers €5-7; entrees €7-11. Open daily 1-3:45pm and 8:30-11:30pm.

TAPAS, 24 TAPAS ❷

C. Diputació, 269 ☎93 488 09 77 www.carlesabellan.com

Climb down the stairs and into the den of delicious tapas. Chef Carles Abellan, formerly of El Bulli, serves food that you can actually afford at this alternative to his acclaimed Comerç 24. Marble countertops and colorful paintings of the menu spruce up this cafeteria-esque alcove. Try a plate of *patatas bravas (€3.75)* with either a glass of *cava (€3)* or their house sangría*(€3.75)*.

Ⓜ Passeig de Gràcia. Walk away from Plaça Catalonia. Tapas, 24 is on the corner of C. Diputació and Pg. de Gràcia. Ⓢ Tapas €2.50-8. Raciones €9-12. Wine and cava €3. Open daily 9am-midnight.

TXAPELA (EUSAKI TABERNA) TAPAS ❶

Psg. de Gràcia, 8-10 ☎93 412 02 89 www.angrup.com

If you're looking for tapas then Txapela's got 'em, along with enough seating to fit however many people may be in your entourage. Two floors of warm-colored wood floors and tinted walls let you have some of the perks of a small mom-and-pop place (cheap, interesting tapas) without all of that small talk and physical contact.

Ⓜ Passeig de Gràcia. Walk toward Plaça de Catalonia on Psg. de Gràcia. Txapela is on the left. Ⓢ Tapas €1.40-2. Wines by bottle €5.25-18.10. Cava by bottle €19.35-26.20. Open M-Th 7:45am-1:30am, F 7:45am-2am, Sa 8:45am-2am, Su 10:45am-1am.

RODIZIO GRILL BRAZILIAN GRILL, CATALAN ❸

C. Consell de Cent, 403 ☎93 265 51 12

Not only is this buffet food delicious, fresh, and of high-quality, but some of the fare, including Brazilian meats, make their way around to each of the tables. The buffet will cost you €18-20, so come hungry enough to eat the entire blue-and-white cow looking down from overhead.

Ⓜ Girona. Walk along C. de Girona toward C. Consell de Cent and turn right onto the road. Rodizio Grill is to the left. Ⓢ M-Th lunch buffet €18.20; nights and F-Sa €20.50. Desserts €3.24-4.30. Cocktails €5. Open M-Th 1-4:30pm and 9pm-midnight, F-Sa 1-4:30pm and 9pm-1am, Su 1-4:30pm and 9pm-midnight.

EL RAIM TAPAS, CAFE ❷

C. Muntaner, 75 ☎93 453 59 53

Authentic Catalan tapas and *bocadillos* without any affectation. Bare walls and ceramic tile paintings remind you of your favorite retro, rock-studded hole-in-the-wall back home, with prices to match. If you're sick of building a meal out of little orders of stuffed eggplant and chicken legs with stewed plum *(€2-3)*, then feel even more eerily close to home with a platter of bacon, eggs, and potatoes *(€5.65)*.

Ⓜ Universitat. Face the university. Take a left onto Gran Vía and a right onto C. Muntaner. Walk for 3 blocks, El Raim will be on the left. Ⓢ Entrees €5.45-9.75. Sandwiches €2.90-6.40. Open M-Sa 9am-1am.

YAMAMOTO JAPANESE, BUFFET ❸

C. Aragó, 197 ☎93 451 87 02

One of the many buffet-style Japanese restaurants in this area of the Eixample, Yamamoto is pretty similar to its horde of competitors. White walls and cafeteria-style seating let you gorge your face in the appropriate setting as you return plate after plate to the buffet to grab sushi, croquettes, dumplings, and maybe even some fruit so your bowels don't hate you. You can also assemble your own mix of fresh seafood, meats, and veggies before sending it off to the chef to be stir-fried.

Ⓜ Universitat. Walk down C. Aribau, to the left of the University, and take a left onto Aragó. Ⓢ Buffet only: M-F midday €8.80, M-Th night €13.25; F night, Sa-Su all day €14.25. Open daily 1-4pm and 8:30pm-midnight.

BARCELONETA

BOMBETA TAPAS ❸

C. Maquinista, 3 ☎93 319 94 45

Take heed of the warning scrawled above the bar, "No hablamos inglés, pero hacemos unas bombas cojonudas"—or, for the non-Spanish speaking set, "We don't speak English, but we make *bombas* that are out of this world." A retro facade with windows plastered with menu listings offers typical Spanish fare like *tostadas*, tortillas, and tapas, but really—just get the *bombas*.

Ⓜ Walk down Psg. Juan de Borbó (toward the beach) and take a left onto C. Maquinista. Ⓢ Appetizers €3-9.50; entrees €5-18. Open M-Tu 9am-11:45pm, Th-Su 9am-11:45pm.

SOMORROSTRO SEAFOOD ❸

C. Sant Carles, 11 ☎93 225 00 10 www.restaurantesomorrostro.com

This eatery is one of the few restaurants that is a part of Barceloneta's restaurant association, a recently established organization dedicated to making the inflated prices of Barceloneta actually worth the cost while bringing the best of the port to its tables. Somorrostro is also one of the best priced of this group, with reasonable seafood dishes, *paella*, and curries *(€13-19)* and a nighttime *menú (€15)*. The real draw for the restaurant comes midday on weekdays—a seafood buffet lets you pay for fish, prawns, and more fresh from the port and cooked to your liking for unbelievably cheap prices *(€13 per kg)*.

Ⓜ Barceloneta. Walk on Plà del Palau over Ronda Litoral to follow the harbor. Take the 5th left after crossing Litoral, onto C. Sant Carles. Ⓢ Weekday lunch buffet €13 per kg. Dinner menú €15. Appetizers €5.50-10; entrees €13.60-18.50. Open Tu-Sa 8-11:30pm, Su 2-4pm and 8-11:30pm.

CAN MAÑO SEAFOOD ❷

C. Baluart, 12 ☎93 319 30 82

A no-frills bar-restaurant that has been serving fresh seafood for good prices to a never-ending crowd of locals for years. Tile floors, white paint, and a random assortment of old framed newspaper clippings provide a refreshing break from those restaurants that make any attempt at interior decoration. If you had any doubts about just how little pretension this place harbors, just ask Tommy the Trout to start singing, "Take Me to the River" to you from his wall plaque.

Ⓜ Barceloneta. Walk on Plà del Palau over Ronda Litoral to follow the harbor. Take the first left after crossing Litoral, onto C. Balboa. Take the 2nd right onto C. Baluart. Ⓢ Meat and fish dishes €3-10. Combination plates €6-8. Open M-F 8am-5pm and 8-11pm, Sa 8am-5pm.

SEGONS MERCAT SEAFOOD ❷

C. Balboa, 16 ☎93 310 78 80 www.segonsmercat.com

Don't be misled by the cartoonish kitchen disasters painted all over its walls—Segons Market serves seriously fresh seafood for reasonable prices, with no worry of a culinary catastrophe. Dark wooden floors paired with orange and white school-style plastic chairs may make you feel as if you're in a child's version of a classy restaurant, but the food is nothing but refined.

Ⓜ Barceloneta. Walk on Plà. del Palau over Ronda Litoral to follow the harbor. Take the 1st left after crossing Litoral, onto C. Balboa. Ⓢ Tapas €4-7.50. Entrees €8-17. Open M-Sa 1-4pm and 9pm-midnight.

GRÀCIA

LA NENA CAFE, ORGANIC ❶

C. Ramon i Caja, 36 ☎93 285 14 76

An extensive menu of gourmet chocolates, ice creams, crêpes, sandwiches, and quiches with ridiculously low prices. Don't try ordering a cold beer to beat the heat, though—the huge banner overhead alerts visitors that they may be the only spot in Barcelona that doesn't serve alcohol. Chill jazz plays over the speakers and kids' games and books line the tall, bright walls. For a filling treat, try one of their *tostadas*, like the goat cheese (goat cheese, tomato, and mushroom on bread), that will have you wishing you too had an extra stomach for more room.

ⓂFollow C. d'Asturies, the one-way road leading from the Metro stop and take a right onto Torrent de l'Olla. Walk a few blocks and take a left onto C. Ramon i Caja. Ⓢ Sandwiches €3.50. Quiches €5.50. Open daily 1pm-1am.

GAVINA — PIZZA ❷

C. Ros de Olano, 17 ☎93 415 74 50

Although there's not yet a market for pizza places where you can dine under life-sized patron saints, Gavina is just ahead of the curve. Don't misinterpret their slant, though—George Washington and a plethora of other nations' money serve to secularize this sanctuary of informal Italian cooking. The big draw is the gigantic, delicious pizzas. Try their namesake the Gavina (potatoes, ham, onion, and mushrooms), but be sure to bring friends or an otherworldly appetite.

ⓂFontana. Walk on Gran de Gràcia away from C. d'Asturies and take a left onto C. Ros de Olano. Ⓢ Pizza €6.50-14. Wine €8.50-15. Open M-Th 1pm-1am, F-Sa 1pm-2am, Su 1pm-1am.

L'ILLA DE GRÀCIA — VEGETARIAN ❷

C. St. Domenec, 19 ☎93 238 02 39 www.illadeGràcia.com

A haven for vegetarians, this classy modern eatery serves real meatless meals worlds away from the *queso bocadillos* you've been downing when your friends had *jamón*. The restaurant offers vegetarian versions of Catalan classics, including spinach *cannoloni* and delicious seitan dishes served in personal crocks *(€6-7)*. Expect more Whole Foods than bohemian chic—this restaurant's decor is slick, minimal, and modern.

ⓂFontana. Take a right onto C. Gran de Gràcia and walk about 5min. Left onto L'illa de Gràcia. Ⓢ Salads €5-6. Entrees €3.60-7.80. Open M-Th 1-4pm and 9pm-midnight, F-Su 2-4pm and 9pm-midnight.

IKASTOLA — BAR, CAFE ❶

C. Perla, 22

If you don't like the specials, just make your own alternate menu on their blackboard—but don't expect the cook to take heed. Every night young locals gather at Ikastole (Basque for "nursery school") to chat, pound out tunes on the upright piano, and scribble everything from love notes to apartment listings on the walls of this laid-back nighttime cafe. Lively, bright, and quick with cheap *bocatas*, Ikastola is the perfect place to start the night before embarking on more mature shenanigans.

ⓂFontana. Follow C. Asturies, the one-way road leading from the Metro stop. Take a right onto C. Torrent de l'Olla and a left onto Perla. Ⓢ Sandwiches €4.50, half €3. Salads €7. Beer €1.70-2.30. Wine €2. Open M-Th 7pm-midnight, F-Sa 7pm-1am, Su 7pm-midnight.

CAFE DEL TEATRE — CAFE, BAR ❷

C. Torrijos, 41 ☎93 416 06 51

If all of the gardens of earthly delights were to be contained in one bowl, it would look and taste like a Cafe del Teatre salad. Pictures of Gràcia line the red walls, while stained-glass windows cast patterns over a chill but perky intellectual clientele. Drop by for dinner and grab a Cocktail del Cafe del Teatre *(€6)* as you wait to start off the night.

ⓂJoanic. Take a right onto C. de l'Escorial and a left onto C. de Sant Lluis after a block. Cafe del Teatre is in the plaça after C. del Torrent d'en Vidalet. Ⓢ Entrees and sandwiches €4.90-6.50. Menú €5.80-6.50. Open daily until 3am.

CHIDO ONE — MEXICAN ❷

C. Torrijos, 30 ☎93 285 03 35 www.chidoone.es

This Mexican restaurant has more *luchador* mettle than Strong Bad, complete with brightly painted walls splattered with murals, crafty animals, and other knick-knacks brought from the homeland. Try one of their handmade tortillas in their delicious quesadillas *(€8.50-10)*, and grab a Mexican beer to wash them down.

Ⓜ Joanic. Take a right onto C. de l'Escorial and a left onto C. de Sant Lluis after a block. Left onto C. Torrijos. Ⓢ Appetizers €8.50-9.50; entrees €9.50-11. Open M-Th 1-5pm and 7pm-midnight, F-Su 1pm-2am.

L'ARMARI

FRENCH ❷

C. Montseny, 13 ☎93 368 54 13

Relaxed French cuisine including *foie gras*, truffles, cheeses, and a range of tartars fill this bistro. Young locals gather under delicate lighting for a midday meal with friends on mismatched chairs (some of which are somehow sporting a classy zebra stripe), while the black-and-white photos and French books on the walls set an appropriately refined scene. But with €4 cocktails before 10pm, don't feel as if you need to stay straight-laced.

Ⓜ Fontana. Walk on Gran de Gràcia away from C. d'Asturies and take a left onto C. Montseny. Ⓢ Tapas €3.50-6. Entrees €5.50-12. Cocktails €4, after 10pm €5.50. Open M-F 9am-2:30am, Sa-Su 6pm-2:30am.

BARCELONA REYKJAVÍK

BAKERY ❶

C. Astúries, 20 ☎93 237 69 18 www.barcelonareykjavik.com

This difficult-to-pronounce bakery is perfect for the discerning backpacker that's tired of white bread and sugary, mass-produced *magdalenas*. This eatery bakes mindblowing breads—if you've been in Spain long enough you'll find their sourdough a godsend—as well as delicious muffins, brioche, and other baked goods. Ingredients and potential flags for each are listed, making people with dietary restrictions' lives a little easier, if only for a short second before they venture back out into the world of meat, cheese, sugar, and gluten. Be prepared to eat on your feet or save it for later—this little storefront has no seating.

Ⓜ Follow C. d'Asturies, the one-way road leading from the Metro stop. i Each item labeled for gluten, dairy, eggs, sugar. Ⓢ Items sold by weight. Breads normally €3-5. Baked goods €1-2. Open M-Sa 11am-9:30pm.

LAILA

LEBANESE, PIZZA ❷

C. d'Asturies, 17 ☎93 415 52 70

Gourmet pizzas and a selection of tasty Lebanese dishes draw in a young and hip crowd, while low, black couches and comfy pillows keep them around. Expect to see a forest of laptops during the chill daytime hours, with the sunset ushering in groups of friends here to literally get their fill.

Ⓜ Fontana. Follow C. d'Asturies, the one-way road leading from the Metro stop. Ⓢ Salads €9-10.50. Entrees and pizzas €8-11. Menú €9.80. Open daily 10am-midnight.

DIAMANT

CAFE ❶

C. d'Asturies, 67 ☎93 217 02 18

A student-laden cafe offering cheap meals, chill atmosphere, and interesting *bocadillos*—try the chicken and vegetable curry *(€3.80)* or the *cabra*, a mix of goat cheese, lettuce, tomato, and eggplant *(€3.50)*. Not hungry? Feel free to whip out your David Foster Wallace and kick back with a *cafe con leche* to pass the afternoon.

Ⓜ Fontana. Follow C. d'Asturies, the one-way road leading from the Metro stop, for a few blocks. Diamant is located on your right as you enter Plaça d'Or. Ⓢ Salads €5.80. Sandwiches €3-4. Tapas €2.10-3.50. Open daily 9am-3am.

ASKA DINYA

MIDDLE EASTERN ❸

C. Verdi, 28 ☎93 368 50 77

Garden views abound in this crumbling rock-walled oasis. Pesky cats look down from overhead as an intoxicating smell of incense fills the nostrils. Afraid of a feline messing with your meal? Well, don't fear—it's all a painted ruse (or at least the cats are), but the serious quality of their food isn't. Loads of Palestinian-inspired options fill the menu, including *babaganoush (€6.50)*, hummus, falafel, and tons of vegetarian options. In fact, this is one of the few places where you're given the option to *add* meat to your liking instead of trying to keep it out.

Follow C. d'Asturies, the one-way road leading from the Metro stop and take a right onto C. Verdi after crossing Torrent de l'Olla. Appetizers €6.50-8.50; entrees €9-13.50. Menú €8. Open daily 1pm-1am.

nightlife

BARRI GÒTIC AND LAS RAMBLAS

BARCELONA PIPA CLUB — BAR, CLUB

P. Reial, 3 — ☎93 302 47 32 www.bpipaclub.com

With pipes from four continents, smoking accoutrements decorated by Dalí, and even an "ethnological museum dedicated to the smoking accessory," the only pipe-related article missing from this club—albeit somewhat appropriately—is Reneé Magritte's *"Ceci n'est pas une pipe."* Despite its cryptic lack of signage and an ambience of a secret society, the combination bar, pool room, and music lounge boasts a surprising number of travelers. The dark wood, low lights, and provincial furnishings make for a perfect place to transport yourself from the more collegiate nightlife of the P. Reial, even if the only experience you have with smoking is toting a candy cigarette.

Liceu. Walk on Las Ramblas toward water. Left onto C. Ferran and first right to enter P. Reial. Pipa Club is an unmarked door to the right of Glaciar Bar. To enter, ring the bottom bell. ***i*** *Rotating selection of tobacco available for sale. Special smoking events. Tango and salsa lessons M and Tu 8:30-10:30pm. Jam session Su 8:30pm. Beer €4-5. Wine €4-5. Cocktails €7.50-9. Open daily 6pm-6am.*

HARLEM JAZZ CLUB — MUSIC CLUB, BAR

C. Comtessa de Sobradiel, 8 — ☎93 310 07 55 www.harlemjazzclub.es

With two live music performances each night and a drink included with admission, Harlem Jazz Club promises to beat those empty-wallet blues. A performance schedule online and on their door lets you choose whether you'll drop in to hear lovesick English crooning or a little saucier Latin flavor. With acts ranging from Bossa Nova to gypsy punk, blues to funk, and soul to salsa, the club is a fantastic place for any music lover to spend the evening.

Liceu. Walk toward the water on Las Ramblas. Left onto C. Ferran. Right onto C. Avinyó. Left onto C. Comtessa de Sobradiel. ***i*** *Live music M-Th 11:30pm and midnight, F-Sa 11:30pm and 1am, Su 11:30pm and midnight. Calendar of events for the month available online or at door. Cover M-Th €5, includes 1 drink; F-Sa €8, includes 1 drink; Su €5. Beer €3.80. Cocktails €7.80. Open M-Th 9pm-4am, F-Sa 9pm-5am, Su 9pm-4am.*

SMOLL BAR — BAR

C. Comtessa de Sobradiel, 9

The chic '60s decor and friendly, burly bartenders combine to please an ever-present hip, gay-friendly, and young crowd. When there's room at the bar, squeeze in tight and try one of over 25 cocktails or a signature shot. The Rasmokov (vodka shot with a lime wedge topped in sugar and espresso powder) will leave you caffeinated, sugar-buzzed, and full of fuzzy, extroverted feelings.

Liceu. Walk toward the water on Las Ramblas. Left onto C. Ferran. Right onto C. Avinyó. Left onto C. Comtessa de Sobradiel. Beer €3.50. Cocktails €5.60. Open M-Th 9:30pm-2:30am, F-Sa 9:30pm-3am.

MANCHESTER — BAR

C. Milans, 5 — ☎66 307 17 48 www.manchesterbar.com

The long listing of bands on the exterior—Joy Division, The Cure, Arcade

Fire, The Smiths, and many, many more—leaves little to the imagination. After passing the turning record table on the interior, you'll find a dark world of intimate seating, band references, and people who love both chatting and drinking the night away. A 7-10pm happy hour with €1.50 Estrellas gets the night started off right, and a vending machine selling tobacco is open until closing.

*ⓂLiceu. Walk toward the water on Las Ramblas, left onto C. Ferran. Right onto C. d'Avinyó. Left onto C. Milans before hitting C. Ample. Manchester is located where the street curves. **i** Happy hour beer €1.50. Ⓢ Beer €2-4. Shots from €2.50. Cocktails €6. Open M-Th 7pm-2:30am, F-Sa 7pm-3am, Su 7pm-2:30am. Happy hour daily 7-10pm.*

TRECE BAR

C. Lleona, 13

If you can fight your way through the crowd of international 20-somethings into this pocket-sized hangout, Trece offers some of the best mojitos in Barcelona *(€6)*. Bare walls with exposed brick show off local artwork and an assorted selection of dismembered body parts, including a set of mannequin legs sticking out over the restroom door and a torso functioning as the primary light source. Hits from the '80s abound, and a projector plays a selection of music videos and YouTube clips over the heads of the clientele.

ⓂLiceu. Walk on Las Ramblas toward the sea, left onto C. Ferran. Right onto C. d'Avinyó and left onto C. de la Lleona. Ⓢ Beer €3. Cocktails €6-7. Open M-Th 7pm-3am, F-Sa 7pm-5:30am, Su 7pm-3am.

SINCOPA BAR

C. Avinyò, 35

At night this music-themed bar plays hosts to as many nationalities as it has currencies and second hand instruments on its walls. Stop by midday for a change of pace—mostly filled with locals, the house boasts a big screen dedicated solely to *fútbol*. On slow days, the sculpture band of musicians hanging from the ceiling provides heartwarming company.

ⓂLiceu. Walk on Las Ramblas toward the water and take a left onto C. Ferran. Right onto C. d' Avinyò. Ⓢ Beer €2-3. Cocktails €7. Juices €2.50. Open M-Th 6pm-2:30am, F-Sa 6pm-3am.

SOUL CLUB BAR, NIGHTCLUB

C. Nou de Sant Francesc, 7 ☎93 302 70 26 www.soulclub.es

Pink mood lighting and a soundtrack of soul, blues, and jazz will leave even the most painfully awkward social outcast feeling as suave and overtly sexual as the voice of Barry White. A small dance floor boosts the intimacy, and leather couches and chairs give you a classy place to court your dance partner (or just sit down for a breather after the music picks up).

ⓂDrassanes. Walk on Las Ramblas toward P. Catalonia. Turn right onto C. Escudellers, and then right onto C. Nou de Sant Francesc. Ⓢ Cover F-Sa €5. Beer €3.50. Cocktails €7.50. Open M-Th 10pm-2:30am, F-Sa 10pm-3am, Su 10pm-2:30am.

ANDÚ BAR

C. Correu Vell, 3 ☎64 655 39 30

A wall of well-stocked wine nestled in a wrought-iron grid lies underneath a bare brick arch behind the bar, perfectly summing up what this bar aims to project. Reliquaries of vintage instruments, tennis rackets, and armarios create a setting for refined 20-somethings to imbibe their fine selection of vino *(€4 for a glass, or by bottle up to €21)* in class.

ⓂJaume I. Walk on V. Laietana towards the water. Turn right onto C. d'Àngel Baixeras. Ⓢ Wine €4. Cocktails €6. Tapas €3-5. Open M-Th 6pm-1am, F-Sa 6pm-3am, Su 6pm-1am. Kitchen open until 1am.

OVISO CAFE, BAR

C. Arai, 5 www.barnawood.com

Cafe Oviso is where ancient Roman villa meets bohemian dive bar. A myriad of frescoes adorn the walls, including images of peacocks, myths, and a curious scene in which a man appears to be putting the moves on a lion. Benches and larger tables invite clients to continue the theme and lounge at their discretion like a drunken Bacchus. A delicious variety of food and juices are served during the day, while at night the bar fills up quickly with a mix of locals from the Plaça Trippy.

ⓂLiceu. Walk toward the water on Las Ramblas. Left onto C. Ferran. Right onto C. Avinyó. Left onto C. Arai; Oviso is on the right as you enter the plaça. ***i*** *Food and juice served during the day. Beer €3. Cocktails €7. Open M-Th 10am-2:30am, F-Sa 10am-3am, Su 10am-2:30am.*

LA RIA TAVERN

C. Milans, 4

Bright white interior, upright seating, and an almost-entirely Catalan clientele makes for cheap booze, cheap food, and a refreshing—albeit grittier—alternative to the dressed up faces in the Plaça Reial. Relaxed and refreshingly authentic, La Ria is exactly the tavern it claims to be.

ⓂJaume I. Walk on Via Laietana towards the water and take a right onto C. d'en Gignàs. La Ria will be on the corner of Gignàs and C. Milans. Beer €1-2.50. Wine €1.50-1.80. Copas €3. Tapas €4-12. Menú €4. Open M-Th 6:30pm-2am, F-Sa 6:30pm-3am.

JAMBOREE NIGHTCLUB, MUSIC CLUB

P. Reial, 17 ☎93 319 17 89 www.masimas.com/jamboree/

A hall-of-fame assortment of jazz musicians on the walls of the lower level will leave you with no guesses as to where this club's allegiances lie, even when its grotto-like halls are filled with Americans singing Aaliyah. The club offers nightly performances by jazz and blues musicians and opens to a younger set after these shows end at midnight. After this witching hour, be prepared for everything from hip hop to Shania Twain.

ⓂLiceu. Walk on Las Ramblas toward the water. Left onto C. Ferran, then right to enter Plaça Reial. ***i*** *Music club performances usually daily 9, 11pm. Full list of upcoming events and concerts on website. Flyers provide discounts. Event tickets €4-12. Dance club cover €10. Beer €5. Cocktails €9-10. Tarantino (upstairs, mostly flamenco) cover €6. Nightclub open M-Th 12:30-5am, F-Sa 12:30-6am, Su 12:30-5am. Music club open daily 9pm-1am. Tarantino open daily 8-11pm.*

SHANGÓ BAR

C. d'en Groch, 9 ☎66 210 51 65 www.shangolatinbar.com

Tucked down a poorly lit alley, Shangó's bright yellow and black door provides a warm, sunny beacon that beckons to revelers throughout the night. Free salsa lessons and a neverending supply of saucy Latin tunes complement the cheap mojitos *(€4.50)* and beer. Meanwhile, the comfortably full level of chairs and couches provides a relaxing place to grab a drink, meet some strangers, and soak in the sensation of being inside a big, sugary lemon.

ⓂJaume I. Walk down V. Laietana toward the water. Take a right onto C. d'En Gignàs and right onto C. d'En Groch. ***i*** *Free salsa lessons Tu-W. Beer €1.50-3. Mojitos €4.50. Cocktails €5-6. Open daily 9pm-3am.*

MARGARITA BLUE BAR

C. Josep Anselm Clavé, 6 ☎93 412 54 89 www.margaritablue.com

Surprisingly, Margarita Blue has margaritas and—surprise #2!—they're blue. Mexican platters complement the vaguely Mexican drink selection as colorful paintings of musicians paired with a mirrored wall keep loving watch over the bar. For those not needing supervision, a bright blue daisy wall in the back offers fluorescent cheer.

Ⓜ Drassanes. Walk toward the water on Las Ramblas and take a left onto C. Josep Anselm Clavé. i Magic show W and Su 10pm. Ⓢ Food €5.80-9, cocktails €7-8. Open M-W 7pm-2am, Th-Sa 7pm-3am, Su 7pm-2am.

EL BOSQ DE LES FADES — CAFE, BAR

Psg. de la Banca, 16 ☎93 317 26 49 www.museocerabcn.com

If you have ever wondered what it's like to be a hobbit and drink a whole pitcher of sangria *(€12)*, Bosq de les Fades provides the perfect opportunity to settle your burning curiosity. A wooded canopy creates an enchanted forest deserving of the bar's name. If you're not the outdoorsy type and prefer something more domestic, you can hang out in a haunted bedroom, so long as you don't mind a woman behind a false mirror dropping in on your conversation. Be prepared for as many gawkers as diners, as the fantastical facade across from the Wax Museum is a popular photograph point.

Ⓜ Drassanes. Walk briefly along Las Ramblas toward the water. Turn left onto Psg. de la Banca. El Bosq de les Fades is at the end of the road, in front of the Museu de Cera. Ⓢ Cava glass €3, bottle €16. Sangria €3.50, pitcher €12. Wine €2.30. Cocktails €6.10-7.20. Open daily 10:30am-1am.

BOULEVARD CULTURE CLUB — NIGHTCLUB

Las Ramblas, 27 ☎93 301 62 89 www.boulevardcultureclub.com

With three rooms, dizzying lights, and a clientele that borders on barely legal, Boulevard Culture Club plays host to the nightclubbers of the traveler-laden Las Ramblas. Promoters draw in dancers with discount fliers along the street. If you don't like the techno playing in the first room, just move on to the next to hear some Missy Elliott instead.

Ⓜ Liceu. Walk on Las Ramblas toward the water, destination on right. i Reduced admission with flyer distributed along Las Ramblas. Calendar of special events and theme nights on website. Ⓢ Cover €15; includes 1 drink. Open daily midnight-6am. Free for men before 1am and women before 2:30am.

KARMA — NIGHTCLUB, BAR

Pl. Reial, 10 ☎93 302 56 80 www.karmadisco.com

Karma: for those who dream of disco in a partified subway station. A bizarre mix of blues, soul, and '80s music plays for a largely uninterested older set while rainbow lights wrap around two barrel vaults that mark the bar and dancefloor. You may be better off living your actual dream by grabbing a boombox, some streetside beer, and a Metro ticket—not that *Let's Go* suggests (illegally) drinking in public.

Ⓜ Liceu. Walk on Las Ramblas toward the water. Left onto C. Ferran, Right to enter Plaça Reial. Ⓢ Club cover €10; includes 1 drink. Beer €4. Cocktails €6-8. Club open Tu-Th midnight-5am, F-Sa midnight-6am, Su midnight-5am. Bar open daily 6pm-2:30am.

LA RIBERA

ALMA — BAR

C. de Sant Antoni dels Sombrerers, 7 ☎93 319 76 07

A quieter alternative for those too cool to bother with the packed houses and inflated prices of nearby Psg. del Born. Cheap drinks provide bait for any traveler, while relaxed seating, rotating art exhibitions, and a bartender that stays surprisingly laid-back even when drunkenly berated about the lack of mojitos give solid reasons to stay for the night.

Ⓜ Jaume I. Walk down C. de la Princesa and take a right onto C. Montcada. Upon entering Psg. del Born, take a right onto C. dels Sombrerers and then take a right again onto the 1st street on your right, C. de Sant Antoni dels Sombrerers. Ⓢ Cava €1.80. Beer €2. Cocktails €6. Open Tu-Th 8:30pm-2:30am, F-Sa 8:30pm-3am.

EL BORN

BAR

Psg. del Born, 26 ☎93 319 53 33

Shed the pretense and shabby themes and stop in to El Born for a straight-up bar—no more, no less. Marble tables and a green palette provide game-time seating and trenches for those brave enough to claim them on weekend nights. With cheap beer *(€2-2.50)* and ambient music, it's no wonder this place is always full.

Ⓜ Jaume I. Walk down C. Princesa and take a right onto C. Montcada. Follow until you hit Psg. del Born. ***i*** *Free Wi-Fi. Beer €2-2.50. Cocktails €6. Open Tu-Su 10am-2:30am.*

LA FIANNA

BAR

C. Banys Vells, 15 ☎93 315 18 10 www.lafianna.com

A glass partition divides the restaurant and bar, but be prepared to push your way through on weekend nights no matter where you choose to stay. Unlike in most places in the area, finding a seat at the bar is a distinct possibility. Patience pays off with mojitos as large as your fist, made with special bitters to set it apart *(€7)*. An elevated lounge area keeps it loose—stretch out on the pillows and survey the pack.

Ⓜ Jaume I. Walk down C. de la Princesa and take a right onto C. Montcada. Upon entering Psg. del Born, take a right onto C. dels Sombrerers and then take a right onto C. dels Banys Vells. Beer €2.50-3.40. Cocktails €4-7. Tapas €2-4.75. Open M-W 6pm-1:30am, Th-Sa 6pm-2:30am, Su 6pm-1:30am. Happy hour with discount tapas on M-Th 7pm-12:30am, F-Sa 7pm-11:30pm, Su 7pm-12:30am.

BERIMBAU

LATIN BAR

Psg. del Born, 17 ☎93 319 53 78

This Brazilian *copas* bar, reportedly the oldest Brazilian bar in Spain, offers a range of drinks you won't easily find this side of the Atlantic. Try the *guarana* with whiskey *(€8)* or an orange and banana juice with vodka *(€9)*. Relaxed, beachy beats fill the air, with wicker chairs to let you live out the summer dream.

Ⓜ Jaume I. Walk down C. Princesa and take a right onto C. Montcada. Follow to Psg. del Born. Cocktails €8-10. Open M-Th 6pm-2:30am, F-Sa 6pm-3am, Su 6pm-2:30am.

CACTUS BAR

BAR

Psg. del Born, 30 ☎93 310 63 54 www.cactusbar.cat

This little bar thankfully bears little resemblance to its vaguely Mexican-themed name. Instead, expect a packed house and an interior like a subdued carnival. A huge selection of gin and tonics and overtly friendly staff light up the night, while a calmer crowd and all-day breakfast specials create a vibrant atmosphere even before happy hour kicks in at 6pm.

Ⓜ Jaume I. Walk down C. Princesa and take a right onto C. Montcada. Follow until you hit Psg. del Born. Breakfast €1.50. Sandwiches €2.50-3.70. Tapas €1.80-6.50. Beer €3. Cocktails €8. Open M-Th 9am-2pm, F-Sa 11am-3pm. Happy hour daily 6-8pm.

NO SÉ

BAR

Psg. del Born, 29 ☎67 148 59 87

One of the many popular bars along Psg. del Born, No Sé aims for nothing in particular. Artwork lines the walls and a young crowd fills its floor, but don't expect a theme. Shiny vinyl paintings, bright walls, scattered seating, and loud electronic music make the potential for an upbeat dance floor on weekday nights when there's actually room to breathe.

Ⓜ Jaume I. Walk down C. Princesa and take a right onto C. Montcada. Follow until you hit Psg. del Born. Cocktails €8-10. Open daily 8pm-2:30am.

PITIN BAR

BAR

Psg. del Born ☎93 319 59 87 www.pitinbar.com

With copious outdoor seating and a lounge upstairs, Pitin Bar offers a more relaxed and mature alternative to the nightclub-in-your-pocket bars that dot the

Psg. del Born. This is where the non-20-somethings come out to play, so expect a more relaxed and mature audience.

Ⓜ Jaume I. Walk down C. Princesa and take a right onto C. Montcada. Follow to Psg. del Born. Beer €2.50-4. Cocktails €6.50-7. Open M-Th noon-2:30am, F-Sa noon-3am, Su noon-2:30am.

BARROC CAFE BAR

C. del Rec, 67 ☎93 268 46 23 www.barroc-cafe.com

Velvet heart-shaped booths, baroque golden frames, and medieval ironwork set the sight for romance while flying cherubim lining the walls move in for the kill. Throbbing techno produces a little confusion, but a little of the house special *mojito barroc (€8)* will clear away any doubts (or inhibitions).

Ⓜ Jaume I. Walk down C. de la Princesa and take a right onto C. Flassanders. Follow over the Psg. del Born as it becomes C. del Rec. Beer €3-3.20. Cocktails €8. Open M-Th 3pm-2-:30am, F-Sa 3pm-3am, Su 3pm-2:30am.

LA HACIENDA BAR, MEXICAN

C. del Rec, 69

This Mexican bar serves semi-authentic Mexican food and drink under plaster walls, colorful Christian flags, and a vividly colored Aztec mural. Cool the spices of the burritos and *enchiladas (€7)* with a Mojito Mexicano *(€4)*. Although most come to dine more than wine, the place still gets busy and bumping on weekend nights.

Ⓜ Jaume I. Walk down C. de la Princesa and take a right onto C. Flassanders. Follow over the Psg. del Born as it becomes C. del Rec. Appetizers €3.50-6.50; entrees €7. Cocktails €4-6. Open daily noon-3am.

EL RAVAL

MARSELLA BAR BAR

C. de Sant Pau, 65 ☎93 442 72 63

Walls lined with antique mirrors, cabinets, old advertisements, and dusty bottles will have you waiting to witness your first saloon brawl. Luckily, the crowd is genial and friendly, even after a few absinthes *(€5)*—not that there's room to fight in this crowded place anyway. Crackling paint and fuzzy chandeliers will have you feeling every month of the bar's 190 years of business.

Ⓜ Liceu. Walk down C. Hospital and take a left onto C. Junta de la Comerç. Take a right at the end of the street onto C. de Sant Pau. Beer €3.50. Absinthe €5. Cocktails €5-6. Open M-Th 11pm-2am, F-Sa 11pm-3am.

PLASTIC BAR BAR

C. Sant Ramón, 23 www.myspace.com/plasticobar

This hip bar is big enough to host as many people as are cool enough to enter. Dark paisley walls with a green lit bar let you squeeze through to the back portion, where the real life awaits. The upper level is for lounging, while the scratchy soundsystem of the lower portion pumps a mix of modern indie and '60s rock to a crowd excited to dance the night away.

Ⓜ Liceu. Walk on Las Ramblas toward the sea. Take a right onto C. Nou de la Rambla and right onto C. de Sant Ramón. Shots €3. Beer €3-3.50. Cocktails €6. Open M 11pm-2:30am, W 11pm-2:30am, Th 11pm-2:30am, F-Sa 11pm-3am.

BAR BIG BANG BAR, MUSIC CLUB

C. Botella, 7 www.bigbangbcn.net

The back room attracts a collegiate crowd to watch free nightly performances like the jazz acts, standup comedy, and vaudeville-esque theater. Out front, customers are serenaded by big band favorites—both local and national—over the stereo and black-and-white projector screen. Creepy eyes look down from every corner, whether from the frames of outsider art or from the jazz star photos lining the dark walls.

♯ Ⓜ Sant Antoni. Walk down C. de Sant Antoni Abad (in the corner of the square where C. del Comte d'Urgell and C. de Manso meet) and take a hard right onto C. Botella. *i* Schedule of performances and special events on website. Variety show on Tu, DJ on F and Sa at midnight. Ⓢ Shots €3. Beer €3-4. Cocktails €6.50. All cheaper before 11pm. ⏰ Open Tu-Sa 9:30pm-2:30am, Su 10:30pm-2:30am.

VALHALLA ROCK CLUB BAR, MUSIC CLUB

C. Tallers, 68 www.myspace.com/valhallaclubderock

Be prepared to see burly men air-guitaring Slayer in the place where a normal dance floor should be. At times serving as a concert hall, this dark and industrial-esque nightclub is a haven for those sick of flashing lights and throbbing techno. Free cover on non-show nights means you can use the saved cash to try their entire selection of *chupitos del rock*, specialty shots named after bands from Elvis to Whitesnake *(€1)*.

♯ Ⓜ Universitat. Walk down C. Tallers. i Draught beer €1.50-2.50 daily until 10pm. Check myspace for calendar of concerts and special events. Ⓢ Shots €1-2. Sangria €2.50. Beer €2.50-5. Cocktails €6-7. ⏰ Open daily 6:30pm-2:30am.

SANT PAU 68 BAR

C. Sant Pau, 68 ☎93 441 31 15

An absurdist bar with an identity crisis. The Van Gogh-esque wall of ears is paired with gas tank-inspired lights and a metal chandelier with circuit board cutouts casting geeksheek patterns of light across the stairwell. If you're looking to get away from the crowd, grab a Bloody Mary *(€6)* and head upstairs to scrawl your regards on the graffiti wall.

♯ Ⓜ Liceu. Walk down C. Hospital and take a left onto C. Junta de la Comerç. Take a right at the end of the street onto C. de Sant Pau. Ⓢ Beer €2. Cocktails €6. ⏰ Open M-Th 8pm-2:30am, F-Sa 8pm-3:30am, Su 8pm-2:30am.

BETTY FORD BAR

C. Joaquín Costa, 56 ☎93 304 13 68

This small bar and restaurant hosts local students coming in to chow down on their relatively cheap burgers. Join in and listen to a mix of funky music while being surrounded by '20s flapper flare. Happy hour *(6-9pm)* provides cheap drinks, and the bathroom size guarantees some intimate encounters.

♯ Ⓜ Universitat. Walk down Ronda de Sant Antoni and take a slight left onto C. de Joaquin Costa. Happy hour cocktails €4. Ⓢ Burgers €6.50. Fries €2. Shakes €3.50. Beer €3. Cocktails €5-6. ⏰ Open M-Th 2pm-1:30am, F-Sa 2pm-2:30am, Su 8pm-1:30am. Kitchen open M-Sa 2-4pm and 7-10pm, Su 7-11pm. Happy hour daily 6-9pm.

ODDLAND BAR

C. Joaquín Costa, 52 ☎93 412 00 49

Not as alienatingly bizarre as the name would imply, this quirky bar gets dancier as the night goes on, thanks to a live DJ playing electro hits. Painted butteflies cover the walls and a trippy blacklit wonderland at the bar allows for an otherworldly experience. Stop in for a weekday cocktail—at only €3.50-4, you might get to see the butterflies take flight.

♯ Ⓜ Universitat. Walk down Ronda de Sant Antoni and take a slight left onto C. de Joaquin Costa. Ⓢ Snacks €1-4.50. Beer €2.30-4. Cocktails M-F €3.50-7. ⏰ Open M-W 7pm-2am, Th-Sa 7pm-2:30am, Su 7pm-1am.

CAFE DE LES DELÍCIES CAFE, BAR

Rambla del Raval, 47 ☎93 441 57 14

Light from the Rambla outside filters in through the French-doors-turned-windows, and after a few drinks the fully furnished house jutting out over the bar will have you wondering whether you're actually inside. Serving a small selection of *bocadillos* during the day to a sparse crowd, the cafe's book and art-lined walls fill up quickly at night.

Liceu. Walk on C. L'Hospital and take a left onto Rambla del Raval. Cafe de les Delícies will be on the righthand side of the Rambla. Sandwiches €1.50-3.50. Beer €2-3.50. Cocktails €5.50-6. Open M-Th 9am-2:30am, F-Sa 9am-3am. Kitchen closes at 1am.

LA ROUGE BAR

Rambla del Raval, 10 ☎93 329 54 45

Push your way through the crowded bar area to lounge in the dark seating in back, or look down on the masses from its loft area. No matter where you stand, be sure to check out the chandelier made of little liquor bottles hanging above the entrance—just don't expect to drink them for free. Cocktails start at €5, while the house shot *chupito la rouge* will cost you €3.50. Electronic dance music plays over the stereo to please the younger crowd.

Liceu. Walk on C. L'Hospital and take a left onto Rambla del Raval. La Rouge will be on the right side of the Rambla. Tapas €1.50-6.50. Appetizers €5-6. Cava €4. Cocktails €5-6. Open M-Th 8pm-2am, F-Sa 8pm-3am.

L'OVELLA NEGRA BAR

C. Sitges, 5 ☎93 317 10 87 www.ovellanegra.com

Think Viking beer hall without the possibility of a funeral pyre burning into the night. Cheap beer flows freely, which makes stomaching the kitsch—anyone care to take a picture with the drunken black sheep cutout?—possible. Split-log benches and a selection of foosball, pool tables, and TVs provide all the charm of a frathouse in Valhalla.

Catalonia. Walk toward the sea on Las Ramblas and take a hard right onto C. dels Tallers. Then take a hard left onto C. Sitges. Tapas €1.50-4. Shots €2.30-3. Beer €1.20-3.60. Pitchers of beer and sangria €10.70-12.50. M-Th 9am-2:30am, F 9am-3am, Sa 5pm-3am, Su 5pm-2-:30am. Drinks cheaper before 11pm.

TRA.LLERS BAR

C. Trallers, 39-41 ☎93 412 78 43

A mural of a foreboding, twisted desert paired with the accompanying spray-painting of a **communist** woman soldier serve to supplement the tone that the heavily tattooed female owner and younger clientele have served to set. Multiple TVs, a wraparound bar, and an excellent selection of imported beer allow you to get surly the way it should be done—by the bottle.

Universitat. Walk down C. Tallers. Tra.llers is just past the intersection of C. Tallers and C. Ramelleres. Sandwiches €2.50-3.80. Beer and wine €2.50-5. Cocktails €6. Open M-Th 11am-2am, F-Sa 11am-3am, Su 11am-2am.

RITA BLUE CAFE, RESTAURANT

Pl. Sant Agustí ☎93 481 36 86 www.ritablue.com

Bright rainbow chairs on the patio match the saturated interior, from the obnoxiously vibrant blue and pink walls to the orange Christmas lights. Rita Blue whips up a mix of cafe-style dishes with a Tandoori twist—try the *bacalao* or tandoori chicken fajitas *(€9.70)*. A student *menú (€6)* keeps the crowd young, as if the strange mosaics and funky paintings of fat old ladies weren't enough to keep away the more mature set. Live house music and a mix of DJs, poetry slams, and other performances spice up the after hours downstairs.

Liceu. Walk down C. l'Hospital and take a left onto C. Junta de la Comerç to enter the plaza. i Live house music M-Sa 11pm. Entrees €9.70-18. Salads and starters €4-8. Lunch menú €6, dinner menú €10. Beer €2.20. Cocktails €5.50-8. Open M-Th 6pm-2am, F-Sa 6pm-3am, Su 6pm-2am.

BAR CENTRIC CAFE, BAR

C. Ramelleres, 27 ☎93 301 81 35

Bar Centric serves cheap comfort foods during the day, including pork sticks, french fries, pastas, and tapas. In the evening, the dark wooden, parlor-like interior fills up with locals looking to chat or catch the game. Come early, but don't expect to stay late—get your fill of the €2 beer and €5-9 cocktails while they last, as this bar only stays open until 10:30pm at the latest.

Ⓜ Universitat. Walk down C. Tallers. Bar Centric will be on the corner of C. Tallers and C. Ramelleres. Tapas €1-6. Specials €4.50-9.50. Beer and wine €2-2.50. Cocktails €5-9. Open M-F 8:30am-10pm, Sa 11am-10:30pm.

MOOG CLUB

C. Arc del Teatre, 3 ☎93 301 72 82 www.masimas.com/moog

One of Spain and Europe's premiere clubs for electronic music, Moog caters both to electrotrash afficionados and lost souls just trying to find a place to dance in Raval. Come on Wednesdays and weekends for the crowd, or drop in earlier during the week for house DJ sets. If you're looking for older hits or just want to get away from the throbbing mass on the dance floor, check out the upper portion, which plays a mix of older electro, disco, and techno.

Ⓜ Drassanes. Walk away from the water on C. de Guardia and take a right onto C. de l'Arc del Teatre. i Discount flyers often available on Las Ramblas. Cover €10. Open M-Th midnight-5am, F-Sa midnight-6am, Su midnight-5am.

BAR RESTAURANT ELISABETS BAR, RESTAURANT

C. Elisabets, 2-4 ☎93 317 58 26

Serving a delicious array of tapas and homemade dishes during the day, Bar Restaurant Elisabets gets to business on weekend nights. Get the night started early for cheap drinks with a younger, mostly local clientele, and soak in the bar's history as an agricultural cooperative by looking at pictures along the wall.

Ⓜ Universitat. Walk down C. Tallers and take a right onto C. Elisabets. Starters and sandwiches €2.40-3.45. Tapas €2-3.55. Lunch menú €8.50. Entrees €6-12. Beer €1.40-2.15. Cocktails €5-7. Open M-Th 7:30am-11pm, F-Sa 7:30am-2am.

L'EIXAMPLE

LES GENTS QUE J'AIME BAR

C. Valencia, 286 ☎93 215 68 79

Come down the stairs into this sultry red velvet underworld for antique photographs, jazz covers of "Tainted Love," and vintage chandeliers that set the mood for you to partake in their sinful pleasures. Not sure where to head for the rest of the night? Cozy up next to the palm reader, or have your tarot cards read to keep from indecision.

Ⓜ Diagonal. Turn right onto Psg. de Gràcia and walk for 3 blocks. Take a left onto C. Valencia. Les Gents is downstairs next to Campechano. i Palm reading and tarot cards M-Sa, €30 and €25. Wine €3. Beer €3.50. Cocktails €7. Open M-Th 7pm-2:30am, F-Sa 7pm-3am, Su 7pm-2:30am.

LA FIRA CLUB

C. Provença,.171 ☎65 085 53 84

Decorated entirely with pieces from the old Apolo Amusement Park in Barcelona, this club is like a debaucherous family reunion without having to worry about the faux pas of incest. The walls act as a mausoleum to innocent years past, sporting dioramas of the fair, fortune tellers, and masks of questionable racial politics. Dance away under the big top, and try not to get too creeped out while downing *Espit Chupitos* under the glare of the knowing sphynx.

Ⓜ Hospital Clinic. Walk away from the engineering school on C. del Rossello and take a right onto C. de Villarroel when it dead-ends. Take the 1st left onto Provença; La Fira is a few blocks down. i Often hosts shows or parties, sometimes with entrance fee or 1-drink min. Beer €5. Cocktails €8. Open Th-Sa 11:30pm-3am.

ZELTAS

BAR

C. Casanova, 75 ☎93 450 84 69 www.zeltas.net

Like a story lifted from a sultry romance novel about an all-male harem with impeccable taste, Zeltas pleases the eyes in more ways than one. An all black interior draped in white, flowing fabric sets the tone, while chic white couches and a bar seemingly dedicated to those looking to dance shirtless sets the mood. Musky cologne floats through the air, and beefy male dancers in tight black spankies make the air somehow thicker.

Ⓜ Universitat. Face the university building and walk left on Gran Vía. Turn right onto C. Casanova. Zeltas is down 2 blocks. ***i*** *Male dancers nightly.* Ⓢ *Beer €5. Cocktails €7.50.* *Open daily 11pm-6am.*

LA CHAPELLE

BAR

C. Muntaner, 67 ☎93 453 30 76

A wall of devotional figurines and paintings with mostly nude men in front allows La Chapelle to show a gayer side of the sacrament. Solemn red lighting mixed with modern bubble lights cut through the veil of testosterone—apparently debaucherous religious imagery is bait for bears. Get a little closer to God while getting a lot closer with some grizzly guys.

Ⓜ Universitat. Face the university building and walk left on Gran Vía. Turn right onto C. Muntaner. La Chapelle is 2 blocks down. Ⓢ *Beer €2.50. Cocktails €5.* *Open daily 4pm-2:30am.*

ATAME

BAR

Consell de Cent, 257 ☎93 434 92 73 www.facebook.com/bar.atame

Dietrich Gay Teatro Cafe's life partner, Atame's sleek minimalist interior pulses with '80s hits and a mostly male crowd that loves to sing along (and encourages you to sing with them). The dance floor in back is packed when drag shows aren't in session, while the front of the bar provides a lush hunting ground with diverse prey for those on the prowl.

Ⓜ Universitat. Face the university building and walk left on Gran Vía. Turn right onto Aribau and walk 2 blocks. Take a left onto Consell de Cent. Atame is a block away. ***i*** *Happy hour cocktails €4. Drag shows and other events nightly. Call for more info.* Ⓢ *Cocktails €5.* *Open daily 7pm-3am. Happy hour 6pm-11am.*

DOW JONES

BAR

C. Bruc, 97 ☎93 476 38 31 www.bardowjones.es

During the day this English-centric bar has enough television screens to keep every fútbol fan happy, no matter his allegiance. At night, the bar lights up with raucous foreigners trying desperately to order their favorite drink before the price spikes—like the stock market, drinks' prices vary based on their popularity during the day. Wait for the prices to crash if you're counting on a winner, or keep buying low and be glad the staff speaks English fluently for when you're slurring your Spanish.

Ⓜ Girona. Walk toward C. Aragó on C. Girona and take a left onto C. Valencia after passing Arago. Walk 1 block and take a left onto C. del Bruc. Dow Jones is close to the corner. Ⓢ *Food €2.75-7.50. Beer €2-5.50. Cocktails €4-7.* *Open M-F 7am-2:30am, Sa-Su noon-3am.*

AIRE

CLUB

C. Valencia, 236 ☎93 454 63 94 www.arenadisco.com

If you're looking for a queer-centric party spot that isn't overwhelmingly male (i.e. the rest of l'Eixample), check out Aire for all of the non-guy company the neighborhood seemed to be lacking. This huge club is packed nearly as soon as its doors open and continues to party with a mix of pop hits, R and B, and electronica well into the night. Don't worry about feeling left out—no matter your gender or orientation, unless you show up at one of their women-only strip shows *(6-10pm 1st Su each month)*—the owner says the club is, "for girls...and friends."

Ⓜ Universitat. Face the university building and walk down the street that runs along its right side, C. Balmes. Turn left onto C. Valencia, 1 street after crossing Arago. Ⓢ Cover €5-10; includes 1 drink. Open Th-Su 11:30pm-3am.*

PLATA BAR BAR

C. Consell de Cent, 233 ☎93 452 46 36 www.facebook.com/platabar

Four flatscreens play a simulcast of Lady Gaga videos in an interior chic enough that sculptural water bottles can parade convincingly as art. Colored lights spice up the chic interior with rainbow flags in the window to match. Order a mojito *(€9.50)* from one of the ripped bartenders, and settle into this classy gay bar before heading over to shake your tail elsewhere.

Ⓜ Universitat. Face the university building and walk down the road that runs along its left side. After 2 blocks, turn left onto C. Consell de Cent. Plata Bar is 2 blocks down. Ⓢ Beer €3.50. Cocktails €9.50. Open daily 7pm-3am.

ESPIT CHUPITOS (ARIBAU) BAR

C. Aribau, 77 www.espitchupitos.com

If you want shots, they've got 'em—580 different delectable little devils will let you party as if you'd gone to Cancun on vacation instead of the Mediterranean. Be prepared for a little more than just drinking, though. Spectacle shots such as the *Harry Potter* literally light up the night, while others have the bartenders getting down and dirty. If you can't get enough, Espit Chupitos has gotten so popular that it now has two other locations in the city, a sister store in l'Eixample called Gato Negro, and an outpost inside La Fira.

Ⓜ Universitat. Walk on C. Aribau to the left of the university building. Espit Chupitos is 4 blocks down. Ⓢ Shots €2. Cocktails €8.50. Open M-Th 8pm-2:30am, F-Sa 8pm-3am, Su 8pm-2:30am.

MOJITO CLUB CLUB

C. Rosselló, 217 ☎65 420 10 06 www.mojitobcn.com

A salsa-inspired club for the younger set, Mojito can't be as easily defined as its Latin beat-blasting genre-mates. Low black leather couches and semi-private alcoves dot the foyer, while the dance floor pulses to everything from hip hop to rumba, depending on the night. Stop by during the day to take a salsa lesson from the **Buenavista Dance Studio** *(☎93 237 65 28)* or go for a cheaper option on Wednesday nights with free Samba lessons during their Brazil party, starting at 11:30pm.

Ⓜ Diagonal. Walk away from Psg. de Gràcia on C. Rossello. Mojito is near the intersection of C. Balmes, on the far side. i Th salsa night, F-Sa salsa until 1:30am. Special events info on website. Ⓢ Cover F-Sa €12; includes 1 drink. Th and Sa 1-drink min. Beer €7. Cocktails €9. Open Th -F 11pm-4:30am, Sa 11pm-3:30am, Su 8:30pm-4:30am.

LUZ DE GAS CLUB, CONCERT HALL

C. Muntaner, 244-256 ☎93 209 77 11 www.luzdegas.com

The most well-known club in the city, and for good reason. Red velvet walls, gilded mirrors, and sparkling chandeliers will have you wondering how you possibly got past the bouncer. Big name jazz, blues, and soul performers occasionally take the stage during the evening hours, while after 1am it becomes overrun by swanky partygoers. Ritzy young things dance to deafening pop, from Outkast to Nancy Sinatra, pounding through the lower area, while the upstairs lounge provides a much-needed break for both your feet and ears.

Ⓜ Diagonal. Take a right onto Rambla de Catalonia, walk 1 block and take a slight left onto Av. Diagonal. Walk 5min. and take a right onto C. de Muntaner. i For show listings and times check the Guía del Ocio or their website. Ⓢ Club cover €18. Beer €7. Cocktails €10. Dance club open daily 11:30pm-5:30am.

DBOY/LA MADAME/DEMIX CLUB

Ronda Sant Pere, 19-21 ☎93 453 05 82 www.matineegroup.com

Three clubs in one, this single spot hosts a downright confusing variety of nightlife options depending on the night. **DBoy** is no-girls allowed, with a young and lively gay crowd dancing in a laser-lit wonderland. **La Madame** fems it up, offering a hetero-centric alternative geared mostly towards women, and **Demix** supplies just like what it sounds—a mixed crowd. Check the website beforehand to see which way the club swings.

Ⓜ Urquinaona. With your back to Plaça Urquinaona, Ronda Sant Pere runs to the right from the P. Follow it a few short steps and look for the LED sign. Ⓢ Cover varies €10-15. DBoy open in summer F-Sa midnight-6am. La Madame open in summer Su midnight-5am. Demix open Jan-July F-Su midnight-6am; Sept-Dec F-Su midnight-6am.

DIETRICH GAY TEATRO CAFE BAR

C. Consell de Cent, 225 ☎93 451 77 07 www.facebook.com/dietrichcafe

Rainbow flags, a cheery staff, and an unquestionably classy portrait of an old, saggy, fishnet-clad Marlene Dietrich wait to greet you as you walk in the door. Despite the cheery atmosphere, a serious dance floor lies waiting in back, complete with a Bacardi-cooler-turned-sculpture along the bar. Some nights are hit-or-miss—a packed house during their special events is countered by an echoing shell on nights off. If the bar seems too empty for your tastes, hop next door to the club's other portion, Atame, for a guaranteed full house.

Ⓜ Universitat. Face the university building and walk left on Gran Vía. Turn right onto Aribau and walk 2 blocks. Take a left onto Consell de Cent. Dietrich is 1 block away. i Drag shows, acrobatics, and dancing on some nights. Check with restaurant for event schedule. Ⓢ Beer €3.50. Cocktails €4.50-7.50. Open Th-Sa 10:30pm-2:30am.

BAR CENTRIK BAR

C. Aribau, 30

One of the newest additions to gay-friendly nightlife in l'Eixample, Bar Centrik caters to a mix of sexualities about as convoluted as its interior decoration—prepare to be engulfed by lush purple walls clad with '60s logos sitting under the bar's straw hut overhang. Super friendly regulars will have you sharing your secrets in no time (as well as listening to some of their own), and just one of their delicious but potent cocktails will have you confessing more than you may have wanted.

Ⓜ Universitat. Face the university building and walk left on Gran Vía. Turn right immediately onto C. Aribau. Bar Centrik is 1 block away. Ⓢ Beer €4. Cocktails €6-8. Open daily 11pm-3am.

EL GATO NEGRO BAR

Consell de Cent, 268 ☎69 977 36 74 www.espitchupitos.com

All of the shocking variety of Espit Chupitos, now with half-hearted attempts at a spooky theme (look for the black cat in the corner). Luckily, this young and bustling bar is a favorite for lively travelers, and the atmosphere (paired with the cheap, often incredibly amusing, shots) makes up for its lack of ambience. Check out Espit Chupitos just down the street if the pocket-sized bar gets too packed for your refined tastes.

Ⓜ Universitat. Face the university building and walk left on Gran Vía. Turn right onto Aribau and walk 2 blocks. Take a right onto Consell de Cent and it's 1 block away. Ⓢ Shots €1.50-3. Beer €1.60-2. No credit cards after 11pm. Open M-Th 8am-2:30am, F-Sa 8am-3am, Su 8am-2:30am. Kitchen closes at 11pm.

SNOOKER BAR BAR

C. Roger de Llúria, 42 ☎93 317 97 60 www.snookerbarbarcelona.com

With award-winning interior decoration in front and an equally impressive pool hall in back, Snooker Bar is like what your smokey-bowling-alley-pool-hall back home would look like after an episode of "Pimp My Snooker." Sit back in one of the red velvet chairs with one of their many scotches and try to figure out why anyone ever decided that pool tables should be neon-lit.

*Ⓜ Passeig de Gràcia. Face Plaça Catalonia and walk left on Gran Vía for 2 blocks. Take a left onto C. Roger de Lluria. **i** Singles night W 8pm. Ⓢ Cocktails €8. Open M-Th 6pm-2:30am, F-Sa 6pm-3am, Su 6pm-2:30am.*

MOMO'S BAR Y COPAS BAR

C. Consell de Cent, 268 ☎93 487 33 14

A sleek interior lit with old Victorian lanterns and a more upbeat string of rainbow-colored lights around the bar. Candles along the bar warm the place up, while low couches along the back provide ample seating for the young crowd that trickles in later during the night. Don't come here expecting a rager—a calm and sparse clientele keeps it classy.

Ⓜ Universitat. Face the university building and walk down the road that runs along its left-hand side. After 2 blocks, turn right onto C. Consell de Cent. Ⓢ Beer, wine, and shots €3. Cocktails €7. Open M-Th 8pm-2:30am, F-Sa 8pm-3am, Su 8pm-2:30am.

BARCELONETA

ABSENTA BAR

C. Sant Carles, 36

Not for the easily spooked, Absenta is like an episode of *The Twilight Zone* if you were trapped inside the television looking out. Staticky TV sets with flickering faces dot the walls, and a life-sized angel hovers above while you sinfully sip your absinthe *(€4-7)*. A young crowd brings this *modernisme*-inspired beauty up-to-date in an appropriately arts manner.

Ⓜ Barceloneta. Walk down Psg. Joan de Borbó toward the beach and take a left onto C. Sant Carles. Ⓢ Beer €2.30. Cocktails €7. Absinthe €4-7. Open Tu-F 11pm-2am, Sa 11am-3am, Su 6pm-2am.

KE? BAR

C. del Baluart, 54 ☎93 224 15 88

Pull up a keg chair—they're comfier than they sound. This small bar attracts a gathering of internationals and provides an alterative to the crowded beaches and throbbing bass of the *playa*. Shelves hanging as tables, fruit decals along the bar, and a playful group of faces peering down from overhead may not be weird enough to have you wondering "whaaat?" but they'll at least remind you not to take yourself too seriously.

Ⓜ Barceloneta. Walk down Psg. Joan de Borbó toward the sea and take a left onto C. Sant Crles. Take a left once you enter the plaza onto C. del Baluart. Ⓢ Beer €2.50. Cocktails €6. Open M-Th 11:30am-2:30am, F-Sa 11:30am-3am, Su 11:30am-2:30am.

CATWALK NIGHTCLUB

C. Ramón Trias Fargas, 2-4 ☎69 264 14 29 www.clubcatwalk.net

Though you'll only get access to the ritzy elevated walk above if you're a VIP, there's enough glam below to ward off your jealousy, so be sure to leave your T-shirts and sneakers back in your hostel. Beautiful people deck the lounges and dancefloor, while the brave (or possibly drunk) take advantage of the lit dancing boxes to strut their stuff to a mix of pop, electro, and R and B.

*Ⓜ Port Olímpic. **i** No T-shirts, torn jeans, or sneakers permitted. Events listing on website. Ⓢ Cover €18. Beer €7. Cocktails €12. Open Th midnight-5am, F-Sa midnight-6am, Su midnight-5am.*

OPIUM MAR NIGHTCLUB, RESTAURANT

Psg. Marítim de la Barceloneta, 34 ☎90 226 74 86 www.opiummar.com

Slick restaurant by day and an even slicker nightclub by night, this lavish indoor and outdoor party spot still knows how to kick it up a notch despite its facade of decorum. Seafood is served until 1am, after which a mix of electronica and American pop pounds from the stereo and lures dancers out of the fashionable white chairs and onto the dance floor.

Ⓜ Port Olímpic. i Events listing on website. DJs every W. $ Cover €20; includes 1 drink. Restaurant open daily 1pm-1am. Club open M-Th midnight-5am, F-Sa 1-6am, Su midnight-5am.

GRAN CASINO CASINO

C. Marina, 19 ☎93 225 78 78 www.casino-barcelona.com

The most beautiful casino in Barcelona, nestled within the requisite amount of glitz and glam surrounding Port Olímpic. Slot machines above in the Sala Americana start the night off slowly, while things get more serious (and addictive) below with tables of blackjack, American and French roulette, a theater hosting Vegas-esque shows, and a killer buffet. Admission to the main floor will cost you *(€4.50)* unless you bring a flyer, but don't worry, that's nothing compared to the money you'll be lured into gambling away the entire night.

Ⓜ Port Olimpic. Under the Fish. i Must be 18 to play. No sneakers or beach clothes allowed; collared shirt recommended for men. Passport required. Live jazz in Sala Principal F-Sa. $ Entrance to Sala Principal €4.50 Sala Americana (slot machines and bar) open M-Th 10am-5pm, F-Sa 10am-5:30pm, Su 10am-5pm. Sala Principal (theater, game tables) open daily 3pm-5am.

MONTJUÏC AND POBLE SEC

ROUGE CAFE BAR

C. Poeta Cabanyes, 21 ☎93 442 49 85

When you walk into a sultry rouge-lit lounge decked in leather chairs and a cavalcade of vintage decor (including a shoddy copy of the Arnolfini wedding portrait), you know you're doing something right. Luckily, a crowd of hip, friendly locals are there to join you. The prettiest, most stereotypically girly drinks in the city are some of the most delicious, so try the melon Absolut Porno *(€6)* or the vodka-based Barcelona Rouge *(€6.50)*.

Ⓜ Parallel. With Montjuïc to your left, walk along Av. Parallel. Take a left onto C. Poeta Cabanyes. Rouge Cafe will be on your left before Mambo Tango Youth Hostel. Open daily in summer 7pm-3am in winter 8pm-3am.

TINTA ROJA BAR

C. Creu dels Molers, 17 ☎93 443 32 43 wwww.tintaroja.net

Named after the 1941 tango "Tinta Roja" by Cátulo Castillo and Sebsatián Piana, this cafe bar mixes literal Latin flavor with the flair of the theater. Argentine drinks are their specialty, ranging from a little boost of *mate (€4.80)* to a full range of the country's liquors and beer. Scattered seating under questionably erotic Impressionistic paintings populate the front, while a back stage plays host to popular tango classes on Wednesday nights at 9pm. Don't mind the mannequins looking down over your footwork—chances are they're just admiring your dance steps.

Ⓜ Poble Sec. With Montjuïc to your right, walk along Av. Parallel. Take the 2nd right onto C. de la Creu dels Molers; Tinta Roja will be on the left. i Tango classes W 9-11:30pm. $ Beer €2.30-4. Wine €2.50-3.70. Mate €4.80. Argentine liquors €5.50-6. Cocktails €7. Open Th 8:30pm-2am, F-Sa 8:30pm-3am.

242 CLUB

C. Entença, 37 ☎93 228 90 73 www.myspace.com/club242

Fearing a hangover after that massive night of partying? One of the longest running after-hours clubs in the city of Barcelona, 242 lets you skip right over those painful waking hours and relive the night you already enjoyed. A crowd trickles in after 6am as the other clubs close to enjoy drinks, electronica, A/C, and movies. If you find yourself winding down, they even have food for breakfast.

Ⓜ Espanya. Walk away from Montjuïc on Gran Vía and take a right onto C. de' Entença. 242 is

right before the intersection with Sepúlveda. ℹ *Special events listed on Myspace.* Ⓢ *Cover €15; includes 1 drink. Beer €5. Cocktails €10.* ⏰ *Open F-Su 6am-whenever the party stops.*

MAU MAU BAR

C. Fontrodona, 35 ☎93 441 80 15 www.maumaunderground.com

The ground zero of the cultural underground in Barcelona, Mau Mau is best known for its online guide to art, film, and other hip happenings around the city. Expect to see artsy 20-somethings lounging on this warehouse-turned-lounge's classy couches before and after concerts at the nearby Sala Apolo, or maybe for the screening of a Herzog flick *(movies every Th-Sa at 10pm).*

ⓂParallel. When facing Montjuïc, walk right along Av. Parallel and take a left onto C. Fontrodona. Follow the street as it zigzags—Mau Mau is just a few blocks down. Ⓢ *Year-long membership €12. Visitors free. Beer €2-3. Cocktails €6-8.* ⏰ *Open Th-Sa 11pm-2:30am. Open other days of the week for special events.*

SALA APOLO CLUB

Nou de la Rambla, 113 ☎93 441 40 01 www.sala-apolo.com

Looking for a party, but lamenting that it's Monday? Sulk no longer—for the last number of years Sala Apolo has been drawing locals to start the week off right with Nasty Mondays, featuring a mix of rock, pop, indie, garage, and '80s *(€11).* In fact, the night is so popular that it spawned an equally persuasively named Crappy Tuesdays *(indie and electropop; €10-12),* which take over after the American one-woman Broadway-esque show "Anti-Karaoke." Stop by later in the week to catch a varied crowd, and check the website for the latest bigger-name indie concerts rolling through the venue.

ⓂParallel. Walk along Parallel with Montjuïc to your right. Take a hard right onto Nou de la Rambla. Not to be confused with Teatre Apolo, which is on Av. Parallel. Ⓢ *Anti-karaoke €8. Nasty M €11. Crappy Tu €10-12. W Rumba €6-10. Other tickets €15-23.*

GRÀCIA

EL RAÏM BAR

C. Progrés, 48 www.raimbcn.com

Though a little farther from Gràcia's roaring plazas, this time capsule with an identity crisis is well worth the short trek. A mix between a Catalan bodega and '50s Cuban bar, this traditional winery has been in business since 1886, when it served as the diner for the old factory across the street. Since then, the owner has transformed the place into a shrine to Cuban music and memorabilia, rum, and incredible mojitos. It consistently attracts a flock of down-to-earth locals looking for one (or all) of the three.

ⓂFontana. Walk down C. Gran de Gràcia and make a left on C. Ros de Olano. Walk for about 4 blocks and take a right onto C. Torrent de l'Olla. Take the 4th left onto Siracusa, and El Raïm is on the corner of its intersection with C. del Progrés. Ⓢ *Beer €2-3. Cocktails €5.50.* ⏰ *Open daily 8pm-2:30am.*

VINIL BAR

C. Matilde, 2 ☎66 917 79 45 www.vinilus.blogspot.com

Those expecting a fetish club—whether for LPs or something of a kinkier persuasion—may be disappointed. Though this is certainly no shrine to a musical era past (or present), the warm lighting and comfy pillows make the perfect place to kick back and watch their daily screened movie. Feel free to geek out over their giant phonograph or the Velvet Underground song playing over the speakers—chances are the hip clientele will perfectly understand.

ⓂDiagonal. Ⓢ *Beer €3-3.50. Cocktails €5.* ⏰ *Open in summer M-Th 8pm-2am, F-Sa 8pm-3am; in winter M-Th 8pm-2am, F-Sa 8pm-3am, Su 8pm-2am.*

ASTROLABI BAR

C. Martinez de la Rosa, 14

Pirate decor with bartenders to match. Maps, clocks, and miniature ships all help to explain away your drunk dizziness as "seasickness." Drop in earlier in the night for some entertainment, with a small and dedicated following cozying up in the watering hole to watch acoustic acts croon over lost loves and anachronisms. If you need an ear to listen, shrunken heads dangle over the bar for your disposal.

*Ⓜ Diagonal. Walk toward Psg. de Gràcia and take a left onto it. Follow the street as it crosses Av. Diagonal and becomes Psg. de Gràcia. Turn right onto C. de Bonavista before Psg. de Gràcia turns into C. Gran de Gràcia. Left onto C. Martinez de la Rosa. **i** Live music daily at 10pm. Ⓢ Beer €2.60. Wine €1. Cocktails €6. Open M-Th 8pm-2:30am, F-Sa 8pm-3am, Su 8pm-2:30am.*

LA CERVERSERA ARTESANA BAR, BREWERY

C. Sant Agustí, 14 ☎93 237 95 94 www.lacervesera.net

When you visit the only pub in Barcelona that makes its own beer, you better order their beer no matter what vows you've taken with PBR. With a huge variety of brews—dark, amber, honey, spiced, chocolate, peppermint, fruit-flavored, and more—there's literally something for everyone, along with seasoned bar snacks to encourage your thirst. If beer isn't your thing, at least come to hear the music—you probably won't hear Pink Floyd and Phil Collins played back-to-back anywhere else in the city.

Ⓜ Diagonal. Take a left onto Psg. de Gràcia and a right (exact right, 90 degree angle) onto C. Corsega at the intersection of Psg. de Gràcia and Via Diagonal. C. Sant Agustí is the 3rd street on the left. Ⓢ House brews €4.80-5. Open M-Th 6pm-2am, F-Sa 6pm-3am, Su 6pm-2am.

DEDUES COCKTAIL AND BAR BAR

C. Torrent de l'Olla, 89 ☎93 416 14 96 www.dedues.es

Cheap beer, free bar snacks, daily specials, and incredible €4 cocktails will keep you in your chairs and in the money at this snazzy orange floral-clad *cocteleria*, whether you're looking for a day drink or a nightcap. Drop by with a new friend during weekday evenings *(M-Th 9-11pm)* to grab two cocktails with natural fruit juice for €8, though they're so good that you may just want them both for yourself.

Ⓜ Fontana. From the metro, walk down C. Asturies until you hit C. Torrent de l'Olla. Walk 5½ blocks down C. Torrent de l'Olla. Ⓢ Sandwiches €1.80-4. Food €3-4. Cañas of beer €1 daily 4-7pm. Cocktails €4. Open M-Th 4pm-2:30am, F 4pm-3am, Sa 6pm-3am.

VELCRO BAR BAR

C. Vallfogona, 10 ☎61 075 47 42

Though Velcro Bar is a bit farther from Gràcia's popular plazas, its screenings of nightly movies attract a young and hip clientele that ends up paying little attention to the moving pictures. True to its name, this is a bar where bright green and pink velcro waits to hold the bottom of your drink.

Ⓜ Fontana. Follow C. Asturies to C. Torrent de l'Olla and make a right. Follow for 3 blocks, make a left onto C. Vallfogona. Ⓢ Cocktails €5-8. Open daily 7pm-2:30am.

LA BAIGNOIRE CAFE BAR, CAFE

C. Verdi, 6 ☎60 633 04 60

More cafe-bodega than bar, the vintage chic interior of this dollhouse-sized establishment attracts a sophisticated younger crowd unafraid of sporting T-shirts. Treat yourself to some fancy wine and a cheese platter before heading back to the life of drinking six-packs of Estrella in the plaza.

Ⓜ Fontana. Take a right onto C. Gran de Gràcia toward C. Montseny. Take the 3rd left onto C. Ros de Olano and follow as it changes into C. Terrol. Take a left onto C. Verdi and it'll be on your right. Ⓢ Wine from €2.70. Cheeses €3.60-3.90. Open M-Th 7pm-1:30am, F-Sa 7pm-2am, Su 6pm-1am.

FLANN O'BRIEN'S BAR

C. Casanova, 264 ☎93 201 16 06 www.flannobrienbcn.com

One of Barcelona's thousands of Irish Bars and one of the few in which you'll actually find any Irish, this sprawling den has been a local and English-speaking favorite for almost 20 years. Nightly live music draws a crowd around 9pm, but grab a Guinness, throw on your rugby shirt, and stick around after the show to see if the expats get surly.

*ⓂDiagonal. Walk for 10min. on Av. Diagonal away from Psg. de Gràcia. Take a right onto Casanova before the round Placa de Francesc Macia. **i** Live music nightly 9pm. Ⓢ Beer €3.50-5. Cocktails €6. Open daily 5:45pm-3am.*

OTTO ZUTZ CLUB

C. Lincoln, 15 ☎93 238 07 22 www.ottozutz.com

Like a tiered layer cake with an impeccably designed party inside (or maybe a portion of Dante's Inferno, depending on the night), three floors of dancing and drinks await. At least four different DJs pound out a huge variety of music to a chic and shiny crowd, with a reprieve from the throbbing masses only available up top. Watch out—during the summer this heaven gets hellishly hot.

ⓂFontana. Walk along Rambla de Prat and take a right as it dead-ends into V. Augusta. Take the first right onto C. Laforja and the first right again to reach C. Lincoln. Ⓢ Cover €10-15; includes 1 drink. Beer €6. Cocktails €6-12. Open W-Su midnight-6am.

KGB CLUB ❸

C. Alegre de Dalt, 55 ☎93 210 59 06 www.salakgb.net

In Soviet Russia, KGB dances you. No, but really—the only indications of the eastern block are the oppressive KGB posters hanging from the walls like propaganda and the sheer utility of the decorations—expect lots of black, lots of metal, and little glitz or bourgeois sparkle. Scrappy youth join the bartenders and live DJ and VJ in a sweaty countdown to get down. Entrance is free with a flyer; otherwise you'll be paying €12-15 to join this **Communist party.**

ⓂJoanic. Walk along C. Pi i Maragall and take the 1st left. To get a cab home, come back to Pi i Maragall. Ⓢ Cover €12 with 1 drink, €15 with 2 drinks until 3am. Free with flyer. Open Th 1-5am, F-Sa 1-6am.

MI BAR BAR

C. de les Guilleries, 6

With chill alternative tunes and graffitied walls lit by crystal chandeliers, it's only fitting that one of Mi Bar's fans has scrawled in Spanish, "it's better that I stay here." A pool table and cheap drinks keep locals coming back to this steadfast hangout.

ⓂFontana. Walk down C. Gran de Gràcia and make a left onto C. Montseny. Continue for 6 blocks, then make a right onto C. de les Guilleries. Ⓢ Wine €1. Beer €1.50-2. Cocktails €5-7. Open M-Th 10pm-2am, F-Sa 10pm-3am.

CAFE DEL SOL CAFE, BAR

Pl. del Sol, 16 ☎93 237 14 48

One of the many tapas bars lining the Pl. del Sol, the Cafe del Sol offers cheap and delicious eats in an ambience well-suited to the square's unbeatably chill nightlife. Giacommeti-esque figures line the wall along the bar, while a back room provides a cozy shelter for those looking for respite from the square.

ⓂFontana. Walk down C. Gran de Gràcia, make a left on C. Ros de olano and the a right on C. Cano/C. Leopoldo Alas. Ⓢ Beer €2.20-2.80. Tapas €3.50-7.50. Entrees €3.50-5.80. Open M-Th noon-2:30am, F-Sa noon-3am, Su noon-2:30am.

EL OTRO BAR BAR, CAFE

Travessera de Gràcia, 167 ☎93 323 67 59

Hopping cafe-restaurant by day and a popular local hangout at night, El Otro

Bar has industrial metal walls in back that fade into a cheerier Tetris-like bar up front. Otherworldly dioramas decorate each of the tables, with a neon color palette that might distract you from your conversation.

Ⓜ Fontana. Walk down C. Gran de Gràcia until you reach Trav de Gràcia. Take a left—El Otro Bar is on the corner. Wine and beer €2.50-3. Cocktails €6.40. Food €2.10-4.50. Open M-Th 8:30am-2:30am, F 8:30am-3am, Sa 9:30am-3am, Su 10:30am-1:30am.

MOND BAR BAR

Pl. del Sol, 21 ☎93 272 09 10

Tattoos, v-necks, and fedoras form the trifecta of hip gear you'll need to fit in here. A well-stocked jukebox lets you pick the hits without bartender intervention, with space to sprawl out on the amphitheater-style stacked benches in back.

Ⓜ Fontana. Take a right onto C. Gran de Gràcia toward C. Montseny. Take the 3rd left onto C. Ros de Olano until you reach Pl. del Sol. Beer €2-4. Cocktails €5-6. Open M-Th 7pm-2:30am, F-Sa 7pm-3am, Su 7pm-2:30am.

NICTALIA BAR

C. St. Domenec, 15 ☎93 237 23 23

A 13-year-old girly-girl's dream—lilac purple walls, white furniture, and colorful chalkboards create a more innocent-feeling place to knock back a few, while some chic modern touches make it feel mature enough for your imbibing not to be debaucherous. Settle in for a few cheap shots *(€2)* with the locals.

Ⓜ Fontana. Walk down C. Gran de Gràcia to C. St. Domenec and make a left. Nictalia is 2 blocks down on the left. Shots €2. Beer €2.50. Cocktails €5-7. Open M-Th 8:30pm-2am, F-Sa 8pm-3am.

CAFE DEL TEATRE CAFE, BAR

C. Torrijos, 41 ☎93 416 06 51

Black cats, white, French doors, stained glass, big green bubble lights, and lots o' locals dot this bustling creep-meets-provincial cafe -bar day and night. Order a mindblowing salad to pad your stomach before downing their signature *Cocktail del Cafe del Teatre (€6).*

Ⓜ Joanic. Take a right onto C. de l'Escorial and a left onto C. de Sant Lluis after a block. Cafe del Teatre is in the plaça after C. del Torrent d'en Vidalet. Beer €1.50-3.60. Shots €2.50-4. Sandwiches €5-6. Open M-Sa 8am-3am, Su 5pm-3am.

TIBIDABO

MIRABLAU BAR, NIGHTCLUB ❷

P. Dr. Andreu ☎93 418 58 79 www.mirablaubcn.com

With easily the best view in Tibidabo and arguably the best view in Barcelona, Mirablau is a favorite with posh internationals and the younger crowd. It also happens to be near the top of Collserola mountain range's highest peak. Reasonable drinks for the area *(cocktails €7-9.50)* and a view that will leave you feeling like you've ascended to heaven—a heaven that plays the Village People—earns this bar a *Let's Go* thumbpick. A relaxed bar and lounge area upstairs changes into an energy-filled dance floor on the lower level, leaving those with two left feet room to spill out onto the terrace.

*Take the L7 to Ⓜ Avinguda de Tibidabo or the Tramvia Blau to Pl. Dr. Andreu. From the metro, walk up the mountain on Av. de Tibidabo to Pl. Dr. Andreu. From the tram, it's to your left when facing the city. **i** Credit card min. Th-Sa €4.70. Drinks discounted M-Sa before 11pm, Su before 6pm. Beer and wine €1.80-6. Cocktails €7-9.50. Open M-Th 11am-4:30am, F-Sa 11am-5:45am.*

MERBEYÉ BAR ❷

Pl. Dr. Andreu ☎93 434 00 35

More like a den than the clifflike Mirablau on the opposite side of the road, Merbeyé provides a classy, red-velvet atmosphere for those looking to embrace the romantic side of the picturesque surroundings. With a lounge whose lights are so low that seeing your companion may be a problem, Merbeyé creates the perfect setting to bring a date or possibly find another at the seemingly never-ending bar. Smooth jazz serenades throughout, and with just one Mirabeyé *(Cava Brut, cherry brandy, and Cointreau; €9-10)* you'll be guaranteed to find yourself at the requisite level of chill.

Take the L7 to Ⓜ Avinguda de Tibidabo or the Tramvia Blau to Pl. del Doctor Andreu. From the metro, walk up the mountain on Av. de Tibidabo to Pl. Dr. Andreu. From the tram, it's to your back when facing the city. Ⓢ Non-alcoholic drinks €8-9. Cocktails €9-10. Food €2-7.60. Open W 7pm-1am, Th noon-2am, F-Sa noon-4am, Su noon-2am.

arts and culture

MUSIC AND DANCE

For comprehensive guides of large events and information on cultural activities in the city, contact the **Institut de Cultura de Barcelona (ICUB)** *(Palau de la Virreina, La Rambla, 99 ☎93 316 10 00 www.bcn.cat/cultura Open daily 10am-8pm)* or the **Guía del Ocio** *(www.guiadelociobcn.com).*

More guide options exist online for those able to glean basic information from Catalan: **www.butxaca.com** is the best of the bunch, with comprehensive bimonthly agenda with film, music, theater, and art listings. The website **www.maumaunderground.com** lists local music news, reviews, and a daily agenda of shows and events, while **www.infoconcerts.cat/ca** provides even more concert listings. For tickets, check out **ServiCaixa** *(☎90 233 22 11 www.servicaixa.com Open M-F 8am-2:30pm)*, available at any branch of the Caixa Catalonia bank, **TelEntrada** *(☎90 210 12 12 www.telentrada.com)*, or **Ticketmaster** *(www.ticketmaster.es)*.

Although a destination for musicians year-round, Barcelona especially perks up during the warmer months with an influx of touring bands and impressive music festivals. The biggest and arguably baddest of these is the three-day electronic music festival **Sónar** *(www.sonar.es)* taking place in mid-June, which attracts internationally renowned DJs, electronica fans, and party people from all over the world. The **Grec** summer festival *(www.bcn.cat/grec)* takes place throughout the summer months, using multiple venues throughout the city to host international music, theater, and dance. The indie-centric **Primavera Sound** *(www.primaverasound.com)* at the end of May is also quickly becoming a regional must-see. More information on local festivals is available in the *Mondo Sonoro*, which lists happenings across the world.

High Class(ical) and Opera

PALAU DE LA MÚSICA CATALANA — L'EIXAMPLE

St. Francesc de Paula, 2 — ☎90 244 28 82 www.palaumusica.org

Although the Bach- and Verdi-studded stage still hosts primarily classical concerts, this *modernista* structure also hosts a surprising variety of musical acts almost every night. Over 300 performances of choral and orchestral pieces, pop, acoustic, jazz, and flamenco grace its stage every year, including those from its very own **Orfeo Català** (Catalan choir) for which the building was constructed. If you're just looking for an excuse to see the breathtaking Secret Garden-esque interior without a tour (or you really like giant air-driven, tubed instruments), drop by for one of their frequent and cheap organ performances—they need them to keep the organ pipes clean.

Ⓜ Jaume I. Facing V. Laietana from the Pl. de l'Àngel exit, take a left onto the road. Walk for 10min. and take a right onto the plaza-like C. Sant Pere Mas Alt. i Check the Guía del Ocio for listings. Ⓢ Concert tickets €8-175. Box office open M-Sa 10am-9pm, Su from 2hr. before show time. No concerts in Aug.

L'AUDITORI GRAN VÍA

C. Lepant, 150 ☎93 247 93 00 wwww.auditori.com

Built in 1999 by world-renowned architect Rafael Moneo, this modern auditorium is now home to the Symphonic Orchestra of Barcelona (OBC). Glass, steel, and concrete house a variety of music types, including classical, chamber, world music, contemporary, and more. Check the website to browse the performances by type. A number of festivals are held here throughout the year in addition to their regular programming, including the World Music Festival, International Percussion Festival of Catalonia, Festival of Old Music of Barcelona, and even the electronic Sònar for those tired of actual instruments.

Ⓜ Monumental. Walk on C. Marina toward Gran Vía. Walk 2 blocks and take a left onto C. d'Ausiàs March, then take the 1st right onto C. Lepant. i Tickets available by phone, through ServiCaixa or TelEntrada, or at box office. Ⓢ Tickets €4-40. Box office open M-Sa noon-9pm, Su 1hr. before show starts.

GRAN TEATRE DEL LICEU LAS RAMBLAS

La Rambla, 51-59 ☎93 485 99 13 www.liceubarcelona.com

A Barcelona institution since its founding in 1847, the Gran Teatre del Liceu is actively reclaiming its role as the premier venue for upscale performances after being closed due to fire in 1994. Classical, opera, and ballet grace the stage of its impressively restored auditorium, while a smaller reception room hosts discussions about the pieces and smaller events. If you're afraid of committing to a ticket, drop in for a tour and hope to catch a sneak peak of the rehearsal for the night's performance.

Ⓜ Liceu. Face the plaza and the house with umbrellas on its side and walk to your right down La Rambla. Teatre is about a block away. i Tickets available at box office, online, or through ServiCaixa. Box office open M-F 1:30-8pm.

Pop and Rock 'n' Roll

RAZZMATAZZ LAS RAMBLAS

C. Pamplona, 88 and Almogàvers, 122 ☎93 272 09 10 www.salarazzmatazz.com

This massive, converted warehouse hosts big-name popular acts from reggae to electropop and indie to metal. The big room packs the popular draw (bands like Motorhead, Alice in Chains, and Gossip), while the smaller rooms hide up-and-comers like the Vivian Girls. Whenever there isn't a throng of people for the concerts, you'll find a young crowd pulsing to the beat of one of their nightly DJs. The labyrinthine nightclub spans across multiple floors in two buildings, connected by industrial stairwells and a rooftop walkway—definitely not intended for the navigationally deficient.

Ⓜ Bogatell. Walk down the diagonal street (C. Pere IV) away from the plaza and take the 1st slight left onto C. Pamplona. Razzmatazz is immediately on the right. i Tickets available online through website, TelEntrada, or Ticketmaster. Ⓢ Tickets €12-22.

SIDECAR LAS RAMBLAS

Pl. Reial, 7 ☎93 317 76 66 www.sidecarfactoryclub.com

Though bigger indie bands may tour here from time to time, Sidecar's real specialty is local fare. Pop, rock, punk, and alternative acts with an edge grace the smallish stage downstairs in a setting much more intimate than other clubs of the same caliber in town.

Ⓜ Liceu. Facing the house with the **dragon** *and umbrellas on it, walk down La Rambla to your right and take a left onto C. Ferran. Take the 1st right to enter P. Reial. Sidecar is in the corner to your left. i Tickets often available through Ticketmaster via the club's website, or www.atrapalo.com. Ⓢ Tickets from €12.*

Folk and All That Jazz

JAMBOREE
LAS RAMBLAS

Pl. Reial, 17 ☎93 319 17 89 www.masimas.com

The black-and-white portraits of jazz musicians lining the walls tell of the club's long-standing history. Jamboree has been hosting jazz acts for over 50 years, and manages to mix this rich history with a surprising dose of relevant contemporary artists—expect to hear a Billie Holiday tribute one night and the Markus Strickland Quartet the next. If you're looking for something a little less predictable, their WTF Jam Sessions are popular with local musicians and will only cost you €4 to peep.

Ⓜ Liceu. Facing the house with the **dragon** *and umbrellas on it, walk down La Rambla to your right and take a left onto C. Ferran. Take the 1st right to enter Pl. Reial. Jamboree is in the far corner to your right.* ***i*** *Tickets available through TelEntrada.* *Jazz tickets €10-25 (normally €10-15), Su jam session €4, flamenco €6.* *Jazz performances Tu-Su 9 and 11pm, check site for exact times as some performances start at 8pm. WTF Jam Sessions M 9pm-1:30am. Upstairs Tarantos holds flamenco shows daily 8:30, 9:30, 10:30pm.*

HARLEM JAZZ CLUB
LAS RAMBLAS

C. Comtessa de Sobradiel, 8 ☎93 310 07 55 www.harlemjazzclub.es

With two live music performances each night and a drink included with admission, Harlem Jazz Club promises to beat those empty-wallet blues. A performance schedule online and on their door lets you choose whether you'll drop in to hear crooning in English over a lost love or a little saucier Latin flavor. With acts ranging from Bossa Nova to gypsy punk, blues to funk, and soul to salsa, the club is a perfect place for any music lover to spend the evening.

Ⓜ Liceu. Walk toward the water on Las Ramblas. Left onto C. Ferran. Right onto C. Avinyó. Left onto C. Comtessa de Sobradiel. ***i*** *Calendar of events for month available online or at door.* *M-Th €5, includes 1 drink. F-Sa €8, includes 1 drink. Su €5. Beer €3.80, cocktails €7.80.* *Open M-Th 9pm-4am with live music at 11:30pm-midnight; F-Sa 9pm-5am with live music at 11:30pm, 1am; Su 9pm-4am.*

CENTRE ARTESÁ TRADICIONÀRIUS
GRÀCIA

Tr. de Sant Antoni, 6-8 ☎93 218 44 85 www.tradicionarius.com

A mini-convention center of sorts that serves as a one-stop shop for traditional Catalan music in a relaxed setting. Whether you're looking to drop in for a Barcelonan singing on a ukelele, or just to track down the next outdoor rumba session or Catalan folk festival, C.A.T. can provide. Each winter they help to organize the Festival Tradicionàrius, which highlights a smorgasbord of Catalan music, dance, and art over the course of January to March.

Ⓜ Fontana. Take a right onto C. Gran de Gràcia, then turn left onto C. del Montseny. Take a left onto Travessia de Sant Antoni. ***i*** *Events often located in other locations throughout the city, check site for details.* *Events €6-20.* *Office open M-F 11am-2pm and 5-9pm.*

barcelona

Flamenco

GUASCH TEATRE
LAS RAMBLAS

C. Aragó, 140 ☎93 323 39 50 or 93 451 34 62 www.guaschteatre.com

If you stop by during the early evening hours, chances are you'll wonder why all the spectators are pint-sized. Half children's theater and half adult shows, the Guasch's stage shows everything from Heidi to the comedic Sex and Jealousy. If the dramatic arts aren't your thing, they frequently showcase *flamenco*—just check the website or call to learn about upcoming events.

Ⓜ Hospital Clinic. Face the engineering school and walk right down C. Comte d'Urgell for 5min. Cross the diagonal Av. de Roma and take the next left onto C. Aragó. ***i*** *Tickets available through TelEntrada or box office.* *Adult tickets €18-20. 25% student discount available.* *Children's theater generally shown Th 6pm, F-Sa 12:30pm, Su 5:30pm; adult theater Th 9pm, F-Sa 10pm, Su*

7:30pm. Box office opens 2hr. prior to performance.

EL PATIO ANDALUZ L'EIXAMPLE

C. Aribau, 242 ☎93 209 33 78

Rumba, *flamenco*, *sevillano*—El Patio provides dinner and an authentic and saucy show, no matter what southern flavor you choose. Entrance includes your choice of drink, tapas, or a full *menú* (depending on which option you choose), with the earlier show lasting about an hour and the later show normally approaching 2hr. Sick of sitting by the sidelines? Performers often encourage diners to try their luck at the floor, so be sure to wear your dancing shoes and most eager expression.

Ⓜ Diagonal. Take a left onto Av. Diagonal and walk for 10min., then take a right onto C. Aribau. Patio Andaluz is before the next block. ***i*** *Call 9am-7pm for reservations or buy tickets at www.flamencotickets.com. Ⓢ Show and 1 drink €30; show and menú €54-67. Daily shows at 8, 10pm.*

THEATER

TEATRE LLIURE LA RIBERA

Pl. Margarida Xirgu, 1 ☎93 218 92 51 www.teatrelliure.com

Established in 1976 by the artsy inhabitants of Gràcia, the Teatre Lliure has become known for presenting works in Catalan, including contemporary pieces and classics from around the globe, and many original Catalan pieces birthed from its own theater cooperative. The present location at the foot of Montjuïc has housed the theater since 2001 but still maintains the feel of its bohemian homeland. Most tickets are more than reasonably priced, and many include entrance to a discussion after the show with the crew and theater critics.

Ⓜ Espanya. Face Montjuïc and go right on Av. Parallel. Take a right onto C. de Lleida and a left through the gate to enter the plaza. ***i*** *Tickets available by box office or ServiCaixa. Some original productions include talk with the artists and critics afterward; check website for info. Language of performance listed on website. Art exhibitions relating to current shows. Ⓢ Tickets €15-24. Art exhibitions on view on days of performances Tu-F 6-8:30pm, Sa-Su 4-6pm.*

TEATRE GREC LA RIBERA

Passeig de Santa Madrona, 36 ☎93 316 10 00 www.bcn.cat/grec

No, this theater isn't left over from the good ol' days, no matter what its name may imply. This open-air Grecian-style amphitheater instead dates just from 1929, when it was carved out of an old stone quarry for the International Exhibition that gave birth to many of Montjuïc's existing spectacles. These days the theater hosts a range of theater, opera, dance, and music performances during the summer months and is the main venue of the city's annual Festival Grec, which takes place from mid-June to early August. Be sure to bring mosquito repellent—being nestled in the Jardins Amargós comes with a price.

Ⓜ Espanya. Head through the 2 bell towers marking the entrance to Montjuïc and follow the escalators to the top. When facing the palace-like art museum, walk along the street to the left and be sure to stay left as it breaks. Teatre Grec is on this road (Passeig de Santa Madrona) just after the Ethnological Museum. ***i*** *Tickets available at Tiquet Rambles (Rambla, 99 ☎93 316 11 11) Tiquet Rambles open daily 10am-8:30pm), Telentrada, and ServiCaixa. Most theater performances in Catalan or Spanish.*

TEATRE NACIONAL DE CATALONIA BARCELONETA

Pl. de les Arts, 1 ☎93 306 57 00 www.tnc.es

This modern structure designed by Ricardo Bofill is a confusing steel and glass nod to the Parthenon. Inaugurated on September 11, 1997, the National Day of Catalonia, it has since been posed as the next cultural center of Barcelona, with an adjacent auditorium with a capacity of 36,000 slated to be completed in the near future. The two performance halls of the main building host contemporary

Catalan and foreign plays, classics, and traditional Catalan dances and music from time to time, while the second building of the complex houses all of the workshops that make the stage tick. Take advantage of youth, if you have it—tickets for shows start from €12 if you're under 25.

*Ⓜ Glories. Face the rocket-shaped Torre Agbar and take the 1st road to your right, Av. Meridiana. Teatre Nacional de Catalonia will be on your right. **i** Tickets available through TelEntrada, ServiCaixa, Tiquet Rambla, and box office. Ⓢ Tickets €15-32, under 25 from €12. Box office and info open W-F 3-8pm, Sa 3-9:30pm, Su 3-6pm.*

CINEMA

CINEMA VERDI — GRACÍA

C. Verdi, 32 ☎93 238 78 896 www.cines-verdi.com/barcelona

This is Barcelona's first theater to run movies in their original language and still the most popular of the few. Together, the cinema and its annex a few streets over make a cinephile's mecca in the city, with 10 screens featuring independent and foreign films. Perfect for any aspiring Ebert, or just a lonely American who's sick of subtitles.

*Ⓜ Fontana. Walk down C. d'Asturies for 5min. and take a right onto C. Verdi. **i** Movie and special events schedule available on website. Ⓢ Tickets €5-7.50; special events €12-16.*

FESTIVALS

Barcelona loves to party. Although *Let's Go* fully supports this endeavor to its fullest extent, we still need to include some nitty-gritty things like accommodations and, you know, food, so we can't possibly list all of the annual festivals around Barcelona. For a full list of what's going on during your visit, be sure to stop by the **tourist information office** once you arrive in the city. As a teaser, here are a few of the biggest, most student-relevant shindigs:

FESTA DE SANT JORDI

La Rambla

This provides a more intelligent, civil alternative to Valentine's Day. Celebrating both St. George (the city's patron saint) and the deaths of Shakespeare and Cervantes, Barcelona gathers along Las Ramblas in search of flowers and books to gift to lovers.

April 23.

FESTA MAJOR

Pl. Rius i Taulet

Festa Major is a community festival in Gràcia in which the artsy intellectuals put on performances and fun happenings in preparation for the Assumption of Mary. Expect parades, concerts, floats, arts and crafts, live music, dancing, and parties.

End of Aug.

LA DIADA

Fossar de les Moreres

This festival is Catalonia's national holiday celebrating the end of the city's siege in 1714 as well as reclaiming national (whoops, we mean regional) identity after Franco. Celebrations will be had and flags will be waved.

Sept 11.

FESTA DE SANT JOAN

The beachfront

These days light a special fire in every pyromaniac's heart as fireworks, bonfires, and torches light the city and waterfront in celebration of the coming of summer.

June 23-24.

FESTA MERCÈ

Pl. de Sant Jaume

This multi-week celebration of Barcelona's patron saint Our Lady of Mercy is the city's main annual celebration. More than 600 free performances and 2000 entertainers cloak the city in multiple venues, all of which are free. There is a contest in the Pl. de Juame every year in which contestants have to build a human tower and have a small child climb up it.

Weeks before and after Sept 24.

BARCELONA PRIDE

Parade ends in Av. Maria Cristina

This week is the Mediterranean's biggest GLBT celebration and takes place throughout Catalonia. Multiple venues throughout the city and surrounding region take active part throughout the festival, culminating with a parade and festival on the final weekend.

Last week of June.

FOOTBALL

Although Barcelona technically has two football teams, **Fútbol Club Barcelona (FCB)** and the **Real Club Deportivo Español de Barcelona (RCD),** you can easily pass a stay in the city without ever hearing about the latter. It is impossible to miss the former, however, and for good reason. Besides being a really incredible athletic team, FCB lives up to its motto as "more than a club."

During the years of Francisco Franco, FCB was forced to change its name and crest in order to banish any nationalistic references to Cataluña, and thereafter became a rallying point for oppressed Catalan separatists. Once the original name and crest were reinstated after Franco's fall in 1974, the team retained its symbolic importance and is still seen as a sign of democracy, identity, and pride for the region.

This passion is not entirely altruistic, however—FCB has been one of the best teams in the world in recent years. In 2009 they were the first team to win six out of six major competitions in a single year. Their world-class training facilities (thanks in part to the 1992 Olympics) supply many World Cuppers each year, leaving many Barcelonans annoyed that they are not permitted to compete as their own nation, similar to Ireland or Wales in the United Kingdom. Much to the chagrin of some hard-headed FCB fans, Spain won the World Cup in 2010.

Because FCB fervor is so pervasive, you will not need to head to Camp Nou to join in the festivities—almost every bar off the tourist track boasts a screen dedicated to their games. Sit down, kick back with a brew, and just don't root for the competition.

essentials

PRACTICALITIES

- **TOURIST OFFICES: Plaça de Catalonia** is the main office along with Pl. de Sant Jaume. *(Pl. de Catalonia, 17S ☎93 285 38 34 www.barcelonaturisme.com Ⓜ Catalonia, underground across from El Corte Inglès. Look for the pillars with the letter i on top.* ***i*** *Free maps; brochures on sights, transportation, tours, and about everything else you could want to find; booking service for last-minute accommodations; gift shop; money exchange; and box office (Caixa de Catalonia). Open daily 9am-9pm.)* **Plaça de Sant Jaume** *(C. Ciutat, ☎93 270 24 29 Ⓜ Jaume I, located in the Ajuntament building in Pl. Sant Jaume. Open M-F 9am-8pm,*

Sa 10am-8pm, Su and holidays 10am-2pm. Closed Jan 1 and Dec 25.) **Oficina de Turisme de Barcelona** *(Palau Robert, Pg. de Gràcia, 107 ☎93 238 80 91, ☎012 in Catalonia www.gencat.es/probert Ⓜ Diagonal. Open M-Sa 10am-7pm, Su 10am-2pm. Closed Dec 25-26, and Jan 1 and 6.)* **Institut de Cultura de Barcelona (ICUB)** (Palau de la Virreina, La Rambla, 99 ☎93 316 10 00 www.bcn.cat/cultura Ⓜ Liceu. Info office open daily 10am-8pm. **Estació Barcelona-Sants** *(Pl. Països Catalans ☎90 224 02 02 Ⓜ Sants-Estació i Info and last-minute accommodation booking. Open June 24-Sept 24 daily 8am-8pm; Sept 24-June 23 M-F 8am-8pm, Sa-Su 8am-2pm.)*

- **TOURS: Self-guided tours** of Gothic, Romanesque, *modernista,* and contemporary Barcelona available; pick up pamphlets in tourism offices. A wide variety of **paid walking tours** also exist, with information available in the brochures at the tourism office. The **Place de Catalonia tourist office** hosts its own walking tours and has information about bike tours. *(☎93 285 38 32. €12, ages 4-12 €5). Ⓜ Catalonia, underground across from El Corte Inglès. Look for the pillars with the letter i on top. i 2hr. walking tour of the Barri Gòtic. Tours daily at 10am (English) and Sa at noon (Catalan and Spanish).* **Picasso tours** *(☎93 285 38 32)* of Barcelona (Ⓜ Catalonia. i Check for English, Spanish, and Catalan tour availability. Includes entrance to **Museu Picasso.** $ €19, ages 4-12 €7. *Tu, Th, Sa 4pm (English) and Sa 4pm (Spanish or Catalan) with pre-booking.)*
- **LUGGAGE STORAGE: Estació Barcelona-Sants** *(Ⓜ Sants-Estació. $ Lockers €3-4.50 per day. Open daily 5:30am-11pm.)* **Estació Nord** *(Ⓜ Arc de Triomf. $ Lockers €3.50-5 per day, 90-day limit.)* **El Prat Airport** *($ €3.80-4.90 per day.)*
- **GAY AND LESBIAN RESOURCES: GLBT tourist guide** includes a section on GLBT bars, clubs, publications, and more *(Pl. de Catalonia tourist office).* **GAYBARCELONA** *(www.gaybarcelona.net.)* and **Infogal** *(www.colectiugai.org).* have up-to-date information. **Barcelona Pride** has annual activities during the last week of June *(www.pridebarcelona.org/en).* **Antinous** specializes in gay and lesbian books and films *(C. Josep Anselm Clavé, 6 ☎93 301 90 70 www.antinouslibros.com Ⓜ Drassanes Open M-F 10:30am-2pm and 5-8:30pm, Sa noon-2pm and 5-8:30pm).*
- **INTERNET ACCESS: Barcelona City Government** offers free Wi-Fi access at over 500 places including some museums, parks, and sports centers. *(www.bcn.es.)* **Easy Internet Cafe** *(Las Ramblas, 31 ☎93 301 75 07 Ⓜ Liceu. $ Decent prices and around 300 terminals. €2.10 per hr. i 1-day unlimited pass €7; 1 wk. €15; 1 mo. €30. Open daily 8am-2:30am.)*
- **POST OFFICE:** *(Pl. d'Antoni López ☎90 219 71 97 www.correos.es Ⓜ Jaume I or Ⓜ Barceloneta. $ Open M-F 8:30am-9:30pm, Su noon-10pm.)*
- **POSTAL CODE:** ☎08001.

barcelona

EMERGENCY!

- **EMERGENCY NUMBERS:** ☎061.
- **POLICE: Local police:** ☎092. **National police:** ☎091. **Tourist police** *(La Rambla, 43 ☎93 256 24 30 Ⓜ Liceu. Open 24hr.)*
- **LATE-NIGHT PHARMACY:** Rotates. Check any pharmacy window for the nearest on duty, contact the police, or call **Información de Farmacias de Guardia** *(☎93 481 00 60).*
- **HOSPITALS/MEDICAL SERVICES: Hospital Clínic i Provincal** *(C. Villarroel, 170 ☎93 227 54 00 Ⓜ Hospital Clínic. Main entrance at C. Roselló and C. Casanova.)*

Hospital de la Santa Creu i Sant Pau *(☎93 291 90 00; emergency ☎91 91 91 ⇟ Ⓜ Vall d'Hebron.)* **Hospital del Mar** *(Psg. Marítim, 25-29 ☎93 248 30 00 ⇟ Ⓜ Ciutadella or Ⓜ Vila Olímpica.)*

GETTING THERE

By Plane

AEROPORT DEL PRAT DE LLOBREGAT BCN

☎93 478 47 04 for Terminal 1, ☎93 478 05 65 for Terminal 2B

To get to Pl. Catalonia, take the **Aerobus** *(☎92 415 60 20)* in front of terminals 1 or 2 *(Ⓢ €5, round-trip ticket valid for 9 days €8.65. ⏰ 35-40min.; every 6-15min. to Pl. Catalonia daily 6am-1am, to airport 5:30am-12:14am).* To the airport, the A1 bus takes you to Terminal 1, A2 bus to Terminal 2. For early morning flights, the Nitbus **N17** runs from Pl. Catalonia to all terminals *(Ⓢ €1.40. ⏰ from Pl. Catalonia every 20min. daily 11am-5am, from airport every hr. 9:50pm-4:50am).* Cheaper, and usually a bit faster, than the Aerobus is the **RENFE train** *(☎90 224 34 02 Ⓢ €1.40 or free with T10 transfer from metro. ⏰ 20-25min. to Estació Sants, 25-30min. to Psg. de Gràcia; every 30min., from airport 6am-11:38pm, from Estació Sants to airport 5:35am-11:09pm).* To reach the train from Terminal 2, take the pedestrian overpass in front of the airport (it's on the left when your back is to the entrance). For those arriving at Terminal 1, a shuttlebus is available outside the terminal to take you to the train station. *⇟ Ⓜ Sants-Estació. ℹ Info and last-minute accommodation bookings, as well as transport connections from the airport to the city center and other locations. ⏰ Open daily 9am-9pm.*

AEROPORT DE GIRONA GRO

☎90 240 47 04 🖳www.girona-airport.net

Transport to Barcelona is available from the airport by **Barcelona Bus** *(Ⓢ €12, round-trip €21. ⏰ 1hr. 10min. from Girona to Estacio d'Autobusos Barcelona Nord. ℹ Buses from the airport to Estacio d 'Autobusos Barcelona Nord are timed to match flight arrivals. Buses from Estacio d 'Autobuses arrive at Girona Airport approximately 3hr. before flight departures. ⏰ Open 24hr.*

By Train

Depending on the destination, trains can be an economical option. Travelers may find trains at **Estació Barcelona-Sants** in Pl. Països Catalans *(Ⓜ Sants Estació)* for most domestic and international traffic, while **Estació de Franca** on Av. Marques de l'Argentera *(Ⓜ Barceloneta)* serves regional destinations and a limited number of international locations. Note that trains often stop before the main stations; check the schedule. **RENFE** *(reservations and info ☎90 224 02 02, international ☎24 34 02 🖳www.renfe.es)* runs to **Bilbao, Madrid, Sevilla,** and **Valencia** in Spain. Trains also travel to **Milan** (via **Turin** and **Figueres**) in Italy and **Montpellier** in France, with connections to Geneva, Paris, and the French Riviera. There's a 20% discount on round-trip tickets. Call or check website for train times and seasonal schedules.

By Bus

Buses are often considerably cheaper than the train and should be considered for those traveling within the region on a budget. The city's main bus terminal is **Barcelona Nord Estació d'Autobuses** *(☎902 26 06 06 🖳www.barcelonanord.com ⇟ Ⓜ Arc de Triomf or #54 bus),* with buses also departing from the Estació Sants and the airport. **Sarfa** *(ticket office at Ronda Sant Pere, 21 ☎90 230 20 25 🖳www.sarfa.es)* is the primary line, but **Eurolines** *(☎93 265 07 88 🖳www.eurolines.es)* also goes to **Paris** via **Lyon** and offers a 10% discount to travelers under 26 or over 60. **ALSA/ENATCAR** *(☎90 242 22 42; www.alsa.es)* goes to **Alicante, Bilbao, Madrid, Sevilla, Valencia,** and **Zaragoza.**

By Ferry

Ferries to the **Baleares Islands, Majorca,** and **Ibiza** leave daily from the port of Barcelona at **Terminal Drassanes** *(☎93 324 89 80)* and **Terminal Ferry de Barcelona** *(☎93 295 91 82 Ⓜ︎Drassanes)*. The most popular ferries are run by **Transmediterránea** *(☎902 45 46 45 www.transmediterrana.es)* in Terminal Drassanes.

GETTING AROUND

By Metro

The mode of transportation used most in the city is the Barcelona **Metro** *(☎93 318 70 74 www.tmb.cat)*. Get to know it well—the extensive train and bus system provides cheap, easy access to nearly the entire city. Different lines are identified by L and then their number *(L1, L2, L3, L4, L5, L8, L10, L11)*. **Trains** run Monday through Thursday and Sundays from 5am to midnight, Friday and days prior to holidays 5am to 2am, and Saturday all day. Stops are marked by a red sign with a white capital M.

By Bus

For more remote or hard-to-access places, the bus may be an important complement to the Metro during your journey. Barcelona's tourist office also offers a **Tourist Bus** *(bcnshop.barcelonaturisme.com $ 1 day €22)* that frequents sights of particular interest in the city and allows riders to hop on and off for a 24hr. period. Depending on how much you plan to use the route (and how much you loathe hopping off of a red double decker labeled "Tourist Bus" when you're traveling), the bus may be a worthwhile investment upon arriving in the city.

Rentals

Motocicletas (motos for short—scooters, and less frequently motorcycles) are a common sight, and **bicycles** are also becoming more popular. Many institutions rent motos by hour, day, and month, but you need a valid driver's license recognized in Spain in order to rent one for personal use. Many places also offer bike rental. If you will be staying in the city for an extended period, it is possible to buy a bike secondhand or register for **Bicing** (*☎90 231 55 31 www.bicing.cat)*, the municipal red and white bikes.

By Taxi

When all other cheaper and more exciting options fail, Barcelona offers a taxi service to get you back home safely on those nights when revelry lasts after Metro hours. The official taxi service is **Radio Taxi** *(☎93 225 00 00)* and is identifiable by the black and yellow cars.

SITGES

There is a reason why this tiny town (pop. 27,000) has a population like an elastic waistband. Situated just 50km south of Barcelona, the town's sandy beaches serve as a refuge for those fleeing the city to seek crystalline water, 300 days of sun, and rocky alcoves. However, the city is much more than a sandy second. Its gorgeous architecture tells the story of a time of farming and fishing long past, while the lush interiors of its museums hint at its rise to prominence in the late 19th century as a center of the *modernisme* art movement. This bohemian flavor still remains in spirit with its thriving arts community, and its role as a premier gay destination in the Mediterranean.

greatest hits

- **CARNE-VALE.** Before Lent kicks in and all good Catholics have to give up meat on Fridays, pig out and thrown down at Sitges's crazy Carnivale (p. 275).
- **A PROFUSION OF PLAYAS.** There are fifteen beaches in Sitges. *Fifteen* (p 273).
- **MOVE OVER, BARCELONA.** Yeah, yeah, the capital of Catalonia's covered in Gaudí's works, but Sitges has just as much *modernisme* to offer.

orientation

Most people arrive at Sitges by train or bus, and both methods of transportation let off at different spots along **Calle Carbonell/Passeig de Vilanova**—buses to the east, at the intersection of Psg. de Vilanova and Psg. de Vilafranca, and trains at the train station to the east on C. Carbonell. Going left along C. Carbonell from the bus stop or right from the train station, turn onto **Calle Sant Francesc** and walk for 5min. to find the heart of the old town, intersected by **Calle de les Parellades.** Any street off **Parellades** will land you at the waterfront after a 5min. walk, with **Passeig de la Ribera** wrapping around the closest (and most popular) beaches.

accommodations

HOSTAL PARELLADES — HOSTAL ❸

C. Parellades, 11 ☎93 894 08 01

Ceilings that reach to the sky house bed-and-breakfast-worthy rooms just big enough to get around in comfortably. Singles are the cheapest in the area, and the sunny terrace with a shaded arcade provides a nice place to curl up with a book after a day spent a block away on the beach. For those musically inclined, a piano awaits your fingertips in the sunny common room.

On C. Parelledes between C. San Pedro and San Pablo. i Sheets included. Ⓢ Singles €30; doubles €60; triples €75.

HOSTAL BONAIRE — HOSTAL ❸

C. Bonaire, 31 ☎93 894 53 26 www.bonairehostalsitges.com

With the beach in full view at the end of the street, chances are that you won't want to spend too much time lounging in front of the TV. If you do, though, or if you prefer A/C, or even a terrace, just ask—the hostal contains a mix-and-match assortment of amenities fitting the laid-back, house-like feel.

From C. Parellades, walk toward the beach on C. Bonaire. i Complimentary Wi-Fi. Ⓢ Singles €30-42; doubles €45-70; triples €65-90.

HOSTAL ESPALTER — HOSTAL ❸

C. Espalter, 11 ☎93 894 28 63 www.pensionespatler.com

Nestled inside the Sauna Sitges behind a door framed by rainbows, this pension offers cheap rooms near the heart of Sitges's (specifically gay) nightlife. Those rooms that don't have balconies have a fullblown patio-size terrace, a fact that'll distract you from the questionable taste in bright pink and blue wall coloring. Have any questions? The super friendly owners and staff will be more than happy to enthusiastically help you with whatever you may need.

Take a right onto Carbonell from the train station and a right onto C. San Francesc at the roundabout. Take a left onto C. Espalter. Hostal Espalter is in the Sauna Sitges. i Free Wi-Fi. Each room has fridge and ensuite bathroom. Ⓢ Singles €35; doubles €60.

HOTEL CID — HOTEL ❹

C. Sant José, 39 ☎93 894 18 42 www.hotelsitges.com

A cheap hotel with an ambience appropriate to its name—good-sized rooms are furnished with pieces that scream of the Inquisition, with large impressionistic paintings to keep you from feeling oppressed. It's not often you'll be offered a view over a pool for this price, much less be able to use the pool it overlooks. Wi-Fi is only available in the lower level, but luckily it's decked with enough leather couches, stone pillars, iron fixtures, and even a piano, making it worth some of your time.

Take a right onto C. Carbonell from the train station, pass the rotunda, and take the 4th left off C. Carbonell. Ⓢ Singles €54-60; doubles €68-79; triples €99-115. Rooms with pool view more expensive. Open May-Oct.

CAU FERRAT MUSEUM, MARICEL MUSEUM, ROMANTIC MUSEUM ART

C. Fonollar; C. Sant Gaudenci, 1 ☎93 894 03 64 www.diba.es/museus/sitges.asp

Although Sitges's museums may not all be housed under one roof, the city couldn't have made visiting them any easier: all have the same hours and ticket prices, and the combination tickets providing entrance to all three museums are a deal. Overlooking the waterfront by the church, on C. Fonollar, the **Cau Ferrat Museum** is the former home of *modernista* big shot Santiago Rusiñol (1861-1931) and provides a snapshot into the area's artistic, star-studded past with works from Picasso, Zuloaga, Casas, and more.

Next door sits the **Maricel Museum,** a palace built in 1910 for the American millionaire Charles Deering. True to the American way, the interior is nothing short of sumptuous, with incredible halls and rooftop terraces. Art from medieval to modern decks the walls, providing a chronology of Catalan art and influences from the romantic period onward for those willing to make the mental leap. These museums are currently undergoing renovations, so you should call ahead or sneak a peak at the website to check opening information.

The **Romantic Museum** is located a bit further inland at C. Sant Gaudenci, 1, off C. de les Parellades, and provides a literal snapshot of the town's past where the other museums only hint around it. This perfectly preserved 19th-century house is filled with ceramics, music boxes, and fantastic furniture, and the special collections boast over 400 antique dolls from around the world and over 25 intricate, though somewhat creepy, dioramas of life at the time in Sitges.

i Cau Ferrat Museum and Maricel Museum currently undergoing renovations. Ⓢ Single tickets €3.50, students and seniors €1.75; combined ticket for all museums €6.40/3.50. Open July-Sept Tu-Sa 9:30am-2pm and 4-7pm, Su 10am-3pm; Oct-June Tu-Sa 9:30am-2pm and 3:30-6:30pm, Su 10am-3pm. Hourly guided tours in Museu Romàntic.

BEACHES

Fifteen different beaches and over 3km of coast along the city center make Sitges a clear alternative to Barcelona's nearby crowded shores. That being said, don't expect to find your own spot near the beaches close to downtown during the summer months. To flee the crowds, try **Platja de la Barra** and **Platja de Terramar** a few kilometers away or take the **L2** bus from the train station to the stop next to Hotel Terramar, and walk for a few minutes back towards the city center *(Ⓢ €1. Every 30min. 9am-9pm.)*

What with Sitges being a top gay resort, it only makes sense that there are some beaches catering to the crowd—**Platja de la Bassa Rodona** is the most popular and just a short walk from downtown, located in front of Hotel Calipolis, though in the past years its tight bronzed bodies and little Speedos have been infiltrated by a more mixed crowd. A rocky outcropping makes for a shallow bathing area secluded from the waves. For some clear water ideal for snorkeling and just gawking, head to **Platja de las Balmins.** To get there, take a left and pass the church and **Platja Sant Sebastia.** Go around the first restaurant you come to, and then take the dirt walkway between the coast and walls of the cemetery—the beach is the quiet cove before the port right after the little hill.

If tan lines aren't your thing, try one of Sitges's many renowned nude beaches—the farther out they are, the less likely getting your picture snapped will be. A 50min. walk to the right along the seafront past Terramar, rocks, and a golf course (or, conversely, taking a cab to Club Atlàntida and walking 10min.) will get you near **Platja de l'Home Mort,** though the small cove itself is located just behind the hills where the train tracks run along the coast. This cove also houses Sitges's only exclusively gay beach, with a neighboring forest known for its debauchery. Literally on the other side of the track (and the city) is **Caia Morisca**—to get there, just walk past the church and **Platja d'Aiguadolç.**

food

IZARRA BASQUE TAPAS ❷

C. Major, 24 ☎93 894 73 70

Izarra offers some of the best Basque food this side of Catalonia with surprisingly reasonable prices, especially for the area. Miniature stools line the walls and bar, but don't expect to get a seat unless you show up early. Order from their daily *menú* or snag a white plate from the back and pile on the tapas yourself.

Walk down C. Major from C. Parralledes. Izarra will be on your left. Tapas €3-11. Open daily 8:30am-midnight. Menú available 1:30-4pm and 8:30-11pm.

CAFE DEL MON CAFE ❶

C. Francesc Gumá, 7 ☎93 811 11 04

An all-day cafe harboring two rarities near the Sitges center—local youth and cheap prices. Sunny yellow walls and rainbow mosaic cafe tables capture a glowing crowd of sunbathed shoulders serenaded by beats from around the world. A menu of cheap *bocadillos*, pizza, and filing *platos* even caters to vegetarians—try the *bocadillo completo* with lettuce, tomato, carrot, asparagus, and cheese *(€4)*. Spice up your meal with one of the cafe's cocktails *(€4.50)*.

Walk along Parellades away from Pl. Espanya and veer left to stay on C. Jesús. Turn left onto C. Francesc Gumá; the cafe is on the left before the next street. Salads €4.50. Platos €5.80-7.50. Tapas and bocadillos €1-7. Cocktails €4.50. Open daily 9am-10pm.

ALFRESCO CAFE MEDITERRANEAN ❸

C. Major, 33 ☎93 894 73 70

Pull up a white modern bowl stool under the stained glass and geometric tile and whip out one of their *Sotheby's* or *Barcelona Style* magazines for some light reading. This bright, stylish cafe mixes Mediterranean sun with modern chic, both in ambience and in cuisine. Chalkboard menus change regularly and consistently offer fresh, exciting options. Although entrees start at €16 and salads at €15, you'll certainly get your money's worth.

Walk down C. Major from C. Paralledes. Alfresco Cafe will be on your right. Appetizers €15; entrees €16. Midday menú €17.50; night menú €22. Open daily 9am-11pm.

nightlife

TRAILER CLUB

C. Àngel Vidal, 36 ☎69 355 94 40 www.trailerdisco.com

Shed those heavy clothes, shoes, and inhibitions for Trailer's incredibly popular Wednesday foam parties, and don't be surprised if you see fellow revelers (or pairs of revelers) with nothing to hide. One of the oldest gay danceclubs in Spain, Trailer boasts 30 years in the game and will easily have you understanding why. Though a sausagefest most nights, this club becomes nothing but men on Thursdays—during "After Dark" the colored lights are flipped off and anything goes.

Take a left onto C. de l'Hort Gran from the train station and take a right onto C. de San Sebastién right before the elbow. Take the 3rd right onto C. San Damian and the 90° right at the 1st intersection onto C. de Angel Vidal. ***i*** *Foam parties on W, After Dark on Th. Cover €15; includes 1 drink. Use a flyer for free admission. Open May-Sept daily 1-6am; Oct-Apr Sa 1-6am.*

ATLÁNTIDA CLUB

Platja les Coves ☎93 453 05 82 www.clubatlantida.com

This expansive beach-bar and nightclub has it all—beautiful sand, chic lighting, and a crowd not afraid to take it off. Sweaty bodies slide past each other to electronic hits during the summer months, spilling into the open air in a half-hearted attempt to cool down. Regular themed nights abound—check the events schedule to see which way the night swings.

Free bus runs from Calipolis hotel in Sitges center. *i* *Listing of events on website. VIP list available on facebook page.* *Cover €15-20.* *Open June-Sept M-Th midnight-5am, F-Sa midnight-6am.*

arts and culture

In the 19th century, Sitges was a hangout of *modernisme* artists ranging from Rusiñol to Picasso; however, you won't need to visit the Cau Ferrat Museum to be reminded of their influence. Morell's **Modernista Clocktower** *(corner of C. d les Parellades and C. Sant Francesç)* looms over a city that has embraced a vibrant cultural community in its own right, with the **Sitges Music Festival** *(July and Aug)* and **Sitges Film Festival** *(Oct)* attracting thousands to its sandy shores every year. Almost nearly as long as the city has been known for its arts, it has also been known as a gay mecca. The **Sitges Gay Pride** *(mid-July)* attracted over 60,000 people from across the world in its first year in 2010, packing the beaches and over 20 gay bars in the city. True to its (arguably) Spanish roots, **Corpus Christi** clothes the streets with flower blankets, while the **Festa Major** *(week of Aug 23)* unites the city under flames and fireworks to celebrate Sant Bartolomé, the city's patron saint. The city's **Carnivale** *(1st week of Lent)* celebrations are some of the most famed in the region. True to Mediterranean fashion, Sitges is also proud of their booze—September brings the **Festa de la Verema,** or grape harvest, where competitors fight to squash grapes along the beach. Despite its small size, Sitges knows how to party hardy, and the rest of the world knows it should follow.

FILM FESTIVAL

Since 1968, sci-fi geeks, scary movie buffs, and really, really famous people have flocked to the sandy shores of Sitges in early October to catch the world's foremost film festival specializing in fantasy and horror. This 10-day extravaganza has seen the special screening of movies from *Final Fantasy VII (2005)* to *Hellraiser (1987), The Bourne Identity (2002)* to *Aliens (1986),* and *Kill Bill (2003)* to *Mulholland Drive (2001),* the best of which each year receive the **Midnight X-Treme Award.** Besides being a fantastic place to catch a flick, the festival also attracts a star-studded crowd of directors, actors, and producers ready to receive their awards, known as **Marias,** for the best of their categories, as determined by international jury. Like a doomsday scene from one of the movies being screened, the city becomes swarmed with a sea of the living undead during the festival's annual **Zombie Walk.**

CARNIVALE

By now, it should come as no surprise that Catalonians know how to party. So, what can you expect when the somber legacy of Lent threatens to take away revelry for 40 days? One giant, ridiculous party. Boasting one of the biggest and baddest Carnivales in all of Europe, the small town of Sitges fills with over 250,000 visitors for the week's festivities, held the seven days preceding Lent during February. The week kicks off with *Dijous Gras* (Fatty Thursday), with the King of the Carnival marking the start of the party. Other highlights of the week include Sunday's **Rua de la Disbauxa** (Debauchery Parade), which includes over 40 floats and 2500 participants. Masked and masqueraded festivities continue throughout the week, with Tuesday's **Rua de l'Extermini** (Extermination Parade) solemnly marking the end of the party week with drag queens dressed in mournful black to grieve of the death of the King of the Carnival. After nearly a full week of revelry, Carnivale is symbolically put to rest with Wednesdays' **Burial of the Sardine,** where a large effigy of the little fish is buried along the beach to mark the end of debauchery and the start of more somber ways. Get your hotel reservations early if you prefer not to sleep on the beach—not surprisingly, this is the local hotel industry's busiest time of year.

essentials

PRACTICALITIES

- **TOURIST OFFICES:** Contact the **Sitges tourist office** for free maps, the monthly agenda of events **Sitges Agenda,** and help booking accommodations. *(Pl. Eduard Maristany, 2 ☎93 810 93 40 www.sitgestur.com From station, turn right onto the street running in front of the station, C. Carbonell, and take the next right at the roundabout, onto Pg. de Vilafranca. The office is 1 block up on the left. i Additional branches at the train station and near the beach, below the church. Open mid-June to mid-Sept M-Sa 9am-8pm; late Sept-early June M-F 9am-2pm and 4-6:30pm.)*
- **LAUNDRY: Net i Sec** provides the opportunity for you to wash that two-week-old T-shirt, if you wish. No pressure. *(C. Artur Carbonell, 8 ☎93 894 98 11 Take a right onto Carbonell from the train station; it's on your left. Open daily 7am-midnight.)*
- **INTERNET: Cafe Cappuchino** provides internet access and phone services. *(C. Sant Francesc, 44 Turn right onto Carbonell from the train station and take the 3rd left onto C. San Francesc. €1 per 15min. Open daily 9am-11pm.)*
- **POST OFFICE:** *(Pl. d'Espanya ☎93 894 12 47 www.correos.es Take a right onto Carbonell upon exiting the train station. Continue through the roundabout as it turns to Psg. de Vilanova and take a left onto C. d'Europa. Follow as it takes a slight right and take a slight right onto Espatler to enter the plaza. Open M-F 8:30am-2:30pm, Sa 9:30am-1pm. No package pickup Sa.)*
- **POSTAL CODE:** 08870.

EMERGENCY!

- **EMERGENCY NUMBER:** ☎112.
- **POLICE: Local police** *(Pl. Ajuntament ☎93 811 00 16; 93 810 97 97.)*
- **HOSPITAL/MEDICAL SERVICES: Hospital Sant Camil** provides medical assistance so your friends don't have to. *(Ronda De Sant Camil ☎93 896 00 25 www.hrsantcamil.es)*

GETTING THERE

By Train

Cercanías RENFE trains *(☎90 224 02 02 www.renfe.es/cercanias)* run from **Estació Barcelona-Sants** to **Sitges** *(€3 i Line 2 toward St. Vicenç de Calders or Vilanova. Use machines to left of ticket queue to shorten your wait. Ticket booth open until 10pm. 45 min., every 25-40min. 7:05am-10:21pm)* and from Sitges to **Barcelona.** *(€3 Every 25-40min., 6:15am-10:54pm.)* Trains also run from **Sitges** to **Cambrils.** *(€5.70 1hr. via* ***Tarragona.****)*

By Bus

Mon Bus *(☎93 893 70 60 www.monbus.cat)* connects the Barcelona **airport** to Pg. de Villafranca in Sitges. *(€3. Every hr. M-F 7:40am-11:40pm.)* Late-night buses operate from Pg. de Villafranca to Ronda Universitat in Barcelona and back. *(€3. Every hr. 12:13-3:13am.)*

By Taxi

Taxis *(☎93 894 13 29)* run between **Barcelona** and **Sitges.** *(€50-60.)*

GETTING AROUND

Sitges is first and foremost a walking city with the main sights being just a 5-10min. walk from each other. If you're adventurous and looking to head to **Atlántida** for some partying, a **free bus** runs from the center of Sitges to the Platja de les Coves, right in front of the club.

If you're looking to venture outside the center, **Bus Urbà** operates within the city. All three lines start their route at the train station and travel outward, with the **L1** covering the north, **L2** covering the west (both ending at Psg. Vilafranca), and **L3** covering the east, ending at C. Emili Picó. *(☎93 814 49 89 1 ride €1.40, 10-ride pass €7.85. Every 30min. M-F 6:45am-8:45pm, Sa-Su and holidays 8:45am-8:45pm.)*

LAS ISLAS BALEARES

This Western-Mediterranean archipelago is the perfect place for any summer vacationer. The primary islands of the Balearics—Majorca, Menorca, Ibiza, and Formentera—may lie only a short flight or **boat ride** apart, but each island maintains a unique personality and culture that complements the others in exciting and wonderful ways. Witness the industry and commerce of Majorca's capital **Palma,** the peace and quiet of **Formentera's** small villages and resorts, the pride of **Menorca's** traditional summer festivals and rich wildlife, and the shamelessness of **Ibiza's** crazy club scene.

While you're welcome to visit during any time of year, your best bet for fun is from June to August. While the accommodations may be pricier, they'll at least be open, and you'll get clear skies, warm waters, and tons of traditional foods and fresh fish to enjoy. While you may not have the convenience of hopping on a bus to get between these hotspots, you can save tons of money by booking flights and ferries in advance.

Since prehistoric times, the islands have been home to countless travelers who have stopped over from Africa and the Iberian Peninsula to see what all the talk is about on the Balearic Islands. Now it's your turn.

greatest hits

- **PARTY PEOPLE, PUT YOUR HANDS IN THE AIR.** Head to Ibiza for the best seaside celebration in the Mediterranean (p. 288).
- **GOODNESS GRACIOUS, GREAT BALLS OF FIRE!** The island of Majorca lights up with bonfires and barbeques during the Fiestas de Sant Sebastia every year (p. 286).

student life

Say Ibiza and everyone thinks the same thing: *discotecas*. Ibiza is a mecca for people who want cavernous clubs that pound beats spun by world-famous DJs until the sun has more than come up. With all this prestige, things can get pricey quickly. But students know that you can still have a wild 24hr. (let's be honest, you didn't come here to sleep) on the cheap. First of all, stay in **Sant Antoni** rather than Ibiza City—it's cheaper and has way more young people. Before you hit the clubs, buy alcohol from a liquor or convenience store and share it with your friends, which is so much cheaper than €10+ cocktails. Then, groove your cheapskate student ass on over to **Soul City,** a fantastic hip-hop and R and B club that has no cover!

majorca *mallorca* ☎971

Since 7000 BCE, people have been using Majorca as an island pit stop in the Mediterranean. Whether it was the Romans, the Byzantines, the Arabs, or the Catalonians, it was always take, take, and more take. Majorca was convenient. It was the biggest island of the Balearics. It had a varied landscape. But over the past 9000 years or so, Majorca has taken a stand, and it isn't going to be pushed around any longer.

We're not going to suggest that Majorca is a spiteful up-and-comer. On the contrary, its rich, multicultural history contributes to the island culture today. Sights like the **Catedral** and **Castell de Bellver** are glowing reminders of all the people who were lucky enough to visit centuries ago, while museums like the **Fundacio Pilar i Joan Miró** suggest that even some of the most talented greats of our time proudly called Majorca home. This "island of calm," as famous Spanish poet Rubén Darío described it, now offers luxurious resorts, delicious local cuisine, abundant shopping options, and a thriving athletic culture centered around biking and aquatic sports. You can tan beside the turquoise waters of this summertime gem by day, and check out the clubs, bars, and restaurants around Palma's port all night. Majorca is mature—it wants to give you relaxation and fun, with some education along the way.

ORIENTATION

The city of Palma is organized around its major plazas. **Plaza Espanya** is the major transit center where the train and Metro stations can be accessed and where many of the tour buses congregate. **Plaza Mayor** has some patio restaurants, street performers, and small kiosk shops, and is surrounded by small streets open only to traffic. **Calle San Miguel** and **Calle Sindicat** near the plaza are packed with small restaurants, cafes, and shops. **Plaza Rei Joan Carles I** is the center of the high-end, expensive shopping in Palma that extends onto **Avenida Jaime III, Calle Unio,** and **Passeig des Born.** The **Paseo Maritimo** curves around the port, where you'll find many of the most popular clubs and nightlife destinations.

ACCOMMODATIONS

While the city of Palma is definitely the center of the island, this center isn't necessarily catering to budget travel. If you're looking for cheaper rooms, inexpensive and thriving nightlife, and some beach time, the nearby town of **Arenal** is only a 25min. bus ride out of Palma on the Playa de Palma.

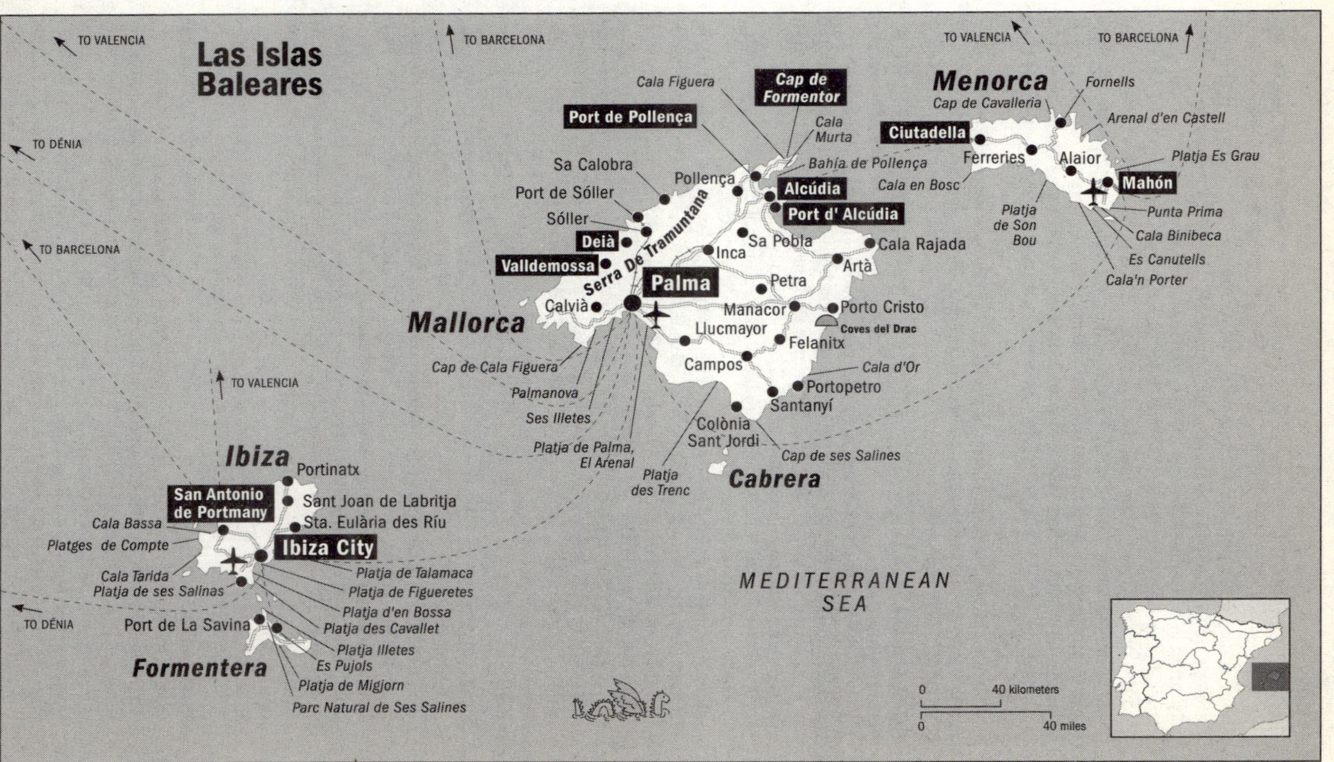
Las Islas Baleares
TO VALENCIA
TO BARCELONA
TO DÉNIA
TO BARCELONA
TO VALENCIA
TO DÉNIA
TO VALENCIA
TO BARCELONA
Menorca
Cap de Cavalleria
Fornells
Arenal d'en Castell
Ciutadella
Ferreries
Alaior
Platja Es Grau
Mahón
Cala en Bosc
Platja de Son Bou
Punta Prima
Cala Binibeca
Es Canutells
Cala'n Porter
Cala Figuera
Cap de Formentor
Port de Pollença
Cala Murta
Bahía de Pollença
Sa Calobra
Pollença
Alcúdia
Port d' Alcúdia
Port de Sóller
Sóller
Serra De Tramuntana
Deià
Valldemossa
Sa Pobla
Inca
Cala Rajada
Artà
Palma
Petra
Calvià
Mallorca
Manacor
Porto Cristo
Coves del Drac
Llucmayor
Felanitx
Campos
Cala d'Or
Cap de Cala Figuera
Portopetro
Palmanova
Santanyí
Ses Illetes
Colònia Sant Jordi
Platja de Palma, El Arenal
Cap de ses Salines
Platja des Trenc
Cabrera
Ibiza
Portinatx
San Antonio de Portmany
Sant Joan de Labritja
Sta. Eulària des Ríu
Cala Bassa
Platges de Compte
Ibiza City
Platja de Talamaca
Cala Tarida
Platja de Figueretes
Platja de ses Salinas
Platja d'en Bossa
Platja des Cavallet
Port de La Savina
Platja Illetes
Es Pujols
Formentera
Platja de Migjorn
Parc Natural de Ses Salines
MEDITERRANEAN SEA
0
40 kilometers
0
40 miles

In Arenal

HOSTAL TIERRAMAR

HOSTAL ❸

C. Berlin, 9 ☎971 262 751 www.hostaltierramar.com

One of the most popular accommodations in Arenal (and that's saying something—this whole town is packed with hostels), Hostal Tierramar knows how to provide a comfortable stay for the beach-minded. Enjoy sizable rooms with tiled floors and colorful sheets that light up when you open up your window to the ocean views. Your massive bathroom is the perfect place to scrub the sand and sunscreen from your body, and the first-floor cafeteria will give you the opportunity to get a book from the library, shoot some pool, or enjoy basic snacks and sandwiches 24hr. a day. At Tierramar, you're steps from the shining blue waters of the Playa de Palma—as well as a direct bus ride into the city *(lines #15 and #25).*

Take bus #21 from the airport to the last stop at Playa de Palma and walk back 2 blocks from the stop to C. Berlin. *i* *Breakfast, sheets, and towels included.* *Singles €26-32; doubles €38-47; triples €57.* *Reception 24hr.*

HOTEL LEBLON

BUDGET HOTEL ❷

C. Trasimero, 67 ☎971 490 200 hotel-leblon@hotmail.com

Hotel Leblon would be an easy bet in a boxing match—it's a hotel-quality accommodation that keeps its prices competing in the budget ring. The rose-colored sheets near your large closet and decorative art is just the beginning. Make your way down to the first-floor bar, colorfully decorated with liquors and syrups, and order up a cocktail *(€3.50)* or snack all day long. The pool out back is decorated with nautical tiles and overflowing with neon floatie toys, so hopefully you'll still have time to swim a lap or two after spending the day at the nearby Playa de Palma. You can also stay at the nearby **Sol de Mallorca** that shares the reception at Leblon, but offers even cheaper singles *(€30)*, doubles *(€34)*, triples *(€39)*, quads *(€45)*, and quints *(€65)*.

Take bus #21 from the airport to the last stop at Playa de Palma and walk back two blocks from the stop to C. Berlin, which intersects C. Trasimero. *i* *Breakfast, sheets, and towels included. Pool available. Restaurant. Bike rentals €6.* *Doubles €40; triples €45.* *Reception 24hr.*

In Palma

HOSTAL RITZI

HOSTAL ❸

C. Apuntadores, 6 ☎971 714 610 www.hostalritzi.com

Hostal Ritzi is a prime cut of convenience—you're steps from one of Palma's main plazas and paying a price that's more suited for a room in Arenal. This hostal totally embraces the bed-and-breakfast vibe: you'll get a warm welcome from the friendly staff, a spacious but homey room, and comfy green couches in the common area. Enjoy a full breakfast in the morning in the bright dining room or on the outdoor patio, and then make your way out onto the town.

C. Apuntadores branches off Pl. Reina. *i* *Breakfast, sheets, and towels included.* *Singles €30; doubles €55-70. Extra bed €20.* *Reception 8:30am-midnight.*

HOSTAL APUNTADORES

HOSTAL ❹

C. Apuntadores, 8 ☎971 713 491 www.palma-hostales.com

Although the prices are getting a bit higher, Hostal Apuntadores definitely provides you with a comfortable stay. Your neat and tidy room will smell fresh, the green-and-beige sheets and wood panels provide a classy and traditional look, and the spacious closet will be manna from heaven for you not-so-light packers. You can grab a coffee or snack from the first-floor cafe and enjoy it on the leather couch, or take the elevator up eight stories to sip and chat on the rooftop terrace that overlooks beautiful city sights like the port and Catedral.

C. Apuntadores branches off Pl. Reina. i Sheets and towels included. Rooftop terrace. Singles €35, with bath €50; doubles €50/€64; triples €75. Reception 24hr.

HOSTAL REGINA HOSTAL ❹

C. San Miguel, 77 ☎971 713 703 www.hostalreginapalma.com

Located right near the transit center of Plaza Espanya, Hostal Regina isn't necessarily a social place, but you'll get a good night's sleep in the extremely comfortable rooms. The bright pink walls decorated with tasteful paintings and lined with greenery will guide you to your cute and quiet room, where floral sheets and wooden furniture will probably remind you of granny's house (now we just need to find some warm chocolate-chip cookies and milk). You can also enjoy convenient services like the airport car hire, bike rental, and full-service laundry.

From Pl. Espanya, take C. Juan March to C. San Miguel and turn left. i Towels and sheets included. Laundry €10. Pets allowed. Singles €35, with bath €50; doubles €60/€70; triples €90. Bike rental €10 per day. Reception 24hr.

SIGHTS

CASTELL DE BELLVER HISTORICAL SIGHT, CASTLE, PRISON

C. Camilo Jose Cela, 17 ☎971 735 065

Every kid dreams of visiting a castle—especially one nestled up in the mountains with stone towers, a deep moat, and high ceilings. However, the Castell de Bellver didn't last as a castle for long. Although intended to be a royal residence for the Catholic kings when visiting the island, this structure has actually spent much of its history serving as a fortified, high-security prison. Exploring the grounds, you'll enjoy the best views of all of Majorca, the colorful tapestries and marble statues filling the rooms, and a fascinating exhibit about one of Bellver's most famous prisoners, Gaspar Melchor Jovellanos, the Enlightenment thinker locked up for simply being "different." While this Euro-Gothic sight may require quite the hike to arrive at the main gates (unless you take the bus which drops you at the doorstep), enjoy the exercise and climb the steps—we promise it's worth the trek.

Take bus #3 or #46 to Pl. Gomila and take C. Bellver to the top. Tour bus takes you directly to the sight. i Information in English and Spanish. €2.50, students under 18 €1. Open June-Sept M-Sa 8:30am-8:30pm, Su 10am-5pm; Oct-May M-Sa 8am-7:30pm, Su 10am-5pm.

FUNDACIO PILAR I JOAN MIRÓ MUSEUM

C. Saridakis, 29 ☎971 701 420 miro.palma.cat

There are many people in this world who have a strong pride in their home town—how else would we end up with songs like *I Love LA* or *Cleveland Rocks?*—but not many people can turn that pride into something as fascinating and beautiful as the Fundacio Pilar. Creator Juan Miró spent his childhood summers in Majorca with his grandmother, escaped to the island during the Nazi invasion of France, and permanently moved to Palma in 1956. Even though he wasn't a resident until later in life, Miró still had an attachment to the capital and decided to donate his entire studio space and much of his collection to the city. Today, the Fundacio Pilar i Joan Miró not only holds about 2500 pieces by the artist, but also provides you with the chance to see his studios. You'll see easels and paintings in the *Taller Sert*, designed by exiled architect and close friend Josep Sert, as well as a large collection of original graffiti in the *San Boter*.

Take bus #3 or #46 to Marivent and then follow the signs up to the Fundacio. i Information in English and Spanish. €6, students €3, free on Sa. Open May 16-Sept 15 T-Sa 10am-7pm, Su 10am-3pm; Sept 16-May 15 T-Sa 10am-6pm, Su 10am-3pm.

PALACIO REAL DE LA ALMUDIANA PALACE

C. Palau Reyal ☎971 214 134 www.patrimonionacional.es

Although this massive stone structure right on the shores of Majorca was originally constructed for Muslim royalty during the 10th century, Jaime II's arrival in Majorca marked a time for change. This first Catholic monarch of the island left a few remnants of the Arab constructions, but from the second he placed the cross-holding angel on top of *Torre de Angel*, it was clear that no one would be praying towards Mecca in this house. While many couples settle for the his-and-hers towels or coffee mugs, Spanish monarchs took things a step further—the Palacio Real has separate residences, orchards, and chapels for the Queen and King, all wonderfully decorated with pointed ceilings, colorful tapestries, and furniture. You can even wander through the original Arab baths used more for luxury than hygiene.

Take the steps near Pl. Reyna. Entrance is between the palace and the Catedral. ***i*** *Information available in English and Spanish. Tours arranged based on demand.* *€3.20, students €2.30. Tours €4. Audio tours €2.50.* *Open Apr-Sept M-F 10am-5:45pm, Sa 10am-1:15pm; Oct-Mar M-F 10am-1:15pm and 4-5:15pm, Sa 10am-1:15pm.*

CATEDRAL MUSEU CHURCH

Pl. Almoina ☎902 022 445

Unlike many other Mediterranean and Iberian cities, Majorca has a strong Christian heritage dating back to the 5th century. While such tolerance was definitely not reciprocated in the years of the Inquisition, the Arab monarchs of Majorca allowed the Catalonian bishops to maintain the Christian community of the island throughout the years of Muslim rule. Such tolerance was the savior of the enormous and picturesque main Catedral. Whether you're entering Palma by bus, bike, or foot, it's impossible to miss this massive structure, with thick stone columns up to 24m tall and over 60 stained-glass windows. Fifteen centuries of wear and tear definitely warrant some renovation, so during the 20th century, Antonio Gaudí arrived to save the day. This famous Spanish architect and designer constructed the stunningly beautiful canopy at the front of the church which hangs from the ceiling, glowing with lanterns.

Take the steps from Pl. Reyna and the entrance is around the back of the Catedral. ***i*** *Informational pamphlets in English and Spanish.* *€4.* *Open June-Sept M-F 10am-6:15pm, Sa 10am-2:15pm; Nov-Mar M-F 10am-3:15pm, Sa 10am-2:15pm; Apr-May M-F 10am-5:15pm, Sa 10am-2:15pm.*

FOOD

Majorca has quite the selection of international cuisine. Walking the streets of Palma, you'll come across many tapas bars and Spanish restaurants, but there are also tons of ethnic options. This island makes the most of its coastline—if you're looking for fresh seafood, just explore the larger restaurants on the **Paseo Maritimo** or leading up to **Plaza Reina.** You should also take advantage of the traditional Majorcan dishes. Fried *mallorqui* (fried offal, potatoes, tomatoes, and onions), vegetable *trumbet* (eggplant, peppers, potatoes, tomatoes, and onions), toasty *pa amb oli* (bread topped with tomato, oil, and salt with cheese, fish, or meats), and savory *sabrosada* (pork and pepper pâté) are some of the local specialties.

LA CUEVA TRADITIONAL ❸

C. Apuntadores, 5 ☎971 724 422

While La Cueva (the cave) lives up to its name with an underground location and low ceilings, this bright, traditional destination wouldn't suit any stalagtites, pirates, or even Batman. La Cueva's menu is simple, with a long list of classic Spanish tapas served up at full *ración* sizes. You can see all your options sitting behind the bar, and the chef constantly cooks up more food to refill these deep-dish platters. Locals devour the *gambas al ajillo, (shrimp with garlic sauce; €12)* and massive platters of traditional *jamon jagubo (€14, large €22).* You may have to fight your way through the crowd congregating outside the door, but it's worth the wait.

C. Apuntadores branches off Pl. Reina. Raciones €5-18. Open M-Sa noon-midnight.

CAFE COTO
INTERNATIONAL, MAJORCAN ❷

Pl. Drassana, 12 ☎636 096 126 www.bar-coto.com

Cafe Coto certainly knows how to be bold—the hot pink exterior, massive flowers growing up the gates, burning red interior walls, golden tables, and giant Frida Kahlo paintings certainly make a statement. However, the decor isn't the only thing making a statement at this cute patio-cafe. The international menu provides a wide array of homemade options to cure any craving. Indian dishes like the goat cheese with homemade mango chutney *(€6.50)* and Sri Lankan soups *(€5.50)* can transport you to anywhere on the globe. If you'd prefer some local flavor classic Majorcan *pa amb olis (€6.50)* or a Spanish tapa tasting platters *(small €8; large €15).* Freshly baked desserts like the warm apple strudel make the daily *menú (€10)* even more tempting.

From Pl. Reyna, take C. Apuntadores and make a left into the plaza. Entrees €5.50-9.50. Salads €8.50. Sandwiches €3-4. Desserts €2-8. Menú of the day €10. Open M-F 8am-1am, Sa-Su 9am-1am.

SAMBFAL
ORIENTAL ❸

Pl. Progress, 15 ☎971 220 122 www.restaurantesambal.com

Sambal describes itself as a "kitchen with emotion," and we bet your taste buds will get pretty emotional after experiencing their food. This Asian fusion restaurant featuring Thai, Japanese, Chinese, and Mediterranean fare is a prime example of Majorca's thriving multicultural cuisine options. The menu is overflowing with tempting dishes designated with symbols of spiciness and meat-content. Hopefully the golden Siddhartha sitting cross-legged in the corner will help guide you to a decision, as choosing three styles of curry with 5 options of meat and veggies *(€12-17)* can cause quite the existential crisis.

Take bus #3 to Pl. de Progress. ***i*** *Vegetarian options available. Appetizers €2-6; entrees €9-17. Salads €7-11. Open M-Sa 11am-4pm and 8-11:30pm.*

FORN DES TEATRE
TRADITIONAL ❷

Pl. de Weyler, 8 ☎971 727 383

Forn des Teatre is the perfect place to grab some traditional Spanish cuisine while staying smack in the city center. You can enjoy those warm summer nights on an outdoor patio overflowing with locals and bustling with the combination of conversation and tunes played by the street performers standing steps away, or make your way into the relaxed, two-story restaurant with Wi-Fi access and TVs. While you can enjoy the long list of tapas-style *raciones (€3.50-10.90)* or Majorcan classic *pa amb olis (€6.50),* the signature of Forn des Teatre is the wide selection of *pinxtos (€1.50).* The 14 daily options do change, but the classics hold strong. The *sobrasada* is a spicy pâté, classic to the island and one of the most popular *pinxtos* at the bar, but the smoked salmon, eggplant, tortilla, and serrano-and-sunny-side-up-egg varieties are equally tantalizing.

In front of the theater between Pl. Rei Juan Carles I and Pl. Mayor. Raciones €3.50-11. Salads €7-9.25. Entrees €9.75-13. Desserts €3-4.50. Open daily 9am-1am.

THE GUINESS HOUSE
CAFE, BAR ❷

Parc de la Mar

Disclaimer: we understand that The Guiness House is innately touristy and that the menu isn't exactly creative, but the location and ambience make this spot one that you just can't skip. Located right on the waters of the Parc de la Mar with the city's best view of the Catedral, there's no better place to enjoy a summer afternoon snack. Busiest during the open hours of the Catedral, as visitors work up quite the appetite after gazing at Gaudí's glorious canopy, it also draws a crowd in summer evenings with open-air movies *(9pm July-Aug).* For all you beer connoisseurs out there, The Guinness House lives up to its name with a lengthy list of international *cervesas* on tap or by the bottle *(€2.60-4.60),* served up at the outdoor patio bar or the even larger tavern bar inside the restaurant.

*On Parc de la Mar across from the Cathedral. **i** Outdoor movies available July-Aug. Sandwiches €4.85-6. Entrees €6.70-13. Salads €6.50-7.80. Pizzas €6.50. Burgers €4.75-7.25. Open daily 8am-2am.*

ECO-VEGETARIA VEGETARIAN ❸

C. Industria, 12 ☎971 282 562

Eco-Vegetaria may very well be Palma's best destination for a fresh, creative, vegetarian meal. While your only option is the multi-course menú, which changes on a daily basis, you get some freedom of selection with the appetizer, two entrees, and dessert *(€13.50).* You'll feel its comfortable ambience in the toasty pumpernickel bread, the refreshing A/C, and the mellow soundtrack. Don't be embarrassed if you find yourself coming back for more. You'll fit right in with the local regulars waiting to get their frequent visitor cards stamped while they pay the bill *(buy 5 meals, get 1 free).*

Take C. Industria from Plaza Progress toward C. Argentina. Menú of the day €13.50. Open M-Th 1:15-4pm, F-Sa 1:15-4pm and 8:30-11pm.

NIGHTLIFE

Around the streets of Palma, near the main plazas and city center, you'll come across a few late-night, loungey cafes and mellow bars, but the real nightlife is concentrated along the **Paseo Maritimo.** Take a walk along this pathway, checking out all those fancy yachts in the harbor as you go, and 10min. away from the Catedral, things will start to heat up.

MOJITO SOUL BAR

Paseo Maritimo, 27 www.mojitosoul.com

You may currently associate nature, envy, and marshmallow breakfast cereals with the color green, but one night out on the Paseo Maritimo and you may start to think of Mojito Soul every time you encounter that portion of the color wheel. That's because the entire place is lit by glowing green lights. The DJ spins a mix of soul and R and B hits to entertain the young, international crowd as they try to answer the eternal question—another daiquiri *(€8)* or another dance. While 75% of bars and clubs in Spain will tell you that they specialize in *mojitos* and *caipirinas*, here's a spot that actually deserves that accolade. You can try 7 varieties of each of these drinks *(€8),* whether in their classic form or with a fruity twist like strawberry, peach, or passionfruit.

On Paseo Maritimo on the inland side. Cocktails €8. Open daily in summer 9pm-4am; in winter 10pm-3am.

GIBSON BAR

Pl. Mercat, 18 ☎971 716 404

Unless you've spent quite a few years at bartending school, Gibson will likely be a learning experience. The lengthy menu (five pages of whiskeys alone) lists drinks in varieties you never knew existed, but at least it features detailed explanations and histories at the bottom of each page. The house specialty dry martinis come in 14 styles, but the Gibson Dry is definitely the most popular, combining gin, vermouth, a small onion, and lemon zest *(€6.50).* Cockails like the "bull shot" *(€7)* may be a test of testosterone levels, but you can also enjoy a simple caipirinha with or without alcohol *(€7)*. Gibson's open all day long, and we won't judge if you're looking for that 8am Bloody Mary *(€7)*, but you can also enjoy a simple coffee *(€1.50)* on the outdoor patio.

Pl. Mercat branches off C. Unio between Pl. Rei Joan Carles I and Pl. Weyler. i Non-smoking area available. Beer €2. Cocktails €6-7. Coffee €1.50. Open daily 8am-3am.

SA RIBELLETA BAR, CAFE

C. Boteria, 1 ☎971 722 489

Sa Ribelleta may be small, but it rakes in locals and tourists of all ages with a vengeance. This mellow, outdoor bar simply screams Majorca—you have the laid back island attitude from the chill waitstaff to the lounge-style chairs, the simple menu of all the classic snacks including *pa amb olis (€4-€8)*, fried *mallorquines*, refreshing *trampo* (salad with oil, tomato, onion, and green peppers), and healthy *tumbet* (vegetables), and a selection of exclusive house wines and island cocktails. From your small, candle-lit wooden table, order up any dish in a small *(€4.50)* or large *(€8)* size (accompanied with bread), and sip the shockingly sweet, alcoholic, Majorcan *hierbas (€4)*. While the closing time is technically 1am, they often stay open later on the weekends to enjoy the warm evening into the late night hours.

On C. Boteria, off Pl. Llotja. Beer €2.50-4.80. Wine €3. Hierbas €4. Cocktails €7.50. Snacks €4-8. Coffee €2-3. Open M-Th 11am-1am, F-Su 8pm-1am.

JAZZ VOYEUR CLUB JAZZ BAR

C. Apuntadores, 5 ☎971 720 780 www.jazzvoyeur.com

This small, dark club lined with photos of jazz greats and low chairs that put you right up at the base of the velvet-curtained stage plays a huge role in Palma's live music scene. In addition to holding concerts almost every night of the week (the shows are free to make up for the pricey drinks), it also orchestrates the annual jazz and music festival in July and over the course of November and December. You can find any type of music at Jazz Voyeur—Thursdays are jam sessions, Wednesdays are Cuban and Blues nights, and the rest of the lineup *(check the website)* fills up with jazz, reggae, and a fine selection of cover bands. The club often offers discounts early in the night *(30% off your drinks)*, so hope to get lucky and save a few euro, and maybe even catch a wink from that dashing Elvis look-alike.

C. Apuntadores branches off Pl. Reina; the club is on the left. i Jam session on Th 8-10pm. €5 minimum F-Sa. Beer €3.50. Wine €4. Cocktails €10. Open Tu-W 9pm-1am, Th 8pm-1am, F-Sa 9pm-3am, Su 9pm-1am.

THE SOHO BAR

Avenida Argentina 5

You're not having a hallucination of Doc Brown picking you up in the De Lorean. You're not reliving your mom's senior prom. You've just stepped into The Soho, Palma's indie bar with quite the '50s decor. From the velvet couches to the bar cluttered with Rubik's Cubes and big sunglasses, to the patterned wallpaper and old-school TV's, you may subconsciously feel your pants tightening in the thighs and belling out at the ankles. Such novelty themes aren't to be enjoyed by the people who actually lived through the '60s; instead, you'll find yourself cozying up at one of the low coffee tables and watching projections of black-and-white TV shows with a student-dominated crowd. Depending on your mood, you can order up a "Woodstock 1969," with vodka, spring, soda, and lemon *(€7)*, an "Audrey Hepburn," with vodka, *cava*, Bailey's, milk, and canela *(€7)*, or one of the many others off the long list of house cocktails. Bring a student ID on Tuesdays to grab a €5 cocktail, or just show up on Thursdays for €1.50 beer.

Off Paseo Maritimo on Avenida Argentina on the left side. i Credit card min. €10. Beer

€2-4.80. Cocktails €7. Open M-Th 6:30pm-2:30am, F-Sa 6:30pm-3am, Su 6:30pm-2:30am.

MISTRAL BAR, CLUB

Paseo Maritimo, 28

You'll have tons of club options along Paseo Maritimo, but Mistral isn't one to skip. You'll know just from walking by and scoping out the attractive locals on the outdoor patio that this is a crowd you want to be dancing against. The dark navy walls, accented by the two glistening, silver bars, may portray a night sky, but this doesn't signal bedtime—it signals a long night of groovin' and movin' to blasting mash-ups of commercial hits. Prismatic cocktails and colorful strobe lights will keep your energy up until the sun comes up to help you with a tan on your walk home.

On Paseo Maritimo on the inland side. Beer €4. Cocktails €7. Open daily 10pm-5am.

FESTIVALS

Most of the events and festivities held in Palma are music and art festivals. While they are greatly attended and enjoyed, these aren't saints' days or folk festivals: they are modern, changing celebrations that don't necessarily hold much historical significance. One of the most popular is the **Fira del Ram** in March and April, which brings in the newest, most high-tech amusement park rides to the city. The most historical event of the year (and one of the most historical in all of Spain) is the **Festa de l'Estendard,** or Banner Day, that honors Majorca's inclusion into the Christian Spanish kingdom under King James in 1229. The *Ayuntamiento* publishes pamphlets and also has an online calendar detailing the city festivities, with a special calendar for the **Fiestas de Sant Sebastia.**

FIESTAS DE SANT SEBASTIA

This festival, beginning annually in mid-January, is Palma's biggest party of the year. It honors the patron saint of the city, Sant Sebastia, who took on his honorable role as the plague ended in 1524. Millions of people are suddenly no longer dying—there's gotta be someone to thank, right? Taking over all the major plazas of Palma, including the **Plaza Mayor, Plaza Rei Carles I,** and **Plaza Espanya,** this celebration is filled with constant concerts and performances, bike and foot races, guided tours, and parties. At the start of the week on January 16, the festivities begin with the lighting of bonfires and barbeques and the procession of dancing devils through the streets. The festivities build until January 20th, the day good old Sebastia was actually dubbed a saint. A grand mass is held in the **Catedral,** major artistic and musical awards are presented at the **Teatre Principal,** competition brews at the *diada* cycling race, and a spectacular fireworks display is set off in the evening.

ESSENTIALS

The official language of Majorca is **Catalan,** not Spanish, and so the city's streets, plazas, and structures have Catalonian names. Luckily, almost everything is translated into Spanish, and often English as well.

Practicalities

- **TOURIST OFFICES:** There are four main tourist offices available in Palma. The **Majorca Tourist Information** service has two locations, the Head Office at Parc de las Estacions and the Casal Solleric Office at Psg. des Born, 27 *(☎902 102 365 wpalmainfo@a-palma.es).* The **Palma City Council** has also established two offices, one at **Placa de la Reina 2** *(☎971 712 216)* and one at the **Airport** *(☎971 789 556).*
- **TOURS:** The **Town Council** runs walking tours from Plaça de Cort, next to the olive tree *(☎971 720 720 i Given in English and Spanish M-Sa 9am-6pm).* Other

city tours are available from **Palma on Bike** *(3½hr.; daily 10am from Av. Gabriel Roca, 15; 10:30am from Av. Antoni Maura, 10 €25.)* There are also **taxi tours.** *(Look for designated signs on city cabs €30 per hr.)* The **tourist bus** picks up from 16 stops all over the city. *(Tours last 1hr. 20min. Leave every 20min. Mar-Oct 10am-8pm, Nov-Feb 10am-6pm. €13.)*

- **CURRENCY EXCHANGE:** There's a currency exchange office with an admittedly inconsistent schedule. *(Av. d'Antoni Maura, 28 Usually open in summer daily 10am-5pm; in winter M-F 10am-5pm.)*
- **INTERNET:** Free city Wi-Fi is available at Plaça Joan Carles I, the Parc de Llevant, S'Escorxador, and the Cultural Centre Flassaders. It can be accessed in 30min. increments by activating your computer's bluetooth. Many restaurants and cafes also offer Wi-Fi with more forgiving time limits. The **public library** also has Wi-Fi. *(Palau Reial, 18 ☎971 711 122 Open M 9:30am-2pm, T 4-8pm, W 9:30am-2pm, Th 4-8pm, F 9:30am-2pm.)*
- **POST OFFICE:** The **central post office** is located at C. Constitución, 6 *(☎902 197 197 www.correos.es Open M-F 8:30am-8:30pm, Sa 9:30am-2pm.)*

Emergency!

- **POLICE: Local police** can be found at C. Sant Fernan. *(☎971 225 500 www.palmademallorca.es).* **National police** are at C. Ruiz de Alda, 8 *(☎971 225 200 www.policia.es).*
- **HOSPITAL:** The **general hospital** is located at Plaza Hospital, 3. *(☎971 212 000 www.gesma.org).*
- **LATE-NIGHT PHARMACY:** You'll find pharmacies all over the city, and a **24-hour pharmacy Bagur** at C. Aragon, 70 *(☎971 272 501).*

Getting There

By Plane

The **Palma de Mallorca Airport** *(☎971 789 000)* is located 11km southeast of Palma and runs flights from tons of international and domestic airlines including **Air Berlin** *(☎902 320 737 www.airberlin.com),* **Easy Jet** *(☎08 712 882 236 www.easyjet.com),* **Iberia** *(☎902 400 500 www.iberia.com),* **Lufthansa** *(☎49 696 960 www.lufthansa.com),* **Spanair** *(☎971 916 047 www.spanair.com),* and **Vueling Airlines** *(☎807 001 717 www.vueling.com).* The **Aena** website *(www.aena.es)* and **Amadeus** website *(www.amadeus.net)* are particularly helpful in consolidating information from all the major airlines. As many of the flights are short and run very consistently, prices vary immensely depending on booking, day of the week, and time of day of the flight. The **Empresa Municipal de Transportes** runs an **airport bus line** *(€2. #1, every 12-15min. M-F 6am-1:50am, Sa-Su 6am-1:10am)* taking your right into Palma, stopping along C. Gabriel Alomar, Porta de Camp, and Av. Alexandre Rosello. You can use bus line **#21** if you're staying in Arenal.

By Ferry

You can also travel to Majorca on a **boat** *(general information Autoritat Portuària de Balears www.portsdebalears.com)* from the Spanish mainland or between Islands. **Acciona-Trasmediterránea** *(☎902 454 645 www.trasmediterranea.es)* runs to Palma from **Barcelona** *(7½hr., M-Th 1, 11pm, F-Su 11pm)* and **Valencia** *(7hr., M-Sa 11:45am, Su 11:59pm)* on the mainland, as well as to **Ibiza** *(4hr.; M 7pm, F 7pm, Su 7pm)* and **Menorca** *(5½hr., Su 5:30pm).* **Baleària Eurolínies Marítimes** *(☎902 160 180 www.balearia.com)* runs to **Ibiza** *(€52.20-65.40 3½hr.; M 2:45am, 8pm; Tu 12:30am, 8pm; W 12:30am, 2:45am, 8pm; Th-F 12:30am, 8pm; Sa-Su 2:45am, 8pm.)* or **Formentera** *(€52.20 4hr., daily 1:15pm).*

Getting Around

By Bus

Public buses within the city of Palma are run by the **Empresa Municipal de Transportes (EMT)** Urbanas de Palma de Mallorca *(C. Josep Anselm Clave, 5 ☎971 214 444)*. There are 35 lines *(€1.25, 10 rides €8.)* that run daily from as early as 6am until as late as 2am. Lines **#1** and **#21** run to the **airport** *(€2. May-Oct 6am-1:50am, every 12min; Nov-Apr 6am-1:10am, every 15min.)*, and line **#50** runs a circular route. *(May-Oct 9:30am-7pm, Nov-Apr 10am-4:40pm; stops every 20min.)* Line **#41** is the overnight line. *(€1. F-Sa 11:45pm-7am; every 15min.)* Also useful are lines **#15** *(€1.25. Daily 5:45am-1:20am, every 10min.)* and the faster **#25** *(€1.25. M-F 6:25am-9:25pm, Sa-Su 6:30am-9:30pm; every 10-13min.)* to Playa de Palma, and lines **#3** *(€1.25. Daily 5:45am-12:35am, every 9-10min.)* and **#46** *(€1.25. M-Sa 6:30am-11:10pm, Su 7:18am-11:30pm, every 20-35min.)* which travel along the port, stopping at major sights like Castell de Bellver and Fundacio Pilar i Joan Miró.

By Taxi

You can also take the city taxis *(M-F 9pm-7am and weekends. €4 plus €1 per km.)*, designated as available by a green light on the top of the car from **Taxi Palma Radio** *(☎971 755 440)* or **Radio Taxi** *(☎971 755 414)*. There are major taxi stops at **Plaza Weyler, Plaza Forti, Avenida Jaime III, Plaza Reina,** and **Passieg de Sagrera.**

To get to other parts of Majorca beyond Palma, **Transport de les Illes Balears (TIB)** *(☎900 177 777 tib.caib.es)*, or TIB, runs five series of bus lines *(#100, #200, #300, #400, and #500)* from Palma that go clockwise around the island. They are notorious for running late, and their timetables vary significantly, but they are technically scheduled to begin running as early at 6am and until as late as 11pm. TIB also runs a Palma to **Pobles** train *(M-F 5:45am-11:15pm, Sa-Su 6:05am-11:15pm)* and a Metro line between the **Estación Intermodal** and the **Estación UIB.** *(M-F every 30min. 6:30am-10:30pm; every 15min. 6:30-7am, 8:30-10:30pm; Sa-Su every hr. 6:30am-10pm, every 30min. 6:30-7:30am, 9-10pm.)* Tren de Sóller runs the scenic "Western Highlights" route along the coast to **Soller** from **Plaça d'Espanya** *(☎971 752 051 www.trendesoller.com €10. 8am-7:30pm.)* enjoyed by tourists and locals alike.

By Bike

Palma is also a major center for cyclotourism, and getting around on a **bike** is extremely popular, whether on your own or in a guided tour. Rent from **Palma On Bike.** *(Av. Antoni Maura, 10 and Av. Gabriel Roca, 15 ☎971 918 988 www.palmaonbike.com Bikes for 1-2 days €12 per day, 3-7 days €10 per day. Kayak rental doubles €50 per day, singles €30 per day. Rollerblades rental €10 per day.)*

ibiza ☎971

We won't tell Mom and Dad, but we know why you're making the trip to Ibiza. You want the whitest sands, the clearest waters, the hottest sun, and the sexiest clubs. This small, Mediterranean island has a rich history of settlement and exploration, but it's modern status is the real draw. You'll be wearing as little clothing at the beach as is acceptable, stuffing your face with the delicious selection of international eats, and reaping the benefits of the commercial tourist industry.

This is where the young and beautiful come to get tanner and more beautiful on their summer vacations. Take that summer designation seriously—this packed party scene turns into a quaint and empty town during the winter months, so work hard all year to save the cash for this trip. You'll be encountering pricey accommodations,

Ibiza
MEDITERRANEAN SEA
To Barcelona, Palma, Denía, Valencia
ESTACIÓ MARÍTIMA DE FORMENTERA
To Platja Talamanca
ESTACIÓ MARÍTIMA
PL. SA RIBA
PL. D'ANTONI RIQUER
Av. Andenes
Av. Santa Eulària del Riu
C. Diputado J. Rivas
C. Antoni Jaume
C. I.M. Quadrado
C. Carlos III
C. Felipe II
C. Carlos V
C. Pedro Francés
Av. Ignacio Wallis
Av. Bartomeu Rosselló
C. Madrid
de San Cristobel
TAXI
Tur i Palau
C. Lluís
Riambau
C. Guillem Montgrí
C. Bisbe Cardona
LA MARINA
Sa Creu
C. Castelar
C. Mar
C. de San Elmo
C. Barcelona
C. J. Verdera
Emili Pou
D'enmig
C. de M. Sora
C. Garijo
Mare Déu
C. Peña
SA PEÑA
PL. SA DRASSANETA
Sa Pedrera
Mercat Vell
PL. Antoni Palau
SA FONT
Mestre Joan Mayans
C. Sa
Baluard Santa Llucía
Casa Valentín
C. Ramón i Cajal
Vicente y Ramón
Av. Bartomeu Ramon y Tur
Comte Rosselló
Vara de Rey
Pg. Vara de Rey
C. Vicente Cuervo
C. Joan d'Austria
C. B.
C. Pedro de Portugal
Spar Supermarket
C. Pere Sala
PL. DEL PARQUE
R. Antoni Costa
C. Santa Cruz
PL. DE VILA
C. Sant Carles
Museu d'Art Contemporani d'Elvissa
C. Miquel Caletà Soler
C. Jaime I
PL. DEL SOL
C. Sant Lluís
C. Santa Maria
D'ALT VILA
PL. CATEDRAL
Catedral
Baluard Sant Pere
R. Joan Baptista Calvi
Parç de la Reina Sofia
Joan Román
Museo Puget
C. Mayor
Museu Arqueològic d'Elvissa
Casa del Governador
Baluard Sant Bernat
Medieval Walls
Baluard Sant Jaume
Baluard Sant Jordi
C. Joan Xico
0
150 meters
150 yards
PL. ENRIQUE FAJARNÉS Y TUR
C. de Madrid
C. del Bispe Carrasco
BBVA
C. del Bispe Huix
Via Púnica
C. Joan Planells
Via Romana
Sa Capella
C. León
Av. de Espanya
C. Cabrero Tur Pérez
Puig des Molins
C. Visent Serra Orvay
C. Bisbe González Abarca
Av. Isidoro Macabich
BUS TO AIRPORT AND BEACHES (DISCO BUS AT NIGHT)
C. Castella
C. Cataluña
C. Extremadura
C. Aragó
CITY BUS
C. Arxiduc Lluís
Hospital Nuestra Señora del Rosario
Wash and Dry
To Platja Figueretes (125m)
BUS TO ST. ANTONI (DISCO BUS AT NIGHT)
To (75m)
To St. Antoni (14km)
Canaries
Parç de la Pau
C. Balears
C. Agapit Llobet
To Playa D'en Bossa, Aeropuerto Eivissa (7km)

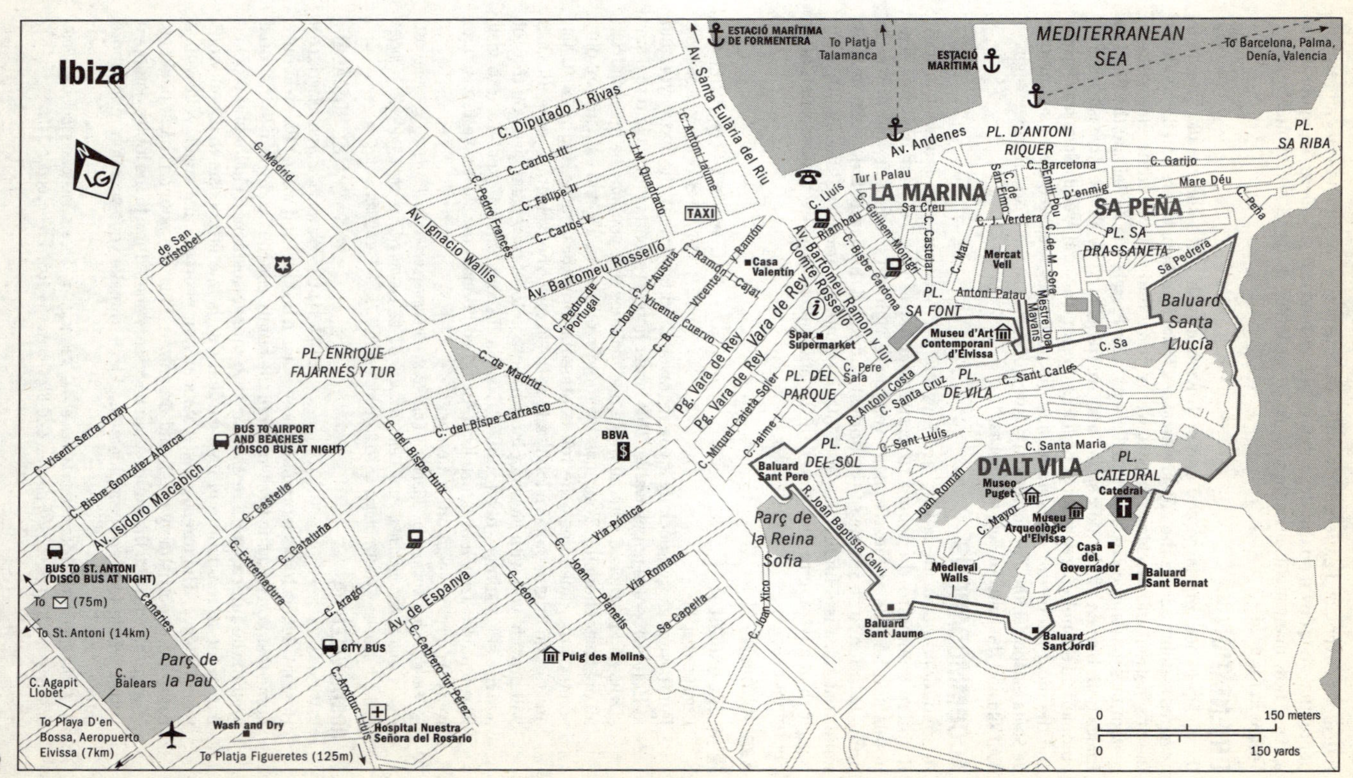

ibiza

ridiculous covers, and expensive mojitos, but memories (assuming you can remember all that goes down on this debauchery-filled island) are priceless. Test your limits and see how many nights straight you can go beaching by day and clubbing by night. You're in for a ride!

ORIENTATION

Ibiza City is not very large and can be traversed with just a short walk. The main avenues running across the city are **Avenida d'Isidor Macabich,** where you'll encounter the bus station, and **Avenida de España,** where you'll find a slew of different markets, restaurants, internet cafes, and small shops. The **Passeig Vara de Rei** and the **Plaza de Parque** both branch off Av. de España and are frequented by all the city visitors. The commerical shopping area is most developed on and around **Avenida Bartolome Roselo,** and the most interesting restaurants line the port along **Avenida Andenes** and **Avenida de Santa Eularia del Riu.** The historical centers of Ibiza are the World Heritage sight of **d'Alt Vila** and the ruins of **Puig des Molins.**

ACCOMMODATIONS

Accommodations in Ibiza City are few and far between and generally pricey. If you're coming to the island to party, **Sant Antoni** may be your best bet. The hotels and hostals are less expensive, you're right on the beach, and you're in prime location to see some of the hottest clubs and the **Sunset Strip.** Also keep in mind that Ibiza is a highly seasonal island—summer prices will be significantly higher than anything in the winter (if the accommodation even stays open after September).

Sant Antoni

HOTEL OROSOL HOTEL ❸

Cami General, 1 ☎971 340 712 www.orosolhotel.com

For these prices (especially if you're traveling with a group), the luxury you find at Hotel Orosol is unbelievable. This larger hotel is scooting its way up to 3-star status and is stacked with all those fine facilities that you may be missing from all the hostel-hopping. Your massive room's red sheets, TV, and balcony are only some of the amenities—the full continental breakfast buffet, big pool (290m away), and bright, modern lobby add to the luxury. The welcoming receptionists will provide you with slews of information on local travel and give you tons of activity suggestions—need a bike? Want a discount club ticket? Care to visit Formentera? They'll organize it all for no additional cost. Just take it easy and relax. You're on vacation, remember?

From the bus station, take Ramon y Cajal to the first intersection to the right. ***i*** *Breakfast, sheets, and towels included. Pool. Cafeteria. A/C €3-12. Laundry €7 wash, €4 dry.* *Singles €26-53; doubles €40-92; triples €57-120; quads €70-172.* *Reception 24hr.*

HOSTAL VALENCIA HOSTAL ❷

C. Valencia, 23 ☎971 341 035 www.ibizahostalvalencia.com

Hostal Valencia looks more like a home than a hostal—and we're talking about a home that you're dying to own. From the comfy couches and warm living room area to the full cafeteria-restaurant with orange-cushioned chairs and stocked bar to the porch-patio and lush garden, this is one little oasis that you won't want to leave. The forest-green sheets in your bedroom and small, yellow-tiled bathroom are pristinely clean and organized. Plus, the pool out back beckons. You can also find all the information necessary about Ibiza in the lobby, equipped with a whole kiosk of pamphlets and ideas to make your vacation much more interesting.

At the intersection of Carrer de Mosen and C. Valencia. ***i*** *Sheets and towels included. Pool. Cafeteria.* *Singles €25-70; doubles €40-80; triples €54-105.* *Reception 24hr.*

HOSTAL MONTANA
HOSTAL ❷

C. Roma, 8 ☎971 340 490 www.montanamarino.com

Hostal Montana knows how to help you make the most of your stay in San Antonio—the friendly staff will point out the best beaches, direct you to the pool at their sister-hostel, **Hostal Marino,** sell you discount tickets to the hottest clubs, or organize a ferry trip to Formentera. You'll enjoy your complimentary breakfast in the morning, but if that night of partying has you sleeping until the afternoon, you can always fight that hangover by grabbing a snack in the cafeteria-bar or wake yourself up with a game of foosball between *bocadillos.* The rooms will make you feel like you've scored a snazzy hotel room, as they come equipped with a mini-fridge (store the mixers), full closet (unpack the stilettos), small balcony (toast to the sunset), and clean, comfy beds (maybe get some—sleep, that is).

From the bus station, take C. Ramon y Cajal and make a left on C. Roma. ***i*** *Breakfast, sheets, towels, mini-fridge, and safe included.* *Singles €17-35; doubles €28-70; triples €42-105.* *Reception 24hr.*

HOSTAL ROSALIA
HOSTAL ❷

Carrer Santa Rosalia, 5 ☎971 340 709 www.hostalrosalia.com

This inexpensive accommodation is packed with partying beachgoers. The simple rooms with white walls and grey tiles get a nice splash of life from the colorful sheets and big windows. You can lounge around the pool and enjoy the TV in the cafeteria during the day, or take the short 10min. walk down to the beaches and port. And if the walk seems too long, Rosalia can get you there faster—the hostal also runs **Top Moto** next door.

Take Carrer del Progress to Carrer Santa Rosalia and turn left. ***i*** *Breakfast €3. Internet available on lobby computer. Pool.* *May-Oct singles €18-20; doubles €30-40; triples €45-60.* *Reception 24hr.*

Ibiza City

HOSTAL LAS NIEVES/JUANITO
HOSTAL ❷

C. Juan de Austria, 17/18 ☎971 190 819 www.hostalibiza.com

Located in the middle of the city center, a short walk from the historic d'Alt Villa and the history-making Playa d'en Bossa, this hostal pair is run out of the same reception on C. Juan de Austuria and gives you a bit of freedom in deciding how much you're going to spend. Simply put, Hostal Juanito is probably the best price you'll find in Ibiza city, but it isn't a point of luxury. You'll enjoy a spacious and clean room but will have to sleep through the heat with no A/C. Las Nieves provides some ventilation and the possibility of ensuite bathrooms, which ups the ante a bit. Either way, they both have the same best feature—the couple that owns the place is one of the nicest you'll encounter on the island, and they are ready to help you plan out your trip.

From the bus stop, take Av. d'Isidor Macabich, turn right onto Av. Ignac Wallis and left onto Juan de Austria. *Nieves singles €30; doubles €60, with bath €75. Juanito singles €25; doubles €50.* *Reception open daily 9am-1pm and 4-8pm.*

EUROPA PUNICO
HOSTAL ❸

Carrer de Aragon, 28 ☎971 303 428 www.hostaleuropapunico.com

This quiet and peaceful hostal, conveniently located near the Parc de la Pau and Av. d'Espanya, may be one of the best deals you'll find in Ibiza City (and believe us, accommodation deals are few and far between). Your bright room with wooden floors and cream sheets only brightens when you open up your sizable window or small balcony. You can pile your plate high at the breakfast buffet, and take your meal out onto the lush patio with shaded picnic tables and comfy seats.

From the bus stop, take C. Extremadura to Carrer de Aragon. i Breakfast, linens, and towels included. Singles €33-66; doubles €40-103; triples €55-139. Reception 24hr.

SIGHTS

The most historic part of Ibiza City is **d'Alt Vila** ("the Walled City"), a UNESCO World Heritage sight. Walking the small, winding streets (or rather climbing, as it's pretty steep), you can enjoy the major sights or follow one of the designated routes described in pamphlets available at the **information offices.** The **bastions** around d'Alt Vila are the perfect look-out points, and the **Baluarte des Porta Neu Sant Pere** holds a small museum exhibit explaining the construction of the city. Also, while the **Museum of Contemporary Art** is currently being renovated (as of summer 2010), the exhibits are available in the Ayuntamiento.

CATEDRAL D'EIVISSA — CHURCH

Pl. de la Catedral, 1

In the year 1234, a group of Catholic monarchs sat down and realized what Ibiza was missing—no, not a new *discoteca*, but a cathedral dedicated to the Virgin Mary. Plans for this classic, Gothic-style cathedral began, and construction continued all the way until the 16th century. The Catedral d'Eivissa takes particular pride in its collection of 14th- and 15th-century artwork and its 16th- and 17th-century bells, which are still rung today. Just a few years back, in 2006, yet another change was made. The small museum in the side of the cathedral now holds paintings and sculptures from Ibiza's religious history.

Across from the information office. Follow signs upon entering d'Alt Vila. i Information available in English and Spanish. Catedral free. Museum €1. Open in summer Tu-Sa 9:30am-1:30pm and 5-8pm; in winter Tu-Sa 9:30am-1:30pm and 4-7pm.

MUSEU PUGET — MUSEUM

C. Major, 18 — ☎971 392 147

Like father, like son—the Museu Puget is dedicated to papa Narcis Puget Vinas and son Narcis Puget Rique, two artists from the island of Ibiza who together compiled quite the collection. The permanent exhibition is composed of 130 pieces by this talented pair, including Vinas' drawings and oil paintings and Rique's watercolors. If this isn't enough island pride for you, the building itself has been a point of interest on the island since the 15th century. This classic Ibizan house passed through the hands of some of the island's most powerful families over the years, including the Laudes of the 1700s and the Comasemas of the 1800s, before becoming a museum in 2007.

Near the information office. Follow signs upon entering d'Alt Vila. i Information available in English and Spanish. Free. Open May-Sept Tu-F 10am-1:30pm and 5-8pm, Sa-Su 10am-1:30pm; Oct-Apr Tu-F 10am-1:30pm and 4-6pm, Sa-Su 10am-1:30pm.

MUSEU ARQUEOLOGIC — MUSEUM

Plaza de la Catedral, 3 — ☎971 301 231

You think Ibiza rakes in international visitors today? It only got so good at filling its beaches and clubs because it has 3000 years of practice. The Archaeological Museum takes you through six major periods in Ibiza and Formentera's history: Prehistoric, Phoenician, Punic, Early Roman, Late Roman and Late Antiquity, and the Islamic Medieval. Each exhibit provides a clear timeline, maps, and images to really send you back in time—and of course lots of ceramics, statues, and currency.

Next to the information office. Follow signs upon entering d'Alt Vila. i Information available in English and Spanish. €2.40, students €1.20. Open Apr-Sept Tu-Sa 10am-2pm and 6-8pm, Su 10am-2pm; Oct-Mar Tu-Sa 9am-3pm, Su 10am-2pm.

BEACHES

While it depends on how you divide it up, there are at least 50 distinct beaches surrounding the island of Ibiza. They all have their own character and pros and cons. You can endure the biggest crowds and enjoy the biggest parties at beaches closer to the city, or you can battle the bus schedule to reach Ibiza's nature reserves and smaller coves. Pick your poison, pick your pleasure. No matter what you choose, you'll be under that same Mediterranean sun, sipping the (essentially) same mojitos.

PLATJA DE SES SALINES — BEACH

10min. drive from Ibiza Town in the Salines Nature Reserve

There's a reason Platja de Ses Salines is one of Ibiza's most popular beaches. Here in the Salines Nature Reserve, you'll find clean, soft sands, and warm, clear waters. With barely any waves, you'll see tourists and locals wading out into the sea to test their skills at paddle ball or just floating around on an inflatable tube. While Ses Salines is the perfect place to relax and work on that summer tan, it's also going to provide you with some of the biggest, most-established beach restaurants on the island. **The Jockey Club** and **Malibu** will serve cocktails right to your lounge chair, spray you with their mist machines, and have their DJs spinning hot tunes all day long.

Take bus #11 from Ibiza City to Salines. ***i*** *First aid available. Lounge chair and umbrella rentals €6-10. Lifeguard on duty daily noon-7pm.*

CALA BASSA — BEACH

Near Sant Antoni

If you say its name fast, "Cala Bassa" may remind you a touch of the *The Teenage Mutant Ninja Turtles'* "cowabunga!" While you can definitely enjoy pizza and sea creatures (and a life free of bad guys) while relaxing at this small cove getaway, there's way more to the Cala Bassa than any '80s cartoon can provide. Whether you want to leap off the rocky cliffs into the warm waters below, play some paddle ball right on the waveless shore, or enjoy the multi-tiered sand levels under the shade of the trees, you'll reap the benefits of smooth sand and clear waters. Cala Bassa is also perfect to test your wits at some water sports—**Ski Pormany** *(11am-7pm, summers only)* offers waterskiing *(€20)*, banana-boating *(€10)*, and tubing *(€15)*, and **Pheonix Dive Center** *(971 806 374 www.pheonixdive.de 10am-6pm, summers only)* offers snorkeling *(from €15)* and SCUBA *(€34)* adventures. Both companies work best with walk-ins, so just show up and hop in the water!

Take the #7 bus from Sant Antoni. ***i*** *Showers and bathrooms available. No camping. Chair rentals €4. Lifeguard on duty daily July-Sept 11am-7pm; Oct 1-June noon-6pm.*

PLATJA D'ES CAVALLET — BEACH

A short walk from Salines to the coast.

Platja d'es Cavallet's free-spirited vibe stems from a few factors: groups of locals frequently make the switch from swimsuits to birthday suits, masseuses perform aggressive and artistic massages right on the sand, the few restaurants sprinkled along the beach (like the huge **Chiringay**) play mellower tunes than the average Ibizan beach-bar, and any tourists who arrive via public transit have just made the 30min. walk through the stunning Salines Nature Reserve to arrive at this peaceful paradise. Along the coast you'll find tons of rocky coves being settled by savvy locals looking for some private tanning and even pass by the 15th-century **Torre de ses Portes.**

Take bus #11 from Ibiza City to Salines and then walk on the coast to D'es Cavallet. ***i*** *First Aid available. Nudity permitted. Lifeguards on duty daily 11am-7pm.*

PLATJA D'EN BOSSA BEACH

Lounging around Platja d'en Bossa you'll hear bottles popping, lighters clicking, and the repeated "Amigo, wanna come to (insert disco here) tonight?" of promoters offering free and discounted club tickets. While you may not get the pristine cleanliness of removed nature reserve beaches, you'll get lines of huge hotels, tall palm trees, and Ibiza's biggest seaside parties. Major beach bars like **Bora Bora** serve drinks and food all day before turning into raging discos after dark. If you go up one block from beach, you'll find tons of bars, pubs, supermarkets, internet cafes, gyms, and restaurants, making Platja d'en Bossa a tourist hub of total convenience.

Take bus #14, summer bus #10B, or the discobus to Platja d'en Bossa. i First aid, showers, and lockers available. Jet-ski and banana boat rentals. On-beach massages. Lockers €3 per 10hr. Lounge chairs €7.

FOOD

BAR 43 TAPAS INTERNATIONAL, OPEN LATE 2

Av. de España, 43 ☎971 300 992 www.ibiza-43.com

Some numbers hog all the attention: lucky (or unlucky) 13, fab 4, and sweet 16. But what ever happened to good old 43? Luckily, Bar 43 Tapas is here to boost this poor, neglected number's self-esteem by serving 43 varieties of international tapas to an equally international clientele. You can test your knowledge of international flags or chat with the owners about the decorations on the walls, all of which have been collected over the course of their world travels. These tapas are the perfect size for sharing, so grab a group to try some Spanish *albondigas* in mustard sauce *(€5)*, a Mexican *quesadilla (€4.50)*, a Greek salad *(€4.80)*, and some Indian chicken curry *(€6.50)*. You can add to the party by tasting one of their refreshing cocktails, like the fruity, tropical "Ibiza 43" that mixes rum, apricot brandy, various juices, and blackberry liqueur *(€7)*.

Near the bus stop on Av. de Espana. Tapas €4-6.50. Open Tu-Sa 1-5pm and 8pm-1am.

BON PROFIT TRADITIONAL 2

Pl. del Parque, 5

If we learned anything from David and Goliath, *Stuart Little*, or *The Princess and the Pea*, it's that even the little guy can have a huge impact—and Bon Profit fits right in with those small-but-strong competitors. Located right on the Plaza del Parque, this classic Spanish restaurant may only cover a small space, but it serves huge portions at shockingly low prices. You can enjoy a full plate of steaming *paella (€3.80)* for lunch any day of the week, or the selection of local fish like the specialty *dorada (€9.50)*. Even any selection off the lengthy wine list will only cost you €1.90 per glass. The friendly staff will serve you with a smile in this old-time establishment, where the plaster has been artistically removed from parts of the walls to uncover the warm brick below.

On the Pl. del Parque, on the side closest to d'Alt Vila. i No smoking. Entrees €3.80-11. Desserts €1.20-2.70. Open daily 1-3pm and 8-10pm.

BAR SAN JUAN TRADITIONAL 3

C. de Montgri, 8 ☎971 311 603

This Ibiza classic is a family establishment, passed down through three generations over the past 60 years. Just don't think that Bar San Juan is stuck in some outdated ways. You'll find a lengthy list of daily options every time you walk in to this small restaurant packed with chatty locals. It may not look too exciting from the outside, but the moment you walk in and see the massive portions passing under your nose, you'll understand why you're lost in the sound of bustling conversation and clinking glasses. On a menu that's all about choices, you'll find a slew of fresh options like dorada, salmon, sepia *(€5-10.80)*, six different types of tortillas *(€3.50-5)*, and a hefty mixed *paella (€4.80)*.

From Psg. Vara de Rei, take either of the side streets to C. de Montgri. i Smoking and non-smoking areas available. Appetizers €4.50-8. Salads €3-6.50. Fish and meat €4-12. Desserts €1.80-2.50. Wine €1-1.70. Open M-Sa 1-3:30pm and 8:30-11:30pm.

KE KAFE FUSION, MEDITERRANEAN, INDIAN, MOROCCAN 3

C. Bisbe Azara, 5 ☎971 194 004 www.kekafe-ibiza.com

Ke Kafe is truly international—you'll find a menu full of Mediterranean, Spanish, Moroccan, Indian, and Thai classics—but it also understands the multicultural universal of good eats. No matter what you're in the mood for, whether it's warm couscous with veggies, chicken, or lamb *(€11-14)*, or a refreshing "7 Pekados" salad *(€7)* topped with fresh strawberries, goat cheese, nuts, and a fruity vinaigrette, Ke Kafe will soothe your cravings. It will also soothe your mind with a mellow soundtrack, Tibetan peace flags on the walls, and the warm glow of orange lamps.

On one of the small side streets between C. Compte Rossello and C. de Montgri. Salads €7. Appetizers €6-7; entrees €10-15. Open M-Sa 1-4pm and 9pm-midnight.

ANCIENT PEOPLE INDIAN, OPEN LATE 2

Av. de España, 32 ☎971 306 687 www.ancientpeopleibiza.com

You've spent the day climbing the streets of D'alt Vila, and now we're throwing more ancient people at you? Don't fret—we're giving you a break from cathedrals and museums (for the moment). This traditional Indian restaurant and tea shop overflows with the smell of classic spices and booming conversation. Take a seat on one of the sequined pillows, among the colorful drapes, or even lie down at a low table on the small platform in back. You'll find all those classics you've missed while traveling Spain: one part of the menu allows you to select chicken *(€9)*, lamb *(€10)*, or prawns *(€10.50)* and match that up with a preparation of your liking, whether it be *korma*, *kashmiri*, or *vindaloo*. The reasonably priced vegetarian section of the menu, including the recommended veggie curry *(€6.50)*, will definitely not disappoint.

On Av. de Espana near the intersection with Carrer Extremadura. i Vegetarian options available. Wait possible on weekend. Appetizers €4-5.75; entrees €9-12. Vegetarian dishes €5.50-6.75. Desserts €3.25. Open M-Th 1pm-midnight, F-Sa 1pm-2am, Su 6pm-midnight.

LA CANELA BAKERY 1

Carrer Aragon, 54 ☎971 305 040

We hate to be a "Debbie Downer," but you may want to collect your best powers of self-restraint before entering La Canela. Take one step into this classic Ibiza bakery and you'll have to keep check of your saliva levels. Behind the glass case, you'll find shelf upon shelf of glistening tarts, colorful mousses, and flaky *empanadas*. Every day, La Canela cooks up 22 varieties of homemade savory treats, and 24 types of fresh, tempting sweets. You'd be foolish to leave this island without trying the traditional Ibizan *flao (€1.90)*, a sweet tart of three fresh cheeses and mint, or *graxionera (€1.55)*, a pudding-like cake. The smiling staff, adorned in striped aprons and white caps, will gladly help you make your selection or even grab you something from their cheese, meat, and wine market.

On Carrer Aragon between the Parc de la Pau and Iglesia de Santa Cruz. Pastries €0.65-3.50. Artisan cakes €14-19 per kg. Open M-Sa 6:30am-9pm.

NIGHTLIFE

Nightlife is Ibiza's pride and joy. Whether you're an Ibiza virgin or a proud veteran, the enormous, packed *discotecas* will never cease to shock and impress. While you need to be prepared for big covers and pricey drinks, you can find discounts from the street promoters in all the city centers and along the beaches as well as at many hostel receptions. The major clubs are generally located outside the cities, splashed all over the island, including **Eden** and **Es Paradis** in Sant Antoni, **Pacha** at the Ibiza port, and **Privilege** and **Amnesia** near San Rafael. But don't fret, as Ibiza has made club transport particularly convenient with the **discobus** *(€3)* which runs lines from midnight to 6:30am, dropping you right at the doors to the major clubs. There are also options for some less expensive partying. The **Sunset Cafes** and smaller clubs along **Calle Santa Anges** in Sant Antoni are some favorite spots, and there are also late night bars all over Ibiza City.

SPACE

CLUB

Playa d'en Bossa ☎971 304 432 www.spaceibiza.com

You may be wondering how they came up with the name Space. Maybe it's because this enormous club with over 4 dance floors, a bar around every corner, and various lounges will move the crowds to new spaces as the night gets busier and busier. Maybe it's because while you're dancing on the crowded dance floor among go-go girls and costumed performers on stilts, a little extra room would be desirable. Or maybe it's just because this club is out of this world. This top Ibiza disco is ready to party any night of the week, but you should make sure to check out the "We Love Sundays" parties and top DJ Carl Cox's hard techno beats every Tuesday.

Take the Discobus from the Ibiza port to Space, or bus #14 during the day to Playa d'en Bossa. Beer €10. Cocktails €13-17. Open M 10pm-6am, Tu 8pm-6am, W 10pm-6am, Th 8pm-6am, F-Sa 10pm-6am, Su 4pm-6am.

EDEN

CLUB

C. Salvador Espriu, 1 ☎971 340 212 www.edenibiza.com

This is one debauchery-filled garden of Eden that could only have been created by the party gods—you've got massive flatscreens playing the hottest music videos, a giant warehouse-sized space, multiple levels of circular dance floors, and a VIP guest list stacked with some of the world's hottest DJs and celebs. Eden is all about temptation, and the glistening red apples all over the dance floor just remind you of all those things that you're dying to have, from that sexy dance partner across the room to those pricey spirits behind the bar. As major clubs on Ibiza go, every night is something special. For the past decade, Eden has created a name for itself with its "Judgment Sundays" of intense techno, and more recently, the "Wonderland" Fridays with world-class DJ sets that bring in stars like Lady Gaga. That apple's just sitting there—take a bite.

Take Discobus line #1 or #4 to Sant Antoni or take C. Ramon y Cajal to the rotunda and follow C. Dr. Fleming. Cover €20-55. Beer €10. Cocktails €12. Open daily midnight-6am.

ES PARADIS

CLUB

C. Salvador Espriu, 2 ☎971 346 600 www.esparadis.com

The title doesn't lie—you have found Ibiza's party paradise (and we doubt it was hard, considering its ad posters absolutely blanket the island). Take one step inside this enormous pyramid of party glory and scope out the multiple levels of circular dance floors and stages decorated with sparkling disco balls and spiraling vined terraces. The fog and strobe lights will get you lost in the line-up of house and electronic hits, and you'll dance until your feet are sore at Wednesday's "Clubland," whip out that leather for Tuesday's "Ibiza Rocks," bob your head along on the calmer Sunday "Jukebox," and then make use of Es Paradis's signature, deep dancefloor-gone-pool at the Monday and Friday "Fiesta del Agua" (pool fills up at 5am).

Discobus line #1 or #4 to Sant Antoni or take C. Ramon y Cajal to the rotunda and follow C. Dr. Fleming. i GLAS (gay, lesbian, and straight) night on Th. Cover €30-45. Beer €6-7. Cocktails €11-13. Open daily midnight-6am.

CAFE DEL MAR — BAR

C. Vara de Rey, 27 ☎971 342 516 www.cafedelmarmusic.com

There seems to be a striking similarity between the vibe in *Aladdin*'s "A Whole New World" and that in Cafe del Mar. This bar makes you feel like you're soaring through the clouds with its pillowed ceiling, white, pink, and blue decor, mellow tunes, and amorphous design. The cafe is a classic that's been around way longer than that street rat and his monkey friend (since 1980 to be exact). Head down on any summer night around sunset, and there's no doubt that you'll find an absolutely packed outdoor patio right on the water. Don't let all this talk of dreams and genies get you sleepy—while Cafe del Mar may be the perfect, laid-back alternative to the Ibiza club scene, it is also one of the island's most popular pre-clubbing spots.

Sunset Strip. Take Vara de Rey in Sant Antoni down to the water. Coffee €4-10. Beer €4.50-7.50. Wine €5.50. Liquors €5-15. Cocktails €10-11. Open daily 5pm-1am.

CAFE SAVANNAH — CAFE, BAR, CLUB

C. Balanzat, 38 ☎971 348 031 www.savannahibiza.com

Coming to Ibiza, your priorities are likely partying, tanning, drinking, and eating—and Savannah can give you everything that you're looking for. This chic cafe-bar-club, right on Sant Antoni's sunset strip, is impossible to miss—from its hot pink drapes to its white globe lamps to its tiled, arching interior and pink bar. You can enjoy the large, beautifully presented portions off their menu, including international hits like Asian woks *(€13-14)*, Spanish Iberian pork *(€16)*, or the multicultural mini-burger combo *(€13)* with lamb-mint, beef-cheddar, and chicken-curry varieties for you to taste. Once you've filled up and watched the Ibiza sunset on the outdoor patio, the whole mood changes. The DJs' mellow tunes turn into commerical dance beats, and the club in back opens up to get you moving, whether hosting their notoriously popular pre-club parties *(W-Sa)*, or holding their own until the early morning *(M-Th, Sa)*.

Sunset Strip. Take Vara de Rey in Sant Antoni down to the water. Wine €4. Cocktails €8-9. Appetizers €8.50-10.50; entrees €13-22. Desserts €6.50-7.50. Cafe open daily 11am-midnight. Bar open M-Th midnight-6am, Sa midnight-6am.

TEATRO PEREYRA — LIVE MUSIC, JAZZ BAR

C. Conde Rosello, 3 ☎971 304 432 www.teatropereyra.com

We don't want to knock the talent and popularity of the international DJs that spin at the hottest Ibiza clubs, but there's definitely something different and special about seeing and hearing music boom from bass drum or spill from a saxophone rather than just make its way out of a speaker. Teatro Pereyra prides itself on providing live international music every night from its small stage and huge speakers. Whether it's the winter Cuban line-up or the mix of jazz, blues, and soul in the summer, you can enjoy the swanky ambience with big chandeliers, colorful paintings, and tables decorated with assorted business cards under the glass. The drinks are pricey, but the shows and entry are free.

From the info office on Passeo Vara de Rey, take Conde Rosello toward D'alt Vila. Wine €8. Beer €8-9. Cocktails €12-15. Prices lower during daytime hours. Open in summer daily 8am-4am; in winter M-Sa 8am-4am. Concerts around 11:30pm.

SOUL CITY CLUB

C. Santa Agnes, 2 ☎971 340 509 www.digitalibiza.com/soulcity

We're about to have your wallet jumping for joy—it's possible to party like crazy in Ibiza without dropping more on a cover than on your accommodation. Soul City will let you in for free, provide the hottest dance beats for free, and even project movies all over their flatscreen TVs and projection screens without asking for an additional dime. Ibiza's original, exclusive hip-hop and R and B club has DJs spinning songs that are sure to get you moving. Ironically, while this is supposedly a city, it's actually far smaller than many of Ibiza's school-sized discos. Think of it this way: pack the same amount of people into a much smaller space, and you have a steaming, sticky, overflowing dance floor of party animals.

Take Discobus line #1 or #4 to Sant Antoni and C. Santa Agnes runs down to the port. ***i*** *No cover.* *Beer €3-4. Spirits €5-6. Cocktails €7.* *Open daily 10pm-6am.*

ESSENTIALS

Practicalities

- **TOURIST OFFICES:** There are **information offices** *(www.ibiza.travel)* all around the island, including at the **port** *(C. Antoni Riquer, 2 ☎971 191 195 Open Apr-Oct M-Sa 9:30am-6pm, Su 10am-1pm; Nov-Mar M-F 9:30am-3:30pm, Sa 9:30am-2:30pm.)* Another convenient location is at the **airport** *(☎971 809 118 Open May-Oct M-F 9am-8pm, Sa 9am-7pm; Nov-Apr M-F 9am-3pm, Sa 8am-1pm)*. There are multiple offices in Ibiza City, including at **Vara de Rey** *(Psg. Vara de Rey, 1 ☎971 301 900 info@ibiza.travel Open Apr-Oct M-Sa 9am-8pm, Su 9am-3pm; Nov-Mar M-F 9am-7pm, Sa 10am-6pm, Su 10am-2pm)*, in **Dalt Vila** *(Plaza Catedal s/n ☎971 399 232 Open June-Sept M-Sa 10am-2pm, 5pm-9pm, Su 10am-2pm; Oct-Mar daily 10am-3pm)*, and at **Parc de la Pau** *(Av. d'Isidor Macabich Open Apr-Oct M-Sa 10am-1:30pm and 5-8pm, Su 10am-2pm; Nov-Mar M-Sa 10am-2pm)*. There are also offices in **Sant Anotoni** *(Psg. de Ses Fonts s/n ☎971 343 363 Open May-Oct M-F 9:30am-8:30pm, Sa 9am-1pm, Su 9:30am-1:30pm; Oct-Apr M-F 9:30am-2:30pm, Sa 9:30am-1:30pm)*, **Santa Eularia des Rui** *(C. Caria Riquer Wallis ☎971 330 728 Open May-Oct M-F 9:30am-1:30pm and 5-7:30pm, Sa 9:30am-1:30pm; Nov-Apr M-F 9am-2pm, Sa 9am-1:30pm)*, and beaches **Cala Llonga** *(Open May-Oct daily 9:30am-2pm and 3:30-8pm)* and **Es Canar.** *(May-Oct daily 9:30am-2pm and 3:30-8pm.)*
- **INTERNET:** You can get **Wi-Fi** access at the **public library** in the Espacio Cultural Can Ventosa *(C. Ignasio Wallis, 26 Open fall-spring M-F 8am-3pm; in summer Tu 8am-3pm)*, or at **Telecentro** internet cafe *(Carrer de Castilla, 10 ☎971 394 269 daily 10am-11:30pm)* that offers internet for €1 per hr. and printing and copying for €0.20 per page.
- **LAUNDROMATS:** You can do your laundry at **Wash and Dry Ibiza** *(Av. de España, 53 ☎971 394 822)*, which also has ironing services and internet access.
- **POST OFFICE:** The central **Post Office** of Ibiza City *(Av. Isodor Macabich 67 ☎971 399 769 Open M-F 8:30am-8:30pm, Sa 9:30am-2pm.)* also has an ATM, photocopy and fax services, and an Ebay desk.

Emergency!

- **EMERGENCY NUMBER:** ☎112.
- **POLICE: National.** *(☎091; 971 398 831)* **Local** *(☎092; 971 315 861 for Ibiza)*
- **HOSPITALS: Can Misses.** *(☎971 397 000)* **Red Cross Ibiza.** *(☎971 390 303)*

- **LATE-NIGHT PHARMACIES: Pharmacies** around each city rotate being open 24hr. You can visit any pharmacy during the day, and they can give you the schedule of which pharmacies are next in line to stay open. Within Ibiza City, there are pharmacies all over, including at **Parque de la Pau,** at **Paseo Vara de Rey,** along **Avenida Espanya,** and three near the border of **D'alt Vila.**

Getting There

By Plane

The **Ibiza Airport**, Sant Jordi *(☎971 809 900)*, is located 7km from Ibiza City and 5km from Sant Jordi. Over 50 airlines connect through the airport including **Air Berlin** *(☎902 320 737 www.airberlin.com)*, **Air Europa** *(☎902 401 501 www.aireuropa.com)*, **British Airways** *(☎902 111 333 www.britishairways.com)*, **Aer Lingus** *(☎952 105 488 www.aerlingus.com)*, **Iberia** *(☎902 400 500 www.iberia.com)*, **Ryan Air** *(☎353 124 80 856 www.ryanair.com)*, **SpanAir** *(☎971 916 047 www.spanair.com)*, and **Vueling** *(☎807 001 717 www.vueling.com)*. There is also Wi-Fi access throughout the airport. From the airport, city bus line **#9** *(€3.20. June and Sept only every 1½hr. 7am-11:30pm.)* runs to Sant Antoni, and **#10** *(€3.20. Apr-Oct 6am-midnight every 20min., Nov-Mar 7am-11:30pm every 30min.)* and **#10B** *(€3.20. July-Aug 12:30am-5:30am every hr.)* run to the Ibiza City. **Radiotaxi** *(☎971 800 080)* can take you by cab for €0.90 per km during the day and €1.10 over night, plus a €1.50 airport supplement fee. Cabs from the airport to Sant Antoni are generally €25-€30, and €15-€20 to Ibiza City. The Aena website *(www.aena.es)* and Amadeus website *(www.amadeus.net)* are particularly helpful in consolidating information from all the major airlines. As many of the flights are short and run very consistently, prices vary immensely depending on how far in advance you book, and the day of the week and time of day of the flight.

By Ferry

You can arrive via boat to Ibiza from the Spanish mainland or between other islands in the Mediterranean. **Acciona-Trasmediterránea** can take you from **Barcelona** *(8hr., M-Tu 1per day, Th-Su 1 per day.)*, **Valencia** *(4hr. 20min., F-Sa 5pm)*, and **Majorca** *(3hr. 45min.; M, F, Su 7pm)*. **Baleària Eurolínies Marítimes** can also take you from **Barcelona** *(8hr.; M, W 10:30pm, F 10:30pm, 11pm, Su 11pm €62.40.)*, **Valencia** *(€78. 3-5hr.; M, W 4:30pm, Tu, Sa 9pm, F, Su 4:30pm, 9pm.)*, and **Majorca** *(€52.20-65.40. 2-3hr.; M-Sa 8am and 10am, Su 8am and 9am)*, but also offers travel from **Fromentera.** *(M-F 12 per day 7:30am-9pm, Sa-Su 17 per day 7:30am-9pm. €23.)*

Getting Around

By Bus

Izabus is the main bus company for the city, running 34 lines to all different parts of the island. Lines **#9** *(€3.20. June and Sept only every 1hr. 30min., 7am-11:30pm)*, **#10** *(€3.20. Apr-Oct every 20min. 6am-midnight; Nov-Mar every 30min. 7am-11:30pm)*, and **#10B** *(€3.20. July-Aug every hr., 12:30am-5:30am)* run to the airport from Sant Antoni and Ibiza City, respectively. Line **#0** *(Sept-June M-Sa every 15min., 7:30am-9am, 1:30-3:30pm, 7-8:30pm; July-Aug last leg runs until 2am)* circles Ibiza City and **#3** *(June-Oct 15 every 30min., 7am-11:30pm; Oct 15-May every 30min., 7am-10:30pm)* runs between Ibiza and Sant Antoni. Fares and line schedules vary, but generally range between €1 and €2.50. The main **bus stop** in Ibiza City is located on Av. d'Isidor Macabich, near the Pac de la Pau. As far as nightlife travel goes, the summer **Discobus** *(☎971 313 447 www.discobus.es)* runs 4 lines that stop at Ibiza's major clubs, including **Space, Pacha, Amnesia,** and **Privelege,** from approximately midnight-6:30am. *(€3.)*

By Taxi

There are also multiple **taxi** companies on the island, including Radio Taxi Ibiza *(Ibiza City ☎971 398 483)* and Radio Taxi Sant Antoni *(☎971 343 764)*. There are taxi points in Ibiza City along the **port,** near **Parque de la Pau,** off **C. Galicia,** and off **Avenida Bartomeu Rossello.** You can rent a **motor scooter** *(Ⓢ €38-65 per day.)* or **bike** *(Ⓢ €6-10 per day.)* from **Extra Rent A Car** in Ibiza City *(Av. Santa Eulalia s/n ☎971 190 160 www.extrarent.com)*. **Top Moto** also rents scooters. *(☎971 344 266 Ⓢ €24-29 per day.)*

las islas baleares

VALENCIA AND ALICANTE

From the craggy mountain backdrop of Alicante to the hypermodern playground of Valencia and everywhere along the Costa Blanca in between, the Mediterranean Coast boasts exactly what you would expect—beautiful sandy beaches peppered by hidden alcoves, stretches of water as blue as lapus lazuli, and practically endless white umbrellas. However, the coast is more than a place where you'll have to empty some sand from your shoes. The southwest corner of Spain boasts a little bit of everything, including cheap museums, thriving contemporary culture, booming nightlife, and serene mountain views. With a history dominated by Phonecians, Carthaginians, Greeks, Romans, and Moors, the area offers a surprising mix of influences that invade plates, palaces, and parties everywhere you turn. A Moorish stronghold from 1094 until 1238 when it was reconquered by Castile, the area still has an Arab influence that sets it apart from its northern neighbors. The next conquest came in the 1930s, when the *Valencianos* became the last region incorporated into Franco's Spanish empire.

Since regaining its autonomy in 1977, Valencia and its surrounding areas have experienced a resurgence of local pride and culture. All along the middle Mediterranean Coast signs and pamphlets sport the local dialect, *valencià*, and killer **paella** and **agua de Valencia** brighten every menu. Charming **cascos antiguos** brim with small, quirky bars, while the brilliant architecture of churches and palatial abodes are converted into sleek new museums. Though Valencia and Alicante are the metropolises along the coast, party destinations such as **Benidorm** and **Sitges** attract hordes of clubhoppers looking to party on the waterfront until the break of dawn.

No matter your destination, expect the possibility of a relatively cheap stay, and plan to use both your Spanish skills and your *siesta* wisely.

greatest hits

- **GARDEN STATE OF MIND.** Alicante's got a great group of gardens where you can escape from the heat and hustle of city life (p. 313).
- **THE REST IS HISTORY.** The archaeological and art museums in Valencia might not help with your tan, but they'll make you look a lot more cultured (p. 302).

student life

Since Spaniards who work regularly take at least a month off in August, it should come as no surprise that students have even more time off, often beginning in July and going through September. And when they're off, they're off—no resumé-padding internships here. Thus, many students go down to the Costa Blanca beaches in Valencia and Alicante to enjoy the virtually rain-free weather, delicious seafood, and beautiful beaches. While on vacation, students wake up late and head to the beach, often lunching on *paella*, a dish emblematic of Spain that originated in Valencia. Watersports are available for the active types, or you can just sleep off your hangover in the sand. During the summer, the party goes all night long at the discos.

valencia ☎96

With the energy of Madrid, the warmth of Sevilla, and the artsy spunk of Barcelona, Valencia is a smaller city that combines the best of its neighbors through a mix of extremes. Layers of history unfold with a short walk through the city, whether from the almost year-round extravagant costumes and sword slinging of the Moors-and-Christians celebrations or from the menus dotted with regional dialect *valencià*, both of which are remnants from the clash of Moorish invaders and Catalan crusaders that left an indelible mark both on the city's culture and architectural landscape. Old city gates overlook the plethora of church bell towers scattered throughout the city, while incredible ever-changing street art and quirky architecture like the Art Deco theater shake up the antique charm of plazas in the **Ciutat Vella.** Winding around the northern boundary of the old city is the lush **Jardín del Turia,** and it's hard to believe that not long ago these grassy paths were instead the Río Turia, which was diverted after the river flooded the city with 2m of water in 1957. Located along its former banks is a mix of the best of the old city's artistic treasures, a young and hip university area bustling with student life, and the ultramodern, ultra-contrasting architectural marvel of the **City of the Arts and Sciences.** Despite its beauty and respectable pedigree, the town is anything but a reliquary of heartwarming buildings. Cuisine and culture are matched with incredible beaches, and oranges and Valencian tomatoes will have any produce-lover in rapture for weeks. Sticky *paella* dots nearly every table in town (as it should; Valencia is its birthplace), while flamenco fills the smallest clubs. With all of this authentic flair, be prepared to practice your Spanish—fewer tourists means fewer English menus.

ORIENTATION 

The most convenient way to enter the city is via the Metro to the **Xátiva** or **Calle Colon** Metro stations or the train to **Estación del Norte. Avenida Marqués de Sotelo** runs from the train station and **Plaza del Toros** through the **Plaça del Ajuntament,** the center of town. Taking a slight right once you get to the end of this triangle-shaped plaza will have you walking along **Calle San Vicente Martir,** leading you to the most bustling areas of town, including the center of architecture, restaurants, and tourism, **Plaza Reina.** To the left upon entering this plaza is a land of shops and pedestrians around **Plaza Doctor Collado,** and continuing inward will take you past the **Mercat Central** into the old city. Plan on bringing a map if you'll be spending time on these confusing streets. To the right upon entering Pl. Reina is **Calle Paz,** a big and bright road leading to impressively

Valencia
Campo de Beisbol
Jardín del Turia
Jardines del Real
EL CARME
CIUTAT VELLA
MERCAT CENTRAL
To (350m)
Bike Path
Pte. San José
PL. PORTAL NUEVO
C. Blanquerías
PL. SANTA MÓNICA
C. Guadalaviar
C. Cronista Rivelles
FEVE
C. Santa Amalia
C. Poeta Borda
C. Alboraya
C. Flora
To Av. Primado Reig (300m)
To Ciutat Universitaria, Av. Blasco Ibañez (500m), (1km)
Real Monasterio de la Trinidad
Museo de Bellas Artes
Cuidad De Las Artes Y Las Ciencias (3km), Palau De Música (700m),
C. San Pío V
To (100m), Estació Marítima (5km)
Pte. Serranos
Pte. de Fusta
Pte. Trinidad
PL. DE LOS FUEROS
C. Conde Trenor
Torres de Serranos
To Ivam (800m)
To Jardín Botànic (1.5km)
C. Salvador Giner
C. Padre Huérfanos
C. Moret
C. Gatellaso
C. de Roteros
C. Museo
C. Na Jordana
C. Marqués de Caro
C. Sogueros
C. Zapateros
C. Pintor Lopez
Pte. del Real
PL. SANTA CRUZ
C. Serranos
C. Navellos
C. del Salvador
C. Trinitarios
PL. POETA LLOREMÉ
PL. DEL TEMPLO
Palacio del Templo
To Ave. Del Puerto (300m), Duna Viajes (50m)
C. Ripalda
C. Sant Ramón
C. Corona
C. Alta
C. Baja
C. Salinas
Palau de la Generalitat
C. Almudín
PL. DE LA VIRGEN
Basílica Virgen dels Desamparats
C. Dr. Beltrán Bigorra
Laundry Stop
C. Pinzón
PL. VINCENTE IBORRA
C. Pintor Zariñena
C. S. Miguel
C. Caballeros
C. Alvarez
San Nicolás
PL. Blanises
C. Calatrava
Santa Iglesia Catedral de Valencia
C. Micalet
PL. DEL NEGRITO
Toledano
Miguelete Tower
C. Palau
PL. NAPOLES Y SICILIA
San Juan del Hospital
C. Viejo Gobernador
C. en Gordo
Poeta Liern
To Calle Guiem Castro (100m)
PL. TOSSAL
PL. MARQUÉS DE BUSIANOS
C. Cadires
C. Correjería
C. Bordadores
PL. DE LA REINA
C. Cabillers
C. del Milagro
C. San Cristobal
PL. SAN VICENTE FERRER
C. Ntra. Sra. Nieves
Montornes
Bonaire
C. Quart
Conquista
C. Moro Zeit
C. Bolsería
Do You Bike
C. Tundidores
C. Zurradores
C. Tapinería
C. Lonja
Iglesia de los Santos Juanes
PL. DR. COLLADO
PL. SARA CATALONA
C. Mar
C. Comedias
To (1.2km)
C. Murillo
C. Carda
Lonja de la Seda
C. Castellvins
C. Tejedores
Orange Bikes
C. en Sendra
C. Santa Teresa
C. Exarchs
PL. del Mercat
Ercilla
Iglesia Santa Catalona
C. Sombrerería
US
C. Paz
C. Tertulia
C. Pintor Domingo
C. Lope de Rueda
PL. JUAN DE VILARRASA
C. Trench
C. Cerrajeros
PL. MARIANO BENLLIURE
Palacio Marqués de Dos Aguas
C. Ruiz
C. En Sala
C. San Andrés
C. Cruz Nueva
C. de la Soledad
C. Universidad
Av. María Cristina
C. San Fernando
C. Embajador Vich
Museu de Cerámicas
Colegio de Patriarcha
Universidad
C. Carniceros
C. Pie de la Cruz
C. Balmes
Av. Barón de Carcer
C. Calabazas
C. Moratín
C. Peydro
To (8km)
C. Camarón Viana
C. Maldonado
Torno Del Hospital
C. Linterna
Ono
Iglesia de San Juan de la Cruz
C. Poeta Querol
C. Salvá
C. Pintor Sorolla
El Corte Inglés
To Amex (800m)
C. Miñana
C. Guillem Sorolla
C. Recaredo
C. Esponosa Bany
C. Escolano
C. Música Peydro
C. San Vicente Martir
Av. Marqués de Sotelo
C. Transits
C. Don Juan de Austria
C. En Lop
Grabodor Selma
C. Barcas
C. Pérez Pujol
C. Pascual y Genís
C. Sagasta
C. Pérez Bayer
C. Sangre
C. En Sanz
C. Correos
El Corte Inglés
PL. DEL AJUNTAMENT
Ayuntamiento
C. Roger de Lauria
To (100m)
C. Periodista Azzati
C. Padilla
C. Mossen Femades
C. Colón
C. Pizarro
C. Martínez Cubells
C. Convento Sta. Clara
C. de Ribera
Paseo Ruzafa
C. San Pablo
C. Quevedo
C. Félix Pizcueta
Work Station
Soriano Librerías
C. Guillem de Castro
C. Xàtiva
C. Espartero
C. Jesús
Cervantes
C. Pelayo
C. de Bailén
Estación del Norte (RENFE)
C. Alicante
To For El Salér and L'abufera (100m)
Plaza de Toros
Museo Taurino
C. Ruzafa
0 200 meters
0 200 yards

ritzy architecture and higher-end shops. Continuing straight to the end of the Pl. Reina, past the cathedral, will eventually get you to the old riverbed-now-turned-park **Jardín del Turia,** and with a right and a 3km walk (or bike or bus ride) you'll make your way along the university area to the modern marvel of the **City of Arts and Sciences.**

ACCOMMODATIONS

RED NEST HOSTEL

HOSTEL ❶

C. La Paz, 36 ☎96 342 71 68 www.nesthostelsvalencia.com

Bright and vibrant, this hostel is so popular—and rightfully so—that it has two locations within a 5min. walk. A mix of large private and dormitory-style rooms features modern decor, windows with beautiful views to the street, and even a convenient cubby for the upper bunks. The inside of the hostel is decorated like a cheery Rubik's cube, only with copious bathrooms and a fully stocked kitchen. air-conditioning in the rooms is sometimes spotty, but a huge fifth-floor lounge keeps things chilly for those afraid of melting away.

From the train station, walk along Marqués de Sotelo and follow it as it takes a slight right and turns into C. San Vicente Martir. Once you enter the Pl. Reina, take a right onto C. Paz. Red Nest is a 5-10min. walk. i Sheets included. Free Wi-Fi; computer with internet €1 per 15min. Kitchen available. Dorms €18-25; doubles €60-65. Towel and padlock deposit €5 each.

HOME BACKPACKERS HOSTEL

HOSTEL ❶

Pl. Vicente Iborra, 46 ☎96 391 37 97 www.likeathome.net

Four floors of rooms range from cozy six-person dorms to expansive 12-person jungle gyms. The social life centers on the equipped kitchen and the sunny terrace. Though the price is bare-bones, it includes everything you need—sheets, towels, Wi-Fi, and a safebox, as well as a vibrant social scene and pop-art murals to link it to its slightly more mature brother, Home Youth Hostel. Centered in the Old City, the hostel is a little bit farther from the bustling life of Pl. Reina, but this just means more authentic places and cheaper prices for those not already swayed by an entirely English-speaking staff.

From C. de Caballeros turn onto C. de San Miguel. Take the 2nd left onto C. del Doctor Beltran Bigorra and look for Home Backpackers sign. i Linens and towels included. Lockers and safety boxes available. 12-bed dorms €12.50; 6-bed €16. Reception 24hr.

HOME YOUTH HOSTEL

HOSTEL ❷

C. de la Lonja, 4 ☎96 391 62 29 www.likeathome.net

All the perks of a *pensión* (large, private rooms without having to climb up to the top bunk) with the perks of a youth hostel (a crowd that's actually fun, an equipped kitchen, and punchy decor that will amuse rather than lull you to sleep). Young and social clientele populate the funky leather chairs of the pop-art-clad living room. Rooms facing outward offer an incredible in-your-face view of the Baroque La Lonja across the street.

From the train station, walk along Av. del Marqués de Sotelo and follow it to take a slight right onto C. Vicente Martir. Take the 3rd left onto C. de los Derechos. Home Youth is located in the plaza. i Linens and towels included. Luggage storage and security boxes. Equipped kitchen available. 3- to 4-bed dorms in summer €23; in winter €15-17. Doubles €30.

HOSTAL EL CID

HOSTAL ❸

C. Cerrajeros, 13 ☎96 392 23 23 www.hostalelcid.es

Besides the charming tiled staircase leading to reception, nothing in this quaint, stylish *pensión* is befitting of the rustic plaster and dark-wood imagery that the name provokes. Homey doubles are decorated with everything from German design magazines to wire dress forms and old card catalogs. Recently transferred to new management, the hostel may be undergoing renovation in the near future.

From the train station, walk along Av. del Marqués de Sotelo and follow it to take a slight right *onto C. Vicente Martir. Take the 2nd left onto C. Cerrajeros and look for El Cid's sign. i Linens and towels included. $ Doubles €30-37, with bath €35-47. Reception 9am-7pm.*

PENSIÓN PARIS PENSIÓN ❷

C. Salvá, 12 ☎96 352 67 66 www.pensionparis.com

Sleep like you're in a crib in the large, immaculately kept rooms with a color palette befitting a cheesy baby shower at Pensión Paris. Quiet rooms with some huge corner suits (think two sets of windows) are perfect for those looking for a calm, cheap, and private refuge from the city while still being in the middle of it all.

From the train station, walk along C. Marqués de Sotelo. Take a right onto C. de las Barcas halfway through the Pl. del Ayuntament. Take a hard right onto C. del Poeta Querol at the theater and the 1st right onto C. de Miñana. Pensión Paris will be on the left, as the street dead-ends onto C. de Salvá. $ Singles €23; doubles with sink €34, with shower €40, with full bath €42; triples with sink €50, with shower €54.

RESIDENCIA ALICANTE PENSIÓN ❸

C. de Ribera, 8 ☎96 351 22 96

Standard *pensión*-style rooms with TV. Think twice before opting to pay more for a private bathroom—you might have to climb over the toilet to get to the shower.

From the train station, walk along C. Marqués de Sotelo and take the 1st right onto C. del Convento de Santa Clara. Take a left onto C. de Ribera–Residencia Alicante is located next to a busy cafe. $ Singles €25-35; doubles €35-45; triples €60.

SIGHTS

The old city and the area around **Plaza Reina** are dotted with beautiful architectural works and older sights. Lovers of early architecture should be sure to visit **La Lonja** and tour the various **churches** scattered throughout the area, all of which have free admission. The steel and ceramic wonder of the **Mercat Central,** Europe's largest food market, is not to be missed, while the city's top-rated (and dirt-cheap, often free) museums are worth the lost beach time. Of those not listed here, the **Museu de les Bells Arts** and **Ceramic Museum** are top-notch.

CIUDAD DE LAS ARTES Y LAS CIENCIAS ARCHITECTURE, MUSEUM

Av. Autopista del Saler, 1 ☎90 210 00 31 www.cac.es.

Like a set from a science-fiction film, the futuristic blue and white citadel that comprises the City of the Arts and Sciences may feel like a world away from the rest of the antique charms, winding streets, and shaded plazas of Valencia. And, in all seriousness, it is—designed almost entirely by architect Santiago Calatrava, the white near-algorithmic designs and eerily blue reflecting pool encase a 350,000 sq. m mini-city entirely of its own. The Boba Fett-helmet-esque **Palau de les Arts** begins the complex, housing opera, dance, and musical performances, and is only available with tickets to a performance or through one of their infrequently offered guided tours. Next is the eye-shaped **l'Hemispheric,** housing an IMAX theater, laser shows, and a planetarium. From here, to the left is the honeycomb-meets-postmodernism crib of the hands-on **Museu de les Ciències Princip Felipe,** while the expansive white spine of the **Umbracle** stretches along the street to the right, innocuous by day, but springing into a thriving club at night. Last but not least is Spain's largest aquarium, **L'Oceanogràfic,** with over 45,500 aquatic creatures. Prices for admission to the ocean complex are steep, but the dolphin shows are top-notch.

Bus #35 runs from near Pl. de Toros. $ Museum entrance €7.50, students and children €5.80; special exhibits €2 more. L'Hemispheric tickets €7.50, students and children €5.80. L'Oceanogràfic €23.30, students and children €17.20. Combination tickets €19-30.50; can be bought at train station through Cercanias trains or at box office. Museum open daily Sept 13-June 30 10am-7pm;

July 1-Sept 12 10am-9pm. L'Hemisphéric runs shows daily every 45-60min. 10am-midnight except during siesta (2:30-4pm). L'Oceanogràfic open in high season daily 10am-midnight. Guided tours of Palau de les Arts M-F at 11am, noon, 2pm.

SANTA IGLESIA CATEDRAL DE VALENCIA ARCHITECTURE

Pl. de la Reuina Cathedral ☎96 391 01 89, Museum ☎96 392 43 02

Though many bell towers dot the skyline of Valencia, the Catedral's 70m **Micalet** (cathedral tower) is the biggest and baddest of them all. For €2 you can make the 202-stair trek to the top and see the view from above—Victor Hugo once counted 300 bell towers from the city, and if you stick around until the top of the hour then you will get to hear them in surround sound. The Catedral itself was begun in 1238, after the original Catedral was replaced by a mosque during Muslim rule in the eighth century. Though stepping inside is free, getting an up-close view of the ornate Gothic **Capilla de Sant Caliz** will cost you. It's a small price to pay for getting up close and personal with a chalice purported to be the **Holy Grail** used by Christ at the Last Supper.

Located at the northern end of Pl. de la Reina. €4.50 (includes audio tour and museum), children and seniors €3. Tower €2, under 14 €1. Cathedral open daily 7:30am-1pm and 4:30-8:30pm. Tower open daily 10am-7pm. Museum open Mar-Nov M-Sa 10am-1pm and 4:30-7pm, Su 10am-1pm and 4:30-5:30pm. Guided visits of cathedral in high season daily 10am-6:30pm; in low season M-F 10am-5:30pm, Su 2-5:30pm.

INSTITUT VALENCIÀ D'ART MODERN (IVAM) MUSEUM

C. Guillém de Castro, 118 ☎96 386 30 00 www.ivam.es

Come see a huge amount of contemporary art for less than you'd pay to rent a towel at your hostel. Permanent galleries house a famed collection of abstract works by 20th-century sculptor Julio González and artist Ignacio Pinazo, while temporary exhibits fill the remaining galleries with avant-garde works from the 20th and 21st centuries, including sculpture, painting, video, and architectural works. Even if only a few galleries are open during your visit (which may happen—this museum's exhibits are constantly in flux), it's well worth the trip.

Leaving the Basilica, take C. Caballeros until it turns into C. Quart. Walk under the Torres de Quart and take a right down C. Guillem de Castro; the museum is on the right. Bus #5 from Pl. del Ajuntament. €2, students €1; free on Su. Open Tu-Su 10am-10pm. Library open M-Th 10am-2pm, F 10am-3pm.

PLAZA DE TOROS AND MUSEO TAURINO DE VALENCIA MUSEUM

C. Xàtiva ☎96 388 37 38 www.museotaurinovalencia.es

A permanent exhibition offers a peek both behind and in front of the scenes of Valencian bullfighting. Articles in the permanent collection range from *El Morenillo* Juan Jimenez's 1852 waistcoat to a life-size stuffed bull ready to spring into action. Look for the multilingual briefers on the history, traditions, and methods of the sport, from the training of a young *picador* to the path of a bull from birth to (possible) pardoning in the ring. If you're not planning on attending a show, sneak peeks of the ring are also offered every half hour.

ⓂXàtiva. In covered area to left of Pl. de Torros when facing the rink from C. Xátiva; museum is halfway down to the right. Free. Open Tu-Su 10am-8pm. Guided tours of bullring every 30min.

THE GREAT OUTDOORS

Beaches

Chances are if it's summer and you're in Valencia, then your hostel will empty out midday as beach bums make the pilgrimage to the city's shores. The cream-colored sand fills with white umbrellas during the peak season, with sunbathers and outdoor enthusiasts splashing in the azure water and walking, biking, and running along the boardwalk that creeps along the expansive beach. If you're planning on walking or biking to the beach, **Avenida del Puerto** runs from the riverbed to the port, after which the beach is just a few blocks north; otherwise, buses #20, 21, and 22 will drop you off seaside. *(About 15min. from city center.)* **Las Arenas** is the most popular beach and is connected by the boardwalk to **La Malvarossa,** which provides water to the sea creatures of L'Oceanogràfic in the **City of Arts and Sciences.** Although you won't get any alone time by heading the 14km south to **Salér,** the view will be much more attractive, including a beautiful pebbled beach, white sand dunes, and a calm lagoon. The **Autocares Herca** bus runs to **Salér** *(On the way to El Perello. 30min., every hr. 7am-9pm. €1-1.10, depending on destination)* from the intersection of Gran Vía de Germanías and C. Sueca. To get to the bus stop, exit the train station and take a right down C. Xàtiva, then turn right onto C. Ruzafa to Gran Vía. Look for a yellow MetroBus post. The ride to Salér can be jammed on weekends, and be sure to leave an entire day to make it worth the trip. For those adventurers seeking the beauty of Salér without the crowds, continue 10min. further on the bus for Salér and walk for another half hour along the shore—the undeveloped **La Devesa** sports a luxurious beach with a nudist section, as well as an incredible forest and lake. However, don't expect the beach bars and capitalist comforts of the city beaches—be sure to bring your own food, and be prepared to use the forest to take care of business. When looking for the return bus, look toward the intersection of the main road and the beginning of the forest trail.

Parks

JARDÍN DEL TURIA

Jardín del Turia is easy to stumble upon, wrapping around the northern portion of the old city where the river used to be before being diverted. Lined with lush grass, pedestrian paths, and stray kittens, this park is now a favorite with casual athletes and bike tours.

Just north of the cathedral.

JARDINES DEL REAL

Near the Museo de Bellas Artes and off C. Sant Pío are the Jardines del Real, with maze-like paths dotted by modern sculpture, equally abstract ponds, and a fountain resembling a big rubber ducky dedicated to Walt Disney to keep things from getting too intellectual.

Walk to the river on C. del Salvador behind the cathedral and continue to Ptg. Trinidad. Take a right onto C. Sant Pio V and enter just past the museum.

JARDÍN BOTÀNIC

C. Quart, 80 ☎96 315 68 17 www.uv.es/jardinbotanic

Jardín Botànic is the most impressive of the parks, with over 43,000 kinds of plants of 300 international species blossoming with reckless abandon. Budding horticulturists should be sure to bring along your dichotomy chart, while others can simply kick back and relax under the shade on one of their many benches.

Go left out of the Po. de Pechina, exit down Gran Vía, and take a left onto C. Quart—the gardens are on the western end of Río Turia near Gran Vía Fernando el Católico. €0.60. Open Tu-Su May-Aug 10am-9pm, Sept-Oct and Mar-Apr 10am-8pm; Nov-Feb 10am-6pm.

FOOD

Paella, paella, paella, agua de Valencia. These are the words that will be pounded into your skull as you trek the paths of the city, with large black pans of yellow rice and seafood splayed out on nearly every table and jars of the area's famed alcoholic drink being offered at every bar. If you're looking for something lighter, try grabbing some fresh fruits and veggies from the gorgeous Art Nouveau **Mercat Central,** the largest food market in Europe since 1928. *(☎96 382 91 00 Open M-Sa 6am-2:30pm.)* For **groceries,** try **El Corte Ingles** *(C. Pintor Sorolla ☎96 315 95 00)* or the smaller **Mercadona.** *(C. el Poeta Open M-Sa 9:15am-9:15pm.)*

SAGARDI

TAPAS ❷

C. San Vicente Martir, 6 ☎96 391 06 68 www.sagardi.com

Delectable Basque-inspired tapas wallpaper the bar—be prepared to fight for a seat, or join the locals and stand as you fill your plate with *pinxos*. Inventive bread-bottomed **boats** of love float into your mouth on a sea of nectarly sangria.

On San Vicente Martir on the left shortly before Pl. Reina. Pinxos €1.80. Sangria €3. Open daily 11:30am-3:30pm and 7:30pm-1:30am.

SOL I LLUNA

CAFE ❷

C. del Mar, 29 ☎96 392 22 16 www.solilluna.net

A two-story interior with A/C offers a relaxed, shabby-chic alternative to the peaceful but sunny plaza seating outside. White wooden wicker chairs and black tables provide the perfect place to take advantage of free Wi-Fi during slower hours. Delectable tapas and smaller entrees please business lunchers, while a bustling nightlife scene brings a crowd of laid-back locals. Get the falafel if it's on the menu for the day—you'll never want to eat from another kebab stand again.

Take a right onto C. del Mar from Pl. Reina when facing the cathedral from the far end near C. San Vicente Martir. Sol i Lluna is located in the small plaza. Tapas €3.50-5.50. Entrees €6.50-13.50. Midday menú half €7, full €10. Open M 2-4pm, Tu-Sa 2-4pm and 9pm-last customer.

LA LLUNA

VEGETARIAN, VALENCIAN ❷

C. San Ramón, 23 ☎96 392 21 46

A taste of traditional Valencia, *sin carne*. This tucked-away vegetarian eatery serves fresh, delicious seafood-less *paella*, gazpacho, *creama catalana*, and more to a pack of dedicated locals and map-carting travelers. A bohemian, dark-raftered interior is splattered with moon memorabilia, while the lone waiter struggles to stay afloat in the crowded sea of tables.

From Pl. Tossal in the old city, walk on C. Alta and take a left onto C. Corona. Follow C. San Ramon as it curves to the right; La Lluna is on the left. Appetizers €4-6; entrees €4-6. Dessert €3.50-4. Midday menú €7.20. Hours vary; call for weekly schedule.

ZUMERIA NATURALIA

CAFE ❶

C. del Mar, 2 ☎96 141 45 03

Incredible crepes and *bocadillos* spotlight the thing that keeps customers coming back—over 50 fresh, tasty fruit drinks are at your disposal, served in huge crystal goblets. Perfect for a light dinner. Get the night started with a smoothie mixed drink *(€5-6.50)*, and don't be surprised if you can't stop at just one. Outdoor seating on the calm street outside provides overflow for when the tightly packed wicker chairs get too full for comfort.

When facing the cathedral in Pl. Reina, C. del Mar is about halfway through the square on the right. Zumeria Naturalia is immediately on the right, tucked into the lower level on the marble facade. Look for chairs and their sign. Juices €3-4, with alcohol €5-6.50. Open M-Th 5pm-1am, F-Sa 5pm-3am, Su 5pm-midnight.

EL RALL

VALENCIAN ❸

C. Tundidores, 2 ☎96 392 20 90 www.elrall.es

A popular *paella* eatery with a lively crowd that spills out onto their secluded plaza. Rice dishes are brought out in skillets based on the size of the group, though parties of one will be left ordering a la carte. If the passing guitar and accordion players aren't properly setting the mood, intimate seating is also available inside.

From the Mercado Central, take the road to the right of Lonja de la Seda (C. Pere Compte) and follow as it becomes Estameñería Vieja. Once in the plaza, El Rall is to the right, on C. Tundidores. ***i*** *Reservations recommended. Appetizers €8.50-15; meat and fish entrees €13-16. Paella €12-15 per person (min. 2 people). Picaditas €8.50-15. Open daily 1-4:30pm and 8-11:30pm.*

LA PAPPARDELLA

ITALIAN ❸

C. Bordadores, 5 ☎96 391 89 15 www.ciciositalianos.com

A huge selection of tasty pastas from gnocchi to rigatoni, as well as the crostini-like *piadine*, offer a taste of something (comparatively) exotic in the tourist haven around Pl. de la Reina. Two levels with bright modern decor and wooden floors offer ample seating and sometimes impeccable views, though if you fight for an outdoor spot, you'll likely be serenaded by accordion songs from next door while looking out over the construction site behind the cathedral.

When facing the cathedral in Pl. Reina, take the road to the left that runs in front of the church, C. de la Correjería. The first right is C. Bordadores—turn onto it, Pappardella is on the left. ***i*** *Gluten-free options available.* ⑤ *Salads €6.80-10. Entrees €7-13. Midday menú €14.* *Open daily 2-4pm and 9pm-midnight.*

NIGHTLIFE

There is a reason why hostels are littered with bodies sleeping through the siestas during midday. Valencia's nightlife starts off late, with bars and pubs not hitting their stride until around midnight. Check the pedestrian areas around **Plaza de la Virgen** and **C. de Caballeros** for big, bright places and crowds of fellow travelers to start off the night with the region's famed *agua de Valencia*. The old city hides a plethora of smaller, quirkier bars and nightclubs, especially around **Plaza Tossal** and **Collado,** attracting hordes of clubhoppers. **Dance clubs** remain painfully empty until 1 or 2am and become packed shortly thereafter. For calmer destinations, check around plazas in the old quarter, and for some more intense action, scout out the university area around **Avinguda Blasco Ibañez.** For a list of events, check out *Valencia City (€0.50),* available at newsstands and tourist offices, and the free monthly *24/7 Valencia* available at internet cafes, tourist booths, and some hostels.

CAFE DEL DUENDE

BAR, FLAMENCO

C. Turia, 62 ☎63 045 52 89 www.cafedelduende.com

Intimate, upbeat bar dedicated to its dance and drink. This local favorite gives the best deal in town, bringing together flamenco so close you can touch the performers, a crowd that knows how to clap and sing along, and beer, all for just €7. Show up early to get a seat; otherwise, stand, stomp, and join the show.

From the center of town, take a left onto C. de Quart and a right onto C. del Turia at the Jardín Botànic. Cafe del Duende is at the far end of the garden. ***i*** *Flamenco Th-F, some Sa at 11:30pm. Distributes Alma 100 and Flama, free monthly publications about flamenco. Schedule of performances on website.* ⑤ *Flamenco show €7; includes 1 drink.* *Open Th 10pm-2:30am, F-Sa 10pm-3:30am, Su 6-11pm.*

RADIO CITY

CLUB

C. Santa Teresa, 19 ☎96 391 41 51 www.radiocityvalencia.com

One bar up front and two on the dance floor keep the youth moving to alternative American pop like Gnarls Barkley and Gorillaz with cheap mini-mojitos flowing freely. Kitschy painted tiles cover the ceiling, and a small border running around the club gives free karma sutra lessons for those looking to pick up some moves.

From the Mercado Central, take a left onto C. de Belluga across from the church. Take a right onto C. Santa Teresa. ***i*** *Flamenco Tu 11pm, Bass City W nights 12:30am.* ⑤ *€7 min. drink purchase. Cocktails €5-7. Beer €3-4.* *Open daily 10pm-2:30am.*

L'UMBRACLE TERRAZA

CLUB, BAR

Av. de Saler, 5 ☎67 166 80 00 www.umbracleterrazza.com

Nestled right next to the dazzling white and geometric modern architecture of the City of Arts and Sciences, the open-air L'Umbracle Terraza offers dazzling views of the city's unnaturally striking (and illuminated) setting. The nightclub is more than just a place to do some sightseeing—swanky white tables and chairs dot the patio, while lower couch-beds invite bedazzled guests to kick back, relax, take in some hookah, and prepare for the move to **Mya,** the bustling nightclub below.

#35 bus to City of Arts and Sciences from near Xàtiva. Located in outside garden parallel to the city. i List of events available on website. Cover €15. L'Umbracle open Apr-Sept M-Sa 11:30pm-late. Mya open daily Th-Sa 1am-later.

JOHNNY MARACAS BAR, CLUB

C. de Caballeros, 39 ☎96 391 52 66

The maracas and miniature bongos lining the bamboo walls aren't just for show—you might hear a beat from the bartenders if the feeling is right. A relaxing cave-dweller-meets-Havana-chic atmosphere that's more classy than kitsch provides a chill alternative to the often-suffocating bar dance floors elsewhere, with killer mojitos and a fish tank under your drink to sweeten the deal. Latin beats serenade drinkers every night of the week, and don't be surprised if you stumble across a salsa lesson.

From the Mercado Central, follow C. de Maria Cristina past the church and take a slight right onto C. Bolsería. At the plaza, take a right onto C. Caballeros and walk just a few seconds. Johnny Maracas is on the right before Fox Congo. Beer €3-4. Cocktails €6-7. Open M-Th 7pm-3am, F-Su 7pm-4am.

AKUARELA CLUB, BAR

Pub at C. Juan Llorens, 48; disco at Eugenia Viñes, 152 ☎96 385 93 85 www.akuarela.es

Located along Malvarrosa Beach, Akuarela isn't an easy stumble from your hostel—plan on paying for a ride to get to the party. Once you arrive on your magical steed, plan to stay the night (and morning). During the summer this party center boasts a pub, club, and a beachside party zone, and during the winter the pub and club still wait at your disposal. Four floors of dancing with remarkably classy decor, complete with bars and plush seating at each level, make for a hard but tasteful night, with a huge rooftop terrace to catch a breather. Expect a mix of every danceable music imaginable, with a focus on Spanish styles—from Valencia's own artists to electronica, R and B, and salsa.

Taxi ride to Pl. Malvarossa. i Flyer gains free entrance until 3am and €3 discounts on drinks after. No cover at pub, but 1-drink min. Free entrance to club with €7 purchase at pub; otherwise Th-Sa €13, after 3am €16. Pub open daily 6pm-3:30am. Club open Sa midnight-7:30am. Beach club open daily in summer midnight-7:30am.

BOLSERIA CAFE CAFE

C. Bolsería, 41 ☎96 391 89 03

Terraced seating hosts an upscale cafe and a chic bar by night—expect button-up shirts, shiny tops, and dismissal at the door if you're wearing a threadbare, ratty T-shirt. Dancing takes place in the nautical-themed, steel-clad, and rose-decked back room, though you will be lucky if there is standing room as the cafe gets packed later in the night.

From the Mercado Central, follow C. de Maria Cristina past the church and take a slight right onto C. Bolsería. The cafe is on the corner in the plaza. i Free agua de Valencia before 12:30am. Salsa on M, 1-drink min. Americana night on W. Beer €4.50. Cocktails €6. Open daily 7pm-3:30am.

FOX CONGO CLUB

C. Caballeros, 35 ☎96 391 85 67

Hop up onto the back benches and shimmy your hips to get the night started off right. Fox Congo fills up quick and early for those looking to get into their groove before others have stopped their barhopping. Chemically lit marble and metal walls set the stage while dancey pop plays to an open, international crowd of hostelers and locals who move to equally diverse (and sometimes clashing) rhythms.

From the Mercado Central, follow C. de Maria Cristina past the church and take a slight right onto C. Bolsería. At the plaza, take a right onto C. Caballeros and walk just a few seconds. Fox Congo is on the right. Beer €4. Cocktails €7. Open Tu-Sa 8pm-3:30am.

FESTIVALS

Like virtually any Spanish city, Valencia literally lights up during the **Fogueres de San Juan** with bonfires, fireworks, and all the other sorts of fires you can imagine. The **Semana Santa,** in the week preceding Easter, litters the city with children's theater and monks reenacting biblical scenes, while **Virgin de los Desamparados (Our Lady of the Forsaken)** (May 11) brings masses of worshippers to follow the flower-blanketed path of the Virgin Mary's likeness from the Basilica in the Plaza de la Virgen to the cathedral.

LAS FALLAS — SPRING

Spaniards love their fire, so how could a festival dedicated to San José, the patron saint of carpenters, disappoint? Reportedly following the tradition of local 16th-century carpenters to burn wood that had accumulated over the year, Valencia's citizens erect *fallas* (huge wooden cardboard and papier-mâché figures) across the city just to burn them down. The real party begins the last Sunday in February just outside of the Torres de Serranos, after which *mascletas* (fireworks displays) are shown daily at 2am in the Pl. del Ayuntamiento until the festival's conclusion. Nightly showers of light illuminate the Turia Gardens, culminating in the appropriately named *Nit del Foc* (night of fire) on March 18 and the burning of the *fallas* at midnight, ringing in San José's day with a bang.

Mar 12-19.

BATTLE OF THE TOMATOES — SUMMER

This isn't your average middle-school food fight. Now in its 65th year, the Battle of the Tomatos in nearby Buñol brings a flock of locals and travelers alike armed with goggles, strong arms, and a change of clothes. The day kicks off on the last Wednesday in August at 11am with a brave soul snatching a ham from the top of a greased pole, after which hundreds of tons of tomatoes pour from the back of a truck and the hurling begins. Parades of the city's *gigantes* (giants) and *cabezudos* (masked figures who carry a stick or pig bladder and chase people) add a regal spin to the veritable mess.

Train to Buñol from Estación del Norte. Last W in Aug.

FIESTIU DE JULIOL — SUMMER

Originally a flower and produce fair devised in 1871, Fiestiu de Juliol (July Fest) has come a long way from old ladies and fruit stands. Concerts and open-air cinema dot the city's gardens and the Palau de la Música, while regular events on beaches and parties keep the festivities rolling well into the night. Bullfights occur daily, and the festival concludes with a float-filled parade along Paseo de la Alameda and the 120-year-old *batalla dels flors* (battle of the flowers), in which young girls shower the crowd with flowers from their stately carriages.

July 8-24.

ESSENTIALS

Practicalities

- **TOURIST OFFICES:** The **Regional Office** provides information on events, lodging, and other points of interest and can also help you find a place to stay. *(C. de la Paz, 48 ☎96 398 64 22 www.comunitatvalenciana.com Open M-F 9am-8pm, Sa 10am-8pm, Su 10am-2pm.)* **Branch at Estación del Nord** *(C. Xátiva, 24 ☎96 352*

85 73 www.turisvalencia.es Open M-Sa 9am-7pm, Su 10am-2pm.) **Branch at Plaza Reina.** *(Pl. Reina, 19 ☎96 315 39 31 Open M-Sa 9am-7pm, Su 10am-2pm.)*

- **LUGGAGE STORAGE:** The **bus and train stations** provide 24hr. storage of your stuff for a small fee. *(€2.50-5, depending on size of luggage. Open daily 5am-1am.)*
- **LAUNDROMAT:** The **L@undry Stop** provides internet so you can Facebook away the hours while your clothes get clean. *(C. Baja, 17 ☎96 391 35 28 www.myspace.com/thelaundrystop i Wi-Fi available. Wash €4. Dry €3. Soap €0.50. Internet €0.50 for 20min. Open daily 9:30am-10pm.)*
- **INTERNET ACCESS:** The **Work Center** provides an entire range of services and supplies for any businessperson or rogue backpacker, from printing to pens to computer stations. *(C. Xàtiva, 19 ☎96 112 08 30 www.workcenter.es Internet access €3 per hr. Wi-Fi available. Open M-Th 24hr., F 7am-11pm, Sa 10am-2pm and 5-9pm, Su noon-2pm and 5-11pm.)*
- **POST OFFICE:** The main branch offers a step above the normal services, with Western Union and call center in a locale fit for a king. *(Pl. del Ajuntament, 24 ☎96 351 23 70 www.correos.es Open M-F 8:30am-8:30pm, Sa 9:30am-2pm.)*
- **POSTAL CODE: Center** 46002; **Renfe** 46007; **Ruzafa** 46005.

Emergency!

- **EMERGENCY NUMBERS:** ☎112 or ☎96 152 51 59.
- **POLICE:** Contact the **police** near Pg. de Alameda *(Pg. de Alameda, 17 ☎96 360 03 50 Ⓜ Alameda.)* or C. Maestre. *(C. Maestre, 2 ☎96 315 56 90 Ⓜ Avenida del Cid.)*
- **CRISIS LINES:** Call the **Red Cross Ambulance.** *(☎96 367 73 75.)*
- **LATE-NIGHT PHARMACIES: Late-night pharmacies** rotate by night—check listing in local paper *Levante (€1)* or the *farmacias de guardia* schedule posted outside any pharmacy around the Pl. de la Reina and Pl. de la Virgen. *(☎96 391 68 21)* **Info Salud** provides health info *(☎96 391 68 21).*
- **HOSPITAL/MEDICAL SERVICES:** Contact the **Hospital Clínico Universitario.** *(Av. Blasco Ibáñez, 17 ☎96 386 39 00)*

Getting There

By Plane

If you are flying to Valencia, you are probably flying on **Aena** into the **Aeropuerto de Manises/Airport of Valencia** *(☎96 159 85 00 www.aena.es)*, 8km from the city. **Bus #150** *(☎96 150 00 82)* runs between the airport and the bus station. *(€1.20. 35min., every 30min. 5:25am-11:55pm.)* The **Metro** line #3 or #5 goes straight from the airport to C. Xàtiva, on the outskirts of Valencia by the *Ajuntament.* *(€1.80.)* You can also take a **taxi** from the airport to city center. *(About €15.)*

By Train

RENFE runs from **Estación del Norte.** *(C. Xátiva, 24 ☎96 352 02 02 www.renfe.es)* Trains from: **Alicante** *(€13-28. 2hr., 11 per day 7am-9pm.)*; **Barcelona** *(€24-43. 3-5hr., every 1-2hr. 5am-8pm.)*; **Granada** *(€51. 8hr., 12:44am.)*; and **Madrid.** *(€25-48. 3½-6hr., every hr. 6:50am-8:20pm.)* Allot time to go through security.

By Bus

Take buses to the **Estación Terminal d'Autobuses.** *(Av. Menéndez Pidal, 11 ☎96 346 62 66 ✢ Across the riverbed, a 20min. walk from the city center.)* Municipal bus #8 runs from Pl. del Ajuntament and the bus station. *(Ⓢ €1.10.)* **ALSA** *(☎90 242 22 42 🖳www.alsa.es)* has bus services from **Alicante** *(Ⓢ €18-21. ⏰ 2½-5hr., every hr. 6am-9pm.)*, **Barcelona** *(Ⓢ €25-30. ⏰ 4-6hr., every 2-3hr. 7am-8pm.)*, and **Málaga** *(Ⓢ €52. ⏰ 11-13hr., 5 per day 8am-11:30pm.)*, **Autores** *(☎96 349 22 30 🖳www.auto-res.net)* goes to **Madrid.** *(Ⓢ €23. ⏰4hr., 10 per day 10:30am-3am.)*

By Ferry

Trasmediterránea offers a ferry service to Valencia. *(Muelle de Poniente ☎90 245 46 45 🖳www.trasmediterranea.es)* Take bus #4 from Pl. del Ajuntament or #1 or 2 from the bus station. Reserve through a travel agency or risk inconvenience by buying tickets at the port on the day of departure.

Getting Around

For complete information and routes for Valencia's public transportation, contact the **Municipal Transport of Valencia (EMT) Office.** *(Pl. Correo Viejo, 5 ☎96 315 85 15; 96 315 85 25 🖳www.emtvalencia.es ⏰ Open M-F 9am-2pm and 4:30-7:30pm.)*

By Bus

Bus schedules depend on day and route. The **tourist routes** are 5, 5B, 25, and 95, while **Bus #8** *(⏰ Every 9-11min. 6am-10:30pm.)* runs to the bus station. Buses #20, 21, and 22 *(⏰ Every 10-12 min. 9am-8:40pm.)* go to **Las Arenas** and **Malvarrosa** along Pg. Marítim. Buy tickets *(€1.25)* on board or a one-day pass at newsstands *(€3.50)*. **Late-night buses** N1, N2, N3, N4, N5, N6, and N7 go through **Pl. del Ajuntament** *(⏰ Every 45 min. M-W 11pm-1am, Th-Sa 11pm-3am, Su 11pm-1am.)*

By Metro

The Metro *(Pl. de Xirivelleta ☎96 397 40 40 🖳www.metrovalencia.com)* service loops around the *casco antiguo* (old quarter) and into the outskirts. The most central stop is on C. Xàtiva across the street from the train station or on C. Colón by El Corte Inglés. Buy tickets from machines in any station. *(Ⓢ €1.25-1.70 depending on distance. 10-ride pass €7.45-10.)*

By Taxi

Contact **Radio Taxi** *(☎96 370 33 33)*, **Tele Taxi** *(☎96 357 13 13)*, **Onda Taxi** *(☎96 347 52 52)*, and **Buscataxi** *(☎90 274 77 47)* for pickup and rates.

By Bike

Rent bikes from **Orange Bikes** *(C. Santa Teresa, 8 ☎96 391 75 51 🖳www.orangebikes.net ✢ From the main entrance of the Mercado Central, walk down Av. María Cristina away from Pl. Ajuntamiento and turn down the 2nd street, continuing on to the end. From Pl. de la Virgen, take C. Caballeros until it turns into C. Santa Teresa. Ⓢ Bikes €9-12 per day, €45-55 per week. ⏰ Open M-F 9:30am-2:30pm and 4:30-8pm, Sa 10am-2pm and 7-7:30pm.)* or **Doyoubike** *(Corner of C. Musico Magenti and Puebla Larga ☎96 337 40 24 🖳www.doyoubike.com Ⓢ M-Th €2 per hr., €10 per day, F-Su €4 per hr., €15 per day. Weekend €25, week €40.)*

alicante ☎96

The most iconic image of Alicante—the craggy Castillo Santa Barbara rising above the bustling nightlife and brilliant beaches of the modern city—is also the reason Alicante's become such a huge tourist destination. Surrounding mountains and lush pine forests make an outdoorsy complement to lazy days in the sand, while loads of free museums and attractions grab those looking to pack up their beach bags and beat the heat—the only site that charges admission is the world-famous **MARQ,** which is well worth the €3 price tag.

Just after sunset, the streets in the old city teem with groups of young things crawling to fill restaurants, cozy bars, and hopping clubs, while the bright *discotecas* of the port fill with tourists and locals as the night marches on. Though a busy party and sunbathing destination in its own right, Alicante has also become the home base for those looking to tap all of the summer resources of the **Costa Blanca,** or "White Coast," that stretches from Dènia to Alicante, named for the color of the fine sand that pads its shores. While the other towns along the water, such as Altea and Dénia, make for more relaxed, secluded, and clean beachgoing, Alicante boasts cheap, sometimes quirky, and incredibly social accommodations just a short TRAM ride away that trump the rising prices of those developing resort destinations.

ORIENTATION

For those traveling from afar, trains arrive at the **Estación Central,** located on the western edge of the city on **Avenida Salamanca.** A short walk down this road will take you to **Plaza Luceros,** which intersects with **Avenida Federico Soto,** which runs straight to the beach (becoming **Avenida Doctor Gadea** near the water) and close to the **bus station** on C. Portugal. Continuing straight through Pl. Luceros will have you walking along **Avenida Alfonso X el Sabio,** the main artery of the city. Walking 10-15min. will drop you off in front of the Mercat Central and **TRAM Station** (where trains from Costa Blanca arrive), while a right just past the market onto **Rambla Méndez Núñez,** known simply as La Rambla, provides a plethora of huge shops and restaurants as well as easy access to the cozier and more interesting options of the *casco antiguo.* If you decide to take the pedestrian **C. Casaños** between La Rambla and Av. Frederico Soto, a world of ritzy restaurants awaits, with cheap shops and food located on any of the side streets. If sand and sun is your destination, the red marble floors and shop-laden path of the **Explanada d'Espanya** run nearly 2km across the port, linking the **Parque de las Canalejas** to the beach and providing access to the looming **Castillo Santa Barbara's** elevator.

ACCOMMODATIONS

Quality hostels and pensions with good prices abound in the *casco antiguo*—if you feel overwhelmed by the selection, stop by the tourist office to get an extensive brochure on accommodations in the area. If you have a specific place in mind, be sure to book at least a week ahead of time, as the appeal of sandy beaches fills up the better hostels during the summer months. If arriving during the **Fogueres de Sant Joan** *(June 18-25),* be sure to book well in advance or risk sleeping on the beach.

PENSIÓN VERSAILLES — PENSIÓN ❷

C. Villavieja, 3 — ☎96 521 47 93, 96 532 98 00

A laid-back, beach-appropriate tropical paradise just minutes from the water and in the heart of the old city's bumping nightlife. Pensión Versailles mixes the two perfectly—12 quirky, bare-bones rooms sport bright, breezy decor while lacking work-related things like outlets. A communal kitchen and gorgeous open terrace contribute to a family feel, with an owner that seems more like a fun-loving grandpa than a business owner. Like any family arrangement, he'll be sure to know your name before you leave (and will be sure to greet you by it when you return on your next trip).

From La Rambla, walk toward the mountain on C. San Isidro and follow it as it becomes C. San Pascua and then C. Villavieja; it's on your left. ***i*** *Linens and towels included. Free Wi-Fi, but it doesn't often work. Free internet.* *4-bed dorms €23; singles €25; doubles €50.* *Terrace open until midnight.*

HOSTAL LES MONGES PALACE — HOSTAL ❸

C. San Agostín, 4 — ☎96 521 50 46 www.lesmonges.es

With a name like "Les Monges Palace," you should expect nothing less than palatial, and that's exactly what Les Monges provides. Chic rooms with modern

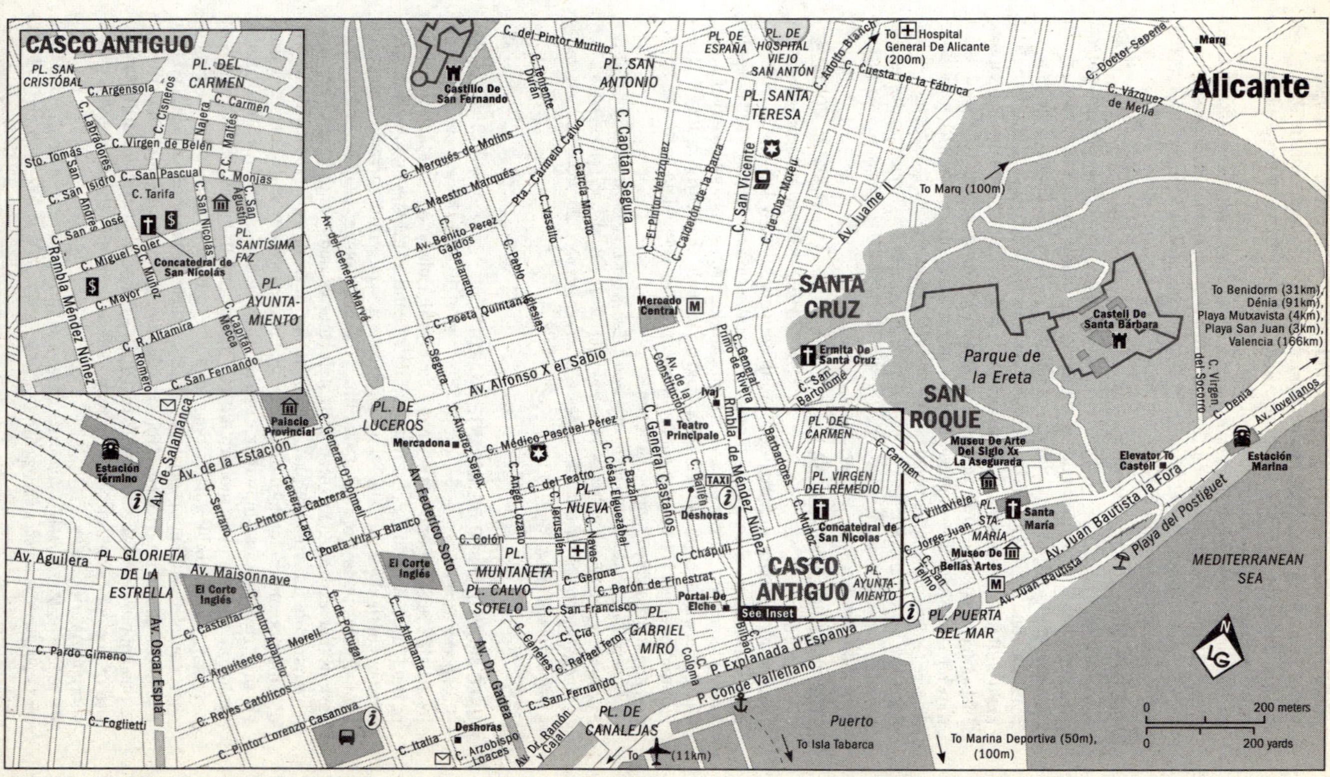
Alicante
CASCO ANTIGUO
PL. SAN CRISTÓBAL
PL. DEL CARMEN
C. Argensola
C. Cisneros
C. Carmen
Najera
C. Maltés
C. Labradores
Sto. Tomás
C. Virgen de Belén
San Andrés
C. San Isidro
C. San Pascual
C. Monjas
C. Tarifa
C. San Agustín
C. San José
C. San Nicolás
PL. SANTÍSIMA FAZ
C. Miguel Soler
Concatedral de San Nicolás
C. Muñoz
Rambla Méndez Núñez
C. Mayor
PL. AYUNTA-MIENTO
C. Capitán Mecca
C. R. Altamira
Romero
C. San Fernando
Castillo De San Fernando
C. del Pintor Murillo
PL. SAN ANTONIO
PL. DE ESPAÑA
PL. DE HOSPITAL VIEJO SAN ANTÓN
PL. SANTA TERESA
C. Adolfo Blanch
To Hospital General De Alicante (200m)
C. Cuesta de la Fábrica
C. Doctor Sapena
C. Vázquez de Mella
Marq
To Marq (100m)
C. Teniente Durán
C. Marqués de Molins
C. Maestro Marqués
Pta. Carmelo Calvo
C. Vasallo
C. García Morato
C. Capitán Segura
C. El Pintor Velázquez
C. Calderón de la Barca
C. San Vicente
C. de Díaz Moreu
Av. Juame II
Av. Benito Perez Galdos
C. Belaneto
C. Pablo Iglesias
C. Poeta Quintana
Av. del General Marvá
Mercado Central
SANTA CRUZ
Ermita De Santa Cruz
C. San Bartolomé
Castell De Santa Bárbara
Parque de la Ereta
SAN ROQUE
C. Virgen del Socorro
C. Denia
Av. Jovellanos
To Benidorm (31km), Dénia (91km), Playa Mutxavista (4km), Playa San Juan (3km), Valencia (166km)
C. General Primo de Rivera
Av. de la Constitución
Ivaj
C. Segura
Av. Alfonso X el Sabio
PL. DE LUCEROS
Teatro Principale
Rmbla. de Méndez Núñez
PL. DEL CARMEN
Barbadores
C. Carmen
Museu De Arte Del Siglo Xx La Asegurada
Elevator To Castell
Estación Marina
Palacio Provincial
Mercadona
C. Álvarez Sereix
C. Médico Pascual Pérez
C. General Castaños
PL. VIRGEN DEL REMEDIO
C. Muñoz
Concatedral de San Nicolás
C. Villavieja
PL. STA. MARÍA
Santa María
Av. Juan Bautista la Fora
Playa del Postiguet
Estación Término
Av. de Salamanca
Av. de la Estación
C. Serrano
C. General Lacy
C. Pintor Cabrera
C. General O'Donnell
Av. Federico Soto
C. Ángel Lozano
C. del Teatro
C. César Elguezábal
C. Bazán
C. Bailén
Deshoras
PL. NUEVA
C. Jerusalén
C. Navas
C. Chápuli
C. Jorge Juan
C. San Telmo
Museo De Bellas Artes
C. Poeta Vila y Blanco
C. Colón
PL. MUNTAÑETA
C. Gerona
C. Barón de Finestrat
Portal De Elche
CASCO ANTIGUO
PL. AYUNTA-MIENTO
See Inset
Av. Juan Bautista
MEDITERRANEAN SEA
Av. Aguilera
PL. GLORIETA DE LA ESTRELLA
Av. Maisonnave
El Corte Inglés
PL. CALVO SOTELO
C. San Francisco
PL. GABRIEL MIRÓ
C. Cid
C. Bilbao
PL. PUERTA DEL MAR
C. Castellar
C. Pintor Aparicio
C. de Portugal
C. de Alemania
C. Canelles
C. Rafael Terol
C. Coloma
P. Explanada d'Espanya
C. Pardo Gimeno
Av. Oscar Esplá
C. Arquitecto Morell
C. Reyes Católicos
Av. Dr. Gadea
C. San Fernando
P. Conde Vallellano
Puerto
C. Foglietti
C. Pintor Lorenzo Casanova
C. Italia
Deshoras
C. Arzobispo Loaces
Av. Dr. Ramón y Cajal
PL. DE CANALEJAS
To (11km)
To Isla Tabarca
To Marina Deportiva (50m), (100m)
0
200 meters
0
200 yards

decor, low Japanese-style beds, and anti-kitsch wicker furniture make for a world away from the ascetic monastery it faces. All rooms include A/C, plush towels, and sleek TVs, and for those willing to splurge, two of the doubles even come with an ensuite sauna and hot tub.

From La Rambla, walk toward the mountain on C. San Isidro and follow it as it becomes C. San Pascual. The hostal is on the corner of C. San Pascual and C. San Agostin. ***i*** *Continental breakfast €6. Towels included. Internet €3 per hr.* *Singles €36; doubles €52, with private bath €59, with sauna and hot tub €98; triples €68, with bath €70.* *Reception 24hr.*

CALDERON 41

HOSTEL ❶

C. Calderon, 41 www.hostelworld.com

You get what you pay for, and, considering the comfy beds, clean rooms, and pleasant, youthful decor, Calderon is allowed to have its faults. A helpful, accommodating staff will lend you whatever they lack, whether a hotplate for a makeshift kitchen, a spot in their room to store your bag, or time on their laptop. Just don't expect them to make another shower magically appear—one is all they have for the whole hostel—and be sure to insist on a room with a window.

Face the front of the Mercado and take the road that runs to its left (C. Calderón de la Barca). Follow as it bends to the right and continue walking until just before the Pl. Espanya. The hostel is behind an unmarked door immediately after the casino Calderon 41. ***i*** *Linens included. Luggage storage available. Free Wi-Fi.* *Dorms €15.*

HOSTAL-PENSIÓN LA MILAGROSA

HOSTAL ❶

C. Villavieja, 8 ☎96 521 69 18 www.hostallamilagrosa.com

Pristine rooms with minimal decoration (hope you enjoy looking at yourself; only a mirror serves to spruce things up), but the view speaks for itself—ask for a room facing the Baroque Basilica Santa Maria. Even if you don't get your pick, you can always scope out the view (and a fantastic shot of the craggy fortress looming overhead) from the roomy rooftop terrace, complete with sun, shade, and an impressively equipped kitchen.

From La Rambla, walk toward the mountain on C. San Isidro and follow it as it becomes C. San Pascua and then C. Villavieja; the hostel is on your right. ***i*** *Towels included. Laundry wash €3, dry €2. Kitchen and terrace available.* *Singles €20, with private bath €30; doubles €35/45; triples €45/60; 2-person apartment €60.* *Reception 24hr.*

SIGHTS

MUSEO ARQUEOLÓGICO DE ALICANTE (MARQ)

MUSEUM

Pl. del Doctor Gómez Ulla ☎96 514 90 00 www.marqalicante.com

Inside this pristine and expansive villa lays the ultramodern exhibition halls of the Museo Arqueológico Provincial de Alicante (MARQ)—named European Museum of the Year in 2004. Step inside to see the beautifully arranged and catalogued collections from the Paleolithic, Iberian, Roman, Islamic, and modern periods that are brought to life with tasteful murals, audio, and videos. More than a moratorium for a distant past, the MARQ includes informative and interactive dioramas on methodology and the practice of archaeology, transporting visitors via time capsule to a shipwreck, through the years of a church's architectural evolution, and even to a modern dig site. Temporary traveling exhibits give you a reason to keep coming back. Snag an audio tour for a comprehensive experience, complete with appropriately dramatic music, or tag along on a guided tour if your *castellano* is up to par. If the fake dig sites have struck your fancy, arrange to head out to one of the museum's real ones—tickets to nearby **Tossal de Manises,** site of ancient Lucentum, come cheap, and the realm of the ancients is just a short TRAM ride away.

Take the TRAM to the MARQ stop for the museum and to Lucentum for the dig site. ***i*** *Tickets can be purchased in advance through ServiCAM (☎90 244 43 00 www.servicam.com).* *€3,* students €1.50. Tossal entrance €2, students €1.20. Combined MARQ-Tossal entrance €4; good for 1 month. Guided tour €1.50. Museum open July-Aug Tu-Sa 11am-2pm and 6pm-midnight, Su 11am-2pm; Sept-June 15 Tu-Sa 10am-7pm, Su 10am-2pm. Tossal open June 16-Sept 14 Tu-Sa 9am-noon and 7-10pm, Su 9am-noon; Sept 18-June 15 Tu-Sa 10am-2pm and 4-6pm, Su 10am-2pm.*

MUSEO DEL BELLES ARTES GRAVINA (MUBAG) — MUSEUM

C. Gravina, 13-15 ☎96 514 67 80 www.mubag.org

The 18th-century Palacio Gravina has housed the Museo del Belles Artes Gravina (MUBAG) since the palace's restoration in 2001. Two floors house over 500 paintings, sculpture, drawings, and ephemera from the 2000-piece collection of the local *Diputación* (provincial council) from in and around Alicante. High ceilings and dark-wood floors organized around a grand central staircase play host to occasional concerts and more informal exhibits, while the upper two floors house the real goods. Up one set of stairs will land you among religious works, portraiture, and lots of still-lifes from the 16th to 19th centuries, while the upper floor houses the modern collection, often featuring temporary themed exhibits. Nestled in between the Postiguet city walls and the Santa Maria basilica, the museum is just a short walk from the heart of the *barrio*, and the price (free) can't be beat. Sacrifice an hour or two at the beach to soak in some local culture from the time before tourists flocked to the umbrella-ed shore.

Walk along the Esplanade toward the castle. Take a left onto the road right after the Luxembourg Consulate and a right onto the next road, C. Gravina. The museum is on the left. Free. Open May-Sept Tu-Sa 10am-2pm and 5-9pm, Su 10am-2pm; Oct-Apr Tu-Sa 10am-2pm and 4-8pm, Su 10am-2pm.

CASTILLO SANTA BARBARA — CASTLE

☎96 516 21 28

Perched above the city, the Castillo Santa Barbara may be one of two castles in the city, but it's the only one you'll remember after you leave. Although the structure as a whole dates as far back as the 10th century under Moorish rule, the primary portions visitable today were constructed in the 15th century and have seen their fair share of conflict since, including a damaging blow during the Spanish Civil War that threatened to tumble its now-flag-bearing side off the mountain. Today, the castle itself offers breathtaking panoramic views of the city and the devastatingly blue water, with the cannon-sprinkled top offering the best comprehensive panorama over the narrow streets and stony plazas of the *casco antiguo*. A more direct route to the top is the sometimes functioning elevator located just across from Postiguet Beach. However, if you make the climb to the top, a splattering of cafes and a museum exhibit await to provide some shade, sustenance, hydration, and maybe even a stiff drink.

Walk along the Esplanade along the beach to reach the elevator (on the left), or climb to the top via the pedestrian path that snakes up the mountain. Free. Open Apr-Sept daily 10am-10pm with elevator running 10am-7:40pm, last ride up 7:20pm; Oct-Mar daily 10am-8pm with elevator running 10am-7:40pm, last ride up 7:20pm; exhibition halls open daily 10am-2:30pm and 4-8pm.

BEACHES

Alicante's **Playa del Postiguet** is just a stumble away from the *casco antiguo*, located directly across from the Ajuntament and running by the base of the mountain. The picturesque beach is a fan favorite and always crowded during the summer months, but it's usually possible to find a spot to plant your umbrella. Restaurants, ice cream shops, and makeshift tents line the Esplanada just minutes away, leaving the consumer world at the fingertips of swimmers and sunbathers. To get a little further away from civilization (and the crowds and litter that accompany it), consider taking the TRAM out to the more tranquil **Playa de Sant Joan** or **Playa del Mutxavista.** (*For Playa* *de Sant Joan or Playa del Mutxavista, take the TRAM to the stops of the same name. Runs every 20min. in summer; every hr. in winter. €1.20.)*

FOOD

RESTAURANTE VILLAHEMY — VALENCIAN ❸

C. Major, 37 ☎96 521 25 29 www.villahemy.com

With an interior this loud, an eatery needs to cook up some serious cuisine for the bite to match up to the bark. Luckily, Villahemy follows through (and then some)—their daily *menú* will have you wishing you'd taken it easy on the bread beforehand, with delectable, mind-blowing specialties including cold melon soup, *paella*, and the local favorite—*bacalao*.

From La Rambla, turn onto C. Major, a few blocks away from the water. Restaurant is right after the plaza. Appetizers €5-10.50; entrees €10-18. Menú midday on weekdays €11, midday on weekends €13, nights €15. Open Tu-Sa 1-4pm and 8pm-midnight, Su 1-4pm.

KEBAP — KEBAB ❶

Av. Dr. Gadea, 5 ☎96 514 10 20

Chances are, if you've been traveling, you've probably succumbed to questionable döner kebabs for a cheap meal, and Kebap manages to right these wrongs in one fell swoop. Seriously fresh ingredients make for huge, tasty wraps with perfect ergonomics for the haul. Though locations are scattered throughout the city, the one right next to the port is the most welcoming, with a kitschy neon sign and a lush, warm interior.

Walk down Av. Federico Soto or Av. Dr. Gadea toward the sea. Kebap is near the start of the boulevard. Other location at C. San Fernando, 12. Salads €2.90-3.40. Appetizers €2.90-4.20; entrees €5-7.30. Wraps €3-3.50. Open daily 1:30-4pm and 8pm-midnight.

LA BARRA DE CÉSAR ANCA — TAPAS ❷

Pl. Gabriel Miró at C. Ojeda ☎96 520 15 80

La Barra de César Anca pleases fat and slim wallets alike—snag some cheap *pinxos (€1.50)* to fill up before ordering one of their signature tapas. Inventive dishes like artichoke stuffed with cuttlefish in their ink with garlic aioli, or tart apple *millefeuilles* with foie, smoked cod, and goat cheese *(both €3.90)* are artfully served on little slate tablets, a step above the normal white plate. Locals and tastefully dressed beachgoers fill its lively bar below, while seating above caters to those desiring a more reserved setting.

Walk down Av. de Frederico Soto or Av. Dr. Gadea toward the water and take a left onto C. del Cid. Take a right to enter Pl. Gabriel Miró; the restaurant is on the side closest to the water. Pinxos €1.50. Appetizers €6.50-12.50; entrees €8.50-10. Inventive tapas €3.75-8.50. Open M 1-4pm, Tu-W 1-4pm and 9-11pm, Th-Sa 1-4pm and 9pm-midnight.

MAMMA LOLA — ITALIAN ❸

C. Castaños, 16 ☎96 514 40 69 www.restaurantemammalola.es

Of the ritzy restaurants lining the pedestrian C. Castaños, Mamma Lola will give you the most chic for your money, with a tiered interior of bright wood, stone walls, lush couches, and exposed duct work. The loving Mamma herself keeps watch over waiters serving fresh, mouthwatering gourmet pasta, pizza, and salad.

Walk toward the water on La Rambla and take a right onto C. de Girona about halfway down. Take another right onto the pedestrian C. Castaños. Appetizers €5-11; entrees €10-18. Salads €9-13. Open M-Th 8-11:30pm, F-Sa 8pm-12:30am, Su 8pm-11:30pm.

TABERNA IBÉRICA — VALENCIAN ❷

C. Toledo, 18 ☎96 521 62 58 www.tabernaiberica.com

If you're going to be surrounded by Valencian cuisine, why not visit some place that does it justice? This mom and pop (or grandmom and grandpop) bodega serves authentic local favorites with quality ingredients that put the picture-menu restaurants lining La Rambla to shame. If you can manage to catch it open (there are few advantages to restaurant chains, but regular hours seem to be one of them), plan to part your way through gossipy older locals.

Where the two prongs form to make La Rambla, walk toward the mountain on C. de Argensola. Follow around the base and walk down the narrow stairs of C. de Toledo; Taberna Ibérica is on the right. Tapas €2-8. Paella €6. Menú €14. Open Tu-W noon-6pm, Th-Sa noon-4pm and 8pm-midnight, Su noon-last customer.

LIZARRAN TAPAS ❶

La Rambla, 18 ☎96 520 68 30 www.lizarran.es

For the indecisive, Lizarra's 300 different types of *pinxos* and tapas can either serve as a panic-attack-inducer or a godsend. The ambience is lacking—think warm orange walls scattered with farming memorabilia, with lots of tourists to top it off—but at least you're almost guaranteed a seat in its expansive interior. Waiters whip around trays of savory tapas, or you can snag your own at the bar. Branches exist throughout the city and offer a cheap option for when you're sick of *bocadillos* and kebab.

Located on La Rambla about halfway between Av. Alfonso X el Sabio and the water. Pinxos €1.25-1.50. Beer €1.70. Open daily 1pm-midnight.

NIGHTLIFE

The most popular area in the evenings is **El Barrio,** a spot full of crooked pedestrian-filled streets between La Rambla and the base of the mountain in the *casco antiguo.* Intimate bars and enormous clubs pack nearly every street as confused hordes of foreign clubhoppers fill whatever place suits their fancy for the night. Interestingly, a ragingly popular place one night may be embarrassingly empty the next.

Bars get bigger and brighter as you near the water, with a range of restaurants and bars with floor-to-ceiling windows lining the tent-lined Esplanade after sunset. To the left of the **Port** at the water's edge sits a huge complex of bars and raging *discotecas,* almost all of which don't charge a cover (though some may require a minimum order). Though it's mostly a top destination on weekends, a decent following fills the places that remain open during weekdays as well. Plan to show up late—most places don't get moving until 2am.

EL COSCORRÓN BAR

C. Tarifa, 2 ☎96 521 27 27

Head through the miniature door and past the padded rafter (there's a good reason why the bar is named after the Spanish word for "bump on the head") and into this den that time seems to have forgotten. Cave-painting-like graffiti covers every possible surface, from windowsills to plaster to cigarette machines, and jazz flows over two floors of buzzing chatter. Grab one of their mojitos *(€3)* from the mint-stuffed watering can—just be sure to ask for some sugar if you fear sour pucker.

From La Rambla facing the water, take a left onto C. San José and another left onto the narrow C. Tarifa. Coscorrón is the miniature door to the left. Beer €2. Mojitos €3. Cocktails €5-6. Open daily 7pm-last customer.

ARTESPIRITU BAR

C. Labradores, 26 ☎67 501 99 94

Since you'll probably trip over their sea of outdoor seating while swimming from C. Labaradores to Pl. San Cristobal, you may as well pull up a seat while they're free. A crowd of locals sporting tattoos and Chelsea cuts fill this bohemian joint as reggae and groove hits play over the stereo. Drink specials for students draw in bar crawlers early, with dancing erupting later in the night.

Take a left when facing the water where La Rambla joins with C. Tomas Lopez Torregrosa to enter the plaza. Artespiritu is up the stairs and to the right on C. Labradores. Teas €2. Beer

€3, students 1L for €3.50. Cocktails €5. Open daily 10am-4am.

ASTRONÓMO CLUB, BAR

C. Virgen de Belén at C. Padre Maltés ☎96 514 35 22

Spanish pop, dance, and electronica pound through two floors in this ever-popular club in the *casco antiguo.* Although crowds can be unpredictable in the area, Astrónomo is a safe bet. Recharge with a Red Bull and vodka at their chill gated terrace across the street, filled with little tables and wrapped in greenery.

Walking along La Rambla toward the sea, take a left onto C. Miguel Soler to run by the Cathedral of Saint Nicolas. Continue and take the left at the elbow, then take the 1st right and the 1st left onto C. Padre Maltés. Beer €3. Cocktails €5-8. Open Th-Sa 11pm-4am.

LA BIBLIOTECA CLUB

C. Muelle de Poniente, 6

One of the many nightlife hotspots in the port's Panoramis complex, La Biblioteca packs its three floors with college students that have put away the books for the night to dance to a mix of Spanish pop, reggaeton, and electronica. If you show up too late, be prepared to perform a canonization-worthy miracle to get to the bar—shoving through the stifling crowds will be more difficult than trying to part the Red Sea.

Face the sea and walk along the Esplanade to the right until reaching the port. Located within the huge Panoramis complex. Beer €4. Cocktails €5-6. Open F-Sa midnight-6am.

JOPLIN BAR

C. Tarifa, 7

Work your way through the crowd lining the little path in front of this small alternative club and its saucy sister La Jarana. A disco ball sprinkles light over a crowd of music-loving youth, and upstairs past a mural of the bar's namesake, Janis Joplin, is another more sparsely populated bar—perfect for chatting about that killer show you just missed. A mix of '60s, pop, rock, hip hop, and whatever else strikes the bartender's fancy, spins throughout the night.

From La Rambla facing the water, take a left onto C. San José and another left onto the narrow C. Tarifa. Beer €2-3. Cocktails €4-6. Open daily 10pm-3am.

LA JARANA BAR

C. Tarifa, 9

Stop into this little bar on any night of the week and you might find Latin beats, body paint, fake dreads, or some mix of the three. A brightly muraled *mestizaje*, or meeting point, La Jarana boasts a small crew dedicated to dancing in a decor unabashedly geared toward the younger set.

From La Rambla facing the water, take a left onto C. San José and another left onto the narrow C. Tarifa. i Samba Th 11pm. Beer €2-3. Cocktails €4-6. Open daily 10pm-3am.

ROUTE 66 BAR

C. Labradores, 5 www.facebook.com/routesixtysixbarrio

Though a far cry from the tough-as-nails biker bar it half-heartedly attempts to emulate, this small bar offers a hard-rock alternative to the pop and electronica of surrounding bars. The eagle-clad walls and vintage advertisements mimic the legendary badboy trail that gives the bar its name, with black-haired bartenders singing along to alt rock hits providing the entertainment until barhopping travelers start to trickle in.

Take a left when facing the water where La Rambla joins with C. Tomas Lopez Torregrosa to enter the plaza. Walk up the stairs and take a right onto C. Labradores. Beer €2. Mojitos €3. Cocktails €5. Open M-Th 4pm-3am, F-Sa 4pm-4am, Su 4pm-3am.

UNDERGROUND BAR

C. Padre Maltés, 2

Out of the ashes of reggae bar Marley rose Underground, *casco antiguo's* den-like home to house and trance. A miniscule dance floor lets you get up close and intimate, and the music will never leave you looking for a dance partner.

Walking along La Rambla toward the sea, take a left onto C. Miguel Soler to run by the Cathedral of Saint Nicolas. Continue and take the left at the elbow, then take the 1st right and the 1st left, near Astronomo's beer garden. Underground is on the right. Beer €2. Cocktails €5. Open M-Th 10pm-3am, F-Sa 10pm-4am, Su 10pm-3am.

FESTIVALS

MOORS AND CHRISTIANS — SPRING, SUMMER

Though Alicante is not the only city in Spain to celebrate the *Reconquista*, its almost endless festivities make it one of the best. Each district throws its own festival throughout the months between March and August, with the largest taking place in mid-June in the San Blas district. Townspeople don elaborate period dress and take up arms, fireworks, and their skirts for a reenactment of the capture of the castle, with parades, parties, and feasts filling the streets before the dust even settles.

FOGUERES DE SANT JOAN — FALL

Pyromaniacs delight in Alicante's Fogeres de San Joan, as fireworks, firecrackers, bonfires, and effigies on fire light the streets, plazas, and beaches. The city prepares itself starting September 20, with a parade in traditional clothing to start off the festivities. Daily firework shows in the Plaza de los Luceros *(2pm)* prep the crowd until the arrival of the evening of September 23, when locals and internationals take part in parades and gorge themselves on open-air feasts. With stuffed tummies and a good buzz, the crowds gather to watch midnight fireworks displayed atop Mt. Benacantil, and then they come to watch the *cremàs* (giant bonfires) in Pl. de Ayuntamiento burn the *fogueras* (giant papier-mâché creatures). After some serious pyrotechnics, the drunken masses move to the beach for the *banyà* (group swim) before partying until sunrise.

Sept 20-23.

LA VIRGEN DEL REMEDIO — SUMMER

On August 5, the city joins to celebrate their matron saint, la Virgen del Remedio (Our Lady of Remedy), with parades and music. Festivities are kicked off on August 3, with the *Alborada*, a traditional choral concert.

Aug 3-5.

ESSENTIALS

Practicalities

- **TOURIST OFFICES:** The **Main Tourism Office-Bus Station** provides tourist information, including brochures and event guides. *(Estación de Autobuses, C. Portugal, 17 ☎96 592 98 02 www.alicanteturismo.com i Other branches by Esplanada d'Espanya and Playa San Juan. Open M-F 9am-2pm and 5-8pm, Sa 10am-2pm.)* For more information, check with **Tourist Info Rambla** *(Rambla Méndez Núñez, 23 ☎96 520 00 00 Open M-F 9am-8pm, Sa 10am-8pm, Su 10am-2pm.)*, **Tourist Info RENFE** *(Estación de Tren RENFE, Av. Salamanca ☎96 513 56 33 Open M-F 9am-2pm and 5-8pm, Sa 10am-2pm.)*, and **Tourist Info Airport.** *(At the Airport ☎96 528 50 11 Open M 9am-3pm, Tu-F 9am-8pm, Sa 10am-8pm.)*
- **LUGGAGE STORAGE:** *(C. Portugal, 17 ☎96 510 72 00. At the bus station. €4-8 per bag. Open daily 8am-9pm.)*
- **INTERNET:** **Internet Cafe Xplorer** provides access to 30 computers, printing, fax, Skype, and breakfast. *(C. San Vicente, 47 ☎96 521 46 24 €0.70 per 30min. Open daily 10am-2am.)*

- **POST OFFICE:** *(C. Bono Guarner, 2 ☎96 522 78 71 www.correos.es* ***i*** *Branch on corner of C. Arzobispo Loaces and C. Alemania ☎96 513 18 87 Open M-F 8:30am-8:30pm, Sa 9:30am-1pm.)*
- **POSTAL CODE:** 03002.

Emergency!

- **POLICE:** *(Av. Julián Besteiro, 15; C. Médico Pascual Pérez, 21 ☎091; 96 510 72 00.)*
- **CRISIS LINES: Red Cross.** *(☎96 525 25 25)* **Hope Hotline.** *(☎96 513 11 22)*
- **HOSPITAL/MEDICAL SERVICES: Hospital General.** *(C. Maestro Alonso, 109 ☎96 593 83 00 www.dep19.san.gva.es)* **Emergency Medical Services.** *(☎96 524 76 00)*

Getting There

By Plane

If you are flying, you will land at the **Aeroport Internacional de El Altet** *(☎96 691 91 00, 96 691 94 00 www.aena.es)*, 11km south of the city center. **Iberia** *(☎90 240 05 00)* and **Air Europa** *(☎90 240 15 01)* have daily flights from **Madrid, Barcelona,** and the **Islas Baleares,** among other destinations. **Alcoyana** *(☎96 526 84 00)* bus #C-6 runs to the airport from Pl. Luceros. *(€1.20. Every 40min.)* Buses also leave from Pl. Puerta Mar.

By Train

RENFE trains run from Estación Central *(Av. de Salamanca ☎90 224 02 02 www.renfe.es Open daily 7am-midnight.)* to **Barcelona** *(€50-55. 5-5½hr., every 1-2hr. 7am-6:20pm.)*, **Madrid** *(€44.70. 4hr., every 2-4hr. 7am-8pm.)*, and **Valencia.** *(€14-28. 1½-2hr., every 1-2hr. 7am-7pm.)* The **Ferrocarrils de la Generalitat Valenciana (TRAM)** to the right of the Mercado Central has service along the *Costa Blanca. (Estació Marina, Av. Villajoyosa, 2 ☎90 072 04 72 www.fgvalicante.com.)* In summer, the **Transnochador** runs to beaches including **Altea** and **Benidorm.** *(€1.20-5.60. Every hr. 11:25pm-3am.)*

By Bus

Estación d'Autobuses *(C. Portugal, 17 ☎96 5 13 07 00 www.alicante-ayto.es/trafico)* has bus lines running to Alicante. **ALSA** *(☎90 242 22 42; 96 598 50 03 www.alsa.es)* runs to: **Altea** *(€4.80. 1½hr., every hr. 7am-7pm.)*; **Barcelona** *(€41-46. 7-9hr., 6 per day 1-10pm.)*; **Benidorm** *(€4-5. 45min-1hr., every 30min. 6:30am-10:30pm.)*; **Denía** *(€10. 2-3hr., 13 per day 7am-9pm.)*; **Granada** *(€28. 5½-7hr., 3 per day 11:36am-9:46pm.)*; **Madrid** *(€27-38. 5-6hr., every hr. 10:45am-7:45pm.)*; **Málaga** *(€38. 7½-9½hr., 11:35am-9:46pm.)*; **Sevilla** *(€37. 9½hr., 9:25am.)*; **Valencia.** *(€18-21. 2½-5hr., every 30min.-1hr. 6:30am-10:30pm.)*

Getting Around

The easiest way to get around in Alicante is with the **TAM-Alicante Metropolitan Transport.** *(C. Díaz Moreau, 6 ☎96 514 09 36; 90 072 04 72 www.subus.es)* Buses **#21** and **22** run from near the train station in Alicante to Playa San Juan. *(€1.20.)* The **TRAM** also provides access to the MARQ and various places within the city. *(€1.20.)* **Taxis** are also a popular way to get around town, so contact Radio Taxi *(☎96 525 25 11)*, Tele Taxi *(☎96 510 16 11)*, or Área Taxi *(☎96 591 05 91)* for estimates.

COSTA DEL SOL

The Costa del Sol, or "Coast of the Sun" is one of the premier beach destinations along the Mediterranean. From the white-sand beaches and famous caves of Nerja to the urban ambience and Cubist history of Málaga, you'll never want to end your trek bouncing between the cities of this southern region. Both travelers looking for their next historic tour and sunbathers just looking for a place to put up an umbrella will enjoy this region's major cities. This is the perfect area to get inspired by the sand, surf, and sights—after all, it's the place that produced Pablo Picasso. Still not sold? If you don't believe us, just ask the groups who fought for it—any place that the Moors, Visigoths, Arabs, and Christians all wanted has to be pretty awesome.

greatest hits

- **DITCH YOUR CUBICLE FOR SOME CUBIST WORK.** Stay at Picasso's Corner Backpackers, smack dab in the middle of all things Cubist (p. 325).
- **GO GREEN.** Head to Rucala for the freshest ingredients and produce. Seriously, the place is named after lettuce (p. 328).
- **BRAVE THE CAVE.** Visit the gigantic Cueva de Nerja for a prehistoric lesson on the Iberian Peninsula (p. 332).
- **SWIM WITH THE FISHES.** Come face-to-fin with some new underwater friends as you scuba dive with Buceo Costa Nerja (p. 334).

student life

The Moors' beautiful *la Alhambra* is matched by the architectural beauty and splendor of the rest of the city. Can't quite afford to stay in such high quality digs? Can't really afford to stay anywhere? If you don't have the cash for a hostel, head for the hills, literally. If you're OK with no running water or electricity, you can join the legions of student travelers and others who take up residence in the **caves of Sacromonte.** Obviously, this is not the safest option, but if you want to relive the lives of cave-painting ancestors, go ahead. Just know that at this point the stuff on the cave walls probably isn't paint.

málaga ☎968

Málaga may be located right on the water, but don't show up looking for puka shells, ukuleles, or any muppets singing *Kokomo*. With an airport, bus and train stations, and a major coastal port, Málaga has become a center for both tourists and urban living. If you turn your back to the waves, you'll get lost in the tall buildings, popular plazas, and wide avenues. With so many people coming down to Málaga, you can benefit from a wonderful array of restaurants, some of the most comfortable accommodations around, and the hopping variety of student-filled late-night destinations.

The hometown of Pablo Picasso, this city takes a great deal of pride in their Cubist, and you can enjoy plenty of sights and references to the artist around every corner. The rich Moorish and Roman history may not be as prevalent as in the nearby cities of Granada or Córdoba, but the combination of Arab, Christian, and Jewish cultures still provides a richness and variety that can only be found in Andalucia.

Málaga essentially wraps up a nice collection of vacation destinations all in one. Get a tan, stuff a shopping bag, and sip some sangria—this is the real deal.

ORIENTATION

The city center of Málaga is bordered by the **Río Guedalmedina** to the west, the **Alameda Principal** to the south, the **Alcazaba** and **Catedral** to the east, and **Plaza de la Merced** to the north. The main shopping and commercial part of the city, where you'll also encounter many banks and ATMs, branches off around **Calle Marques de Larios.** The primary sights generally cluster around **Calle San Augustín** and **Calle Alcazabilla.** You'll find a strong selection of restaurants, bars, and clubs, generally populated by a younger crowd, near **Plaza de la Merced** and **Calle Alamios.** The **Tunnel Alcazaba** will take you from Plaza de la Merced to the popular **Malagueta Beach,** or you can take a bus to the quieter, more family-oriented **Padregalejo Beach.**

ACCOMMODATIONS

CASA BABYLON — HOSTEL ❷

C. Pedro de Quejana, 3 ☎952 267 228 www.casababylonhostel.com

Only a 7min. walk from Plaza de la Merced, Casa Babylon is a glowing beacon of hope for the free-spirited backpacker. The shirtless, gaucho-pant-wearing receptionist will greet you warmly at the front gates and happily sit you down in the "chill out" lounge, where you'll sink into the big leather couches beside a collection of guitars and psychedelic murals. But just because the hostel has this hippie vibe doesn't mean you need to fully give in to that persona—shower in your spacious bathroom and snuggle up in your sleeping bag in the large, pristinely clean, tiled dorm rooms. At Casa Babylon, you can grab a drink at the bar, make dinner in the spacious kitchen, take some "you time" in the hammocks out front, or even watch local soccer games with the young staff.

From Pl. de la Merced, take C. Victoria to C. Compas de la Victoria and make a right onto C. Louis Maceda and continue onto Pedro de Quejana. i Breakfast, towels, and linens included. Laundry €2. 2- to 8-bed dorms €18-19. Reception 24hr.

PICASSO'S CORNER BACKPACKERS — HOSTEL ❷

C. San Juan de Letran, 9 — ☎952 212 287 www.picassoscorner.com

The name isn't just a tourist ploy—this backpacker's getaway is located smack dab in the center of the main sights of Málaga (we're talking minutes from Picasso's house, the Picasso Museum, and the Catedral) and right in the middle of the hottest nightlife. It honors the artist with colorful, bright rooms all equipped with balconies overlooking good ol' Pablo's beloved hometown. Picasso's corner knows how to make you comfy at home and informed while out and about. Feel free to browse its massive amount of information on all the local sights and restaurants, or just make conversation with the all-knowing bartenders behind the large, tiled bar in the lounge. You can make yourself dinner on the rooftop barbecue or in the well-equipped communal kitchen, or enjoy nightly homemade meals *(€5)*. Keep in mind the 10% discount if you've stayed at Funky or Pilar in Córdoba.

C. San Juan de Letran branches off Plaza de la Merced near the information point. i Breakfast and sheets included. Female-only dorms available. Laundry €3. Luggage storage available. 6-bed dorms €18; 4-bed €19. Doubles €44. Towels €2. Beach umbrella €3. Reception 24hr.

HOSTEL BABIA — HOSTEL ❷

Pl. de los Martires, 6 — ☎952 222 730 www.babiahostel.com

Sometimes even the smallest of conveniences can brighten your day—isn't it nice to have a full restaurant at your feet, a foosball table in your giant living room, and some friendly Spaniards offering to teach you how to SCUBA dive *(€50)?* Hostel Babia has clean, modern, and bright facilities, from it's fully equipped kitchen with colored picnic tables to its sizable TV screen in the lounge. Even if the communal bathrooms (curtained stalls) aren't a point of full luxury, the high-ceilinged rooms with colorful walls, metal-framed bunks, and small balconies will definitely provide a good night's sleep for the tired traveler.

From C. Carreteria, take C. Andres Perez to Pl. de los Martires. i Breakfast, towels, and sheets included. Luggage storage available. 10-bed dorms €16; 8-bed €17; 6-bed €18. Doubles €44.

SIGHTS

While Málaga is a top beach destination, there's definitely more to it than just sun and sand. As the birthplace of **Pablo Picasso,** it has to have quite a few sights dedicated to the artist. You'll also find traces of the Roman, Phoenician, and Moorish heritage of the city, whether you're just passing by the **Roman Amphitheater** or roaming the paths of the **Alcazaba.** Most of the major sights are clustered around **Plaza Obispo, Calle San Augustín,** and **Calle Alcazabilla,** but there are also many smaller, special spots worth seeking out.

MUSEO DE PICASSO — MUSEUM

C. San Augustin, 8 — ☎902 443 377 www.museopicassomalaga.org

While you can feel the presence and history of Pablo Picasso throughout the city of Málaga, there is no better place to truly capture the aura of the artist than the museum dedicated to the man himself. The building's pale marble floors and white walls allow the creative and wonderful collection to speak for itself. The rooms are organized in chronological order, allowing you to trace the changes and stages of the artist's style to better understand his passionate views on politics, education, the human body, bullfighting, and (of course) women. You'll find quotes along the walls by Picasso with repeated examples of that oh-so-famous signature. Aside from the main collection, you can enjoy the permanent basement archaeological sight of 7th- and 8th-century Phoenician, Roman, and Moorish constructions, and the temporary exhibitions that hone in on one aspect of Picasso's work and supplement his art with media from modern artists.

*Off C. San Augustin between the Catedral and Plaza de la Merced. **i** All information in English and Spanish. Collection €6. Temporary exposition €4.50. Combined ticket €8, students €4. Open Tu-Th 10am-8pm, F-Sa 10am-9pm, Su 10am-8pm.*

ALCAZABA FORTRESS

C. Alcazabilla ☎630 932 287 www.ayto-malaga.es

If you've been to Granada, you'll probably view the Alcazaba as a smaller version of the Alhambra. From the views to the gardens to the fountained passageways, there's no doubt that this building is another flavor of Moorish fortress. But even if you've seen the Alhambra (and also if you haven't), Málaga's Alcazaba is still worth a visit. Walking between the numbered stops on the grounds, you'll visit sights like the **Puerta de las Columnas** (Gate of the Columns) that perfectly signal the Arab additions to Roman structures. In the **Nazarith Palace,** built between the 11th and 14th centuries, you'll see three main courtyards, including the **Torre de Maldonado,** which is decorated with manmade marble columns. If you're a real go-getter (and have good walking shoes), you can make the trek up to the **Gibralforo** *(combined ticket €3.95),* the additional hideout and viewpoint used by Moorish royalty.

*Next to Roman Amphitheater off C. Alcazabilla. **i** Tour pamphlets in English and Spanish. €2.10, students €0.60. Free Su after 2pm. Combined ticket with Gibralforo €3.95. Open daily in summer 9:30am-8pm; in winter 8:30am-7pm.*

CATEDRAL MÁLAGA CHURCH

C. Molina Lario s/n ☎952 228 491

The Catedral Málaga is often facetiously called the "one-armed lady" because one of its towers was never completed, but you can't really blame them for not finishing—this structure is enormous! After knocking down a mosque and a smaller church, the city took on the huge task of constructing this Renaissance-style cathedral in 1527. While they were able to build enough by 1588 to open up for mass, the financial struggle, including failed harbor taxes and cancellations, continued over the next two centuries. Even though the church may never be an emblem of architectural perfection, you can still stare in awe at the massive, green organs overlooking the choir, the Chapel of the Incarnation dedicated to the patron saint of Málaga, and the main altar decorated with marble podiums and stained glass.

*Entrance at Pl. del Obispo. **i** Audio tour available in English included in ticket price. €4. Open M-F 10am-6:45pm, Sa 10am-5:45pm.*

MUSEO DE ARTES Y COSTUMBRES POPULARES MUSEUM

Pasillo de Santa Isabel, 10 ☎952 217 137 www.museoartespopulares.com

The world is full of museums detailing ancient history and modern developments, but sometimes those guys in the middle get overlooked. The Museo de Artes y Costumbres Populares is a traditional 17th-century inn converted into a museum honoring Málaga lifestyle. It's organized a bit like a game of *Clue*—learn about the blacksmith in the stable with the carriages, or the bourgeoisie in the bedroom with the wooden birthing chair. You'll get a glimpse of all the top professions from every social class and learn the folklore and religion that flooded their minds. You can even trace back time through posters for the *Grandes Fiestas en Málaga*, still celebrated every August to date.

*Make a left off C. Cisneros onto Pasillo de Santa Isabel and the museum is on the left. **i** Information in English and Spanish. €2, students €1. Open in summer M-F 10am-1:30pm and 5-8pm, Sa 10am-1:30pm; in winter M-F 10am-1:30pm and 4-7pm, Sa 10am-1:30pm.*

BEACHES

While the beaches closest to the city center are generally very crowded and not necessarily picturesque, you'll find more peaceful terrain and better photo ops as you move east along the coast. While we know you want to show off those washboard abs in your swimsuit, you'll really have to struggle to resist the freshly grilled and fried local seafood, or the steaming *paellas*, from the restaurants lining the boardwalks.

PLAYA DE PEDROGALEJOS — BEACH

While it may require a little extra travel to get there, the quick bus ride is definitely worth the trip down to Playa de Pedrogalejos. This lengthy, 1200m strip of beach has finer sand and finer views along the small, curled up, *w*-shaped coves that protect you from the bigger waves and colder water. You can rent a lounge chair *(€2.50-3.50)* and enjoy a free drink or snack with the rental, or just picnic like a local under the clusters of colorful beach umbrellas. The boardwalk is packed with restaurants of varying prices, grilling up fresh fish right on the sand out of old tin **boats** converted into fire pits. You can even burn off those *paella* calories with some pickup soccer on the enclosed sand pitches. As you make your way further east toward **Playa de Palo-Pedrogalejos** and **Playa Palo**, you'll encounter the *caseta* (canvas booth) flea market, selling everything from *Dora the Explorer* towels to fresh fruits and discounted underwear—Christmas shopping, anyone?

Take bus #11 or 34 to Av. Juan Sebastian Elcano and make a right onto any side street down to the beach. i Information kiosk, showers, and bathrooms available. Lounge chairs €2.50-3.50. Lifeguards on duty 11am-8pm. Lounge chair rentals 9:30am-8:30pm.

PLAYA DE LA MALAGUETA — BEACH

This 1200m beach stretching from the harbor and curling into a cove may not be the most picturesque pairing of sand and sea that you've ever encountered, but it's definitely Málaga's most popular and convenient spot to laze around. You're steps from the busy city streets, 10min. on foot from Pl. de la Merced, and a stone's throw from some aquatic relaxation. Playa de la Malagueta sucks in tourists and locals alike, whether they're lounging under a rented umbrella *(€4 with chair, €8 with 2 chairs)*, exploring the rock-bar at the end of the *caleta* (cove), resting under a plum tree on a grassy knoll, or curling up in one of the stone letters of the "malagueta" statue (the "L" probably isn't your best choice). You can grab a bite at one of the many restaurants right on the sand, grilling up fresh fish and fragrant *paellas*, or just cool off with an ice cream cone from one of the many kiosks along the boardwalk.

From Pl. de la Merced, walk through the tunnel and take Paseo de la Farola down to the end of the beach. i Showers, bathrooms, and playgrounds available. Information kiosk near intersection of Pl. de la Malagueta and Paseo Maritimo Pablo Ruiz Picasso. Lounge chair and umbrella €4; 2 lounge chairs and umbrella €8. Lifeguards on duty 11am-8pm. Lounge chair rentals 10am-8pm.

FOOD

As you're never more than about 20min. from the ocean, it's no surprise that coming across fresh seafood is pretty easy in Málaga. Whether you want a thick tuna steak *a la plancha* (grilled), or some *calamaritos fritos* (fried calamari), the options are seemingly endless. But Málaga doesn't stop at seafood—this industrial tourist center also offers a wide selection of international, modern, and creative cuisine that will satiate even the most critical of foodies. If you're looking for something fresh and simple, the **marketplace** *(M-Sa 8am-3pm)* offers a wide selection of local fish, produce, meat, cheese, and baked goods.

RUCALA

MODERN, INTERNATIONAL ❷

C. Carreteria, 73 ☎952 222 883 www.rucala.es

Who needs a gym? Take one step into Rucala, and you'll immediately feel refreshed and healthy (it's named after a type of lettuce for goodness sake!). The green walls, plants, and nature decor are constant reminders of the freshness of the food, and the modern, international menu is a constant reminder of the stylistic freshness of the kitchen staff. Their extensive salad selection, starring the popular goat cheese, raisin, apple, and honey mustard option *(€6.50)*, is based in a collection of crisp mixed greens, but the rest of the menu is ready to hit any ingredient from anywhere on the planet. Warm up with duck confit with risotto and mango chutney *(€12)* or a teriyaki chicken wok with coconut milk and rice *(€8)*. The *menú* of the day *(€8)* is an awesome deal and constantly changing to include funky variations of world classics—ever seen a "caprese" prepared with mozarella pearls floating in chilled tomato soup with basil leaves and honey? Yeah, neither had we.

On the right if coming from the river on C. Carreteria. **i** *Vegetarian options available. Appetizers €4-7. Salads €6.50-7; entrees €8-€12. Desserts €4-4.50. Menú of the day €8. Wine €2.40-2.60. Open daily 1:30pm-12:30am.*

TAPERIA PEPA Y PEPE

TAPAS, TRADITIONAL ❶

C. Caldereria, 9 ☎650 821 316

Pepa and Pepe must have made a lovely match if they were going to spearhead their own timeless Andalucian restaurant. The menu is filled with a great selection of inexpensive wine and beer, fried and grilled seafood *(ration €4.80-5.50, half-ration €2.90-3.80)*, and classic dishes at shockingly low prices. Walk into this small restaurant, and you'll be able to see the entire kitchen staff working under the brick archway in the corner next to the ham, sausage, and wine bottles that decorate the walls. Feel free to grab a rickety wooden table inside or a barrel and stool in the plaza, and order up some traditional bacon-wrapped dates *(ration €4.80, half-ration €2.90)* or chicken, shrimp, or pork *pinchos (skewers; €1.80 each)*, marinated and grilled to perfection. Because it's small, Pepa y Pepe is always overflowing with locals pouring out of the open glass doors. Just be glad for the lightning-fast service—spots open up quick!

Cross Plaza de Uncibay from C. Mendez Munez and make a left. Rations €3-7.50; half-rations €1.80-3.80. Tapas €1-1.80. Beer €1-1.60. Wine €1.20-1.80. Open M-Th 1-4pm and 7:30pm-midnight, F-Sa 1-4pm and 7:30pm-12:30am, Su 1-4pm and 7:30pm-midnight.

CLANDESTINO

INTERNATIONAL ❸

C. Nino de Guevara, 3 ☎952 219 390 www.clandestino.com

Clandestino just puts you in a sharing mood. Maybe it's because of the friendly waitstaff or the warm, homey feeling of yellow walls decorated with kitchen-themed paintings. Maybe it's the 12-page drink menu of quality, international wines *(€2.20-2.60)*, beer *(€1.60-4.50)*, and cocktails *(€4-6)* that may require you to team up to make a selection, or maybe it's the absolutely massive portions of fresh, unique, and delicious dishes that will stuff a solo eater to the brim. Consider splitting some comfort food like the pumpkin ravioli stuffed with *foie gras* and goat cheese *(€11)* or a huge, refreshing Kazuo Salad overflowing with grilled asparagus, bamboo shoots, avocado, tomato, buffalo mozzarella, and topped with a light, soy vinaigrette *(€10)*.

From C. Mendez Nunez, take C. Belgrano and make a right onto Nino de Guevara. Appetizers €10-15. Pasta €10-11.40. Salads €10-11.20. Meat and fish entrees €15-18. Desserts €5.50-5.60. Menu of the day €9. Open daily 1pm-1am. Menu of the day available M-F 1-5pm.

NIGHTLIFE

Nightlife in Málaga is clustered into the area between **Calle Mendez Nunez** and **Calle Alamios** near **Plaza de la Merced,** but that doesn't mean your options are limited. You'll find a wide selection of student-populated bars and clubs, all with their own musical tastes and types of patrons. Don't even think of requesting *Baby One More Time* at a rock club or some Zeppelin at a commercial club, or risk receiving derisive laughter. Pick your mood and your spot, and let the good times roll.

SALA CAIRO

CLUB, BAR

C. Juan de Padilla, 15 www.salacairo.es

Sala Cairo is Málaga's spot for your high-profile night out. Sit on their shiny, patent-leather stools, watch videos on one of their multiple flatscreen TVs, sip pricey cocktails *(€6)* at one of the two glowing bars, and maybe even reserve a spot at the elevated VIP area equipped with sleek white couches. Coming here means you'll be hanging out with the hottest, most stylish 20-somethings in town, all dressed and ready to dance to Sala Cairo's poppy, '80s Spanish music into the early hours. If you're ready to go out a bit earlier, you can enjoy €2 off any drink until 1:30am or even catch the Thursday night concerts around midnight.

Juan de Padilla is between Mendez Nunez and Beatas. Cover Sa night €6-7. Beer €4. Cocktails €6. Open Th-Sa 11pm-4am.

BUNKER BAR

BAR, CLUB

C. Mariblanca, 9

You don't need to duck and cover to enter this bunker, but you should be ready for something a little rougher around the edges. Walk into this small bar and club and lean up against the metal grating on the walls and funky, dark murals in the corners. Bunker says they play a little bit of everything from anywhere in the world, but they maintain a strict policy against playing commercial pop or anything that could be found on *Perez Hilton.* Instead, Bunker is the place to rock out to some alternative beats and grab a beer *(€2-2.50)* with a mix of tourists and local students. You can party hard at the bi-monthly Saturday night concerts and DJ sets, or chill during Tuesday movies and Wednesday night storytelling.

From Pl. de la Merced, take C. Alamos and make a right onto Mariblanca. Beer €2-2.50, half-liters €3.50. Cocktails €5-6. Open M-Th 11pm-3am, F-Sa 11pm-4am. Movies and storytelling 9:30pm.

LA BOTELLITA

CLUB

C. Alamos, 36 www.labotellita.com

La Botellita is any MTV viewer's dream, offering pop and commercial hits on its dance floors as four flatscreens display music videos. This club knows how to rake in the students with flashy, silver-and-black patterned walls and namesake bottles along its bar. Early birds beware: La Botellita wouldn't even consider getting a crowd until after 2:30am. You can sit and drink at the tables along the walls, or get grooving down in the center of the dance floor. Thursday nights during the school year are student-only, so get ready to release your academic stress with all the other bookworms.

Take C. Alamos from Pl. de la Merced and the club is on the left. Beer €3. Cocktails €3.50. Open Th-Sa 11pm-4am.

ESSENTIALS

Practicalities

- **TOURIST OFFICES:** There are multiple tourist information points throughout the city, including the **central municipal tourist office.** *(Pl. de La Marina, 11 ☎952 122 020 www.malagaturismo.com Open daily Oct-Feb 9am-6pm; Mar-Sept 9am-8pm.)* There are also smaller **information points** throughout the city at Pl. de la Merced.

(Open daily 10am-2pm.), near the **Post Office.** (Open daily 10am-2pm.), and at the train and bus stations (Open daily 10am-8pm.), and near the Picasso Museum. *(C. Granada, 70 Open daily 9am-6pm).*

- **TOURS:** The city runs **guided walking tours** from the Info Office *(Plaza de la Marina Nov-Mar M-Sa 10am, noon, 5pm; Apr-Oct M-Sa 9, 11am, 6pm. €5.)* that stop at such sights as the Cathedral, Picasso Museum, Alcazaba, and Roman Theater. You can also rent **audio tours** from the Pl. de la Marina tourist office on one of eight themes including traditional, religious, Picasso, and contemporary. **Málaga Bike Tours** *(C. Trinidad Grund, 1 ☎606 978 513 www.malagabiketours.eu €23. 4hr., 10am.)* will show you the city and offer a free drink. Tour in a *bicitaxi* (rickshaw) with **Tricosol.** *(☎657 440 605 www.tricosol.com Full tour €18, half tour €10. Open daily 8am-10pm; duration varies upon request.)* from Plaza de la Constitución, the Cathedral, or the Roman Theatre, or even get picked up from your accommodation.
- **CURRENCY EXCHANGE:** You can **exchange money** at Barclay's Bank *(C. Marques de Larios s/n ☎952 220 425 Open M-F 8:30am-2:30pm.)* or at El Corte Ingles *(Av. Andalucia, 4-6 ☎952 076 500 Open M-Sa 10am-10pm.)* department store, which also has one of the city's largest **supermarkets** and a post office point.
- **INTERNET:** The **public library** *(C. Ollerias, 34 ☎952 133 950 Open M-F 9:30am-8pm)* is also a cultural center, restaurant, and a **free Wi-Fi** point. Many restaurants and cafes around the city also supply free free Wi-Fi.
- **POST OFFICE:** The main **post office** *(Av. Andalucia, 1 ☎902 197 197 www.correos.es Open M-F 8:30am-8:30pm, Sa 9:30am-2pm)* also has an ATM and photocopy services.

Emergency!

- **EMERGENCY NUMBERS:** ☎012. Ambulance and Emergency Healthcare: ☎061. Red Cross: ☎952 222 222. Information: ☎010.
- **POLICE:** National ☎091 or ☎952 046 200. Local: ☎092 or ☎952 126 551. The police station is located at Av. de la Rosaleda, 19.
- **LATE-NIGHT PHARMACIES:** There's a **24hr. pharmacy** *(Alameda Principal, 2 ☎952 212 858)* that closes its doors in the evening but will open if you ring the bell.

Getting There

By Plane

The **Málaga Airport** *(Avenida García Morato ☎902 404 704 www.aena.es)* is located about 8km outside the city and runs international and domestic flights on many airlines including **Air Berlin** *(☎952 105 520 www.airberlin.com)*, **Air France** *(☎952 048 192 www.airfrance.com)*, **Aer Lingus** *(☎952 105 488 www.aerlingus.com)*, **British Airways** *(☎902 111 333 www.britishairways.com)*, **Iberia** *(☎952 136 166 www.iberia.com)*, and **Virgin Airlines** *(☎952 048 349 www.virgin-atlantic.com)*. **Bus #19** from Plaza del General Torrijos is a direct airport shuttle that runs every 30min. from 6:30am-midnight. You can also take a Renfe train to the airport on line C-1 from Málaga-Centro Station or Málaga Railway Station every 30min. from 5:45am to 11:45pm.

By Train

The **Málaga Railway Station** *(Explanada de la Estación s/n ☎902 24 02 02 6:10am-11pm)* runs **Renfe** trains *(www.renfe.com)* from: **Barcelona** *(€138.80. 5hr. 50min.; 10:20am, 3:50pm.)*; **Córdoba** *(€39.60. 1hr., 11 per day 8:30am-12:25am.)*; **Sevilla** *(€36.40. 2hr., 6 per day 6:50am-7:35pm.)*; **Madrid** *(€76.40. 2hr. 50min., 12 per day 9:25am-12:25am.)*; **Valencia.** *(€54.80. 9hr. 40min., 11:30am.)* You can take either of the circular routes or buses #1, #3, or #4 to the train station.

By Bus

The **bus station** *(Paseo de los Tilos, s/n ☎952 350 061 www.estabus.emtsam.es)* is located near Pl. de la Marina and en route to the airport. It runs lines from multiple companies to destinations all over Spain, and connecting throughout Europe and North Africa. **Diabus** *(☎902 277 999 www.daibus.es)* runs from **Madrid.** *(€21.80. 6hr., 7 per day 7:30am-midnight.)* **Alsa** *(☎913 270 540 www.alsa.es)* runs from: **Sevilla** *(€15.80. 3½hr., 7 per day 7am-8:30pm.)*; **Córdoba** *(€12.70. 2½hr., 4 per day 8:30am-5pm.)*; **Granada** *(€9.80. 2hr., 17 per day 7am-9:30pm.)*; **Barcelona.** *(€77.81. 17hr., 3 per day 5:30pm-midnight.)* **Los Amarillos** *(☎952 363 024 www.losamarillos.es)* runs from **Ronda.** *(€9.20. 1hr. 45min, 8 per day 8am-8pm.)*

Getting Around

By Taxi

Much of Málaga, especially in the historic quarter, is composed of small passway streets accessible only by foot. But don't fret: walking is extremely manageable. Even from the bus station to the nightlife center around Pl. de la Merced is only a 15min. walk. Taxis are better at navigating the small streets than the public buses. **Unitaxi** *(☎952 333 333)* and the **Taxi Union** *(☎952 040 804)* are the city's recommended companies. It costs about €20 to take a cab to the airport. *(15min.)* If you're traveling the larger streets and longer distances, the city buses run by **Empresa Municipal de Transportes** *(Alameda Principal, 15 ☎902 527 200 www.emtmalaga.es Single ride €1.10, 10 rides €7.)* can easily get you to all points in the city. Buses **#11** and **#34** from Paseo de los Curas are perfect for getting to the more eastern beaches farther from the city center, **C-1** and **C-2** run circular routes around the city, and **N-1, N-2,** and **N-3** are the "noctural," late-night lines. From Paseo del Parque **#4, #3,** and **#19** run to the bus and train stations and **#19** *(40 min.; M-F 6:25am-11:30pm, Sa-Su 6:30am-11:30pm.)* runs to the airport. The **A Express** *(€2)* runs more directly to the airport, getting you from the train station to the airport in about 15min. All city buses stop on the **Alameda Principal**.

By Bike

You can also **rent bikes** from **Cyclo Point** *(Av. Juan Sebastián Elcano, 50 ☎952 297 324 www.cyclo-point.com Open Tu-F 10am-8pm, Sa 10am-5pm. €10 per day, €50 per week.)* or **Bike 2 Málaga.** *(C. Victoria, 15 ☎952 211 296 www.bike2malaga.com €5 per half day, €10 per day. Open daily 10am-2pm and 4-8pm.)*

nerja ☎952

The tourist capital of the Costa del Sol, Nerja clearly knows how to entertain with the awe-inspiring Cueva de Nerja, the high-energy party harbor at Plaza Tutti Frutti, and over 13km of Spain's hottest beaches. Even though Nerja may seem more amusement park than historical sightseeing haven, its culture is far better than its cotton candy. This ancient Moorish town is actually named for the Arab word *narixa*, meaning "abundant spring," describing the beautiful but menacing limestone waterfalls pouring down from the surrounding Sierra. Nerja prides itself on its untouched ocean coves, temperate and sunny climate, and relaxed, beachy attitude. This small town is the perfect place to get a tan, snack on the catch of the day, and rejuvenate in a Spanish paradise.

ORIENTATION

Avenida de la Pescia is the street you'll take upon entering Nerja and that you'll use to visit the Cueva de Nerja. It has more of an industrial feel, but it's also extremely efficient, packing in a police station, multiple supermarkets, a gas station, and bus stops all within a 5-10min. walk. **Calle Pintada** and **Calle Almirante Fernandiz** take you from Av. la Pescia down to the beach, and you'll find lots of shops, accommodations, and restaurants along them. C. Almirante Fernandiz, with the help of **Calle Los Huertes** and **Calle Rodriguez Acosta,** also borders the historic center of the city. The "beach town" part of Nerja is found near the **Balcón de Europa, Plaza Cavana,** and **Calle El Barrio** and **Calle Diputación.**

ACCOMMODATIONS

HOSTAL MARISSAL — HOSTAL ❸

Paseo Balcón de Europa, 3 ☎952 520 199 www.hostalmarissal.com

Hostal Marissal puts you smack-dab in the beach center of Nerja. Your room's sea-foam green sheets and curtains and dark wooden furniture will leave you thinking it's time for sunshine and sand, and the bustling cafeteria-style restaurant on the ground floor will keep you (and every other beachgoer around) happily fed. Located on the boardwalk to the Balcón de Europa, Hostal Marissal also provides unbeatable views and an ocean breeze. If you're lucky enough, your room's balcony will face the sea and be a perfect spot to reenact some Kate and Leo moments.

On the boardwalk to Balcón de Europa. ***i*** *Towels and sheets included. TV and bathroom ensuite. Singles €30-45; doubles €40-60. Reception 9am-midnight.*

HOSTAL ABRIL — HOSTAL ❷

C. Pintada, 124 ☎952 526 124 www.hostalabril.com

Hostal Abril is the perfect way to relax on your beach getaway. This family-run establishment will make you feel right at home as the young kids come kiss Mom goodbye while she checks you in at reception. The bright, spacious rooms with white sheets, marble floors, and sunflowers will provide you with some rest (and with some free tea on the side table), while the patio-garden with full lounge chairs and benches will give you some sun without the sand. It's located just steps from the bus stop, so you can drop off your belongings and take a trip to the Cueva de Nerja without any hassle. For a slightly higher price, you can also check out of the **Apartamentos Abril** *(C. Cristo esquina C. San Juan, 1),* whose rooms come equipped with full kitchen and living room space.

From the bus stop and facing the beach, C. Pintada is to the left of the park; the hostal is on the left. ***i*** *Towels and sheets included. TV, safes, and bathroom ensuite. Singles €25-33; doubles €33-42; triples €36-55; quads €43-75; quints €47-82. Reception 9am-11pm.*

SIGHTS

As Nerja is detached from the **caves,** aqueduct, and small historic towns beyond the city border, many of the sights are just that—things you will see from afar. The **Balcón de Europa** was used as a fortress in the ninth century but today is a great spot to catch some ocean views and grab a bite to eat with your fellow tourists. The **Barco de Chanquete** featured all over the popular '80s TV series *Verano Azul* symbolizes the recent increase in Nerja's tourism. The **La Dorada I** boat housed the character Chanquete on the show and would do Gilligan, the Professor, and even the Millionaire proud.

CUEVA DE NERJA — CAVE

Caretera de Maro, s/n ☎952 529 520 www.cuevadenerja.es

You've got two million years of rainwater and bicarbonate to thank for this puppy. The 264,279 cubic m Cueva de Nerja (Cave of Nerja) is one of Spain's best tools for studying the prehistoric era on the Iberian Peninsula and has become one of the largest draws to the tourist capital of Costa del Sol. The caves' history sounds like Steven Spielberg's 1985 classic *The Goonies*, but we promise this is no Hollywood feature. Five young boys discovered the Cueva in 1959, and within two years the sight was converted into a national point of historic interest.

Today, there exist three primary cavities of the cave, including the touristic **lower gallery** as well as the upper and new gallery only open to speleologists for research. Don't be disappointed by the security, though. The touristic cave boasts massive stalagmites, threatening stalactites, and a ton of other forms like "soda straws," "pearls," and "pineapples," whose names may remind you more of a beach resort than of the cool shadows you'll be exploring. While the Shaquille O'Neals of the world may have to crouch a tiny bit to descend down the steps, everyone will find an open, underground, natural palace that's perfect for getting a cheesy tourist photo taken *(€8)*. Hopefully you won't encounter any of your childhood nightmares in the **Sala de las Fantasmas** (Hall of Ghosts), and you can get a flashless photo with the world-record-holding **Gran Columna del Catacismo** (central column of the Hall of Catacism). You'll walk by the main stage where the annual **Festival de Cueva de Nerja** *(mid-July; shows at 10pm; €50)* holds its ballet, orchestra, tango, and flamenco performances. You can also visit the **Centro de Interpretación** *(open daily 10am-2pm and 4-6:30pm)*, where you'll find further details about the history and structure of the cave as well as a full-scale model and various films. Ready for some relaxation? Enjoy a picnic on the shaded tables at **Plaza de los Descubridores** or head into the **restaurant** *(Pl. de los Descubridores, 1 ☎952 529 558 www.lorenzoreche.net $ Buffet €8.80.)*, where you can get a table on the patio overlooking the beach and the picturesque town of Maro.

Take the Nerja-Cuevas bus or drive to Exit 295 off Autovia del Mediterráneo or Hwy. N-340. i Cave info in English and Spanish; interpretation center only in Spanish. $ €8.50. Open daily in summer 10am-7:30pm; in winter 10am-2pm and 4-6:30pm.

EL ÁGUILA AQUEDUCT — LANDMARK

Hwy. N-340

While the El Águila (The Eagle) Aqueduct may look like it was built in Roman times, this 19th-century structure with four stories and 37 arches is actually a mere stylistic model—but that doesn't mean it's not awesome! The aqueduct was originally intented to irrigate the orchards around Maro and Nerja and provide water to the city's old sugar factory. Today, much of its practical use has been shut down, but it still holds some irrigation purpose, and its original "pure and clean contraception" inscription on one of the lower arches makes for an awesome photo op. Whether you're walking back from the Cave of Nerja or making the drive into the city, it's definitely worth pulling over to snap a shot or two.

Off Hwy. N-340 between Nerja and the Cueva along the panoramic pull-over point.

MARO — HISTORIC TOWN

The tiny town of Maro (if you can even call it a town—city maps refer to it as an "Andalucian corner") is only a few steps from the Cueva de Nerja and even closer to the beaches and farmland surrounding it. Walking the streets among the white houses, blue waters, and green orchards, you won't hear much other than chirping birds, flowing fountains, and maybe a tourist or two blasting Bob Marley from a parked car taking in the **panoramic viewpoints.** While there are a few small accommodations and scarcely populated restaurants, Maro is more about picturesque relaxation than five-star establishments. The **beaches** are smaller than those found within the city lines of Nerja, and this same simplicity carries over into the town's main sight, **Iglesia Nuestra Señora de las Maravillas** (Church of Our Lady of Wonders). This small church was completed in the 17th century, but its structure holds remnants of a much older design. The eclectic architectural stylings, including wooden beams and pointed arches, house some cluttered religious artwork and small electric fans, all honoring the patron saint of Maro.

Off Autovia del Mediterraneo of Hwy. N-340, adjacent to the Cueva de Nerja. Take the Nerja-Cuevas bus or drive to Exit 295 off Autovia del Mediterraneo or Hwy. N-340. It's a 5min. walk from Cueva de Nerja along the green path.

THE GREAT OUTDOORS

Scuba Diving

BUCEO COSTA NERJA

Playa Burriana ☎952 528 610 www.nerjadiving.com

This family-run diving company is Nerja's only dive center and is equipped to take you out for a quick dive trip or teach you all you need to know for certification. PADI courses for one to four people are available for many types of snorkel, scuba, emergency, and rescue certification for both adults (over 14) and teens (over 12), and TDI technical diving courses are offered for those trying to test their limits. Rent all the necessary equipment for a daytime or evening dive or snorkel session. While the shop itself is located on Playa Burriana, the dive sights extend further east along the Costa del Sol, handpicked to bring you the best chance of seeing an octopus, dolphin, or swordfish face-to-face (or face-to-fin).

Office on Playa Burriana. ***i*** *Medical forms to be completed available on website. All guides speak English. PADI courses €100-420; PADI Professional €180-625. Snorkel tours €30. Scuba with guide and equipment: tours €50, night €62 (10% off if 3 or more). Scuba with just guide (bring your own equipment) €35/42. Insurance €6 per day, €24 per month. Regular dives at 9:30am, 1:30, 4pm. Night dives after 7pm. Make reservations a few days in advance.*

Beaches

PLAYA BURRIANA

☎952 522 156

This stretch of sand along **Paseo Maritimo Antonio Mercero** is one of Nerja's most popular beaches and one of the main tools for raking in all the summer visitors to this sunny city. The boardwalk is packed with **gift shops, snack stands,** and **ice cream parlors** that are ready to soothe that sweet tooth or equip you with a new umbrella or boogie board. Tons of **restaurants** and **bars** serve up any type of cuisine you could imagine, with a heavy emphasis on fried fish and barbecue. Most of the restaurants are large with busy outdoor patios, generally offering Wi-Fi and plenty of TV screens. There are also a few nicer restaurants along **C. Filipinas,** all with their own bit of character—some have ridiculous, decorative flags draping their ceilings, some present the most luxurious breakfast options in town, and others hold dance performances on a nightly basis. On the sandy shore, you'll find everything from volleyball courts and playgrounds to a **police station** and **public changing rooms.** You can rent a **lounge chair** *(€4)* from any of the small, umbrella-shaded podiums along the beach. Before you head back to your car or your hotel, make sure to check out the **viewpoints** along the switchbacks branching off **Calle Bajamar.**

i *Pets and loud music are not permitted. Lifeguard station and police station open daily 11:30am-8pm. Beach open June 15-Sept 15.*

Hiking

The Sierra Almijara and the Sierra de Tejada mountain ranges, including the 1832m peak of Navachica, overlook Nerja. The most eastern part of the Sierra Almijara is referred to by locals, maybe a bit self-obsessively, as the **Sierra de Nerja.** Even if the people of Nerja are vain in naming their mountain range, we can't blame them for wanting to establish this namesake because of the beautiful hiking options through these sierras. One of the most popular full-day hikes passes through the **Rio Chillar,** giving you the chance to swim in the Vado de los Patos (Ford of the Ducks), explore the Cueva de las Palomas (Cave of the Doves), smell the eucalyptus forests and apricot trees, and catch sight of the main dam and irrigation channels. You'll find the start of the route and base of the riverbed at **Calle El Picasso,** near the sports complex, or at **El Playazo Beach.** You'll find multiple other routes starting from the **Fuente del Esparto.** From the fountain, the two most popular routes are the challenging, 36km (round-trip) climb to the top of **Navachica** and the shorter half-day trip to the **Almendron Cliff.** Both hikes are notorious for their spectacular views and memorable visits to two of the old city mines, **Mina del Uno** (Mine of One) and **La Furia** (The Fury).

Updated and more detailed information on hiking routes is available from the **information center,** but even those pamphlets warn that trails are often a bit ambiguous and that permanent, natural structures are your best bet as directions. **Adventura** also leads guided hiking trips *(€35 per person)* along Rio Chillar and through the Sierra Almijara.

Other Outdoor Activities

ADVENTURA

Paseo Burriana, 2 or C. Mediterraneo, 3 ☎952 520 471 www.adventuranerja.com

Adventura is ready to find you all that its name describes: an adventure. Whether by mountain, land, or sea, this company has the facilities and guides to help you get your adventurous fix. Their land department offers such activities as horseback riding *(€25 per hr., €45 per 2hr.)* and off-road biking *(€20 for bike, €40 with guide),* the mountain department can get you hiking *(½ day €35 per person)* or canyoning *(€60 per person; min. 4 people; 4-5hr.),* and the water section will get you drenched with a windsurf *(from €10 per hr.)* or a kayak trip *(€20 per person; 3hr. guided tour).* They also serve as a scuba booking agent for **Buceo Costa Nerja,** but they don't provide guides, equipment, or facilities of their own.

Office at the far end of Playa Buriana. ***i*** *Insurance forms and packed lunches available upon request. Free Wi-Fi; computers €4 per hr. Headsets and webcams also available.* *Office and clubhouse open daily in summer 10am-8pm; in winter 10am-6pm.*

FOOD

Since Nerja is a beach town, all traditional Spanish restaurants feature tons of fresh seafood at great prices. Since Nerja is also a top tourist destination, you'll come across various international cuisine options, especially British and Italian restaurants. Along **Playa Buriana** and **Plaza Fabrica de los Cangrejos,** you'll find great views and outdoor patios but few things authentically Spanish. Don't be turned off by restaurants run out of hotels and *hostals*—with such a bustling tourist industry, many of these spots will be the most established, popular dining destinations in town.

LAS PEINATAS MODERN, SPANISH ❷

C. San Miguel, 18 ☎952 526 397 www.peinatablanca.com

Las Peinatas is kind of like MTV's *Pimp My Ride*—it's all about taking something classic and making it new and fresh (without the fuzzy dice or flame decals). With the decor, you'll immediately notice the glistening *peinatas* (traditional hairpins often worn for flamenco) decorating almost every inch of wall space in this modern restaurant. The menu follows this vibe as well, including the sweet cherry gazpacho *(€4.50)* and the *pastel de rabo de toro con foie y setas*, or bull's-tail pie with *foie gras* and mushrooms *(€9.50),* which both take a unique spin on Andalucian classics. Take advantage of some timeless money-savers like a free tapa with any drink off the extensive wine list *(€1.80-2.20 per glass)* or the tasty, marinated olives and warm bread that come with your meal. Many of the rations are easily large enough to split, so don't be thrown off by the surprisingly low prices—this place is just a steal.

From the bus stop, make a right on C. San Miguel and walk about 3min.; the restaurant is on the left. *Rations €3.50-11.50. Desserts €4.50-5.90.* *Open daily 10am-4pm and 7pm-midnight.*

ANAHI DINER ❷

Puerta del Mar, 6 ☎952 521 457

Don't fret—you may be getting some of the best ocean views off Balcón de Europa, but your wallet won't feel a thing. Anahi is one of Nerja's top diners, and its simple, inexpensive menu will make you smile almost as much as the sea breeze off the small patio or the beautiful view through the huge glass doors of its interior dining room. If you're sick of standard Spanish breakfasts like toast and jam (or just looking for some gluttony), Anahi will make sure you're too full to function. Try the savory asparagus omelette *(€5.20)* or steak-and-eggs platter *(€7)*. Or give into temptation and order the waffles topped with chocolate and vanilla ice cream, chopped walnuts, and honey *(€4.20)*. The fresh-fruit tarts, croissants, and quiches *(€1-2)* can easily be taken to go for a sightseeing snack. Anahi also boasts an array of toasty sandwiches *(€1.60-3.50)*, including their signature Anahi burger, piled high with lettuce, tomato, onion, bacon, and eggs *(€3.50)*.

Located to the left of Balcón de Europa as you face the water. **i** *Ocean-view balcony.* Ⓢ *Pastries €1-2. Eggs €3.70-7. Pancakes and waffles €3.50-4.20. Sandwiches €1.60-3.50. Lunch and dinner entrees €6.30-11.* *Open daily 8am-12:30am.*

AYO — BEACH RESTAURANT ❷

Playa Buriana s/n — ☎952 522 289 www.ayonerja.com

Everyone in Nerja has heard of Ayo—this restaurant owner not only opened up one of Playa Buriana's top eateries over 40 years ago, but he also was one of the first people to ever explore the Cueva de Nerja (he'll humbly tell you how he wasn't one of the five *descubridores* honored at the sight, but will make sure you know that it was Ayo and comrades who first came across the entirety of the cave). Don't think Ayo's personal celebrity is what rakes in the clientele to the checkered tablecloths right on the sand. While Ayo has a full menu of entrees, with some of the best freshly grilled fish *(€12.75)* and lamb *(€13.75)* in town, this spot is famous for its overflowing plates of *paella (€6)*. In the corner of the sandy plot, it's impossible to miss the massive iron pan atop a wooden fire being attended to by multiple chefs. They'll be making up fresh seafood-and-chicken *paella* all day long, so stop in at any time and get one of the warmest, freshest, and tastiest samplings on the Costa del Sol.

At the end of the Antonia Mercero boardwalk. **i** *Flamenco July-Sept W 9-11pm.* Ⓢ *Appetizers and eggs €2-8.25. Paella €6. Meat and fish €5-14.50. Beer €1.80. House wine €7 per bottle.* *Open daily noon-10pm.*

LA PUNTILLA — SEAFOOD ❷

C. Bolivia, 1 — ☎952 528 951 lapuntillanerja@hotmail.com

Even in a beach town, you may find yourself frustrated with all those deep-fried, breaded menu items that you can't even identify (it's popcorn something, right?). Well, that's definitely not the case at La Puntilla. Walking by the outside street patio, you'll see all the fresh catches of the day in the window, from the thick tuna steak to the whole local *dorada* and *chuta*. Based on the market price, the chefs behind the bar will gladly prepare these seafood treats however you like and serve them up piping hot. You can also take your pick of the white clams or mussels *(half-ration €4.50, full ration €8)*, or the absolutely massive *langostinos (market price)*. You can even abandon basic simplicity with the house recommendation of *zarzuela*, a whole fried fish served in a deep dish of marinated vegetables *(€36; serves at least 2)*. The local regulars might share their favorites (not just verbally—they may very well pass a plate) with you at the metallic bar and may even usher you up the stairs to catch the views off the summer rooftop terrace.

From C. Ruperto Anduez, turn onto C. San Pedro, and it becomes C. Bolivia. **i** *Rooftop terrace open July-Aug. Fresh seafood based on market price and weight.* Ⓢ *Eggs €2.20-4.20. Fish half-ration €3.50-5.30, full €6-11.60. Meat €2.50-11.50. Desserts €3-3.30.* *Open daily 11:30am-4:30pm and 7:30pm-midnight.*

NIGHTLIFE

Nightlife in Nerja, like all other aspects of the city, changes from season to season. The sunnier it is, the more tourists you'll find. As far as lingo goes, keep in mind that the "pubs" will have lengthy drink menus but aren't just for sitting and sipping—they'll often have dance floors in addition to their large, outdoor terraces. Along **Playa Buriana,** you'll come across lots of English-run pubs that are popular but overflowing with every tourist in town. **Plaza Tutti Frutti** is the heart of the night scene, lined with pubs and clubs on all sides. Keep your eyes peeled for promoters handing out **two-for-one drink deals** and other specials along the plaza. All establishments on the plaza open at 10pm and close between 3 and 4:30am. There are a few designated *discotecas* just outside the plaza, the most popular of which is **Jimmy's** *(C. de Antonio Millón),* but these dance havens don't even open until 2am.

LA EMBAJADA — PUB, DISCOTECA

Pl. Tutti Frutti 2 — www.publaembajada.com

Walking around Plaza Tutti Frutti, you'll notice that La Embajada is one of the few places bringing in more locals than tourists. The reason's simple: this card-themed, black-and-red bar and dance floor is a total ace. You can enjoy the comfy white couches on the outdoor terrace while checking out the flatscreen TV or make your way inside (where you'll find yet another bar, another flatscreen, and an elevated DJ booth) to dance, and maybe find that lucky king or queen (or jack?). While the drinks aren't necessarily cheap, you do get to choose from quite the cocktail selection *(€5)*—the sex on *la embajada* (vodka, grenadine, peach liquor, and orange juice) is one of the biggest sellers. If you're visiting in July or August, the Friday-night themed parties make La Embajada one of the hottest spots in town.

If entering Pl. Tutti Frutti from Av. Castilla Perez, it's one of the 1st bars on the right. Beer €3. Cocktails €5. Open daily 10pm-4:30am.

BAR BLANCO Y NEGRO — BAR

C. Pintada, 35 — ☎606 853 352 — www.myspace.com/blackandwhitebarnerja

You're walking up C. Pintada any night of the week. You start to hear the drumbeat of your favorite '90s hit. As you keep walking, some of the melodies join in, too. Then you get really close to the marbled hallway leading to Bar Blanco y Negro, and you realize that the lyrics are totally tone deaf. The stereo isn't broken—you have arrived at Nerja's top "entertainment bar." Inside, the checkered tiles covering the steps lead to the colorfully lit stage where there is karaoke every night of the week *(10pm)* except Saturdays, when the spotlight shifts to high-energy live concerts. Pick from the selection of creatively titled shots like the "lollipop" (Amaretto, grenadine, and lime) or wild and fruity cocktails like the bar's most popular, the "fat hooker" (vodka, peach schnapps, Malibu, and orange juice). If none of their combos tempts your wild side, they're happy to mix up anything upon request.

As you face the water, it's on the right-hand side of C. Pintada down a small hallway. Beer €1.50. Shots €2.50; 6 for €12.50. Cocktails €6. Jugs €17. Open daily 11am-5am.

H2O — BAR, LOUNGE

Playa Buriana s/n — ☎952 525 971 — www.h2onerja.com

Coming off your day in a lounge chair on Playa Buriana, you may be ready for a cold cocktail...or 50. H2O is Playa Buriana's most packed evening destination, and this massive cocktail bar will mix up over 50 varieties of fruity combos, stretching your alcoholic imagination to new lengths. The Hawaiian Deluxxe *(€7.50),* made with Malibu, Cointreau, Brugal rum, grenadine, and various juices, is their most popular signature drink, but they can make you an assortment of alcoholic drinks by the glass or pitcher. You can also cool off with a non-alcoholic option *(€3.50; pitcher €10)* like the Green Summer Cooler (pineapple juice, lemon juice, hierba buena, and ginger ale). H2O is even the perfect place to snag some Wi-Fi or a fresh salad *(€8)*, sandwich *(€4.50)*, or homemade cake *(€4)* over the course of the day. Check out the website for announcements about occasional free dance parties, celebrating any occasion from "school's out" to the bar's fifth anniversary.

Up C. Filipinas from Playa Buriana. i Non-customers may use Wi-Fi for €2. Cocktails €6-7.50; pitchers €17-19. Non-alcoholic cocktails €3.50; pitchers €10. Beer €1.90-4. Appetizers and desserts €2.50-8. Open daily Apr-Sept 10am-1am; Oct-Mar 1pm-1am.

ESSENTIALS

Practicalities

- **TOURIST OFFICES:** The tourist information office is located on the ground floor of the Ayuntamiento *(C. Carmen 1 ☎952 521 531 tourismo@nerja.org Open M-Sa 10am-2pm and 5-9pm, Su 10am-2pm.)* and can provide maps, guides, schedules, and general information in English and Spanish.
- **CURRENCY EXCHANGE:** You can exchange money at the **La Caixa Bank** *(i 24hr. ATM available. Open M-F 8:15am-2pm.)* at Pl. Cavana or visit the exchange office a few doors down *(C. El Bario s/n ☎670 035 922 www.easynerja.com Open M-Sa 10:15am-1:30pm and 5:30-8:30pm.)*, which will also help you to book a taxi *(€65)* or minibus *(€100)* to the **Málaga Airport.**
- **INTERNET:** The **public library Salvador Rueda** *(☎952 528 252 biblioteca@nerja.es Open M-F 10am-2pm and 5-8pm)* is located at Pl. la Ermita, behind the church, and offers free Wi-Fi and three computers. There is a **Time Sport Fitness Center** *(Av. de Pescia, 21 ☎952 522 882 1-day pass €8, 1-week €38; sauna free Tu for men, Th for women. Open M-F 8am-11pm, Sa 9am-2pm.)* on Av. la Pescia just beyond the intersection with C. Rodriguez Acosta that offers equipment, classes, sauna, and internet access.
- **POST OFFICE:** The post office *(C. Almirante Fernandiz, 6 ☎902 197 197 www.corres.es Open M-F 8:30am-8:30pm and Sa 9:30am-1pm.)*, also offers a bank, a **Western Union,** and **Telecor** phone services.

Emergency!

- **EMERGENCY NUMBER: Ambulance:** ☎902 505 061.
- **POLICE: Local police.** *(C. Virgen de Pilar, 1 ☎091, 952 521 545 policialocal@nerja.org)*.
- **LATE-NIGHT PHARMACIES:** While there is not a specific 24hr. pharmacy in Nerja, the six city pharmacies rotate staying open 24hr. on a six-day cycle.

Getting There

Traveling directly to Nerja is limited to buses and cabs. If you need to fly, the nearest **airport** is in Málaga, and you can then take a bus from there. *(€4. Every 30min. 7am-midnight.)* You can also take a RadioTaxi cab *(€70)* between Nerja and the airport. The tourist website *(www.nerja.org)* has time tables for trips from all nearby cities.

By Bus

You can connect from the bus station *(Av. Pescia s/n ☎902 422 242)*, which is actually more of a busline stop, on **Alsa** buses *(www.alsa.es)* to: **Málaga** *(€4. 1hr., 23 per day 7am-11pm.)*; **Granada** *(€9. 2hr., 7 per day 7am-8pm.)*; **Almeria** *(€12. 4hr., 6 per day 7:45am-7pm.)*; **Córdoba** *(€16. 4½hr.; 3, 5pm.)*; **Sevilla** *(€20. 5hr.; 7, 8am, 6pm.)*; **Madrid** *(€20. 7½hr.; 8, 8:30am, 3, 3:30pm.)*; **Barcelona.** *(€75. 15hr., 9:30pm.)*

costa del sol

ESSENTIALS

You don't have to be a rocket scientist to plan a good trip. (It might help, but it's not required.) You do, however, need to be well prepared, and that's what we can do for you. Essentials is the chapter that gives you all the nitty-gritty you need to know for your trip: the hard information gleaned from 50 years of collective wisdom (and that phone call to Europe the other day that put us on hold for an hour). Planning your trip? Check. Staying safe and healthy? Check. The dirt on transportation? Check. We've also thrown in communications info, meteorological charts, and a **phrasebook,** just for good measure. Plus, for overall trip-planning advice from what to pack (money and as little underwear as possible) to how to take a good passport photo (it's physically impossible; consider airbrushing), you can also check out the Essentials section of www.letsgo.com.

We're not going to lie—this chapter is tough for us to write, and you might not find it as fun of a read as 101 or Discover. But please, for the love of all that is good, read it! It's super helpful, and, most importantly, it means we didn't compile all this technical info and put it in one place for you (yes YOU) for nothing.

greatest hits

- **GOT A VISA?** You won't need one if you're going to be in Europe for less than 90 days. If you will be, though, put it on your spring-cleaning list, since you'll need to apply six to eight weeks in advance (p. 340).
- **GET MONEY.** Paper, plastic, traveler's checks. Which works for you? Each has benefits, don't get screwed on the exchange rate, though (p. 341).
- **BUY A RAILPASS.** Great way to meet people, and one of the cheapest ways to see the Riviera. What could be better (p. 348)?
- **SHIP SOUVENIRS HOME BY SURFACE MAIL.** Our scintillating "By Snail Mail" section will tell you how. You'll laugh, you'll cry (p. 351).
- **CALL YOUR FAMILY.** Your mother will worry if you don't (p. 351).

planning your trip

entrance requirements

- **PASSPORT:** Required for citizens of all countries.
- **VISA:** Required of non-EU citizens staying longer than 90 days.
- **WORK PERMIT:** Required for all foreigners planning to work in EU countries.

DOCUMENTS AND FORMALITIES

You've got your visa, your invitation, and your work permit, just like Let's Go told you to, and then you realize you've forgotten the most important thing: your passport. Well, we're not going to let that happen. **Don't forget your passport!**

Visas

EU citizens do not need a visa to globetrot through the Riviera. Citizens of Australia, Canada, New Zealand, and the US do not need a visa for stays of up to 90 days, but this three-month period begins upon entry into any of the countries that belong to the EU's **freedom of movement** zone. Those staying longer than 90 days may purchase a visa at your local consulate. A visa costs €99 and allows the holder to spend up to 90 days within a six-month period in any Schengen countries.

one europe

The EU's policy of freedom of movement means that most border controls have been abolished and visa policies harmonized. Under this treaty, formally known as the Schengen Agreement, you're still required to carry a passport (or government-issued ID card for EU citizens) when crossing an internal border, but, once you've been admitted into one country, you're free to travel to other participating states. Most EU states are already members of Schengen (excluding Cyprus), as are Iceland and Norway. For more consequences of the EU for travelers, see **The Euro** feature later in this chapter.

Double-check entrance requirements at the nearest embassy or consulate of the countries in the Riviera you plan to visit for up-to-date information before departure. US citizens can also consult travel.state.gov.

Entering the Riviera countries to study requires a special visa. For more information, see the **Beyond Tourism** chapter.

Work Permits

Admittance to a country as a traveler does not include the right to work, which is authorized only by a work permit. For more information, see the **Beyond Tourism** chapter.

TIME DIFFERENCES

The countries in the Riviera are 1hr. ahead of Greenwich Mean Time (GMT) and observe Daylight Saving Time. This means that it is 6hr. ahead of New York City, 9hr. ahead of Los Angeles, 1hr. ahead of the British Isles, 8hr. behind Sydney, and 10hr. behind New Zealand.

french consular services

- **AUSTRALIAN EMBASSY IN PARIS:** *(4 rue Jean Rey 75015 Paris, France ☎+01 40 59 33 06 www.france.embassy.gov.au Open M-F 9am-5pm.)*
- **CANADIAN EMBASSY IN PARIS:** *(35 av. Montaigne, 75008 Paris, France ☎01 44 43 29 00 www.france.gc.ca Open M-F 9am-noon and 2-5pm.)*
- **IRISH EMBASSY IN PARIS:** *(4 rue Rude, 75116 Paris, France ☎01 44 17 67 00 www.embassyofireland.fr Open M-F 9:30am-noon.)*
- **NEW ZEALAND EMBASSY IN PARIS:** *(7ter rue Léonard da Vinci, 75116 Paris, France ☎01 45 01 43 43 www.nzembassy.com/france Open July-Aug M-Th 9am-1pm and 2-4:30pm, F 9am-2pm; Sept-June M-Th 9am-1pm, 2-5:30pm, F 9am-1pm and 2-4pm.)*
- **UNITED KINGDOM EMBASSY IN PARIS:** *(2 av. Gabriel 75382 Paris, France ☎01 43 12 22 22 ukinfrance.fco.gov.uk/en/ Open M-F 9:30am-1pm and 2:30-6pm.)*
- **UNITED STATES EMBASSY IN PARIS:** *(35, rue du Faubourg St. Honoré 75363 Paris, France ☎01 44 51 31 00 french.france.usembassy.gov/ Open M-F 9:30am-1pm and 2:30-6pm.)*
- **FRENCH CONSULATE IN AUSTRALIA:** *(Level 26, St. Martins Tower, 31 Market St., Sydney NSW 2000 ☎02 9268 2400 www.ambafrance-au.org Open M-F 9am-1pm.)*
- **FRENCH CONSULATE IN CANADA:** *(1 pl. Ville Marie Montréal, QC H3B 4S3, Canada ☎514 878 3485 www.consulfrance-montreal.org Open M-F 9:30am-4:30pm.)*
- **FRENCH EMBASSY IN IRELAND:** *(36 Ailesbury Rd., Dublin 4, Ireland ☎+353 1 277 5000 www.ambafrance.ie/ Open M-F 9:30am-noon.)*
- **FRENCH EMBASSY IN NEW ZEALAND:** *(34-42 Manners St. PO Box 11-343 Wellington, New Zealand ☎43 84 25 55 www.ambafrance-nz.org/ Open M-Th 9am-6pm, F 9am-4pm.)*
- **FRENCH CONSULATE IN UNITED KINGDOM:** *(21 Cromwell Rd., London SW2 2EN ☎020 7073 1250 www.ambafrance-uk.org/ Open M-Th 8:45am-noon, F 8:45-11:30am.)*
- **FRENCH CONSULATE IN UNITED STATES:** *(4101 Reservoir Rd. NW, Washington, DC 20007-2151 ☎202 944 6000 www.ambafrance-us.org Open M-F 8:45am-12:45pm.)*

money

GETTING MONEY FROM HOME

Stuff happens. When stuff happens, you might need some money. When you need some money, the easiest and cheapest solution is to have someone back home make a deposit to your bank account. Otherwise, consider one of the following options.

Wiring Money

Arranging a **bank money transfer** means asking a bank back home to wire money to a bank in Europe. This is the cheapest way to transfer cash, but it's also the slowest and most agonizing, usually taking several days or more. Note that some banks may

spanish consular services

- **AUSTRALIAN EMBASSY IN SPAIN: Embassy.** *(Torre Espacio, Paseo de la Castellana, 259D, Planta 24, Madrid 28046 ☎34 91 353 6600 www.spain.embassy.gov.au Open M-Th 8:30am-5pm, F 8:30am-2:15pm.)*
- **BRITISH EMBASSY IN SPAIN: Embassy.** *(Torre Espacio, Paseo de la Castellana 259D, 28046 Madrid ☎34 91 714 6300 www.mae.es/Embajadas/Ottawa/en/Home Open M-Th 8:30am-5pm, F 8:30am-2:15pm.*
- **CANADIAN EMBASSY IN SPAIN: Embassy.** *(Torre Espacio, Paseo de la Castellana, 259D, Madrid 28046 ☎34 91 382 8400 www.canadainternational.gc.ca/spain-espagne/ Open Sept-July M-Th 8:30am-2pm and 3-5:30pm F 8:30am-2:15pm; Aug M-F 8:30am-2:15pm.)*
- **IRISH EMBASSY IN SPAIN: Consulate.** *(Gran Vía Carlos III, 94, Barcelona 08028 ☎34 93 49 15 021 www.irlanda.es Open M-F 10am-1pm.)*
- **NEW ZEALAND EMBASSY IN SPAIN: Embassy.** *(Pinar 7, 3rd fl., Madrid 28046 ☎34 91 523 0226 www.nxembassy.com/spain Open July-Aug M-F 8:30am-1:30 and 2-4:30pm; Sept-June M-F 9am-2pm and 3-5:30pm.)*
- **USA EMBASSY IN SPAIN: Embassy.** *(c. de Serrano 75, Madrid 28006 ☎34 91 587 2200 www.embusa.es Open M-F 8:30am-1pm.)*
- **SPANISH CONSULATE IN AUSTRALIA: Consulate General.** *(Level 26, St-Martins Tower, 31 Market St., Sydney NSW 2000 ☎+61 2 9261 2433 www.ambafrance-au.org Open M-F 9am-1pm.)*
- **SPANISH EMBASSY IN BRITAIN: Embassy.** *(39 Chesham Pl., London SW1X 8SB ☎20 7235 55 55 www.maec.es/Embajadas/Londres Open M-F 9:30am-noon.)*
- **SPANISH EMBASSY IN CANADA: Embassy.** *74 Stanley Ave., Ottawa, Ontario, Canada, K1M 1P4 ☎613 747 2252 www.mae.es/Embajadas/Ottawa/en/Home Open M-Th 8:30am-5pm F 8:30am-2:15pm.)*
- **SPANISH EMBASSY IN IRELAND: Embassy.** *(3rd fl., Block E, Iveagh Ct., Harcourt Rd., Dublin Ireland ☎352 1 26 08 066 www.mae.es/Embajadas/dublin Open M-F 9:30am-1:30pm.)*
- **SPANISH CONSULATE IN NEW ZEALAND:** in Canberra, Australia.
- **SPANISH EMBASSY IN USA: Embassy** *(2375 Pennsylvania Ave., Washington DC 20037 ☎+01 202 452 0100 www.maec.es/embajadas/Washington).*

only release your funds in local currency, potentially sticking you with a poor exchange rate; inquire about this in advance. Money transfer services like **Western Union** are faster and more convenient than bank transfers—but also much pricier. Western Union has many locations worldwide. To find one, visit www.westernunion.com or call the appropriate number: in Australia ☎1800 173 833, in Canada and the US 800-325-6000, in the UK 0800 735 1815. To wire money using a credit card in Canada and the US, call ☎800-CALL-CASH; in the UK, 0800 833 833. Money transfer services are also available to **American Express** cardholders and at selected **Thomas Cook** offices.

italian consular services

- **AUSTRALIAN EMBASSY IN ITALY:** (*V. Antonio Bosio 5, Rome 00161 ☎06 85 27 21, emergency ☎800 87 77 90 🖳www.italy.embassy.gov.au ⏰ Open M-F 9am-5pm.)*
- **BRITISH EMBASSY IN ITALY:** (*V. XX Settembre 80a, Rome 00187 ☎06 42 20 00 01 🖳www.britain.it ⏰ Open M-F 9:15am-1:30pm.)*
- **CANADIAN EMBASSY IN ITALY:** (*V. Zara 30, Rome 00198 ☎06 85 444 🖳www.canadainternational.gc.ca/italy-italie/index.aspx ⏰ Open M-Th 8:30-11:30am.)*
- **IRISH EMBASSY IN ITALY:** (*P. di Campitelli 3, Rome 00186 ☎06 69 79 121 🖳www.ambasciata-irlanda.it ⏰ Open M-F 10am-12:30pm and 3-4:30pm.)*
- **NEW ZEALAND EMBASSY IN ITALY:** (*V. Clitunno 44, Rome 00198 ☎06 85 37 501 🖳www.nzembassy.com/italy ⏰ Open M-F 8:30am-12:45pm and 1:45-5pm.)*
- **USA EMBASSY IN ITALY:** (*V. Vittorio Veneto 121, Rome 00187 ☎06 46 741 🖳rome.usembassy.gov ⏰ Open M-F 8:30am-12:30pm.)*
- **ITALIAN EMBASSY IN AUSTRALIA:** (*12 Grey St., Deakin, Canberra ACT 2600 ☎02 6273 3333 🖳www.ambcanberra.esteri.it ⏰ Open M-F 9am-noon.)*
- **ITALIAN EMBASSY IN CANADA: (***275 Slater St., 21st fl., Ottawa, ON K1P 5H9 ☎613-232-2401 🖳www.ambottawa.esteri.it ⏰ Open M-Tu 9am-noon, W 9am-noon and 2-4pm, Th-F 9am-noon.)*
- **ITALIAN EMBASSY IN IRELAND:** (*63/65 Northumberland Rd., Dublin 4 ☎01 660 1744 🖳www.ambdublino.esteri.it ⏰ Open M-W 10am-noon, Th 1:30-3:30pm, F 10am-noon.)*
- **ITALIAN EMBASSY IN NEW ZEALAND:** (*34-38 Grant Rd., PO Box 463, Thorndon, Wellington ☎04 4735 339 🖳www.ambwellington.esteri.it ⏰ Open M-Tu 9am-1pm, W 9am-1pm and 3-4:45pm, Th-F 9am-1pm.)*
- **ITALIAN CONSULATE GENERAL IN UK:** (*38 Eaton Pl., London SW1X 8AN ☎020 7235 9371 🖳www.conslondra.esteri.it ⏰ Open M-F 9am-noon.)*
- **ITALIAN EMBASSY IN USA:** (*3000 Whitehaven St. NW, Washington, DC 20008 ☎202-612-4400 🖳www.ambwashingtondc.esteri.it ⏰ Open M 10am-12:30pm, W 10am-12:30pm, F 10am-12:30pm.)*

US State Department (US Citizens only)

In serious emergencies only, the US State Department will forward money within hours to the nearest consular office, which will then disburse it according to instructions for a US$30 fee. If you wish to use this service, you must contact the Overseas Citizens Services division of the US State Department *(☎+1-202-501-4444, from US 888-407-4747).*

TIPPING AND BARGAINING

In France, service is added to bills in bars and restaurants, called "*service compris.*" Most people do, however, leave some change (up to €2) for drinks and food, and in nicer restaurants it is not uncommon to leave 5% of the bill. For other services, like taxis and haircuts, 10-15% tip is acceptable.

In Italy, tips of 5-10% are customary, particularly in restaurants. Italian waiters won't cry if you don't leave a tip—just get ready to ignore the pangs of your

pins and atms

To use a debit or credit card to withdraw money from a cash machine (ATM) in Europe, you must have a four-digit Personal Identification Number (PIN). If your PIN is longer than four digits, ask your bank whether you can just use the first four or whether you'll need a new one. Credit cards don't usually come with PINs, so if you intend to hit up ATMs in Europe with a credit card to get cash advances, call your credit card company before leaving to request one.

Travelers with alphabetic rather than numeric PINs may also be thrown off by the absence of letters on European cash machines. Here are the corresponding numbers to use: 1 = QZ; 2 = ABC; 3 = DEF; 4 = GHI; 5 = JKL; 6 = MNO; 7 = PRS; 8 = TUV; 9 = WXY. Note that if you mistakenly punch the wrong code into the machine multiple (often three) times, it can swallow (gulp!) your card for good.

conscience later on. Taxi drivers expect the same kind of tip, but lucky for you alcoholics, it is unusual to tip in bars.

Native Spaniards rarely tip more than their spare change, even at expensive restaurants. However, if you make it clear that you're a tourist—especially an American one—they might expect you to tip more. Don't feel like you have to tip, as the servers' pay is almost never based on gratuity. No one will refuse your money, but you're a poor student so don't play the fool.

In the Riviera, bargaining is acceptable (and advised!) at open air markets, but it's less appropriate in regular shops. Looks like you'll be paying retail...

TAXES

The European Union requires that member countries add a value added tax (VAT) of 19.6%, which is applied to a variety of goods and services (e.g. food, accommodations), though it is less for food (5.5%). Non-European Economic Community visitors to France who are taking these goods home may be refunded this tax for purchases totaling over €175 per store. When making purchases, request a VAT form, and present them at the détaxe booth at the airport. These goods must be carried at all times while traveling, and refunds must be claimed within six months.

safety and health

GENERAL ADVICE

In any type of crisis, the most important thing to do is **stay calm.** Your country's embassy abroad is usually your best resource in an emergency; registering with that embassy upon arrival in the country is a good idea. The government offices listed in the **Travel Advisories** feature at the end of this section can provide information on the services they offer their citizens in case of emergencies abroad.

Local Laws and Police

Who ya gonna call? It is unlikely that you'll unintentionally break the law while in the Riviera, but should you find yourself behind bars you can phone the local embassy. They probably won't get you released, but they can help you secure counsel. In Italy, the two law enforcement bodies are the *polizia (☎113)* and the *carabinieri (☎112).* If you need assistance in Spain, the **Policía Nacional** *(☎092)* deal with crime investigation and theft, while the **Policía Local** *(☎091)* deal specifically with local issues. In France, **La Police Nationale** is the branch of French law enforcement that is most often seen in urban areas, and they can be reached by calling ☎17.

the euro

Despite what many dollar-possessing Americans might want to hear, the official currency of 16 members of the European Union—Austria, Belgium, Cyprus, Finland, France, Germany, Greece, Ireland, Italy, Luxembourg, Malta, the Netherlands, Portugal, Slovakia, Slovenia, and Spain—is the euro.

Still, the currency has some important—and positive—consequences for travelers hitting more than one eurozone country. For one thing, money-changers across the eurozone are obliged to exchange money at the official, fixed rate (below) and at no commission (though they may still charge a small service fee). Second, euro-denominated traveler's checks allow you to pay for goods and services across the eurozone, again at the official rate and commission-free. For more info, check a currency converter (such as www.xe.com) or www.europa.eu.int.

Drugs and Alcohol

Recreational drugs are illegal in all countries in the Riviera, and the laws are taken quite seriously. The legal blood alcohol content in Spain, Italy, and France is .05, which is lower than most other countries, so think twice before getting behind the wheel.

SPECIFIC CONCERNS

Travelers with Disabilities

Those in wheelchairs should be aware that travel in Italy will sometimes be extremely difficult. Many cities predate the wheelchair—and sometimes it seems even the wheel—by several centuries and thus pose unique challenges to disabled travelers. Venice is particularly difficult to navigate in a wheelchair given its narrow streets and numerous bridges (many with steps). Be aware that while an establishment itself may be wheelchair-accessible, getting to the front door in a wheelchair might be virtually impossible. **Accessible Italy** *(☎+378 941 111 www.accessibleitaly.com)* is an organization that offers advice to tourists of limited mobility heading to Italy, with tips offered on subjects ranging from finding accessible accommodations to organizing wheelchair rental.

Natural Disasters

Italy is liable to occasional earthquakes and volcanic eruptions. If Vesuvius decides to become active during your trip (this could actually happen), your best resource will be your country's embassy.

Demonstrations and Political Gatherings

The French Revolution may have been in 1789, but the spirit of the revolution certainly hasn't died. Protests and strikes are frequent in France, but violence does not often occur. You may find yourself in Grenoble on the day of a transit strike (as one *Let's Go* researcher did), but who hasn't always wanted to see France by Vespa?

PRE-DEPARTURE HEALTH

Matching a prescription to a foreign equivalent is not always easy, safe, or possible, so if you take **prescription drugs,** carry up-to-date prescriptions or a statement from your doctor stating the medications' trade names, manufacturers, chemical names, and dosages. Be sure to keep all medication with you in your carry-on luggage.

The names in France, Italy, and Spain for common drugs are quite similar to English, and most pharmacists speak at least a little English so you should have little trouble finding the drugs that you need.

travel advisories

The following government offices provide travel information and advisories by telephone, by fax, or via the web:

- **AUSTRALIA: Department of Foreign Affairs and Trade** *(☎+61 2 6261 1111 www.dfat.gov.au).*
- **CANADA: Department of Foreign Affairs and International Trade (DFAIT).** Call or visit the website for the free booklet *Bon Voyage...But (☎+1-800-267-8376 www.dfait-maeci.gc.ca).*
- **NEW ZEALAND: Ministry of Foreign Affairs** *(☎+64 4 439 8000 www.mfat.govt.nz).*
- **UK: Foreign and Commonwealth Office** *(☎+44 20 7008 1500 www.fco.gov.uk).*
- **US: Department of State** *(☎888-407-4747 from the US, +1-202-501-4444 elsewhere travel.state.gov).*

Immunizations and Precautions

Travelers over two years old should make sure that the following vaccines are up to date: MMR (for measles, mumps, and rubella); DTaP or Td (for diphtheria, tetanus, and pertussis); IPV (for polio); Hib (for *Haemophilus influenzae* B); and HepB (for Hepatitis B). For recommendations on immunizations and prophylaxis, check with a doctor and consult the **Centers for Disease Control and Prevention (CDC)** in the US or the equivalent in your home country *(☎+1-800-CDC-INFO/232-4636 www.cdc.gov/travel).*

getting around

For information on how to get to the Riviera and save a bundle while doing so, check out the Essentials section of **www.letsgo.com.** (In case you can't tell, we think our website's the bomb.)

BY PLANE

Commercial Airlines

For small-scale travel on the continent, *Let's Go* suggests **budget airlines** for budget travelers, but more traditional carriers have made efforts to keep up with the revolution. The **Star Alliance Europe Airpass** offers low economy-class fares for travel within Europe to 220 destinations in 45 countries. The pass is available to non-European passengers on Star Alliance carriers, including Lufthansa, bmi, Spanair, and TAP Portugal *(www.staralliance.com).* **EuropebyAir's** snazzy FlightPass also allows you to hop between hundreds of cities in Europe and North Africa. *(☎+1-888-321-4737 www.europebyair.com Ⓢ Most flights US$99.)*

In addition, a number of European airlines offer discount coupon packets. Most are only available as tack-ons for transatlantic passengers, but some are standalone offers. Most must be purchased before departure, so research in advance. For example, **oneworld,** a coalition of 10 major international airlines, offers deals and cheap connections all over the world, including within Europe *(www.oneworld.com).*

budget airlines

The recent emergence of no-frills airlines has made hopscotching around Europe by air increasingly affordable. Though these flights often feature inconvenient hours or serve less popular regional airports, with ticket prices often dipping into single digits, it's never been faster or easier to jet across the continent. The following resources will be useful not only for crisscrossing Europe but also for those ever-popular weekend trips to nearby international destinations.

- **BMIBABY:** Departures from multiple cities in the UK to Paris, Nice, and other cities in France *(☎0871 224 0224 for the UK, +44 870 126 6726 elsewhere www.bmibaby.com).*
- **EASYJET:** London to Bordeaux and other cities in France. *(☎+44 871 244 2366, 10p per min. www.easyjet.com Ⓢ UK£50-150.)*
- **RYANAIR:** From Dublin, Glasgow, Liverpool, London, and Shannon to destinations in France *(☎0818 30 30 30 for Ireland, 0871 246 0000 for the UK www.ryanair.com).*
- **SKYEUROPE:** Forty destinations in 19 countries around Europe *(☎0905 722 2747 for the UK, +421 2 3301 7301 elsewhere www.skyeurope.com).*
- **STERLING:** The first Scandinavian-based budget airline connects Denmark, Norway, and Sweden to 47 European destinations, including Montpellier, Nice, and Paris *(☎70 10 84 84 for Denmark, 0870 787 8038 for the UK www.sterling.dk).*
- **TRANSAVIA:** Short hops from Krakow to Paris. *(☎020 7365 4997 for the UK www.transavia.com Ⓢ From €49 one-way.)*
- **WIZZ AIR:** Paris from Budapest, Krakow, and Warsaw *(☎0904 475 9500 for the UK, 65p per min. www.wizzair.com).*

BY TRAIN

Trains in the Riviera are generally comfortable, convenient, and reasonably swift. Second-class compartments, which seat from two to six, are great places to meet fellow travelers. Make sure you are on the correct car, as trains sometimes split at crossroads. Towns listed in parentheses on European train schedules require a train switch at the town listed immediately before the parentheses.

You can either buy a **railpass**, which allows you unlimited travel within a particular region for a given period of time, or rely on buying individual **point-to-point** tickets as you go. Almost all countries give students or youths (under 26, usually) direct discounts on regular domestic rail tickets, and many also sell a student or youth card that provides 20-50% off all fares for up to a year.

BY BUS

Though European trains and railpasses are extremely popular, in some cases buses prove a better option. Some Italian regions, particularly the Amalfi Coast, as well as some rural regions in Spain do not have rail service, and therefore can only be reached by bus. Travel in France though, is generally much easier by other forms of transportation. Often cheaper than railpasses, **international bus passes** allow unlimited travel on a hop-on, hop-off basis between major European cities. **Busabout**, for instance, offers three interconnecting bus circuits covering 29 of Europe's best bus hubs. *(☎+44 8450 267 514 www.busabout.com Ⓢ 1 circuit in high season starts at US$579, students US$549.)* **Eurolines**, meanwhile, is the largest operator of Europe-wide coach

rail resources

- **WWW.RAILEUROPE.COM:** Info on rail travel and railpasses.
- **POINT-TO-POINT FARES AND SCHEDULES:** www.raileurope.com/us/rail/fares_schedules/index.htm allows you to calculate whether buying a railpass would save you money.
- **WWW.RAILSAVER.COM:** Uses your itinerary to calculate the best railpass for your trip.
- **WWW.RAILFANEUROPE.NET:** Links to rail servers throughout Europe.
- **WWW.LETSGO.COM:** Check out the Essentials section for more details.

services. We get misty-eyed just thinking about their unlimited 15- and 30-day passes to 41 major European cities. *(www.eurolines.com High-season 15-day pass €345, 30-day pass €455; under 26 €290/375. Mid-season €240/330; under 26 €205/270. Low-season €205/310; under 26 €175/240.)*

BY BOAT

Most European ferries are quite comfortable; the cheapest ticket typically still includes a reclining chair or couchette. Fares jump sharply in July and August. Ask for discounts; ISIC and Eurail Pass holders get many reductions and free trips. You'll occasionally have to pay a port tax (under US$10).

Spain offers ferries for three major destinations: from Andalusian coastal towns to Morocco, between the Canary Islands in the Atlantic, and from Barcelona or Valencia to the Balearic Islands (read: Partytown, Ibiza).

Ferries are also a great budget option for travel in the south of France. **Corsica Ferries** runs from Nice and Toulon to Corsica. For the traveler with a little more money to burn, there are also ferries to St-Tropez from St-Raphaël. They run more frequently during July and August, check www.bateauxsaintraphael.com for more information.

If you want to travel to Sicily or Sardinia, a ferry will probably be the best option. **Tirrenia** *(www.tirrenia.it)* is Italy's largest ferry company, running routes to and from Sicily, Sardinia, Albania, and Tunisia. Check their website when you plan your trip since most routes only run on certain days of the week.

BY BICYCLE

Some youth hostels rent bicycles for low prices, and in France and Spain there are often on-street terminals where you can rent bikes and drop them off elsewhere. In addition to **panniers** (US$40-150) to hold your luggage, you'll need a good **helmet** (US$10-40) and a sturdy **lock** (from US$30). For more country-specific books on biking through the Riviera, try **Mountaineers Books** *(1001 SW Klickitat Way, Ste. 201, Seattle, WA 98134, USA ☎+1-206-223-6303 www.mountaineersbooks.org).*

keeping in touch

BY EMAIL AND INTERNET

Hello and welcome to the 21st century, where you can check your email in most major European cities, though sometimes you'll have to pay a few bucks or buy a drink for internet access. Although in some places it's possible to forge a remote link with your home server, in most cases this is a much slower (and thus more expensive) option than taking advantage of free **web-based email accounts** (e.g.,

www.gmail.com). **Internet cafes** are listed in the **Practicalities** sections of cities that we cover. For lists of additional cybercafes in the Riviera, check out www.cybercaptive.com and www.netcafeguide.com.

Wireless hot spots make internet access possible in public and remote places. Unfortunately, they also pose security risks. Hot spots are public, open networks that use unencrypted, unsecured connections. They are susceptible to hacks and "packet sniffing"—the theft of passwords and other private information. To prevent problems, disable "ad hoc" mode, turn off file sharing and network discovery, encrypt your email, turn on your firewall, beware of phony networks, and watch for over-the-shoulder creeps.

BY TELEPHONE

Calling Home from the European Riviera

Prepaid phone cards are a common and relatively inexpensive means of calling abroad. Each one comes with a Personal Identification Number (PIN) and a toll-free access number. You call the access number and then follow the directions for dialing your PIN. To purchase prepaid phone cards, check online for the best rates; www.callingcards.com is a good place to start. Online providers generally send your access number and PIN via email, with no actual "card" involved. You can also call home with prepaid phone cards purchased in Europe.

If you have internet access, your best—i.e., cheapest, most convenient, and most tech-savvy—bet is probably our good friend **Skype.** *(www.skype.com)* You can even videochat if you have one of those new-fangled webcams. Calls to other Skype users are free; calls to landlines and mobiles worldwide start at US$0.021 per minute, depending on where you're calling.

Another option is a **calling card,** linked to a major national telecommunications service in your home country. Calls are billed collect or to your account. Cards generally come with instructions for dialing both domestically and internationally.

Placing a collect call through an international operator can be expensive but may be necessary in case of an emergency. You can frequently call collect without even possessing a company's calling card just by calling its access number and following the instructions.

Cellular Phones

The international standard for cell phones is **Global System for Mobile Communication (GSM).** To make and receive calls in countries in the European Riviera, you will need a GSM-compatible phone and a **SIM (Subscriber Identity Module) card,** a country-specific, thumbnail-size chip that gives you a local phone number and plugs you into the local network. Many SIM cards are prepaid, and incoming calls are frequently free. You can buy additional cards or vouchers (usually available at convenience stores) to "top up" your phone. For more information on GSM phones, check out www.telestial.com. Companies like **Cellular Abroad** *(www.cellularabroad.com)* and **OneSimCard** *(www.onesimcard.com)* rent cell phones and SIM cards that work in a variety of destinations around the world.

BY SNAIL MAIL

Sending Mail Home from the European Riviera

Airmail is the best way to send mail home from the countries in the Riviera. **Aerogrammes,** printed sheets that fold into envelopes and travel via airmail, are available at post offices. Write "airmail," "*par avion,*" in French, "*per posta aera,*" in Italian, or "*por avion,*" in Spanish) on the front. Most post offices will charge exorbitant fees or simply refuse to send aerogrammes with enclosures. Surface mail is by far the cheapest and slowest way to send mail. It takes one to two months to cross the Atlantic and one to three to cross the Pacific—good for heavy items you won't need for a while, like souvenirs that you've acquired along the way.

international calls

To call countries in the Riviera from home or to call home from countries in the Riviera, dial:

- **1. THE INTERNATIONAL DIALING PREFIX.** To call from Australia, dial ☎0011; Canada or the US, ☎011; Ireland, New Zealand, the UK, France, Italy, or Spain ☎00.
- **2. THE COUNTRY CODE OF THE COUNTRY YOU WANT TO CALL.** To call Australia, dial ☎61; Canada or the US, ☎1; Ireland, ☎353; New Zealand, ☎64; the UK, ☎44; France, ☎33; Italy ☎39; Spain ☎34.
- **3. THE CITY/AREA CODE.** *Let's Go* lists the city/area codes for cities and towns in the Riviera opposite the city or town name, next to a ☎, as well as in every phone number. If the first digit is a zero (e.g., ☎04 for Cannes), omit the zero when calling from abroad (e.g., dial ☎4 from Canada to reach Cannes).
- **4. THE LOCAL NUMBER.**

Sending Mail to the European Riviera

In addition to the standard postage system whose rates are listed below, **Federal Express** handles express mail services from most countries to France, Italy, and Spain (*☎+1-800-463-3339 www.fedex.com*). Sending a postcard within France costs €0.56, while sending letters (up to 20g) domestically requires €0.56. Sending a postcard within Spain costs €0.78 while sending letters up to 20g domestically requires €0.34.

There are several ways to arrange pickup of letters sent to you while you are abroad. Mail can be sent via **Poste Restante** (General Delivery; *Lista de Correos* in Spanish, *Fermo Posta* in Italian) to almost any city or town in the Riviera with a post office, but it is not very reliable in all parts of the Riviera.

Address Poste Restante letters like so:

Napoleon BONAPARTE
Poste Restante (in your language)
Cannes, France

The mail will go to a special desk in the central post office, unless you specify a post office by street address or postal code. It's best to use the largest post office, since mail may be sent there regardless. It is usually safer and quicker, though more expensive, to send mail express or registered. Bring your passport (or other photo ID) for pickup; there may be a small fee. If the clerks insist that there is nothing for you, ask them to check under your first name as well. *Let's Go* lists post offices in the **Practicalities** section for each city.

American Express has travel offices throughout the world that offer a free **Client Letter Service** (mail held up to 30 days and forwarded upon request) for cardholders who contact them in advance. Some offices provide these services to non-cardholders (especially AmEx Travelers Cheque holders), but call ahead to make sure. For a complete list of AmEx locations, call ☎+1-800-528-4800 or visit www.americanexpress.com/travel.

climate

With the Riviera bordering the Mediterranean Ocean, the weather is what you might expect. Winters tend to be pretty mild, with summers having that balmy Mediterranean air you know and love (or you soon will after you visit).

AVG. TEMP. (LOW/ HIGH), PRECIP.	JANUARY			APRIL			JULY			OCTOBER		
	°C	°F	mm	°C	°F	mm	°C	°F	mm	°C	°F	mm
Barcelona	5/13	42/56	32	9/18	49/64	28	19/28	67/82	12	14/22	57/71	58
Marseille	2/10	36/50	43	8/18	46/64	42	17/29	63/84	11	10/20	50/68	76
Naples	4/12	39/54	116	9/18	48/94	62	18/29	64/82	19	12/22	54/72	107

To convert from degrees Fahrenheit to degrees Celsius, subtract 32 and multiply by 5/9. To convert from Celsius to Fahrenheit, multiply by 9/5 and add 32.

°CELSIUS	-5	0	5	10	15	20	25	30	35	40
°FAHRENHEIT	23	32	41	50	59	68	77	86	95	104

measurements

Like the rest of the rational world, France, Italy, and Spain use the metric system. The basic unit of length is the meter (m), which is divided into 100 centimeters (cm) or 1000 millimeters (mm). One thousand meters make up one kilometer (km). Fluids are measured in liters (L), each divided into 1000 milliliters (mL). A liter of pure water weighs one kilogram (kg), the unit of mass that is divided into 1000 grams (g). One metric ton is 1000kg. In Italy, you might find food items measured by *ettos*, which are equivalent to 100g.

MEASUREMENT CONVERSIONS	
1 inch (in.) = 25.4mm	1 millimeter (mm) = 0.039 in.
1 foot (ft.) = 0.305m	1 meter (m) = 3.28 ft.
1 yard (yd.) = 0.914m	1 meter (m) = 1.094 yd.
1 mile (mi.) = 1.609km	1 kilometer (km) = 0.621 mi.
1 ounce (oz.) = 28.35g	1 gram (g) = 0.035 oz.
1 pound (lb.) = 0.454kg	1 kilogram (kg) = 2.205 lb.
1 fluid ounce (fl. oz.) = 29.57mL	1 milliliter (mL) = 0.034 fl. oz.
1 gallon (gal.) = 3.785L	1 liter (L) = 0.264 gal.

language

Bienvenida! Bienvenue! Benvenuto! Depending on what part of the Riviera you're in, you will (hopefully) be welcomed warmly in either Spanish, French, or Italian. If you're used to speaking Spanish in America, you'll find that "real" Spanish is a little different: *c*'s and *z*'s sound like a *"th"*-sound rather than an *"s"*-sound. Fear not; the entire country doesn't have a speech impediment, promise. Throughout the Riviera though, you'll be likely to find an English speaker where you want one the most (hospitals, hotels, police stations) so even if you aren't a romance language scholar, you'll get by.

PRONUNCIATION

Though French, Italian, and Spanish use the same phonetic sounds as English, they're all represented differently (just to shake stuff up, naturally). As funny as tourists struggling through languages can be, here are a few pointers to sounding things out during your stay in the Riviera.

French

PHONETIC UNIT	PRONUNCIATION	PHONETIC UNIT	PRONUNCIATION
au	o, as in "go"	ch	sh, as in "shoe"
oi	ua as in "guava"	ou	oo, as in "igloo"
ai	ay as in "lay"	å	ah, as in "menorah"

Spanish

PHONETIC UNIT	PRONUNCIATION	PHONETIC UNIT	PRONUNCIATION
a	aw, as in "law"	u	oo, as in "boo"
e	ey as in "ray"	ll	y-, as in "year"
i	ee as in "fee"	j	h- as in "hat"
o	oh as in "oval"	v	a mixture of v/b

Italian

PHONETIC UNIT	PRONUNCIATION	PHONETIC UNIT	PRONUNCIATION
a	"a" as in "father" *(casa)*	o (closed)	"o" as in "bone" *(sono)*
e (closed)	"ay" as in "gray" *(sera)*	o (open)	"aw" as in "ought" *(bocca)*
e (open)	"eh" as in "wet" *(sette)*	u	"oo" as in "moon" *(gusto)*
i	"ee" as in "cheese" *(vino)*		

PHRASEBOOK

ENGLISH	SPANISH	FRENCH	ITALIAN
I am from (the US/ Europe).	Soy de (los Estados Unidos/Europa).	Je suis de (USA / Europe).	Io sono di (USA / Europa).
I have a visa/ID.	Tengo una visa/identificación.	J'ai un visa/ID.	Ho un visto/ID.
I will be here for less than six months.	Estaré aquí por menos de seis meses.	Je serai ici pour au moins six mois.	Sarò qui per meno di sei mesi.
What's the problem, sir/ madam?	¿Cuál es el problema, señor/señora?	Quel est le problème, monsieur/madame?	Qual è il problema, signore/signora?
I lost my passport/ luggage.	Se perdió mi pasaporte/ equipaje.	J'ai perdu mon passeport/bagages.	Ha perso il mio passaporto/bagaglio.
I have nothing to declare.	No tengo nada para declarar.	Je n'ai rien à déclarer.	Non ho niente da dichiarare.
Help please!	Ayúdame por favor!	Aidez-moi s'il vous plaît!	Aiuto per favore!
Where is the nearest hospital?	¿Dónde está el hospital más cercano?	Où est l'hôpital le plus proche?	Dove si trova l'ospedale più vicino?
I am hurt.	Estoy herido.	Je suis blessé.	Sto male.

let's go online

Plan your next trip on our spiffy website, www.letsgo.com. It features full book content, the latest travel info on your favorite destinations, and tons of interactive features: make your own itinerary, read blogs from our trusty Researcher-Writers, browse our photo library, watch exclusive videos, check out our newsletter, find travel deals, follow us on Facebook, and buy new guides. Plus, if this Essentials wasn't enough for you, we've got even more online. We're always updating and adding new features, so check back often!

EUROPEAN RIVIERA 101

history

FROM THE CAVES TO THE BEACH

The Southern Coast of Europe has historically been pretty sunny and warm. Given that these two things have always been (and always will be) attractive to humans, this area has been continuously inhabited since **prehistoric times.** Legend has it that **Hercules** stopped by here for a little R and R in what is today **Monaco,** establishing a reputation for ignoring the Gods and kicking ass. This attitude persists in Monaco today, be it the IRS or OECD financial regulations that seek to intervene.

facts and figures

- **NUMBER OF CITIZENS ALLOWED TO GAMBLE IN MONTE CARLO:** 0.
- **JAMES BOND FILMS SHOT IN MONACO:** 3.
- **SOLDIERS IN MONEGASQUE ARMY:** 112.
- **MAN MADE SAND BEACHES IN NICE:** All of them.
- **NUMBER OF FRENCH AT THE BEACH IN WINTER:** None; the French think it's too cold in winter.
- **NAME OF MOST PRESTIGIOUS AWARD IN CANNES FILM FESTIVAL:** Palme d'Or, or "Golden Palm."
- **MAJORITY RELIGION:** Roman Catholic.
- **PERCENT OF MEGA YACHTS THAT VISIT THE RIVIERA IN THEIR LIFETIME:** 90%.
- **PORTS ON THE ITALIAN RIVIERA:** 5.

THANKS GREECE, WE'LL TAKE OVER FROM HERE

After Greek colonization in the seventh century BCE, when the port cities of Nice, Antibes, and St. Pierre-de-l'Almanarre were constructed and populated, **Julius Caesar** took over the area during the **Gallic Wars.** Augustus continued the trend of land acquisition by kicking the **Carthaginians** out of Barcelona and Spain in 19 BCE. By the second century CE, Rome reached the peak of its expansion with the aid of its extensive Southern ports.

ANGSTY TEENAGERS: GOTHS AND VANDALS

Around the fifth century CE, **Germanic tribes** decided that they liked sun and trade routes, and subsequently invaded the Southern Coast. After some internal fighting among the **Visigoths** (the leader **Ataulf's** style wasn't jiving, so his troops killed him in 414), most of the warfare...well...actually continued. The **Vandals** lived up to their name, sacking Roman cities along the coast until the Empire ceased to strike back in 476 CE. With Ostrogoths occupying Genoa and Visigoths in Barcelona, the Riviera seemed doomed to dressing in black and hating their parents forever. Adding to the mix, the **Saracens** decided they'd take **France,** since that wasn't claimed yet.

GIVE PEACE A CHANCE, OR NOT

In 975, the **Goths** were kicked out of the Riviera, and replaced with a steady system of feudalism. Genoa, Monaco, and **Provence** became independent states, while **Barcelona** was annexed by the **Kingdom of Aragon.** During this time, land changed hands many times in a less-than-peaceful manner between the **Italian States**, **French Monarchy** and its **Independent Principalities,** and the **Spanish Monarchy.** Linguists and map makers were beside themselves until the longest game of Risk ever came to a relative end when **Louis XI** of France captured **Provence** in 1486. Monaco was ahead of the game by 200 years, and won its independence when a renegade group lead by **François Grimaldi** disguised themselves as monks and captured the Rock of Monaco in 1297. It just so happens that the Italian word for "monk" is "monaco." The Kingdoms existed in relative peace with each other, with breaks for the **Spanish and Austrian Wars of Succession.** Punished for supporting Spain during the Austrian War of Succession, the French bombarded **Genoa** with 13,000 cannonballs, and forced them to cede **Corsica** to France.

NAPOLEON: OVERALL BADASS

In a flurry of revolutionary fervor, Monaco was quickly engulfed by the volatile state of France in 1793. Not long after, **Napoleon** rose to power and asked Genoa nicely if it would relinquish its political independence. They complied. **Tolstoy** commemorated this occurrence in the first sentence of **War and Peace**: "*Eh bien, mon prince*, so Genoa and Lucca are now no more than private estates of the Bonaparte family." Napoleon annexed **Barcelona** in 1812, and officially incorporated it into the **First French Republic.** All but unknown outside of the city today, Genoa actually mounted a successful revolt against France in 1814, only to be annexed by the **Kingdom of Sardinia** a year later during the

950,000 BCE: Nomadic people known for gambling and not paying income tax settle in Roquebrune-Cap-Martin, near Monaco.

SOMETIME AFTER THAT, BCE: Hercules kicks some Godly ass in Monaco, and a Temple is built in his honor.

58 BCE: Julius Ceasar stops in Monaco after winning Gallic Wars. Decides that he wants Greece too.

8 BCE: Not having enough space for his mega-yacht, Augustus continues to conquer the southern coast of Spain.

1 CE: Romans can finally stop counting their years backwards.

Congress of Vienna. In addition to Genoa, Sardinia was given **Monaco** (as well as the Southern Coast of what it today, France) as a protectorate. Monaco would remain under Italian control until France finally admitted to Monaco's sovereignty, in exchange for 95% of its land. Good deal, no?

IT'S GOOD TO BE THE KING

The Southern Coast of Europe became a popular travel destination for the extremely wealthy around the mid-1800s. Surprisingly, after 800 years of constant warfare, the Riviera wasn't so economically productive. Despite its lack of wealth, there was enough of a demand to build a dinky railroad between the Riviera and the rest of Europe. By 1865, 100,000 visitors were coming every year, mostly from Britain. Seeking to capitalize on the tourism, the **Prince of Monaco** legalized gambling and built the **Monte Carlo Casino**. Meanwhile, the Côte d'Azur became a popular hangout for **Napoleon III, Leopold II,** and **Tsar Alexander II.** Even **Queen Victoria** caught some sun here, accompanied by her entourage of 100 chefs, ladies in waiting, and Indian servants; she also brought her own bed. The **Prince of Wales** went clubbing in **Cannes** every spring for three weeks at a time; he couldn't fit it in his schedule once he became King in 1901, and he never again visited the Riviera while on the throne.

PARTY'S OVER, MAN

With the outbreak of **World War I,** Europe's aristocracies began to disintegrate, and with them the parties as well. With the **European Aristocracy** in shambles, more and more famous **Americans** started visiting the region in the summer months. While Europe was recovering, the dollar was strong (ah, the good 'ol days), allowing poor, alcoholic writers like **F. Scott Fitzgerald** and **Hemingway** to enjoy the high life along the coast. In 1923, **Coco Chanel** took Paris by storm by showing off her dark tan, thus making topless sunbathing popular in the Riviera. You're welcome, gentlemen.

WORLD WAR II

WWII posed another debilitating drain on the Riviera's life, wealth, and culture. Just as prosperity had begun to return to the region, Spain fell to fascism in 1939 after a grueling, three year fight against it in the **Spanish Civil War**. Barcelona was hit particularly hard, as demonstrated by the bombing of the **Cathedral of Barcelona;** 1000 people were killed, most of whom were children. By contrast, France put up a valiant effort for five *whole* weeks before Paris fell to the **Nazis** in 1940. Italy also succumbed to fascism under **Benito Mussolini,** who went ahead and invaded **Monaco.** When Mussolini couldn't keep up, the German Army occupied the state, and attempted to deport its **Jewish population.** At the secret orders of Prince Louis, the Monaco police warned those whom the **Gestapo** planned to arrest in advance. The Riviera remained a fascist stronghold until the **US invasion** of St-Raphaël in 1944. **German** resistance fell quicker than you can say *sieg heil.* Unfortunately for Spain, the fascist dictator **Francisco Franco** did not die until 1975, and actively suppressed the nation's minorities.

4TH CENTURY CE:
Jesus becomes popular, and the first cathedrals are built in Côte d'Azur.

313 CE:
Edict of Milan grants religious freedom in the Roman Empire. Religion is never a problem in Europe ever again.

5TH CENTURY CE:
Goths and Vandals sack Riviera, ending Roman rule as well as dressing in all black and spraypainting the city walls.

1100 CE:
Genoese crusaders mistake green goblet from Middle East as Holy Grail. Monty Python continues search after crusaders proved wrong.

13TH CENTURY CE:
The House of Grimaldi takes over Monaco and begins

uninterrrupted rule for 800 years.

1492 CE: Columbus donates 1/10th of income from New World discovery to Genoese Bank of St. George, marking the first bank bailout.

1765 CE: John Brown recommends that British upperclasses pursue "climo-therapy" to cure tuberculosis. Nice becomes flooded with gold digging women and dying nobles.

1923 CE: Coco Chanel aquires dark tan on the beach, which is all the rage in Paris.

1956 CE: Grace Kelly marries Prince Ranier III of Monaco, infusing some fresh chromosomes into an aesthetically challenged royal family.

TURN THE MUSIC BACK UP!

1946 saw the premier of the **Cannes Film Festival,** making snooty French movies available to hipsters around the world. Keeping in theme with royalty, the **Festival Palace** was built on the **Cercle Nautique,** where the **Prince of Wales** used to meet his mistresses in the 19th century. The Riviera soon became the epicenter for modern royalty, and a popular hang out for **Grace Kelly,** the **Kennedys,** and **Princess Diana** with her lover (shhhh!) Dodi Fayed. St-Tropez became a new place to park your yacht, and Monaco became an even better place to park your money, tax free! Even today, the **Riviera** is an expensive, outlandish destination for the super rich to race cars, gamble, and enjoy wealth. Spain finally caught up to the rest of the region when hosting the 1992 **Summer Olympics** in **Barcelona** with its subsequent rapid urbanization.

customs and etiquette

FIRST IMPRESSIONS

The first time you meet someone in the Riviera, shaking hands is expected, although friends will greet one another with a kiss on the cheek. This is the same in all areas of Italy, Monaco, France, and Spain. If you're planning on eating in a restaurant or heading out clubbing, dress it up—the easiest way to stand out as a tourist is to wear shorts and a T-shirt out to dinner. Don't expect to be let into the club wearing sneakers. At restaurants, the tip is included in the bill, but feel free to leave a 5-10% tip for exceptional service.

WHAT NOT TO SAY

Never discuss money in private or public company. Its seen as tasteless. In restaurants, arguing over who had what when the bill comes up is even more shameless. The host is usually expected to pay; however, among friends it is more common to split the bill by the number in your party. In addition to money, talking about business is also seen as boring. It may seem strange in such a money-infused culture, but keep in mind that there are still some left over cultural quirks from aristocracy.

MAÑANA/DEMAIN/DOMANI

Being late to things is normal. If you're invited to dinner at someone's house, you'll find them unprepared if you show up "on time." Try aiming for 15-30min. late. The attitude of "do it later or tomorrow" is one that Southern Europe embraces. While a German meeting might work differently, a cafe rendez-vous typically never starts at the agreed time.

WE'RE CLOSED

In Spain and especially Barcelona, everything closes between 2 and 4pm, for an official siesta. If it's Sunday, stores stay closed after 2pm. In France and Monaco, businesses that usually continue service on Sundays, such as restaurants and cafes, are closed the day after, on Monday. Keep in mind if you're planning a hot date on a Monday; make sure to reschedule for later in the week. Plus, who want's to go on a date on Monday night?

art and architecture

SPAIN AND BARCELONA

Gaudí is everywhere in Barcelona. If you see something that resembles a melting sand castle, or something out of an acid trip, you can be sure that this Catalan architect crafted it. **Casa Milà,** better known as **La Pedrera,** was built between 1906 and 1910. A wealthy widow's wedding gift to her second husband, the corner building is defined by its undulating and detailed tile work, two of Gaudí's trademarks. Gaudí's also had a hand in Barcelona's most recognizable symbol: **La Sagrada Familia,** the dreamlike church that you see under construction. It's been under construction since 1882, with the expected day of completion in the year 2026 (the 100th anniversary of Gaudí's death). The Church was officially consecrated in November of 2010. The third of Gaudí's most famous structures is the **Parc Güell.** Situated on the el Carmel hill in Barcelona, this trippy park is covered in curvy, 3D mosaics, a massive colonnade, and a mosaic **dragon. Picasso** was also a famous resident of Barcelona. While you'll have to go to Madrid to see Guernica, the **Museu Picasso** has one of the largest collections of mixed-up faces and cubist images in the world. Picasso started painting in 1901, and dabbled in cubism and **communism,** having been awarded the Lenin Peace Prize by the Soviet Government. His movements can be separated into four periods: the **Blue Period** (1901-1904), **Rose Period** (1905-1907), the **African-Influenced Period** (1908-1909), and **Cubism** (1909-1919).

FRANCE AND CÔTE D'AZUR

In France, you can see everything from **Roman Aqueducts** to the **Belle Époque** in the 20th century. In the towns of **St-Raphaël** and **Frejus,** you can still see the Roman aqueducts that still carry water to the cities. In 9 BCE, Augustus built himself a Trophy (**La Turbia**) for conquering the region; part of the structure still stands in nearby **Beausoleil.** Also built by the Romans, the **baths at Cimiez** include an amphitheater, thermal baths and a basilica. Conveniently enough, you can also see the **Henri Matisse** modern art collection in the same city. You can continue your march through art history with the **Gothic Cathedrals** in Grasse and Nice. The **Chappelle de l'Oratoire** in Grasse uses ornate Gothic doors and windows to decorate this high-ceilinged place of worship. Nice is rife with **Baroque cathedrals,** like the **Cathedrale Sainte-Reparate**. In **Saint-jean-Cap-Ferrat**, you can see a perfect example of the beginning of the **Belle Époque** in the **Villa Ephrussi de Rothschild.** The Villa overlooks the Mediterranean, and is surrounded by different themed gardens, including the **Spanish Garden,** and the **Stone Garden.** Back in Nice, the **Hotel Negresco** is another example of the Belle Époque. Built in 1912 by then-famous architect **Eiffel,** the hotel has every extravagant feature you can hope for to attract wealthy clients, including the 16,309 crystal chandelier commissioned by **Czar Nicholas II.** He did not get to deliver it due to the **October Revolution.**

MONACO

Monaco's architectural history is very similar to that of **Côte d'Azur**, only with a little more Italian and Monegasque influence. Most buildings were specially designed to attract recreational tourists at the turn of the century. For the musically inclined, you can visit the **Ópera de Monte-Carlo** and the inner **Salle Garnier**. **Puccini** debuted his *La rondine* here, as well as 45 other world premiers since its opening. A very different sort of attraction, the **Casino Monte-Carlo** is not your average casino. Constructed by architect **Charles Garnier,** who also constructed the **Paris Opera,** the casino is one of the many examples of Beaux Arts, an empire style popular around the time of **Napoleon III.** In case you were afraid there weren't any churches, you can breath a sigh of relief when you reach the **Saint Nicolas Cathedral.** The retable is from 1500, while the whole cathedral was consecrated in 1875. Most of the **Grimaldis** and **Grace Kelly** are buried here.

ITALY

The art and architecture of Italy really need no introduction, and while you won't see as many famous Renaissance masterworks on the Riviera as you will in other areas of the country, this area is still home to some masterworks. First off, it is the site of **Herculaneum** and **Pompeii.** These two cities were leveled in 79 CE after the eruption of Mount Vesuvius, and today they provide some of the clearest examples of Roman architecture and urban planning remaining. Whatever artifacts have been removed from the sites themselves are in **Naples,** a city with its own vibrant artistic and architectural history. In the Middle Ages, the first ever king of Naples built the **Castel Nuovo,** a sturdy, sandstone symbol of Neapolitan power that's seen everything from assassination plots to sacks by the Spaniards. Later on, Bonapartists and Bourbons tricked out the city with newer, grander, buildings that had less of a defend-us-from-invaders aesthetic. The **Piazza del Plebiscito** is an excellent example of city planning, from its opulent royal palace to **San Francesco di Paola,** a church whose Ionic pillars and 52m dome are reminiscent of the Pantheon in Rome.

food and drink

SPAIN

Catalan cuisine is different from the *chocolate con churros* you'll get in the capital city. The food of Barcelona is much more influenced by the Mediterranean and mountains of the Pyrenees, and you'll find a lot of innovative dishes with cod, anchovies, and sardines. If fish isn't your thing, there are also heavy pork dishes as well. Vegetarians, don't go running away just yet. The food is also heavily influenced by tomatoes, red pepper, and Arbequina olive oils. For dessert, try a *creme catalana,* a yellow custard-like creme which can be its own dessert, or stuffed in pastries.

FRANCE

You'll never get tired of citrus and fruits, unless you go to the South of France. This area is also the main supplier of herbs for the country, as well as for a lot of Europe. Honey is a staple and prized ingredient in this region, as well as goat cheese, sausages, and lamb. Making use of the sea as well, there are also many dishes that include garlic anchovies. Try drinking **Pastis,** a yellow anise-flavored alcoholic drink. Hemingway coined the term, "Death in the Afternoon" as a mix of Pastis and Champagne, reminding all of us how much a hangover sucks at 5pm.

MONACO

Similar to Southern French cuisine, Monaco has its own specialty dishes to try. **Barbagiuan** is a pastry that is prepared from pumpkin or spinach with rice, cheese, and leek added for flavoring. **Socca** is a pancake made from chickpea flour. A special main dish native to Monaco is Stocafi, which is dried cod cooked in tomato sauce. Well, its a good thing you can always just get a steady supply of French food while in Monaco.

ITALY

Pesto is an abundant ingredient in any Italian cuisine. Another popular dish is **minestrone,** a thick soup made with potatoes, aubergines, and courgettes. Again, making use of the sea (you see a theme here) there are many dishes that include *stoccafisso,* or stockfish, that is sun-dried and wind-dried on wooden racks. It was a popular method for preserving fish when salt was not commonly available.

BEYOND TOURISM

If you are reading this, then you are a member of an elite group—and we don't mean "the literate." You're a student preparing for a semester abroad. You're taking a gap year to save the trees, the whales, or the dates. You're an 80-year-old woman who has devoted her life to egg-laying platypuses and figuring out what the hell is up with that. In short, you're a traveler, not a tourist; like any good spy, you don't observe your surroundings—you become an active part of them.

Your mission, should you choose to accept it, is to study, volunteer, or work in Europe as laid out in the dossier—er, chapter—below. More general wisdom, including international organizations with a presence in many destinations and tips on how to pick the right program, is also accessible by logging onto the Beyond Tourism section of www.letsgo.com. We leave the rest (when to go, whom to bring, and how many changes of underwear to pack) in your hands. This message will **self-destruct** in five seconds. Good luck.

greatest hits

- **FREE WILLY.** Enjoy life on the high seas, sailing in the Bay of Naples while researching the ecology of dolphin and whale habitats (p. 365).
- **STOP FIXING GRANDMA'S COMPUTER.** Use that computer science major to get yourself an overseas internship instead (p. 367).
- **START FIXING GRANDMA'S HOUSE.** Help out the elderly and disabled in Italy (p. 365).
- **KEEP IT CLASSIC.** Study the classics in Naples, Italy (p. 362).

studying

UNIVERSITIES

Most universities in big European cities have opened their doors to English-speaking exchange students, either directly or through outside programs. While you'll still have to jump through lots of bureaucratic hoops and do your I'm-a-helpless-foreigner song and dance a few times, it is totally possible to enroll directly in a local university. That being said, while most international programs will have instruction in both the native language and English, local universities are likely to keep classes romance-language-only.

visa information

If you're lucky enough to have an EU passport, stop reading and count your blessings. Non-EU citizens hoping to study abroad in Europe, on the other hand, should read on for some visa wisdom. The visa is what makes you a legal, official person in your country, your "get out of jail free and don't get deported" card. The acquisition process can be complicated and requires more pieces of identification than you knew existed, so give yourself at least two and a half months. Visa applications also often have **fees** attached to them, which can range from $30-$100, so use those two and half months to save your paychecks. For every country, the best and most up-to-date information can be obtained from your local consulate, but below are some general guidelines.

In France, short-stay visas are good for up to 90 days, but if you're studying for a semester, you'll need one of two long-stay visas. Prospective long-term travelers must fill out two to four applications–depending on the consulate–for the appropriate visa and provide a passport valid for at least three months after the student's last day in France, plus two extra passport photos. Additionally, students must give proof of enrollment in or admission to a French learning institute, a letter from the home university or institution certifying current registration as a student, a financial guarantee with a monthly allowance of US$600 per month during the intended stay, and proof of medical insurance. When in France, students with long-stay visas must obtain a *carte de séjour* (residency permit) from the local Préfecture de Police; students should file to obtain the card as soon as possible upon arrival. They will be required to undergo a medical examination (including x-rays) in addition to providing proof of residency (if your name's not on the electricity/gas bill, the bill of your host family or landlord and a copy of their French identity card will do). You'll also need to bring two passport photos, proof of financial resources and €55, which is the cost of the carte de séjour.

All non-EU citizens visiting Italy must obtain a visa for any stay **longer than three months.** You can apply for a student visa at your local Italian embassy or consulate. Make sure to bring a valid passport, visa application form, a passport photo, proof of residency, documentation of the course or program in which you are participating, proof of health insurance coverage, and (if you are under the age of 18) an affidavit of financial support from your parents as well as your parents' most recent bank statement. Within eight days of your arrival in Italy, you will need to obtain a **Permesso di Soggiorno** (residency permit) from your local police station.

International Programs

- **AMERICAN INSTITUTE FOR FOREIGN STUDY (AIFS):** With programs in 17 different countries and over 50,000 participants each year, AIFS is one of the oldest and largest cultural exchange organizations out there. In France, AIFS offers semester, year-long, and summer programs in Paris, Cannes, and Grenoble (term-time only) in both French and English. Also offers 4- to 6-week summer programs in Barcelona. *(☎800-727-2437 www.aifs.com i 2.7 min. GPA for Barcelona program. Ⓢ Semester $13,495-16,495; summer $4995-8495. Prices vary depending on location and length.)*
- **INSTITUTE FOR THE INTERNATIONAL EDUCATION OF STUDENTS:** IES offers a summer program in Arles, a semester or academic year program in Nantes, and summer, semester, and academic year programs in Paris. Business students can earn a Certificate in International Management by enrolling in a full-time master's program with French and international students. Otherwise, students take some of their classes on-site at the IES Abroad Center but are encouraged to take one or two courses at one of the French IES partner institutions. *(☎800-995-1750 or312-994-1750 www.iesabroad.org ⓈSemester $16,700-18,215; summer $6500-6675.)*
- **CULTURAL EXPERIENCES ABROAD (CEA):** CEA offers summer, semester, trimester, short-term, or academic-year programs in Paris, Aix-en-Provence, Grenoble (in the French Alps), and the French Riviera. Most students live in shared apartments, but there is the option to "upgrade" to a homestay or independent living arrangement. *(☎800-266-4441 www.gowithcea.com Ⓢ Fees range from $4395 for a 4-week session to $25,995 for an academic year.)*
- **CCIS STUDY ABROAD (CEA):** The College Consortium for International Studies (CCIS) is a partnership of colleges and universities that sponsors a number of study-abroad programs around the world. In France, students can choose between many location, including Nice. *(☎800-453-6956 or 202-223-0330 www.ccisabroad.org Ⓢ Semester $6490-10,861; summer $2617-5484. Estimates do not include room and board and vary depending on length and location of program.)*
- **COUNCIL ON INTERNATIONAL EDUCATIONAL EXCHANGE:** The classical studies program in Naples offers a mix of English- and Italian-language instruction to beginners or complete novices of the language. A liberal arts program taught entirely in Italian is also available. Available for either semester or the full academic year. *(300 Fore St., Portland, ME ☎207-553-4000 www.ciee.org i College students; 2.75 min. GPA; liberal arts program in Ferrara requires 4 semesters of college-level Italian, Naples requires 5. Classical studies program in Naples only open to students majoring in classical studies. Ⓢ Semester $13,900; academic year $26,500, includes 2 meals per day with homestay option.)*
- **GLOBAL LEARNING SEMESTERS:** Choose from their plethora of multi-country summer and semester programs. Summers focus on the Mediterranean, with programs in art and photography, early Christianity, Greek heritage, international marketing, and music, all of which make stops in Rome. You can also do a semester across the Mediterranean or throughout Europe that will include stays in most of Italy's major cities (Florence, Rome, and Venice) and may be thematically organized. *(14525 SW Millikan Way, #32004 Beaverton, OR ☎877-300-7010 www.globalsemesters.com i College students with min. sophomore standing, 2.5 min. GPA. Ⓢ Summer $6250-6500, depending on when confirmation deposit is made; semester $12,950-16,950, depending on program and time of confirmation deposit. Does not include meals, except breakfast at hotels during travel.)*
- **INTERNATIONAL STUDIES ABROAD:** Studying abroad during the summer, over a

semester, or during an academic year in International Studies Abroad (ISA)'s Rome or Florence programs means you'll be in an international university filled largely with other Americans, but trips (included in the program fees) to places like Pompeii, Capri, Cinque Terre, and Orvieto may help you escape your English-speaking peers. *(1112 W Ben White Blvd., Austin, TX ☎800-580-8826 www.studiesabroad.com i 2.5-3.3 min. GPA, depending on program. $ Summer $4100-8900, depending on program; semester $14,500-15,500, depending on program; academic year $26,000-29,800, depending on program. Does not include meals.)*

- **ACADEMIC PROGRAMS INTERNATIONAL:** Through this program you will be enrolled at a local university, but don't fret—there are some classes offered in English. With locations in Barcelona, Bilbao, Cadiz, Granada, Madrid, Salamanca, and Sevilla. *(301 Camp Craft Rd., Suite 100, West Lake Hills, TX. ☎800-844-4124 www.academicintl.com i 18+. College or graduate students. Housing provided. $ $4800-21,500.)*
- **ACADEMIC STUDIES ABROAD:** This small program provides lots of amenities including health insurance and a cell phone. Summer and semester-long programs offered in Barcelona, Madrid, Salamanca, and Sevilla. *(4 Belgrade Ave., Suite 5, Roslindale, MA, ☎888-845-4272 www.academicstudies.com i Eligibility depends on the requirements of the host university. $ Semester $8495-13,495; summer $3995-5100; Prices depend on location and length.)*
- **ARCADIA UNIVERSITY FOR EDUCATION ABROAD:** Summer, semester- and year-long academic programs in Barcelona, Granada, Majorca (summer only), and Toledo. Some courses taught in English, some in Spanish. Toledo program fee includes four-day field study in Morocco. Internship program also offered in Toledo. *(450 South Easton Rd., Glenside, PA, ☎866-927-2234 www.arcadia.edu/abroad i 3.0 min. GPA for most but not all programs. $ Semester $14,825-15,210.)*

Local Programs

- **EUROPEAN UNIVERSITY BARCELONA:** One of the world's top business schools just happens to be in Barcelona. Perfect for all those future world-dominators out there. *(Ganduxer 70, Barcelona ☎+34 93 201 81 7 www.euruni.edu $ Semester approx. $7000.)*
- **UNIVERSITAT DE BARCELONA:** Founded in 1450, boasting 18 "faculties" (majors, in America-speak), and eight graduate schools, UB gives you your pick of classes, and may even teach you to say "*Dondé está la biblioteca?*" in *Catalá*! *(Gran Vía de les Corts Catalanes 585, Barcelona ☎+34 934 021 100 www.ub.edu.)*

volunteering

If you're that glutton for punishment who can't help feeling a pang of guilt while on vacation (Must offset the carbon emissions of my plane flight! Think of the whales I could be saving while I'm at this beautiful beach! etc.), perhaps it's time to consider traveling in Europe as a volunteer. In the listings below, you'll find a mix of organizations, some of which you can contact directly and others that are umbrella organizations with sweet hook-ups to local projects. In some cases, you will pay a fee for this service, but consider what a less altruistic vacation would cost you and then evaluate volunteer prices in that light. When choosing an organization with which to volunteer, always make an effort to speak with past participants, investigate how your participation fee is spent, and check out the group's reputability in order to ensure that your efforts are serving the people, creatures, or issues you signed up to help in the first place.

The International Volunteer Programs Association has a user-friendly website (*www.volunteerinternational.org)* that should help you as you plan your volunteering vacay.

ENVIRONMENTAL AND WILDLIFE CONSERVATION

- **ECOVOLUNTEER, COMMON DOLPHINS:** Sleep on a 17.7m cutter in the Bay of Naples, and save the whales (dolphins too!) with this international volunteer organization. *(☎31 74 2508250 www.ecovolunteer.org)*
- **GLOBAL VISION INTERNATIONAL:** Help research the ecology of the Pelagos Cetacean Sanctuary (meaning it's time to live out your Flipper and Free Willy fantasies) on a 21m sailing **boat** in the Ligurian Sea in this company's Italy program. *(☎888 653 6028 www.gviusa.com)*
- **PCT TOURS:** Help undo the damage of tourism in Cinque Terre by working to repair stone walls, clean trails, or even harvest crops in Vernazza. (*www.protectcinqueterre.com* ***i*** *In July and Sept 10-person min. per session. Meals included.* $ *€145 per person per day.)*
- **CENTRES PERMANENTS D'INITIATIVES POUR L'ENVIRONNEMENT (CPIE):** With 80 offices throughout France as well as in Corsica, Guadeloupe, Guyana, Martinique, and Réunion, CPIE works on environmental education for sustainable development. *(26 rue Beaubourg, Paris ☎+33 1 44 61 75 35 www.cpie.fr)*
- **EARTHTRUST:** Interested in oceanographic research and conservation? Contact this group and make sure they're currently active in your area. *(☎808-261-5339 www.earthtrust.org)*
- **EARTHWATCH:** This program takes on volunteers to help with fieldwork and data collection. Family and teen expeditions are available. *(3 Clock Tower Pl., Ste. 100, Box 75, Maynard, MA ☎800-776-0188 www.earthwatch.org)*

COMMUNITY ACTIVISM

- **STOP SIDA:** Works to increase AIDS prevention in Spain. *(Muntaner, 121 Entlo.1ª, Barcelona ☎902 10 69 27 www.stopsida.org)*
- **CENTRES PERMANENTS D'INITIATIVES POUR L'ENVIRONNEMENT (CPIE):** With 80 offices throughout France as well as in Corsica, Guadeloupe, Guyana, Martinique, and Réunion, CPIE works on environmental education for sustainable development. *(26 rue Beaubourg, Paris ☎+33 1 44 61 75 35 www.cpie.fr)*
- **UNITED PLANET:** This international non-profit organizes "volunteer quests" in partnership with local programs in need of volunteers. Several such projects are available in Italy for lengths of four weeks to three months and offer the opportunity to experience a high level of cultural immersion while assisting disabled people or the elderly. *(☎800-292-2316 www.unitedplanet.org)*

working

LONG-TERM WORK

It can be tricky to find long-term work in Europe. Countries like Italy suffer from a relatively high level of unemployment, and so local firms aren't exactly desperate for foreigner employees. American firms abroad, however, are a more likely bet. A listing of American firms in France is available for purchase from the American Chamber of Commerce in France. Go to www.amchamfrance.org or e-mail amchamfrance@amchamfrance.org for more information. For the student working in Italy, an internship or au pair position are probably the most reliable long-term options. In Spain, you can begin your job search at the **Oficinas de Empleo,** the national employment service that controls the job market.

Teaching English

If you are not an EU citizen, getting a job teaching English in Europe will likely be a daunting task. Use the sites listed below to conduct your own investigation into the possibilities available to you. In the end, a long-term position may not be in the cards. Instead, consider a summertime camp counselor gig or dabble in freelance tutoring.

- **ESL BASE:** This site is a helpful resource for those investigating the possibility of traveling through Italy on the strength of their English. *(www.eslbase.com)*
- **OXFORD SEMINARS:** Provides a ton of helpful information, including detailed explanations of how to obtain work visas for citizens of all different countries hoping to teach in Europe. *(www.oxfordseminars.com)*

more visa information

Any non-EU citizen working in Europe must have a work visa. Any non-EU citizen traveling in Italy to work must possess a work visa, a *permesso di soggiorno per lavoro* (permission to stay for those with a work visa), and a work permit. Both the permission to stay and an interim work permit (good for 90 days) can be obtained at the police station of the town in which you are residing once you have received your work visa. While there are many types of work visas, it is quite difficult for most **non-EU citizens** to obtain one of any kind because, in order for the visa to be issued, prospective employers must initiate the process by providing evidence that their foreign employee is both an expert in the field and that his or her employment does not take away a job from an EU citizen. As you might imagine, this process involves lots of paperwork and takes time—basically, it's a bureaucratic nightmare. If you want to give it a shot, your best bet is to bring your passport, proof of residency, a letter explaining the purpose and nature of your trip, your round-trip ticket to Italy, proof of financial means in Italy, and the necessary information from your employer to your local Italian embassy or consulate... and grovel. Visit the Italian **Ministry of Foreign Affairs** website (*www.esteri.it)* or the US Embassy site *(italy.usembassy.gov)* for more information.

Those hoping to work in France for less than 90 days must apply for an Autorisation Provisoire de Travail at a local branch of Direction Départementale du Travail, de l'Emploi et de la Formation Professionnelle (D.D.T.E.F.P.). A passport and proof of short-term employment are necessary to secure authorization; a short-term, or Schengen visa (US$82) is also sometimes required. Non-EU citizens wishing to work in France for more than 90 days must have an offer of employment authorized by the French Ministry of Labor (www.travail.gouv.fr/) before applying for a long-stay visa (US$136) through their local French consulate. Within 8 days of arrival in France, holders of long-stay visas must apply for a carte de séjour. International students hoping to secure a job must possess a carte de séjour d'étudiant (student residency card) and apply for an Autorisation Provisoire de Travail at a D.D.T.E.F.P. office. Students in France are permitted to work up to 19½hr. per week during the academic year, and full time during summer and holidays. Special rules apply for au pairs and teaching assistants; see www.consulfrance-washington.org for more info.

- **TRANSITIONS ABROAD:** This site's section on teaching English contains a mother lode of tips on finding teaching positions, many of them the result of the writers' first-hand experiences. *(www.transitionsabroad.com/listings/work/esl/index.shtml)*

Au Pair Work

If you find a family that will take you on for three months or less, you should be free to Mary Poppins your heart out as an au pair in Europe. Women are more likely to find au pair work than men. Non-EU citizens hoping to take a job longer than three months will have to apply for a Long-Stay Au Pair Visa.

- **AU PAIR.COM:** Families post listings directly to this site. *(www.aupair.com)*
- **AUPAIRCONNECT:** Potential au pairs and families can sign up to this service that matches them up for free. *(www.aupairconnect.com)*
- **AUPAIR WORLD:** Free access to au pair listings. Includes information about au pair and host family responsibilities. *(www.aupair-world.net)*
- **CHILDCARE INTERNATIONAL:** Lists au pair opportunities throughout Europe, including Italy. *(www.childint.co.uk)*
- **GREAT AU PAIR:** American website with au pair listings by location and country in English. *(www.greataupair.com)*
- **NEW AUPAIR.COM:** Lots of free listings for prospective au pairs and info about visas and (out of date) average au pair salary listings. *(www.newaupair.com)*

Internships

Why do one at home when you could pad your résumé in Europe?

- **INTERNATIONAL ASSOCIATION FOR THE EXCHANGE OF STUDENTS FOR TECHNICAL EXPERIENCE (IAESTE):** This program provides paid overseas internships to full-time university students studying in technical fields. If you're unsure whether you're studying in a "technical field," see the website for a detailed list of eligible disciplines. Most programs run 8-12 weeks in the summer. Placement is available in many European countries, but you may not be placed in your preferred country. *(www.iaeste.org $1000 program fee for placement. Cost of living covered by salary.)*
- **INTERN ABROAD:** Part of the Go Abroad.com network that remains a jack-of-all trades. *(www.internabroad.com)*
- **GLOBAL EXPERIENCES:** Like a study abroad-type program for internships, meaning you get a support system and housing. *(www.globalexperiences.com Programs fees $7000-8000.)*

Other Long-Term Work

- **ESCAPE ARTIST:** This listings website allows employers to post right on its directory and allows you to search listings by location, employment type, and your work experience. Also posts many articles on living and working abroad. *(www.escapeartist.com/Overseas_Jobs)*
- **EXPAT EXCHANGE:** Includes an Italy forum with articles by Italian expats on everything from having a baby in Italy to where to find the best pizza. Also includes international job listings. *(www.expatexchange.com)*
- **WORKAWAY:** Site lists opportunities for work exchange (you work, they provide room and board) that can be searched by region and type of work. Lots of options to turn your man- or woman-power into a "vacation" of sorts at bed and breakfasts and farms. *(www.workaway.info)*

SHORT-TERM WORK

Let's get one thing straight: as much as we like a little rule-breaking every now and then, *Let's Go* does not recommend working illegally in a foreign country. It may have nice perks like a paycheck and free food, but your end-of-year bonus is probably going to be deportation and **prison food.** Not that the natives take any heed: illegal short-term hires are very common in resort areas of France, and it's estimated that southern Italy pays up to 50% of its wages under the table. Itinerant workers in these areas are most commonly employed as bartenders or restaurant staff, construction workers, farmhands, tour guides or souvenir vendors, domestics, or language tutors. Some hostels will hire you in exchange for free or discounted room and board. But, again, *Let's Go* encourages you to work legally. Non-EU citizens on the right side of the law can obtain a work permit.

- **TRANSITIONS ABROAD:** General site for moving abroad to the Iberian Peninsula. Lots of listings for student work, internships, and general short-term deals. (*www.transitionsabroad.com*)
- **EASY EXPAT:** This site offers diverse opportunities for the traveler looking to make some coin in the near future.(*www.easyexpat.com*)
- **BACK DOOR JOBS:** This site advertises "short-term job adventures." Make sure you navigate to the international page. (*www.backdoorjobs.com*)
- **RESORT JOBS:** Site with worldwide listings about recent resort openings and employment opportunities. (*www.resortjobs.com*)
- **SEASONWORKERS.COM:** Lots of different opportunities, from childcare to ski resort employment. Site also includes information on work visas and permits. (*www.seasonworkers.com*)
- **WORLD WIDE OPPORTUNITIES ON ORGANIC FARMS:** Organizations like this thrive more on volunteers working for lodging than short-term workers, but it never hurts to ask about compensation. Not available in Morocco. (*www.wwoof.org*)

tell the world

If your friends are tired of hearing about that time you saved a baby orangutan in Indonesia, there's clearly only one thing to do: get new friends. Find them at our website, www.letsgo.com, where you can post your study-, volunteer-, or work-abroad stories for other, more appreciative community members to read. There's also a Beyond Tourism section that elaborates on non-destination-specific volunteering, studying, and working opportunities. If you liked this chapter, you'll love it; if you didn't like this chapter, maybe you'll find the website's more general Beyond Tourism tips more likeable, you non-likey person.

INDEX

r

s

t

u

v

w

MAP INDEX

MAP LEGEND
Sight/Service
Airport
Arch/Gate
Bank
Beach
Bus Station
Capital City
Castle
Church
Consulate/Embassy
Convent/Monastery
Ferry Landing
347
Highway Sign
Hospital
Internet Cafe
Library
M
M
Metro Station
Mountain
Mosque
Museum
Pharmacy
Police
Post Office
Skiing
Synagogue
Telephone Office
Theater
Tourist Office
Train Station
N
LG
The Let's Go compass always points NORTH.
Pedestrian Zone
Stairs
Park
Water
Beach

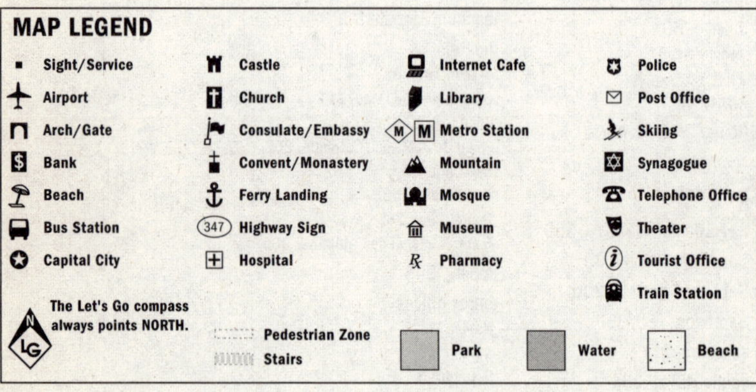

ACKNOWLEDGMENTS

BRONWEN THANKS: Chris. Tried to hold down the fort without you—sorry we couldn't fit in more pretty pictures. Marykate. Whatever Chris says, you really are the hardest-working person at LGHQ. Julia and William, for their enthusiastic and energetic prose. Rossi, Anna, Teresa, and Joe, for this book. Conor, for putting up with me all summer. My parents, who deserve to retire to Cinque Terre.

JONATHAN THANKS: In no particular order: Anna Boch, Marykate Jasper, the whole Let's Go office, the RWs my family, all the food establishments in Harvard Square, the Los Angeles Lakers, and the Kevin & Bean radio show.

ANNA THANKS: In a very particular order: all the kick-ass RW's, Jonathan Rossi, Marykate Jasper, the Snuggie, Caturday, Iya Megre, honey-stung fried chicken, the Winthrop-Eliot Dramatic Society, Marcel Moran, friends-list, Lucy, Waffle, and Moustafa the smoothie guy in the T-stop.

JOE THANKS: The Let's Go office team and his RWs for their hard work. Special thanks go out to the Starbucks staff for keeping me well caffeinated, Bolt Bus for taking me back to Dix Hills, my brother and sisters for always being down to party, and to my mother for her continued support. The ladies of Harem Pod. Lady Gaga should also be thanked for her part in our bad romance.

THERESA THANKS: Veggie Planet pizzas and Petsi Pies coffee, Liza Flum's kitchen and bootleg TV and the rickety machines at the Central Square Y. I thank Joe Gaspard and my pod-mates for having my back, and my parents, bad music, and David Foster Wallace for getting me through. My uncle's '80s comic books and my grandpa's Chicago sundaes helped too.

CHRIS THANKS: **Bronwen,** for being the hardest-working person at LGHQ and an awesome person at the same time. Marykate, for remarkable patience in the face of an avalanche of questions. William and Julia, for beautiful photos, great writing, and a whole load of amity. Finally, the most special thanks to Area 51, for three years of happiness; my family, for 22 years of the same; and PJ, for everything.

ABOUT LET'S GO

THE STUDENT TRAVEL GUIDE

Let's Go publishes the world's favorite student travel guides, written entirely by Harvard students. Armed with pens, notebooks, and a few changes of clothes stuffed into their backpacks, our student researchers go across continents, through time zones, and above expectations to seek out invaluable travel experiences for our readers. Because we are a completely student-run company, we have a unique perspective on how students travel, where they want to go, and what they're looking to do when they get there. If your dream is to grab a machete and forge through the jungles of Costa Rica, we can take you there. If you'd rather bask in the Riviera sun at a beachside cafe, we'll set you a table. In short, we write for readers who know that there's more to travel than tour buses. To keep up, visit our website, www.letsgo.com, where you can sign up to blog, post photos from your trips, and connect with the Let's Go community.

TRAVELING BEYOND TOURISM

We're on a mission to provide our readers with sharp, fresh coverage packed with socially responsible opportunities to go beyond tourism. Each guide's Beyond Tourism chapter shares ideas about responsible travel, study abroad, and how to give back to the places you visit while on the road. To help you gain a deeper connection with the places you travel, our fearless researchers scour the globe to give you the heads-up on both world-renowned and off-the-beaten-track opportunities. We've also opened our pages to respected writers and scholars to hear their takes on the countries and regions we cover, and asked travelers who have worked, studied, or volunteered abroad to contribute first-person accounts of their experiences.

FIFTY-ONE YEARS OF WISDOM

Let's Go has been on the road for 51 years and counting. We've grown a lot since publishing our first 20-page pamphlet to Europe in 1960, but five decades and 60 titles later, our witty, candid guides are still researched and written entirely by students on shoestring budgets who know that train strikes, stolen luggage, food poisoning, and marriage proposals are all part of a day's work. Meanwhile, we're still bringing readers fresh new features, such as a student-life section with advice on how and where to meet students from around the world; a revamped, user-friendly layout for our listings; and greater emphasis on the experiences that make travel abroad a rite of passage for readers of all ages. And, of course, this year's 16 titles—including five brand-new guides—are still brimming with editorial honesty, a commitment to students, and our irreverent style.

THE LET'S GO COMMUNITY

More than just a travel guide company, Let's Go is a community that reaches from our headquarters in Cambridge, MA, all across the globe. Our small staff of dedicated student editors, writers, and tech nerds comes together because of our shared passion for travel and our desire to help other travelers get the most out of their experience. We love it when our readers become part of the Let's Go community as well—when you travel, drop us a postcard (67 Mt. Auburn St., Cambridge, MA 02138, USA), send us an email (feedback@letsgo.com), or sign up on our website (www.letsgo.com) to tell us about your adventures and discoveries.

For more information, updated travel coverage, and news from our researcher team, visit us online at www.letsgo.com.

THANKS TO OUR SPONSORS

HELPING LET'S GO. If you want to share your discoveries, suggestions, or corrections, please drop us a line. We appreciate every piece of correspondence, whether a postcard, a 10-page email, or a coconut. Visit Let's Go at **www.letsgo.com** or send an email to:

feedback@letsgo.com, subject: "Let's Go European Riviera"

Address mail to:

Let's Go European Riviera, 67 Mount Auburn St., Cambridge, MA 02138, USA

In addition to the invaluable travel advice our readers share with us, many are kind enough to offer their services as researchers or editors. Unfortunately, our charter enables us to employ only currently enrolled Harvard students.

Maps © Let's Go and Avalon Travel
Design Support by Jane Musser, Sarah Juckniess, Tim McGrath

Distributed by Publishers Group West.
Printed in Canada by Friesens Corp.

ISBN-13: 978-1-59880-741-7

First edition
10 9 8 7 6 5 4 3 2 1

Let's Go European Riviera is written by Let's Go Publications, 67 Mt. Auburn St., Cambridge, MA 02138, USA.

LEGAL DISCLAIMER. For 50 years, Let's Go has published the world's favorite budget travel guides, written entirely by students and updated periodically based on the personal anecdotes and travel experiences of our student writers. Although every effort was made to ensure that the information was correct at the time of going to press, the author and publisher do not assume and hereby disclaim any liability to any party for any loss or damage caused by errors, omissions, or any potential travel disruption due to labor or financial difficulty, whether such errors or omissions result from negligence, accident, or any other cause.

ADVERTISING DISCLAIMER. All advertisements appearing in Let's Go publications are sold by an independent agency not affiliated with the editorial production of the guides. Advertisers are never given preferential treatment, and the guides are researched, written, and published independent of advertising. Advertisements do not imply endorsement of products or services by Let's Go, and Let's Go does not vouch for the accuracy of information provided in advertisements.

If you are interested in purchasing advertising space in a Let's Go publication, contact Edman & Company at ☎1-203-656-1000.

quick reference

YOUR GUIDE TO LET'S GO ICONS

☎ Phone numbers	Not wheelchair-accessible	Has A/C
Websites	Has internet access	Directions
Takes credit cards	Has outdoor seating	Other hard info
Cash only	Is GLBT or GLBT-friendly	Prices
Wheelchair-accessible	Serves alcohol	Hours

PRICE RANGES

Let's Go includes price ranges, marked by icons ❶ through ❺, in accommodations and food listings. For an expanded explanation, see the chart in How To Use This Book.

SPAIN	❶	❷	❸	❹	❺
ACCOMMODATIONS	under €20	€20-29	€30-37	€38-50	€ 50+
FOOD	under €6	€6-12	€13-17	€ 18-25	€25+

FRANCE	❶	❷	❸	❹	❺
ACCOMMODATIONS	up to €25	€25-€40	€40-€60	€60-€80	€80 or above
FOOD	up to €15	€15-€25	€25-€35	€35-€45	€45 or above

ITALY	❶	❷	❸	❹	❺
ACCOMMODATIONS	Under €20	€20-30	€31-45	€46-65	Above €65
FOOD	Under €7	€7-15	€16-25	€26-33	Above €33

IMPORTANT PHONE NUMBERS

SPAIN EMERGENCY: POLICE ☎091, FIRE ☎080			
Ambulance	☎061	To Report a Crime	☎902 102 112
Directory Assistance	☎11822	Operator	☎1008

FRANCE EMERGENCY: POLICE ☎17, FIRE ☎18, MEDICAL ☎15			
European emergency	☎112	Directory assistance	☎118 218
English-language crisis line	☎01 47 23 80 80	SNCF train reservations and information	☎08 92 30 83 08

ITALY EMERGENCY: POLICE ☎112, FIRE ☎113, AMBULANCE ☎118			
Canadian Embassy	☎06 85 444	British Embassy	☎06 42 20 00 01
Irish Embassy	☎06 69 79 121	US Embassy	☎06 46 741

USEFUL PHRASES

ENGLISH	SPANISH	FRENCH	ITALIAN
Hello!/Hi!	Hola!	Bonjour!	Ciao!
Please.	Por favor.	S'il vous plait.	Per fevore
Sorry!/Excuse me!	Perdón !	Pardon!	Perdono!

MEASUREMENT CONVERSIONS

1 inch (in.) = 25.4mm	1 millimeter (mm) = 0.039 in.
1 foot (ft.) = 0.305m	1 meter (m) = 3.28 ft.
1 mile (mi.) = 1.609km	1 kilometer (km) = 0.621 mi.
1 pound (lb.) = 0.454kg	1 kilogram (kg) = 2.205 lb.
1 gallon (gal.) = 3.785L	1 liter (L) = 0.264 gal.